1-2-3® BEYOND THE BASICS

Richard Cranford
Greg M. Perry
Brian Underdahl

1-2-3® Beyond the Basics

Copyright © 1992 by Que® Corporation.

Library of Congress Catalog No.: 90-62962

ISBN 0-88022-620-X

94 93 92 91   4 3 2 1

Interpretation of the printing code: the rightmost double-digit number is the year of the book's printing; the rightmost single-digit number, the number of the book's printing. For example, a printing code of 91-1 shows that the first printing of the book occurred in 1991.

Screen reproductions in this book were created with Collage Plus from Inner Media, Inc., Hollis, NH, and Inset from Inset Systems, Brookfield, CT.

1-2-3 Beyond the Basics is based on Lotus 1-2-3 Releases 2.01, 2.2, 2.3, 3, and 3.1, but can be used with Releases 1A and 2.

Publisher: Lloyd J. Short

Associate Publisher: Karen A. Bluestein

Acquisitions Manager: Terrie Lynn Solomon

Project Development Manager: Mary Bednarek

Managing Editor: Paul Boger

Book Designer: Scott Cook

Production Team: Jill Bomaster, Phil Kitchel, Bob LaRoche, Sarah Leatherman, Anne Owen, Howard Peirce, Tad Ringo, Louise Shinault, Dennis Sheehan, Bruce Steed, Suzanne Tully, Christine Young, Mary Beth Wakefield

This book is dedicated to my wife, Laura Jennings-Cranford, for her support, encouragement, and love.

—R. C.

Product Directors
Joyce J. Nielsen
Shelley O'Hara

Production Editor
Robin Drake

Editor
Leigh Davis

Technical Editors
Robert J. Murtha
Jerry Ellis
Shelley O'Hara

Editorial Assistant
Patty Brooks

*Composed in New Century Schoolbook and Macmillan
by Que Corporation*

Richard Cranford

Since 1986, **Richard Cranford** has contributed articles to *LOTUS* Magazine describing techniques and ready-to-run applications for 1-2-3 and Symphony. He has been an editor at *LOTUS* since 1987. He was a contributing author for Que's *1-2-3 Macro Library*, Third Edition (1990). He recently developed, for Lotus Development Corporation, a series of 1-2-3 templates for insurance agents to be distributed as *The Lotus Solution for Insurance*. He holds a degree in Management Information Systems from Northeastern University, and lives in Cambridge, Massachusetts.

Greg M. Perry

Greg M. Perry is a Professor of Computer Science at Tulsa University in Tulsa, Oklahoma, a consultant, lecturer, and author of seven books on computer applications. He has published several articles in such publications as *PC World*, *Data Training*, and *Inside First Publisher*. He holds degrees in Computer Science and Finance.

Brian Underdahl

Brian Underdahl is an independent consultant based in Reno, Nevada. He is the author of *Upgrading to MS-DOS 5*, as well as a coauthor of *Using Symphony*, Special Edition, *Using 1-2-3 Release 3.1*, Second Edition, and a number of other books from Macmillan Computer Publishing. He was the technical editor of *Using 1-2-3 for DOS Release 2.3*, Special Edition and several other fine Que books. His background in engineering and business gives him the ability to present complex subjects in a clear and concise manner.

Trademark Acknowledgments

Que Corporation has made every effort to supply trademark information about company names, products, and services mentioned in this book. Trademarks indicated below were derived from various sources. Que Corporation cannot attest to the accuracy of this information.

@BASE, Instant Analyst, Look & Link, Macro Editor/Debugger (MED), SeeMORE, and Ultra-Vision are trademarks of Personics Corporation.

@EASE is a trademark of Spreadsheet Solutions Corporation.

@Functions III, 3D-Graphics, Beyond 640, Financial Toolkit, and JetSet are trademarks of Intex Solutions, Inc.

@Tools is a trademark of PC Publishing, Inc.

1-2-3, DataLens, Freelance, Lotus, Lotus Developer Tools, Lotus HAL, Magellan, Symphony, and VisiCalc are registered trademarks, Allways is a trademark, and PrintGraph is a product of Lotus Development Corporation. (Lotus HAL is distinguished from HAL, which is a trademark of Qantel for its Hotel & Leisure software.)

3-2-1 GOSUB, Decision Analyst, Project Calc/Resources, and What-If Solver are trademarks of Frontline Systems, Inc.

Applause II, dBASE, dBASE III, and dBASE IV are registered trademarks of Ashton-Tate Corporation.

Apple II is a registered trademark of Apple Computer, Inc.

AT&T is a registered trademark of American Telephone & Telegraph Company.

Baler is a trademark of Baler Software Corporation.

Borland, Paradox, Paradox Application Language (PAL), and Quattro Pro are registered trademarks of Borland International, Inc.

CorelDRAW! is a trademark of Corel Systems Corporation.

Draw Partner and Professional Write are trademarks and Harvard Graphics is a registered trademark of Software Publishing Corporation.

Epson is a registered trademark of Seiko Epson Corporation.

ForeCalc is a trademark of Business Forecast Systems, Inc.

Hercules Graphics card is a trademark of Hercules Computer Technology.

HP and LaserJet are registered trademarks of Hewlett-Packard Company.

IBM and OS/2 are registered trademarks of International Business Machines.

Impress is a product of PC Publishing.

King Jaguar is a trademark of Sheng Labs, Inc.

Microsoft Excel, Microsoft Word, Microsoft Word for Windows, and MS-DOS are registered trademarks of Microsoft Corporation.

NEC is a registered trademark of NEC Corporation.

NetWare and Novell are registered trademarks of Novell, Inc.

OKIDATA is a registered trademark of Oki America, Inc.

PageMaker is a registered trademark of Aldus Corporation.

PFS: First Publisher is a registered trademark of Spinnaker Software.

Q&A is a registered trademark of Symantec Corporation.

Quicken is a registered trademark and Transfer Utility is a trademark of Intuit.

R:BASE is a registered trademark of Microrim, Inc.

Sideways is a registered trademark and Noteworthy, The Worksheet Utilities, and InWord are trademarks of Funk Software.

SNAPSHOT is a trademark of Design Software.

TurboTax is a registered trademark of ChipSoft, Inc.

Ventura Publisher is a registered trademark of Ventura Systems, Inc.

WordPerfect is a registered trademark of WordPerfect Corporation.

Acknowledgments

As principal author, I want to acknowledge and thank the following people who made important contributions to this book:

Brian Underdahl, who wrote Chapter 12 and the portion of Chapter 11 that deals with external database operations.

Greg Perry, who wrote Chapters 13 through 16 and the Appendix.

Terrie Lynn Solomon, Que's Acquisitions Manager, and **David Paul Ewing**, formerly Que's Publishing Director, for their guidance and assistance in getting the project started.

Joyce Nielsen, Product Director for Parts I, II, and III, and **Shelley O'Hara**, Product Director for Part IV.

Rob Murtha, Technical Editor for Parts I, II, and III, **Jerry Ellis**, Technical Editor for most of Part IV, and **Shelley O'Hara**, Technical Editor for Chapter 14.

Robin Drake, Production Editor.

Leigh Davis, Copy Editor.

Karen Bluestein, Associate Publisher, who (with **Scott Cook**) developed the design for this book and future books in Que's Beyond the Basics series.

Patty Brooks, Editorial Assistant, for whom the electronic age was no great advantage; Ms. Brooks retyped all of Chapter 10 when it was learned that all three disks were corrupted.

And **Daniel Gasteiger**, who helped me get past a few tricky macro problems.

—R.C.

Contents

Introduction, 1

What Is Contained in This Book, 1
Who Should Read This Book?, 2
Which Versions of 1-2-3 Are Covered?, 2
How Is This Book Organized?, 2
    Part I: Reviewing 1-2-3 Basics, 2
    Part II: Optimizing 1-2-3, 3
    Part III: Creating 1-2-3 Applications, 4
    Part IV: Using 1-2-3 with Other Programs, 4
Appendix, 5
How Can You Learn More about 1-2-3?, 5
Conventions Used in This Book, 6
    Special Typefaces and Representations, 6
    Macro Conventions, 7
    General Conventions, 8

I Reviewing 1-2-3 Basics

1 An Overview of 1-2-3 Basics, 11

Starting 1-2-3, 11
Getting Started with the Worksheet, 12
    Elements of the 1-2-3 Screen, 14
    Moving Around the Worksheet, 15
    Entering Labels, 17
    Entering Values, 19
Working with Formulas, 20
    Establishing Cell References by Pointing, 21
    Using Functions To Create More Powerful Formulas, 21
Using 1-2-3 Menu Commands, 22
    Using Commands To Format Cells, 23
    Using Commands To Copy Cells, 23
    Using Commands To Format Entire Worksheets, 24
Saving and Retrieving 1-2-3 Files, 25
    Preparing To Save Your Work, 25
    Saving the Worksheet, 26
    Retrieving Files and Starting New Files, 27

    Modifying the Worksheet, 27
        Setting Column Widths, 28
        Performing What-If Tests, 29
        Understanding Displayed versus Actual Values, 30
        Using Manual Recalculation, 31
        Editing Cells, 32
        Using Automatic EDIT Mode, 33
        Erasing Cells, 34
    Working with Ranges, 34
        Using Three-Dimensional Ranges, 36
        Preselecting Ranges, 36
        Using Range Names, 37
        Using the Mouse To Specify Ranges with Releases 2.3 and 3.1, 38
    Printing the Worksheet, 38
    Using 1-2-3 Graphics, 38
    Working with Databases, 40
    Using Macros, 43
        Creating a Simple Keystroke-Replacement Macro, 44
        Using Macro Key Names, 45
        Considering More Complex Macros, 46
    Summary, 47

II Optimizing 1-2-3

2 Designing Applications, 51

    Understanding the Importance of Design Issues, 51
    Using Labels To Document Worksheets, 53
        Determining Where To Use Labels, 53
        Avoiding the Use of Too Many Labels, 54
    Arranging Worksheet Sections To Fit on One Screen, 54
        Designing Worksheets with Several Rows, 56
        Using Menu Macros To Navigate Large Worksheets, 57
    Recognizing When To Use Macros, 58
    Designing Worksheets That Protect Formulas, 59
        Creating a Restricted Zone with /Worksheet Titles, 61
        Arranging a Worksheet Diagonally, 63
        Combining a Restricted Zone with a Diagonal Worksheet Arrangement, 64
        Recognizing When To Use Other Worksheet Arrangements, 65
    Designing Applications in Release 3.x, 67

Using Multiple Worksheets for a Single Application, 67
Using GROUP Mode To Format Multiple Worksheets Concurrently, 68
Storing Macros in a Separate Worksheet, 70
Using Macros in GROUP Mode Applications, 70
Using an Opening Screen To Document Multiple Worksheet Applications, 71
Summary, 72

3   Working with Data, 73

Entering Labels, 73
Deciding When To Enter Label Prefixes, 74
Assigning a Label Format with Release 3.x, 75
Entering Values, 75
Using the Numeric Keypad, 76
Using a Macro To Automate Value Entry, 76
Entering Numeric Series with /Data Fill, 77
Finding the Right Stop Value, 78
Filling Rectangular Ranges with Numeric Series, 78
Using Dates and Times with /Data Fill, 80
Formatting Values, 82
Understanding General Format, 82
Using /Range Format Reset, 83
Changing the Appearance of Currency and Comma Formats, 83
Changing the Currency Symbol, 84
Changing the Appearance of Date and Time Formats, 84
Using /Range Format Other with Release 3.x, 84
Creating Entry Forms That Restrict Data Input, 85
Creating the Input Area with /Range Input, 86
Entering Data into an Entry Form, 87
Using a Macro with Entry Forms, 87
Using the FORM Command with Releases 2.3 and 3.x, 87
Using Optional Arguments in the FORM Command, 88
Using the FORM Command with the APPENDBELOW Command, 89
Entering Dates and Times with Release 3.x, 90
Copying Worksheet Data, 92
Specifying Ranges, 92
Understanding the Implicit Size of the Target Range, 92
Adding the Depth Dimension with Release 3.x, 93
Using Relative, Absolute, and Mixed References, 95
Changing the Addressing Mode with the Abs Key (F4), 95
Mixing Relative and Absolute Cell References, 96
Copying Formulas without Inserting Dollar Signs, 97
Copying Absolute References Relatively, 98

Using /Range Search To Change Addressing in Formulas, 99
Using Worksheet Relative Addressing with Release 3.x, 101
Copying Near the Edges of the Worksheet, 101
Copying Cell Formats and Protection Status, 102
Copying Allways Formats with Release 2.2, 102
Copying Wysiwyg Formats with Release 2.3 and 3.1, 103
Using /Copy To Recalculate a Range, 104
Using /Range Value To Convert Formulas to Values, 104
Using /Range Trans To Copy and Transpose, 105
Using the /Move Command, 108
Understanding How /Move Differs from /Copy, 108
Exercising Caution with the /Move Command, 109
Copying between Files and Worksheets with Release 3.x, 110
Copying from a File on Disk, 110
Copying to or from Files in Memory, 111
Copying Data between Files without Using Coordinates, 111
Copying to Noncontiguous Cells, 112
Using the Undo Feature, 115
Understanding How Undo Works, 116
Using Undo To Experiment in Releases 2.2 and 2.3, 117
Using Undo with Macros, 117
Adding the Undo Feature to Earlier Releases, 118
Searching Ranges for Characters, 118
Using /Range Search To Find Characters, 118
Using /Range Search To Change Characters, 118
Using /Range Search in Macros, 119
Summary, 119

4   Managing Files, 121
Changing the Directory, 121
Retrieving Files, 122
Using the Name Key (F3), 122
Searching for Specific Files, 123
Searching Subdirectories, 123
Opening Multiple Files with Release 3.x, 123
Saving Files, 124
Protecting Existing Files, 124
Creating a New File from an Old File, 124
Saving Files by Highlighting, 125
Tracking the Default File Name, 125
Saving Files with Passwords, 125

Saving Files with the Backup Option, 126
Saving Part of a Worksheet, 126
Combining Files, 127
  Using /File Combine Copy, 127
  Using /File Combine Copy with Formulas, 128
  Using /File Combine Add, 130
    Advantages of /File Combine Add, 133
    Tracking the /File Combine Operation, 133
    Understanding the Difference between /File Combine Add and /File Combine Copy, 134
    Using /File Combine Add with Portions of Worksheets, 134
  Using /File Combine Subtract, 134
  Using /File Combine Subtract To Analyze Worksheets, 135
Using /File Import, 137
  Preparing Word Processing Text, 137
  Importing Word Processing Text, 138
  Formatting Imported Text, 138
  Importing Data from Other Programs, 138
  Using /File Import Numbers, 141
Linking Files, 143
  Linking with Releases 2.2 and 2.3, 143
    Linking with the Viewer Add-In (Release 2.3), 144
    Linking to Named Cells and Ranges, 145
    Using File Linking for Base Assumptions, 146
    Using File Linking in Modular Applications, 147
    Updating Linked Files, 150
    Checking for File Links, 151
  Linking with Release 3.x, 151
    Linking Open Files, 152
    Modifying Linked Files, 153
    Using Compound File Linking Formulas, 153
    Updating File Links, 154
    Checking for File Links, 155
Summary, 155

5   Printing Reports, 157
Understanding Default Print Settings, 157
Controlling the Printer, 158
  Understanding Control Codes, 158
  Sending Control Codes from 1-2-3, 158
Setting Margins, 160
Printing Wide Ranges on Multiple Pages, 161

Using Headers and Footers, 161
   Using Dates in Headers and Footers, 162
   Adding Page Numbers to Headers and Footers, 162
   Using a Cell Reference as a Header or Footer, 162
Using Border Columns, 163
Using Border Rows, 166
Maximizing the Number of Rows Per Page, 168
Printing Cell Formulas, 168
Printing to Disk Files, 170
Printing to Encoded Files with Releases 2.3 and 3.x, 171
Background Printing with Release 2.3, 171
Exporting Data with /Print File, 173
Printing Solid Dividing Lines with Release 3, 174
Creating Presentation-Quality Printouts with Add-In Programs, 177
   Printing with Allways (Release 2.2), 178
      Adjusting the Layout for Allways Printing, 178
      Setting the Allways Print Range, 179
      Selecting a Printer for Allways Printing, 180
      Selecting Pages To Print, 181
      Printing the Range, 181
      Printing an Encoded Allways File, 181
   Printing with Wysiwyg (Releases 2.3 and 3.1), 182
      Setting the Print Range, 182
      Setting Margins, 183
      Setting Headers, Footers, and Borders, 183
      Selecting Pages To Print, 184
      Printing the Range, 184
Summary, 185

6   Working with Formulas and Functions, 187

Understanding Operators and Operator Precedence, 187
   Considering Operator Precedence in Detail, 188
   Applying the Rules of Precedence, 189
Understanding Boolean Expressions, 190
   Using Boolean Expressions in Database Criteria Ranges, 190
   Using Independent Boolean Expressions, 191
   Creating Boolean Expressions with #AND# and #OR#, 192
Creating Shorter Formulas with @MIN and @MAX, 193
Simplifying Formulas, 193
Using Noncontiguous Ranges with Statistical Functions, 194
Avoiding Problems with @AVG and @COUNT, 195
Calculating Cube Roots and nth Roots, 197

Using the @MOD Function, 197
    Exercising Caution with @MOD, 198
    Using @LOG To Compute the Magnitude of Numbers, 199
Avoiding Repetition in @IF Formulas, 199
Creating Nested @IF Formulas, 200
Using Special Functions To Control the Flow of Macros, 200
    Using @CELL To Test for Cell Entries, 200
    Using @CELLPOINTER To Store the Current Cell Address, 201
Using Variations on Lookup Functions, 201
    Using Lookup Functions in Incremental Applications, 202
    Using Lookup Functions with Character Strings, 202
Using @DATEVALUE To Speed Up Date Entry, 203
Summary, 204

7   Creating and Printing Graphs, 205

Understanding Graphs, 205
    Understanding Graph Types, 207
    Using Release 2.3 and 3.x Graph Types, 210
Using the Graph Key (F10), 211
Creating Graphs Quickly with /Graph Group, 212
Using Automatic Graphing with Release 3.x, 212
Graphing Numbers of Different Magnitudes, 213
    Using Two Y-Axes with Release 3.x, 214
    Using Formulas To Compare Data with Releases 2.01, 2.2, and 2.3, 215
Using Composed Characters in Graphs, 217
Naming Graphs, 217
    Using Named Graphs, 218
    Displaying Named Graphs with Macros, 218
Saving Graphs, 219
Enhancing Graphs with Wysiwyg, 220
Printing Graphs, 223
    Printing Graphs with Allways (Release 2.2), 223
    Printing Graphs with the /Print Menu (Release 3.x) , 224
    Printing Graphs with Wysiwyg (Releases 2.3 and 3.1), 225
Summary, 226

8   Writing Macros, 227

Naming and Starting Macros, 227
    Starting Macros with the Run Key (Alt-F3), 227
    Using the Run Key (Alt-F3) in Macro Development, 228
    Simulating the Run Key (Alt-F3) in Release 2.01, 228

Organizing Macro Names, 229
Creating Macros with the Learn Key in Release 2.2 and 2.3, 230
Shortening Recorded Macros in Release 2.2, 231
   Arranging the Macro, 232
   Using the Repeat-Eliminating Macro, 232
Creating Macros with the Record Feature in Release 3.x, 234
   Clearing the Buffer, 235
   Editing the Buffer, 236
   Copying Buffer Contents, 236
Using Numeric Arguments with Key Names, 237
   Using Cell References for Repeating Key Names, 237
   Using Formulas for Repeating Key Names, 238
Using Advanced Macro Commands, 239
   Using GETLABEL and GETNUMBER, 239
   Accepting Single Characters without the Enter Key, 240
   Displaying Messages, 240
Understanding Subroutines, 241
   Creating Commands with Subroutines, 241
   Using Subroutines To Organize Programs, 242
   Using Subroutines To Replay Stored Characters, 243
   Avoiding the use of QUIT and RETURN, 244
Techniques for Using Menu Macros, 245
   Making Custom Menus Safer To Use, 245
   Organizing Menu Macro Code Effectively, 246
   Creating Menu Trees, 247
Using the Macro Library Manager with Releases 2.2 and 2.3, 248
Running Macros in Open Release 3.x Files, 249
   Saving the Current Worksheet, 249
   Abandoning a Worksheet, 250
Summary, 250

III   Creating 1-2-3 Applications

9   Using 1-2-3 for Business Presentations, 253

Creating Text-Only Charts, 253
   Creating Simple Text Charts, 254
   Creating Text-Only Charts with Allways (Release 2.2), 255
   Creating Text-Only Charts with Wysiwyg (Releases 2.3 and 3.1), 257
Creating Graphs for Presentations, 258

Choosing the Correct Graph Type, 259
Adding Text to Graphs, 261
Combining Graphs and Text with Release 3.x /Print Commands, 262
Combining Graphs and Text with Allways (Release 2.2), 262
Combining Graphs and Text with Wysiwyg (Releases 2.3 and 3.1), 263
Preserving the Shape of a Graph, 263
Adding Graphics to Existing Text, 264
Mixing Text and Graphs with Allways (Release 2.2), 264
Mixing Text and Graphs with Wysiwyg (Releases 2.3 and 3.1), 266
Summary, 269

10   Using 1-2-3 for Financial and Accounting Applications, 271

Modifying Financial Functions for Annuity-Due Calculations, 271
Using Financial Functions in Unusual Ways, 272
Calculating the Term of a Loan, 272
Calculating the Deposit Needed To Reach a Future Value, 273
Computing the Principal of a Loan, 273
Computing Financial Values without a Designated Function, 273
Using the Release 3.x @VDB Function, 274
Calculating Variable Depreciation with Releases 2.01 and 2.2, 276
Creating an Amortization Table, 277
Creating Self-Sizing Financial Tables, 279
Controlling the Size of a Table with Formulas, 279
Controlling the Size of a Table with Macros, 281
Dating Financial Tables Automatically, 282
Creating Date Values at Weekly Intervals, 282
Creating Date Values at Monthly Intervals, 284
Using Formulas To Age Receivables, 287
Creating Bullet-Proof Financial Models, 288
Summary, 292

11   Using 1-2-3 as a Database Manager, 293

Selecting Criteria Ranges, 293
Ensuring Accurate Record Selection, 294
Specifying Multiple Criteria, 295
Connecting Criteria with AND, 295
Connecting Criteria with OR, 298
Using Combinations of AND and OR, 299
Creating Safe Output Ranges, 299
Using Field Names in Database Functions, 300
Managing Disk-Based Databases with Release 3.x, 300

Accessing External Data Tables, 301
Using /Data External List, 302
Listing External Tables, 302
Listing Fields from External Tables, 302
Using /Data External Create, 303
Creating External Databases from 1-2-3 Databases, 304
Exporting Data to an External Table, 306
Adjusting Worksheet Data To Match Driver Field Lengths, 306
Using /Data External Other Refresh, 307
Creating Reports, 308
Creating Summary Reports with /Data Table, 309
Creating One-Way Data Tables, 310
Creating Two-Way Data Tables, 311
Creating Three-Way Data Tables with Release 3.x, 312
Creating Summary Reports with Formulas, 313
Creating Multilevel Summary Reports, 314
Creating Detailed Reports, 315
Creating Detailed Extracts by Sorting, 316
Creating Detailed Reports with Subtotals, 317
Creating Subtotaled Reports with Formulas, 318
Using Macros To Create Subtotaled Reports, 320
Creating Formatted Reports, 322
Setting Up the Report Format and Macro, 323
Printing the Report, 324
Summary, 325

IV   Using 1-2-3 with Other Programs

12   Using Add-Ins with 1-2-3, 329

Understanding Add-Ins, 329
Using the Standard 1-2-3 Add-Ins, 332
Macro Library Manager (Releases 2.2 and 2.3), 332
Loading Macro Libraries, 334
Editing Macro Libraries, 334
Allways (Release 2.2), 336
Wysiwyg (Releases 2.3 and 3.1), 336
Auditor (Release 2.3), 336
Viewer (Release 2.3), 341
Using Other Add-Ins with 1-2-3, 342

Macro Editor/Debugger (MED), 347

SeeMORE, 349

Look & Link, 352

What-If Solver, 356

Project Calc/Resources, 358

The Worksheet Utilities, 360

   The CELLWKS Add-In, 361

   The FILEWKS Add-In, 366

Sideways, 367

InWord, 368

ForeCalc, 370

@EASE, 371

Developing Your Own 1-2-3 Add-Ins, 373

  The Lotus Add-In Toolkit (Release 3.x), 373

    Toolkit Modules, 374

    Toolkit Considerations, 374

  The Lotus Developer Tools for Release 2.x, 375

Using Other Developer Tools with 1-2-3, 375

  @Tools, 375

  King Jaguar, 376

Summary, 377

13   Using 1-2-3 with Presentation Programs, 379

Using 1-2-3 with Freelance Plus, 380

  Creating a Sample 1-2-3 Worksheet To Import, 381

  Importing 1-2-3 Data, 383

  Importing 1-2-3 PIC Files, 388

Using 1-2-3 with Harvard Graphics, 389

  Creating a Sample 1-2-3 Worksheet To Import, 390

  Importing 1-2-3 Data, 392

  Streamlining the Importing Process, 395

  Importing Named 1-2-3 Graphs, 396

Using 1-2-3 with CorelDRAW!, 398

  Creating a Sample 1-2-3 Graph To Import, 398

  Importing 1-2-3 PIC Files, 401

Using 1-2-3 with First Publisher, 404

  Importing 1-2-3 Data, 404

  Importing 1-2-3 PIC Files, 407

    Creating a Sample 1-2-3 Graph To Import, 407

Taking a SNAPSHOT of the Graph, 408
Importing the Graph, 409
Using 1-2-3 with PageMaker, 410
Creating a Sample 1-2-3 Worksheet To Import, 410
Importing 1-2-3 Data, 412
Importing 1-2-3 PIC Files, 416
Using 1-2-3 with Ventura Publisher, 416
Importing 1-2-3 Data, 417
Creating a Sample 1-2-3 Worksheet To Import, 417
Preparing the PRN File, 419
Importing the Data, 420
Importing 1-2-3 PIC Files, 422
Summary, 424

14 Using 1-2-3 with Word Processing Programs, 425

Using 1-2-3 with WordPerfect, 425
Importing 1-2-3 Data, 426
Linking a Worksheet to a Document, 429
Changing the Link Options, 430
Importing 1-2-3 PIC Files, 431
Creating a Sample 1-2-3 PIC File To Import, 431
Preparing the Text for the Imported Graph, 432
Adjusting the Graph, 434
Editing the Graph, 435
Using 1-2-3 with Microsoft Word, 436
Importing 1-2-3 Data, 436
Adjusting the Column Alignment, 438
Updating the Imported Data, 439
Importing 1-2-3 PIC Files, 439
Creating a Sample 1-2-3 PIC File To Import, 440
Importing the PIC File, 441
Previewing the Graph in the Document, 442
Adjusting the Graph, 442
Using 1-2-3 with Word for Windows, 443
Importing 1-2-3 Data, 443
Adjusting the Column Alignment, 445
Updating the Imported Data, 446

Importing 1-2-3 PIC Files, 447
   Creating a Sample 1-2-3 PIC File To Import, 447
   Preparing To Import the PIC File, 449
   Importing the PIC File, 450
   Adjusting the Graph, 450
Using 1-2-3 with Professional Write, 452
Summary, 454

15   Using 1-2-3 with Financial Programs, 455

Using 1-2-3 with Symphony, 455
   Creating a Sample 1-2-3 Worksheet To Import, 456
   Importing Symphony Worksheets with 1-2-3, 457
   Using 1-2-3 Release 3.x with Symphony, 457
   Using 1-2-3 Release 2.x with Symphony, 459
Using 1-2-3 with Quattro Pro, 460
   Creating a Sample 1-2-3 Worksheet To Import, 460
   Using 1-2-3 Menus in Quattro Pro, 461
   Importing and Exporting Files, 462
Using 1-2-3 with Excel, 463
   Creating a Sample 1-2-3 Worksheet, 463
   Understanding 1-2-3 and Excel Differences, 464
   Using the Excel Help Lotus 1-2-3 Menu System, 465
   Importing Files from 1-2-3, 467
   Exporting Files to 1-2-3, 468
Using 1-2-3 with Quicken, 468
   Using Quicken Reports in 1-2-3, 469
   Using the Transfer Utility, 470
     Detail Transfers, 470
     Summary Transfers, 472
Using 1-2-3 with TurboTax, 474
   Preparing the Data, 475
   Using Multiple Copy Forms, 476
   Importing Data into TurboTax, 477
Handling Import Errors, 479
Summary, 479

16   Using 1-2-3 with Database Programs, 481

Using 1-2-3 with dBASE, 481
   Preparing the Data, 481
   Importing 1-2-3 Release 3.x Data with dBASE, 482
   Importing 1-2-3 Release 2.x Data with dBASE, 484
   Importing 1-2-3 Release 2.x Data from the dBASE Dot Prompt, 486
   Exporting Data from dBASE to 1-2-3, 487
Using 1-2-3 with Paradox, 488
   Preparing the Data, 488
      Column Labels, 489
      Data Formats, 489
   Importing the Data, 490
   Exporting Paradox Tables to 1-2-3, 492
Using 1-2-3 with Q&A, 493
   Preparing the Data, 494
   Creating the Database File, 495
   Importing the Data, 497
   Exporting Q&A Data to 1-2-3, 498
   Using the Exported Q&A Data, 500
Summary, 502

A   Using 1-2-3 on a Network, 503

Understanding Networking, 503
Installing 1-2-3 on a Network, 505
   Creating Server Directories, 506
   Assigning Access Rights, 507
   Mapping the 1-2-3 Directory, 508
   Initializing the Disk, 509
   Copying the Files, 510
   Initializing the Count, 510
      Specifying the Count, 511
      Modifying the License Overflow Message, 511
      Viewing the 1-2-3 Log File, 512
Using 1-2-3 on a Network, 512
   Creating Personal Directories, 512
   Installing 1-2-3, 514
   Changing the Directory, 515
   Printing on a Network, 516
   Ending the 1-2-3 Session, 516

Index, 517

INTRODUCTION

A decade ago, *VisiCalc*, the first electronic spreadsheet, was introduced for the Apple II family of computers. Almost immediately the computer press pronounced VisiCalc the software that legitimized the desktop computer in the American office. VisiCalc's creators developed a version for the IBM PC but, before it caught on, Lotus Development Corporation released a similar but superior product called *1-2-3*. Lotus 1-2-3 quickly became the spreadsheet software of choice for the PC hardware platform. 1-2-3 has evolved since its first version in 1983, adding features that users wanted and needed.

The 1-2-3 core program has constantly improved, adding features such as character-string manipulation, a way to recover from mistakes, and an environment for creating three-dimensional worksheets. Many add-in programs also have appeared, designed by Lotus and by third-party developers. Using one or more of these add-ins, you can customize 1-2-3 to suit your needs.

1-2-3's users also have evolved. All over the world, legions of enthusiastic spreadsheet designers continually develop applications with 1-2-3's new and long-standing features and with the growing number of add-ins. *1-2-3 Beyond the Basics* is for everyone who wants to join the ranks of experienced users by learning 1-2-3's sometimes hidden capabilities.

What Is Contained in This Book?

1-2-3 Beyond the Basics goes beyond the material covered in Que Corporation's *Using 1-2-3* books. The *Using* series of 1-2-3 books serves the needs of beginning and intermediate users, covering the basics of performing a task (for example, creating a graph) and ways to improve on the basic skills. The aim of *1-2-3 Beyond the Basics* is to help you improve on what you have learned and to teach you to use features found only in the newer 1-2-3 versions. This book doesn't concentrate on teaching the keystrokes for creating a pie graph or for totaling a column of numbers with @SUM; instead, it discusses ways to establish all graph ranges in one operation and how to use several range arguments in one @SUM formula.

Who Should Read This Book?

The majority of this book is written from the assumption that you have used 1-2-3 for some time, are comfortable with its basic operations, and have created useful, functional applications with 1-2-3. Starting with this base of knowledge, you can use this book to learn more advanced but lesser-known techniques for coaxing extra value from the software.

If you are a relatively new or infrequent 1-2-3 user, however, begin by reading Chapter 1, "An Overview of 1-2-3 Basics." This chapter is especially helpful if you start 1-2-3 and work through the examples as you read.

For more experienced users, this book provides advice designed to help you get more out of your software. It demonstrates intermediate and advanced techniques for handling data, using the /File and /Print commands, designing useful and efficient formulas, and working with graphs and macros. This book also provides guidelines for developing different types of 1-2-3 applications and for using 1-2-3 in conjunction with other software programs.

Which Versions of 1-2-3 Are Covered?

This book specifically covers Lotus 1-2-3 Releases 2.01, 2.2, 2.3, 3, and 3.1. Some sections concentrate on the new features of later versions, but most of the material in this book also applies to Release 2.01. In some cases, alternative approaches are provided for accomplishing the same objective with different versions of 1-2-3.

How Is This Book Organized?

This book is composed of four major parts. Part I contains only the first chapter, which explains the basics of starting and using 1-2-3. Part II contains seven chapters describing effective ways to use and optimize several areas of 1-2-3's capabilities. Part III contains three chapters that help you to create different types of 1-2-3 applications. Part IV contains five chapters that detail ways to add to 1-2-3's power by using it with other PC software. The Appendix addresses the special considerations of using 1-2-3 on a local area network.

Part I: Reviewing 1-2-3 Basics

Chapter 1, "An Overview of 1-2-3 Basics," guides you through starting 1-2-3—providing a tour of the 1-2-3 environment, defining terms such as *worksheet*, *frame*, *control panel*, and *cell*, and explaining how to move the cell pointer around the worksheet and how to enter data. As the chapter progresses, you learn how to develop a simple application and the significance of each step. The chapter shows you how to create formulas, save a worksheet, adjust formats, define ranges, create graphs, and develop database applications. All of the beginning material in this book is found in Chapter 1; you can skip this chapter if you have already mastered the basics of 1-2-3.

Part II: Optimizing 1-2-3

Chapter 2, "Designing Applications," discusses concepts to consider before creating your first formula or macro. It compares the process of using macros to handle a worksheet's mathematical operations with using formulas that perform the same task. It also illustrates ways to manage the appearance of worksheets and to make them more user-friendly, and demonstrates ways to lay out a worksheet to allow for later modifications.

Chapter 3, "Working with Data," shows some faster ways to enter large volumes of data into a worksheet and suggests ways to avoid problems when entering labels beginning with numerals (such as street addresses). This chapter also discusses ways to assign formats to ranges or to entire worksheets and considers in detail the workings of the /Copy, /Move, /Range Value, and /Range Transpose commands.

Chapter 4, "Managing Files," goes beyond saving and retrieving worksheet files; you learn how to manipulate parts of files with the /File Xtract and /File Combine commands and ways to create applications spanning several worksheet files by using /File Combine and the file-linking feature.

Chapter 5, "Printing Reports," covers advanced techniques for core-program printing in the various 1-2-3 versions—including changing printer styles within a print range, adjusting margins, and using headers, footers, and print borders—and it shows you how to print the worksheets you have enhanced with the Allways and Wysiwyg add-ins.

Chapter 6, "Working with Formulas and Functions," discusses ways to create formulas that save memory and speed up recalculation. You see how to create efficient formulas by applying the rules of operator precedence, using Boolean algebra, and planning formulas carefully. Chapter 6 also discusses several of 1-2-3's functions and some unexpected uses for them.

Chapter 7, "Creating and Printing Graphs," explains why graphs are useful tools for presenting data and tells you which graph types to use for different purposes. The chapter identifies quick ways to convert worksheet ranges to graphs in the various 1-2-3 versions. You learn how to plot data of different magnitudes on the same graph, enhance 1-2-3 graphs with the Allways and Wysiwyg add-ins, and print graphs.

Chapter 8, "Writing Macros," covers ways to name and run macros, create macros by recording keystrokes, and use the advanced macro commands (those that do not duplicate keys on the keyboard). This chapter also discusses the importance of subroutines and shows you how to create and use them. Finally, it shows you how to create macros that exist outside the current worksheet—in macro libraries or in open Release 3.x files.

Part III: Creating 1-2-3 Applications

Chapter 9, "Using 1-2-3 for Business Presentations," helps you use 1-2-3 to create visually appealing printouts that you can convert to transparencies or handouts. It progresses from simple text charts to effective graphical presentations, annotating graphs with short passages of text and illustrating textual reports with graphs. You learn to create presentations using 1-2-3 alone and using 1-2-3 with Allways or Wysiwyg.

Chapter 10, "Using 1-2-3 for Financial and Accounting Applications," focuses on tools you need when using 1-2-3 to track dollars and cents. You learn ways to work with the financial functions and how to compute financial values that have no designated functions. The chapter discusses simple ways to create loan-amortization tables for a variety of situations, how to assign dates to the rows of a financial table, and how to create tables that are always the right size for the span of time covered. Finally, you learn how to create financial models that are easy to use and resistant to user error.

Chapter 11, "Using 1-2-3 as a Database Manager," discusses ways to use criteria ranges effectively, how to set up output ranges that don't corrupt worksheet data, how to use the database statistical (@D) functions, how to create and use disk-based databases with Release 3.x, and how to use your 1-2-3 database to generate reports.

Part IV: Using 1-2-3 with Other Programs

Chapter 12, "Using Add-Ins with 1-2-3," examines the alternatives available if 1-2-3 doesn't offer the built-in features you need. The chapter discusses many different types of add-ins, including tools that help you debug and improve your current worksheets, find optimal solutions to complex problems, and use 1-2-3 for word processing or project management. Methods for creating your own add-ins and functions are considered, for situations where no existing add-in product offers a solution.

Chapter 13, "Using 1-2-3 with Presentation Programs," shows you ways that 1-2-3 can be used with the graphics programs Freelance Plus,

Harvard Graphics, CorelDRAW!, First Publisher, Ventura Publisher, and PageMaker. 1-2-3 has graphing capabilities, but you can add flair to your 1-2-3 graphs with these programs.

Chapter 14, "Using 1-2-3 with Word Processing Programs," discusses how you can integrate 1-2-3 worksheets with text from WordPerfect, Microsoft Word, Word for Windows, and Professional Write. When you want to describe worksheet data, importing the worksheet into your word processing software's text file format is easier than retyping it.

Chapter 15, "Using 1-2-3 with Financial Programs," explains how you can use 1-2-3 with Symphony, Quattro Pro, Excel, Quicken, and TurboTax. You occasionally may want to exchange worksheet data with someone who uses another spreadsheet program; most of these programs read and write 1-2-3 worksheets easily. At tax time, you may need to use information stored in 1-2-3 with your tax-preparation software or your financial management program. This chapter shows you how to accomplish these objectives.

Chapter 16, "Using 1-2-3 with Database Programs," describes using 1-2-3 with dBASE, Paradox, and Q&A. 1-2-3's built-in database commands sort and retrieve data, but you occasionally may need a database program with more extensive data management and reporting capabilities than those offered by 1-2-3.

Appendix

The Appendix, "Using 1-2-3 on a Network," discusses installing, managing, and using 1-2-3 on a network. Installation takes time and requires some help from a network supervisor; however, the Appendix provides a guide to the important concepts of network installation, configuration, and protection.

How Can You Learn More about 1-2-3?

Using 1-2-3 for DOS Release 2.3, Special Edition (covering Releases 2.01, 2.2, and 2.3) and *Using 1-2-3 Release 3.1*, Second Edition (covering Releases 3 and 3.1) are Que's most comprehensive guides to the latest versions of 1-2-3. These books introduce the program's basic worksheet, database, and graphics capabilities, showing how to set up a worksheet, use 1-2-3 commands and functions, and create and print reports and graphs. Installation instructions, a complete Command Reference, and a pull-out command chart are provided.

1-2-3 Database Techniques, which covers Releases 2.01, 2.2, and 3, explains the basic concepts behind database management and acquaints you with 1-2-3's capabilities as a database management system. The book covers the principles for designing efficient, powerful data management systems, and teaches you how to link external and multiple databases.

1-2-3 Graphics Techniques, which covers Releases 2.01, 2.2, and 3, contains the concepts and techniques you need to produce the most effective graphics with 1-2-3. Practical examples take you step-by-step through the process of creating a range of graph types, using macros for graphing, printing presentation-quality graphs, and even making slides and annotating graphs.

The first half of *1-2-3 Macro Library*, Third Edition (Releases 2.01, 2.2, and 3) covers creating macros from the fundamentals to advanced techniques. The second half presents an arsenal of ready-to-use macros (also included on disk) for many 1-2-3 operations, such as database management and file operations. The book focuses on macros, assuming that the reader has some experience with 1-2-3's worksheet environment, basic commands, functions, and formulas.

All of these books can be found in better bookstores worldwide. In the United States, you can call Que at 1-800-428-5331 to order books or obtain more information.

Conventions Used in This Book

Certain conventions are used in *1-2-3 Beyond the Basics* to help you understand the techniques and macros described in the text.

Special Typefaces and Representations

Words printed in uppercase include range names (SALES), functions (@FIND), mode (READY) and status (END) indicators, and cell references (A:B19). Also presented in uppercase letters are DOS commands (CHKDSK) and file names (STATUS.WK1).

In most cases, keys are represented as they appear on the keyboard. The arrow keys are represented by name (for example, "the up-arrow key"). The Print Screen key is abbreviated PrtSc, Page Down is PgDn, Insert is Ins, and so on; on your keyboard, these key names may be spelled out or abbreviated differently.

Ctrl–Break indicates that you press and hold down the Ctrl key while you press the Break key. Other hyphenated key combinations (such as Alt–A, Alt–B, and Ctrl–Alt–Del) are performed in the same manner. If key combinations are not hyphenated, don't hold down any of the keys; press each key once in the order listed (for example, End Home).

Words or phrases defined for the first time appear in *italic*. Characters that you are to type appear in **boldface**. Words and prompts appearing on-screen are printed in a `special typeface`.

In the text, the slash and the first letter of each menu selection from 1-2-3's main menu system are in boldface; for example, **/R**ange Format Currency or "Select the Global option." When abbreviated, the command appears in lowercase, such as **/rfc**. Commands from the Wysiwyg menu begin with a special colon; for example, **:Graph Edit**.

This book refers to the function keys (F1 through F10) by the names of the functions performed during a 1-2-3 session. The text says, for example, "Press the Name key (F3)" or "Press Name (F3)." Several of the function keys produce a different result when used in combination with the Alt key, and the available Alt-function key combinations have their own names. The text refers to these combinations by name as if they were separate keys; for example, by saying "Press the Run key (Alt–F3)" or "Press Alt–F3 (Run)." Keeping track of 1-2-3's names for the function keys is a good idea because you use those key names when writing macros. If you want a macro to move the cell pointer to a certain location, for example, the command to use is {GOTO}, not {F5}.

Macro Conventions

Conventions pertaining to macros deserve special mention:

1. Macros named with Alt-*letter* combinations appear with the backslash (\) and single-character name in lowercase: \a. In this example, \a indicates that you hold down the Alt key while you press the A key.

2. 1-2-3's advanced macro commands are enclosed within braces, such as {WINDOWSOFF}, when used in a syntax line or within a macro but appear without braces in the text itself, as in the following statement: "The WINDOWSOFF command suppresses updating of the screen."

3. 1-2-3 menu keystrokes in a macro line appear in lowercase: /rnc.

4. Range names within macros appear in uppercase: /rncTEST~.

5. In illustrations and within the text, representations of direction keys, such as {DOWN}; function keys, such as {CALC}; and editing keys, such as {DEL}; appear in uppercase and are enclosed in braces.

6. The Enter key is represented in macros by the tilde (~). Note that throughout the text, the term *Enter* is used instead of *Return* for the Enter key.

General Conventions

Text that refers to 1-2-3 Releases 2.01, 2.2, and 2.3 may be summarized as Release 2.x. Similarly, text referring to 1-2-3 Releases 3 and 3.1 may be summarized as Release 3.x.

 This paragraph format beginning with the word "Caution" warns the reader of hazardous procedures (for example, activities that delete files).

 This paragraph format beginning with the word "Tip" suggests easier or alternate methods of executing a procedure, or shortcuts to simplify or speed up the processes described in the text.

Part One

REVIEWING 1-2-3 BASICS

Chapter One

AN OVERVIEW OF 1-2-3 BASICS

The purpose of this book is to give you some intermediate and advanced skills—to move you, as the book's title implies, beyond the basics of entering labels and values and adding them up with @SUM formulas. The book is written from the assumption that you have been using 1-2-3 for a while and are familiar with the program but may not know how to use all of the commands or functions, how to work efficiently, or how to design useful and efficient worksheet applications.

If you are a new 1-2-3 user and many of the concepts presented in this chapter are unfamiliar to you, consider consulting Que's line of *1-2-3 QuickStart* or *Using 1-2-3* books. The *1-2-3 QuickStart* series is intended for beginning 1-2-3 users and provides a step-by-step tutorial approach to learning 1-2-3 basics. Each of the books in Que's *Using 1-2-3* series is a comprehensive reference and tutorial aimed at beginning to intermediate 1-2-3 users. At the time this book was printed, the following books in these two lines were available: *1-2-3 Release 2.2 QuickStart*, Second Edition; *1-2-3 for DOS Release 2.3 QuickStart*; *1-2-3 Release 3.1 QuickStart*, Second Edition; *Using 1-2-3 Release 2.2*, Special Edition; *Using 1-2-3 for DOS Release 2.3*, Special Edition; and *Using 1-2-3 Release 3.1*, Second Edition.

If you already use 1-2-3 on a regular basis and you feel comfortable starting the program and devising simple worksheets, you can skip this chapter and proceed to Part II: Optimizing 1-2-3. If you're relatively new to 1-2-3 or use 1-2-3 infrequently, however, read Part I and work through the exercises. When you understand the material in Part I, the value of the intermediate-to-advanced material in Parts II, III, and IV increases.

Starting 1-2-3

Typically, the files comprising the 1-2-3 program are copied to a hard disk and are in a subdirectory. You can make that directory current by entering the operating system command **CD\123** (substitute the correct directory name for **123** if necessary).

When the 1-2-3 directory is current, you can start the program in one of two ways. The first method is to start the Lotus Access System, which enables you to start the 1-2-3 worksheet program and the utility programs that come with 1-2-3, such as the Install program or the Translate utility. When you start the Access System from the operating-system prompt by typing **LOTUS** and pressing Enter, an Access System screen appears. If you use 1-2-3 Release 2.2, the Access System screen looks like figure 1.1. The screen looks like figure 1.2 for 1-2-3 Releases 3 and 3.1.

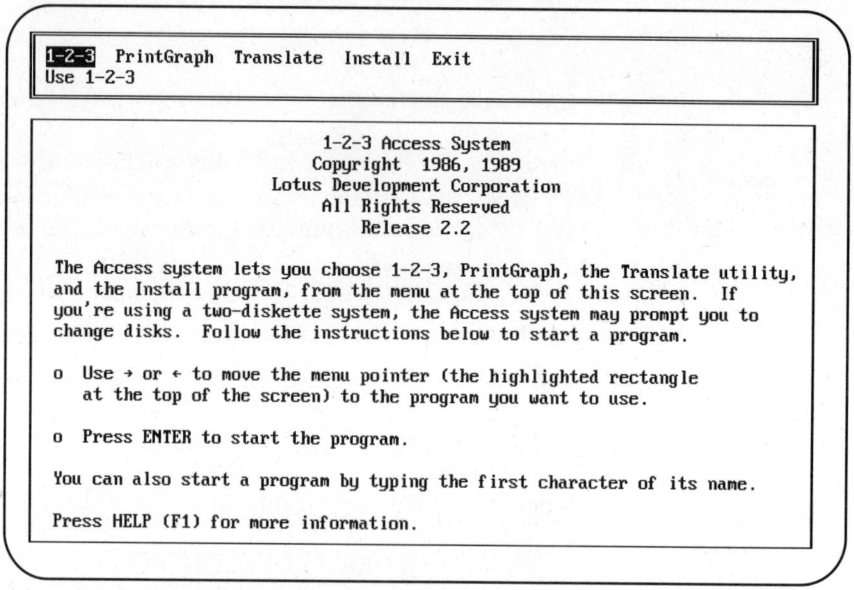

```
┌──────────────────────────────────────────────────────────────┐
│ 1-2-3  PrintGraph  Translate  Install  Exit                    │
│ Use 1-2-3                                                      │
└──────────────────────────────────────────────────────────────┘

                    1-2-3 Access System
                    Copyright  1986, 1989
                 Lotus Development Corporation
                    All Rights Reserved
                       Release 2.2

   The Access system lets you choose 1-2-3, PrintGraph, the Translate utility,
   and the Install program, from the menu at the top of this screen.  If
   you're using a two-diskette system, the Access system may prompt you to
   change disks.  Follow the instructions below to start a program.

   o  Use → or ← to move the menu pointer (the highlighted rectangle
      at the top of the screen) to the program you want to use.

   o  Press ENTER to start the program.

   You can also start a program by typing the first character of its name.

   Press HELP (F1) for more information.
```

Fig. 1.1. The access screen for 1-2-3 Release 2.2.

The top two rows of the Access System screen consist of a menu. To select an option from the menu, you can use the right- or left-arrow keys to highlight the desired option (then press Enter), or you can type the first character of the option. Because the **1-2-3** option is always highlighted when you start the Access System, just press Enter to start 1-2-3.

The second way to start 1-2-3 is directly from the operating system prompt—by typing **123** and pressing Enter. This procedure starts the 1-2-3 worksheet without going through the Access System menu.

Getting Started with the Worksheet

When you start 1-2-3 Release 2.01 or 2.2, you usually see a blank worksheet like the one shown in figure 1.3. The Release 2.3 screen is similar but lines separate the row numbers and column letters in the worksheet frame. Releases 3 and 3.1 display an opening screen like the one shown in figure 1.4.

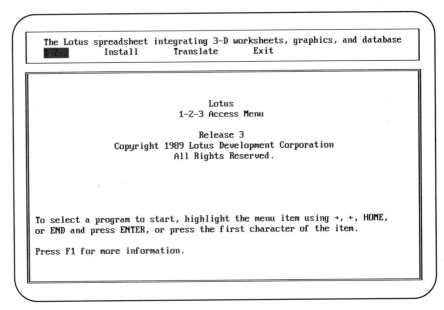

Fig. 1.2. *The access screen for 1-2-3 Releases 3 and 3.1.*

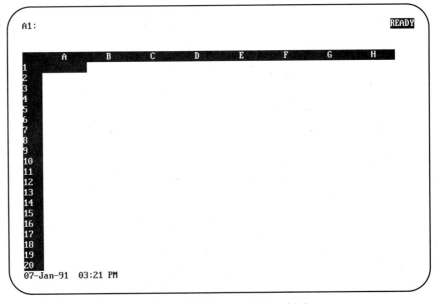

Fig. 1.3. *The blank worksheet in 1-2-3 Releases 2.01 and 2.2.*

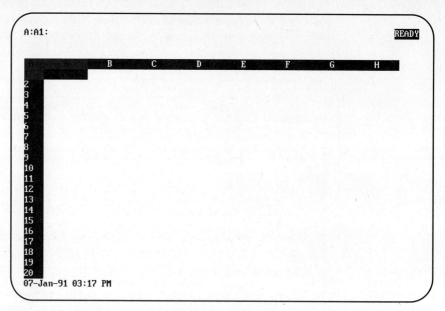

Fig. 1.4. *The blank worksheet in 1-2-3 Releases 3 and 3.1.*

The 1-2-3 opening screen differs from figures 1.3 and 1.4 if your system has an auto-loading worksheet file, or an add-in program that is attached and invoked automatically upon starting 1-2-3. You can reset 1-2-3 to "bare-bones" to follow this discussion by pressing / (slash) and then pressing **W** to select **W**orksheet, **E** to select **E**rase, and **Y** to select **Y**es. (Remember that you also can select a menu option by highlighting it and pressing Enter.) If your screen still looks different from figure 1.3 or 1.4, an add-in probably is attached. In this case, hold down the Alt key and press the F10 key; then press **C** to select **C**lear and **Q** to select **Q**uit. This process clears all add-ins from memory.

Elements of the 1-2-3 Screen

The most noticeable feature of the 1-2-3 worksheet is the inverse-video border appearing along the left side and across the top of the screen. This border (the *frame*) indicates which of the 8,192 *rows* and 256 *columns* are displayed on-screen. In each figure, the numbers 1 to 20 appear down the left side of the frame and the letters A to H along the top of the frame. The numbers correspond to the top 20 rows and the letters to the first 8 columns of the worksheet. Figure 1.4, which illustrates the blank worksheet in Release 3.x, displays an additional letter A at the top left corner of the frame to indicate that the first worksheet is being displayed. The worksheet is much larger than the area you can see at any one time.

The 1-2-3 worksheet is divided into units called *cells*. A cell is the intersection of a column and a row. Cells are designated by a combination of the column letter and the row number. Directly below the letter A at the top of the frame and at the same level as the number 1 on the side of the frame is cell A1. Below the letter D and at the same level as the number 15 is cell D15. With Release 3.x, the designation also includes the worksheet letter. The cell in column D, row 15 of the first worksheet is designated as A:D15. The combinations of worksheet letters, column letters, and row numbers are called *cell addresses*, *cell coordinates*, or *cell references*.

Inside the corner of the frame is a rectangle that normally is the same color as the frame. This is the *cell pointer*. The cell pointer indicates which cell is *current*—which cell will be affected when you enter a value or label. The cell pointer is often (incorrectly) called the cursor. The cursor is different from the cell pointer; it appears as an underscore, usually in the middle of the cell pointer but sometimes elsewhere on-screen.

The three rows above the frame are the *control panel*. At the extreme left of the top row you see the characters A1 (Release 2.x) or A:A1 (Release 3.x). These characters tell you which cell is current. At the extreme right of the top row is the *mode indicator*. In figures 1.3 and 1.4, 1-2-3 is in READY mode. The second and third rows of the control panel are used for menus, or for information about a cell being edited or a range being modified.

Below the frame at far left is the *date-and-time indicator* (in Release 3.x, the *file indicator*), which shows the date and time currently stored in your computer. The remainder of the bottom row of the screen is used for various indicators that tell you if UNDO mode is enabled, if 1-2-3 is currently running a macro, or if certain keys, such as Num Lock or Scroll Lock, have been pressed.

Moving around the Worksheet

When you access the 1-2-3 program, the current cell is cell A1. You can use the arrow keys to move the cell pointer to another cell. On many keyboards, the arrow keys are the same as the numeric keypad. You can use the arrow keys of the numeric keypad if the keyboard's number lock is turned off. If Num Lock is turned on, the word NUM appears in inverse video at the bottom of the 1-2-3 screen.

If you have Release 2.3 and want to use a mouse, the mouse software must be loaded before you start 1-2-3 (the AUTOEXEC program that runs automatically when you turn on the computer usually handles the loading of mouse software). With the mouse, you can make menu selections, select groups of cells, and move the cell pointer around the worksheet. When you click the left mouse button with the mouse pointer in a cell, the cell pointer jumps to the position of the mouse pointer. The arrow icons on the right side of the screen also can move the cell pointer in all directions, when you select them using the mouse. With Release 2.3, you can use the mouse with or without the Wysiwyg add-in attached. With Release 3.1, you can move the cell pointer with the mouse only if Wysiwyg is attached.

In all versions of 1-2-3, you can move the cell pointer on a two-dimensional plane—up and down or left and right. Release 3.x can create worksheets with the third dimension, depth. The simple worksheet models described in this chapter use two dimensions (height and width). Later chapters of this book discuss the use of three-dimensional worksheets in detail, but you must understand how to move the cell pointer between worksheets. (If you use Release 2.x, skip the following paragraph.)

Press / to access the 1-2-3 menu. Press **W** to select **Worksheet**, **I** to select **Insert**, **S** to select **Sheet**, **A** to select **After**, press **2**, and press Enter. You have added worksheet B and worksheet C to your original worksheet (A). The cell pointer is in worksheet B, as indicated by the worksheet letter at the upper left corner of the frame. Within each new worksheet, you can move the cell pointer up, down, left, and right just as you did in worksheet A. You also can move the cell pointer forward and backward through the worksheets. To move the cell pointer from worksheet B to worksheet A, hold down the Ctrl key and press the PgDn key. Hold down the Ctrl key and press PgUp to move the cell pointer back to worksheet B and then to worksheet C. Press Ctrl–Home to move the cell pointer back to worksheet A before continuing with this section.

Another way to move the cell pointer is to press the GoTo key (F5) and enter the cell coordinates. To move the cell pointer to cell E15, press F5, type the characters **E15**, and press Enter. When you complete the GoTo operation by pressing Enter, the cell pointer moves directly to cell E15.

Throughout this book, the verb enter *means to press the Enter key after typing characters. The instruction* enter **E15** *is the same as* type **E15** *and* press Enter.

You can move the cell pointer back to cell A1 by pressing the Home key. If you move the cell pointer beyond column H or row 20, the visible portion of the worksheet moves. Moving the cell pointer one column at a time to the right shifts the worksheet so that columns B to I and then C to J are displayed, and so on. When you move the cell pointer one row at a time below row 20, rows 2 to 21 and then 3 to 22 are visible, and so forth.

When you press the Tab key, your view of the worksheet shifts to the next full screen to the right. If columns A to H are currently visible, and you press Tab from any column in A through H, columns I to P become visible. The cell pointer stays in the same row but moves to column I. If you create a large worksheet application, you can scan it using the Tab key. As you continue to press Tab, you see all of the columns of the worksheet without skipping and without overlapping.

If you hold a Shift key and press Tab, the opposite happens: the column just to the left of the screen becomes the far-right column of the screen. If columns I to P are visible, for example, when you press Shift–Tab, columns A to H become visible.

Holding down the Ctrl key and pressing the right-arrow key has the same effect as pressing Tab. Hold Ctrl and press the left-arrow key to get the Shift–Tab effect.

Pressing PgDn (the Page Down key) shifts the worksheet to show you the next screen down. If Rows 1 to 20 are visible and you press PgDn, rows 21 to 40 become visible. If the cell pointer is in row 7 when you press PgDn, it ends up in row 27 (note that the cell pointer appears to stay in one place on-screen). Pressing PgUp reverses the process, displaying the 20 rows above the top row currently on-screen.

Entering Labels

A cell can contain a label, a value, or a formula (a value computed by 1-2-3). This discussion focuses on how text and numbers are represented as a label or a value. Suppose that you want to set up a worksheet like the one in figure 1.5. If you move the cell pointer to cell B3 and press **S**, the mode indicator (at the upper right corner of the screen) changes from READY to LABEL, as shown in figure 1.6. This change indicates that 1-2-3 treats the entry you're typing as a label, making this determination from the first character typed. Typing a letter of the alphabet or certain other characters shifts 1-2-3 from READY mode to LABEL mode. Note also that the letter S appears on the second line of the control panel.

If you type the label **Sales Report** and press Enter, the label appears in the worksheet. Notice in figure 1.5 that the label is too long to appear entirely in cell B3 and extends into cell C3. The entire label is still part of cell B3, however—even the three characters that appear to be in cell C3. The top line of the control panel shows the contents of cell B3 as 'Sales Report. 1-2-3 placed the apostrophe at the beginning of the label. The use of the apostrophe is discussed next.

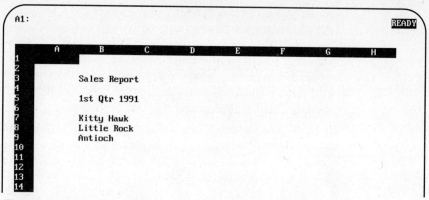

Fig. 1.5. A worksheet with labels entered for a sales-reported model.

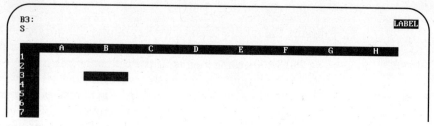

Fig. 1.6. A typed letter in the control panel (upper left), which changes the mode indicator (upper right) to LABEL.

When you type a numeral as the first character of a cell entry, 1-2-3 shifts to VALUE mode. Typing an entry such as **1st Qtr 1991** and pressing Enter causes 1-2-3 to beep. The entry is not accepted because 1-2-3 cannot treat the combination of numerals and letters as a value. Press Esc to cancel the entry and return 1-2-3 to READY mode.

A label that uses a numeral or a mathematical symbol as the first character must begin with a *label prefix*. The most common default label prefix is the apostrophe. If you begin a cell entry by typing an apostrophe, the mode indicator changes to LABEL. You then can type the characters **1st Qtr 1991** and press Enter. This time 1-2-3 accepts the entry.

All labels have label prefixes. The difference between the label entries in the previous examples is that 1-2-3 added the prefix to the label (in cell B3) beginning with a letter. You *must* type a label prefix when the label's first character is one that shifts 1-2-3 to VALUE mode.

To speed up your work, you can type the characters of a label, **Kitty Hawk** in this example, and press the down-arrow key instead of the Enter key. This action enters the label in the cell and moves the cell pointer down one cell. When you enter data in cells, you can complete an entry and move the cell pointer to another cell by pressing the left-arrow, up-arrow, right-arrow, or down-arrow keys.

Entering Values

The other type of cell entry is a value. Many people think of values as being divided into simple numbers and formulas, but 1-2-3 generally doesn't make that distinction. Figure 1.7 shows the sales report worksheet with three values in column D. If you move the cell pointer to cell D7 and begin typing the characters **4200**, 1-2-3 shifts to VALUE mode as soon as you press **4**. You can complete the entry by pressing Enter or the down-arrow key.

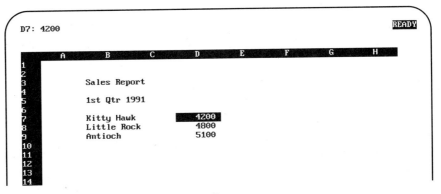

Fig. 1.7. Three values entered in column D.

If you type **\ –** and press Enter, you create a label that forms an underline—separating the numbers from the formula that sums them. Like all labels, this entry has a label prefix. In this case, the prefix is a backslash, which is the *repeat-character prefix*. Cell D10 displays nine hyphens, exactly enough to fill the cell.

What the cell *contains*, however, is a backslash and one hyphen (\ –). When a label is preceded by a backslash, 1-2-3 repeats the character(s) following the backslash until the cell is filled. Entering \ – in a cell is different from entering an apostrophe followed by nine hyphens. A cell containing a backslash as a label prefix always fills the cell completely without extending into the next cell, no matter how wide the column is. Changing the column width doesn't affect a label beginning with the backslash, as it does a label beginning with an apostrophe.

Working with Formulas

If you enter the characters **+D7+D8+D9** into cell D11, the cell displays the value 14100, as shown in figure 1.8. As the control panel shows, however, the cell contains the characters you just entered. The first plus sign causes 1-2-3 to treat the entry as a positive value. (Without the plus sign, the entry is a label, because the first character of the entry is a letter.) The other two plus signs perform the addition.

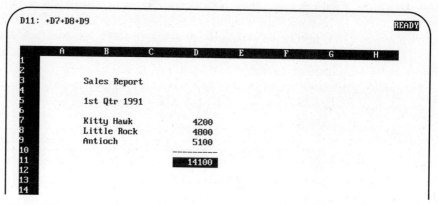

Fig. 1.8. *The underline (cell D10) and a formula that sums the three values entered.*

If you move the cell pointer to cell D7 and replace its current entry with **4201**, cell D11 displays the new total 14101. (You need not erase the cell first; the new entry replaces the existing one.) The power of 1-2-3 formulas is that the formulas change to reflect changed values in other cells on which they depend. Change cell D7 back to **4200** and cell D11's result changes back to 14100.

You also can create formulas that perform subtraction, division, multiplication, and exponentiation (raising a number to a power). The formula +D8–D7, for example, *subtracts* the value in cell D7 from the value in cell D8. The formula +D9*2 *multiplies* the value in cell D9 by 2. The formula +D9/2 *divides* the value in cell D9 by 2. Finally, +D9^2 raises the value in cell D9 to the second power. The caret (^) is the *exponentiation* character. Note that all of these formulas use a constant (the value 2) instead of being composed entirely of cell references.

You can mix operations together in the same formula; +D7*2+D9 multiplies the value in cell D7 by 2 and then adds the value in cell D9. 1-2-3 applies the generally accepted rules governing which mathematical operations are performed first. The formula +D7*2+D9 performs the multiplication first, rather than adding the 2 to the value in cell D9 and then multiplying that sum by the value in cell D7. You can add parentheses to formulas to ensure that the formulas perform operations in the order you prefer. Chapter 6 of this book discusses operator precedence and the use of parentheses in more detail.

Establishing Cell References by Pointing

You can enter the formula in cell D11 in another way—by moving the cell pointer instead of typing cell addresses to tell 1-2-3 which cells to add. Move the cell pointer to cell D11 and type a plus sign. Press the up-arrow key four times to move the cell pointer to cell D7, and type another plus sign. The cell pointer returns to cell D11 and the control panel says +D7+. Move the cell pointer to cell D8 and type a plus sign. The cell pointer returns to cell D11 again and the control panel reads +D7+D8+. Complete the formula by moving the cell pointer to cell D9 and pressing Enter. (You also can use the mouse to move the cell pointer.)

This method for creating formulas is useful if you don't know the address of another cell, or if a cell you want a formula to refer to is outside the area displayed on your computer screen.

Using Functions To Create More Powerful Formulas

Adding the values in three cells with a formula like the one in the preceding example isn't unreasonable, but adding the values in a block of 50 cells by typing cell addresses and plus signs is tedious.

Fortunately, 1-2-3 has a way to enter a formula that adds all of the values in a large area of the worksheet. The formula begins with the characters @SUM. The @ (pronounced "at") character is used by 1-2-3 to indicate that the characters following the @ constitute a specific operation. The combination of @ and the name of an operation is a *function*. The @SUM function, as its name implies, calculates the sum of a series of values. @SQRT computes the square root of a value. @CELL provides information about a specific worksheet cell. Other functions exist to handle many kinds of operations.

To add the values in cells D7, D8, and D9, you can enter the formula @SUM(D7..D9) in cell D11. The characters D7..D9 indicate a *range*, a rectangular area of the worksheet. Here the range extends from cell D7 to cell D9, inclusive. The formula adds all of the values in that range.

You can enter this formula using the arrow keys just as you did with the original formula. With the cell pointer in cell D11, type the characters **@SUM** and move the cell pointer to cell D7. When the cell pointer is at cell D7, type a period to *anchor* the cell pointer. At this point, the formula in the control panel reads *@SUM(D7..D7*. To complete the formula, move the cell pointer down two cells (to highlight the range D7 to D9), type a closing parenthesis, and press Enter. To highlight the range with the mouse, type **@SUM(**, point to cell D7, and move the mouse to D9 while holding down the left mouse button. Type a closing parenthesis and press Enter.

Using 1-2-3 Menu Commands

Entering labels, numbers, and formulas into cells is not the only way to build a worksheet application. 1-2-3 also provides a set of powerful commands that modify cells, ranges, or the entire worksheet.

When you press the slash (/) key while 1-2-3 is in READY mode, you call up the 1-2-3 *command menu*, as shown in figure 1.9. (If you use a mouse with Release 2.3 or 3.1, you can move the mouse pointer above the top frame of the worksheet into the control panel to call up the menu. In Release 3.1, you must attach Wysiwyg to use the mouse.) The menu fills the second and third rows of the control panel. The first line of the menu contains individual *menu options*. The second line lists details of the highlighted menu option. Some of the menu options, when selected, display yet another menu. When you press the slash key, for example, 1-2-3 highlights the **Worksheet** command. The menu's second line lists **Global, Delete, Insert,** and several other commands appearing in the subsequent menu if you select **Worksheet.** For menu options that don't call up another menu, a phrase is displayed explaining the highlighted option. The second-line display for the **Copy** command, for example, reads `Copy a cell or range of cells`.

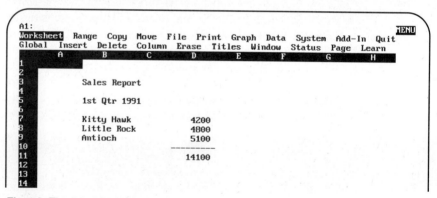

Fig. 1.9. *The 1-2-3 main menu.*

You can select a menu option in one of three ways. You can use the left- or right-arrow key or the space bar to highlight the desired option and select it by pressing Enter. You can move the mouse pointer to the option and press the left mouse button. Or you can type the first character of the option. In 1-2-3's command menus, each option has a unique first character. Selecting options with the first-character method is usually fastest. The following three sections provide some practice with the command menu.

In this book, instructions to use menu options start with the word *select*, followed by a slash and the complete name of the menu option. You may be directed to select **/R**ange **F**ormat **R**eset and press Enter. This instruction tells you to press the slash key, select **R**ange (by typing **R** or by highlighting **R**ange and pressing Enter), select **F**ormat, select **R**eset, and press Enter. Note that the first letter of each menu item is printed in bold to indicate that you can use the item by typing its first letter. You can select **/R**ange **F**ormat **R**eset, for example, by typing **/RFR** (or **/rfr**). Pressing the Esc key returns the menu pointer to the preceding menu, or the cell pointer to the worksheet in READY mode when pressed from the main menu. The right mouse button also functions as the Esc key. Pressing Ctrl Break always returns 1-2-3 to READY mode from a menu.

Using Commands To Format Cells

The formula **+D7/D$11** divides the value in cell D7 by the value in cell D11. (The meaning of the dollar sign is discussed later.) The formula's result, 0.297872, is mathematically equivalent to 29.79%, meaning that the value in cell D7 is 29.79% of the total in cell D11. You can tell 1-2-3 to display a percentage by using the 1-2-3 commands to assign a *format* to the cell.

The second menu line that appears when you highlight **R**ange on the 1-2-3 main menu includes **F**ormat, **L**abel, **E**rase, and several other commands. To assign a format, select **R**ange by pressing Enter. The items that appeared on the second line of the preceding menu are now on the first line as menu options; a new set of items appears on the second line. The **F**ormat command is highlighted. Select **F**ormat by pressing Enter and a third menu appears. Each option describes a format for worksheet cells. Press the right-arrow key until the **P**ercent command is highlighted and press Enter. 1-2-3 displays the prompt `Enter number of decimal places (0..15):` followed by 2. To accept the suggested value of 2, press Enter. Pressing Enter a second time accepts the current cell as the range to format—and cell D7 now displays 29.79%.

Using Commands To Copy Cells

After you have assigned a format to one cell, you can copy the formula in that cell, along with its format, to other cells (cells E8 and E9 in this example). To copy the cell, select **/C**opy and press Enter to select the current cell at the prompt `Enter range to copy FROM: (Copy what?` in

Release 2.3). At the succeeding prompt `Enter range to copy TO:` (`To where?` in Release 2.3), move the cell pointer down one cell, type a period to anchor the cell pointer, move the cell pointer down one more cell (cells E8 and E9 are now highlighted), and press Enter. The worksheet resembles figure 1.10. The three numbers in column E indicate that the sales from the three stores in this example represent 29.79%, 34.04%, and 36.17% of the total sales of $14,100.

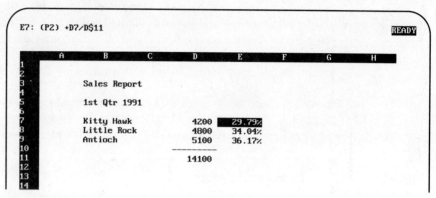

Fig. 1.10. *The result of using menu commands to format cell E7 and copy the formula to cells E8 and E9.*

What is the purpose of the dollar sign in the formula in cell E7? Dollar signs in formulas make the row or column portion of a cell reference *absolute*. Move the cell pointer to cell E8 and then to E9; the formulas (as listed in the control panel) are +D8/D$11 and +D9/D$11, respectively. The original formula is a division operation using the value in the cell to the left as the numerator. When you copy the original formula, the resulting formulas also use the values in cells to the immediate left as numerators. The dollar sign before the 11 means that you want the denominator in all of the copies to be from row 11. When 1-2-3 copies the formula, it doesn't change the reference to row 11 in the denominator as it changes the reference to row 7 in the numerator. Chapter 3 of this book provides more information on the /Copy command and absolute references.

Using Commands To Format Entire Worksheets

The command menu can be used to assign a format to the entire worksheet. This format applies to all cells except those to which you assign a range format (as in the preceding example, with range E7..E9). Select /Worksheet Global Format Currency and press **0**. Your worksheet resembles figure 1.11. The values in column D now include a dollar sign and commas between thousands but no decimal point or decimal places. If you enter another value in the worksheet (other than in range

D7..D11), the new value also has the Currency format with no decimal places. You can override this format (before or after entering values) by selecting /Range Format, choosing a different format, and specifying a range where the format will be applied.

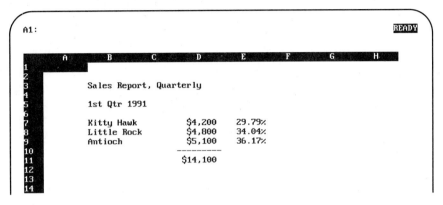

Fig. 1.11. *The result of using a global format to display values with a dollar sign and no decimal places.*

Saving and Retrieving 1-2-3 Files

If you want to use your 1-2-3 worksheets again at a later time, you must *save* them. Saving a worksheet means storing the data in a disk file from which 1-2-3 can retrieve the worksheet, including its contents and formatting specifications.

You don't have to start from scratch each time you begin a new 1-2-3 session; just retrieve your saved worksheet. You retrieve a worksheet when you want to add new data to it, modify it, or continue work on a larger project than you can complete in one session.

Preparing To Save Your Work

Before you save a worksheet as a file, you must decide *where* to store the file. Most people use 1-2-3 on a computer equipped with a hard disk drive (also called a fixed disk drive), which is usually designated as *drive C*. Hard disks typically are divided into *directories*—artificial divisions of the disk, each containing its own set of files.

It's a good idea to establish a directory just for the worksheet files you create using 1-2-3. You can set up a directory while working in 1-2-3 by selecting /System. This command temporarily stops your 1-2-3 session and gives you access to operating-system commands (DOS or OS/2).

Type **MD C:\123FILES** and press Enter. (*MD* is the DOS command for *make directory*.) If you prefer, substitute a different name (up to eight characters) for **123FILES**. To return to your 1-2-3 session, type **EXIT** and press Enter.

You can make 123FILES the *current* directory (1-2-3 normally saves files in the current directory) by selecting /**F**ile **D**irectory. The prompt `Enter current directory:` appears, followed by the name of the default directory. To change this directory, type the name of the directory you use for 1-2-3 files—for example, **C:\123FILES**—and press Enter. (If you prefer, you can save 1-2-3 files on floppy disks instead of the computer's hard disk.)

Saving the Worksheet

When you have created and selected a directory for your 1-2-3 files, you can save worksheets in that directory by selecting /**F**ile **S**ave and entering a file name of up to eight characters. To save the sample worksheet you have created, select /**F**ile **S**ave and enter a name such as **SAMPLE**. If a file with that name already exists, a menu appears with the choices **Cancel**, **R**eplace, and **B**ackup. (Backup doesn't appear in all versions.) If you don't want to eliminate an existing file, select Cancel, reissue the /**F**ile **S**ave command, and try a different name.

When you save a worksheet the first time, you establish a file name for it. The next time you select /**F**ile **S**ave, the prompt is followed by the new name you provided for the file. Press Enter to accept the existing file name. When the Cancel/**R**eplace/**B**ackup menu appears, select **R**eplace.

Save your worksheets before you finish them. The more often you save, the less work lost if an accident occurs. If you save every 10 minutes while developing a worksheet, an unexpected power failure results in a maximum loss of 10 minutes of work.

Saving the same worksheet under more than one name is occasionally useful. Suppose that you need to develop two similar worksheets for tracking office supplies expenditures and maintenance supplies expenditures. Start by creating the office supplies worksheet, saving it (frequently) under the name **OFCSUPP**. When the first worksheet is finished, save it one last time as **OFCSUPP**. Then select /**F**ile **S**ave and enter **MTSUPP** at the `Enter name of file to save:` prompt. The existing file name disappears when you type the first letter. This process creates a new file and establishes **MTSUPP** as the current file name. Make the changes to convert the office supplies worksheet to a maintenance supplies worksheet. When you select /**F**ile **S**ave again, the `Enter name of file to save:` prompt is followed by `MTSUPP`.

Releases 3 and 3.1 can read and write Release 2.x files. Files saved in Release 3.x have a WK3 extension instead of WK1. To save a file in Release 3.x that can be shared with 2.x users, type the file name with a WK1 extension. Any formatting information not usable in Release 2.x is not saved.

Retrieving Files and Starting New Files

When you have created several 1-2-3 files, you may want to update or modify one file and then (after saving the file) work with a different file. You are not required to clear the existing worksheet from memory before retrieving a new file.

To illustrate this principle, save the file once again in its current state; then select **/F**ile **S**ave, press Enter to accept the existing file name, and select **R**eplace. Then make a change in the worksheet. Select **/R**ange Format **P**ercent, enter **1**, highlight range **E7..E9**, and press Enter. Select **/F**ile **S**ave and enter a new file name (for example, **SAMPLE2**). Select **/F**ile **R**etrieve; the names of the worksheet files in the current directory appear in the control panel. (This list may consist of only the two files you have just created.) To retrieve the original file, highlight its name and press Enter. You also can select a file to retrieve by typing its name; you don't need to type the WK1 or WK3 extension. The original version of the file (with two decimal places in column E) replaces the later version of the file.

Sometimes you may want to use a worksheet, save it, and build a new worksheet from scratch. In that case, you *do* want to remove the existing worksheet from memory. After you have saved your work, select **/W**orksheet **E**rase **Y**es.

Modifying the Worksheet

This section discusses ways to customize your worksheets. 1-2-3 offers many options for controlling the look and functionality of a worksheet. Varying column widths, for example, can enhance the worksheet's appearance or accommodate large values. You can change the way the worksheet displays numbers or recalculates formulas, or try different values in the worksheet to see how the changes affect results. You also can edit the contents of cells and erase cells containing unwanted entries.

Setting Column Widths

Now that you are familiar with some of the basic principles of working with disk files, return to the SAMPLE2 worksheet (select /File Retrieve, type or highlight **SAMPLE2**, and press Enter).

Rather than using currency with zero decimal places as the default format, change the format to two decimal places. Select /Worksheet Global Format Currency and press Enter to accept the suggested value of 2 decimal places. You may expect the formulas in column D to read $4,200.00, $4,800.00, and so forth. Instead, the cells are filled with asterisks. The problem is that column D is not wide enough to display values in the thousands with a dollar sign, a comma, a decimal point, and two decimal places. Values don't extend out of their cells as labels do.

To remedy this problem, widen column D to accommodate more characters. Move the cell pointer to any cell in column D and select /Worksheet Column Set-Width. 1-2-3 displays the prompt `Enter column width (1..240):` followed by the current column width of 9. Use the right-arrow key to widen the column one character at a time. The first time you press the right-arrow key, column D widens to 10 characters and the values in range D7..D9 display the correct values instead of asterisks. The second time, the column widens to 11 characters and the formula in cell D11 displays the correct result. When the column is the desired width, complete the operation by pressing Enter.

To make a column narrower, select /Worksheet Column Set-Width and use the left-arrow key to narrow the column one character at a time. You also can set the width by entering a number. To set the width of a column to 25 characters, select /Worksheet Column Set-Width, type **25**, and press Enter.

You can set a default format for the entire worksheet as easily as you set a format for a range; similarly, you can set a default column width, affecting all columns except the ones you size with /Worksheet Column Set-Width. To set a standard column width of 8, select /Worksheet Global Column-Width, press **8**, and press Enter. All columns except D adjust to 8 characters in width.

To reset a column with a special width to the default width, move the cell pointer to that column and select /Worksheet Column Reset-Width (instead of selecting /Worksheet Column Set-Width and entering a number). When you use the Reset-Width option, the width of the column adjusts to the default width. If the width of a column is set with /Worksheet Column Set-Width, the width does not change even if the global width is changed. If the global width is 9 and you set the width of one column to 9, that column stays at 9 even when you change the global width. Use the Reset-Width option when you want a column to adjust if the global width is changed.

Performing What-If Tests

The sample worksheet reports first-quarter sales for a hypothetical store chain. In the next example, the worksheet is expanded to show projected sales in the second quarter if sales increase by 10%.

To change the worksheet, enter the label **2nd Qtr 1991** in cell B13 (don't forget the apostrophe). Copy range B7..B9 to cell B15. (you need not highlight the entire T0 range.) Enter the label **Projected Increase** in cell E13 and **10%** in cell H13. To assign a percentage format to H13, select /**R**ange **F**ormat **P**ercent, press **0**, and press Enter twice.

The next step is to enter the formula **+D7*(1+H$13)** in cell D15. (The asterisk is the character you use in 1-2-3 formulas for multiplication.) This formula computes the projected second-quarter sales for the Kitty Hawk store by multiplying first-quarter sales by the sum of 1 and the increase percentage in cell H13. Copy this formula to cells D16, D17, and D19. Finally, enter \ – in cell D18 to make the worksheet resemble figure 1.12.

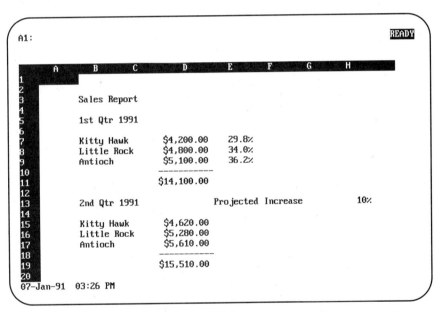

Fig. 1.12. *The SAMPLE2 worksheet, modified to show projected sales data for the second quarter.*

The worksheet shows that, if sales increase by 10% in the second quarter, sales in the three stores will be $4,620, $5,280, and $5,610, for a total of $15,510. But what if the 10% estimated increase is optimistic? How high will the sales be if the increase is 8%? You can find out easily. Highlight cell H13 and replace the existing value with 8%. Instantly, the values in rows 15 to 19 change to $4,536, $5,184, $5,508, and $15,228. If you try a few other percentages in cell H13, the results in rows 15 to 19 change each time you enter a new value.

Understanding Displayed versus Actual Values

When you enter 8% in cell H13, cell D19 returns $15,228. If you enter 7.5% in cell H13, the cell continues to display 8%, but cell D19 returns $15,157.50, as shown in figure 1.13. This value is 7.5% greater than the value in cell D11, because the value in cell H13 is really 7.5%. Cell H13 displays 8% because it is formatted as a percentage with zero decimal places.

Keeping track of the actual values in the worksheet is important. Figure 1.13 seems to indicate that the second-quarter values represent an 8% increase over the first-quarter values. The worksheet thus can be misleading. To remedy the problem, assign cell H13 a percentage format with two decimal places. The cell then conveys accurately the amount by which the second-quarter values exceed the first-quarter values.

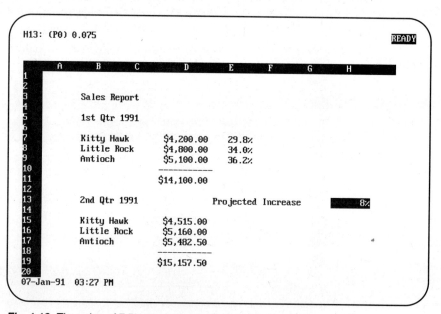

Fig. 1.13. *The value of 7.5% appearing in the worksheet as 8%.*

Using Manual Recalculation

The SAMPLE2 worksheet is extremely simple, containing eight formulas that change instantly when you change one of the values on which the formulas depend. The process of updating formulas is called *recalculating the worksheet*. By default, 1-2-3 recalculates the worksheet automatically. If the version number is earlier than 2.2, 1-2-3 recalculates each time you enter anything in a cell or edit an existing cell entry (the process of editing cells is covered later in this chapter). 1-2-3 Releases 2.2, 2.3, and 3.x recalculate formulas only if the formulas depend on a cell that you have changed. This is called *minimal recalculation*.

As your 1-2-3 skills develop, you can create worksheets containing much more data and using more complex formulas to analyze data. If 1-2-3 recalculates the worksheet automatically, working is harder as your worksheet grows in size. When you enter a number in a cell and try to move the cell pointer, the cell pointer movement is delayed while 1-2-3 updates the worksheet.

To keep 1-2-3 from slowing down, set recalculation to manual by selecting /Worksheet Global Recalculation Manual. Then change the value in cell H13 to 10%. The values in rows 15 to 19 don't change immediately; instead, a CALC indicator appears at the bottom of the screen, as shown in figure 1.14. (Figure 1.14 assumes that the value in cell H13 was 7.5% before it was changed to 10%.)

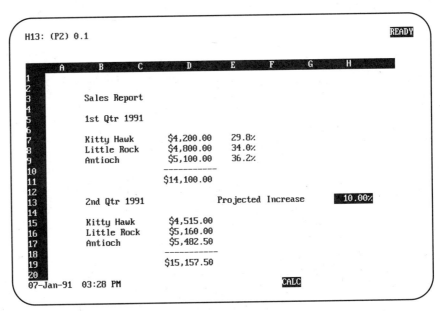

Fig. 1.14. Formulas (in rows 15 to 20) that don't reflect the change made to the projected increase percentage because recalculation is set to **M**anual.

The CALC indicator tells you that the worksheet has been changed and may contain formulas that don't reflect those changes. This distinction can be important. If you print the worksheet as it appears in figure 1.14, the resulting printed copy indicates that if first-quarter sales increase by 10%, sales in the second quarter would be $4,515.00, $5,160.00, and $5,482.50. Unless the recipient is good at math or double-checks the results (many of us are inclined to trust computer printouts) he or she may act inappropriately based on the printed worksheet.

When you set recalculation to manual, you must remember to recalculate the worksheet when you change data or add new data. To recalculate the sample worksheet, press the *Calc key* (F9). The value in cell D19 changes from $15,157.50 to $15,510.00 and the CALC indicator disappears. The formulas in rows 15 to 19 display the correct values based on the percentage in cell H13.

Editing Cells

In the sample worksheet, you have created new entries—labels, numbers, and formulas—in blank cells. If you see that you have made a mistake in an entry, or if you want to change wording or capitalization, you don't have to retype the entire entry. You can edit cells, changing one or a few characters.

Suppose that you want to change the label in cell B3 to *Sales Report – Quarterly*. Highlight cell B3 and press *Edit* (F2); the mode indicator now reads EDIT. The contents of the cell appear in the control panel, followed by a cursor. The next character you type appears at the end of the existing label. To change the label in cell B3, press the space bar once, type a hyphen, add another space, type the word **Quarterly**, and press Enter. The new, longer version of the label appears in cell B3.

You can accomplish more with cell editing than just adding characters at the end of a label. To change cell B3 to read *Sales Report, Quarterly*, press *Edit* (F2) and use the left-arrow key to move the cursor to the space after the word *Report*. Press the Del key twice to delete the space and the hyphen, type a comma, and press Enter.

Besides the left-arrow and right-arrow keys, you can use other keys to move the cursor when editing a cell entry. Home moves the cursor to the beginning of the entry. End moves the cursor to the end. Tab moves the cursor five characters to the right and Shift–Tab moves it five characters to the left.

When you want to replace one set of characters with another (as when you replaced a space and a hyphen with a comma), you usually delete characters. The Backspace key deletes characters to the left; the Del key deletes the character that the cursor is under (additional characters shift to the left once for each character deleted). After you delete any unwanted characters, you can begin typing new characters. Existing characters to the right of the cursor move to accommodate new characters as you type.

An alternative way to replace characters in cell entries is to use overtype mode. As you type each character, 1-2-3 overwrites the character at the current cursor position and moves the cursor one position to the right. Use this method to change the number in cell D7 to $4,217.00. Move the cell pointer to cell D7, press Edit (F2), and press the left-arrow key twice. The cursor is under the first zero. Press the Ins key. The OVR (overtype) indicator appears at the bottom of the screen. Type **17**; the new characters replace the zeros, and you complete the entry by pressing Enter.

Three other keys are useful in editing cells. Esc aborts the editing process and leaves the cell as it was before you pressed Edit. The up-arrow and down-arrow keys complete the editing process (as the Enter key does) and move the cell pointer up or down one cell. This process is similar to the trick (mentioned earlier in this chapter) of using the arrow keys when entering data in cells. When you edit a cell, however, the left-arrow and right-arrow keys move the cursor back and forth within the entry and cannot be used to complete the editing process.

Using Automatic EDIT Mode

At times, 1-2-3 shifts to EDIT mode automatically. Early in this chapter, an example showed what happens if you try to enter the label *1st Qtr 1991* without a label prefix. Because the first character is a numeral, 1-2-3 determines that you are entering a value. When you type an invalid cell entry, 1-2-3 beeps and switches to EDIT mode, so you don't need to press Esc and retype the entry. Instead, press Home to move the cursor to the beginning of the entry, type the required apostrophe and press Enter. 1-2-3 accepts the entry.

When possible, 1-2-3 moves the cursor to the invalid part of the entry. If you try to enter **1102 Main Street** without typing a label prefix, 1-2-3 moves the cursor to the space after the 2, because the space is the first invalid character for a value. Another possible error is the misspelling of a function name. If you enter the formula **2*@SUB(D7..D9)+5**, 1-2-3 beeps and moves the cursor to the @ character because no @SUB function exists. The cursor draws your attention to the error. Because 1-2-3 is in EDIT mode, you can move the cursor to the offending letter B, press Del, press **M**, and press Enter.

Erasing Cells

The sample worksheet now contains two entries (in cells A1 and D1) that need to be erased. Using the proper method for erasing cells is important. Move the cell pointer to cell A1, select **/R**ange **E**rase, press the right-arrow key three times to highlight range A1..D1, and press Enter. You also can use the mouse to highlight the range. To erase one cell, the procedure is the same. Highlight the cell, select **/R**ange **E**rase, and press Enter.

Using **/R**ange **E**rase is the best way to empty individual cells of their contents (in Release 2.3, you can erase a cell by highlighting it and pressing the Del key). It may seem that you can erase a cell's contents by pressing the space bar and then Enter; however, this process enters a space in the cell, rather than erasing the cell. Because a space is invisible, the cell looks empty, but it isn't. The cell contains a label. A cell containing a label and an empty cell behave differently in several ways, as indicated by the following example.

Suppose that you want to use the @AVG function to return the average of all values in a range. This function adds the values and divides the sum obtained by the number of entries in the range. In the formula @AVG(B5..B14), the range consists of 10 cells. If all of the cells in the range contain values, the sum of the values is divided by 10. If one of the cells contains the value 0, the sum is still divided by 10, as you may expect. If one of the cells in the range is empty, the sum is divided by 9. If one of the cells contains a label, however, the @AVG function regards that label as an entry with a value of 0, and the sum of the values is divided by 10. If the label is a space, the @AVG formula gives a misleading result: the result appears to be the average of nine values, when in fact it is the average of 10 values, one of which is 0.

A cell containing an invisible label is different from an empty cell in other ways. Using the **/R**ange **E**rase command helps you avoid problems later on.

Working with Ranges

Early in this section you learned how to assign formats to ranges, and you now know how to erase ranges. Throughout this book, instructions require you to *specify* ranges. The next section discusses several methods for specifying ranges.

To erase the three percentages in column E of the sample worksheet, most 1-2-3 users would move the cell pointer before issuing the erase command. When you move the cell pointer to cell E7 and select **/R**ange

Erase, the prompt Enter range to erase: appears in the control panel. This prompt is followed by the range coordinates E7..E7. The two periods and the second E7 tell you that the cell pointer is anchored. You can specify range E7..E9 by moving the cell pointer down two cells (note that the highlighted area expands each time you press the down-arrow key) and pressing Enter.

To erase a range *without* moving the cell pointer first, select /**R**ange Erase. 1-2-3 displays the prompt Enter range to erase: followed by the address of the current cell, two periods, and the same address. Again, the two periods followed by a cell address indicate that the cell pointer is anchored. Press Backspace or Esc to unanchor the cell pointer. The two periods and the second cell address disappear. Now you can move the cell pointer to cell E7. The cell pointer moves freely instead of highlighting a block of cells. When the cell pointer is at E7, type a period to anchor the cell pointer again. The coordinates after the Enter range to erase: prompt change from E7 to E7..E7. Move the cell pointer down two cells to highlight range E7..E9 and press Enter. The range is erased and the cell pointer moves back to where it was before you started the operation.

Be aware that 1-2-3 is not entirely consistent about anchoring the cell pointer when it prompts you for a range. When you select /**R**ange Search (Release 2.2 and later), for example, you see the prompt Enter range to search: followed by the address of the current cell. To specify a range starting at the current location you must type a period, and to specify a range elsewhere in the worksheet you don't need to press Backspace. As you perform the various operations for which 1-2-3 prompts you for a range, check the coordinates in the control panel to see if you must anchor or unanchor the cell pointer before highlighting the desired range.

A third way to specify a range is to type the range coordinates. With the cell pointer anywhere in the worksheet, select /**R**ange Erase. At the Enter range to erase: prompt, type **E7.E9** and press Enter. Note that you need only type *one* period. References to ranges in this book and in most other material about 1-2-3 use two periods by convention. When you specify ranges by entering coordinates, you can type one or two periods.

Finally, in Releases 2.3 and 3.1, you can specify ranges with the mouse. In Release 3.1, the Wysiwyg add-in must be attached before you can use the mouse. Because Releases 2.3 and 3.1 also enable you to prespecify ranges with the F4 key, you can perform multiple commands on the highlighted range. This method saves you from having to specify the range each time you select a command.

Using Three-Dimensional Ranges

With Release 3.x, a range can add depth to width and height (assuming that you are working with more than one worksheet). You can specify three-dimensional ranges with the arrow keys or by entering coordinates, as with two-dimensional ranges. To specify A:E7..C:E9 as a range to erase, move the cell pointer to cell E7 in worksheet A, select **/R**ange Erase, press the down-arrow key twice, hold down the Ctrl key and press the PgUp key twice, and press Enter. You can specify the range with coordinates by selecting **/R**ange Erase and entering **A:E7..C:E9**.

If you enter coordinates without specifying worksheet letters, 1-2-3 assumes that the desired range is in the current worksheet. If the cell pointer is in worksheet B, for example, entering E5..F10 is the same as specifying range B:E5..B:F10.

Preselecting Ranges

With Release 2.3, you can select a range before you perform an operation on it. You can use the same procedure with Release 3.1 if the Wysiwyg add-in is attached.

To preselect a range, press the F4 key to anchor the cell pointer. Use the arrow keys to highlight a range beginning at the cell pointer's location, or press Backspace to unanchor the cell pointer, move the cell pointer to the range's upper left cell, type a period to reanchor the cell pointer, and use the arrow keys to highlight the range. When the desired range is highlighted, press Enter. You also can press F4 and enter the range coordinates or range name, or preselect with the mouse. 1-2-3 returns to READY mode but the range stays highlighted.

With the range preselected, you can issue a range-related command such as **/R**ange Erase, **/R**ange Format, or **/C**opy. 1-2-3 performs the task without prompting you to specify a range. If you select **/R**ange Erase, for example, 1-2-3 erases the preselected range without displaying the `Enter range to erase:` prompt. If the operation requires more than one range, 1-2-3 treats the preselected range as the operation's first range. If you select **/C**opy, for example, 1-2-3 skips directly to the `To where?` or `Enter range to copy TO:` prompt.

Preselecting a range makes performing several operations on the same range easier. Suppose that you want to erase a range *and* set all of its cells to the worksheet's default format. Preselect the range, select **/R**ange Erase, and then select **/R**ange Format **R**eset. This method also works well when formatting ranges with multiple Wysiwyg commands.

Pressing the Escape key or any direction key deselects the range and clears the highlight from the screen.

Using Range Names

1-2-3 enables you to assign names to various ranges in the worksheet; for example, you can give the name Q1SALES to range D7..D11. Naming a range gives you a fourth way of specifying that range to erase it, assign a different format to it, copy it, etc. When you are prompted to specify a range, you enter the range name.

To assign the name Q1SALES to a range in the sample worksheet, select **/R**ange **N**ame **C**reate, enter **Q1SALES**, and specify range **D7..D11** (using one of the methods described in the preceding section). Using the same procedure, assign the range name **Q2SALES** to range **D15..D19**. Change the format of Q1SALES by selecting **/R**ange **F**ormat **C**urrency, entering **0**, and entering **Q1SALES**.

When your worksheet contains range names, you have still another option for specifying ranges. To use this method, select **/R**ange **F**ormat **C**urrency and enter **0**. Then press the *Name key* (F3). The two range names you have already specified appear in the control panel, as shown in figure 1.15. Specify range D15..D19 as the range to format by highlighting the word Q2SALES and pressing Enter.

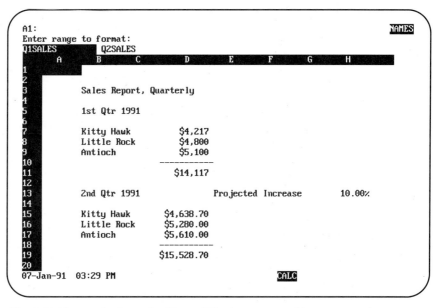

Fig. 1.15. *The result of pressing Name (F3) when prompted for a range to format.*

Because a few changes have been made in the sample worksheet since it was last saved, save the worksheet again.

Using the Mouse To Specify Ranges with Releases 2.3 and 3.1

In Releases 2.3 and 3.1, you can use the *click-and-drag* technique to specify ranges with the mouse. (Remember that in Release 3.1, the Wysiwyg add-in must be attached to use the mouse.) Click-and-drag is a combination of pointing, clicking, and moving (dragging) the mouse. To click-and-drag, move the mouse pointer to the desired beginning location—for example, the upper left corner of a range. Press and hold the left mouse button (don't release the button at this time); this action anchors the cell pointer). Move the mouse pointer to the desired ending location, such as the lower right corner of a range, and release the mouse button. The desired range is highlighted. Click the left mouse button again to finish specifying the range.

To select a range from B5 through D10, for example, point to cell B5, press and hold the mouse button, point to cell D10, release the mouse button, and press the left button again.

Printing the Worksheet

To get a printed copy of your worksheet, your printer must be attached to your computer, turned on, and on-line. To print the sample worksheet, select **/P**rint **P**rinter **R**ange and specify **A1..H19**. If the printer uses continuous-feed (fan-fold) paper, make sure that the top of a sheet is positioned at the print head. Select **A**lign (this tells 1-2-3 to start at the top of a new page) and **G**o to start printing the specified range. Select **P**age to make the printer advance to the next sheet (or eject the paper if you use a page printer, such as a laser or inkjet printer). To return 1-2-3 to READY mode, select **Q**uit.

Always press the Calc key (F9) before printing to ensure that the work-sheet formulas return correct results.

Later in this book, you learn how to use the Allways and Wysiwyg add-ins to enhance your worksheet with different kinds and sizes of type, dividing lines, and shaded areas. You also see how to print an enhanced worksheet and even how to print a graph on the same page with work-sheet data.

Using 1-2-3 Graphics

You have seen how 1-2-3 performs math and enables you to arrange the results in a convenient row-and-column format. If 1-2-3 and other spreadsheet products performed only those functions, the software still would be useful for financial analysis, business planning, and many other areas. But 1-2-3 offers many other features, including the capacity to create graphs illustrating relationships or comparisons between values in the worksheet. Other software products for personal computers include more types of graphs and greater flexibility in sizing, coloring, and annotating the graphs. But 1-2-3 helps you to create graphs on-screen almost effortlessly, without ending your 1-2-3 session and starting another program.

Using the values, formulas, and labels entered in the sample worksheet, you can create a graph like the one in figure 1.16.

To create the graph, begin by selecting **/Graph Type B**ar to access the main graph menu and choose the graph type. Select **X** and specify range **B7..B9** to define the labels that appear along the bottom of the graph (the x-axis). Two ranges of values control the height of the bars. To specify these ranges, select **A** and specify range **D7..D9**; then select **B** and specify range **D15..D17**.

To enhance the graph, select **Options Titles First** and enter **\B3**. The backslash tells 1-2-3 to use the label in cell B3 as the graph's first title. To specify a y-axis title, select **Titles Y-Axis** and enter **Sales**. The word Sales will appear on the left side of the graph. Select **Legend A** and enter **\B5**; then select **Legend B** and enter **\B13**.

You have provided 1-2-3 with all of the information needed for creating a graph. To view the graph on-screen, return to the main **/Graph** menu by selecting **Q**uit and then View. A graph, similar to the one in figure 1.16, appears on-screen. (The exact appearance of the graph depends on your equipment and 1-2-3 configuration.)

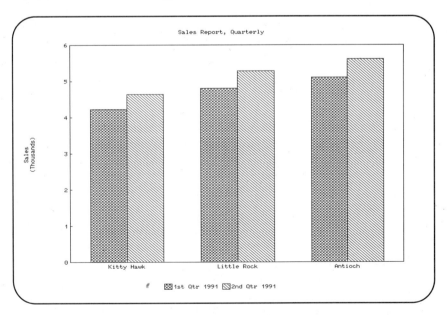

Fig. 1.16. *A 1-2-3 graph of worksheet data created almost effortlessly.*

When you finish looking at the graph, press any key to clear it and return to the /Graph menu; then select **Quit** to return to READY mode.

1-2-3 creates other types of graphs, including line and pie graphs. Releases 2.3, 3, and 3.1 offer the same types of graphs as Releases 2.01 and 2.2, with some additions. The later versions offer variations on the basic types, enabling you to create horizontal bar graphs, area graphs, mixed bar-and-line graphs, and other types of graphs.

Chapter 7 provides more information on creating and printing graphs.

Working with Databases

A database is a collection of information organized for easy retrieval. You can set up a database in your 1-2-3 worksheet and then find the information in the database matching specific criteria. If the database is a list of company employees, for example, you can use a 1-2-3 command to look up the employees who are in management positions. Using a different command, you can copy information on those employees to another area of the worksheet.

In such a database, the information pertaining to any one employee is called a *record*. Because a 1-2-3 database is part of the worksheet, the number of records it can contain is limited by the amount of random-access memory (RAM) in your computer. Even if your computer has plenty of RAM, the number of records in a 1-2-3 database cannot exceed 8,191 (the number of rows in the worksheet, minus one for a row of headings). Dedicated database products for the PC (such as dBASE, R:BASE, and Paradox) store data on a hard disk and can manage databases with hundreds of thousands of records. Obviously, you should use a dedicated database program if you need to handle a great deal of database work, or if you need to create and maintain a large database. 1-2-3 can accommodate a database of a few hundred records and perform basic database operations, which may be all you need for simple tasks.

Before creating a 1-2-3 database, save the sample worksheet again and select /**Worksheet Erase Yes** to clear the worksheet from memory. Then enter the labels and values shown in figure 1.17. Enter the values in column E without typing dollar signs or commas. Format the column by selecting /**Range Format Currency**, entering **0**, and specifying the range **E6..E15**.

Each row below row 5 in the sample database represents a record. Each column is a *field*. A field is a subdivision of a record that is always used for the same kind of information. Saying that Paul B (employee number

A002) is a supervisor is correct but, more to the point, the record for employee A002 contains Supv in the Emp Type field. The labels in row 5 are called *field headings*.

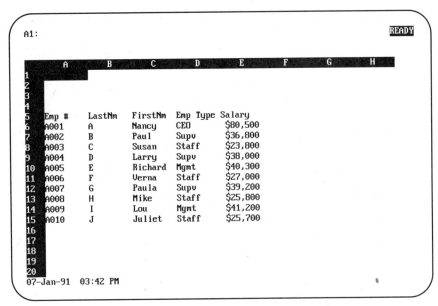

Fig. 1.17. *A 1-2-3 database, arranged in rows and columns.*

Before you actually can use this block of labels and values as a database, you must set up a *criteria range*, a worksheet range in which you place entries that control which records are selected as you perform various database operations. A criteria range must consist of at least two rows and the top row must contain one or more of the field headings from the database range. Because the field headings in the criteria range must match those in the database range exactly, use the /Copy command instead of entering the labels by hand. Copy the range A5..E5 to cell A1. The resulting worksheet resembles figure 1.18.

To make database operations easier, assign some range names. Select /Range Name Create, enter **EMPDATA**, and specify the range **A5..E15**. Then select /Range Name Create, enter **CRIT**, and enter **A1..E2** as the range coordinates.

To search the database for employees who are supervisors (records containing Supv in the Emp Type field), enter the label **Supv** in cell D2 (just below the field heading Emp Type). Then select /Data Query. To specify the input range (the database range), select Input and enter **EMPDATA**. Then select Criteria and enter **CRIT**. To begin the query operation, select Find. 1-2-3 highlights the first record in the database matching the specified criteria, as shown in figure 1.19. If you press the down-arrow key, the next record containing `Supv` in the `Emp Type` field is highlighted. Press the down-arrow key again and the third matching record is highlighted. Press the up-arrow key and the highlight jumps back to the preceding matching record. The **F**ind command enables you to browse through a database, highlighting those records matching the criteria you specify. To stop browsing and return to the **/**D**ata **Q**uery menu, press Enter or Esc; then select **Q**uit to return to READY mode.

```
A1: 'Emp #                                                              READY

         A        B        C        D        E       F       G       H
1  Emp #    LastNm   FirstNm  Emp Type Salary
2
3
4
5  Emp #    LastNm   FirstNm  Emp Type Salary
6  A001     A        Nancy    CEO        $80,500
7  A002     B        Paul     Supv       $36,800
8  A003     C        Susan    Staff      $23,800
9  A004     D        Larry    Supv       $38,000
10 A005     E        Richard  Mgmt       $40,300
11 A006     F        Verna    Staff      $27,000
12 A007     G        Paula    Supv       $39,200
13 A008     H        Mike     Staff      $25,800
14 A009     I        Lou      Mgmt       $41,200
15 A010     J        Juliet   Staff      $25,700
16
17
18
19
20
07-Jan-91  03:42 PM
```

Fig. 1.18. *A criteria range, copied from the field headings of the database to another area of the worksheet.*

You can press Ctrl–Break to stop the query and return to READY mode. Pressing the *Query key* (F7) also stops the query and leaves the cell pointer on the current record. Pressing the Query key again restarts the last query operation with the current criteria.

You also can use **/**D**ata **Q**uery commands to extract records from the database, copying them to another part of the worksheet. Before you can extract records, you must specify an output range. Like a criteria range, the top row of an output range contains field headings. Because the field headings must match the database field headings perfectly, use the **/**C**opy command. Copy the range A5..E5 to cell A17, select **/**D**ata **Q**uery **O**utput, specify the range **A17..E17**, and select Extract. 1-2-3 copies the three records to rows 18 through 20, as shown in figure 1.20. Select **Q**uit to return to READY mode.

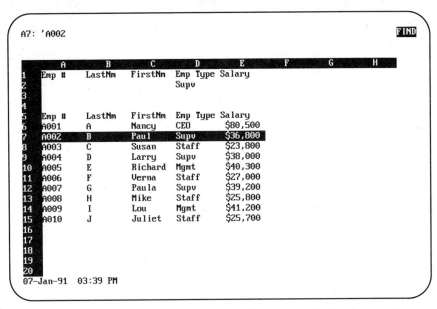

Fig. 1.19. *The result of issuing the /Data Query Find command to find the records in a database matching the specified criteria.*

You can broaden the selection criteria for databases by adding rows to the criteria range. Enter the label **Mgmt** in cell D3 of the sample database. Then select **/R**ange Name Create and enter **CRIT**. 1-2-3 highlights the current coordinates of CRIT (range A1..E2). To enlarge the range by one row, press the down-arrow key once and then press Enter. By enlarging CRIT, you also enlarge the area designated as the criteria range in the **/D**ata **Q**uery menu.

Select **/D**ata **Q**uery **F**ind. 1-2-3 again highlights the second record in the database. As you press the down-arrow key several times, note that records with Supv or Mgmt in the Emp Type field are highlighted. Terminate the **F**ind operation by pressing Enter and selecting **Q**uit.

Using Macros

Macros are like small programs; you use them to give 1-2-3 a series of *instructions* to perform certain functions. The simplest macros—and the easiest to understand—duplicate sequences of keys you type on the keyboard. When you find yourself performing a task repeatedly, consider creating a short macro to handle the job for you.

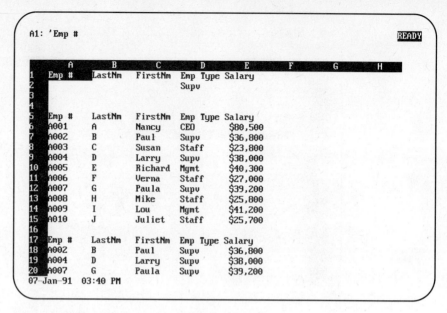

```
A1: 'Emp #                                                              READY

         A          B          C          D          E       F       G       H
1    Emp #      LastNm     FirstNm    Emp Type   Salary
2                                     Supv
3
4
5    Emp #      LastNm     FirstNm    Emp Type   Salary
6    A001       A          Nancy      CEO        $80,500
7    A002       B          Paul       Supv       $36,800
8    A003       C          Susan      Staff      $23,800
9    A004       D          Larry      Supv       $38,000
10   A005       E          Richard    Mgmt       $40,300
11   A006       F          Verna      Staff      $27,000
12   A007       G          Paula      Supv       $39,200
13   A008       H          Mike       Staff      $25,800
14   A009       I          Lou        Mgmt       $41,200
15   A010       J          Juliet     Staff      $25,700
16
17   Emp #      LastNm     FirstNm    Emp Type   Salary
18   A002       B          Paul       Supv       $36,800
19   A004       D          Larry      Supv       $38,000
20   A007       G          Paula      Supv       $39,200
07-Jan-91   03:40 PM
```

Fig. 1.20. *The result of issuing the /Data Query Extract command to copy the records matching specified criteria to another area of the worksheet.*

Creating a Simple Keystroke-Replacement Macro

Earlier in this chapter, you learned how to adjust the width of a column: press / to call up the menu, select Worksheet Column Set-Width, type the number of characters for the desired width, and press Enter. You can make menu selections in one of two ways: highlight the item and press Enter, or type the first letter of the item. Using the second method, you set a column width of 15 by typing /wcs15 and pressing Enter; you easily can create a macro that presses these keys for you.

If the database worksheet described in the preceding section is still on your screen, save the worksheet. Then start a new worksheet by selecting /Worksheet Erase Yes.

To begin creating the macro, move the cell pointer to cell AB1. Type an apostrophe to indicate that the following text is a label. Then type /wcs15~ and press Enter. (The last character is called a *tilde*; it usually is located next to the exclamation point at the top of your keyboard.) This label is a macro program. Like all computer programs, it consists of instructions. Each character is an instruction to "press" one of the keys; the slash key, the W key, and so on. The tilde instructs 1-2-3 to press the Enter key.

Typically, you assign a *macro name* for each macro you create. The macro name consists of the Alt key—represented by the backslash (\)—and one of the letters in the alphabet. You *invoke* (start) a macro by holding down the Alt key and pressing the assigned letter key. The macro name you select should be appropriate to the purpose of the macro. For the width-adjusting macro in this example, use the name \w.

Move the cell pointer to cell AA1. Type '\w and press Enter. With the cell pointer still in cell AA1, select /**R**ange **N**ame **L**abels **R**ight. At the Enter label range: prompt, press Enter to specify cell AA1. When you use the /**R**ange **N**ame **L**abels **R**ight command, 1-2-3 assigns the labels in the specified range as range names for the cells one column to the right. You specified cell AA1 at the range prompt but assigned the name \w to cell AB1.

Now document the macro. Move the cell pointer to cell AD1 and enter the text **Sets the width of the current column to 15**. Figure 1.21 shows the width-adjusting macro, the label used to assign a name to it, and the description of the macro's operation.

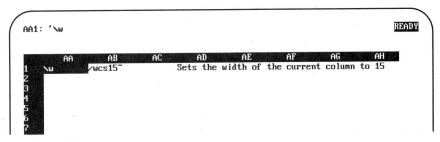

Fig. 1.21. A macro for adjusting the width of the current column.

To try the macro, hold down the Alt key and press **W** (or **w**). Instantly, the column in which the cell pointer is located is widened to 15 characters.

Using Macro Key Names

A number of keys on the keyboard—such as the arrow keys and function keys—produce an action, rather than a character on-screen. To use a macro to press one of these keys, use a *key name*, enclosed in braces ({ }). The instruction {DOWN} in a macro causes the cell pointer to move down a cell, just as if you had pressed the down-arrow key. {GOTO} followed by a cell address or range name and a tilde (for example, {GOTO}B15~) moves the cell pointer to a specified location, as if you had pressed the F5 (GoTo) key and entered the address or range name.

The macro shown in figure 1.22 helps you enter labels with initial capitals. It uses the @PROPER function, which converts all letters in a character string to lowercase except those following a space. The macro also uses the key names {EDIT}, {HOME}, and {CALC}, which tell 1-2-3 to press the F2 (Edit), Home, and F9 (Calc) keys, respectively.

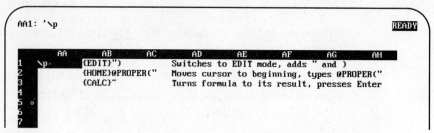

Fig. 1.22. *A macro that converts entries to initial capitals.*

Clear your worksheet with **/W**orksheet **E**rase **Y**es and enter the labels shown in figure 1.22. Assign the name \p to cell AB1 by moving the cell pointer to cell AA1, selecting **/R**ange **N**ame **L**abels **R**ight, and pressing Enter twice.

Move the cell pointer to an empty cell and type **elwood p. dowd** but don't press Enter. Instead, hold down the Alt key and press **P** (or **p**). The macro switches 1-2-3 to EDIT mode and adds the characters ") to what you have typed. Then it presses the Home key (moving the cursor to the beginning of the entry) and types the characters @PROPER(". Then the macro presses Calc (F9) to convert the formula to its result. Finally, it presses Enter to place the entry in the cell. The entry elwood p. dowd thus becomes elwood p. dowd"),@PROPER("elwood p. dowd"), and finally Elwood P. Dowd.

Considering More Complex Macros

The 1-2-3 advanced macro commands enable macros to perform tasks that cannot be performed from the keyboard. These tasks include presenting prompts and accepting information from the user, controlling the flow of macro programs with customized macros, and performing an operation a specified number of times. These advanced commands make 1-2-3 macros as powerful as many dedicated computer languages.

To learn more about macros and how you can use them to create sophisticated applications, see Chapter 8 of this book, the sections on macro programming in your 1-2-3 manual, or one of the many books available on the subject of macros, such as *1-2-3 Macro Library*, 3rd Edition (Que Corporation, 1990).

Summary

If you understand the examples in this chapter, you should feel comfortable with the 1-2-3 environment. You can experiment with 1-2-3 by building some simple models to help with tasks in your office or at home. Don't be afraid to try new things; you probably cannot hurt 1-2-3 or your computer with your experiments.

When you have mastered the basics, you are ready for Part II: Optimizing 1-2-3. Parts II, III, and IV provide helpful advice and demonstrate some interesting shortcuts to make you more productive with 1-2-3.

Part Two

OPTIMIZING 1-2-3

Chapter Two

DESIGNING APPLICATIONS

B y now, you have learned the basic 1-2-3 skills: entering labels and values, creating formulas, using menu commands, and creating simple macros. A thorough knowledge of 1-2-3's capabilities is important, but you also must understand how to use that knowledge to devise worksheet applications that are effective, efficient, and easy to use. Just as an excellent carpenter isn't necessarily qualified to design a house, a 1-2-3 user who is an expert on menu commands, functions, and macro language may not know how to design 1-2-3 applications. Creating a house generally requires the services of an architect and a carpenter. Fortunately, you can be both architect and carpenter for your 1-2-3 applications.

This chapter discusses the following aspects of designing 1-2-3 applications:

- Why every worksheet is really a computer program

- Why design is important

- How labeling helps clarify and document an application

- How and when to arrange a worksheet by "screens"

- How to keep changes made in one area from affecting other areas

Applying the techniques covered in this chapter can help you to eliminate frustration for yourself and for others who use the applications you design.

Understanding the Importance of Design Issues

Any worksheet you create in 1-2-3, no matter how simple, is a computer program even if it contains no macros. The worksheet shown in figure 2.1, for example, is a program for calculating loan payments.

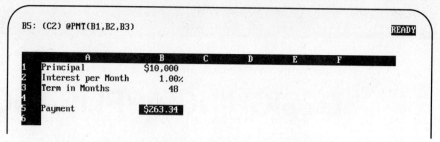

```
B5: (C2) @PMT(B1,B2,B3)                                          READY

          A              B        C        D        E        F
1   Principal         $10,000
2   Interest per Month  1.00%
3   Term in Months       48
4
5   Payment          $263.34
6
```

Fig. 2.1. *A simple worksheet that constitutes a computer program.*

Don't dismiss figure 2.1 as just a worksheet with a few labels and functions; it is a bona fide computer program, functionally identical to the
following program written in BASIC:

```
10 CLS
20 INPUT "Enter Principal",P
30 PRINT
40 INPUT "Enter Interest per Month",I
50 PRINT
60 INPUT "Enter Term in Months",T
70 PRINT:PRINT
80 PT=P*I/(1–(1+I)^(–T)):REM STANDARD FORMULA FOR
     LOAN PAYMENTS
90 PRINT "The monthly payment is";PT
100 PRINT
```

Both programs perform the same task. The worksheet uses three labels
to identify the three input cells and another label to identify the formula
that calculates the result. The BASIC program uses three prompts that
tell the user to enter values, then calculates the payment and prints
some messages before displaying the result.

Because both programs are simple, design is not critical. As long as the
cells are labeled (or the user of the BASIC program sees meaningful
prompts), any design is fine. On the other hand, these programs were
designed with *some* care; the worksheet can operate in the same manner
without labels, but the user would have a hard time figuring out which
value to enter in which cell. In the same way, the BASIC program can
use just the statements INPUT P, INPUT I, and INPUT T for the loan's
principal, interest, and term, respectively, but the user would see only
question marks, not prompts.

Design is always significant, and it becomes more important as the com-
plexity of the program increases. The following sections discuss some
major design issues.

Using Labels To Document Worksheets

Labels are important because they guide the user through the worksheet and because they document the worksheet. Providing detailed technical documentation is an excellent idea (and sometimes a job requirement) for all programmers, including worksheet programmers. Documenting can help other programmers make necessary modifications by explaining the purpose of the formula in cell A17 or how the macro in column V works. Even if you do not need this type of detailed documentation, the very presence of labels in a worksheet is a form of documentation.

Determining Where To Use Labels

Very few cells in a worksheet should be left unlabeled. Exceptions to this rule include cells that use a formula to calculate the current date (if the cell is formatted to display values as dates, it's self-explanatory) and formulas that compute intermediate values needed to calculate a desired result. Individual values do not need labels; if you label all intermediate computations, the user may be confused. You *should* label the block as a whole, however, to tell the user that the results in the individual cells are not relevant. Figure 2.2 shows an example of a worksheet that uses a block of intermediate formulas to convert a value to a dollar amount expressed in words. The range E4..E11 contains intermediate formulas used by the formula in cell A16. Because the results of the intermediate formulas are unimportant, the individual cells containing those formulas need no labels.

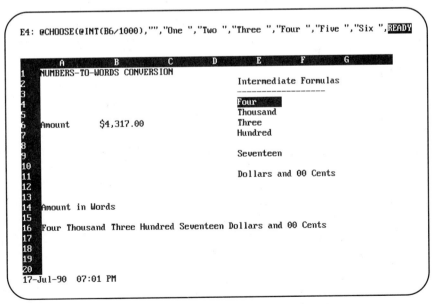

Fig. 2.2. A worksheet with unlabeled cells (E4..E11) containing intermediate formulas.

Avoiding the Use of Too Many Labels

Label cells as a way of documenting their functions, but try not to overdo the use of labels in a worksheet. Using too many labels produces a cluttered effect, as shown in figure 2.3. A better way to display information in a worksheet appears in figure 2.4. Notice that all 12 months now appear on one worksheet screen. Anyone viewing the worksheet (or reading a printout) can look at the annotations for the months without having to separate the important part—the values—from all the verbiage.

```
A1: [W21] 'SALES BY                                                    READY

            A              B              C              D
1  SALES BY            Men's          Women's        Children's
2  MONTH              Clothing       Clothing       Clothing
3                     (L Mango, Mgr) (D Lemon, Mgr) (N Papaya, Mgr)
4  January              $43,112        $44,146        $42,995
5    (Post Xmas Retrns)
6  February             $54,300        $60,913        $57,435
7    (Wash B'day sale)
8  March                $49,524        $47,341        $44,938
9    (No unus. actvty)
10 April                $50,792        $46,324        $49,329
11   (Summr line arrvs)
12 May                  $51,447        $56,181        $47,557
13   (Mothers day)
14 June                 $48,943        $53,590        $58,181
15   (No unus. actvty)
16 July                 $42,103        $40,190        $39,157
17   (Slow)
18 August               $50,403        $48,342        $57,661
19   (Back to School)
20 September            $47,832        $53,803        $47,948
23-Apr-91  05:09 PM
```

Fig. 2.3. A cluttered worksheet, with too many labels mixed in with values.

Arranging Worksheet Sections To Fit on One Screen

When possible, arrange parts of a worksheet that are meant to be viewed together—or used as entry screens rather than printouts—in sections that can fit on one worksheet screen. Figures 2.5 and 2.6 show how inconvenient a worksheet can be when its columns are widened to accommodate labels.

You have to use the Tab key to see all of the columns of attendance numbers and percentages shown in figures 2.5 and 2.6. A better design plan is to use narrow columns with abbreviations and two worksheet rows for the labels, as shown in figure 2.7.

```
A1: [W21] 'SALES BY MONTH                                              READY

           A              B            C            D
 1  SALES BY MONTH     Men's        Women's      Children's
 2                     Clothing     Clothing     Clothing
 3  January            $43,112      $44,146      $42,995
 4  February           $54,300      $60,913      $57,435
 5  March              $49,524      $47,341      $44,938
 6  April              $50,792      $46,324      $49,329
 7  May                $51,447      $56,181      $47,557
 8  June               $48,943      $53,590      $58,181
 9  July               $42,103      $40,190      $39,157
10  August             $50,403      $48,342      $57,661
11  September          $47,832      $53,803      $47,948
12  October            $60,500      $64,930      $59,032
13  November           $48,480      $49,840      $54,490
14  December           $91,844      $88,453      $89,450
15  Average            $53,273      $54,504      $54,014
16  Unusual activities affecting sales:
17  Jan, post Xmas returns; Feb, Wash. B'Day sale; Apr, Summer line
18  arrives; May, Mother's day; Jul, slow month; Aug, back to school;
19  Oct, Col. Day sale; Dec, Christmas. No unus activity Mar June, Sep, Nov.
20
23-Apr-91  05:10 PM
```

Fig. 2.4. *The same worksheet, with notes separated from results to make it easier to read.*

```
A1: [W19] '4th Grade Attendance Record                                READY

           A              B            C            D
 1  4th Grade Attendance Record
 2  February 1990
 3
 4
 5  School             Class Size   Average Attendance   % Attendance
 6  Central            34           29                   85.3%
 7  Martin Luther King 31           29                   93.5%
 8  14th Street        33           30                   90.9%
 9
10
11
12
13
14
```

Fig. 2.5. *The partially-visible worksheet with columns set too wide.*

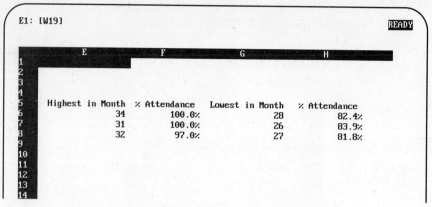

```
E1: [W19]                                                                    READY

        E                 F              G               H
1
2
3
4
5   Highest in Month   % Attendance   Lowest in Month   % Attendance
6              34          100.0%               28            82.4%
7              31          100.0%               26            83.9%
8              32           97.0%               27            81.8%
9
10
11
12
13
14
```

Fig. 2.6. *The other half of the worksheet shown in figure 2.5.*

```
A1: [W12] '4th Grade Attendance Record                                       READY

        A        B      C       D        E        F        G        H
1   4th Grade Attendance Record
2   February 1990
3
4                Class   Avg          Highest/          Lowest/
5   School        Size   Att   % Att   Month   % Att    Month   % Att
6   Central        34    29    85.3%    34     100.0%     28    82.4%
7   M.L. King      31    29    93.5%    31     100.0%     26    83.9%
8   14th Street    33    30    90.9%    32      97.0%     27    81.8%
9
10
11
12
13
14
15
```

Fig. 2.7. *The revised worksheet, all of which is visible on-screen.*

You can overdo the use of abbreviations. Figure 2.8, which shows monthly sales for a hypothetical supermarket chain, is an example of a worksheet using too many abbreviations. The whole report fits on one worksheet screen, but the column headings are too cryptic. The user cannot tell easily that the headings refer to canned goods, beverages, household cleaners, health and beauty aids, and so forth. This worksheet would be easier to read with more meaningful abbreviations, even if it wouldn't fit on one screen. As a worksheet designer, you must find the right balance between descriptive labels and compact abbreviations.

Designing Worksheets with Several Rows

If a worksheet must extend beyond the screen *vertically*, try to break it into sections that fit in 20-row blocks. In other words, the sections begin at rows 1, 21, 41, and so on, enabling a user to find the different sections using the PgDn and PgUp keys.

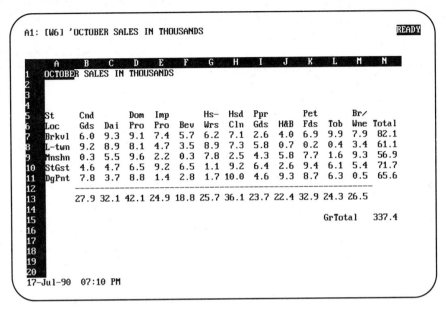

```
A1: [W6] 'OCTOBER SALES IN THOUSANDS                                    READY

      A     B    C     D     E     F    G     H    I     J    K     L    M     N
1  OCTOBER SALES IN THOUSANDS
2
3
4
5  St    Cnd        Dom   Imp         Hs-   Hsd  Ppr        Pet        Br/
6  Loc   Gds  Dai   Pro   Pro   Bev   Wrs   Cln  Gds   H&B  Fds   Tob  Wne   Total
7  Brkvl 6.0  9.3   9.1   7.4   5.7   6.2   7.1  2.6   4.0  6.9   9.9  7.9   82.1
8  L-twn 9.2  8.9   8.1   4.7   3.5   8.9   7.3  5.8   0.7  0.2   0.4  3.4   61.1
9  Mnshn 0.3  5.5   9.6   2.2   0.3   7.8   2.5  4.3   5.8  7.7   1.6  9.3   56.9
10 StGst 4.6  4.7   6.5   9.2   6.5   1.1   9.2  6.4   2.6  9.4   6.1  5.4   71.7
11 DgPnt 7.8  3.7   8.8   1.4   2.8   1.7  10.0  4.6   9.3  8.7   6.3  0.5   65.6
12        ---------------------------------------------------------------------
13        27.9 32.1 42.1 24.9 18.8 25.7 36.1 23.7 22.4 32.9 24.3 26.5
14
15                                                         GrTotal    337.4
16
17
18
19
20
   17-Jul-90  07:10 PM
```

Fig. 2.8. A worksheet that fits on one screen, but uses too many abbreviations.

This suggestion assumes that 1-2-3 displays exactly 20 worksheet rows on the monitor at one time. Some people with EGA or VGA monitors use a 1-2-3 driver set that can display 43 rows at one time. Others use add-ins such as SeeMORE or Impress, and still others use the Wysiwyg add-in for Release 2.3 or 3.1, which enables 1-2-3 to display more than 20 rows. If you use an EGA or VGA monitor or an add-in, divide the worksheet into sections that fit the number of rows displayed.

Release 3.x users also have the option of using multiple worksheets in an application. Depending on the specific application, this method may be easier than breaking a worksheet into whole pages.

Using Menu Macros To Navigate Large Worksheets

Sometimes worksheets become complex, especially when multiple worksheets are used with Release 3.x. If a worksheet has many sections that cannot be arranged vertically, you can set up a menu macro to help the user find the different sections.

Figure 2.9 shows a menu macro that helps users navigate a complicated worksheet. When the user presses Alt–F, the labels in row 7 appear as menu items. The labels in row 8 appear as prompts (restricted by column width in this figure). The labels in row 9 consist of the key name {GOTO} followed by a range name and the macro symbol for the Enter key (~). Figure 2.10 shows the menu in use. Each menu item uses a descriptive name for the section; the prompt explains the section's purpose.

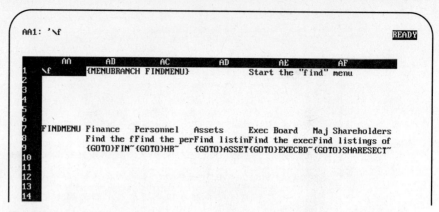

Fig. 2.9. *A macro that is used to create a menu for navigating a complex worksheet.*

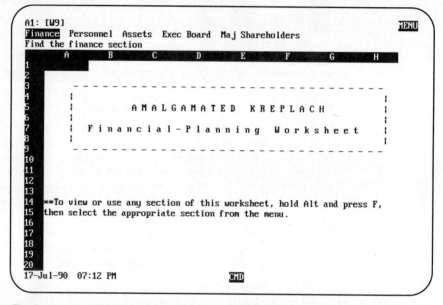

Fig. 2.10. *A menu is displayed when the user presses Alt–F.*

Chapter 8 discusses the mechanics of creating menu macros in more detail.

Recognizing When To Use Macros

Macros get more publicity than other 1-2-3 features. The inclusion of a rudimentary programming language in the original version of 1-2-3 made it a great improvement over its predecessor, VisiCalc, but macros are not always essential for useful, powerful worksheet applications.

Many computer professionals, familiar with traditional procedural languages such as Pascal, C, and BASIC, apply programming knowledge to 1-2-3's macro language without understanding the simple elegance of basic worksheet design. Entire books are devoted to describing worksheet templates driven by macros; some of these applications may as well have been written in Pascal.

Remember the worksheet for calculating loan payments at the beginning of this chapter (fig. 2.1)? Some seasoned procedural-language programmers approach the same problem by creating the macro shown in figure 2.11. This macro is superfluous for two reasons. Displaying user prompts in 1-2-3's control panel is unnecessary if the cells into which the user enters data are labeled clearly. The macro can perform the calculation, but you can place the same formula (or, even better, a function) into a cell.

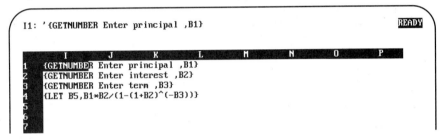

Fig. 2.11. A procedural-language style of macro that computes loan payments.

The macro in figure 2.11 only performs a calculation. When possible, use cell formulas instead of macros for simple calculations. For tasks that cannot be performed simply by making entries in cells—for example, creating menus for worksheet navigation—design an appropriate macro.

Designing Worksheets That Protect Formulas

Most worksheets have separate sections for interacting with the user (data-input areas) and for calculations and other tasks (usually formulas and macros). In some cases, sections that perform calculations also display results. Figure 2.12 shows a worksheet that mixes the sections for data input and calculation. Rows 5 and 7 are for the data input, and rows 6, 8, and 9 contain formulas that compute values based on the input. Because this design (or lack of design) is confusing to the user, the possibility is increased that the user will overwrite a formula by entering a value.

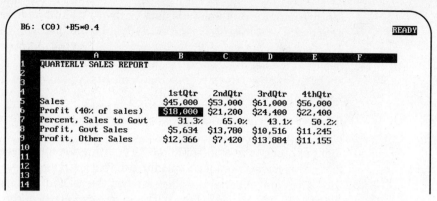

Fig. 2.12. A worksheet that mixes input areas (rows 5 and 7) with calculation areas (rows 6, 8, and 9).

Figure 2.13 shows an improved version of the worksheet. Separating formula areas from input areas makes the worksheet easier to understand and helps users avoid overwriting formulas by accident.

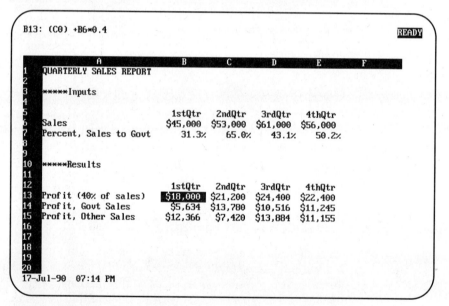

Fig. 2.13. A worksheet that separates input areas from calculation areas.

Some complex worksheets contain sections with macros or intermediate calculation formulas that the end user does not need to see, or sections that the user must see but may not modify. Separating these sections from the data-input area of the worksheet is helpful, but you also can use 1-2-3's built-in protection feature to prevent unintentional modification of cell contents. You activate the protection feature by selecting /Worksheet Global Protection Enable. To assign unprotected status to the cells designated for data input in figure 2.13, select /Range Unprotect and specify range B6..E7. With protection enabled, if the user tries to modify or make an entry in any cell except the unprotected ones, 1-2-3 beeps and displays the message Protected cell.

1-2-3's protection feature discourages modifications but does not protect the worksheet from intentional tampering. Most people who have any knowledge of 1-2-3 know how to disable the protection feature.

In the following sections, you learn ways to restrict areas of the worksheet using Release 2.3 and earlier. Time-saving (and more reliable) protection features added to Releases 3 and 3.1 also are described.

Creating a Restricted Zone with /Worksheet Titles

Many 1-2-3 worksheets are arranged with data-input areas beginning in cell A1; users can find the beginning of the area by pressing the Home key. Macros or intermediate calculations are placed in the columns to the right of the data-input section, perhaps beginning in column AA. The problem with this approach is that the user can corrupt macros by inserting or deleting rows in the worksheet.

If you want users to be able to insert or delete *rows*, you can place macros and calculations *below* the data-input section; however, this method doesn't solve the problem of adding or deleting *columns*. Further, if any macros invoke the commands /Worksheet Insert Row or /Worksheet Delete Row, those macros may fail because named cells in which they store values, labels, cell addresses, and so on may have changed.

To eliminate these problems, place macros and calculations *above* the data-input section. For example, if you need fewer than 100 rows for macros, you can place the macros in the area beginning at cell A1 and start the data-input section in row 101. To enable the user to find the beginning of the data-input section by pressing the Home key, use 1-2-3's /Worksheet Titles command to create a restricted zone for the macros.

Figures 2.14 and 2.15 show a worksheet with a restricted zone. Notice that row 100 is always at the top of the screen. If the user presses the Home key when the cell pointer is in cell J161 (as shown in figure 2.15), the cell pointer moves to cell A101, not to cell A1. If the user presses the up arrow key when the cell pointer is in row 101, 1-2-3 beeps, just as if the cell pointer were in row 1. The restricted zone protects rows 1 to 99 for macros and intermediate calculations. New worksheet rows can be added without affecting anything above row 100.

This approach isn't quite foolproof. If the user presses Home while adding rows, he or she can insert rows above row 100. The cell pointer restriction applies only when 1-2-3 is in READY mode.

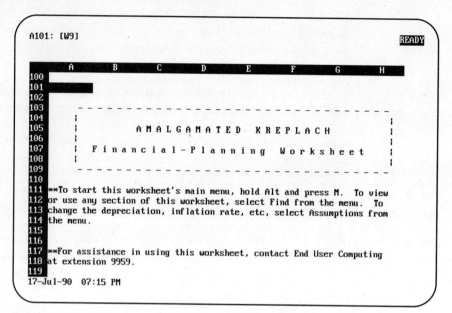

Fig. 2.14. *The data-input section of the worksheet, beginning in row 101.*

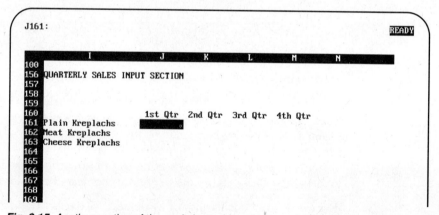

Fig. 2.15. *Another section of the worksheet shown in figure 2.14, with row 100 still visible.*

To set up the worksheet with a restricted zone, begin by arranging the worksheet so that the last row in the protected area (in this example, row 100) is the first row on-screen. You can accomplish this objective by pressing Home followed by F5 (GoTo), and entering **A100**. Then position the cell pointer in row 101 and select **/Worksheet Titles Horizontal**.

At some point after setting up a restricted zone, you may need access to the restricted area. To disable the restriction, select /Worksheet Titles Clear. After making your changes, reset the titles. If you don't want to disable the titles, you can press GoTo (F5) followed by Home to move the cell pointer to cell A1. (In the example, row 100 would still appear on-screen but without affecting the operation of the worksheet.)

Arranging a Worksheet Diagonally

Creating a restricted area above the input area solves the problem of adding rows, but does not enable the user to add columns without risk of corrupting the worksheet. (In many worksheets, adding columns is not an issue. In figure 2.15, for example, more rows may be needed to accommodate more varieties of kreplachs, but no new columns should be required, because a year always has four quarters.)

If a worksheet must allow for additional rows *and* additional columns, however, the best solution is to arrange the worksheet diagonally; that is, with the first section beginning in cell A1, and subsequent sections below and to the right. Figures 2.16 and 2.17 show a worksheet with two independent work areas. Because no entries exist in columns A–G below row 20 or rows 1–20 beyond column G, you can add new rows or columns to either section. If you add rows or columns to the sheet music section (fig. 2.16), the additions affect the location of the instrument section but do not add space between its entries. Adding rows or columns to the in-struments section (fig. 2.17) does not affect the sheet music section. A diagonal arrangement is especially useful for applications with macros in 1-2-3 versions prior to Release 3.x (in which macros can be placed in different, attached worksheets).

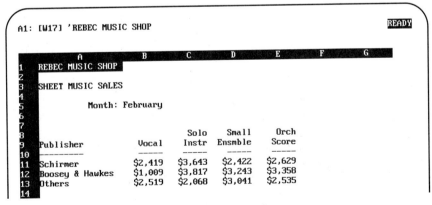

Fig. 2.16. Part of a worksheet arranged in a diagonal pattern.

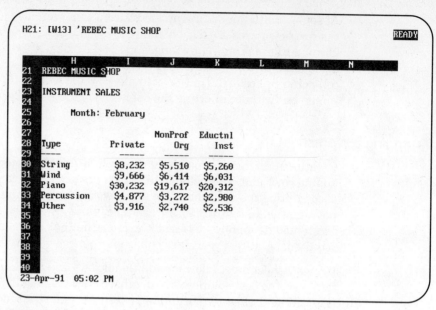

```
H21: [W13] 'REBEC MUSIC SHOP                                              READY

         H          I        J        K        L        M           N
21  REBEC MUSIC SHOP
22
23  INSTRUMENT SALES
24
25        Month: February
26
27                          NonProf   Eductnl
28  Type            Private     Org      Inst
29  ----            -------  -------  -------
30  String           $8,232   $5,510   $5,260
31  Wind             $9,666   $6,414   $6,031
32  Piano           $30,232  $19,617  $20,312
33  Percussion       $4,877   $3,272   $2,980
34  Other            $3,916   $2,740   $2,536
35
36
37
38
39
40
    23-Apr-91  05:02 PM
```

Fig. 2.17. *The section of the worksheet below **and** to the right of the section shown in figure 2.16.*

Combining a Restricted Zone with a Diagonal Worksheet Arrangement

The music shop example demonstrates the diagonal worksheet arrangement in which all sections contain data-input areas, but the diagonal arrangement also can be used in a worksheet with a restricted area. To isolate the restricted section from the data-input section, you can use a variation of the restricted-zone technique discussed earlier in this chapter. The command /Worksheet Titles Both restricts access to the rows above *and* to the columns to the left of the cell pointer.

Suppose that the range A1..F20 of the music shop worksheet contains macros. To restrict the data-input area to cells beginning with H21, start by arranging the worksheet so that cell G20 is the upper left cell on-screen. Then position the cell pointer in cell H21 and select /Worksheet Titles Both. To improve the appearance of the screen, you can hide column G by selecting /Worksheet Column Hide, moving the cell pointer into column G, and pressing Enter. The screen resembles figure 2.18. The cell pointer cannot move up or left of H21 (the new home position), and the user (or any macros in the range A1..F20) can add rows or columns without affecting the data-input area.

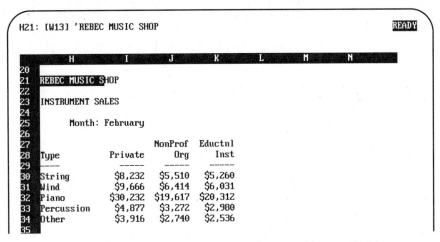

Fig. 2.18. With /Worksheet Titles Both active, and home position at cell H21.

Recognizing When To Use Other Worksheet Arrangements

Before you use the diagonal worksheet arrangement, consider whether you *want* the addition of columns in one section to affect other sections. Figures 2.19 and 2.20 show two sections of a worksheet used by a chain of electronics stores. Notice that the section in figure 2.20 appears directly under the section in figure 2.19. To list car stereo and personal stereo products separately, the user can create a new worksheet column between columns D and E, thus opening space in all sections of the worksheet. The modified worksheet appears in figures 2.21 and 2.22. In this case, arranging sections vertically makes more sense than arranging them diagonally.

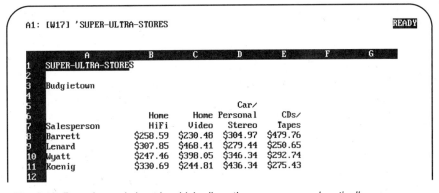

Fig. 2.19. Part of a worksheet in which all sections are arranged vertically.

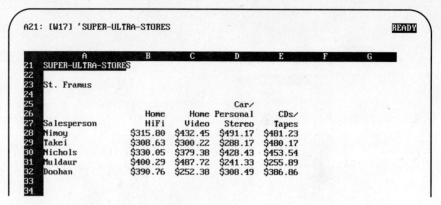

Fig. 2.20. *The second section of the worksheet in figure 2.19.*

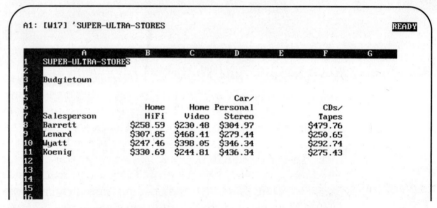

Fig. 2.21. *The worksheet from figure 2.19 with a new column inserted.*

A21: [W17] 'SUPER-ULTRA-STORES   READY

	A	B	C	D	E	F	G
21	SUPER-ULTRA-STORES						
22							
23	St. Framus						
24							
25				Car/			
26		Home	Home	Personal		CDs/	
27	Salesperson	HiFi	Video	Stereo		Tapes	
28	Nimoy	$315.80	$432.45	$491.17		$481.23	
29	Takei	$308.63	$300.22	$288.17		$480.17	
30	Nichols	$330.05	$379.38	$428.43		$453.54	
31	Muldaur	$400.29	$487.72	$241.33		$255.89	
32	Doohan	$390.76	$252.38	$308.49		$386.86	
33							
34							

Fig. 2.22. *The second section of the worksheet, also affected by the inserted column.*

Designing Applications in Release 3.x

Because 1-2-3 Releases 3 and 3.1 are three-dimensional, you can arrange an application requiring different section formats in different worksheets, so that adding rows or columns to one section does not affect another section. You also can keep macros and intermediate formulas in separate worksheets so that adding rows or columns to the data-input sections does not corrupt the programming. When the sections of an application share a common format, the GROUP mode feature enables you to synchronize all worksheets so that adding rows or columns to one worksheet changes all worksheets identically. This three-dimensional feature is ideal for designing both simple and complex worksheet applications.

Using Multiple Worksheets for a Single Application

If a worksheet contains many data-input areas, you can arrange those areas behind each other rather than spreading them across a large two-dimensional worksheet. Figures 2.23 and 2.24 show how the music shop worksheet from the preceding example can be arranged as a three-dimensional worksheet.

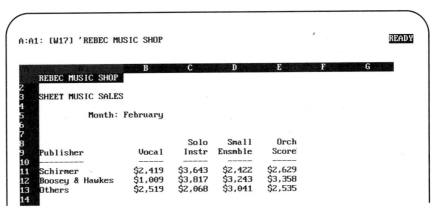

Fig. 2.23. The data-input area of the first worksheet.

The sections arranged in a diagonal pattern in a Release 2.x worksheet avoid problems caused by adding rows or columns to either section, but you must press at least two keys in succession (PgDn and Tab) to move from the first section to the second section. Arranging sections in worksheets A and B of a three-dimensional worksheet enables you to switch between sections using Ctrl–PgUp and Ctrl–PgDn. If you use Release 3.1 with the Wysiwyg add-in loaded and you have a mouse, you can switch between worksheets by clicking on the ↑ or ↓ icons at the far right side of the screen.

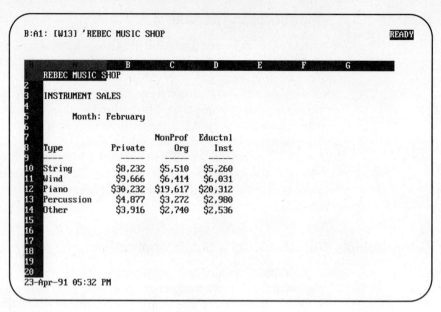

```
B:A1: [W13] 'REBEC MUSIC SHOP                                    READY

            B         C         D         E         F         G
  REBEC MUSIC SHOP
2
3  INSTRUMENT SALES
4
5       Month: February
6
7                         NonProf   Eductnl
8  Type         Private       Org      Inst
9  ----         -------   -------   -------
10 String        $8,232    $5,510    $5,260
11 Wind          $9,666    $6,414    $6,031
12 Piano        $30,232   $19,617   $20,312
13 Percussion    $4,877    $3,272    $2,980
14 Other         $3,916    $2,740    $2,536
15
16
17
18
19
20
23-Apr-91 05:32 PM
```

Fig. 2.24. *The second worksheet, unaffected by changes in the first worksheet.*

With GROUP mode disabled, users can add rows or columns to either worksheet without affecting the other worksheet.

Another advantage of arranging sections of an application in separate worksheets is that each section can have independent column widths. In a two-dimensional worksheet, you must arrange sections horizontally or diagonally if you do not want them to share column widths.

Using GROUP Mode To Format Multiple Worksheets Concurrently

In the electronics store example discussed earlier in this chapter, data-input areas were arranged to allow the /Worksheet Insert Column command to affect all sections. Figures 2.25 and 2.26 show the same work- sheet example as a multiple-worksheet arrangement. When you set up multiple worksheets in which the worksheets are formatted identically, you can enable GROUP mode by selecting /Worksheet Global Group Enable. In GROUP mode, some changes that you make in one worksheet affect all other worksheets. If you add a column between columns D and E in worksheet A, for example, a column appears in the same location in worksheet B. If you change the width of column A in worksheet B, the width of column A in worksheet A also changes.

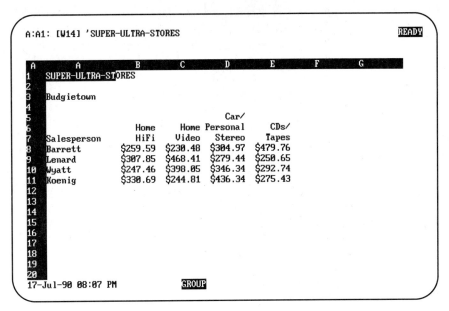

Fig. 2.25. Worksheet A with GROUP mode enabled.

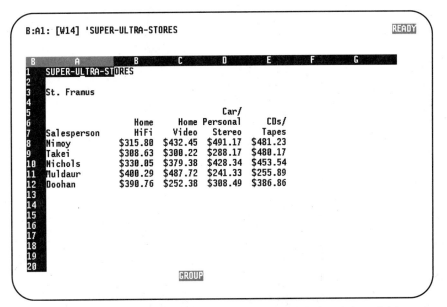

Fig. 2.26. The section of the electronics store worksheet behind worksheet A (shown in figure 2.25).

When GROUP mode is enabled, formats and label prefixes also are shared among worksheets. If you assign a currency format with two decimal places to range B8..E12 in worksheet A, the same format is assigned to range B8..E12 in all other worksheets. Formatting a range in one worksheet as right-aligned labels modifies all existing entries in the same range in other worksheets.

Storing Macros in a Separate Worksheet

Use separate worksheets for macros in an application even if you don't really need a three-dimensional worksheet for other reasons. To add a new worksheet, select /Worksheet Insert Sheet After 1. While GROUP mode is disabled, you can add rows and columns to other sections of open worksheets without danger of corrupting the macros.

When you create macros in a three-dimensional 1-2-3 application, assign names to any cells or ranges that the macros will update and refer to those cells or ranges by name (not coordinates) in the macros. Using cell addresses in macros is not a good idea, especially when multiple worksheets are involved.

Suppose that one of a macro's tasks is to copy the contents of the current cell to cell F35 in worksheet A. If the cell pointer is in worksheet D and the instruction is coded as /c~F35~, the macro copies the current cell to cell D:F35 (cell F35 in worksheet D) instead of cell A:F35. A better approach is to assign a name to cell A:F35—for example, NEWSALES—and to use the macro instruction /c~NEWSALES~. This practice eliminates ambiguity about where cell F35 will be copied, and eliminates the need to modify the macro if you change the arrangement of cells in worksheet A.

Using Macros in GROUP Mode Applications

Sometimes you may need to use macros in a three-dimensional worksheet with several identical data-input areas and with GROUP mode enabled. Suppose that you need some macros with the electronics stores worksheet (fig. 2.25 and 2.26). How can you arrange the application so that you can add rows or columns to the worksheets without corrupting the macros?

One approach is to place the macros in a separate worksheet, below and to the right of the range occupied by the data-input areas in the other worksheets. For example, if you are using five worksheets with entries in range A1..M113, you can place the macros in a sixth worksheet beginning at cell N114.

Another approach is to place macros in a separate file behind the current file. Suppose that you have a five-worksheet template with the file name

STORES.WK3. Add a sixth worksheet by selecting /Worksheet Insert Sheet After and entering 1; you can develop and debug the macros in the sixth worksheet. When the macros are complete, extract the worksheet to a separate file by selecting /File Xtract Formulas, entering a file name (for example, STMACROS), and highlighting the range containing the macros. To remove the sixth worksheet, place the cell pointer in the sixth worksheet, select /Worksheet Delete Sheet, and press Enter. Finally, select /File Open After and specify STMACROS. Now you can enable GROUP mode and add rows or columns to any of the five worksheets in STORES.WK3 without affecting STMACROS.WK3.

You can start macros in a different file by using Alt-*letter* combinations *only* if the corresponding range names do not exist in the current file. If the cell pointer is in worksheet A of STORES.WK3, for example, and you want to start the \d macro located in STMACROS.WK3, STORES.WK3 can contain no cell or range named \d. When you hold down the Alt key and press a letter, 1-2-3 first looks for the range name corresponding to that combination in the current file.

Using an Opening Screen To Document Multiple Worksheet Applications

Complex three-dimensional applications can be intimidating for newer users of Releases 3 and 3.1. An opening screen like the one shown in figure 2.27 can help the user navigate the worksheet, while protecting your programming.

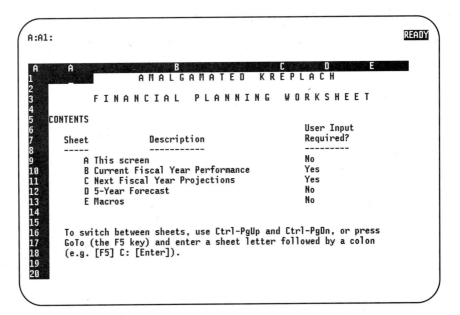

Fig. 2.27. The opening screen for a complex Release 3.x worksheet.

In Release 3.x, you can move the cell pointer to any worksheet by pressing GoTo (F5), entering the worksheet letter followed by a colon, and pressing Enter.

Summary

The best guide for efficient worksheet design is your own judgment. You can tell by looking at your worksheet whether an area designed for data input or producing printed reports is going to be confusing or clear. The only pitfall is your familiarity with the design; as you develop, test, debug, and improve a worksheet, try to take a step back occasionally and see the worksheet through the eyes of the person who will use it.

In this chapter, you have seen why good design is important, how to use labels sparingly but effectively, how to organize worksheets into manageable sections, and how to arrange worksheets so that changing one section modifies or doesn't modify another as desired.

The next chapter discusses various approaches to entering and manipulating data in your worksheets.

Chapter Three

WORKING WITH DATA

The formulas, functions, and macros that are the heart of a 1-2-3 worksheet depend on good information. This chapter discusses important practices for managing your data, including entering data efficiently, changing data appearance with format commands, copying and moving, and changing large blocks of data.

This chapter discusses the following strategies for working with data:

- When to use a label prefix
- How to enter labels that require label prefixes
- Which characters to use when entering values
- How to enter sequential values with /Data Fill commands
- How to create and use entry forms
- How to format values
- Efficient ways to copy data
- How to use /Range Value and /Range Transpose
- How to move worksheet data safely
- How to recover editing mistakes with the Undo key
- How to find and replace characters in ranges

Entering Labels

If you try to enter a label that begins with a number (for example, a street address like 1211 Sycamore Lane), 1-2-3 assumes that the entry is a value entered incorrectly, and switches to EDIT mode. Because the first character of the entry does not tell 1-2-3 that your entry is a label, you need to use a label prefix.

The most common label prefixes are the apostrophe ('), the carat (^), and quotation marks ("), which respectively indicate left-aligned, centered, and right-aligned labels. The backslash (\) creates a label that repeats enough times to fill a cell. The split vertical bar (¦) creates a label that appears on-screen but is not printed.

Deciding When To Enter Label Prefixes

Many keyboard characters can be used at the beginning of a label only if preceded by a label prefix. The following characters switch 1-2-3 to VALUE mode: 0–9, @, #, $, ., (, +, and –.

Because the slash (/) and the less-than symbol (<) access the 1-2-3 menu, neither can be used to begin a label. (The less-than symbol starts the menu because early versions of 1-2-3 ran on computers that did not have a slash key.)

The five label prefixes (', ", ^, \ , and ¦), if used as the first character of a label, appear on-screen and in printouts only if preceded by another label prefix. If you want a cell to display the label "N" Method, for example, and you type only "N" **Method**, the cell displays N" Method, and the cell contents are right-aligned. Instead, type '"N" **Method** to tell 1-2-3 that the following entry is a left-aligned label.

In figure 3.1, the label in cell AA1 indicates that the name \s is assigned to cell AB1. Because the backslash is a label prefix, you need to type '**\s** to enter the label. If you omit the apostrophe, the cell displays SSSSSSSSS.

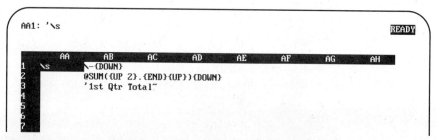

Fig. 3.1. *A label (in cell AA1) preceded by a label prefix.*

The purpose of the macro that begins in cell AB1 is to type a backslash and hyphen (to fill a cell with hyphens) and then move the cell pointer down. If you type the entry in cell AB1 without an apostrophe, cell AB1 displays -{DOWN}-{. Cell AB2 requires a label prefix because the string begins with a mathematical symbol. If you type this entry without a label prefix, 1-2-3 attempts to execute an invalid formula.

When \s is invoked, the entry in cell AB3 enters a label. Because the label begins with a number, the macro must type a label prefix; therefore, you need to enter this cell as **"1st Qtr Total**. The first apostrophe is the cell's label prefix. The second is the apostrophe that the macro types when entering the label 1st Qtr Total.

Assigning a Label Format with Release 3.x

With Release 3.x, you can assign the Label format to a range or to the worksheet. Select **/R**ange Format Other and specify the range in which you want to enter labels, or select **/W**orksheet Global Format Label to format the entire worksheet in label format (except for those cells and ranges that already have a format). Assigning the Label format means that you can enter labels beginning with numerals or math operators without typing a label prefix. Exceptions to this rule include labels beginning with / or <, and labels whose first character is a label prefix.

Entering Values

Any cell entry that is not a label must be a value. 1-2-3 actually considers both simple numbers and formulas to be values. The following sections, however, use the term *values* to mean simple values; these sections discuss ways to enter many values in the worksheet.

The 10 numerals and the decimal point are the characters used most frequently when entering values.

Few 1-2-3 users know how to use the percent sign to enter values. To enter the value 11.9% in a cell, you mentally divide 11.9 by 100; that is, you move the decimal point two places to the left, and enter **.119**. You also can enter **11.9%**, and 1-2-3 divides the number by 100. You may prefer to divide by 100 because you do not have to use a shifted key to enter values. Note that if you enter **11.9%**, the cell displays 11.9% only if you assign it the Percent format with one decimal place or the Automatic format with Release 3.x.

You can use *E* or *e* to enter very large values; E stands for the term *times 10 to the power of*. Enter **5e2** in a cell, and 1-2-3 converts the entry to 500, 5 times 10 to the power of 2. This function is useful in two ways. You can copy printed values in scientific notation into the worksheet by typing them *verbatim*. You also can enter large numbers without having to count zeros. When entering the value 3.2 million, you may lose track of the zeros typing 3200000. If you remember that whole millions have six zeros, you can enter 3.2 million as **3.2e6**. 1-2-3 immediately converts the entry to 3200000.

Using the Numeric Keypad

Using the top row number keys of your keyboard to enter values can be tedious. Learn to use the numeric keypad instead. The keypad is easier to use than you may think, and with a little practice you can use it to enter numbers quickly and accurately.

A problem with using the numeric pad is that on most computers the same keys are used as direction keys. You can solve this problem in one of two ways. One solution is to use a macro (discussed in the next section) that enables you to enter a number and then moves the cell pointer for you. A second and simpler approach, suitable for smaller quantities of numbers, changes the direction keys to numeric keys by using the Shift key. Use your left hand to operate the Shift key while entering numbers with your right hand. When the Num Lock key is on, the Shift key has the opposite effect.

If you are not adept at using the numeric keypad, try entering the numbers you see in column B of figure 3.2. Move the cell pointer to cell B5. Turn off Num Lock. Position your index, middle, and ring fingers on the 4, 5, and 6 keys on the numeric keypad. Hold down the Shift key with your left hand, and press the 5, 6, and 4 keys with your right hand. Release the Shift key and press the down-arrow key (on 2) with your right middle finger. Now the cell pointer is in cell B6. Press the Shift key again, and press the 5, 4, and 9 keys with your right hand. Release the Shift key, and press the down-arrow key (on 2) again. Repeat this process until you have entered all of the numbers down to cell B9 (use your right thumb to press the 0 key). Release the Shift key, press the down-arrow key four times, press the Shift key again, and continue entering the numbers in the range B13..B17.

Using a Macro To Automate Value Entry

If you need to enter many numbers in one column, use the macro shown in figure 3.3. Type the macro and assign the name \n to cell AB1. Move the cell pointer to where you want to enter the numbers, press Num Lock, and start the macro by pressing Alt–N. Type a number on the numeric keypad and press Enter. The cell pointer moves down a cell, and the macro waits for your next entry. When you finish entering numbers, stop the macro by holding Ctrl and pressing the Break key. Be sure to release Num Lock before trying to reposition the cell pointer with the direction keys.

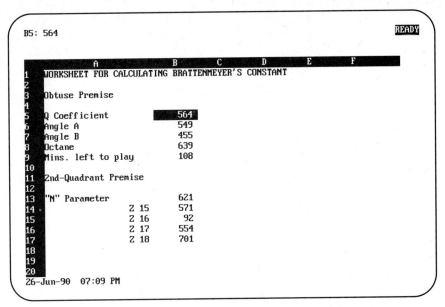

Fig. 3.2. *Some numbers you can use to practice using the numeric keypad.*

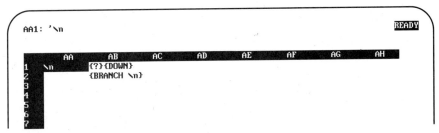

Fig. 3.3. *A macro that enables you to use the numeric keypad to type a column of numbers (without holding the Shift key).*

Entering Numeric Series with /Data Fill

The /Data Fill command provides a quick and convenient way to enter consecutive numbers or numbers separated by a constant interval: 1, 2, 3, 4, 5; 10, 15, 20; 13, 23, 33, 43; etc. You provide this command with a range to fill with values; a starting number; a step number (the interval); and a stop number (the ending value). You can enter the start, step, and stop values as numerals or as formulas. 1-2-3 fills the specified range with values, unless it reaches the specified stop value before the range is filled.

You can fill a range with any series of values, as long as the intervals between values are constant. Some possible combinations include the following: multiples of 5 starting at 1000; dollar amounts between $10 and $20 at intervals of 25 cents, where the start value is 10, step value is .25, and stop value is 20; and numbers ending with 3, where the start value is 3 and the step value is 10. To fill a range with descending values, use a negative number for the step value, and be certain that the stop value is equal to or less than the lowest value you want to use.

/Data Fill eliminates any existing entries in the range, whether or not the entire range fills with values. If you select /Data Fill and specify A1..A100 as the range, and enter 1, 1, and 50 as the start, step, and stop values, existing entries in range A1..A50 are overwritten, and entries in range A51..A100 are erased.

Finding the Right Stop Value

When you use /Data Fill, you must have the correct stop value. Using integers is simple; to fill a range with the numbers 1 to 17, specify a fill range 17 cells high and accept the default stop value (usually 8191), or specify a fill range a bit larger than you need and specify 17 as the stop value.

When you enter formulas as the start, step, and stop values, you sometimes get unwanted results. Suppose that you want to fill a range with 15 values between 0 and π times 2 (approximately 6.283), not including 0. If the range is A1..A20, the start value is 2*@PI/15, the step value is 2*@PI/15, and the stop value is 2*@PI, the /Data Fill operation stops at cell A14, which contains approximately 5.87. The operation cannot reach cell A20 because the value 1-2-3 computes for the 15th number in the series is slightly higher than 2 times π. Instead, use the size of the range and not the stop value to control the last number to be created. Specify A1..A15 as the fill range, use 2*@PI/15 for the step and stop values, and enter a number higher than 2 times π, such as 7, as the stop value.

Filling Rectangular Ranges with Numeric Series

You can arrange the numbers in a column, along a row, or in a rectangular range. Figure 3.4 shows the result of using /Data Fill with a fill range of B4..E10, a start value of 10, and a step value of 10. 1-2-3 fills the range from top to bottom, and then from left to right.

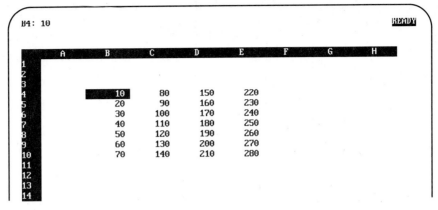

Fig. 3.4. A /*D*ata *F*ill rectangular range filled in column order from top to bottom.

To fill a range with numbers arranged in rowwise order left to right and then top to bottom, you can use the /**D**ata **F**ill command in combination with the /**R**ange **T**ranspose command. The key is to reverse the dimensions of the fill range. Figure 3.4 shows a filled 4–by–7 range, 4 columns wide and 7 rows high. To fill a 4–by–7 range with numbers arranged in rows, start by using /**D**ata **F**ill to fill a 7–by–4 range. Figure 3.5 shows the result of filling such a range. Select /**R**ange **T**ranspose, highlight the range just filled, and move the cell pointer to the upper left corner of an empty area of the worksheet. (The result of this operation is shown in figure 3.6.) Erase the original range and move the transposed range to the desired location.

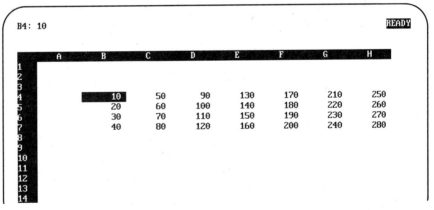

Fig. 3.5. A /*D*ata *F*ill 7–by–4 rectangular range arranged in columns.

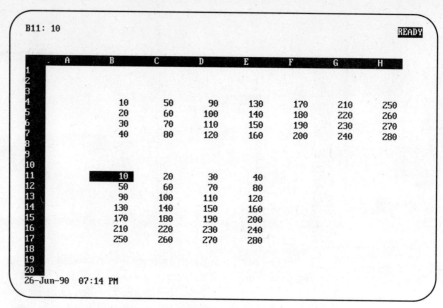

Fig. 3.6. *A 4–by–7 range in rows created by using the /Range Transpose command on a 7–by–4 range in columns.*

Using Dates and Times with /Data Fill

You can enter date formulas as start, step, and stop values to fill a range with a series of dates. In figure 3.7, the entries in column A were created by using /Data Fill with a start value of @DATE(91,4,12), a step value of 1, and a stop value of @DATE(91,4,24). To fill a range with dates a week apart, use 7 as the step value, and use as the stop value a date that you are sure is later than the last date to be created.

In figure 3.8, a range is filled with a series of times at 15-minute intervals. The start value is @TIME(13,0,0), and the step value is @TIME(0,15,0).

If you use 0 as a start value and assign one of the international date formats to the fill range, the resulting entries resemble elapsed times instead of times of day (see fig. 3.9). The start value is 0, and the step value is @TIME(0,5,0). The short international time format, /Range Format Date Time 4, is assigned to range A2..A17.

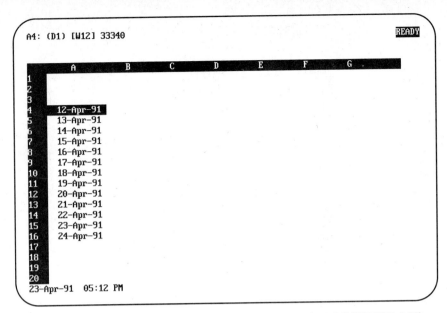

Fig. 3.7. *A filled range created with /Data Fill using a start value of @DATE(91,4,12).*

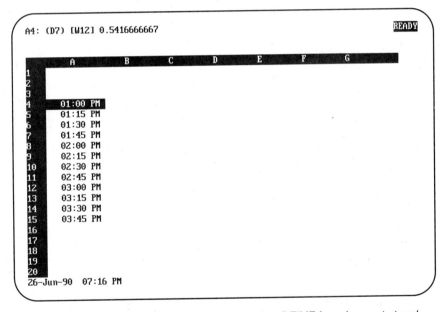

Fig. 3.8. *A series of times in a range created by using @TIME formulas as start and step values.*

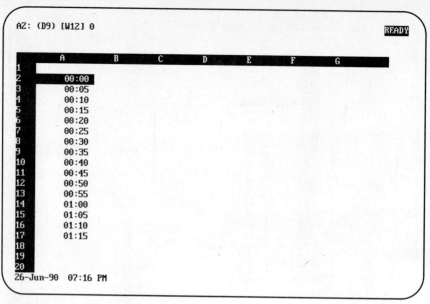

```
A2: (D9) [W12] 0                                              READY

         A         B      C      D      E      F      G
1
2     00:00
3     00:05
4     00:10
5     00:15
6     00:20
7     00:25
8     00:30
9     00:35
10    00:40
11    00:45
12    00:50
13    00:55
14    01:00
15    01:05
16    01:10
17    01:15
18
19
20
26-Jun-90  07:16 PM
```

Fig. 3.9. *A series of elapsed times in a range created by using 0 as a start value and an @TIME formula as the step value.*

Formatting Values

Intermediate 1-2-3 users are familiar with format options that have been constant since the software's first version, such as **Fixed**, **Currency**, **Date**, and **+/−** formats. In the sections that follow, you see how to avoid the problems associated with the General format, how to use **/R**ange Format **R**eset to advantage, how to change the appearance of several formats, and how to use the advanced formatting features of Release 3.x.

Understanding General Format

General is the default format in effect when you start a new 1-2-3 session. Cells assigned the General format display as many decimal places as are needed to express the number. For a value with an infinite number of decimal places, such as 10/3 or π, the cell displays the value with one less character than the width of the cell, up to a maximum of 12 characters. If column A has a default width of 9, for example, the formula 10/2 in cell A1 displays 5, the formula 10/4 displays 2.5, and the formula 10/3 displays 3.333333. In a cell with a width of 40, however, 1-2-3 displays only 10 decimal places; therefore, 10/3 returns 3.3333333333.

General is the only format that displays a decimal point with no numerals after it. If a formula computes 135.9748 in a cell with a column width of 5, for example, the characters 135. display in the cell. Notice that the General format truncates, rather than rounds. The value 135.9748 in a cell with the Fixed 0 format displays as 136. General format displays 135., although the value is closer to 136. If precision is critical, avoid using General format to prevent returning misleading numbers.

General format is useful for displaying high numbers without filling a cell with asterisks. If the column is wider than 6 characters, the General format switches to scientific notation when necessary. The number one billion in a nine-character cell is displayed as 1.0E+09, 1 times 10 to the 9th power.

Using /Range Format Reset

The Reset option of the /Range Format menu removes the format from a cell or a range and makes the cell or range conform to the global format of the worksheet. Suppose that your worksheet has a global format of Currency 0, but one range is formatted as Currency 2. You want the values in this range to display zero decimal places. Don't assign the Currency 0 format to this range; when you format an individual range, 1-2-3 uses memory for each cell in that range. Instead, remove the Currency 2 format with /Range Format Reset to get the Currency 0 setting.

Changing the Appearance of Currency and Comma Formats

You can change the appearance of most formats by changing the punctuation marks 1-2-3 uses to separate digits. In some European countries, for example, the number 4,323.54 is written as 4.323,54. A period separates thousands and a comma separates the integer portion from the decimal portion.

To use this convention in 1-2-3, select /Worksheet Global Default Other International Punctuation B Quit. To make this change permanent, select Update Quit; otherwise, just select Quit. The formats that normally use a decimal point, such as Fixed, Scientific, Currency, , (comma), General, and Percent, will then use a comma. The formats that use commas to separate thousands, Currency and , (comma), will instead use a period.

By default, 1-2-3 displays negative values in parentheses in cells assigned the Currency or comma format. With Releases 2.2, 2.3, 3, and 3.1, you can choose to have such values displayed with a minus sign. Select /Worksheet Global Other Default International Negative Sign Quit. Select Update if you want to make the change permanent, and select Quit.

Changing the Currency Symbol

You also can change the monetary symbol used in the Currency format. Select /Worksheet Global Default Other International Currency. Type the character(s) to use as the currency symbol; for example, type **DM** for deutsche marks or **Fr** for francs. To express currency in pounds, yen, pesetas, or guilder, press the Compose key (Alt–F1) and type **L=**, **Y=**, **PT**, or **FF**, respectively. Select **P**refix or **S**uffix, depending on whether you want the symbol to appear before or after the number. Select **Q**uit, select Update if you want to make the change permanent, and select **Q**uit.

Changing the Appearance of Date and Time Formats

You cannot change the appearances of the Date **1**, Date **2**, and Date **3** formats, but you can change the appearance of international date formats. The date May 15, 1991 can appear in any of the following formats:

05/15/91 or 05/15

15/05/91 or 15/05

15.05.91 or 15.05

91–05–15 or 05–15

To change the characters used in **D**ate formats, select /Worksheet Global Default Other International Date, and select **A**, **B**, **C**, or **D**.

Similarly, you cannot change the first two **T**ime functions, but you can change the punctuation used for Long International and Short International **T**ime formats. You can make 1-2-3 display the time 4:53:32 p.m. in one of the following formats:

16:53:32 or 16:53

16,53,32 or 16,53

16.53.32 or 16.53

16h53m32s or 16h53m

To change the characters used in times, select /Worksheet Global Default Other International Time, and select **A**, **B**, **C**, or **D**.

Using /Range Format Other with Release 3.x

Release 3.x provide four format options not available with Release 2.x. You access these formats by selecting /**R**ange Format Other.

Two options are not formats in the way that **Fixed** and **Currency** are formats. **/Range Format Other Automatic** and **/Range Format Other Label** affect the way 1-2-3 handles data as you enter it, not the way cells display values.

When you assign the **Automatic** format to a range, the manner in which you enter the next value in the cell determines the format assigned to it. If you enter **$520.73**, the cell gets the **Currency 2** format. If you enter **4,301**, the cell gets the comma format with no decimal places. If you enter **15–May–91**, 1-2-3 converts the entry to the value 33373 (this conversion happens whether or not you use the **Automatic** format) and the cell gets the **Date 1** format. The cells no longer have the **Automatic** format; they are permanently formatted according to the manner in which you entered the values.

When you assign the **Label** format to a range, everything you enter in that range is treated as a label. You can enter such labels as **1st Qtr Sales** or **4329 Larsen St.** without typing an apostrophe.

Use **/Range Format Other Color Negative** to make 1-2-3 display negative values in a different color or, if you use a monochrome monitor, a different intensity than positive values. The **Negative** format can coexist with another format in the same cell. Use **/Range Format Other Color Reset** to remove this option from cells.

The **Parentheses** option also coexists with other options, enabling you to enclose values in parentheses to differentiate them from other values in the worksheet. The number inside the parentheses can have any numeric format. A cell can display ($420.19), (38.1%), or (50). If you use the **Parentheses** format and **Currency** or comma format in the same cell, and you have not changed the default settings so that these formats use a minus sign, negative values appear in two sets of parentheses, (($5,000)), for example. Add the **Parentheses** format to cells with **/Range Format Other Parentheses Yes**; remove it with **/Range Format Other Parentheses No**.

Creating Entry Forms That Restrict Data Input

Sometimes you need to enter data in cells separated by no particular pattern (see fig. 3.10). This section of the worksheet enables a user to enter labels and values in the cells indicated by the outlines. Using characters to outline input cells is optional.

Using the Wysiwyg add-in with Release 3.1 or Impress with Release 2.2 enables you to create more attractive entry forms by encasing cells in solid lines.

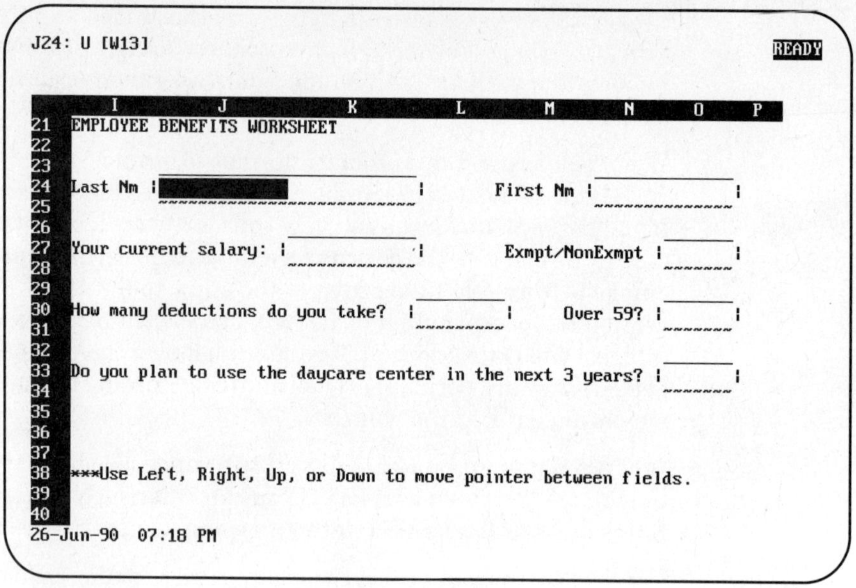

```
J24: U [W13]                                                            READY

        I          J          K          L          M          N     O     P
21  EMPLOYEE BENEFITS WORKSHEET
22
23
24  Last Nm :█████████████████████:          First Nm :_____:
25                                                     ~~~~~~~~~~~~~~
26
27  Your current salary: :_____:          Exmpt/NonExmpt :_____:
28                       ~~~~~~~~~~~~~                           ~~~~~~~
29
30  How many deductions do you take? :_____:     Over 59? :_____:
31                                   ~~~~~~~~~              ~~~~~~~~
32
33  Do you plan to use the daycare center in the next 3 years? :_____:
34                                                              ~~~~~~~
35
36
37
38  ***Use Left, Right, Up, or Down to move pointer between fields.
39
40
    26-Jun-90   07:18 PM
```

Fig. 3.10. *A portion of the worksheet transformed into an input screen using /Range Input.*

By using the keys listed in the label at the bottom of figure 3.10, you can move the cell pointer directly from one input cell to the next with just one keystroke.

Creating the Input Area with /Range Input

With all versions of 1-2-3, you can set up an input screen like the one in figure 3.10 using the /Range Input command. After you select Input and specify a range, 1-2-3 moves the upper left corner of that range to the upper left corner of the screen and positions the cell pointer on the top left unprotected cell in the range. Turning on the worksheet's protection feature by selecting /Worksheet Global Protection Enable is not necessary.

Assume that the name INPRANGE is assigned to range I21..P40 and that cells J24, N24, K27, O27, L30, O30, and O33 are unprotected. No matter where in the worksheet the cell pointer is located, selecting /Range Input and specifying INPRANGE as the data range brings up the screen shown in figure 3.10.

Entering Data into an Entry Form

After selecting **/R**ange **I**nput, execute one of three different procedures: press Enter or Esc to end the input operation and return the cell pointer to its original location; make an entry in the current cell; or press a direction key to move to a different entry cell.

If you make an entry in the current cell, 1-2-3 interprets the first character typed and decides whether the entry is a value or a label. You can use / or < as the first character in a label in an entry form. You finish an entry by pressing Enter, which finalizes the entry but does not end the input operation. Press Enter twice to complete an entry and end the input operation. Similarly, you can cancel a cell entry by pressing Esc. If you are in the middle of an entry, however, Esc does not end the input operation.

Another option is to press a direction key, End, or Home to move to another entry cell. From cell J24, pressing the right-arrow key moves the cell pointer to cell N24, the down-arrow key moves to cell K27, and the left-arrow key, up-arrow key, and End each move to the last unprotected cell in the input range (O33). Pressing Home after moving the cell pointer to another cell causes the cell pointer to jump back to cell J24. Pressing the right-arrow key repeatedly moves the cell pointer to each input cell in succession, and then back to cell J24.

You can use the direction keys, Home, or End to finish an entry and move the cell pointer to the next input cell with just one keystroke. When the cell pointer is in cell J24, for example, you can type the letters **Flintstone** and press the right-arrow key. The label Flintstone is entered in cell J24, and the cell pointer jumps to cell N24.

Using a Macro with Entry Forms

Macros can make the **/R**ange **I**nput command easier to use. Just include the label **/riINPRANGE~** in the macro. Keep in mind that this instruction suspends operation of the macro; instructions that follow the macro are not executed until the user ends the input operation. A macro cannot move the cell pointer or enter data during an input operation; a macro also cannot end an input operation.

Using the FORM Command with Releases 2.3 and 3.x

1-2-3 Releases 2.3, 3, and 3.1 include an advanced macro command that operates like **/R**ange **I**nput with some extra features. The FORM command syntax is as follows:

{FORM *input_area,[call_range],[include_range],[exclude_ range]*}

All arguments except the first are optional. In figure 3.10, you can include the instruction {FORM INPRANGE} in a Release 2.3 or 3.x worksheet, and it functions identically to /riINPRANGE~, with two exceptions. The upper left corner of INPRANGE is not positioned in the upper left corner of the screen, and the screen is not restored to its original state after input is completed.

Using Optional Arguments in the FORM Command

Using optional arguments makes the FORM command much more powerful than /Range Input. You can use the second argument to specify a *call_range* in the current worksheet or in an open file. The *call_range* must be two columns wide. The left column contains a list of characters or key names, such as {CALC} or {TABLE}. The right column contains macro routines to be called if the user presses the key named in the adjacent cell. The third argument specifies a range containing a list of keystrokes that are accepted while the input operation is active. The fourth argument specifies a range containing keystrokes that are not accepted.

Figure 3.11 shows an entry form from a Release 3 worksheet, and figure 3.12 shows the macro that drives the form. The name QUESTIONS is assigned to input range A1..D17. The name KEYS is assigned to range AB4..AC5 (the *call_range*).

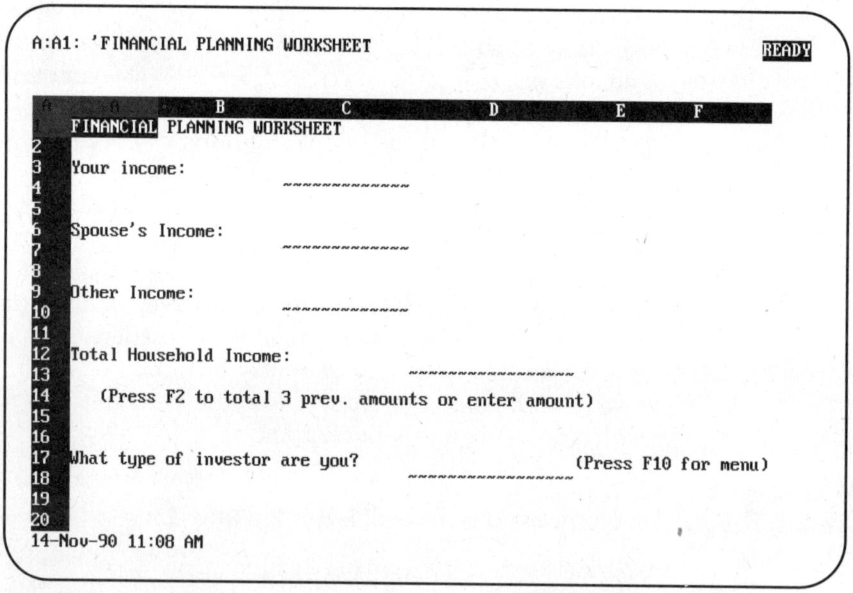

Fig. 3.11. *An entry form that is controlled by the FORM command.*

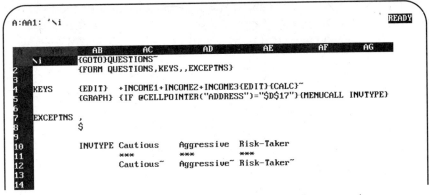

```
A:AA1: '\i                                                    READY

              AB          AC           AD          AE         AF        AG
      \i     {GOTO}QUESTIONS~
2            {FORM QUESTIONS,KEYS,,EXCEPTNS}
3
4     KEYS   {EDIT}  +INCOME1+INCOME2+INCOME3{EDIT}{CALC}~
5            {GRAPH} {IF @CELLPOINTER("ADDRESS")="$D$17"}{MENUCALL INVTYPE}
6
7     EXCEPTNS ,
8              $
9
10           INVTYPE Cautious    Aggressive   Risk-Taker
11                   ***         ***          ***
12                   Cautious~   Aggressive~  Risk-Taker~
13
14
```

Fig. 3.12. A FORM command (in cell AB2) that includes a call_range and an exclude_range.

If the user presses F2 (Edit), the keystrokes in cell AC4 are invoked, typing the formula +INCOME1+INCOME2+INCOME3, converting the formula to a value, and pressing Enter. The label in cell AB5 indicates that F10 (Graph) is intended for use when the cell pointer is in cell D17, but no provision is made to prevent its use at other times.

If the user presses F10 (Graph), the advanced macro commands in cell AC5 are invoked. The IF command prevents the Graph key from having any effect if the cell pointer is not in cell D17. If the cell pointer is in cell D17, the second instruction calls the simple menu in range AC10..AE12. This macro enables the user to select one of three descriptions, and enters the selected description in cell D17.

Because this macro does not specify an *include_range* in the FORM command, two commas are required to separate the *call_range* from the *exclude_range*, which is specified as AB7..AB8. This *exclude_range* prevents the user from making the common mistake of typing commas when entering large numbers. This range also prevents the user from typing $, which is unnecessary.

Using the FORM Command with the APPENDBELOW Command

You can add information to a database using the FORM command followed by the APPENDBELOW command to add the entries from the entry form to the end of the database range. The APPENDBELOW command takes two arguments: *target_location* and *source_location*. The *source_location* can be only one row high and should be as many columns wide as the database (*target_location*). The *target_location* must include all of the records in the database range. Each time you invoke the APPENDBELOW command, the size of *target_location* expands.

Figure 3.13 shows a simple macro that uses the FORM command and an entry form. Figure 3.14 shows a database after APPENDBELOW adds the most recently entered record.

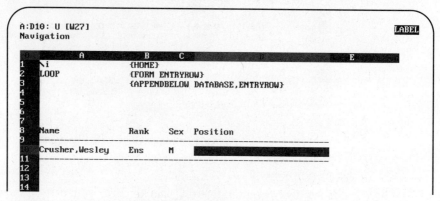

Fig. 3.13. *Using the FORM and APPENDBELOW macro commands to add records to a database.*

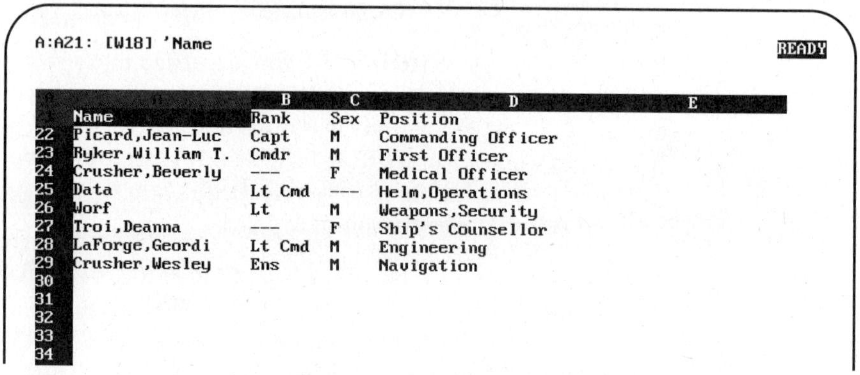

Fig. 3.14. *A new entry added to the database using the APPENDBELOW command.*

The FORM and APPENDBELOW commands are not available with Release 2.2 and earlier. You can use /ri (**/R**ange **I**nput) in place of the FORM command in macros. If you want the macro to add the entries to a database, however, you must add instructions to find the first empty row below the database, copy the entries to that row, and expand the database range.

Entering Dates and Times with Release 3.x

Entering dates is a difficult task with Release 2.3 and earlier. The most efficient method uses a formula, for example **@DATE(91,7,4)** for July 4, 1991. If you forget this format and try to enter a date in the common MM/DD/YY form, for example **7/4/91**, you create a formula that divides 7 by 4 and divides the result by 91, which returns 0.01923.

Releases 3 and 3.1 eliminate the difficulty in entering dates. If you enter three values separated by slashes and the combination can be treated as a date, Releases 3 and 3.1 convert the combination to the serial number corresponding to the date. If you type **7/4/91**, for example, the entry in that cell immediately changes to 33423. If the cell has a date format assigned, the cell displays the date, for example July 4, 1991.

You also can enter dates in the DD–MMM–YY format with Releases 3 and 3.1. 1-2-3 converts the entry **19–nov–41** to 15229. The letters in the month portion of the entry need not be capitalized.

If the combination of characters cannot be treated as a date, Releases 3 and 3.1 treat the entry as a formula. If you enter **6/31/91**, the entry remains 6/31/91, and 1-2-3 returns the value 0.0021269. If the cell has a date format, 1-2-3 displays the date January 00, 1900. If you enter **31–jun–90**, 1-2-3 treats the entry as a subtraction problem and returns ERR, unless the worksheet contains a cell named JUN.

If you omit the year number, 1-2-3 assumes that you want the current year according to your computer's clock. If you enter **7/4** or **4–jul** and the current year is 1991, the entry is converted to the value 33423.

Similarly, you can enter time in one of 1-2-3's time formats. Enter **12:00**, and 1-2-3 converts the entry to 0.5. Enter **4:36:30** pm, and 1-2-3 converts the entry to 0.192013.

Enter dates in the form MM/DD/YY only if 1-2-3 is configured to use that form as its long international date format. 1-2-3 also can be set to display and accept dates in the forms DD/MM/YY, DD.MM.YY, and YY–MM–DD. To learn the current international date format, select **/W**orksheet **G**lobal **D**efault **S**tatus.

If you enter a time in 12-hour format and specify a.m. or p.m., or if you omit the a.m. or p.m. specification but the time is between 1:00 a.m. and 12:59:59 p.m., use colons to separate hours, minutes, and seconds. 1-2-3 uses colons for the Lotus standard long and Lotus standard short time formats. To enter times in 24-hour format—**00:15** for 15 minutes past midnight or **16:00** for 4:00 p.m., for example—your entry must match the international time format for which 1-2-3 is configured. Releases 3 and 3.1 can accept times in the formats HH:MM:SS, HH,MM,SS, HH.MM.SS, or HHhMMmSSs. To identify the current international time format, select **/W**orksheet **G**lobal **D**efault **S**tatus. You cannot enter times in the short international format—hours and minutes only—if the default international date formats use periods.

Releases 2.2 and earlier are not so forgiving about entries resembling dates and times, but you can devise a macro that accepts a variety of different date and time formats. See the discussion of the functions @DATEVALUE and @TIMEVALUE in Chapter 6 of this book.

Copying Worksheet Data

When you develop worksheet applications, your work goes much faster if you copy labels or ranges of values or if you replicate formulas to fill large ranges, rather than creating an entry from scratch for every cell in the worksheet. The following sections discuss some tricks you can use with the /Copy command to save keystrokes.

Specifying Ranges

Many 1-2-3 users move the cell pointer to the upper left corner of the range to be copied before selecting /Copy. You can save time by selecting /Copy without moving to the source range first. One option is to un-anchor the FROM range in the control panel by pressing the Backspace or Esc key. This procedure removes the second cell reference; then you can move the cell pointer to the start of the source range and reanchor it by typing a period.

Another method is to specify the source range by typing the range name or cell coordinates of the range, such as SALES or C23..E30. When you press any key other than a direction key, Backspace, or Esc, the default source range supplied by 1-2-3 disappears.

The advantage of unanchoring the range or entering coordinates is that you can keep the cell pointer in the area in which you are currently working. The cell pointer returns to its starting point when the copy operation is complete.

Understanding the Implicit Size of the Target Range

If the source range has more than one row and more than one column (or more than one worksheet with Releases 3 and 3.1), the target range is the same size as the source range. If you copy a multiple-cell range to another location, therefore, you need not specify the entire target range, only the upper left corner.

If you copy range B15..C20 to range B25..C30, for example, the implicit target range is B25..C30, but you need specify only cell B25 as the target range. With Releases 3 and 3.1, if you copy the multiple-worksheet range A:A10..C:D20 to cell E:A1, the implicit target range is E:A1..G:D11, which you specify as E:A1.

A source range containing only one row can be copied to several rows, but the implicit width of the target range is the same as the width of the source range. Figure 3.15 shows a worksheet with three entries in row 1. You can copy these cells to a range of many rows, but the implicit width of the target range is always three columns. To copy range A1..C1 to range A2..C5, you only need to highlight or specify range A2..A5 as the target range. Figure 3.16 shows the result of the copy command in figure 3.15.

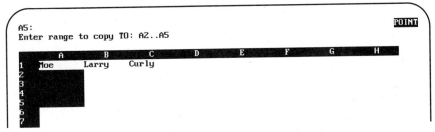

Fig. 3.15. Copying a multiple-column, single-row range to multiple rows.

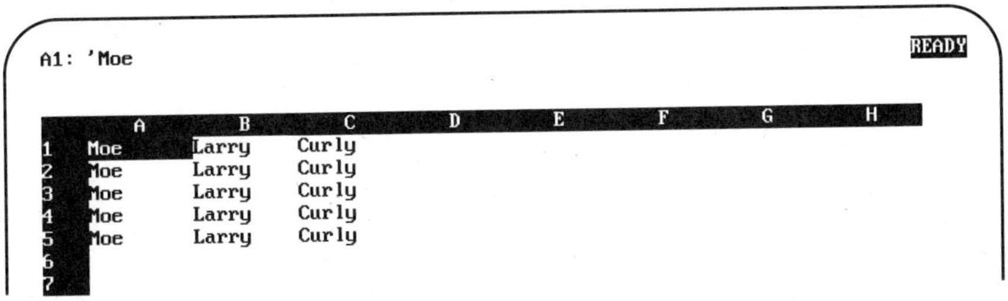

Fig. 3.16. Multiple rows resulting from the /*Copy* command in figure 3.15.

A source range containing only one column can be copied into several columns, but the implicit target range is the same number of rows as the source range.

Figure 3.17 shows a worksheet with five entries in column A. You can copy the cells to a range of any width, but the implicit height of the target range is always five rows. To copy these entries to columns B through F, specify A3..A7 as the source range and B3..F3 as the target range. The result of the /*Copy* command in figure 3.17 is shown in figure 3.18.

Adding the Depth Dimension with Release 3.x

1-2-3 ranges always have two dimensions: width (columns) and height (rows). With Releases 3 and 3.1, ranges have an extra dimension: depth (worksheets).

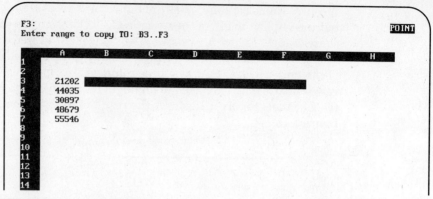

Fig. 3.17. *Copying a single-column, multiple-row range to multiple columns.*

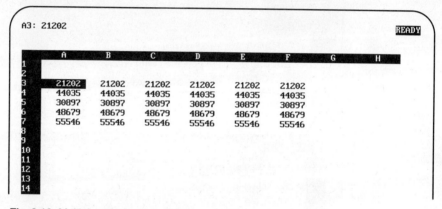

Fig. 3.18. *Multiple columns resulting from the /Copy command in figure 3.17.*

Just as you can copy a one-row source range to many rows, or a one-column source range to many columns, you can copy a one-worksheet source range to a target range several worksheets deep. The target range can be larger than the source range in all three dimensions when the source range consists of one cell. A range several rows high but one column wide and one worksheet deep can be copied to a range several columns wide, several worksheets deep, or both. The target range can be larger than the source range in any dimension where the source range has a size of one. Conversely, a source range several rows high, several columns wide, and several worksheets deep can be copied only to a range of exactly the same size.

Using Relative, Absolute, and Mixed References

How a formula changes when you copy it from one cell to another depends on whether its cell references are relative, absolute, or mixed. When you create cell formulas that you intend to copy later you must use the right kind of cell references, to make the copied cells do what you want them to do.

Relative addresses in a formula refer to cells by their position relative to the current cell—how many rows above or below, how many columns right or left, and (with Releases 3 and 3.1) how many worksheets before or after. If cell B1 contains the formula +A1, for example, the formula says *plus the value of the cell one column to the left in the current row*.

Absolute addresses refer to cells by their worksheet address. Instead of determining the position relative to the current cell, an absolute reference refers directly to the actual cell address. If cell C3 contains the formula +$A$1, its formula means *plus the value of cell A1*.

Mixed cell references are a hybrid of relative and absolute addresses. One part of a mixed reference is relative and the other is absolute. The formula +A$1 in cell B4 means *plus the value of the cell one column to the left in row 1*.

Adding a dollar sign before a component of a cell address in a formula changes that portion of the address from relative to absolute. The formula +A$1 is a mixed reference—relative in column address and absolute in row address.

Changing the Addressing Mode with the Abs Key (F4)

You can type the dollar signs as you enter addresses, but 1-2-3 provides another method for switching among relative, absolute, and mixed addressing modes, the *Abs key* (F4).

Using the Abs key (F4) to change addressing modes is simple. When you enter a formula, press Abs (F4) after you type an address or point to a cell. You also can use the Abs key after positioning the cursor under the cell address in a formula you are editing. Each time you press Abs (F4), 1-2-3 changes the addressing mode to the next mode available in the version you are using. The following tables show the modes in the order presented by 1-2-3, assuming that the existing formula is +B1.

After toggling through the available modes, 1-2-3 starts at the top of the list again.

Table 3.1. Release 2.x Addressing Modes.

Formula	Mode
+$B$1	Column absolute, row absolute
+B$1	Column relative, row absolute
+$B1	Column absolute, row relative
+B1	Column relative, row relative

Table 3.2. Release 3.x Addressing Modes.

Formula	Mode
+$A:$B$1	Worksheet absolute, column absolute, row absolute
+$A:B$1	Worksheet absolute, column relative, row absolute
+$A:$B1	Worksheet absolute, column absolute, row relative
+$A:B1	Worksheet absolute, column relative, row relative
+A:$B$1	Worksheet relative, column absolute, row absolute
+A:B$1	Worksheet relative, column relative, row absolute
+A:$B1	Worksheet relative, column absolute, row relative
+A:B1	Worksheet relative, column relative, row relative

Mixing Relative and Absolute Cell References

Figure 3.19 shows how you can use mixed absolute references to create a financial table by writing one formula and copying it into a large range. Notice the placement of dollar signs in the @PMT formula in cell B7. The first argument always must refer to the principal amount in cell A2; therefore this reference contains two dollar signs. No matter where this formula is copied, the first argument is $A$2 in the resulting formula. The second argument must refer to the row of interest rates and has a dollar sign before the row reference. Wherever the formula is copied, the second argument refers to the cell in the same column and in row 6. Because the third argument must refer to the column of loan terms, it has a dollar sign before the column reference. Wherever the formula is copied, the third argument refers to the cell in the same row and in column A.

To complete the table, copy cell B7 to range B7..G12. Figure 3.20 shows the completed table. Notice that the resulting formula in cell D9 retains references to cell A2 for the principal argument, row 6 for the interest argument, and column A for the term argument.

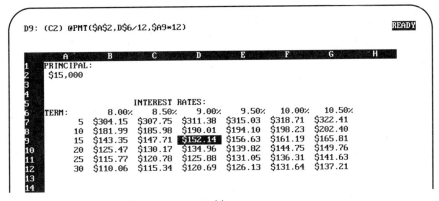

```
B7:  (C2) @PMT($A$2,B$6/12,$A7*12)                          READY

          A        B        C        D        E        F        G        H
 1  PRINCIPAL:
 2    $15,000
 3
 4
 5                        INTEREST RATES:
 6  TERM:        8.00%    8.50%    9.00%    9.50%   10.00%   10.50%
 7           5  $304.15
 8          10
 9          15
10          20
11          25
12          30
13
14
```

Fig. 3.19. *A formula with mixed and absolute references.*

```
D9:  (C2) @PMT($A$2,D$6/12,$A9*12)                          READY

          A        B        C        D        E        F        G        H
 1  PRINCIPAL:
 2    $15,000
 3
 4
 5                        INTEREST RATES:
 6  TERM:        8.00%    8.50%    9.00%    9.50%   10.00%   10.50%
 7           5  $304.15  $307.75  $311.38  $315.03  $318.71  $322.41
 8          10  $181.99  $185.98  $190.01  $194.10  $198.23  $202.40
 9          15  $143.35  $147.71  $152.14  $156.63  $161.19  $165.81
10          20  $125.47  $130.17  $134.96  $139.82  $144.75  $149.76
11          25  $115.77  $120.78  $125.88  $131.05  $136.31  $141.63
12          30  $110.06  $115.34  $120.69  $126.13  $131.64  $137.21
13
14
```

Fig. 3.20. *The completed loan payment table.*

Copying Formulas without Inserting Dollar Signs

If you create a formula whose references are all relative, but you need an identical copy of the formula at some other cell, you can achieve this objective without adjusting all of the references.

The trick is to convert the formula to a label. Move the cell pointer to the formula and press Edit (F2), Home, the apostrophe key, and Enter. Copy the resulting label to another part of the worksheet. Because it is a label, the cell references don't change. Edit the original cell, removing the apostrophe to turn it back into a formula. Edit the copied label in the same way to turn it into a formula. The resulting formula has the same cell references as the original.

Copying Absolute References Relatively

The need to copy absolute references relatively is a sticky problem that sometimes arises when you develop applications (see fig. 3.21). The worksheet contains three tables listing the monthly loan payments for 10-, 15-, 20-, and 25-year loans of $10,000, $15,000, and $25,000.

Create the worksheet in figure 3.21 so that you can follow this example. Set the width of column A to 7 and the width of columns B and C to 4. Enter the labels shown in cells A1, A3, and C3 and the values shown in range B3..B6. Enter \‐ in cell A2, and copy cell A2 to range B2..D2. Format cell D1 as Currency 0. Copy range A1..D13 to cell A8. Finally, enter **10000**, **15000**, and **25000** in cells D1, D8, and D15, respectively.

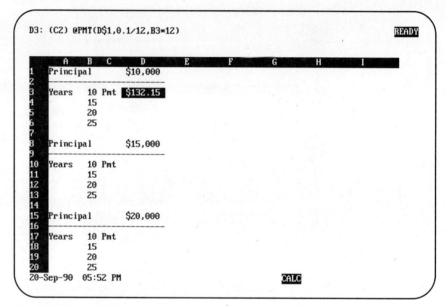

Fig. 3.21. A formula that presents a problem for copying.

Creating the worksheet is relatively simple up to this point. Now you must enter in cell D3 an @PMT formula that uses cell D1 as the principal argument and the cell two columns to the left multiplied by 12 as the term argument. To copy this cell into range D4..D6 and keep the reference to cell D1 in all the copies, include a dollar sign before the row reference in the first argument. Type the formula **@PMT(D$1,0.1/12, B3*12)** in cell D3, format cell D3 as Currency **2**, and copy cell D3 to range D4..D6. Your worksheet should resemble figure 3.22.

You now must copy those four formulas to ranges D10..D13 and D17..D20 in such a way that the D$1 reference is replaced with D$8 and D$15, respectively.

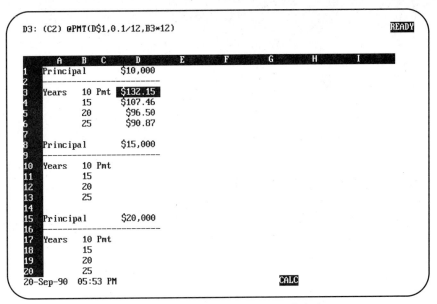

```
D3: (C2) @PMT(D$1,0.1/12,B3*12)                              READY

    A    B    C    D       E      F      G      H      I
1  Principal      $10,000
2  ---------------------------
3  Years    10 Pmt $132.15
4           15      $107.46
5           20      $96.50
6           25      $90.87
7
8  Principal       $15,000
9  ---------------------------
10 Years    10 Pmt
11          15
12          20
13          25
14
15 Principal       $20,000
16 ---------------------------
17 Years    10 Pmt
18          15
19          20
20          25
20-Sep-90  05:53 PM                         CALC
```

Fig. 3.22. The first payment formula copied to the three cells below.

With 1-2-3 Releases 2 and 2.01, you can make this copy by using the
/File Combine command. Assign the name PMTS to range D3..D6 and
save the worksheet using the file name TABLES. To create the appropriate formulas in range D10..D13, position the cell pointer at cell D10,
select /File Combine Copy Named/Specified-Range, type **PMTS**, and
enter or select the file name **TABLES**. This procedure combines the
formulas from the worksheet that you saved as TABLES.

The first of these formulas, however, refers to the cell two rows up, not to
a cell in row 8, despite the dollar sign. The formula that now appears in
cell D10 is @PMT(D$8,0.1/12,B10*12), as shown in figure 3.23.

Similarly, the formula in cell D11 refers to a cell three rows up. To
complete the worksheet, position the cell pointer in cell D17 and repeat
the /File Combine operation. The completed worksheet appears in
figure 3.24.

Using /Range Search To Change Addressing in Formulas

The /File Combine copying technique also works with Releases 2.2, 2.3,
3, and 3.1. You can avoid accessing disk files, however, by using an alternative technique involving the /Range Search command. To use this
technique, create the original formula with the absolute reference, and
use the /Copy command to finish creating the first set of formulas. Then

use the **/R**ange **S**earch command to delete the dollar signs. This procedure enables you to create additional sets of formulas by copying the entire first set.

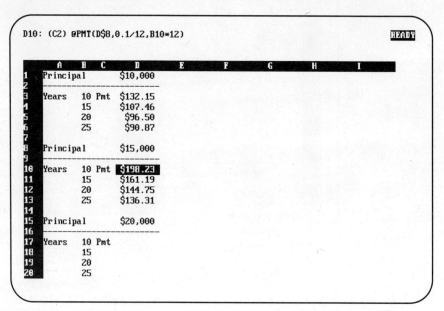

Fig. 3.23. *Formulas combined from a worksheet file, with absolute cell references copied relatively.*

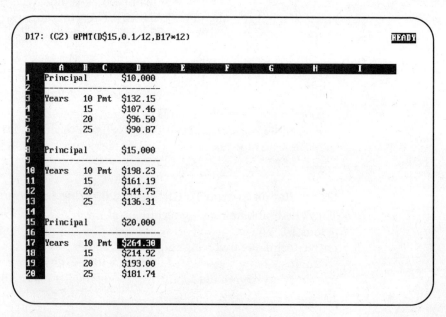

Fig. 3.24. *The completed payment table worksheet.*

To adjust the payments table in figure 3.24, select **/R**ange **S**earch and specify range **D3..D6**. At the prompt `Enter string to search for:` type **D$1**. Select **F**ormulas **R**eplace. At the prompt `Enter replacement string:` type **D1**. Select **A**ll. You have created four formulas containing references to cell D1 without the dollar signs.

To complete the worksheet, copy range D3..D6 to cell D10, and copy the same range to cell D17. All formulas in range D10..D13 refer to cell D8. Similarly, all formulas in range D17..D20 refer to cell D15.

Using Worksheet Relative Addressing with Release 3.x

Because Releases 3 and 3.1 can use multiple worksheets, the problem of copying formulas in the preceding example has a simpler solution. Use stacked worksheets, and place each of the loan payment charts at the same row-column address in a different worksheet. As long as you use a worksheet relative addressing mode, you can copy formulas that are row- or column-absolute to the other worksheets (see fig. 3.25).

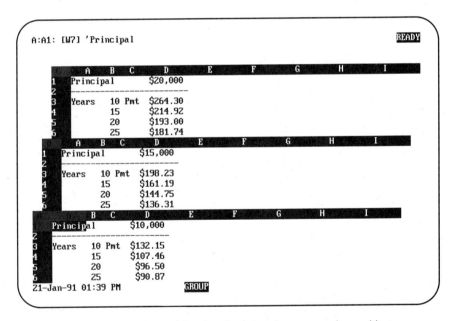

Fig. 3.25. A 3–D approach to solving the absolute reference copying problem.

Copying Near the Edges of the Worksheet

Be careful when you copy formulas containing references to cells near column A, row 1, or the first or last worksheet in a three-dimensional worksheet.

Suppose that cell E10 of a worksheet contains a formula with a reference to cell A1. If you copy that formula to cell E9, the resulting formula contains a reference to cell A8192; if you copy cell E10 to cell D10, the resulting formula contains a reference to cell IV1. With Releases 3 and 3.1, if a file contains five worksheets and a formula in worksheet D contains a reference to a cell in worksheet E, copying the formula to worksheet E creates a formula with a reference to a cell in worksheet A.

Copying Cell Formats and Protection Status

The /Copy command copies a cell's formats and protection status along with its contents. Suppose that you enter a formula in a cell and assign a Currency format. Copying that cell to fill a range ensures that all of the resulting cells have the same format.

Formatting a cell before you copy saves time, especially when you copy a cell to fill a large range. With a preformatted source cell, you highlight the large range only once (when you perform the copy operation) instead of twice (when you copy the cell and again when you format the large range).

You can copy the format or protection status of a cell to other cells even if the original cell is empty. When you copy an empty cell, you also are copying the *emptiness* of the cell, which means that you erase all cells in the target range.

Just as the /Copy command copies formats, it also copies the absence of formats. If you copy a cell that has no format assigned to it—a cell using the global format, for example—all cells in the target range lose their individual formats. You can use /Copy instead of /Range Erase to clear both contents and formats in a range; just find an empty cell using the global format and copy it to the range you want to clear.

Copying Allways Formats with Release 2.2

When you work with Release 2.2 and the Allways add-in program, you may want to copy the attributes assigned to a cell or range—font, color, shading, and lines—to another range without copying the data in that range. You can accomplish this objective by issuing the Allways command /Special Copy, defining a source range and target range as with the regular /Copy command. This procedure copies only the attributes assigned to cells by Allways; the contents of cells and the formats assigned by 1-2-3 are not copied. In figure 3.26, the user is ready to copy the Allways attributes assigned to source range C4..C8 to target range C11..C15. The shading, lines, and underlining visible in the source range (but not the data) will be copied to the destination.

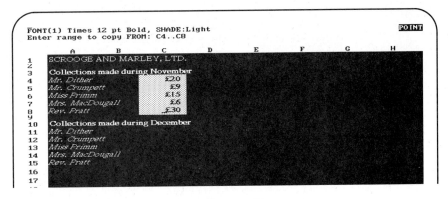

Fig. 3.26. Using the /*Special* **C**opy command in Allways.

Copying Wysiwyg Formats with Release 2.3 and 3.1

With Release 2.3 or 3.1 and the Wysiwyg add-in program, you can copy attributes from one cell or range to another without copying the data, using a process similar to the one just described for Allways and Release 2.2. Issue the command **:S**pecial **C**opy and define a source range and target range. This procedure copies only the attributes assigned to cells by Wysiwyg. To copy the contents of cells with the formats assigned by 1-2-3 and the Wysiwyg attributes, use the normal /**C**opy command. Figure 3.27 illustrates the use of the **:S**pecial Copy command.

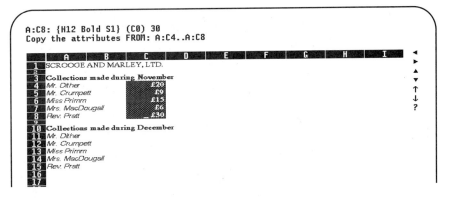

Fig. 3.27. Using the **:S**pecial **C**opy command in Wysiwyg.

*Allways and Wysiwyg also include the command /Special **M**ove or* ***:** Special **M**ove, which moves attributes from one place to another.*

Using /Copy To Recalculate a Range

When you copy a range to itself by selecting /Copy, specifying a source range, and specifying the upper left cell of the source range as the target range, the cell references in the formulas remain unchanged. The values that the formulas return, however, may change in some cases. When you copy a range to itself, 1-2-3 updates the returned values based on the current values of the cells to which the formulas refer. Copying a range to itself recalculates that range without recalculating the entire worksheet.

Suppose that you have a large worksheet (one that takes a few minutes to calculate) where the formulas in range C9..C17 are dependent on the value in cell C7. You want to change the value in cell C7 and find the new values in range C9..C17 without recalculating the entire worksheet. You must first set /Worksheet Global Recalc to Manual to stop the worksheet from recalculating. After changing cell C7, copy range C9..C17 to cell C9. The formulas return values based on the new value in cell C7.

This trick does not always yield accurate results. Suppose that cell C7 is not a value but a formula that depends on a value in cell C23. You change cell C23 and want to know the new results in range C9..C17. Copying that range to itself does not recalculate the range, because the result in cell C7 has not changed and because the formulas in the range refer to cell C7, not to cell C23. Recalculating a range by copying it to itself saves time, but you must be certain that all cells to which the range refers do not need updating.

Using /Range Value To Convert Formulas to Values

Using the /Range Value command is similar to copying, and you see the same prompts in the control panel. The difference is that /Range Value copies only the results of formulas and not the formulas themselves.

After you create an array of formulas, you may want the same numbers to appear in another part of the worksheet. Because values usually use less memory than formulas, you may want the second set of numbers to be values. To convert the second set of numbers to values, select /Range Value, specify the source range, and specify the target range.

You need to specify only the upper left corner of the target range when you use the /Range Value command. You can convert a range of formulas to values by selecting /Range Value, specifying a source range, and specifying the upper left corner of the source range as the target range. Keep in mind that the values in the target range are the current values of the formulas in the source range.

*Be sure to recalculate the worksheet before issuing the /**R**ange Value command or you may create an unchanging table of incorrect values.*

Using /Range Trans To Copy and Transpose

The /**R**ange Trans (transpose) command is similar to /**R**ange Value. The difference is that in the target range with /**R**ange Trans single columns of data are changed to rows. In the source range, single rows are copied to a columnar format.

Creating identical sets of labels down the side and across the top of a matrix is a good use for the /**R**ange Trans command (see fig. 3.28 for an example). After you enter the labels in range B7..B11, you can transpose the same set of labels to range C6..G6.

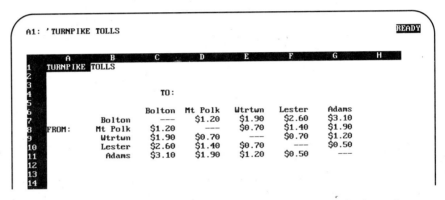

Fig. 3.28. *Using /Range Trans to create the same labels for rows and columns in a range.*

When you transpose a 3–D range using Release 3 or 3.1, you must make some choices. Figure 3.29 shows a range 3 columns wide, 3 rows high, and 3 worksheets deep with the numbers 1 to 27 arranged left to right, top to bottom, and front to back. When you select /**R**ange Trans, specify range A:A1..C:C3, and specify cell A:E1 as the target range, 1-2-3 presents a menu with the choices **R**ows/Columns, **C**olumns/Worksheets, and **W**orksheets/Rows.

Select **R**ows/Columns, and the numbers remain in their original worksheets but are arranged in columns instead of rows (see fig. 3.30).

Select **C**olumns/Worksheets, and all the left columns are arranged in worksheet A, the middle columns in worksheet B, and the right side columns in worksheet C (see fig. 3.31).

Select Worksheets/Rows, and all the top rows are arranged in worksheet A, the middle rows in worksheet B, and bottom rows in worksheet C (see fig. 3.32).

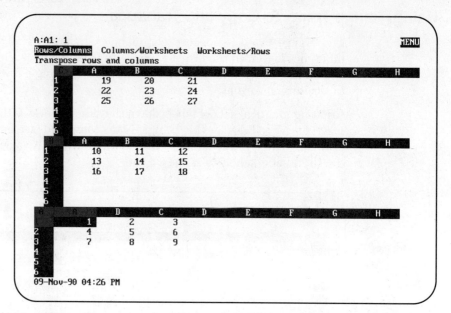

Fig. 3.29. A 3–D range arranged left to right, top to bottom, and front to back.

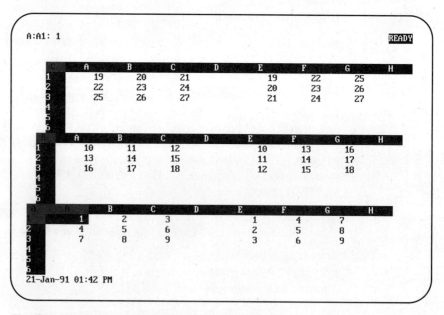

Fig. 3.30. The result of using /Range Trans Rows/Columns.

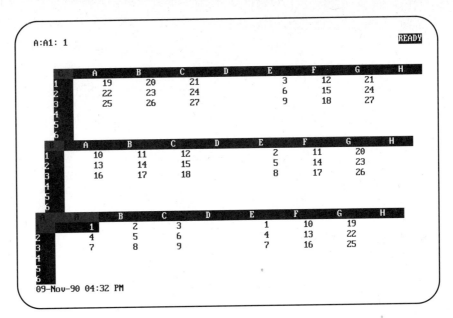

Fig. 3.31. The result of using /Range Trans Columns/Worksheets.

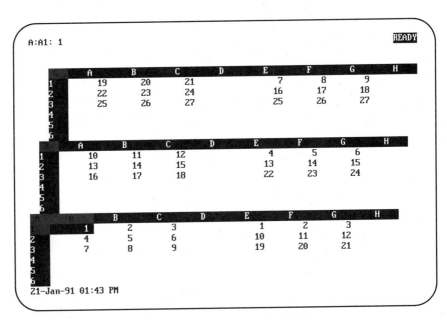

Fig. 3.32. The result of using /Range Trans Worksheets/Rows.

Using the /Move Command

Using the /Move command is like using the /Copy command. When you select /Move, 1-2-3 prompts you for a source range and a target range. To move the contents of range B15..C20 to range B25..C30, for example, position the cell pointer at cell B15, select /Move, highlight range B15..C20, and press Enter. Move the cell pointer to cell B25 and press Enter.

1-2-3 accepts range coordinates at the prompt Enter range to move TO: (or To where? in Release 2.3), but everything other than the upper left cell of that range is superfluous. You need to specify only one target cell for the /Move command.

The same method described earlier in this chapter for using /Copy can save time and keystrokes when using /Move. Don't move the cell pointer to the source range first; just select /Move. When the Enter range to move FROM: *prompt appears, press Backspace to unanchor the range, and specify the source range with the direction keys, cell coordinates, or a range name. Then specify the target range and press Enter. The cell pointer returns to its original location after the move is executed. This technique also works with the /Range Value and /Range Trans commands.*

Understanding How /Move Differs from /Copy

The /Move command and the /Copy command behave differently in two important ways. Cell references in moved formulas still refer to the same cells; and cells having nothing to do with the source or target range can be affected by the move (see fig. 3.33).

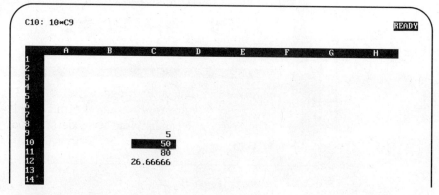

Fig. 3.33. Formulas (in range C10..C12) that refer to the cell above them.

Cell C9 contains the value 5. Cell C10 contains the formula 10*C9. Cell C11 contains the formula +$C$10+30 and cell C12 contains the formula

+$C11/3. If you move range C10..C11 to cell E10, the worksheet resembles figure 3.34.

Cell E10 contains the formula 10*C9. The reference to cell C9 in the original cell was relative, but the formula in cell E10 still refers to the original cell, C9. Cell E11, however, now contains the formula +$E$10+30. Despite the dollar signs, the formula in cell E11 still refers to the cell directly above it, not to cell C10 as it originally did. The original cell reference, C10, was moved to E10. Cell C12, which did not move, is changed to +$E11/3. This formula formerly referred to cell C11, but when cell C11 moved, the reference to cell C11 adjusted despite the dollar sign.

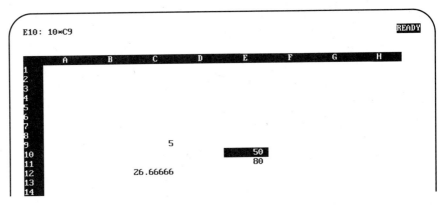

Fig. 3.34. *Formulas that retain correct cell references after being moved.*

Exercising Caution with the /Move Command

If you use the /Move command in a worksheet containing formulas referring to cells in the target range, those formulas are corrupted. Suppose that you enter the value **66** in cell E1 of the worksheet shown in figure 3.33, and move the contents of cell E1 to cell E11. Cell C12 changes to +ERR/3, as shown in figure 3.35.

The /Move command also corrupts range names. Never move a cell or range to another cell or range overlapping the anchor cells of a named range. With this move, the range name still exists but no longer has coordinates assigned to it. Any formulas referring to the affected range name also are corrupted. If a worksheet contains the range SALES and the formula @SUM(SALES), moving a cell to any cell overlapping the upper left or lower right corner of the range SALES cancels the coordinates of the named range and changes the formula to @SUM(ERR).

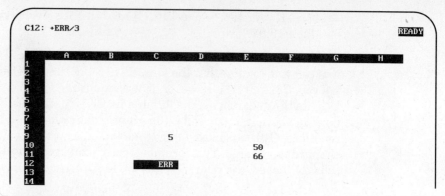

Fig. 3.35. Error caused by moving a value to a cell referenced by a formula.

To avoid these problems, use the /Copy command instead of the /Move command, and erase the original entry.

Look at figure 3.35 again. If cell E1 contains the value 66 and you want to move that value to cell E11, copy cell E1 to cell E11, and erase cell E1. To move a formula to a cell within a named range or used by another formula, change the formula to a label, erase the original entry, and change the resulting label in the target cell back to a formula.

Copying between Files and Worksheets with Release 3.x

With Releases 3 and 3.1, you can copy ranges from one file to another and, for some operations, from files that are not in memory.

Copying from a File on Disk

If you know the coordinates or range name of a range in another file, you can copy that range to the current file without opening the other file. Select /Copy; at the `Enter range to copy FROM:` prompt (or `Copy what?` in Release 2.3), type two less-than signs (<<) followed by the name of the file containing the range you want to copy, two greater-than signs (>>), and the source range. Press Enter, specify the target range, and press Enter again.

Copying a range from a file on disk is like using the command /File Combine Copy Named/Specified-Range. The difference is that formulas are converted to values as they are brought into the current worksheet. This method does not work backward; you cannot copy a range to a file on disk, because you cannot change a 1-2-3 worksheet that is not in memory.

You can use /Range Trans to copy and transpose a range from a work-sheet on disk to the current file. You also can use the /Range Value command to specify a source range in a worksheet on disk, but using the /Copy command gives you the same result.

Copying to or from Files in Memory

When you open more than one file, you can copy ranges from the current file to another file and from other files to the current file. To specify coordinates or range names from another file, type the name of the other file surrounded by greater-than and less-than signs (<< >>), and type the coordinates or range name. If you open the file SALES89 after you open the current file, and you want to copy range A:A5..A:C15 from SALES89 to the current location of the cell pointer, select /Copy, type **<<SALES89.WK3>>A:A5..A:C15** to specify the source range, press Enter, and press Enter again to use the current cell pointer location as the target. To copy range A:M1..A:M10 in the current file to cell A:P1 in SALES89, select /Copy, highlight range A:M1..A:M10, press Enter, type **<<SALES89.WK3>>A:P1**, and press Enter.

When you copy a range from one file in memory to another, formulas are not converted to values. Relative formulas do not change. Suppose that a formula referring to a cell five rows below it is copied to a different file. The resulting formula refers to the cell five rows below the target cell. Absolute or mixed formulas retain their characteristics, although the copied formulas refer to cells in the file to which they are copied, not the file where they originated.

Copying the formula +$E$15*1.05 to any cell in another file multiplies cell E15 in the other worksheet by 1.05. If the current file contains the formula +E$15*1.05 in cell E20 and you copy that formula to cell F30 in another worksheet, the resulting formula is +F$15*1.05.

This rule has one exception: If a formula refers to a named range and the name is preceded by a dollar sign, the copied formula refers to the named range in the original file. If the file SALES89 contains the formula @AVG($JULY) and you copy that formula to another file, for example, the resulting formula reads @AVG(<<SALES89.WK3>>$JULY).

Copying Data between Files without Using Coordinates

When copying data from an unopened file on disk, you must specify the file name and the range coordinates. When two or more files are open, however, you can specify ranges by moving the cell pointer and highlighting as when you are copying within one file.

To copy a cell or range from one file to another, you must open both files. Open the first file with /File Retrieve; to open another file, select /File Open. If the open files contain multiple worksheets, the Ctrl–PgUp and Ctrl–PgDn keystrokes move the cell pointer through the files one worksheet at a time. If the cell pointer is in worksheet A of a 10-worksheet-deep file, and you want to look at the next file, cycling through worksheets B to J can be tedious. To move quickly through a file of many worksheets, press Ctrl–End Ctrl–PgUp. 1-2-3 skips the remaining worksheets and brings the first worksheet of the next file to the screen. Ctrl–End Ctrl–PgDn moves the cell pointer back to the original worksheet location. Pressing Ctrl–End Home moves the cell pointer to the first open file. Ctrl–End End moves the cell pointer to the last open file.

Because copying from one open file to another leaves formulas intact, you must use /Range Value to copy from one file and convert the formulas to values in the process.

Copying to Noncontiguous Cells

The copy operation enables you to copy a formula to a series of noncontiguous cells, but this technique requires a little practice. In figure 3.36, the objective is to copy a formula to every second cell. Rows 4, 6, 8, and so on contain order numbers. Rows 5, 7, 9, and so on contain the sales amounts of the orders. The formula that calculates the commission for the first order is in cell B5. You need to copy that formula to cells B7, B9, B11, B13, and B15. To copy the formula, select /Copy and specify a source range that includes all but the last two cells of the area you want to fill with formulas. In this case, that range is B5..B13, as shown in figure 3.37.

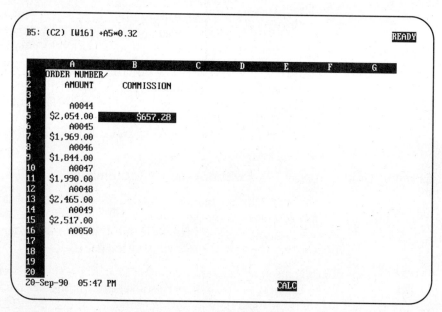

Fig. 3.36. *A worksheet requiring a copy of a formula in every second cell.*

Specify as a target range the cell in which you want the first of the copied formulas to appear. In this case, that cell is B7, as shown in figure 3.38. The completed worksheet resembles figure 3.39.

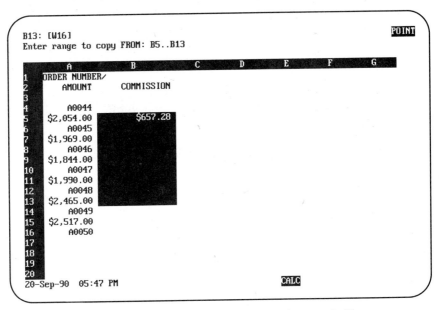

Fig. 3.37. Specifying a source range two cells less than the range to fill.

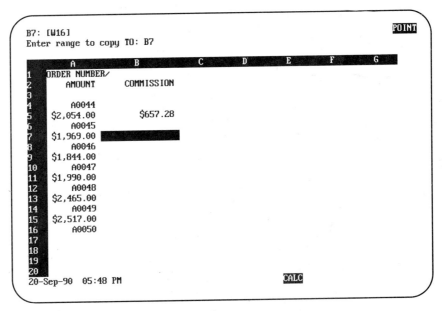

Fig. 3.38. Specifying a target range two rows below the beginning of the source range.

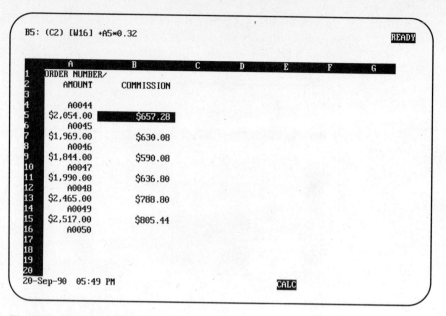

Fig. 3.39. A worksheet in which the formula in cell B5 has been copied to every other cell in range B7..B15.

To understand how this procedure works, you must understand how the /Copy command operates. 1-2-3 copies the first cell of the source range to the first cell of the target range; the second cell of the source range to the second cell of the target range, and so on. In this case, 1-2-3 copies cell B5 to B7, then B6, which is empty, to B8. Cell B7, containing the formula copied from B5, is copied to B9, and the empty cell B8 to B10. The copy process continues in this manner until 1-2-3 copies the last cell in the source range, cell B13, to the last cell in the target range, B17.

To copy a row of entries to every third row, specify a source range three rows less than the range you want to fill, and a target cell three rows below the first row.

The same techniques work for copying ranges wider than one column into alternate rows.

A similar problem with the same solution involves copying a cycle of entries. Figure 3.40 shows a projection worksheet being developed. The sales for the first year are known values. Assume that sales will increase by 12% from the fourth quarter of one year to the first quarter of the next, by 10% from the first to second quarter of any year, by 8% from the second to third quarters, and by 5% from the third to fourth quarters. Based on this assumption, the following formulas appear in range C7..C10:

C7:	+C6*1.12
C8:	+C7*1.10
C9:	+C8*1.08
C10:	+C9*1.05

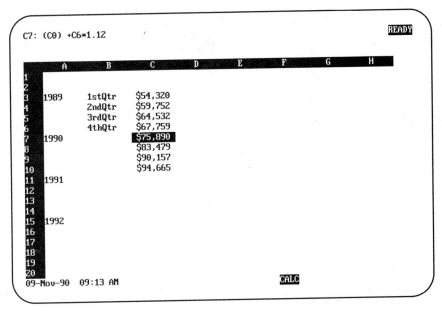

Fig. 3.40. A worksheet requiring additional sets of labels in range B7..B18 and formulas in range C11..C18.

These formulas provide projected sales for the second year. To complete the worksheet, create three more sets of quarterly labels in column B by copying range B3..B14 to cell B7. Create two more sets of projection formulas by copying range C7..C14 to cell C11. The completed projection worksheet appears in figure 3.41.

Using the Undo Feature

As you build worksheet applications, you may make mistakes. You may copy one range to another and overwrite important data in the target range. You may accidentally erase a range or even delete an entire worksheet that isn't saved.

The best protection against mistakes is saving the worksheet frequently. If you inadvertently erase a worksheet, or if you foul up your calculations, and you saved the worksheet 10 minutes earlier, at most you lose 10 minutes of work.

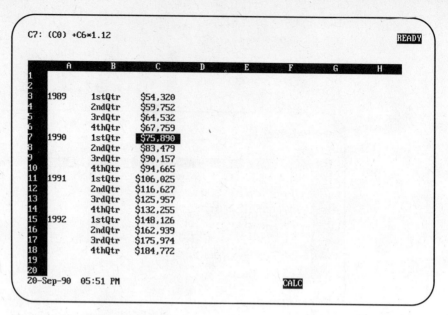

Fig. 3.41. *The completed projection worksheet.*

With Releases 2.2, 2.3, 3, and 3.1, you can recover from most mistakes without losing any work by pressing the Undo key (Alt–F4). You must press Undo (Alt–F4) before you taking any other action in the worksheet. If you overwrite data with /Copy and then enter a label, for example, Undo cannot bring back the important data; it only erases the label. Undo can often thwart a disaster, but is still no substitute for saving your work often.

Understanding How Undo Works

Releases 2.2 and 2.3 enable you to undo mistakes by storing a complete copy of your worksheet in an area of RAM called a *buffer*. When you make a change in the worksheet, such as entering a value, copying a range, or erasing a cell, 1-2-3 replaces the buffer contents with a copy of the worksheet as it appeared before you made the change. If you press Undo (Alt–F4), 1-2-3 swaps the worksheet in its current form with the worksheet in the buffer and makes the buffer version the current version of the worksheet.

1-2-3 requires more and more memory to store a backup copy as your worksheet gets larger. At some point, you may need to save memory by disabling Undo. Select **/W**orksheet **G**lobal **D**efault **O**ther **U**ndo **D**isable.

Releases 3 and 3.1 handle the Undo feature a bit differently. For efficiency, these products store in the buffer only the information needed to restore the worksheet to the state prior to your changes.

Another difference between Releases 3 and 3.1 Undo and Release 2.2 Undo is that Releases 3 and 3.1 display a Yes/No menu after you press the Undo key.

Using Undo To Experiment in Releases 2.2 and 2.3

With Releases 2.2 and 2.3, you can Undo the undo. The first time you press Undo after making a change, the worksheet in its prior state is swapped into the foreground. Press Undo a second time, and the current and backup worksheets are swapped again. You can repeat this process indefinitely, until you make another change in the worksheet. Because the Undo feature toggles in this manner in these versions, you can use it to conduct experiments as you design worksheets.

Enter **PROFIT AND LOSS REPORT** in cell A1 of a Release 2.2 or 2.3 worksheet. Then edit the label, adding spaces between the characters to read P R O F I T A N D L O S S R E P O R T. Press Undo (Alt–F4) several times. You can switch back and forth between the two labels until you decide which one looks better. You also can use Undo in this way to decide whether a Fixed format range looks better with **2** or **3** decimal places.

This experimentation trick does not work with Releases 3 and 3.1 because of the different way the Undo feature is treated; however, simple formatting comparisons can be made by copying the current worksheet to the next worksheet, making the change, and comparing the two by switching worksheets with the Ctrl–PgUp and Ctrl–PgDn keys.

Using Undo with Macros

When you run a macro, 1-2-3 stores the worksheet as it appears before the macro starts, rather than storing it continually as the macro makes changes to the worksheet; therefore, you can use Undo to undo an entire macro. This capability is especially useful when you are developing and debugging macros. A faulty macro sometimes can corrupt a worksheet; you can press Undo (Alt–F4) to restore the worksheet to its pre-macro state. Just the same, to prevent losing much work, save the worksheet before running a macro that you are developing.

Adding the Undo Feature to Earlier Releases

If you own Release 2, 2.01, or even Release 1A, and you have a copy of Lotus HAL, consider loading HAL with 1-2-3. HAL turns the Backspace key into an Undo key that works even when you perform operations with regular 1-2-3 commands. This system even toggles like the Release 2.2 or 2.3 version. The Undo feature alone makes loading HAL worth the effort.

Searching Ranges for Characters

Just as the newest versions of 1-2-3 enable you to recover from mistakes, they also enable you to change your mind about worksheet design. Suppose that you created a worksheet in which several of the labels use the abbreviation Intern'l to stand for International. Then you decide that the abbreviation Int'l would look better. With Releases 2.2, 2.3, 3, and 3.1, you can use the /Range Search commands to find all of the labels in a range or the entire worksheet containing Intern'l and change those characters to Int'l. /Range Search also can find characters without replacing them and can find or change strings in formulas.

Using /Range Search To Find Characters

To locate all of the cells in a range containing a given string, select /Range Search and specify a range to search. If a range is already specified, press Backspace or Esc to clear it. To search the entire worksheet, press Home, the period key, and End Home. Enter the search characters, select Labels or Formulas, and select Find. 1-2-3 finds the first cell containing the search characters and highlights the characters within the cell entry on the control panel. Select Next to find the next occurrence, or select Quit to stop the search operation and leave the cell pointer at its current location.

Using /Range Search To Change Characters

To find and replace strings of characters in a range of cells, you can use /Range Search Labels (or Formulas) Replace. Suppose that you created several different formulas based on cell B4, where you assumed that users would enter negative values. When you finish developing the worksheet, you decide that using positive values in cell B4 would be easier. To change the "polarity" of references to cell B4 in all formulas in the worksheet, you can use /Range Search to replace B4 with -B4.

This procedure places a minus sign in front of each occurrence of B4 in the search range but is likely to leave the expressions +-B4 and --B4 in many of the formulas. You can eliminate the extra minus signs by using

/Range Search Formulas **R**eplace to replace +-B4 with -B4, and then --B4 with +B4. This procedure may leave a few unnecessary plus signs. You may find a formula with the expression 2*+B4, but these extra plus signs do not change the outcome of the formula, and you can remove them as you find them.

Using /Range Search in Macros

To use the **/R**ange **S**earch commands in macros, you must solve the problem of clearing existing search and replace strings that may or may not be present. If you use Release 2.2 or 2.3, have the macro type a dummy character and then press Esc, as in the following macro:

```
/rsx{ESC}AAA~1rx{ESC}BBB~a
```

The advanced macro language in Releases 3 and 3.1 provides the CE (clear entry) command to remove the existing entry at a prompt. To use **/R**ange **S**earch with either version, use a macro instruction such as the following:

```
/rs{CE}AAA~1r{CE}BBB~a
```

Summary

In this chapter, you learned techniques for entering labels and numbers efficiently, filling ranges with sequential numbers, assigning formats to values, creating and using input forms, and copying and moving worksheet data.

Entering and formatting data is perhaps not as glamorous as devising efficient formulas or powerful macros, but managing worksheet data is important, and the skills acquired by practicing the methods discussed in this chapter can be of great benefit as you build worksheet applications.

The next chapter discusses strategies for using directories, storing and retrieving worksheet files, and other file management tasks.

Chapter Four

MANAGING FILES

When you are not using 1-2-3, your worksheets are stored in disk files. Retrieving and saving files is the first skill new 1-2-3 users need to learn, but disk files have many other uses, including sophisticated applications extending beyond the confines of one worksheet.

Most of the techniques discussed in this chapter surpass the two basic operations of retrieving and saving files. Even some intermediate and advanced techniques, however, relate to retrieving and saving files.

This chapter discusses the following file management topics:

- Setting the current directory
- Alternative ways to retrieve and save files
- Saving parts of worksheets
- Combining data from other worksheet files
- Importing data from files created by other software
- Linking files

Changing the Directory

Changing the directory that 1-2-3 uses for storing and retrieving files can save time and keystrokes. You can change the current directory temporarily by selecting **/F**ile **D**irectory and specifying the drive and path. When you change directories without changing drive letters, you can skip typing the drive letter. To switch from C:\123FILES to C:\ACCTG, for example, select **/F**ile **D**irectory and enter **\ACCTG**. If you use a subdirectory of the current directory, you can skip the backslash. To switch from C:\, the root directory, to C:\123FILES, for example, select **/F**ile **D**irectory and enter **123FILES**. You can use the same trick to select a directory within 123FILES. If you switch from drive C to a floppy drive or to a *logical drive*, a partition on a hard disk with its own drive letter, you must include the drive letter and a colon in the path.

If you use one directory most of the time, configure 1-2-3 to make that directory the default. Select /Worksheet Global Default Directory. Press Esc to clear the current path specification. Type the new path specification, press Enter, and select Update. 1-2-3 saves the updated configuration file (123.CNF), and the directory you entered is selected the next time you start the program.

Retrieving Files

When you select /File Retrieve and accept the default *.WK? search specifier, 1-2-3 displays the names of all files in the current directory with extensions beginning with WK—in other words, any file created by any version of 1-2-3. If you use Release 2.x and you have Release 3.x files with the WK3 extension in the directory, you cannot retrieve the Release 3.x files, although the names appear in the control panel. If you use Release 3.x, you can retrieve WK3 extension files, WK1 files created by the Release 2.x series, and WKS files created by 1-2-3 Release 1A.

Using the Name Key (F3)

You can search the files in the current directory by pressing the Name key (F3). 1-2-3 displays a maximum of 105 file names in full-screen format (see fig. 4.1). You can view additional file names by pressing the down-arrow key to scroll the list or End to jump to the last file on the list. To retrieve a file, highlight it and press Enter.

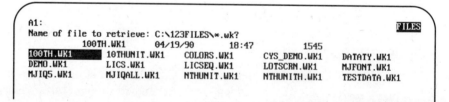

Fig. 4.1. 1-2-3 file names in a full-screen format.

Pressing the Name key (F3) displays most or all of your file names at once and, as you highlight a file, the date and time it was last updated and its size appear above the first row of file names. If you cannot remember the name of the file you want, checking the dates or file sizes may help you make a good guess. You may remember, for example, that you last updated the file you want in early April or that it was a very large file.

Searching for Specific Files

You can narrow the list of files to search by entering a name with wild-card characters. Suppose that the file you want to retrieve relates to hardware and its name begins with HDW. After you select /File Retrieve, enter **HDW*.*** to search for files beginning with HDW.

Searching Subdirectories

If you are searching for a file that may be in any of several directories, use the Backspace key to navigate through the directory tree.

Suppose that the current directory is C:\123FILES, but you keep worksheets in other subdirectories of the root directory. When you select /File Directory and press the Name key (F3), a list of files in C:\123FILES appears. When you press Backspace, your screen may look like figure 4.2. The path and file specifier at the top of the screen, C:\123FILES*.WK, is replaced by C:*.WK. If any 1-2-3 files are in the root directory, the file names appear on-screen followed by the root directory's subdirectories.

Directory names end with a backslash; file names end with the extension WK1. To look for a file in any directory, highlight the directory name and press Enter. If you see the file you want to retrieve, highlight its name and press Enter. To look for a file in a different subdirectory, press Backspace to redisplay the root directory and its subdirectories; highlight a different directory and press Enter.

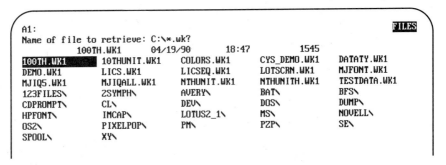

Fig. 4.2. Displaying a root directory's worksheet files and its subdirectories.

Opening Multiple Files with Release 3.x

Releases 3 and 3.1 enable you to open or retrieve files. *Opening* a file is like retrieving a file without losing the active worksheet. You can open a file before or after (in front of or behind) the worksheets you are using.

You can modify the file and establish links between the file and other worksheets and then save the file in its modified state. To open a file, select /File Open, select Before or After, and specify the file to open.

Saving Files

Saving your worksheet with Release 2.3 and earlier versions harbors a potential pitfall. From habit, you may select /File Save, press Enter, and press **R** to confirm the operation. If you have not established a name for a new worksheet, these keystrokes save the current worksheet by using the name of the first file in the current directory. The Undo key (Alt–F4) cannot correct this error. File recovery products such as Norton Utilities usually cannot restore the old file. Unless you backed up the first file to another disk or directory, the file is lost.

Protect yourself by establishing a file for each new project as soon as you start it, or select /Worksheet Erase to clear the current worksheet before starting a new worksheet, and save the empty worksheet with the new file name.

This problem is eliminated with Release 3.x; if you save a worksheet without establishing a file name, 1-2-3 uses the first available file name in a sequence beginning with FILE0001.WK3.

Protecting Existing Files

To provide additional protection for the first file in a directory, create a dummy file by saving an empty worksheet and typing ! when you are prompted for the file name. The !.WK1 file appears first in 1-2-3's list. If you accidently save a worksheet without naming it, you overwrite the dummy file and not something important. In Release 3.x, because the punctuation characters are listed last, use the name **1.WK3**.

Creating a New File from an Old File

Using an existing worksheet to create a new worksheet saves time, but you can accidentally save the new version over the old one. As soon as you retrieve a file that you want to modify, save it using its new name. If you plan to use a worksheet called MAYSALES to create JUNSALES, for example, select /File Retrieve, enter **MAYSALES**, then immediately select /File Save and enter **JUNSALES** to save the worksheet to the new name before you make any changes.

Saving Files by Highlighting

You can save a file by selecting the name from the list of current file names. Suppose that once a month you retrieve a worksheet called PROJCTNS, add new data to it, and save it in a directory on your hard disk and on a floppy disk as a backup. After you make the changes, save the worksheet by selecting **/F**ile **S**ave, pressing Enter, and selecting **R**eplace. Then select **/F**ile **S**ave again. Press Esc three times to clear the file name, the drive, and the path specifiers from the control panel prompt, and enter **A:**. A list of files in drive A appears in the control panel. Press the Name key (F3) to display the files in full-screen mode. Highlight the file name under which you want to save the backup copy of the worksheet and press Enter.

Tracking the Default File Name

If you save a worksheet with a different path or file name, the most recently used path and name become the default. Suppose that you retrieve the file C:\123FILES\PROJCTNS and save the worksheet to **A:\PROJCTNS**. The next time you select **/F**ile **S**ave, the default drive is listed as A:. To return to drive C, press Esc three times (to clear the file name, directory, and drive) and enter **C:**. Highlight the directory name 123FILES\, press Enter, highlight PROJCTNS.WK1, and press Enter.

If you use Releases 2.2, 2.3, or 3.x, you can use the Undo key (Alt–F4) to return the earlier file name as the default. Because Undo cannot undo operations that write data to disk, the file just created in A: is not deleted, but Undo returns everything else to its original condition (before you began the **/F**ile **S**ave operation). If you save the file C:\123FILES\PROJCTNS as **A:\PROJCTNS** and immediately press Undo (Alt–F4), when you next select **/F**ile **S**ave the default is again C:\123FILES\PROJCTNS.

Saving Files with Passwords

You can assign a password to a 1-2-3 file to prevent others from retrieving it. Select **/F**ile **S**ave and type the file name followed by one space and the letter **P**. If the file name already exists, press the space bar and then the letter **P** when the name appears; then press Enter. 1-2-3 displays Enter password. Enter a password of up to 15 characters.

 *You can use uppercase letters, lowercase letters, or a combination in your password. 1-2-3 doesn't regard **Swordfish** to be the same password as **swordfish** or **SWORDFISH**. When you retrieve a password-protected file, you must use the same capitalization as when you saved the file.*

After you enter the password, 1-2-3 displays the prompt `Verify pass-word`. Enter the password exactly as before. This extra step protects you from errors you may make when typing the password. (You may, for example, think that a file's password is *swordfish* when you actually typed **sowrdfish**.) 1-2-3 saves the worksheet and displays the Cancel/Replace menu if the file exists.

When you retrieve a password-protected file, 1-2-3 clears the screen and displays the prompt `Enter password`. You must type the password as you entered it when saving the file. If you forget the password, you probably cannot retrieve the file unless you own a specialized file-utility program that can decipher or bypass passwords.

Saving Files with the Backup Option

The Backup option in Releases 2.2, 2.3, and 3.x enables you to store the second-most-current version and the current version of a worksheet.

Suppose that you are developing a worksheet application that works reasonably well. You saved the worksheet and you want to add an enhancement, but you don't know whether it will work. Make the change and save the worksheet again but select **B**ackup when the Cancel/**R**eplace/**B**ackup menu appears. The worksheet, as it was before you made the enhancement, is copied to a file with the extension BAK. The new version of the worksheet is saved with the extension WK1 or WK3.

If the change you made doesn't work as you had hoped, you can return the worksheet to its previous state by retrieving the BAK file. Select **/F**ile **R**etrieve and type the complete file name, including the **BAK** extension. Then save the file using the regular extension.

The Backup option enables you to keep the two most recent versions only. If you are working with a complex application and you may need to return to earlier versions, save the worksheet at various points in its development using such names as VERSN1, VERSN2, and VERSN3.

Saving Part of a Worksheet

/File **X**tract creates a new 1-2-3 worksheet file containing the entries in a specific range of the current worksheet. Select **/F**ile **X**tract and then select **F**ormulas if you want to save the range with its formulas intact, or **V**alues if you want to convert all formulas in the range to values in the resulting file. Enter a file name or specify a current file name; then specify the range to extract by highlighting the range or by entering its coordinates or a range name. If the file name you specified already exists, select **R**eplace or **B**ackup from the menu.

This operation creates a 1-2-3 file that includes the entries in the range you indicated, in which the upper left corner of the range is located in cell A1. The worksheet's global settings—format, recalculation mode, and default column width—are preserved in the resulting file. The widths of individual columns in the extract range and individual cell formats in the extract range also are preserved. The original worksheet's range names are preserved but, if the coordinates of any ranges extend above or to the left of the extract range, the coordinates of the named ranges are in unexpected places in the resulting worksheet.

If you select **Formulas**, include in the extract range all cells and ranges to which the formulas in the extract range refer. If the extract range includes formulas referring to cells to the right of or below the extract range, the resulting worksheet contains formulas referring to empty cells. If the extract range includes formulas referring to cells to the left of or above the extract range, the resulting worksheet contains formulas referring to cells in the area near cell IV8192.

To create an extracted worksheet relatively free of problematic range names and formulas, save the original worksheet under its own name and select **/R**ange Name **R**eset to eliminate all range names. Convert all formulas referring to cells outside the extract range to values by using the command **/R**ange **V**alue.

Combining Files

The **/F**ile **C**ombine command enables you to bring some or all entries from a worksheet file on disk into the current worksheet. You can use this command to combine two worksheets into one; you also can use values from another file to add or subtract values in the current worksheet. Only the cell contents and individual cell formats from the other worksheet appear in the current worksheet. Global settings and range names are not transferred to the current worksheet.

Using /File Combine Copy

The **/F**ile **C**ombine **C**opy command brings all labels, values, and formulas into the current worksheet verbatim and replaces any current cell entries. Using **/F**ile **C**ombine **C**opy is a simple way to avoid redundant typing. Suppose that the labels in rows 1 to 3 of figure 4.3 must appear in every worksheet created for your company. You need only enter the labels once in a separate worksheet file called CONFID.WK1 or CONFID.WK3. Each time you create a new worksheet, position the cell pointer in the new worksheet where you want the confidentiality statement to appear and select **/F**ile **C**ombine **C**opy Entire-File; then specify the file name **CONFID.WK1** or **CONFID.WK3**.

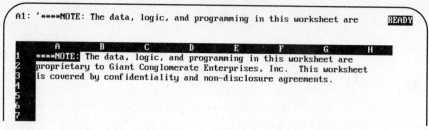

```
A1: '****NOTE: The data, logic, and programming in this worksheet are          READY

      A      B      C      D      E      F      G      H
1  ****NOTE: The data, logic, and programming in this worksheet are
2  proprietary to Giant Conglomerate Enterprises, Inc.  This worksheet
3  is covered by confidentiality and non-disclosure agreements.
4
5
6
7
```

Fig. 4.3. A confidentiality message stored in its own worksheet file for combining into other files.

You don't need to store boilerplate text in a dedicated worksheet. The /File Combine Copy command also enables you to copy data from a specific range in another worksheet. Suppose that you create a worksheet named MARKTG.WK1 containing the confidentiality message. The message appears in range A54..A57, as shown in figure 4.4. Before saving MARKTG.WK1, assign the name CONFIDENTIAL to range A54..A57. When you are ready to combine the text into another worksheet, position the cell pointer where the text is to appear and select /File Combine Copy Named/Specified-Range. At the Enter range name or address: prompt, enter **CONFIDENTIAL**. Then specify the file name **MARKTG**.

If the range you want to combine into the current file has no range name, use the range coordinates (for example, A54..A57).

The confidentiality message in figures 4.3 and 4.4 lies in an area one cell wide and three cells high. This data overwrites any entries in a comparable area in the current worksheet. Of course, the files or ranges you combine into a worksheet may be much larger. Before using /File Combine Copy, be certain that the cell pointer is at the upper left corner of an area large enough to accommodate the incoming data.

Using /File Combine Copy with Formulas

The /File Combine command also enables you to import formulas into the worksheet. Suppose that you enter dates into many of the worksheets you create, and you want 1-2-3 to determine such items as the day of the week and the first and last days of the month in which the date falls. Figure 4.5 shows a worksheet that computes several dates and values pertaining to the date in cell B1. If this worksheet is saved under the name DATEDATA, you can import its formulas into any other worksheet by selecting /File Combine Copy Entire-File and specifying the file name **DATEDATA**.

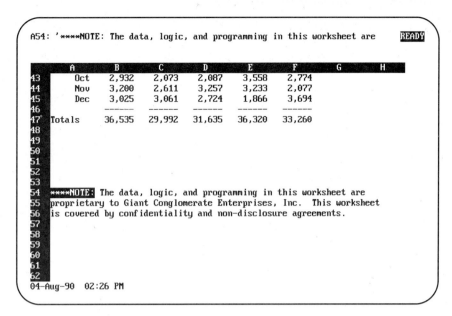

Fig. 4.4. A confidentiality message (A54..A57) that can be combined using /File Combine Copy Named/Specified-Range.

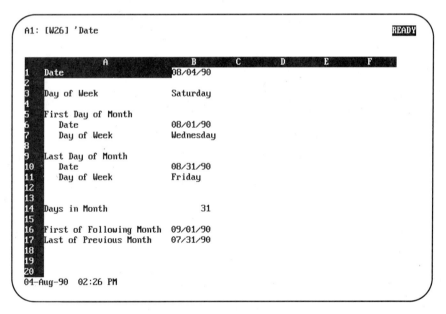

Fig. 4.5. Cell references in formulas that remain relative when copied into a different area of another file.

When you combine formulas, the cell references remain relative. In figure 4.5, the formula in cell B6 is +B1-@DAY(B1)+1. If you combine the entire file into the area of the current worksheet beginning at cell E30, the cell located at cell B6 in the original file appears in cell F35 in the new file and reads +F30-@DAY(F30)+1, even if both cell references in this formula are absolute. If the formula in the original worksheet reads +$B$1-@DAY($B$1)+1, it reads +$F$30-@DAY($F$30)+1 if you copy it to cell F35 using /File Combine.

Using /File Combine Add

Another method of combining data into a worksheet uses /File Combine Add. 1-2-3 brings all numeric data from the other worksheet, or the specified range of the other worksheet, into the current worksheet and adds the values to any values already in the current worksheet.

Figures 4.6 and 4.7 show productivity worksheets for two plants in a manufacturing company. Assume that two other worksheets contain data for plants located in Gadfly and Waldotown.

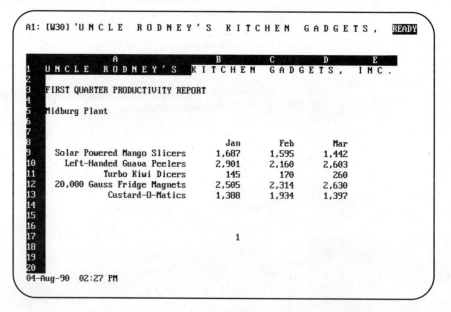

Fig. 4.6. *The first of four individual plant worksheets to be consolidated into a company-wide worksheet.*

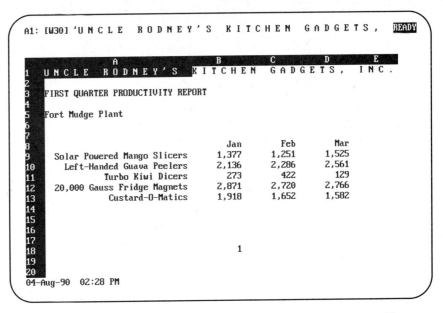

A1: [W30] 'U N C L E   R O D N E Y ' S   K I T C H E N   G A D G E T S ,   READY

```
              A                    B        C        D        E
 1  U N C L E   R O D N E Y ' S   K I T C H E N   G A D G E T S ,   I N C .
 2
 3  FIRST QUARTER PRODUCTIVITY REPORT
 4
 5  Fort Mudge Plant
 6
 7
 8                                 Jan      Feb      Mar
 9  Solar Powered Mango Slicers    1,377    1,251    1,525
10    Left-Handed Guava Peelers    2,136    2,286    2,561
11           Turbo Kiwi Dicers       273      422      129
12  20,000 Gauss Fridge Magnets    2,871    2,720    2,766
13           Custard-O-Matics      1,918    1,652    1,582
14
15
16
17
18                                    1
19
20
04-Aug-90  02:28 PM
```

Fig. 4.7. *The second of four worksheets to be consolidated into a company-wide worksheet.*

At the end of each quarter, the managers of the plants enter the number of kitchen gadgets produced and send the worksheets to Uncle Rodney's corporate headquarters in St. Philomena. There the vice president of production produces a master productivity report consolidating the values from all four plant worksheets.

To consolidate the values, she begins by retrieving the consolidation worksheet, shown in figure 4.8. She positions the cell pointer in cell A1, selects **/F**ile **C**ombine **A**dd **E**ntire-File, and specifies the file **MIDBURG.WK1**. All values from the Midburg file appear in range B9..D13, as shown in figure 4.9. Notice that the 1 from cell B17 of the Midburg worksheet now appears in cell B17. The V.P. then selects **/F**ile **C**ombine **A**dd **E**ntire-File and specifies the file **FTMUDGE.WK1**. All values in range B9..D13 from the Fort Mudge worksheet are added to the values in the corresponding range of the consolidation worksheet, and 1 appears in cell B18. She repeats the process for the Gadfly and Waldotown worksheets.

With all four plant files combined, the consolidation worksheet resembles figure 4.10. The value in cell B9 is the sum of the cell B9 values from the four plant worksheets, the value in cell B10 is the sum of the cell B10 values from the four plant worksheets, and so on.

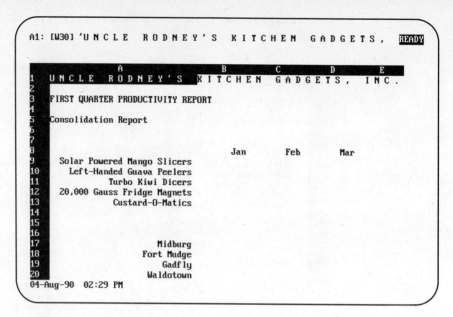

Fig. 4.8. A master consolidation worksheet, prior to combining data from the individual plant files.

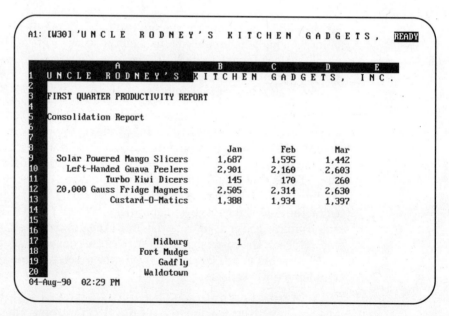

Fig. 4.9. Figures from the first plant file, combined into the consolidation worksheet with /File Combine Add Entire-File.

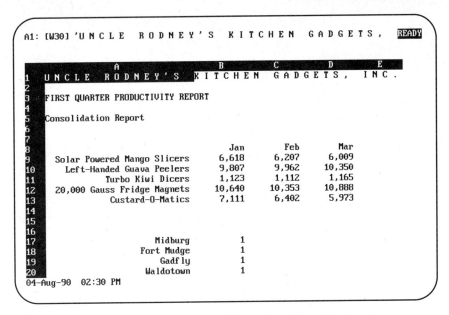

A1: [W30] 'U N C L E   R O D N E Y ' S   K I T C H E N   G A D G E T S ,   READY

```
              A              B        C        D        E
1  U N C L E   R O D N E Y ' S   K I T C H E N   G A D G E T S ,   I N C .
2
3  FIRST QUARTER PRODUCTIVITY REPORT
4
5  Consolidation Report
6
7
8                                Jan      Feb      Mar
9  Solar Powered Mango Slicers   6,618    6,207    6,009
10    Left-Handed Guava Peelers  9,807    9,962    10,350
11          Turbo Kiwi Dicers    1,123    1,112    1,165
12  20,000 Gauss Fridge Magnets  10,640   10,353   10,888
13          Custard-O-Matics     7,111    6,402    5,973
14
15
16
17               Midburg         1
18            Fort Mudge         1
19               Gadfly          1
20            Waldotown          1
04-Aug-90  02:30 PM
```

Fig. 4.10. *The completed consolidation worksheet after all four files have been combined.*

Advantages of /File Combine Add

One benefit of consolidating data with /File Combine Add is that you use less memory. Suppose that the productivity reports for the four plants are 20 or 30 times as large as the ones shown in figures 4.6 and 4.7. Each report's memory requirement approaches the available RAM limit in a typical PC at Uncle Rodney's. Storing all of the individual values and a range of formulas to calculate them is impossible. Instead, the data is stored in a set of disk files. When the disks are sent to headquarters, they are combined into a master file that doesn't increase in size substantially and would not even if 100 plant files were consolidated.

Tracking the /File Combine Operation

The 1s in range B17..B20 of figure 4.10 result from a technique that ensures that every worksheet is added to the consolidation worksheet only once. The Midburg worksheet contains 1 in cell B17 and the Fort Mudge worksheet contains 1 in cell B18. The Gadfly and Waldotown worksheets contain 1s in cells B19 and B20, respectively. When the files are combined, these values are added to the corresponding cells in the master worksheet. If the vice president makes a mistake and combines the Fort Mudge file twice, 2 appears in cell B18.

If 1-2-3 reports a Memory full *error when attempting to add an entire file with* /File Combine Add Entire-File, *use the* Named/Specified-Range *option instead, supplying range coordinates that include all of the data in the worksheet. This strategy works well for macros that perform consolidations.*

Understanding the Difference between /File Combine Add and /File Combine Copy

/File Combine Add differs from /File Combine Copy in several important ways. With the Copy option, incoming data always overwrites data in the current file. With the Add option only values and the results of formulas, not labels, are brought into the current worksheet. /File Combine Add places the incoming values in empty cells or adds them to simple values in the target worksheet but never overwrites labels or formulas in the target worksheet.

Suppose that you place the cell pointer at cell A1 in one of your worksheets, select /File Combine Add Entire-File, and specify the name of another file. If cell A5 of the current file is empty and cell A5 of the incoming file contains the value 10 or a formula that evaluated to 10 when the file was saved, cell A5 in the current worksheet displays the value 10. If cell A7 contains the value 100 and cell A7 of the incoming file contains the value 20, cell A7 displays the value 120.

If cell A10 of the incoming file contains a label, the label is disregarded, and cell A10 of the current file remains unchanged. Finally, if cell A15 of the current file contains a formula or a label, any entry in cell A15 of the incoming file is disregarded and cell A15 remains unchanged. The label Consolidation Report in cell A5 of figure 4.10 is not changed by the labels in the same position of the individual plant worksheets.

Using /File Combine Add with Portions of Worksheets

/File Combine Add, like /File Combine Copy, can be used to import portions of worksheets. An alternative method in the kitchen gadget example is to position the cell pointer at cell B9, issue the command /File Combine Add Named/Specified-Range, enter **B9..D20**, and specify the file name. Because all plant worksheets and the consolidation worksheet are formatted identically, however, using the Entire-File option is easier than specifying a range.

Using /File Combine Subtract

Another option using /File Combine is Subtract. /File Combine Subtract works like /File Combine Add, except that incoming values are subtracted from values in the current worksheet.

In the kitchen gadgets example, each plant worksheet contains 1 in a different cell to confirm that the vice president combines each file only once. If she accidentally combines the Fort Mudge file twice, the consolidation worksheet displays 2 (see fig. 4.11). The 2 in cell B18 indicates that one file was combined an extra time and the values in range B9..D13 are too high. To correct this mistake, she selects /File Combine Subtract Entire-File and specifies the file **FTMUDGE**. This command subtracts the Fort Mudge values from the numbers in range B9..B13 and subtracts 1 from the 2 in cell B18.

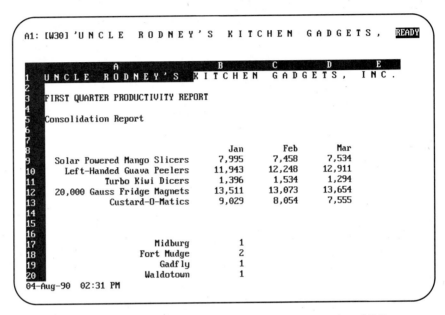

Fig. 4.11. A worksheet with incorrect results, as indicated by the 2 in cell B18.

The File Combine Subtract command also can be used to see how well the company performed without the contribution of one of the plants. Selecting /File Combine Subtract Entire-File and selecting the Midburg file subtracts the Midburg values from range B9..D13. The consolidation worksheet then resembles figure 4.12.

Using /File Combine Subtract To Analyze Worksheets

You can use /File Combine Subtract to determine which cells in a worksheet are formulas and which are values. In figure 4.13, some entries in columns B through E are values and some are formulas. To determine which entries are values, save the worksheet so that you don't lose the most recent changes. Set recalculation to Manual, if necessary

(/Worksheet Global Recalculation Manual). Then select /File Combine Subtract Entire-File and specify the name you used to save the file. Because the incoming values match the values in the cells, all cells containing simple values are set to $0.

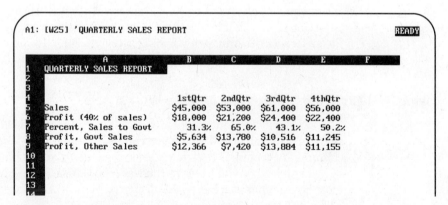

```
A1: [W30] 'U N C L E   R O D N E Y ' S   K I T C H E N   G A D G E T S,   READY

         A                    B          C          D          E
1   U N C L E   R O D N E Y ' S   K I T C H E N   G A D G E T S,   I N C.
2
3   FIRST QUARTER PRODUCTIVITY REPORT
4
5   Consolidation Report
6
7
8                             Jan        Feb        Mar
9   Solar Powered Mango Slicers    4,931      4,612      4,567
10     Left-Handed Guava Peelers   6,906      7,802      7,747
11          Turbo Kiwi Dicers        978        942        905
12   20,000 Gauss Fridge Magnets   8,135      8,039      8,258
13          Custard-O-Matics       5,723      4,468      4,576
14
15
16
17              Midburg            0
18          Fort Mudge             1
19             Gadfly              1
20           Waldotown             1
04-Aug-90  02:32 PM
```

Fig. 4.12. Worksheet first-quarter figures without the Midburg plant data.

Because **File Combine Subtract** doesn't overwrite formulas and recalculation is set to **Manual**, cells containing formulas don't change. After the /File Combine operation, the worksheet resembles figure 4.14, which clearly shows that rows 6, 8, and 9 contain formulas and rows 5 and 7 contain values.

```
A1: [W25] 'QUARTERLY SALES REPORT                                           READY

         A                B          C          D          E          F
1   QUARTERLY SALES REPORT
2
3
4                      1stQtr     2ndQtr     3rdQtr     4thQtr
5   Sales              $45,000    $53,000    $61,000    $56,000
6   Profit (40% of sales)  $18,000    $21,200    $24,400    $22,400
7   Percent, Sales to Govt   31.3%      65.0%      43.1%      50.2%
8   Profit, Govt Sales    $5,634    $13,780    $10,516    $11,245
9   Profit, Other Sales  $12,366     $7,420    $13,884    $11,155
10
11
12
13
14
```

Fig. 4.13. Worksheet entries that may be values or formulas.

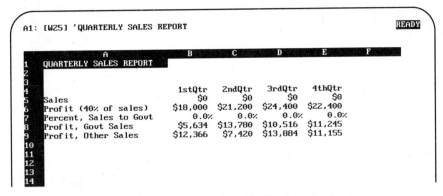

Fig. 4.14. *Simple values identified by* $0 *using* **/File Combine Subtract.**

Using /File Import

The /File Import commands add power to your 1-2-3 applications by enabling you to use data generated by many other kinds of computer programs. If a worksheet must be explained with a passage of text, for example, typing the text in 1-2-3 may be inconvenient. The /File Import commands enable you to add text created with your word processing software. Several financial, accounting, and scientific software packages can export their results to simple ASCII files; /File Import enables you to move this data into your worksheet without retyping it.

Preparing Word Processing Text

By using /File Import Text, you can import into 1-2-3 blocks of text created by word processing software. Your word processing program should *export* rather than *save* the text you want to add to your worksheet. Most word processing software saves text in a *native format*, a file designed to be read only by the program that created it. The file contains the document itself and additional characters that control the format of the document. Most programs, however, can create files without formatting and other extraneous characters. Some programs refer to this procedure as *exporting* or as *printing to a file*. Your software documentation should tell you how to create files without formatting.

When you export a file, the left, top, and bottom margins must be set to 0, and the file should contain no *page breaks* (spaces between pages of text). Each line of text must end with the carriage-return and line-feed characters (ASCII characters 13 and 10). If possible, give the file name the extension PRN.

Importing Word Processing Text

To import text into a 1-2-3 worksheet, position the cell pointer where you want the text to begin and select **/File Import Text**. A list of files with the extension PRN in the current directory appears in the control panel. Pressing the Name key (F3) displays files in full-page format. Select the text file to import from this list by highlighting it and pressing Enter. If the file name doesn't have the extension PRN, type the complete file name and press Enter. If you are not sure of the file name, use wild-card characters; for example, enter ***.TXT** if the file has the extension TXT. Or enter ***.*** to list all files in the current directory.

After you select the file, it appears in the worksheet as a column of long labels beginning at the current position of the cell pointer. You must have an adequate number of empty cells below the cell pointer. Cells in other columns are not affected.

Formatting Imported Text

If the text you import extends beyond the screen, or if you want to arrange the text in a narrower area of the worksheet, you can reformat with **/Range Justify**. Suppose that you created the worksheet shown in figure 4.15, and you want to annotate it with a passage of text generated by word processing software. When you import the text using **/File Import**, most of the text is hidden behind the formulas in columns D through G, as shown in figure 4.16. To make this text fit into the empty space in the lower left corner of the screen, select **/Range Justify** and specify range **A13..C20**. The text is rearranged, as shown in figure 4.17. The labels in range A13..A19 resemble text typed with word processing software.

Importing Data from Other Programs

The **/File Input Text** command transfers data that cannot be converted for use with 1-2-3 or that 1-2-3's Translate utility cannot convert. If your software can output data to a text file, you probably can import it to and convert it in 1-2-3.

Suppose that an accounting package exports to a text file a report consisting of account numbers and the dates, times, and amounts of transactions. You import this data into a 1-2-3 worksheet as a column of labels, as shown in figure 4.18. 1-2-3's parse commands can analyze the first entry and make some shrewd guesses as to how to divide the labels into individual cell entries.

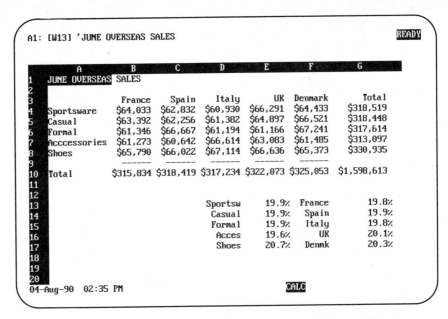

```
A1: [W13] 'JUNE OVERSEAS SALES                                        READY

        A          B          C          D          E          F          G
1  JUNE OVERSEAS SALES
2
3               France     Spain      Italy       UK     Denmark      Total
4  Sportsware  $64,033    $62,832    $60,930    $66,291   $64,433    $318,519
5  Casual      $63,392    $62,256    $61,382    $64,897   $66,521    $318,448
6  Formal      $61,346    $66,667    $61,194    $61,166   $67,241    $317,614
7  Acccessories $61,273   $60,642    $66,614    $63,083   $61,485    $313,097
8  Shoes       $65,790    $66,022    $67,114    $66,636   $65,373    $330,935
9               -------    -------    -------    -------   -------
10 Total       $315,834   $318,419   $317,234   $322,073  $325,053  $1,598,613
11
12
13                                   Sportsw    19.9%   France      19.8%
14                                   Casual     19.9%   Spain       19.9%
15                                   Formal     19.9%   Italy       19.8%
16                                   Acces      19.6%   UK          20.1%
17                                   Shoes      20.7%   Denmk       20.3%
18
19
20
04-Aug-90   02:35 PM                                    CALC
```

Fig. 4.15. A worksheet created in 1-2-3 with an area reserved for imported text.

```
A13: [W13] 'Sales in Spain are highest for the second month in a row. Analy READY

        A          B          C          D          E          F          G
1  JUNE OVERSEAS SALES
2
3               France     Spain      Italy       UK     Denmark      Total
4  Sportsware  $68,442    $66,644    $61,004    $75,464   $74,722    $346,276
5  Casual      $64,307    $79,206    $61,344    $68,271   $66,792    $339,920
6  Formal      $75,674    $78,485    $73,509    $74,061   $66,558    $368,287
7  Acccessories $63,595   $72,907    $68,804    $62,514   $68,011    $335,831
8  Shoes       $40,969    $47,681    $35,431    $41,183   $49,350    $214,614
9               -------    -------    -------    -------   -------
10 Total       $312,987   $344,923   $300,092   $321,493  $325,433  $1,604,928
11
12
13 Sales in Spain are highest for   Sptsw     21.6%   France      19.5%
14 retail activity there is genera  Casual    21.2%   Spain       21.5%
15 this month as the fall season a  Formal    22.9%   Italy       18.7%
16                                  Acces     20.9%   UK          20.0%
17                                  Shoes     13.4%   Denmk       20.3%
18
19
20
04-Aug-90   02:44 PM                                    CALC
```

Fig. 4.16. Imported text partially hidden by columns D through G of the worksheet.

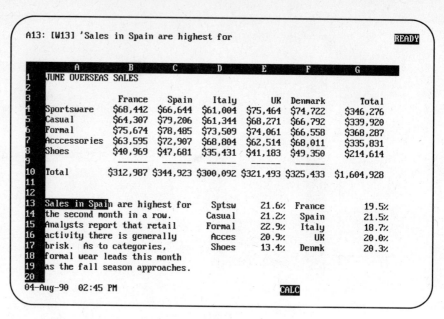

Fig. 4.17. Imported text rearranged with /**R**ange **J**ustify.

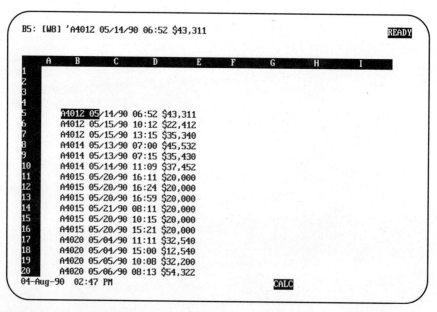

Fig. 4.18. Accounting data imported into a column of labels.

Place the cell pointer in cell B5. Select /**D**ata **P**arse **F**ormat-Line **C**reate. 1-2-3 moves all of the labels down one row and adds the characters shown in cell B5 of figure 4.19. The characters L>>>> indicate that the

first 5 characters are treated as a label. The characters D>>>>>> indicate that the characters immediately below them are converted to date
values. Likewise, the letters T and V indicate the beginnings of time and
value columns, respectively.

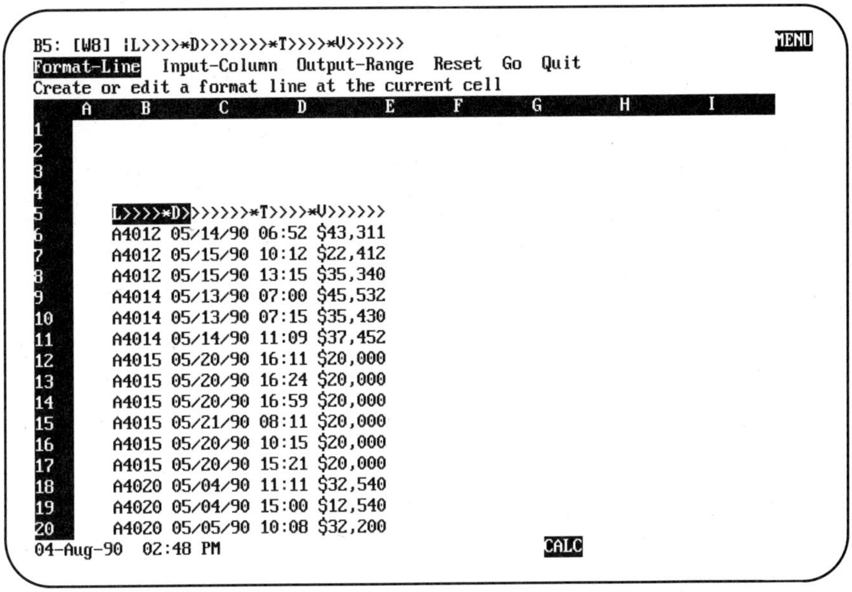

```
B5: [W8] ¦L>>>>*D>>>>>>>*T>>>>*V>>>>>>                                    MENU
Format-Line  Input-Column  Output-Range  Reset  Go  Quit
Create or edit a format line at the current cell
        A      B       C       D       E       F       G       H       I
1
2
3
4
5       L>>>>*D>>>>>>>*T>>>>*V>>>>>>
6       A4012 05/14/90 06:52 $43,311
7       A4012 05/15/90 10:12 $22,412
8       A4012 05/15/90 13:15 $35,340
9       A4014 05/13/90 07:00 $45,532
10      A4014 05/13/90 07:15 $35,430
11      A4014 05/14/90 11:09 $37,452
12      A4015 05/20/90 16:11 $20,000
13      A4015 05/20/90 16:24 $20,000
14      A4015 05/20/90 16:59 $20,000
15      A4015 05/21/90 08:11 $20,000
16      A4015 05/20/90 10:15 $20,000
17      A4015 05/20/90 15:21 $20,000
18      A4020 05/04/90 11:11 $32,540
19      A4020 05/04/90 15:00 $12,540
20      A4020 05/05/90 10:08 $32,200
04-Aug-90  02:48 PM                                       CALC
```

Fig. 4.19. The /Data Parse Format-Line command indicating where and how imported
text is divided.

Continue the parse operation by selecting **Input-Column** and specifying
a range that includes the format line and all of the imported labels.
Select **Output-Range**, specify a cell at the upper left corner of an empty
area of the worksheet, and select **Go**. 1-2-3 creates the entries in columns
F through I of figure 4.20. You then can format the columns, as shown in
figure 4.21.

Using /File Import Numbers

You can use **/File Import** to divide text files into individual values without using **/Data Parse**. Suppose that a software package creates a text
file that looks like the following lines:

```
459 323.1 78432 1
3545 212.18 45090 1
1283 87.43 64640 1
856 94.532764 1
```

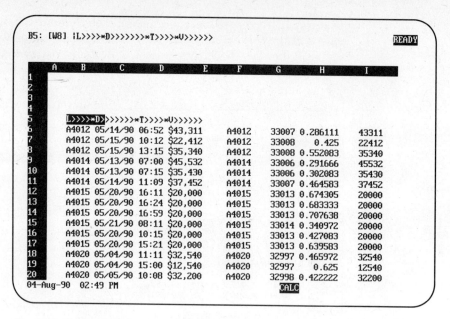

Fig. 4.20. *Columns of labels and unformatted values created by the /Data Parse Output-Range command.*

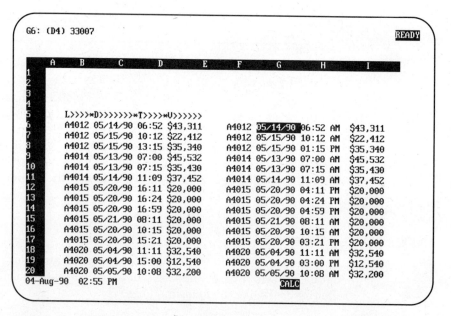

Fig. 4.21. *Unformatted values given an appropriate appearance by the /Range Format command.*

If you import this file into a worksheet with **/**File Import **N**umbers, 1-2-3 treats every uninterrupted block of numerals as a value. Whether numbers are separated by commas, spaces, or Xs makes no difference; 1-2-3 treats most nonnumeric characters as delimiters and disregards them. A period is treated as a decimal point and a hyphen as a minus sign; a percent sign causes 1-2-3 to divide the number preceding it by 100.

Another exception is *E* or *e*, which 1-2-3 treats as an exponentiation character. If a file contains the characters 5E9, 1-2-3 interprets the characters as meaning *5 times 10 to the ninth power*. When you import the file, 5E9 is converted to 5,000,000,000 (five billion).

Suppose that the preceding list of numbers appears in a file named VALS.TXT. If you position the cell pointer at cell A10, select **/**File Import **N**umbers, and specify **VALS.TXT**, the numbers are arranged as values in the worksheet, as shown in figure 4.22. The **/**File Import **N**umbers command also can import text, if the text is enclosed by quotation marks.

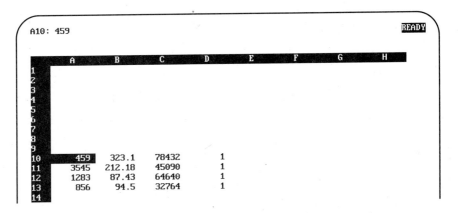

Fig. 4.22. *Numbers in text files converted to individual cell entries using /File Import Numbers.*

Linking Files

Worksheets created in Releases 2.2, 2.3, and 3.x can include values that depend on cells in other worksheet files. These files can be on disks in your own computer or available to your computer via a local area network (LAN).

Linking with Releases 2.2 and 2.3

To create a linking formula with Releases 2.2 and 2.3, type a plus sign (**+**), two less-than signs (**<<**), the path and name of the file that you want to link, two greater-than signs (**>>**), and the address or name of the cell that you want to link. The following formula links the value in cell B15 of the file BACKGRND.WK1 in the root directory of drive C:

$$+<<\text{C:}\backslash\text{BACKGRND.WK1}>>\text{B15}$$

Including a path specifier for the file name is not strictly necessary if the file is in the current directory. If you later retrieve a file with linking formulas, however, and the current directory doesn't contain the file specified in the linking formulas, the linking formulas return ERR. Always specify the path when you use file-linking formulas to prevent this error.

You don't need to specify an extension unless the file name has an extension other than WK1. By specifying the correct extension, you can create links to any file that Release 2.2 can retrieve, including Release 1A (WKS) files, Symphony (WRK or WR1) files, or files created by a non-Lotus spreadsheet product that creates 1-2-3-compatible files.

If you attempt to create a linking formula and the file you specify doesn't exist, 1-2-3 beeps and displays the error message File does not exist. If the file exists but you specify an invalid cell address, 1-2-3 switches to EDIT mode and positions the cursor under the offending characters.

Linking with the Viewer Add-In (Release 2.3)

The *Viewer* add-in (included with Release 2.3) makes linking even more convenient. Using technology developed for Lotus' Magellan software, Viewer enables you to browse through 1-2-3, Symphony, and Lotus-Works files, seeing them as they would appear if you retrieved them.

To use Viewer, select **/Add-In Attach**, specify **VIEWER.ADN**, select an available Alt-function key combination, and select **Q**uit. Move the cell pointer to the cell where you want to create a linking formula. Invoke Viewer with the Alt-function key combination you selected, and select Link from the resulting menu.

On the left side of the screen, Viewer displays a list of the subdirectories and WKS, WK1, WRK, and WR1 files in the current directory. The right side of the screen displays the upper left corner of each file as you highlight it, as shown in figure 4.23.

To move up the directory tree, press the left-arrow key or click on the ◀ symbol (near the upper left corner of the screen) to move up to the parent directory of the current directory (whether the root directory or an intermediate subdirectory). To move to a subdirectory of the current directory, highlight the desired directory name and press the right-arrow key or click on the ▶ symbol.

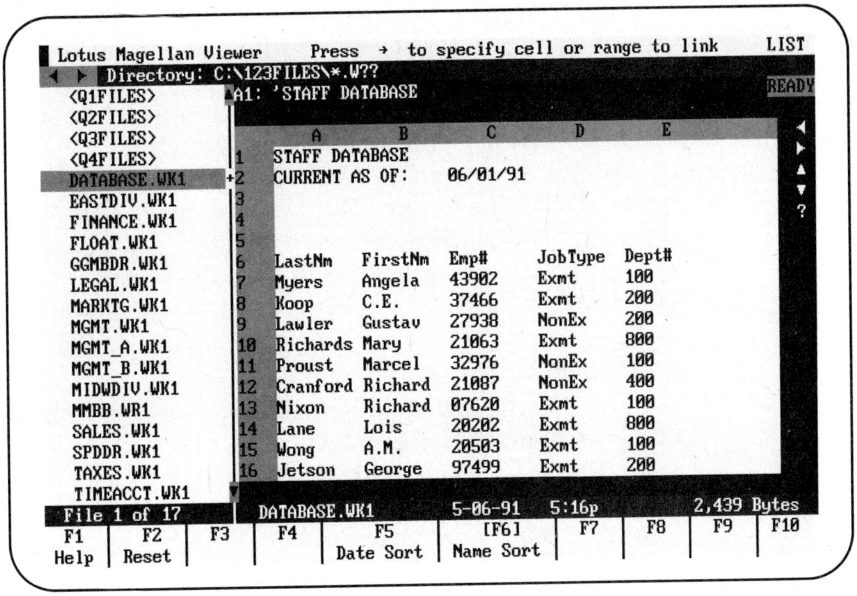

Fig. 4.23. Searching worksheet files in the current directory with the Viewer add-in.

When you find the appropriate worksheet file, move the cell pointer to the exact cell where you want the link and press Enter. When you find the appropriate worksheet file (for example, C:\Q1DATA\Q1SALES), press the right-arrow key or click on the ▶ to move the highlight bar to the right-side window. (The highlight bar now resembles a cell pointer.) Move the cell pointer to the cell you want to link (for example, cell M20). Highlight the cell and press Enter. This procedure instantly creates a linking formula with the following format:

    << path\filename>>address

In this example, the current cell in your worksheet now contains the following formula:

    `+<<C:\Q1DATA\Q1SALES.WK1>>M20`

Linking to Named Cells and Ranges

You can use a range name instead of a cell reference. The following formula is a valid linking formula, if the BACKGRND.WK1 file contains a cell or range named MARKUP:

    +<<C:\BACKGRND.WK1>>MARKUP

If the range name doesn't exist in the specified file, 1-2-3 switches to EDIT mode and positions the cursor under the first character of the range name.

If the named range is larger than one cell, the result of the linking formula is the most recent value of the upper left cell of that range. Using a range name has one advantage over using a cell reference: if you change the location of the named cell or named range in the first worksheet using a /Move or /Worksheet Insert Row or Insert Column command, the linking formula in the second worksheet continues to refer to the named cell or the first cell of the named range. This advantage doesn't hold if the linking formula uses a cell reference. If you move the contents of a cell referred to by address in a linking formula in another worksheet, the linking formula continues to refer to the same address.

Using File Linking for Base Assumptions

You can use file linking to store in a worksheet assumptions underlying other worksheets. Suppose that your job is to create a dozen or more worksheets that produce financial reports for your company. Each worksheet contains calculations based on an estimated inflation rate of 5 percent. You could dedicate one cell in each worksheet for the inflation rate and enter .05 in each cell. If the company's analyst changes the estimate, however, you have to retrieve each worksheet and enter the new value. If you miss any corrections, the results of the worksheets don't agree.

A more efficient method is to create one worksheet with values that are relevant to all of the financial reports. Figure 4.24 shows such a worksheet. If you create this worksheet and save it under the name UNI_VAL.WK1, you can create any number of additional worksheets that depend on the values contained in UNI_VAL.WK1. These worksheets use formulas like the following:

$$+<<C:\backslash FINREPT\backslash UNI\_VAL.WK1>>INF\_RATE$$

Figure 4.25 shows a worksheet with a link to UNI_VAL.WK1. If management wants to see a complete set of reports based on an assumed inflation rate of 6 percent, you need only change the value in cell C16 of the assumptions worksheet and resave the file. The coffee mug worksheet and other worksheets that make projections dependent on the inflation rate show the effects of the higher rate.

Range names are used in the worksheet in figure 4.24. If you need to insert new worksheet rows and add a new value among the current rows, linking formulas in other worksheet files continue to refer to the appropriate cells.

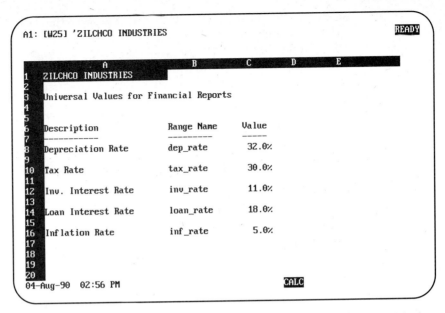

Fig. 4.24. A worksheet with values common to many financial reports that are linked.

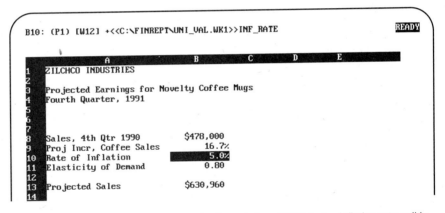

Fig. 4.25. A worksheet linked through the formula in cell B10 to the inflation rate cell in the universal values worksheet.

Using File Linking in Modular Applications

Suppose that a Release 2.2 or 2.3 worksheet contains a very long database listing transactions in three western regions: the Northwest, California and Nevada, and the Southwest. A second worksheet contains a similarly long database for the Midwest, the Northeast, and the South. Combining the transactions from all six regions into one Release 2.2 or 2.3 worksheet is impossible.

Each worksheet contains a table produced with the /Data Table commands summarizing the transaction amounts by account number and region. The table for the western regions worksheet appears in figure 4.26. The task is to combine the summarized data from both worksheets into one place for further analysis, comparison, and graphing.

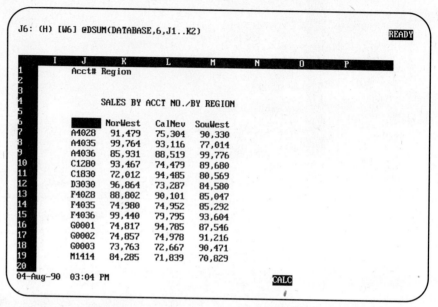

Fig. 4.26. *A worksheet summarizing sales figures for three western regions.*

File linking provides the solution. To create a table of results from all regions, create a worksheet like the one shown in figure 4.27. The labels in column A and row 6 define a master table that will contain values from both database worksheets.

You can create a formula to link the upper left cell in the master table to the upper left cell of the data table in the western regions worksheet, and copy the formula (see fig. 4.27). Copying linked formulas is similar to copying ordinary formulas. The row and column reference shifts as the formula is copied. When the formula in cell B7 is copied to range B7..D19, the formula in cell B8 reads +<<C:\WEST.WK1>>K8 and the formula in cell C7 reads +<<C:\WEST.WK1>>L7 (see fig. 4.28).

The last step is to create a formula linking the first cell in the fourth column to the upper left cell of the data table in the eastern regions worksheet, and copy the formula to fill the three right columns in the master table (see fig. 4.29).

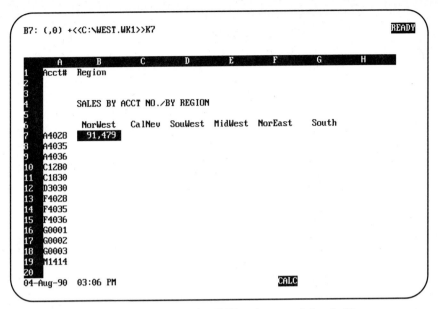

Fig. 4.27. *A master table linked through cell B7 to the upper left cell of the summary table in the western regions worksheet.*

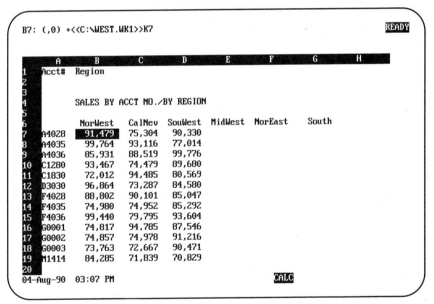

Fig. 4.28. *A range of cells produced by linking the formula in cell B7 to a range of cells in the western regions worksheet.*

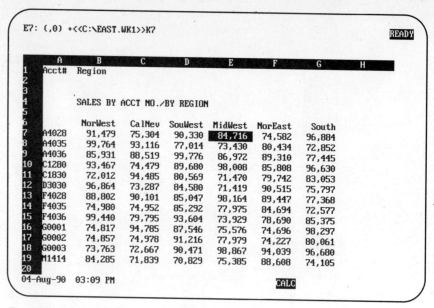

```
E7: (,0) +<<C:\EAST.WK1>>K7                                    READY

         A        B        C        D        E        F        G       H
1    Acct#    Region
2
3
4             SALES BY ACCT NO./BY REGION
5
6             NorWest  CalNev  SouWest  MidWest  NorEast  South
7    A4028     91,479  75,304   90,330   84,716   74,582  96,884
8    A4035     99,764  93,116   77,014   73,430   80,434  72,852
9    A4036     85,931  88,519   99,776   86,972   89,310  77,445
10   C1280     93,467  74,479   89,680   98,008   85,808  96,630
11   C1830     72,012  94,485   80,569   71,470   79,742  83,053
12   D3030     96,864  73,287   84,580   71,419   90,515  75,797
13   F4028     88,802  90,101   85,047   98,164   89,447  77,368
14   F4035     74,980  74,952   85,292   77,975   84,694  72,577
15   F4036     99,440  79,795   93,604   73,929   78,690  85,375
16   G0001     74,817  94,785   87,546   75,576   74,696  98,297
17   G0002     74,857  74,978   91,216   77,979   74,227  80,061
18   G0003     73,763  72,667   90,471   98,867   94,039  96,680
19   M1414     84,285  71,839   70,829   75,385   88,608  74,105
20
04-Aug-90   03:09 PM                                  CALC
```

Fig. 4.29. *Columns E, F, and G produced by linking to the eastern regions worksheet.*

After you save this worksheet, you can retrieve either database worksheet; add, delete, or modify records; and create a revised table by reissuing the /Data Table commands or by pressing the Table key (F8). When you retrieve the master table worksheet, the linking formulas enter the new values found in the data tables of the two database worksheets.

This example uses cell addresses because naming each cell in the data table in each database worksheet is not practical. Even if you name all of the cells, you have to enter each linking formula individually (rather than using /Copy) if you want each formula to reference a name when you view its contents in the control panel. When you copy a linking formula that refers to a named cell, the copied formulas refer to cell addresses, even if the specified cells are named. Copying a linking formula is convenient but precludes using formulas that refer to descriptive cell names and moving cells in the linked worksheets.

Updating Linked Files

When you create or edit a file-linking formula, 1-2-3 accesses the file you specify and finds the current value of the cell you specify. If you retrieve a file containing linking formulas, 1-2-3 accesses all of the files specified by linking formulas and retrieves the current values from the appropriate cells. If your computer is not connected to a local area network, you can rely on the linking formulas to enter the most up-to-date values. If your computer is on a network and the current worksheet has links to shared files, another user can retrieve, modify, and save one of the linked worksheets while you are working with the current file. 1-2-3 doesn't access the linked files constantly to find the most recent values. To be certain that the linking formulas in your worksheet return the most current values before printing part of the worksheet, for example, press slash and select /File Admin Link-Refresh. 1-2-3 accesses all files and finds the values again.

Checking for File Links

To see which files are linked to the current worksheet, select /File List Linked, which displays a screen listing all files referred to by file-linking formulas. The first file on the list is highlighted and the control panel shows the complete path of the file, its size, and the date and time created. By moving the highlight around the screen, you can view the same information for the other files.

Linking with Release 3.x

With Releases 3 and 3.1, you can display entries from other worksheet files and perform mathematical functions or string manipulation. To establish a simple file link, type a plus sign (**+**), two less-than signs (**<<**), the path and name of the file you want to link, two greater-than signs (**>>**), and the cell address or range name of the chosen cell, as in the following example:

+<<C:\R3FILES\TAXRATE.WK3>>A:B5

Unlike Releases 2.2 and 2.3, Release 3.x accepts linking formulas with more than one expression. The following formula multiplies the value in cell H10 of the current worksheet by the value in cell B5 of TAXRATE.WK3:

+H10*<<C:\R3FILES\TAXRATE.WK3>>B5

You also can use values from cells in two different worksheets in one formula, as in the following example:

+<<C:\R3FILES\EARNINGS.WK3>>M8*<<C:\R3FILES\TAXRATE.WK3>>B5

This formula multiplies the value in cell M8 of the EARNINGS file by the value in cell B5 of the TAXRATE file and places the result in the worksheet cell where the formula appears.

Including a path specifier for the file name is not strictly necessary if the file is in the current directory. If you later retrieve a file with linking formulas, however, and the current directory doesn't contain the file specified in the linking formulas, the formulas return ERR. Specify the path in file-linking formulas to prevent this error.

You don't need to specify an extension unless the file name has an extension other than WK3. By specifying the correct extension, you can create links to any file that can be retrieved with Release 3.x, including Release 1A (WKS) files, Release 2.x (WK1) files, Symphony (WRK or WR1) files, or 1-2-3-compatible files created by a non-Lotus worksheet product.

If you attempt to create a linking formula and the file you specify doesn't exist, 1-2-3 beeps and displays the error message File does not exist. If the file exists but you specify an invalid cell address, 1-2-3 switches to EDIT mode and positions the cursor under the offending characters.

You can use a range name instead of a cell reference. The following formula is a valid linking formula if the BACKGRND.WK3 file contains a cell or range named MARKUP:

+COST<<C:\BACKGRND.WK3>>MARKUP

If the range name doesn't exist in the specified file, 1-2-3 switches to EDIT mode and positions the cursor under the first character of the range name. If the named range is larger than one cell, the result of the linking formula is the most recent value of the upper left cell of that range.

Linking Open Files

Establishing links between Release 3.x worksheets is simple when you open the files you want to link and use the direction keys to define the linked cells. Suppose that you want to multiply cell B:D15 by a cell (located in an assumptions file) that computes a markup percentage. The assumptions file, found in directory C:\DATA, is called GLOBALS.WK3, but you don't know the address of the cell.

Open the assumptions file behind the current worksheet by selecting /File Open After and specifying the file **GLOBALS.WK3**. 1-2-3 retrieves the file, places it behind the current worksheet, displays the file, and positions the cell pointer in the file. Press Ctrl–PgDn to return to sheet B in the file you were using. Now you can create a link.

Position the cell pointer where you want to create the formula. Type a plus sign (+), move the cell pointer to cell B:D15, type an asterisk (*), use Ctrl–PgUp to move the cell pointer to the correct worksheet in the GLOBALS.WK3 file, use the direction keys to highlight the cell containing the markup formula, (for example, C:A10), and press Enter. The following formula is the completed link:

+D:B15*<<C:\DATA\GLOBALS.WK3>>C:A10

After you establish links in this manner, the links remain constant, even if both files are not simultaneously in memory. If you remove GLOBALS.WK3 from memory with the commands **/W**orksheet **D**elete

File, the formula you created remains intact. If you save the current worksheet and retrieve it later, the worksheet still contains the link to GLOBALS.WK3.

Modifying Linked Files

Simultaneously opening all linked files provides additional flexibility in modifying applications. Suppose that you created two files called PARTA.WK3 and PARTB.WK3. Formulas in PARTA.WK3 refer to cells in PARTB.WK3 by cell coordinates. The arrangement of PARTB.WK3, however, is not satisfactory, and you must add rows or columns or move some cells. If you retrieve PARTB.WK3 and make these changes, the linking formulas in PARTA.WK3 no longer refer to the correct cells. Instead, retrieve PARTA.WK3 and open PARTB.WK3. Make the necessary changes in PARTB.WK3, and the linking formulas in PARTA.WK3 adjust to match the new cell coordinates.

Using Compound File Linking Formulas

The preceding sections demonstrated that linking formulas supported by Releases 2.2 and 2.3 can maintain—in one worksheet—values common to many worksheets. You also can use linking formulas to create in one file a table of data from other files. Release 3.x can provide links in the same manner or use compound linking formulas that consolidate data from other files without using **/F**ile **C**ombine.

Figures 4.30 and 4.31 show two of the four productivity worksheets used by a manufacturing company, and figure 4.32 shows the worksheet that consolidates the numbers from all four files. The formula shown in cell B9, copied to range B9..D13, returns totals for the entire company without requiring you to issue the commands **/F**ile **C**ombine **A**dd repeatedly.

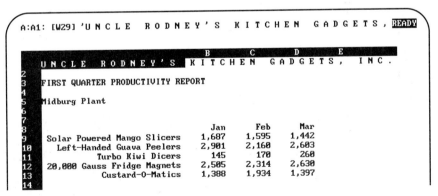

Fig. 4.30. One of four plant worksheets to be consolidated with file-linking formulas.

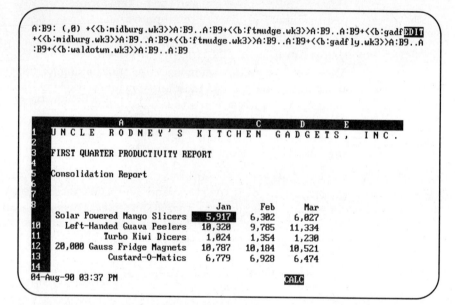

```
A:A1: [W29] 'U N C L E   R O D N E Y ' S   K I T C H E N   G A D G E T S ,  READY
```

```
                           B            C          D         E
U N C L E   R O D N E Y ' S   K I T C H E N   G A D G E T S ,   I N C .
2
3  FIRST QUARTER PRODUCTIVITY REPORT
4
5  Fort Mudge Plant
6
7
8                               Jan      Feb      Mar
9    Solar Powered Mango Slicers  1,377    1,251    1,525
10     Left-Handed Guava Peelers  2,136    2,286    2,561
11          Turbo Kiwi Dicers       273      422      129
12  20,000 Gauss Fridge Magnets  2,871    2,720    2,766
13         Custard-O-Matics      1,918    1,652    1,582
14
```

Fig. 4.31. *A second plant worksheet to be consolidated.*

```
A:B9: (,0) +<<b:midburg.wk3>>A:B9..A:B9+<<b:ftmudge.wk3>>A:B9..A:B9+<<b:gadf EDIT
+<<b:midburg.wk3>>A:B9..A:B9+<<b:ftmudge.wk3>>A:B9..A:B9+<<b:gadfly.wk3>>A:B9..A
:B9+<<b:waldotwn.wk3>>A:B9..A:B9
```

```
                    A                     C          D         E
1  U N C L E   R O D N E Y ' S   K I T C H E N   G A D G E T S ,   I N C .
2
3  FIRST QUARTER PRODUCTIVITY REPORT
4
5  Consolidation Report
6
7
8                               Jan      Feb      Mar
    Solar Powered Mango Slicers  5,917    6,302    6,027
10     Left-Handed Guava Peelers 10,320    9,785   11,334
11          Turbo Kiwi Dicers     1,024    1,354    1,230
12  20,000 Gauss Fridge Magnets 10,787   10,184   10,521
13         Custard-O-Matics      6,779    6,928    6,474
14
04-Aug-90 03:37 PM                                  CALC
```

Fig. 4.32. *Formulas (in range B9..D13) that consolidate data from the four plant worksheets.*

Updating File Links

Like Releases 2.2 and 2.3, Release 3.x accesses the files referenced in linking formulas as you create or edit the formulas. Release 3.x, however, doesn't check all of the linked files for current values when you retrieve a file containing linking formulas.

Suppose that a file named PARTA.WK3 contains a formula that repeats the value in cell B47 of PARTB.WK3. When the linking formula was created, cell B47 returned the value 11,000; therefore, the linking formula returned the same amount. Later, PARTB.WK3 was modified so that cell B47 returned 17,000 and the file was saved. If PARTA.WK3 is retrieved, its linking formula returns 11,000, not 17,000.

To update all of the linking formulas in a worksheet, select /File Admin Link-Refresh. If your computer is not part of a network, issue the Link-Refresh commands as soon as you retrieve a file containing linking formulas to ensure that the results in the current worksheet reflect any changes made in the linked worksheets. If your computer is on a network and the current worksheet has links to shared files, another user can retrieve, modify, and save one of the linked worksheets while you are working with the current file, so issue the Link-Refresh commands just before printing the current worksheet. The printout then is based on the most current data.

Checking for File Links

To determine which files are linked to the current worksheet, select /File List Linked. This command retrieves a screen listing all files referred to by file-linking formulas. The first file on the list is highlighted and the control panel shows the complete path of that file, its size, and the date and time created. By moving the highlight around the screen, you can view the same information for the other files.

Summary

Regardless of which 1-2-3 version you use and no matter how powerful your computer, the amount of data and number of formulas that fit in RAM are limited. By managing files effectively, you can expand the capability and efficiency of your 1-2-3 applications.

In this chapter, you learned ways to retrieve and save worksheet files and methods for creating multiple worksheet applications by using file-combining and file-linking techniques. The next chapter discusses printing reports with 1-2-3.

Chapter Five

PRINTING REPORTS

T his chapter discusses strategies for controlling your printer and producing professional-looking documents from worksheets by using 1-2-3 print commands and add-in programs.

This chapter covers the following important printing topics:

- Controlling the printer using 1-2-3 commands
- Adjusting margins
- Using headers, footers, border columns, and border rows
- Printing to disk files
- Printing with Allways (Release 2.2)
- Printing with Wysiwyg (Releases 2.3 and 3.1)

Understanding Default Print Settings

Most dot-matrix, daisy-wheel, and inkjet printers print six lines of text to every vertical inch. Because 8 1/2-by-11-inch paper thus has room for 66 lines of type, 1-2-3 uses a default page length setting of 66. The page length setting determines, for example, the number of lines necessary to advance the paper to align the next page.

1-2-3's normal page length setting is 66, but a 66-row range doesn't fit on one page. 1-2-3's default margin settings require top and bottom margins of two lines each. Three lines each also are reserved for a header and a footer, even if you don't specify header or footer text. With four lines reserved for margins and six lines reserved for header and footer, therefore, 1-2-3's default setting prints 56 lines to a page. You can adjust the top and bottom margins, but you cannot change the number of lines 1-2-3 reserves for headers and footers. At six lines per inch, you can print 60 lines at most on an 11-inch sheet of paper, with the top and bottom margins set to 0. You can completely suppress the printing of headers and footers, but your documents will have no white space at the tops and bottoms of pages, making your printouts difficult to read and photocopy.

Many laser printers print at a default of 60 lines per page. This setting sometimes produces text that "creeps down" as you print successive pages. To correct the problem, set 1-2-3's page length to 60. Select /Print Printer Options Pg-Length, enter 60, and select Quit.

Controlling the Printer

Most printers can produce text in italics, boldface, letter-quality, and near-letter-quality, with varying numbers of characters per horizontal inch or lines per vertical inch. The mode of printing usually can be changed by a special series of characters sent to the printer by the host computer in the same way that ordinary text is sent to the printer.

Understanding Control Codes

The computer sends characters to the printer as binary numbers composed of electrical pulses. The binary numbers conform to ASCII (American Standard Code for Information Interchange) format, a widely accepted scheme for numbering letters and other characters. If the computer sends the binary equivalent of 65 to the printer, the printer prints capital A, because 65 is the ASCII value for A. If the computer sends the binary equivalent of 27 (the number of the Esc key) followed immediately by the binary equivalent of 77 (the number for the letter M), and the printer is an Epson or compatible, the printer changes to elite mode, 12 characters per inch.

Most printer control codes begin with the Esc key; but exceptions exist. (Some models of Okidata printers, for example, use character number 29 to produce condensed printing, approximately 17 characters per inch.) Epson printers use Esc–1 to set vertical line spacing to 7/72 of one inch. The correct code is the Esc key followed by the numeral 1, not the ASCII character 001. To determine which codes to use, consult your printer manual. The manual should explain clearly which character combination to use.

Sending Control Codes from 1-2-3

1-2-3 enables you to send special codes to the printer before you send the characters found in the print range. Select /Print Printer Options Setup and enter the sequence of characters for the desired printing style. For characters represented on the keyboard, type the character. For characters that you cannot type, type a backslash followed by the ASCII number of the character. You must use three digits; if the ASCII number has one or two digits, use leading zeros. If the code for elite type is Esc–M, for example, select **/Print Printer Options Setup**, type the characters **\027M**, and press Enter. When you specify a print range and select Go, 1-2-3 sends the characters Esc and M to the printer before sending the first character in the print range.

You can apply print attributes to selected rows of the print range by including printer codes in the worksheet. Reserve rows in the worksheet for printer codes. Enter two split vertical bars (¦ ¦) followed by the printer codes in the extreme left column of the print range and leave the remainder of the row empty. Figure 5.1 shows an example of a print range with two attribute changes. The characters in cell A1 engage double-width printing in Epson and compatible printers. The characters in cell A3 disable double-width printing. The result of printing this range appears in figure 5.2. Note that 1-2-3 treats the first of the split vertical bars as a label prefix so that only the second appears in the worksheet.

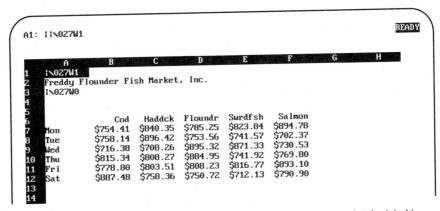

Fig. 5.1. *A printer code (in cell A1) that instructs an Epson printer to print the label in cell A2 in expanded mode.*

	Cod	Haddck	Floundr	Swrdfsh	Salmon
			Freddy Flounder Fish Market, Inc.		
Mon	$754.41	$840.35	$785.25	$823.84	$894.78
Tue	$758.14	$896.42	$753.56	$741.57	$702.37
Wed	$716.38	$708.26	$895.32	$871.33	$730.53
Thu	$815.34	$808.27	$884.95	$741.92	$769.80
Fri	$778.80	$803.51	$808.23	$816.77	$893.10
Sat	$887.48	$758.36	$750.72	$712.13	$790.90

Fig. 5.2. *The printed document resulting from printing the range in figure 5.1.*

Setting Margins

In regular 1-2-3 printing, margins are defined as numbers of characters from the left side of the page or numbers of rows from the top or bottom, rather than in inches. Allways (Release 2.2) and Wysiwyg (Releases 2.3 and 3.1) define margins in inches.

1-2-3's top and bottom margins are set to two lines by default. If you don't change these default settings, 1-2-3 advances the paper two lines before printing the header (or the three rows reserved for the header). 1-2-3 then advances the paper to the next page after printing the number of lines specified in the page length setting minus the footer and bottom margins.

The left and right margins are set, by default, to four characters from the left side and 76 characters from the left side, respectively. At these default settings, you can print ranges whose column widths contain 72 characters maximum—8 columns set to the default width of 9, for example. If the combined widths of the columns in the print range exceed 72, even by one character, 1-2-3 treats the right side columns in the range as too wide to be printed within a 72-character row, and prints the columns that don't exceed 72 characters, advances the paper to the next page, and prints the remaining columns. Figure 5.3 shows an example of a too-wide range continued on a second page.

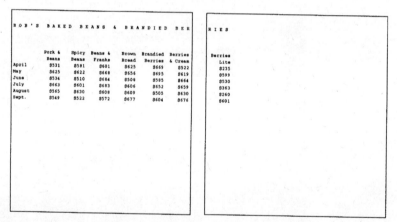

Fig. 5.3. A print range that is too wide to print on one page.

The worksheet range used to create figure 5.3 contains seven nine-character columns and one 10-character column. To print this range on one page, you can decrease the left margin by one or increase the right margin by one. Of course, you cannot accommodate infinitely wider and wider print ranges by continuing to adjust the margins. If you need to print wider ranges, use a printer control code that selects elite mode or condensed mode.

If you are not certain of the number to use as a right margin, you usually can enter something higher than necessary, 100, for example. A high number causes a problem only if you use headers or footers in which text is center-aligned or right-aligned. Headers and footers are discussed in the following section. The best way to determine the correct right margin is to add the widths of the columns in the print range and add the result to the left margin.

Printing Wide Ranges on Multiple Pages

When 1-2-3 splits a printed worksheet on multiple pages, the result can be annoying (if you expected all of the worksheet to print on one page) or advantageous. If you have a wide worksheet to print, you deliberately can specify a wide print range and let 1-2-3 divide it into printable chunks. 1-2-3 can make the row labels—the month names at the extreme left of figure 5.3, for example—appear on every page. For more information on printing row labels on every page, see the discussion later in this chapter on using borders.

Using Headers and Footers

1-2-3 enables you to enter text that appears at the top or bottom of every page in a printout. You can use this text to flag output with the name of your company, for example. You also can use the header or footer feature to number pages and date-stamp printouts.

To add a header, select **/Print Printer Options Header** and enter the text to appear at the top of each page. To add a footer, select **/Print Printer Options Footer** and enter the text to appear at the bottom of each page.

The footer doesn't appear on the last page of the printout unless you select **P***age from the* **/P***rint menu after selecting* **G***o and before selecting* **Q***uit.*

By using split vertical bars (¦) in a header or footer, you can divide the header into portions appearing on the left side, in the center, at the right side, or any combination of these options. The location of the left side, right side and center are determined by the left and right margin settings. If you enter the header string **Sales Report ¦ Wisent Industries ¦ R.C.Fuzwell**, the characters Sales Report appear in the upper left corner of each page, the characters Wisent Industries appear at the top center of each page, and the characters R.C.Fuzwell appear in the upper right corner of each page. You can use other combinations to change the placement of header or footer text, as in the following examples:

¦ ¦R.C. Fuzwell (R.C. Fuzwell appears at the right)

Sales Report¦ ¦R.C. Fuzwell (Sales Report appears at the left, R.C. Fuzwell appears at the right)

¦Wisent Industries¦R.C. Fuzwell (Wisent Industries appears in the center, R.C. Fuzwell at the right)

¦Wisent Industries (Wisent Industries appears in the center)

Using Dates in Headers and Footers

To include the date in a header or footer, use the at sign (@). As 1-2-3 prints the header or footer, the @ is replaced by the current date stored in the computer. If you enter the header string **Earnings report as of @**, 1-2-3 prints the characters Earnings report as of 03-Nov-91 if that is the current system date. Usually, the date in a header or footer appears in standard 1-2-3 format, DD-MMM-YY. 1-2-3 prints dates in the long international format, MM/DD/YY, if you select **/W**orksheet **G**lobal **D**efault **O**ther **C**lock **I**nternational **Q**uit before printing. If your worksheet displays the date at the bottom of the screen, the date format in printed headers and footers matches the format of the screen clock.

Adding Page Numbers to Headers and Footers

To number pages, use the pound sign (#). 1-2-3 replaces # with the appropriate page number as it prints the header or footer. If the footer consists of the characters **¦–#–**, for example, each page is numbered at bottom center; the numbering reads -1-, -2-, and so on.

Using a Cell Reference as a Header or Footer

With Releases 2.2, 2.3, and 3.x, you can store a header or footer in a cell. To use the result of a cell as a header, enter a backslash followed by the cell address. If you enter **\D1** as a header, for example, 1-2-3 prints the current result of cell D1 at the top of each page. You also can use a range name; for example, **\PAGEHEAD**. If the range is larger than one cell, 1-2-3 uses the result of the upper left cell of the range as the header.

You cannot mix cell addresses or range names with other characters in a header or footer. If you enter the header **Wisent Industries¦ \D1**, 1-2-3 prints the characters \D1 instead of entering the result of cell D1. You can use the characters ¦, @, and # in cell D1, however. As 1-2-3 prints the headers, it uses these characters as though you typed them at the header prompt. If cell D1 contains the label ¦ ¦Page #, for example, entering \D1 at the header prompt tells 1-2-3 to number pages at the upper right corner.

By using cell addresses, you can print your worksheet with headers or footers that vary according to the worksheet results. Suppose that cell D1 (the header cell) contains the following formula:

```
@IF(NETDIFF<0,'Decrease','Increase')
    &' in Revenues This Month||Page #'
```

1-2-3 prints `Decrease in Revenues This Month` or `Increase in Revenues This Month` on the left side of the page and the word `Page`, followed by the page number, on the right side of the page.

You can use a cell designated as a header or footer to produce a time indicator. If you enter **@NOW** in cell D1, assigning it a time format and using **\D1** as the header, the header for each page of the worksheet displays the time when the worksheet was last calculated. If cell D1 contains a string-returning formula, part of which computes the current day of the week using the expression @MOD(@NOW,7), the header displays the day of the week on which the worksheet was printed. You also can create formulas that return the current date in any format you choose (such as March 3, 1991 or 3 March'91) and use these formulas in headers.

Figure 5.4 shows a section of a worksheet whose purpose is to calculate a string to use as a header. Cell I17 converts the current date to words using the following formula:

@INDEX(I3..I9,0,@MOD(@NOW,7))&' '
&&@INDEX(J3..J14,0,@MONTH(@NOW)−1)&' '
&&@STRING(@DAY(@NOW),0)&', '
&&@STRING(1900+@YEAR(@NOW),0)

Cell I20 incorporates the string in cell I17 into a longer string resembling a header using the following formula:

+I17&'¦Wisent Industries Financial Report¦Page #'

If you enter the characters **\I20** at the header prompt, the result resembles figure 5.5.

Using Border Columns

The **B**order option of the **/P**rint menu enables you to add ranges from your worksheet to the left side or the top of your printouts. Suppose that you want to print a report (from the worksheet in fig. 5.6) using the sales figures for June and July and the locations listed in column A. Select **/P**rint **P**rinter **R**ange, specify range **G5..H10**, select Options **B**orders **C**olumns, specify any cell in column A, and select **Q**uit **A**lign **G**o **Q**uit.

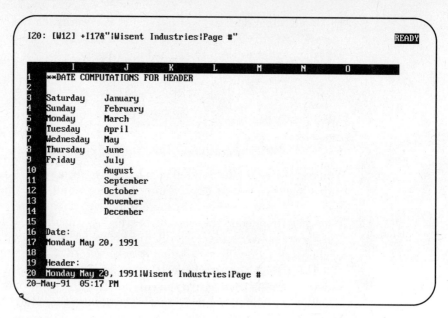

Fig. 5.4. *A worksheet section that produces a computed header displaying the current date in words.*

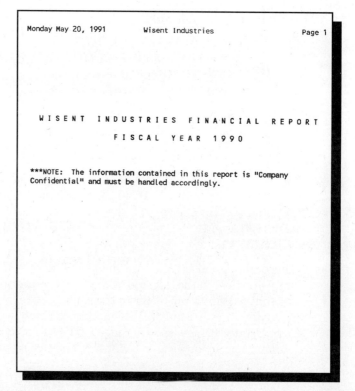

Fig. 5.5. *The printout resulting from the computed header technique in figure 5.4.*

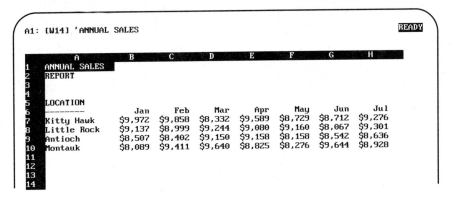

A1: [W14] 'ANNUAL SALES   READY

	A	B	C	D	E	F	G	H
1	ANNUAL SALES							
2	REPORT							
3								
4								
5	LOCATION							
6	-------	Jan	Feb	Mar	Apr	May	Jun	Jul
7	Kitty Hawk	$9,972	$9,858	$8,332	$9,589	$8,729	$8,712	$9,276
8	Little Rock	$9,137	$8,999	$9,244	$9,080	$9,160	$8,067	$9,301
9	Antioch	$8,507	$8,402	$9,150	$9,158	$8,158	$8,542	$8,636
10	Montauk	$8,089	$9,411	$9,640	$8,825	$8,276	$9,644	$8,928
11								
12								
13								
14								

Fig. 5.6. *An annual report worksheet containing figures for 12 months but displaying seven months on-screen.*

When 1-2-3 prints the range, it includes the cells in column A that are in the same rows as the print range; therefore, 1-2-3 prints the labels in range A5..A10 and, to the immediate right, the values in range G5..H10. Figure 5.7 shows the result.

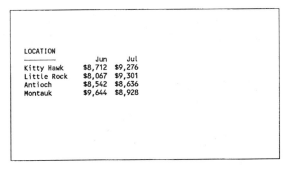

```
LOCATION
-------       Jun      Jul
Kitty Hawk   $8,712   $9,276
Little Rock  $8,067   $9,301
Antioch      $8,542   $8,636
Montauk      $9,644   $8,928
```

Fig. 5.7. *The result of specifying column A of figure 5.6 as the print border and range G5..H10 as the print range.*

You can use the **Border** option to print the entire 12-month report in one operation. Select **/P**rint **P**rinter **R**ange and specify range **B1..M10**. Select **O**ptions **B**orders and designate column A as the border column. Select **H**eader and enter ¦ ¦**Page #**. Then select **Q**uit **G**o **Q**uit. The result resembles figure 5.8.

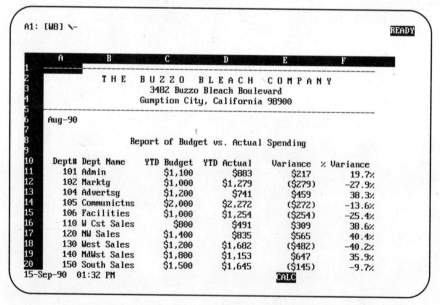

```
                                              Page 1                                                    Page 2

ANNUAL SALES                                             ANNUAL SALES
REPORT                                                   REPORT


LOCATION                                                 LOCATION
........                                                 ........
          Jan    Feb    Mar    Apr    May    Jun    Jul            Aug    Sep    Oct    Nov    Dec
Kitty Hawk  $9,972 $9,858 $8,332 $9,589 $8,729 $8,712 $9,276    Kitty Hawk  $8,410 $9,483 $9,612 $9,369 $8,418
Little Rock $9,137 $8,999 $9,244 $9,080 $9,160 $8,067 $9,301    Little Rock $8,732 $9,001 $9,822 $9,664 $8,779
Antioch     $8,507 $8,402 $9,150 $9,158 $8,158 $8,542 $8,636    Antioch     $8,772 $9,494 $9,736 $9,334 $8,691
Montauk     $8,089 $9,411 $9,640 $8,825 $8,276 $9,644 $8,928    Montauk     $8,628 $9,750 $9,902 $8,180 $8,077
```

Fig. 5.8. *A printed document produced with /Print Printer Options Borders, specifying a print range too wide for one page.*

Using Border Rows

Using border rows is similar to using headers. The rows you specify as borders appear at the top of every page. Using border rows is a more flexible way to present text at the top of each page than using headers. Figure 5.9 shows the first part of a long list of departments and their budgeted and actual spending amounts. Printing the list requires several pages and you need some identifying text to appear at the top of every page.

```
A1: [W8] \-                                                              READY

         A       B          C          D          E          F
1  ----------------------------------------------------------------------
2             T H E   B U Z Z O   B L E A C H   C O M P A N Y
3                      3482 Buzzo Bleach Boulevard
4                      Gumption City, California 98900
5  ----------------------------------------------------------------------
6   Aug-90
7
8                      Report of Budget vs. Actual Spending
9
10   Dept# Dept Name    YTD Budget  YTD Actual    Variance   % Variance
11    101 Admin          $1,100       $883         $217        19.7%
12    102 Marktg         $1,000      $1,279       ($279)      -27.9%
13    104 Advertsg       $1,200       $741         $459        38.3%
14    105 Communictns    $2,000      $2,272       ($272)      -13.6%
15    106 Facilities     $1,000      $1,254       ($254)      -25.4%
16    110 W Cst Sales      $800       $491         $309        38.6%
17    120 NW Sales       $1,400       $835         $565        40.4%
18    130 West Sales     $1,200      $1,682       ($482)      -40.2%
19    140 MdWst Sales    $1,800      $1,153       $647         35.9%
20    150 South Sales    $1,500      $1,645       ($145)       -9.7%
15-Sep-90  01:32 PM                               CALC
```

Fig. 5.9. *A multiple-page worksheet that requires identifying text on each printed page.*

Rows 1 through 5 provide an attractive page header. Cell A6 contains the formula @NOW, formatted in the month-and-year format. (The option of using different date formats is one advantage to using border rows instead of headers, which limit you to the DD-MMM-YY format.) Row 8 identifies the report and the labels in row 10 identify the individual columns. To place these rows at the top of every printed page, select /Print Printer Options Borders Rows, specify any range that extends from row 1 to row 10, select Quit Range, specify the range extending from cell A11 to the last entry in column F, and select Align Go Quit.

You cannot number pages with border rows as you can with headers. You can, however, number pages by entering a header string *and* using border rows.

Don't specify a print range that includes the border rows. If you designate rows 1 to 10 as border rows and begin the print range in cell A1, rows 1 to 10 are printed twice on the first page of the printout.

Suppose that you want the Buzzo Bleach header to appear on the first page only and the date, the report name, and the column headings on every page. 1-2-3 makes no provision for creating a one-time report header, but you can print the report in the following manner.

Clear the existing print range and borders by selecting /Print Printer Clear Range Borders Quit. Specify range **A1..F5** as the print range and select **Align Go**. Specify a new print range extending from cell A11 to the last entry in column F, select **Options Borders Rows**, specify any range that extends from row 6 to row 10, and select **Quit**. Don't select **Align**. Select **Go**; when printing is complete, select **Page Quit**. 1-2-3 prints the border rows and then prints the print range until it fills a page. Then 1-2-3 advances the paper to the next page, prints the border rows again, and continues printing the print range. You must select **Align** before printing the one-time report header, but don't select **Align** before printing the report itself, or 1-2-3 doesn't place the between-page spaces in the correct positions.

You can create a short macro to handle the keystrokes of adjusting the range border settings and issuing the **Align** and **Go** commands in the correct sequence. A macro for the Buzzo Bleach worksheet appears in figure 5.10.

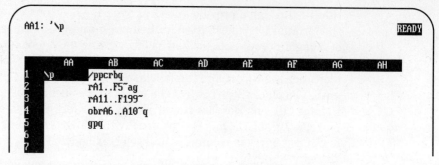

Fig. 5.10. *A macro that prints a long range with a one-time report header.*

Maximizing the Number of Rows Per Page

If you need to fit as many rows as possible on one sheet of paper, suppress headers, footers, and page breaks by selecting the **/Print Printer Options Other Unformatted** command.

If you suppress these options, you will have no white space in your document, making your printouts difficult to read and photocopy. If the paper in your line printer is not aligned, the last rows of each page may print on the perforation between pages. Consider setting the top and bottom margins to 0 and accepting the three lines for headers and footers that 1-2-3 usually reserves. Unformatted print is better suited to printing to a disk file. To reset formatted print, select **/Print Printer Options Other Formatted.**

Printing Cell Formulas

You usually will want to print the results displayed on-screen in your worksheet. 1-2-3 also enables you to print the exact contents of every cell in a range, arranged in one column on the paper. To use this option, select **/Print Printer Options Other Cell-Formulas Quit.** Specify a print range and select **Align Go Quit.** The result resembles figure 5.11. The printout lists the address of every cell containing any kind of entry. Each address is followed by the format of the cell, if different from the worksheet's default format; the column-width of the cell, unless the column conforms to the default width; and the contents of the cell.

```
A1: 'AMORTIZATION WORKSHEET
A3: 'Interest Rate:
C3: (P1) [W11] 0.12
A4: 'Principal:
C4: (C0) [W11] 175000
A5: 'Term:
C5: [W11] 25
A6: 'Payment:
C6: (C2) [W11] @PMT(C4,C3/12,C5*12)
A8: "Period
B8: "Balance
C8: [W11] "Principal
D8: [W10] "Interest
A9: 1
B9: (C0) @PV(C$6,C$3/12,C$5*12-A9)
C9: (C2) [W11] +C4-B9
D9: (C2) [W10] +C$6-C9
A10: 2
B10: (C0) @PV(C$6,C$3/12,C$5*12-A10)
C10: (C2) [W11] +B9-B10
D10: (C2) [W10] +C$6-C10
A11: 3
B11: (C0) @PV(C$6,C$3/12,C$5*12-A11)
C11: (C2) [W11] +B10-B11
D11: (C2) [W10] +C$6-C11
A12: 4
B12: (C0) @PV(C$6,C$3/12,C$5*12-A12)
C12: (C2) [W11] +B11-B12
D12: (C2) [W10] +C$6-C12
A13: 5
B13: (C0) @PV(C$6,C$3/12,C$5*12-A13)
C13: (C2) [W11] +B12-B13
D13: (C2) [W10] +C$6-C13
A14: 6
B14: (C0) @PV(C$6,C$3/12,C$5*12-A14)
C14: (C2) [W11] +B13-B14
D14: (C2) [W10] +C$6-C14
A15: 7
B15: (C0) @PV(C$6,C$3/12,C$5*12-A15)
C15: (C2) [W11] +B14-B15
D15: (C2) [W10] +C$6-C15
A16: 8
B16: (C0) @PV(C$6,C$3/12,C$5*12-A16)
C16: (C2) [W11] +B15-B16
D16: (C2) [W10] +C$6-C16
```

Fig. 5.11. A printout resulting from using the **C**ell-Formulas option.

Printing a range or an entire worksheet using the Cell-Formulas option is a way to document the worksheet. A Cell-Formulas document provides a record of all formulas, values, and labels and may help you correct a worksheet if formulas are overwritten or converted to values. To return to normal printing, select /Print Printer Options Other As-Displayed.

Printing to Disk Files

1-2-3's /Print menu enables you to export the results of a worksheet as a pure ASCII text file. You can use this option to create a file that you can print at a later time or at another location.

You print information to a file in the same manner that you print to the printer, except that you begin the process by selecting /Print File. 1-2-3 prompts you for a file name. If you don't specify an extension, 1-2-3 adds the extension **PRN**. To create a file name with no extension, type the file name followed by a period.

You also can choose an existing file by highlighting it and pressing Enter. If the file exists, you see a two-option menu enabling you to replace the existing file or cancel the operation. After you specify a file (and select **R**eplace if necessary), you see the same menu that you see when printing to the printer.

Suppose that you have selected /Print File and specified a file name. You have used the default margin settings and specified a large print range, and the header consists of **Page #**. When you select **G**o, 1-2-3 creates a text file beginning with two empty lines because the top margin is set to 2. 1-2-3 then prints the characters Page 1 preceded by four spaces (because the left margin is set to 4); two more empty lines (because 1-2-3 reserves three lines for the header); and the characters found in the print range, each line preceded by four spaces. You can see what 1-2-3 has done if you bring the text file into the worksheet by selecting /File Import Text (see fig. 5.12). The imported data resembles cell entries, but it actually consists of long labels, one for each line of text.

You can print this file to almost any printer from the operating system prompt. Use the command **PRINT** followed by the file name. You also can enter the command **COPY** *FILENAME*.**PRN PRN** or **TYPE** *FILENAME*.**PRN>PRN**. The resulting printout looks exactly as it would if you printed it from 1-2-3. The only exception is that printer control codes you enter as a setup string or in the worksheet are not included in the text file. The text files you create with /Print File can include headers and footers, border columns, and border rows. The files also can use different margins or unformatted text, or use Cell-Formulas format.

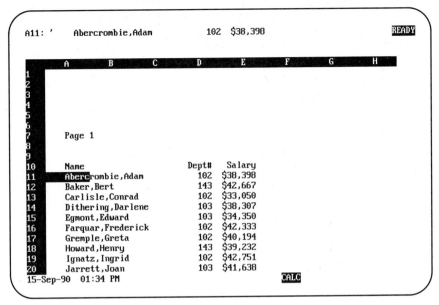

```
A11: '    Abercrombie,Adam        102  $38,398                           READY

        A        B         C        D         E        F        G        H
   1
   2
   3
   4
   5
   6
   7    Page 1
   8
   9
   10   Name                          Dept#   Salary
   11   Abercrombie,Adam               102   $38,398
   12   Baker,Bert                     143   $42,667
   13   Carlisle,Conrad                102   $33,050
   14   Dithering,Darlene              103   $38,307
   15   Egmont,Edward                  103   $34,350
   16   Farquar,Frederick              102   $42,333
   17   Gremple,Greta                  102   $40,194
   18   Howard,Henry                   143   $39,232
   19   Ignatz,Ingrid                  102   $42,751
   20   Jarrett,Joan                   103   $41,638
   15-Sep-90  01:34 PM                                  CALC
```

Fig. 5.12. *A worksheet of undelimited ASCII data, which is created by printing to a file.*

Printing to Encoded Files with Releases 2.3 and 3.x

With 1-2-3 Releases 2.3 and later, you can print a range to an encoded disk file. You can specify printer control codes at the setup string prompt or in the worksheet. Select **/P**rint Encoded and specify a file name. 1-2-3 uses the default extension ENC for encoded files. If the file name exists, select **R**eplace from the Cancel/**R**eplace menu, specify the print range, and select any options you want, including a setup string. Then select Go. This process creates a file tailored to the type of printer for which 1-2-3 is currently configured. To print this file from the operating system prompt, use the command **COPY /B *FILENAME*.ENC PRN**. Replace **PRN** with **COM1** if your printer is attached to the serial port of your computer. The **/B** after **COPY** indicates that you are copying a binary file to the device name PRN. The printout looks exactly as though you printed directly to the printer from 1-2-3.

Be certain that your computer is connected to the same kind of printer specified in the 1-2-3 configuration when you created the encoded file.

Background Printing with Release 2.3

If you use Release 2.3 and find that the mode indicator flashes WAIT for a long time after you select **/P**rint Printer Go, consider using the background printing option. When you use this feature, 1-2-3 sends the print range to an encoded file (extension ENC) and returns control of the computer to you while it copies the encoded file to the printer in the background.

You may not need background printing. Many computers use extra memory as a print buffer. (The command that sets up the buffer is usually found in the AUTOEXEC.BAT or CONFIG.SYS file.) Some printers also have memory chips that serve as buffers. When a print buffer is available, text sent to the printer by applications software is stored in the buffer until the printer can print it; the applications software is free to perform other tasks. If the 1-2-3 mode indicator stops displaying WAIT before printing is complete, your equipment probably uses a buffer, and you need not use background printing.

To use background printing, you must load the BPRINT program (included with your 1-2-3 package) into memory before you start 1-2-3. At the DOS prompt, change to the directory containing 1-2-3, type **BPRINT**, and press Enter; then start 1-2-3. To print a range in the background, select **/P**rint **B**ackground and specify a file name. If the file exists, the **C**ancel/**R**eplace menu appears. To avoid overwriting an existing ENC file, select **C**ancel and reissue the **/P**rint **B**ackground command, specifying a different file name. If you prefer to replace the existing file, select **R**eplace.

The same print menu appears that you see when you select **/P**rint **P**rinter. Select the desired options from this menu and then select **A**lign **G**o **Q**uit (or **A**lign **G**o **P**age **Q**uit). You may notice that 1-2-3 takes a few seconds to create the encoded file. At about the same time that printing begins, the mode indicator changes from WAIT to MENU, indicating that you can use 1-2-3 normally while the range is being printed. You even can abandon the current worksheet by selecting **/W**orksheet **E**rase **Y**es (save the worksheet first if you made any changes in it) and retrieve another worksheet.

To cancel printing, select **/S**ystem to exit 1-2-3 temporarily. At the DOS prompt, issue the command **BPRINT –T**. The **–T** option terminates all printing, including files still waiting to print. Use **BPRINT –C** ***FILENAME*** to remove a specific file from the print queue. Type **EXIT** and press Enter to return to 1-2-3. To halt printing temporarily (for example, to answer the phone), access the operating system with **/S**ystem and issue the command **BPRINT –PA**. BPRINT stops until you enter **BPRINT –R** to resume printing.

Exporting Data with /Print File

The /Print File command often can be used to create files for use by other software, such as a word processing program. Suppose that a worksheet creates a summary table, such as the one in figure 5.13, and you want to include the table in a printed report. Select /Print File and enter a file name. Use the default extension PRN unless your word processing program is selective about file name extensions; in that case, specify an appropriate extension. Select Replace if necessary; then select Range and specify range I6..M10. Select Options Margins None. If you use Release 2.01 or earlier, the Margins None option doesn't exist. Set the top, left, and bottom margins to 0 and the right margin to 240. Select Other Unformatted Quit Go Quit.

When you export data to be used by other programs, suppress page breaks and use no left, top, or bottom margin.

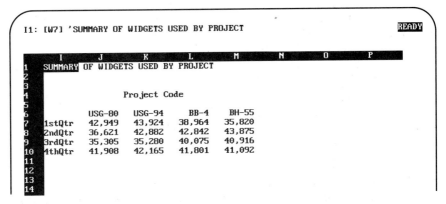

Fig. 5.13. A summary table to be included as text in a printed report.

You also can use /Print File to export data for use with a database program. Most database programs can read each line of a text file and treat (for example) the first 15 characters as the first field, the next 10 characters as the second field, and the next 3 characters as the third field. If you create a database (such as the one in figure 5.14) in 1-2-3, you can export records to a file that can be used to add the records to a new or existing database generated by a database program.

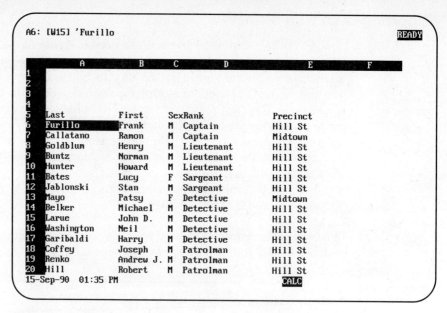

```
A6: [W15] 'Furillo                                                    READY

              A              B        C        D            E            F
1
2
3
4
5     Last           First      SexRank                  Precinct
6     Furillo        Frank      M  Captain               Hill St
7     Callatano      Ramon      M  Captain               Midtown
8     Goldblum       Henry      M  Lieutenant            Hill St
9     Buntz          Norman     M  Lieutenant            Hill St
10    Hunter         Howard     M  Lieutenant            Hill St
11    Bates          Lucy       F  Sargeant              Hill St
12    Jablonski      Stan       M  Sargeant              Hill St
13    Mayo           Patsy      F  Detective             Midtown
14    Belker         Michael    M  Detective             Hill St
15    Larue          John D.    M  Detective             Hill St
16    Washington     Neil       M  Detective             Hill St
17    Garibaldi      Harry      M  Detective             Hill St
18    Coffey         Joseph     M  Patrolman             Hill St
19    Renko          Andrew J.  M  Patrolman             Hill St
20    Hill           Robert     M  Patrolman             Hill St
15-Sep-90   01:35 PM                                     CALC
```

Fig. 5.14. *A 1-2-3 database that can be exported into a database program using the /Print File command.*

To add the records to an existing database, determine the field lengths in use in that database and match the column widths to the field lengths. If you plan to create a new database from the records in the worksheet, do the opposite; jot down the column widths in effect when you export the data and use these widths as field lengths when you create the database in the database program. In either case, all columns must be wide enough that no labels spill out of their cells and no values are displayed as asterisks.

To share the records shown in figure 5.14 with a database program, select /Print File and enter a file name. Select Replace, if necessary. Set the left, top, and bottom margins to 0. Set the right margin to a number high enough to accommodate the length of the records or, for convenience, to 240 (the maximum right margin). Select Unformatted printing and create the file by selecting Go from the /Print menu.

Printing Solid Dividing Lines with Release 3

You probably have used hyphens, split vertical bars, slashes, and back-slashes to create dividing lines in a worksheet. Figure 5.15 shows an example of a 1-2-3 Release 2.2 worksheet created with hyphens and split vertical bars.

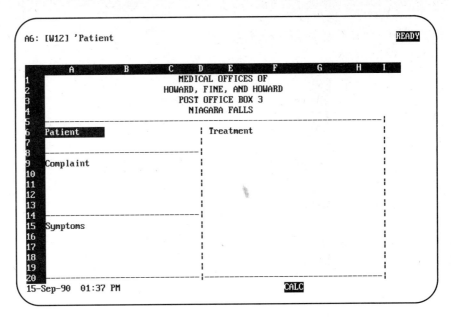

```
A6: [W12] 'Patient                                                    READY

         A      B     C    D    E        F      G        H    I
 1                              MEDICAL OFFICES OF
 2                            HOWARD, FINE, AND HOWARD
 3                              POST OFFICE BOX 3
 4                                NIAGARA FALLS
 5       ---------------------------------------------------------------
 6      Patient                           | Treatment                    |
 7                                        |                              |
 8       ---------------------------------|                              |
 9      Complaint                         |                              |
10                                        |                              |
11                                        |                              |
12                                        |                              |
13                                        |                              |
14       ---------------------------------|                              |
15      Symptoms                          |                              |
16                                        |                              |
17                                        |                              |
18                                        |                              |
19                                        |                              |
20       ---------------------------------|------------------------------|
      15-Sep-90   01:37 PM                              CALC
```

Fig. 5.15. *A conventional 1-2-3 document using hyphens and split vertical bars to create straight dividing lines in a worksheet.*

The Allways add-in program (available separately for Releases 2 and 2.01 and included with Release 2.2) and the Wysiwyg add-in program for Releases 2.3 and 3.1 enable you to create more professional-looking printouts by surrounding ranges with solid lines. No add-in programs like Allways and Wysiwyg are available for Release 3, but you can use IBM-graphics characters in place of dashes and split bars. Figure 5.16 shows what an improvement IBM graphics can make in a 1-2-3 worksheet.

You enter these characters in a worksheet by specifying their ASCII numbers. A horizontal line (–) has the ASCII number 196. To fill a cell with horizontal lines instead of hyphens, press the backslash (\) key; then hold down the Alt key and press the **1**, **9**, and **6** keys on the numeric pad (not on the top row of the keyboard). When you release the Alt key, the horizontal line appears on the control panel. Press Enter. The cell now resembles cell A5 of figure 5.16.

To create a centered vertical bar (|), as in cell D6 of figure 5.16, press the carat (^) key; then hold down the Alt key and press **1**, **7**, and **9** on the numeric pad. Then release the Alt key and press Enter.

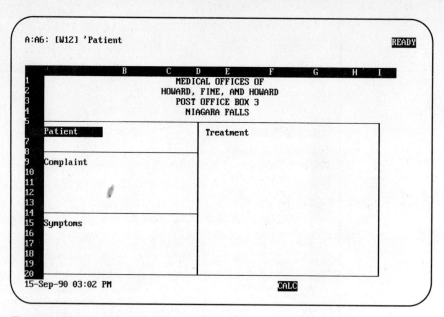

A:A6: [W12] 'Patient   READY

```
                    B         C      D     E         F        G      H    I
1                                    MEDICAL OFFICES OF
2                              HOWARD, FINE, AND HOWARD
3                                  POST OFFICE BOX 3
4                                    NIAGARA FALLS
5
   Patient                                       Treatment
7
8
9  Complaint
10
11
12
13
14
15 Symptoms
16
17
18
19
20
   15-Sep-90 03:02 PM                            CALC
```

Fig. 5.16. IBM-graphics characters creating solid lines in a Release 3 worksheet.

Following is a list of other graphics characters and their corresponding ASCII numbers.

Character	ASCII number
Upper left corner (┌)	218
Upper right corner (┐)	191
Lower left corner (└)	192
Lower right corner (┘)	217
T connector (┤)	180
T connector (┴)	193
T connector (┬)	194
T connector (├)	195

Other characters that you can use for creating dividing lines and boxes are listed in the 1-2-3 Release 3 manual. Adding lines to a worksheet with these characters requires planning and adjusting of column widths, but the results are worth the extra time you spend.

If you print this worksheet in the usual way, however, the printout doesn't look like your screen, even if your printer can print the IBM-graphics characters. 1-2-3 translates the vertical line to a split vertical bar and the horizontal line to a hyphen as it sends the characters to the printer. You must use an unorthodox method for printing these characters.

1-2-3 Release 3 doesn't translate the graphics characters if you print the range to a file instead of to the printer. You must fool 1-2-3 into thinking that the graphics characters are being sent to a file. Select /Print File. Enter **PRN** or **LPT1** (parallel port) or **COM1** or **COM2** (serial port) and select **R**eplace.

PRN, LPT1, COM1 and COM2 are device names reserved by DOS or OS/2. Any activity that usually sends data to a file sends the data to the printer port if the target file name is replaced with PRN, LPT1, or COM1.

After you specify the correct device name and select **R**eplace, the /**P**rint menu appears. Specify the desired range and select print options (such as margins, headers, footers, and borders). Select Go. This procedure produces a printout with solid dividing lines as they appear on-screen.

If the printout from your dot-matrix printer contains many Ds, 3s and other characters instead of the graphics characters, your printer cannot handle the graphics characters or must be switched to IBM-emulation mode. You probably can switch the printer to this mode by sending a control code sequence. In normal printing, you use a setup string to send control characters to the printer. If 1-2-3 thinks it is printing to a file, it ignores the setup string.

Instead of using a setup string, use the macro shown in figure 5.17 to send the control characters to the printer. This macro uses the OPEN command to channel the control characters to the printer port rather than to a disk file. Replace PRN in cell K1 with **COM1** if the printer is connected to a serial port. 1-2-3 writes the characters Esc, t, and 1 to the printer. These characters are appropriate for Epson and other types of printers. Check your printer manual and (if necessary) change the characters following the word WRITE in cell K2. After you run this macro, you can print the graphics characters using the /**P**rint File command.

If you use a LaserJet or similar laser printer, you may see degree signs (°) or foreign-language characters instead of graphics characters when your printer is not using a character set containing graphics characters. Use the buttons on your printer to select a more suitable character set, or use the macro shown in figure 5.17 to send the printer a control code sequence that selects the desired character set.

Creating Presentation-Quality Printouts with Add-In Programs

Release 2.2 includes the Allways add-in program, which enables you to choose different typefaces, add solid lines to worksheets, and incorporate 1-2-3 graphs into worksheets. Allways is available separately for use with Releases 2 and 2.01. Releases 2.3 and 3.1 include Wysiwyg, which has many of the same features as Allways but also enables you to edit and justify text, switch typefaces within lines of text, create graphs from scratch, and incorporate graphics files exported by Lotus Freelance Plus and many other graphics programs.

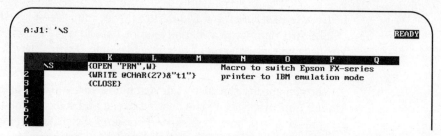

Fig. 5.17. *A macro that sends control characters to an Epson printer to switch the printer to IBM-emulation mode.*

The following sections of this chapter discuss techniques for printing worksheet data formatted and enhanced with Allways or Wysiwyg. For more information on using add-in programs, see Chapter 12 of this book.

Printing with Allways (Release 2.2)

Printing with Allways is very similar to regular 1-2-3 printing. After starting Allways with the Alt-function key combination you assigned to it, select /Print, define a range, and select Go. Allways printing gives you many of the same options as regular printing, such as adjustable margins, headers, footers, border rows, and columns. Selecting and implementing these options in Allways is different in several important ways.

Adjusting the Layout for Allways Printing

Some Allways options that affect printing are not part of the /Print menu. When Allways is active, select /Layout. 1-2-3 displays the screen shown in figure 5.18 and gives you access to the left, right, top, and bottom margins, headers, footers, borders, and page-size settings.

Margins are expressed in inches from their respective sides of the page. The default margin settings are all one inch. To adjust the margins, select Margins and then Left, Right, Top, or Bottom. When you finish adjusting the margins, select Quit.

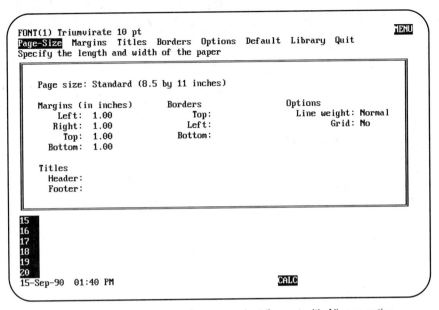

```
FONT(1) Triumvirate 10 pt                                    MENU
Page-Size  Margins  Titles  Borders  Options  Default  Library  Quit
Specify the length and width of the paper


   Page size: Standard (8.5 by 11 inches)

   Margins (in inches)      Borders            Options
       Left:   1.00            Top:               Line weight: Normal
      Right:   1.00           Left:                      Grid: No
        Top:   1.00         Bottom:
     Bottom:   1.00

   Titles
     Header:
     Footer:




15
16
17
18
19
20
15-Sep-90  01:40 PM                          CALC
```

Fig. 5.18. The screen that appears when you select /Layout with Allways active.

To set a header or a footer, select Titles, select Header or Footer, and enter the header or footer text. Follow the same conventions you use with headers and footers in normal printing; use the split vertical bar to divide the text into left-aligned, centered, and right-aligned sections; use # to number pages; and use @ to include the current date. With Allways, you cannot use a backslash and a cell address to display the result of a worksheet cell as the header or footer. You can clear existing headers and footers by selecting Clear and then Header, Footer, or Both. When you finish adding or changing headers and footers, select Quit.

As with regular 1-2-3 printing, you can specify border columns to appear on the left side of each page and border rows to appear at the top of every page. In Allways, however, you also can specify border rows to appear at the bottom of every page. Select Borders and then Top, Left, or Bottom. Specify a range that includes all of the rows or columns that you want on every page. To clear borders, select Clear followed by Top, Left, Bottom, or All. To return to the main /Layout menu, select Quit.

Setting the Allways Print Range

After you make the desired adjustments in the layout settings, select Quit to return to the Allways READY mode. Select /Print. 1-2-3 displays the Allways /Print menu. To set a print range, select Range Set and specify the range by entering coordinates or by highlighting the desired range and pressing Enter.

In regular 1-2-3 printing, the size of the range that fits on a page is controlled by the margin settings. 1-2-3 prints as many entire columns as fit between the left and right margins, advances the paper to the next page, and prints the remaining columns.

Always printing follows the same procedures, but Always shows you by way of its visible page break lines which columns don't fit on the page. After you select a print range and return to the Always READY mode, the print range is encased in a broken red line—black on monochrome screens—and any page breaks within the print range also are marked by broken lines. If the print range you selected is a few characters too wide to be printed within the margins, the far right column in the print range has a broken line on both its left and right sides, indicating that the right column appears on a separate sheet.

To correct the problem before you begin printing, try changing the left or right margins—you can adjust them in increments of 1/100 of an inch— or making the columns narrower. The problem is corrected when the line to the left of the right-hand column disappears.

Selecting a Printer for Allways Printing

Select /Print again. If necessary, change the printer or printer configuration. Select Configuration; a menu appears, as shown in figure 5.19. The number of options in the menu depends on which printer is selected. For most dot-matrix or inkjet printers, the choices are limited to Printer, Interface, and Quit. For laser printers, you can select the font cartridge, the paper bin, resolution, and orientation (vertical or horizontal). Adjust the configuration if necessary and select Quit to return to the /Print menu.

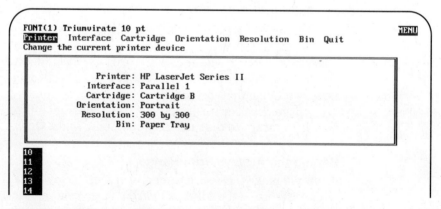

Fig. 5.19. The Allways printing menu, displaying configuration options.

Selecting Pages To Print

If your printing area is small, you probably don't need to use the **Settings** option of the **/P**rint menu; however, if you selected a long range that prints on several pages, you may want to start printing from a page after the first page or stop printing before the last page. If you used the # character in a header or footer, you may want to number the first page with a number higher than one. Or you may want to print more than one copy at a time.

To make such adjustments, select **Settings.** Select **Begin** and enter the number of the page where you want Always to start printing. You can make this selection whether or not you use a header or footer to number pages. The rows between the top of the print range and the first page break comprise the first page, the rows between the first and second page break comprise the second page, and so on. If you select **Begin** and enter **3**, for example, Always starts printing just after the second page break.

Select **End** and enter the page at which to stop printing. The number you enter must be relative to the first page in the print range, not the first page to be printed. To print three pages beginning at the third page of the print range, for example, enter **3** after selecting **Begin** and enter **5** after selecting **End.** If you want Always to print to the last page of the print range, enter **9999.**

Select **First** and enter the number that replaces # in the header or footer of the first page of the print range. To print more than one copy, select **Copies** and enter the desired number. Select **Q**uit to return to the main **/P**rint menu.

Printing the Range

Select **G**o to print the range immediately or **F**ile to create a file you can print later or at another location from DOS. If you select **File,** enter a file name. Always uses the extension ENC for encoded files. If the file exists, Always presents a Cancel/Replace menu. Select **R**eplace if you want to overwrite the existing file. With Always printing, you don't have to select **G**o after selecting **File.** Go and File function the same way, except that Go sends data to the printer and File to a disk file. After Always has finished printing, whether to the printer or to a file, the Always READY mode returns.

Printing an Encoded Allways File

You print an Allways encoded file from DOS the same way that you print a Release 2.3 or 3.x encoded file. Type **COPY /B** and the file name, including the ENC extension. Type the name of the device port to which the printer is attached (PRN or COM1, for example) and press Enter.

Printing with Wysiwyg (Releases 2.3 and 3.1)

Wysiwyg, which stands for *what-you-see-is-what-you-get*, is an add-in program that comes with Releases 2.3 and 3.1. Wysiwyg uses technology developed for Impress, an add-in program for Release 2.x. Lotus Development Corporation acquired the rights to Impress and used it to create an add-in program tailored for Release 3.1, later adapting it for Release 2.3. People who used older versions of Impress with Release 2.x may find Wysiwyg confusing, but people who have used Allways will find Wysiwyg familiar, because Lotus rearranged the menu structure of Wysiwyg to resemble Allways more closely than Impress.

Printing a worksheet range enhanced with Wysiwyg is similar to regular 1-2-3 printing; you select the print menu, specify a range, and select **G**o. The most important difference in Wysiwyg printing is that you start the Wysiwyg menu by typing a colon (**:**) instead of a slash.

Setting the Print Range

When you select **:P**rint, the Wysiwyg setting screen shown in figure 5.20 appears on-screen. Select **R**ange **S**et and specify the range you want to print. Then select **Q**uit.

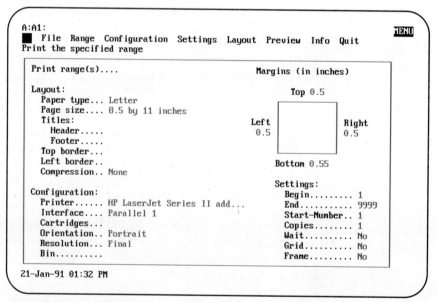

Fig. 5.20. *The Release 3.1 Wysiwyg printing menu that appears when you select the* **:Print** *command.*

In regular printing, the size of the range that fits on a page is controlled by the margin settings. 1-2-3 prints as many entire columns as fit between the left and right margins, advances the paper to the next page, and prints the remaining columns.

Wysiwyg printing follows the same procedures, but Wysiwyg shows you by way of its visible page break lines which columns don't fit on the page. After you select a print range and return to the READY mode, the print range is encased in a broken line and any page breaks within the print range also are marked by broken lines. If the print range that you selected is a few characters too wide to be printed within the margins you set, the far right column in the print range has a broken line on both its left and right sides, which indicates that the right column appears on a separate sheet.

To correct the problem before you start printing, try to adjust the left or right margins or make the columns narrower. You know that you have corrected the problem when the line to the left of the right-hand column disappears.

Setting Margins

Select **:P**rint again and select **L**ayout to gain access to the settings for paper size, margins, headers, footers, and borders.

Margins are expressed in inches from their respective sides of the page. To set the margins, select **M**argins and then **L**eft, **R**ight, **T**op, or **B**ottom, and enter a new setting. The margin settings can be as fine as 1/100 of an inch. When you finish adjusting the margins, select **Q**uit.

Setting Headers, Footers, and Borders

To set a header or a footer, select **T**itles, select **H**eader or **F**ooter, and enter the header or footer text. Follow the same conventions you use with headers and footers in normal printing. Use the split vertical bar to divide the text into left-aligned, centered, and right-aligned sections; use # to number pages; and use @ to include the current date. As with regular 1-2-3 printing, you can enter a backslash and a cell address to use the result of a worksheet cell as the header or footer. You can clear existing headers and footers by selecting **C**lear and then **H**eader, **F**ooter, or **B**oth. When you finish adding or changing headers and footers, select **Q**uit.

To specify rows to appear at the top of every page, or columns to appear at the left of every page, select **B**orders, select **R**ows or **C**olumns, and specify a range that includes all of the rows or columns you want on every page. To clear borders, select **C**lear, followed by **R**ows, **C**olumns, or **B**oth. Wysiwyg doesn't enable you to set border rows for the bottoms of pages as Allways does. To return to the main **:P**rint menu, select **Q**uit.

Selecting Pages To Print

If your printing area is small, you probably don't need to use the **Settings** option of the **:P**rint menu; however, if you selected a long range that prints on several pages, you may want to start printing from a page after the first page or stop printing before the last page. If you used the # character in a header or footer, you may want to number the first page with a number higher than 1. Or you may want to print more than one copy at a time.

To make such adjustments, select **Settings**. Select **Begin** and enter the number of the page you want Wysiwyg to start printing. You can make this selection whether or not you use a header or footer to number pages. The rows between the top of the print range and the first page break comprise the first page, the rows between the first and second page break comprise the second page, and so on. If you select **Begin** and enter **3**, for example, Wysiwyg starts printing just after the second page break.

Select **End** and enter the page at which to stop printing. The number you enter must be relative to the first page in the print range, not the page at which Wysiwyg starts printing. To print three pages beginning at the third page of the print range, for example, enter **3** after selecting **Begin** and enter **5** after selecting **End**. If you want Wysiwyg to print to the last page of the print range, enter **9999**.

Select **First** and enter the number that replaces # in the header or footer of the first page of the print range. If you want more than one copy, select **Copies** and enter the desired number. Select **Quit** to return to the main **:P**rint menu.

Printing the Range

Select **Go** to print the range immediately or **File** to create a file you can print later or at another location from DOS. Select **Preview** to view an image of the range as it would appear on paper. If you select **File**, enter a file name. Wysiwyg uses the default extension ENC. If the file exists, Wysiwyg presents a Cancel/Replace menu. Select **Replace** if you want to overwrite the existing file.

With Wysiwyg printing, you don't need to select **Go** after selecting **File**. **Go** and **File** function in the same way, except that **Go** sends data to the printer and **File** sends data to a disk file. After Wysiwyg has finished printing, whether to the printer or to a file, it returns you to READY mode.

You can print a Wysiwyg encoded file from the operating system prompt in the same way that you print a Release 3.x encoded file. Type **COPY /B** and the file name, including the ENC extension. Specify the name of the device port to which the printer is attached (PRN or COM1, for example) and press Enter.

Summary

Most worksheets are designed to produce printed reports. By understanding the subtleties of 1-2-3 print commands, you can make your printouts as attractive and understandable as possible.

This chapter discussed how to optimize the appearance of printouts with printer control codes and margin adjustments, and how to annotate printouts with header, footer, and border commands. You also learned how to produce presentation-quality documents with the Allways and Wysiwyg add-in programs.

The next chapter discusses the use of functions and methods for streamlining worksheet formulas in 1-2-3.

Chapter Six

WORKING WITH FORMULAS AND FUNCTIONS

F ormulas provide the real power of 1-2-3. People who consider themselves "power users" often write complex macros rather than formulas, but a well-organized array of efficient cell formulas can handle business, financial, or scientific problems almost instantly, and just as quickly provide revised answers when you change any factor of the problem.

This chapter covers the following formula and function topics:

- The rules of operator precedence
- Applying operator precedence rules to create more efficient formulas
- How Boolean algebra applies to 1-2-3 formulas
- Tricks for creating more efficient formulas
- Tricks for using functions

Understanding Operators and Operator Precedence

Except for formulas using only functions (@SUM(A15..A20), for example), 1-2-3 formulas must contain one or more of 17 mathematical operators. The most frequently used operators are addition (+), subtraction (−), multiplication (*) and division (/).

1-2-3 follows the specific rules of operator precedence used by mathematicians for centuries. Multiplication and division, for example, take precedence over addition and subtraction. The expression $4+8\times3$ equals 28 (4 added to the result of 8 multiplied by 3) and not 36 (3 times the sum of 4 and 8).

The following table lists the operators you can use in 1-2-3 formulas, in descending order of precedence.

Operator	Order of Precedence	Definition
( )	1	Parentheses
^	2	Exponentiation (x to the nth power)
+	3	Positive
–	3	Negative
*	4	Multiplication
/	4	Division
+	5	Addition
–	5	Subtraction
=	6	Equal to
< >	6	Not equal to
<	6	Less than
>	6	Greater than
>=	6	Greater than or equal to
<=	6	Less than or equal to
#NOT#	7	Not
#AND#	8	And
#OR#	8	Or

Considering Operator Precedence in Detail

Parentheses take precedence over all other operators. The expression $4+8\times3=28$ is true, but the expression $(4+8)\times3=36$ also is true because the parentheses tell you to solve the addition portion of the expression first.

Exponentiation takes precedence over all operators except parentheses. To find the result of the expression $A*B^n$, raise B to the nth power and multiply the result by A. To raise the product of A and B to the nth power, use the formula $(A*B)^n$.

The positive operator (+) at the beginning of an expression establishes the expression as a value. Typically, you use the positive operator to indicate that the opening expression in a formula is a cell reference. With the expression +E30*10, for example, if you don't use the positive operator, 1-2-3 treats the entry as a label.

The negative operator (–) reverses the sign of a value; positive values become negative and negatives become positive. The negative operator also is used to establish that an expression is a value *and* change its sign, as in the expression –E30*10.

 Don't confuse the positive and negative operators with addition and subtraction operators. Both sets of operators use the same characters, but the positive and negative operators take precedence over multiplication and division, which take precedence over addition and subtraction.

Multiplication and division have equal precedence. 1-2-3 solves problems using the multiplication and division operators from left to right.

Addition and subtraction also have equal precedence. In a formula that adds several values, order doesn't matter (addition, like multiplication, is commutative). With subtraction, order is important.

The *logical* operators =, < >, <, >, <=, and >= are most commonly found in the *test* argument of the @IF function, as in the partial expressions @IF(D13=5, or @IF(F3<=F9,. You also can use logical operators in some interesting formulas that don't involve @IF. A discussion of the specific uses for the logical operators and their position in the order of precedence appears later in this chapter.

The #NOT# operator makes true (or nonzero) expressions false (or 0). It also makes false (or 0) expressions true (or nonzero).

The #AND# and #OR# operators join two or more values together to form an expression that returns 1 or 0, depending on whether the values joined are zeros or nonzeros. The following formula, for example, returns 1 only if all of the referenced cells have values other than 0:

+A1#AND#A3#AND#A5#AND#A7

If even one of the referenced cells is empty or contains 0, the expression returns 0. On the other hand, the following expression returns 1 as long as at least one of the cells named contains a nonzero value:

+A1#OR#A3#OR#A5#OR#A7

Applying the Rules of Precedence

Many 1-2-3 users include too many parentheses in formulas. The extra parentheses often make a formula harder to decipher and take up additional computer memory. Understanding the rules of precedence can help you avoid using unnecessary parentheses.

The following expression is 8 characters too long:

((B7*D3)+F5)/10+(((A$4*G8)*M2)–D6)

The following revised version of the preceding formula performs the same computation:

(B7*D3+F5)/10+A$4*G8*M2–D6

Understanding Boolean Expressions

A Boolean expression returns 1 or 0, depending on whether or not the expression is true. The formula 6=6 returns 1, because 6=6 is true. The formula 6=5 returns 0. Similarly, the formula +A15=C20 returns 1 if the values in cells A15 and C20 are equal, or 0 if the values are unequal. Any formula using =, < >, <, >, <=, >=, #NOT#, #AND#, or #OR# is a Boolean expression and can return 1 or 0 only.

The *test* argument in an @IF formula is a Boolean expression. In the following formula, the argument C30<=400 is the test that @IF performs:

@IF(C30<=400,D18,E18)

1-2-3 evaluates this expression and assigns it the value 1 or 0. If the expression evaluates to 1, the formula returns its second argument. If the expression evaluates to 0, the formula returns its third argument.

1-2-3 always treats the first argument in an @IF formula as a Boolean expression, even if the argument doesn't contain one of the operators mentioned earlier. Any expression that doesn't equal 0 is considered to be true. The following formula checks to see if cell M50 contains a value other than 0:

@IF(M50,400,800)

If the value is other than 0, the formula returns 400. If cell M50 is empty, contains a label or a string-returning formula, or contains a 0 or a formula that currently returns 0, 1-2-3 returns 800.

Users who see a formula like @IF(M50,400,800) for the first time often ask, "If M50 is...what?" The answer is, "If M50 doesn't equal 0." The formula is equivalent to the following expression:

@IF(M50< >0,400,800)

Using Boolean Expressions in Database Criteria Ranges

Boolean expressions are commonly found in criteria ranges for database operations. Suppose that you want to perform an operation to extract from a database all records for which the value in the Age field is less than or equal to 34. Assuming that the first cell containing data in the

Age column is cell B19, enter the formula **+B19<=34** in the first cell of the Age column of the criteria range. The formula returns 1 or 0, but the result of the formula is unimportant. 1-2-3 adjusts the cell reference as it searches through the database looking for values in the Age column that make the formula return 1.

Using Independent Boolean Expressions

Boolean expressions can appear in formulas without @IF. In figure 6.1, the formula in cell B16 adds the food and bar totals and multiplies that sum by the product of 15% and an expression that returns 1 or 0. The last expression returns 1 only if the value in cell B7 is 8 or higher; thus the formula multiplies the food and bar totals by .15 or by 0.

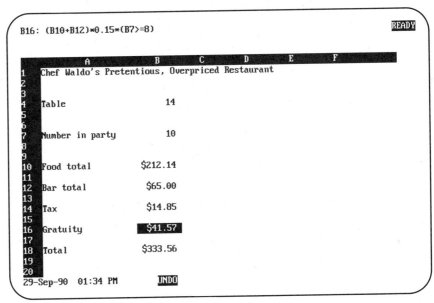

Fig. 6.1. A worksheet using a Boolean expression (in cell B16) to evaluate a condition.

The formula in cell B16 is 21 characters, versus 26 characters in the following @IF formula:

@IF(B7>=8,(B10+B12)*0.15,0)

If the number of characters in a formula seems unimportant in a worksheet like this, consider the worksheet in figure 6.2. This worksheet contains a long list of stock items; Column A shows part numbers, column B inventory numbers, and column C formulas for finding the number of usable parts in stock.

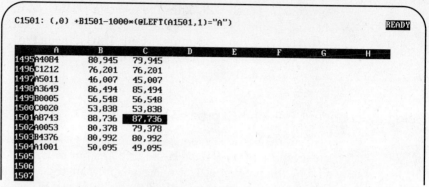

```
C1501: (,0) +B1501-1000*(@LEFT(A1501,1)="A")                           READY

          A           B          C       D        E        F        G        H
1495 A4084         80,945     79,945
1496 C1212         76,201     76,201
1497 A5011         46,007     45,007
1498 A3649         86,494     85,494
1499 B0005         56,548     56,548
1500 C0020         53,838     53,838
1501 A8743         88,736     87,736
1502 A0053         80,378     79,378
1503 B4376         80,992     80,992
1504 A1001         50,095     49,095
1505
1506
1507
```

Fig. 6.2. Formulas (in column C) that are much shorter than equivalent @IF formulas.

This company is required to keep a reserve of 1,000 *A* items for national defense. The column C formulas subtract 1,000 from the column B values if the Boolean expression returns 1 (the label in column A begins with A). This formula uses about 17% fewer characters than the following formula:

@IF(@LEFT(A1501,1)="A",B1501–1000,B1501)

When you can reduce by 17% the number of characters in 1,500 formulas, that reduction is significant. The worksheet uses less of the computer's RAM, recalculates faster, and produces a smaller file when saved.

Creating Boolean Expressions with #AND# and #OR#

Another approach to using Boolean algebra in formulas is to connect values with the operators #AND# or #OR#. Any expression using these operators must return 1 or 0. If you connect two values with #AND#, the expression returns 1 only if both values are nonzero. If you connect two values with #OR#, the expression returns 1 if either of the values is nonzero, or if both are. Values connected with #OR# return 0 only if both values are equal to zero.

Figure 6.3 shows a worksheet used at a company where employees receive overtime for hours worked beyond 40 and a bonus for working both evening and weekend hours in any week. The formula in cell H8 multiplies the total hours worked by the pay rate, multiplies the result by 5%, and multiplies that result by an expression that evaluates to 1 if cells D8 and E8 both contain values other than 0. This formula is more compact than an equivalent @IF formula.

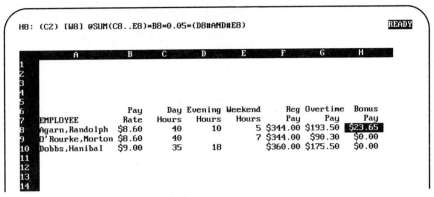

Fig. 6.3. A bonus-pay formula requiring that cells in columns D and E contain nonzero values.

Creating Shorter Formulas with @MIN and @MAX

You may regard @MIN and @MAX as functions for finding the lowest or highest value in a list, but these functions also are useful for setting "ceilings" and "floors." Assume that a mail-order company adds a 5% service charge to orders but never charges more than $5.00 on any order. To compute 5% of the value in a cell named TOTAL but stop at $5.00, you can use either of the following formulas:

@IF(TOTAL*.05>5,5,TOTAL*.05)

@MIN(TOTAL*.05,5)

If using @MIN to set a ceiling seems confusing, remember that you can state the problem as, "The service charge is 5% of TOTAL or $5.00, whichever is less."

Just as @MIN sets ceilings, @MAX sets floors. Suppose that a government agency provides pamphlets, charging 15 cents for each pamphlet to a maximum of $15 for orders over 100. If a cell named NUM contains the number of pamphlets requested, 1-2-3 returns the correct amount with the following formula:

@MAX(15,NUM*0.15)

Simplifying Formulas

The most important part of designing efficient formulas is understanding each formula's function and the mathematical processes required to avoid "overdesigning."

A good example of a problem that invites overdesigning is rounding a dollar value to the nearest fifty cents. Some users create long formulas that test for a remainder when the original value is divided by varying amounts. Some go so far as to create a formula that converts the original value to a character string and evaluates the extreme right character.

Both of these approaches are too complicated. Rounding a dollar value to the nearest half-dollar (or quarter or nickel) is not much harder than rounding to the nearest dollar. Multiply the original value by 2 and round the result to 0 decimal places; $11.47*2 equals $22.94, which rounds to $23.00. Divide the rounded result by 2; $23.00/2 equals $11.50, which is $11.47 rounded to the nearest half-dollar. The following 1-2-3 formula performs the operation as described, assuming that the original amount to be rounded is in cell A1:

@ROUND(A1*2,0)/2

The following formula is a mathematically-equivalent substitute for the preceding formula:

@ROUND(A1/0.5,0)*0.5

Dividing by .5 is mathematically the same as multiplying by 2. This formula bears more resemblance to the original problem, which is stated in terms of half-dollars ($.50). You can apply this technique if you need to round to the nearest quarter or nickel; replace 0.5 with 0.25 for quarters or 0.05 for nickels.

Many mathematical problems can be solved without using a 50-character formula and dozens of functions. If you plan before you type the first function, you can have trim, easy to read, memory-stingy formulas.

Using Noncontiguous Ranges with Statistical Functions

@SUM and the other 1-2-3 statistical functions are typically used with one range, for example, in the expressions @SUM(D10..D30) and @COUNT(J8..M20). These functions, however, can include several different ranges within the parentheses.

The formula in cell B20 of figure 6.4 sums the salaries of the exempt employees in departments 101 and 102. This formula includes ranges B4..B6 and B12..B14, separated by commas, thus replacing the following (longer) formula:

(@SUM(B4..B6)+@SUM(B12..B14))

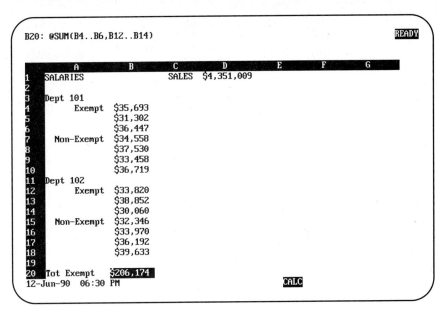

Fig. 6.4. *Two noncontiguous ranges totaled with one @SUM formula.*

You can mix single-cell references or literal arguments with ranges. To add the value in cell C10 to the formula in cell B20, you can add +C10 outside the closing parenthesis, but the following formula achieves the same objective:

@SUM(B4..B6,B12..B14,C10)

You even can mix mathematical operators with ranges, for example, in the following formula:

@SUM(D1*0.15,B4..B6,B12..B14)

This trick works with all statistical functions except @SUMPRODUCT (found in Release 3.x only), which requires two ranges of the same size.

Avoiding Problems with @AVG and @COUNT

When you use the function @AVG, beware of cells in the range or ranges that merely *appear* to be empty. Some 1-2-3 users enter a space to blank a cell. This practice causes problems when you use @AVG, which sums the values in one or more ranges and divides the sum by the number of entries in the range or ranges. If you create a formula to return the average of a range of 10 cells, and one of the cells appears to be empty, you may assume that the formula divides the sum of the values in the other cells by 9. If the "empty" cell contains a space, however, the sum actually is divided by 10.

@COUNT presents a similar problem. Suppose that a range contains more than 100 cells, some of which are empty, and you need an accurate count of the number of entries in the range. Because invisible entries are included in the result, you must make sure that no invisible entries exist in the range before using @COUNT.

Another problem with @AVG and @COUNT is the way that these functions handle ranges consisting of one cell. @COUNT(B7) always returns 1, even if cell B7 is truly empty; @COUNT($B$7..B7) and @COUNT(B$7..B7) return 0 if cell B7 is empty and 1 if cell B7 contains data. To correctly determine whether cell B7 contains an entry, use the following formula, which returns 1 only if cell B7 is not empty:

(@CELL("type",B7..B7)< >"b")

Because this is a Boolean expression, it returns 1 if cell B7's type is not *b* (blank); otherwise it returns 0. Because a cell contains either zero entries or one entry, the formula correctly returns the number of entries in cell B7.

@AVG is the same as an @SUM expression divided by an @COUNT expression referring to the same range. Because @COUNT(B7) always returns 1, @AVG(B7) always returns the value in cell B7 divided by 1. You probably wouldn't use a formula like @AVG(B7), but you may use a formula like the following:

@AVG(A5..A11,B7,C5..C10)

The problem with this formula is that cell B7 always counts as 1 in the denominator. If cell B7 is empty and all of the cells in the other two ranges contain data, you want this formula to divide the sum by 13, but instead 1-2-3 divides by 14. To work around this problem, enter cell B7 in the formula as a range.

To find the average of values in a range, a cell, and another range, use the following formula:

@AVG(A5..A11,B$7..B7,C5..C10)

In Release 3.x, you can use the following format:

@AVG(A5..A11,B7..B7,C5..C10)

 Make only one of the range references absolute. You cannot enter @COUNT(B7..B7) in Release 2.2 or earlier, because 1-2-3 changes the formula to @COUNT(B7). Nor can you enter @COUNT(B$7..B$7); 1-2-3 changes this entry to @COUNT(B$7). Release 3.x, however, accepts the entry @COUNT(B7..B7).

Calculating Cube Roots and *n*th Roots

1-2-3's @SQRT function calculates the square root of a value. No functions exist for cube roots or other roots, but you can compute the *n*th root of a value by raising the value to the reciprocal of *n*.

To compute the cube root of the value in cell M50, use the following formula:

+M50^(1/3)

The parentheses are important because exponentiation takes precedence over division. Without the parentheses, the formula raises the value in cell M50 to the first power and divides the result by 3.

In mathematics, the square root of a negative value is undefined, because no number exists—negative or positive—that can be multiplied by itself to yield a negative number. For this reason, @SQRT(–4) returns ERR. The same is true of any other *n*th root of a negative number where *n* is an even number. A negative number cannot have a square root, a fourth root, a sixth root, and so on. A negative number can, however, have a cube root, a fifth root, a seventh root, and so on, as long as *n* is an odd number, because an odd number of negative values multiplied together returns a negative value. The cube root of –27 is –3, for example, because –3*–3*–3 equals –27.

If you use the formula +M50^(1/4) to find the 4th root of cell M50, you want the formula to return ERR if cell M50's value is negative. You get this result anyway. 1-2-3 returns ERR when it tries to raise a negative number to a power that is not an integer.

If you use the formula +M50^(1/3) to return the cube root of cell M50, however, the formula returns ERR if cell M50 is negative. This is not the result you want, because the cube root of a negative value is a real number. To compute the *n*th root of *x* where *n* is odd, compute the *n*th root of the absolute value of *x* and make the result negative if the original value is negative. To compute the cube root of cell M50, for example, use the following formula:

@ABS(M50)^(1/3)*(M50/@ABS(M50))

Using the @MOD Function

@MOD calculates remainders. Given that 16 divided by 3 is 5 with a remainder of 1, @MOD(16,3) returns 1, but because 15 is evenly divisible by 3, @MOD(15,3) returns 0. The result of @MOD(*x*,*y*) is always greater than or equal to 0 and less than *y*, or less than or equal to 0 and greater than *y* when *x* is negative.

You can use @MOD to determine whether a value is odd or even. @MOD(D20,2) returns 1 if the value in cell D20 is odd and 0 if the value is even. The following formula returns the same information in written form:

@IF(@MOD(D20,2),"Odd","Even")

The result of @MOD(x,y) "cycles" back to 0 when x reaches an exact multiple of y. If you divide the integers 0 to 9 by 3, the remainders are 0, 1, 2, 0, 1, 2, 0, 1, 2, 0. To use vernacular, @MOD tells you where in a cycle a number falls. For this reason, @MOD is useful for some calculations relating to dates and times. You can use @MOD to determine the day of the week of a date value, for example. Remember that 1-2-3 stores dates as serial values starting at 1 for January 1, 1900. The values of dates falling on Saturdays are evenly divisible by 7. The values of dates falling on Sundays, when divided by 7, have a remainder of 1. Date values for Mondays have a remainder of 2, and so forth.

To find the day of the week of the date value in cell G6, use the following formula:

@CHOOSE(@MOD(G6,7),"Saturday","Sunday","Monday",
   "Tuesday","Wednesday","Thursday", "Friday")

This formula doesn't provide the correct day of the week for dates preceding March 1, 1900, because 1-2-3 erroneously treats February 29, 1900 as a valid date.

Exercising Caution with @MOD

With most versions of 1-2-3, @MOD doesn't work correctly if its second argument is smaller than 0.5. The expression @MOD(4,0.05), for example, which should tell you how many pennies are left over if you divide $4.00 into nickels, should return 0. Instead it returns an infinitesimal negative value, −2.2 to the negative 17th power (in Release 2.2). This figure usually is close enough to zero for most applications, but a formula or a macro relying on a 0 result doesn't work. A macro containing the following instruction, for example, doesn't work as expected because 1-2-3 never executes the BRANCH instruction:

```
{IF @MOD(A5,0.05)=0}{BRANCH NEXTRTN}
```

Instead, use the following instruction:

```
{IF @ROUND(@MOD(A5,0.05),2)=0}{BRANCH NEXTRTN}
```

A different @MOD problem occurs with Release 3.x. When the y argument is smaller than .5, @MOD typically returns the value of y itself.

@MOD(4,0.05), for example, returns 0.05. Avoid using @MOD with small
y values with Release 3.x; instead, use a formula like the following:

@ROUND((A5/0.05–@INT(A5/0.05))*0.05,2)

Using @LOG To Compute the Magnitude of Numbers

@LOG returns logarithms and answers the question, "To what power
must 10 be raised to become equal to *x*?" @LOG(100), for example, returns 2, because 10 to the power of 2 equals 100. The integer portion of
@LOG's result, plus 1, is the number of digits in the integer portion of *x*.
Any number "in the hundreds" has a logarithm whose integer portion
is 2; for example, @LOG(413) returns 2.61595.

You can use @LOG to create macros and formulas that accommodate a
number's digits. The following macro command makes a column just
wide enough to accommodate the integer number in the current cell:

/wcs1~/wcs{RIGHT @LOG(@CELLPOINTER("contents"))+1}~

This macro works reliably only if the cell pointer is in a cell containing a
value with **F**ixed **0** format.

Avoiding Repetition in @IF Formulas

One reason that users create long formulas in 1-2-3 is that such formulas
follow human thought processes. You may see the solution to a problem
in the following terms, for example:

If condition A is true, add X, Y, and Z together and multiply by 10.

If condition A is not true, add X, Y, and Z together.

The following formula is an example of the stated solution:

@IF(A15<10000,(D3+F8+F11)*10,D3+F8+F11)

The problem with the preceding formula is that it repeats the expression
D3+F8+F11. Following is a more compact version:

@IF(A15<10000,10,1)*(D3+F8+F11)

This formula doesn't flow in a natural way if you read it aloud, but you
can see that the shorter version produces the same result as the longer
version. With practice and planning, you can devise formulas like this for
large worksheet applications, removing excess characters from formulas,
saving memory, and making your programming more efficient.

Creating Nested @IF Formulas

The @IF function evaluates an expression and chooses between two other expressions depending on whether the first expression is true (non-zero) or false (zero). Somewhat less intuitive is the technique of making the *true* or *false* expression (or both) process another IF test. This technique is called *nesting* @IF expressions.

The following formula evaluates whether the value in cell A5 is greater than 15:

@IF(A5>15,@IF(@MOD(A5,2)=0,"Go","Quit"),"Too Low")

If the value is greater than 15, the formula performs a second test, determining whether the value is an even number. If both conditions are met, the formula returns the string Go. If the value in cell A5 is greater than 15 but odd, the formula returns Quit. If the first test fails (the value in cell A5 is not greater than 15), the formula skips the second test and returns the string Too Low.

The expression @IF(@MOD(A5,2)=0,"Go","Quit") is the true result for the formula's original test (A5>15).

This expression is called a *nested-if test*. The string Too Low is the false result for the formula's original test. Keep in mind that Too Low can be replaced by another @IF function with two possible results, either or both of those can be @IF function(s), and so on. One cell can contain a complex decision tree.

Using Special Functions To Control the Flow of Macros

Special functions like @CELL and @INFO are not as useful as other functions (@SUM or @PMT, for example) for creating formulas that appear on-screen or are printed. These functions are more useful in macros. Use the IF macro command with an expression based on a formula so that a macro executes tasks only if conditions are met.

Using @CELL To Test for Cell Entries

Suppose that you create a worksheet where the user enters several values and uses a macro to produce a table or schedule based on those values. An example of this type of worksheet appears in figure 6.5. You may want the macro to return an error message if the user leaves cell B12 blank. Assuming that the name FREQ is assigned to cell B12, you can use the following instruction:

{IF @CELL("type",FREQ)="b"}{BRANCH ERRMSG}

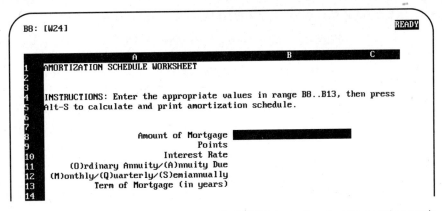

Fig. 6.5. *A worksheet that uses a macro with @CELL to confirm that the user has made an entry in cell B12.*

Using @CELLPOINTER To Store the Current Cell Address

Suppose that you want a macro to "remember" the location of the cell pointer and move the cell pointer back to that location later. Use @CELLPOINTER with the "address" or "coord" attribute. Assign a name, for example STARTADDR, to a cell that the macro can use to store the current cell pointer location. The cell immediately below STARTADDR must be empty. Use the following command to store the address:

```
{LET STARTADDR,@CELLPOINTER("address")}
```

In Release 3.x, replace "address" with "coord". After executing this instruction, the macro can move the cell pointer to other parts of the worksheet. To cause the macro to reposition the cell pointer at the starting address, use the following command:

```
{GOTO}{STARTADDR}~
```

Be sure to encase STARTADDR in braces so that the macro treats its characters as a subroutine. Without the braces, the macro merely moves the cell pointer to the cell named STARTADDR.

Using Variations on Lookup Functions

@VLOOKUP and @HLOOKUP are powerful, convenient functions that return a value from the row or column in a lookup table that is most closely associated with a lookup value. These functions are based on some specific assumptions and are not compatible with all applications, but you can make some adjustments to your models to alter the way these functions work.

Using Lookup Functions in Incremental Applications

Suppose that a company's commission structure dictates that orders less than or equal to $1,000 merit a 4.2% commission, orders greater than $1,000 up to and including $5,000 merit an 8% commission, and so on. A structure like this is not consistent with the way the lookup functions normally operate.

If you adjust the values in the lookup column or row, making them slightly higher than the cutoff points, the lookup function returns values in a way that matches the scheme just described. Figure 6.6 shows an example of such a lookup table. Because each value in range A8..A12 increases the whole dollar amount by one tenth of a cent, the @VLOOKUP formula in cell B17 functions in its normal way but returns 8.0% for an order size of $5,000.

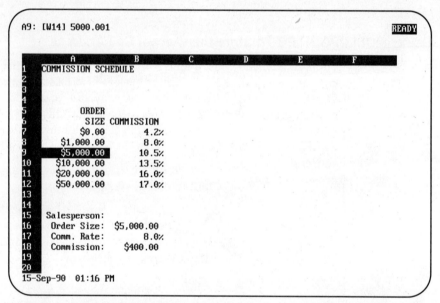

Fig. 6.6. *A lookup table that adds very small amounts to the lookup values, changing the results of an @VLOOKUP formula.*

Using Lookup Functions with Character Strings

If you use @VLOOKUP or @HLOOKUP to find character strings, 1-2-3 looks for an exact match (including capitalization) for the lookup string. If the extreme left column of the range SALARIES contains the label Grant, the following formula returns ERR because the function doesn't find an exact match for GRANT:

@VLOOKUP("GRANT",SALARIES,3)

You can devise a lookup that is not case-sensitive. The key is the fact that, for the most part, 1-2-3 considers character strings equal without regard to case. The logical expression (A1=B1) returns 1 if labels in cells A1 and B1 are identical in every way except the case of letters. If cells A1 and B1 contain the labels Grant and GRANT, (A1=B1) evaluates to 1.

With this principle in mind, you can create a slightly different kind of lookup table, as shown in figure 6.7. The cells in range A4..A10 contain formulas, no more than one of which returns 1. Each formula compares the label at its right to the label in cell D14. Cell A4, for example, contains the formula +B4=$D$14. Cell A11 contains 1 (not a formula). The @VLOOKUP formula in cell D17 looks up the number 1 in column A and returns the salary from its row. Remember that because cell B7 returns 1 whether the label in cell D14 is GRANT, Grant, or grant, the formula works no matter how the name in cell D14 is capitalized. If cell D14 is blank or contains a label not found in column B, all of the formulas in range A4..A10 return 0, so the @VLOOKUP formula finds 1 in cell A11 and returns NA.

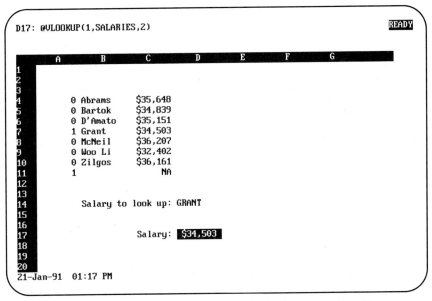

Fig. 6.7. A lookup table for an @VLOOKUP formula that is not case-sensitive.

Using @DATEVALUE To Speed Up Date Entry

With Release 2.2 or earlier, if you try to enter the date April 3, 1991 by typing **4/3/91**, 1-2-3 treats the entry as a division operation. Because Release 3.x converts entries resembling legal dates to date values, the entry **4/3/91** is instantly converted to 33331.

This date entry feature creates some leeway for human inconsistency. You can use or omit leading zeros (entering **3** or **03** for March), leave out the year (if entering a current-year date), or enter dates in Lotus standard date formats (for example, **19–Jan–91**).

If you create macros that prompt the user to enter data, you can get Release 2.x to accept dates with the same level of flexibility. The trick is to use @DATEVALUE to convert labels to date values. The macro routine shown in figure 6.8 provides an example. The macro prompts the user for a date, which can be entered in almost any familiar date format. If the entry cannot be converted to a date, the macro branches to an error routine that alerts the user to the problem and requests another entry.

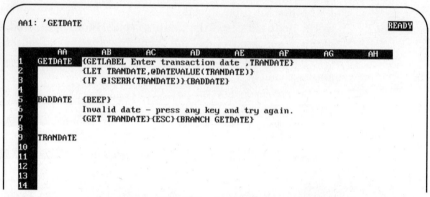

Fig. 6.8. A macro routine that prompts the user for a date and accepts dates in a variety of formats.

Summary

In this chapter, you have gained some understanding of the principles underlying 1-2-3's processing of mathematical formulas. You can use this knowledge to create more efficient formulas in your worksheet applications, using fewer keystrokes. You also have learned some function techniques, ways to put functions to good use, and methods for converting function limitations to advantages.

The next chapter discusses methods for designing, using, and printing graphs in your 1-2-3 worksheets.

Chapter Seven

CREATING AND PRINTING GRAPHS

C onverting streams of numbers to graphs makes the trends or relationships in those numbers instantly clear. The process of producing graphs from labels and numbers in your 1-2-3 worksheet is easy and quick.

Dedicated graphics programs such as Lotus Freelance Plus, Harvard Graphics, or Ashton-Tate's Applause II produce better graphs than 1-2-3 because the graphics programs are designed specifically to create attractive graphs. But all versions of 1-2-3 produce graphs that are acceptable for a variety of uses.

This chapter discusses the following considerations for creating graphs:

- How graphs can be useful
- When to use the different types of graphs
- How to create graphs quickly
- How to mix values of different magnitudes in the same graph
- How to work with named graphs
- Different ways to print graphs

Understanding Graphs

Even if you never print graphs, or if you prefer a dedicated graphics product, learning about 1-2-3's graphics capabilities is worth your time because the software can create *ad hoc* graphs very quickly.

Suppose that you create a worksheet with sales figures from a six-month period for a chain of electronics stores (see fig. 7.1 for an example). You can compare the figures for audio sales at the four locations by looking at range B8..E8, but you get a clearer understanding of the relationships between sales at each location by creating a graph. Graphing this data takes very few keystrokes. Select **/Graph Type Bar X** and specify range

B7..G7, select **A** and specify range **B8..G8**, and select **View** to create and display the graph shown in figure 7.2. This simple graph (created in about 15 seconds) tells you visually about the audio sales figures. The Little Rock location has the highest sales and Kitty Hawk has the lowest, but the spread between highest and lowest isn't very wide.

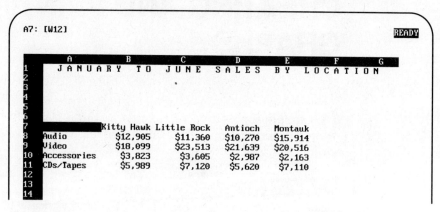

Fig. 7.1. *Raw numbers in a worksheet; discerning relationships between values is difficult.*

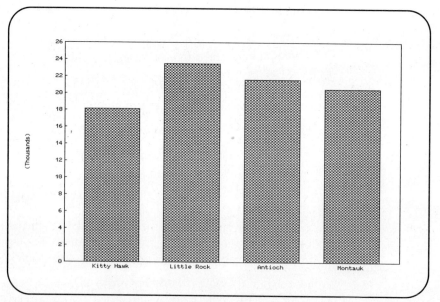

Fig. 7.2. *A graph created from the sales amounts in figure 7.1.*

You can see the difference between Kitty Hawk's and Little Rock's sales by looking at the raw numbers in figure 7.1, but the impact is not the same.

Suppose that you want to see what percentage each product line at the Kitty Hawk store contributes to total sales for that location. One way to accomplish this objective is to create formulas that compute the percentages. Enter the formula **+C8/@SUM(C$8..C$11)** in cell F8 and assign a Percent format to that cell. The result of the formula shows that audio sales made up 31.62% of Kitty Hawk's sales. Copy cell F8 to range F9..F11 to find the percentages for the other product lines.

A pie graph like the one shown in figure 7.3 makes the same information easier to appreciate. Creating the graph is actually easier than setting up the block of formulas to calculate percentages. Select **/Graph Reset Graph Type Pie**, select **X** and specify range **A8..A11**, select **A** and specify range **C8..C11**, and select View. By creating the pie graph, you can see quite clearly that video sales constituted just over half of the sales at the Kitty Hawk location.

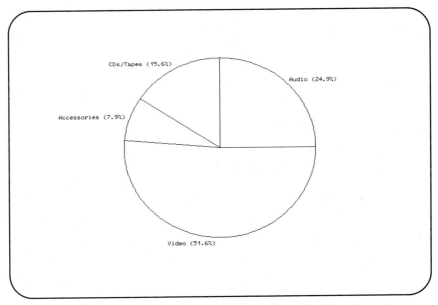

CDs/Tapes (15.6%)

Audio (24.9%)

Accessories (7.9%)

Video (51.6%)

Fig. 7.3. A pie graph showing the breakdown of sales by product line at one store.

Understanding Graph Types

The line, bar, pie, stack-bar, and XY graph types are available in all versions of 1-2-3. The following list describes the general use of each type of graph.

- Line graphs show how data changes over time.
- Bar graphs compare discrete groups of data.

- **P**ie graphs show individual subsets of data as proportions of a whole set of data.

- **S**tack-Bar graphs show comparisons among two or more data ranges plus the contributions of data subsets within each data range.

- **XY** graphs (also called scatter diagrams) show relationships between one variable value and one or more other values.

Examples of bar and pie graphs appeared earlier in this chapter. In figure 7.4, a line graph shows the increase in camcorder sales during eight six-month periods.

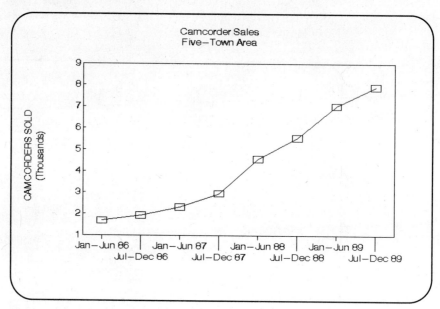

Fig. 7.4. *A line graph showing sales growth.*

Figure 7.5 (a stacked-bar graph) shows that Delmont residents bought more camcorders than the other towns but with a smaller percentage of VHS–C format than most of the other towns.

In figure 7.6 (an XY graph), each square represents a pair of numbers pertaining to a town: the town's median income and camcorders purchased per 1,000 people. The horizontal position of each square represents the median income and the vertical position represents camcorder purchases. The fact that the squares are clustered around a diagonal line seems to indicate a correlation between median income and camcorder purchases.

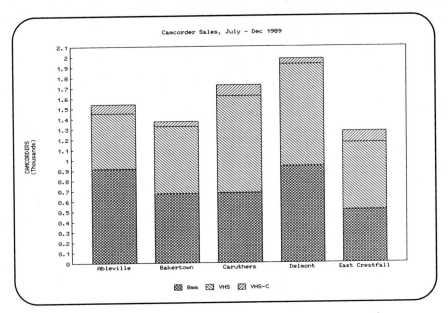

Fig. 7.5. *A stacked-bar graph comparing totals and subtotals at the same time.*

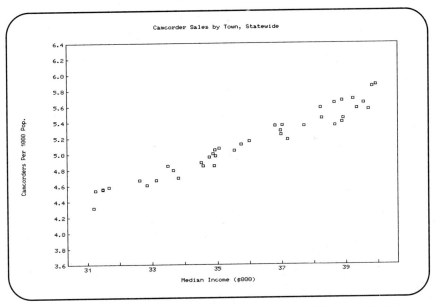

Fig. 7.6. *An XY graph showing the correlation between two variables: median income and camcorders purchased.*

Using Release 2.3 and 3.x Graph Types

Releases 2.3, 3, and 3.1 offer two additional graph types: mixed and HLCO (High-Low-Close-Open). Mixed graphs combine line and bar graphs. HLCO graphs record the prices of a stock or other financial instrument.

Figure 7.7 shows a mixed graph. This style of graph is used here to show how a set of specific values (sales of widgets for a particular area) compares to a background trend (sales of widgets nationwide).

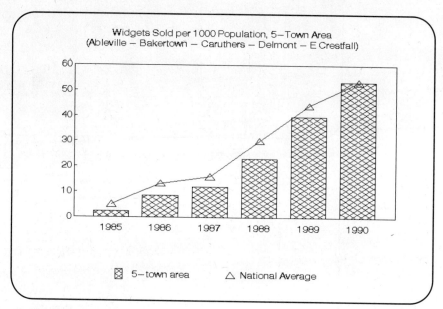

Fig. 7.7. *A mixed graph.*

In a mixed graph, ranges A, B, and C are always plotted as bars and D, E, and F are always plotted as lines. To create a graph with one set of bars and one line, as in figure 7.7, use the first set of data as the A range and the second set as the D range.

Figure 7.8 shows an HLCO (High-Low-Close-Open) graph. The high and low ends of the vertical lines show the high and low prices for each day. The short horizontal lines extending to the left indicate opening prices and the lines extending to the right mark closing prices.

Only seven graph types appear in the /Graph Type menu, but the variations made possible by the /Graph Type Advanced menu and (with Release 3.x) the /Graph Options Format menu increase the "types" of graphs to more than 30. You can arrange bar graphs in horizontal or vertical format, for example. With Release 2.3, you can give bar, stacked-bar, and mixed graphs a three-dimensional effect. With Release 3.x, you can convert line graphs to area graphs. You also can change stacked-bar graphs to 100% stacked-bar graphs (all bars the same height and the relative sizes of the sections indicating portions of the whole).

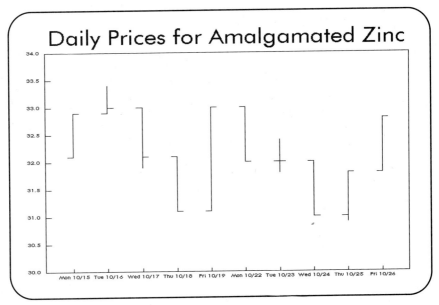

Fig. 7.8. An HLCO graph tracking the fluctuations of stock prices.

Using the Graph Key (F10)

With Release 2.2 and earlier, you can display a graph only by selecting View from the main graph menu or by returning to READY mode and pressing the Graph key (F10). To experiment with different X-scale settings, for example, you must select **Q**uit **Q**uit View to see how the graph looks, and then select **O**ptions **S**cale **X**-Scale to try a different setting.

With Releases 2.3 and 3.x, you can use the Graph key (F10) while any part of the /Graph menu is active. To experiment with different text sizes for graph legends in Release 3.x, for example, you can skip selecting **Q**uit **Q**uit **Q**uit **Q**uit View. Instead, press the Graph key (F10) after changing the text size for the legends with **O**ptions **A**dvanced **T**ext **S**econd **S**ize.

Creating Graphs Quickly with /Graph Group

Releases 2.2 through 3.1 enable you to set a graph's **X** range and several data ranges simultaneously using /Graph Group. Suppose that you want to use the labels in column A of figure 7.9 as the **X** range and the values in columns B, C, and D as the **A**, **B**, and **C** ranges, respectively. Earlier versions of 1-2-3 required that you set each range separately, but with /Graph Group you specify the entire range (in this case, specify **A5..D9**) and select Columnwise.

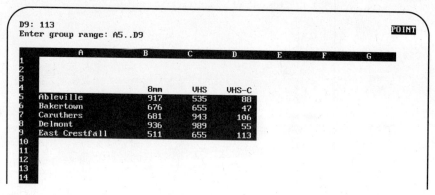

Fig. 7.9. Assigning ranges with /Graph Group.

1-2-3 makes the extreme left column in the specified range the **X** range, the next column the **A** range, and so on. (If you select **R**owwise after specifying the range, the top row becomes the **X** range, the second row becomes the **A** range, and so on.)

If you specify a range more than seven columns wide and select Columnwise, or a range more than seven rows high and select **R**owwise, 1-2-3 ignores data beyond the seventh column or row.

*Remember to clear all ranges (**X** and **A** through **F**) between graphs with /Graph **R**eset.*

Using Automatic Graphing with Release 3.x

The fastest way to set up several graph ranges simultaneously is by using the automatic graph feature with Releases 3 and 3.1. To use this feature, arrange the data you want to graph in adjacent columns. Each column must have the same number of entries (the highlighted range in figure 7.9 is a good example). If you want the extreme left column to become the **X** range, make sure that it contains labels or date-formatted values; otherwise it becomes the **A** range. All other data—except labels above or to the left of the graph range—must be separated from the graph range by at least two rows and two columns. Position the cell pointer anywhere within the graph range and press the Graph key (F10). 1-2-3 displays a graph based on the entries in the graph range.

By default, 1-2-3 assigns graph ranges in a columnwise manner when you use the automatic graph feature. For rowwise orientation, select /Worksheet Global Graph Rowwise. To make the change permanent, select Update. To return to the worksheet, select Quit.

Graphing Numbers of Different Magnitudes

You may need to graph two sets of data where the numbers in one set are hundreds or thousands of times greater than the numbers in the other set. Suppose that you want to create a bar graph showing the selling prices and square footage of some houses that were sold recently. Assuming that the houses generally sold for $100,000 or more and consisted of a few thousand square feet, you cannot use the selling price as a graph's A range and the square footage as the B range, or you get a meaningless graph like the one shown in figure 7.10.

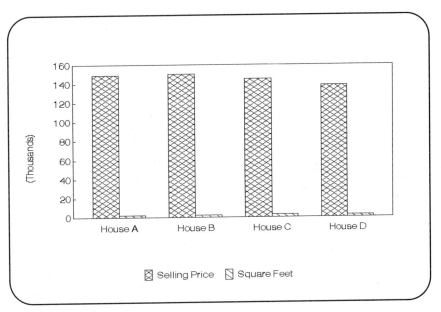

Fig. 7.10. A bar graph that attempts to show two widely different sets of values.

Release 3.x provides a way to graph data of different magnitudes directly, creating a meaningful graph. With Release 2.x, you can create formulas that scale down one set of data so that it matches the other in magnitude, and then use the set of smaller numbers and the scaled-down values to produce an understandable graph.

Using Two Y-Axes with Release 3.x

With Releases 3 and 3.1, you can use bars or lines representing two very different sets of values in the same graph, with two sets of scales (one on each side of the graph).

Figure 7.11 shows a graph with two scales of magnitude. The left bar in each set of two vertical bars represents the number of widgets produced at a specific plant. These bars are scaled against the left y-axis. The right bar in each set represents the number of widgets produced per worker as a measure of efficiency. These bars are scaled against the right y-axis. This graph shows that Midtown produced the fewest total widgets but more widgets per worker than the other two plants.

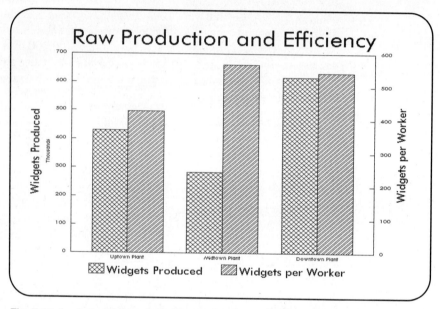

Fig. 7.11. A graph with two y-axes comparing two very different sets of values.

The graph in figure 7.11 is created from the data in figure 7.12. To create the graph, select /Graph Type Bar X and specify range A6..A8, select A and specify range B6..B8, select B and specify range D6..D8, and select Type Features 2Y-Ranges B Quit Quit. When the /Graph menu reappears, select Options Titles First and enter \A3, select Titles Y-Axis and enter \B5, and then select Titles 2Y-Axis and enter \D5. Select Legend A and enter \B5, select Legend B and enter \D5, and select Quit View to see the graph on-screen. Using this cell reference method for selecting graph titles and legends makes the graph easier to update—when the cells with titles change, the graph is updated automatically.

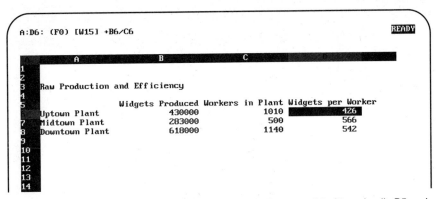

```
A:D6: (F0) [W15] +B6/C6                                          READY

           A              B                C
1
2
3  Raw Production and Efficiency
4
5                Widgets Produced Workers in Plant Widgets per Worker
   Uptown Plant           430000           1010            426
7  Midtown Plant          283000            500            566
8  Downtown Plant         618000           1140            542
9
10
11
12
13
14
```

Fig. 7.12. Numbers (in columns B and D) and labels (in range A6..A8 and cells B5 and D5) used to create the graph in figure 7.11.

Using Formulas To Compare Data with Releases 2.01, 2.2, and 2.3

Release 2.3 and earlier versions don't have the double y-axis capability, but you still can create useful graphs with data sets of different magnitudes. This method uses formulas to make the scale of the two sets of values comparable and legends to make clear the meaning of the bars or lines in the graph. Figure 7.13 shows the widgets graph created with Release 2.2.

The procedure is the same for Releases 2.01 and 2.3 but the appearance of the graph is different.

The graph in figure 7.13 is created from the data in figure 7.14. Note that the formulas in range B16..B18 divide the values in range B6..B8 by 1000, producing results in hundreds to match the widgets-per-worker values in range D6..D8. To create the graph in figure 7.13 from this worksheet, select /Graph Type Bar X and specify range A6..A8, select A and specify range B16..B18, and select B and specify range D6..D8. Select Options Titles First and enter \A3, select Legend A and enter \B15, select Legend B and enter \D5, and select Quit View to see the graph.

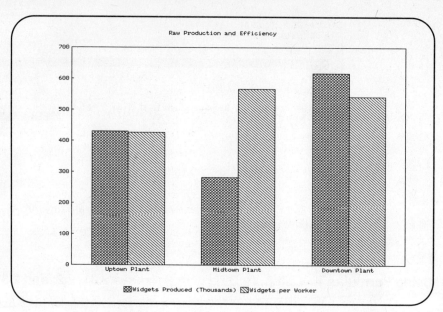

Fig. 7.13. *A Release 2.2 graph that uses a legend and formulas to show data sets with different orders of magnitude.*

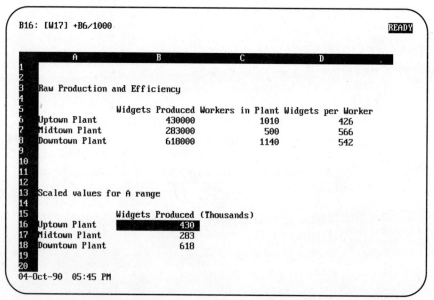

Fig. 7.14. *Formulas (in range B16..B18) that convert the numbers in range B6..B8 to match the values in range D6..D8.*

Using Composed Characters in Graphs

1-2-3 uses a character set that includes many more characters than appear on the keyboard. You add these characters to your graphs using the Compose key (Alt–F1) and a two-character keystroke sequence. To create a Japanese yen symbol (¥), for example, press Compose (Alt–F1) and type **y=** (the **y** can be upper- or lowercase).

You may feel that some composed characters are not very useful with Release 2.2 and earlier. 1-2-3 cannot display some of these characters on-screen (for example, the trademark symbol and copyright symbol) and some text printers cannot print them. These characters appear correctly in the titles and other text that you add to graphs, however, and print properly when you use PrintGraph. The composed characters can add polish to your graphs; in figure 7.15, for example, the superscripted 3 (^{3}) and trademark symbol (™) provide special information. To create the title for this graph, select **/Graph Options Titles First** and type the text shown, using the sequences Alt–F1 **^3** and Alt–F1 **TM** to create the symbols.

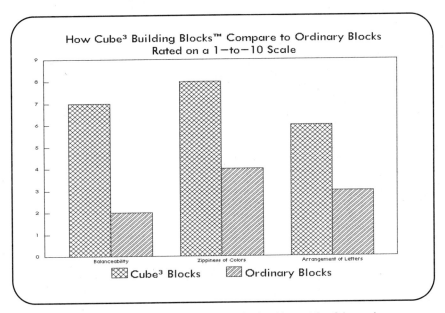

Fig. 7.15. *A graph using composed characters in the title and the **A** legend.*

Naming Graphs

A worksheet can contain several named graph settings, each of which stores the graph options selected to create that graph. The specifications and name for each graph are stored in RAM until you save the host worksheet file, at which time this information is saved as part of the file. Graph names are not stored as separate disk files. The procedure for saving graph files is discussed later in this chapter.

Using Named Graphs

When you finish setting up a graph, assign a name to it by selecting /Graph Name Create and entering a name. Repeat this procedure for each graph as you complete it. You can use the same or similar settings for the next graph in the same worksheet, or select /Graph Reset Graph Quit to restore the default settings.

To make a named set of graph settings the *current graph*, select /Graph Name Use and enter the desired graph name. The graph appears on-screen and remains in place until you press a key. To make another graph current, select /Graph Name Use and enter a different name.

To change the settings of an existing named graph, select /Graph Name Use and change the graph as necessary. Then select Name Create and enter the same graph name (or select the name by highlighting it in the control panel).

Displaying Named Graphs with Macros

A macro can use /Graph Name Use to make a graph current. With all 1-2-3 versions, use the characters /gnu*graphname*~ in the macro. This command duplicates the keystroke process; the graph stays on-screen— and operation of the macro is suspended—until you press a key.

With Releases 2.2 and later, you also can use the GRAPHON command to make a graph current. The string {GRAPHON *graphname*} makes the specified graph current and displays it until the macro ends or processes another GRAPHON command or the GRAPHOFF command, or until the macro "needs" the text screen (for example, to display a prompt and get a response with the GETLABEL command).

The GRAPHON command, if used without arguments, just displays the current graph; {GRAPHON *graphname*} makes a graph current and displays it; and {GRAPHON *graphname*,nodisplay} makes a named graph current without displaying it.

After displaying a graph with the GRAPHON command, a macro can continue to operate *behind* the graph, updating cells or ranges in the worksheet, processing loops or delays, and performing {IF} tests.

You can use the GRAPHON command to create automated *slide shows* in 1-2-3. After each GRAPHON command, use the WAIT command for timed shows or the GET command for user-controlled shows. The following macro, for example, displays a series of graphs on-screen for 10 seconds each:

```
{GRAPHON GRAPH1}
{WAIT @NOW+@TIME(0,0,10)}
{GRAPHON GRAPH2}
{WAIT @NOW+@TIME(0,0,10)}
{GRAPHON GRAPH3}
{WAIT @NOW+@TIME(0,0,10)}
```

The following macro places each graph on-screen and waits for you to press a key:

```
{GRAPHON GRAPH1}
{GET KPRESS}
{GRAPHON GRAPH2}
{GET KPRESS}
{GRAPHON GRAPH3}
{GET KPRESS}
```

Releases 2 and 2.01 don't include the GRAPHON command, but you still can create user-controlled slide shows using the /Graph Name Use command. (You cannot create timed shows in these versions.) The following macro displays a series of graphs and waits for a keypress:

```
/gnuGRAPH1~
nuGRAPH2~
nuGRAPH3~
q
```

Saving Graphs

To print graphs created with Release 2.01 or earlier versions, use the separate PrintGraph program included with your 1-2-3 software package. To print graphs with Release 2.2, you can use the PrintGraph program or the Allways add-in. Both programs require that you save the graph as a PIC file. With Release 2.3, you can use PrintGraph or the Wysiwyg add-in. Wysiwyg doesn't require a PIC file.

To create a PIC file for use with PrintGraph or Allways (and many dedicated graphics programs), use the /Graph menu to set up your graph, select Save, and enter a name for the file.

/Graph Save saves only a binary representation of the lines, shapes, and text in the graph; you cannot modify graphs saved with this command. Save the host worksheet with /File Save after saving the graph for

printing. The worksheet contains the numbers and settings that actually control the graphs.

Releases 3 and 3.1 can print graphs directly from the /**P**rint menu without using PrintGraph; however, you can save graphs as PIC files or CGM (Computer Graphics Metafile) files for use with other graphics programs. The default format for saved graphs is PIC. To save graphs as CGM files, select /**W**orksheet Global **D**efault Graph **M**etafile. To make this change permanent, select **U**pdate. Select **Q**uit to return to the worksheet.

Enhancing Graphs with Wysiwyg

The Wysiwyg **:G**raph **E**dit feature in Releases 2.3 and 3.1 can enhance graphs with interesting visual elements. **:G**raph **E**dit accesses a set of commands similar to those in Lotus' Freelance Plus; you can add lines, arrows, boxes, ellipses, polygons, or additional text, and edit, move, resize, color, or rotate the objects.

The graph ranges are added to the worksheet with the **:G**raph **A**dd commands. A graph range can display the current graph or a named graph in the current worksheet; it also can display a graph created "from scratch" or an image stored on disk as a PIC or CGM file.

Wysiwyg enables you to enhance the contents of an image file or the components of a graph created with 1-2-3's /**G**raph commands. You can enlarge or reduce all of the text in the graph (by entering a font-magnification factor) and change the individual colors in the graph. You also can resize the entire graph.

Wysiwyg can produce a wide variety of colors on a color monitor or color printer. Many of these colors are produced by a process called *dithering*—mixing together pixels of different colors (for example, mixing red and yellow to make orange). These colors appear as shades of grey when printed on a black-and-white printer. You can print bar graphs without using 1-2-3's hatching patterns by assigning colors to the various graph ranges that print as noticeably different greys.

Figure 7.16 shows some of the ways you can dress up a "plain vanilla" graph using Wysiwyg. To create this sample worksheet, begin by creating the graph. Type all of the entries shown in columns A through C. Select /**G**raph **G**roup, specify range A5..C10, and select **C**olumnwise; then select **T**ype **B**ar. Select **O**ptions **T**itles **F**irst, enter **A1**, select **T**itles **Y**-Axis, and enter **Units Sold**. Finally, select **C**olor **Q**uit **Q**uit.

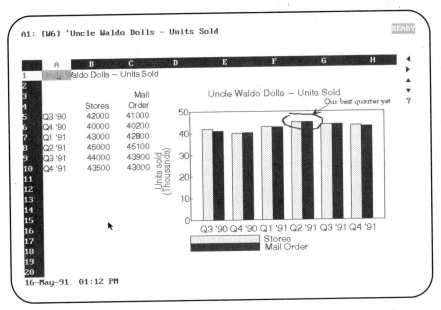

Fig. 7.16. A "plain vanilla" 1-2-3 graph added to a worksheet and enhanced with Wysiwyg's **:G**raph **E**dit commands.

To add the graph to the worksheet, select **:G**raph **A**dd **C**urrent and specify range **D3..H18**. Select **:G**raph **E**dit, move the cell pointer to a cell within range D3..H18, and press Enter. The graphics editing window appears, as shown in figure 7.17.

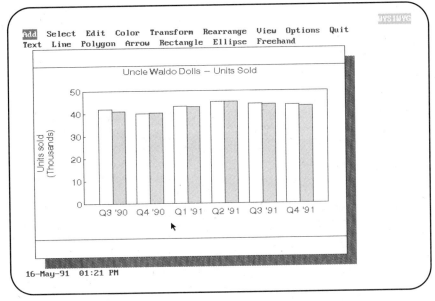

Fig. 7.17. Wysiwyg's graphics editing window.

To use the graphics editing window menu, press the first character of the menu item you want to select, or highlight your choice and press Enter. You also can move the mouse pointer into the menu area and click on your choices.

To change the colors of the two sets of bars in the graph, select **Color Map 2** and specify the desired color (for this example, color 48). To specify the color, enter the color number, use the arrow keys to highlight the square and press Enter, or click on the square with the mouse. Then select **3**, specify color number **1**, and select **Quit**.

Now add the line around the tops of the tallest bars. If you have a mouse, select **Add Freehand** from the menu, move the mouse pointer to the place where you want to start drawing, hold down the left mouse button, and drag the pencil symbol along the path of the line you want to draw. When you finish drawing, release the mouse button.

If you don't have a mouse, freehand drawing with the arrow keys is difficult. You can use Wysiwyg, however, to draw an ellipse around the tops of the tallest bars. Select **Add Ellipse** and move the pointer to the upper left corner of the area that will contain the ellipse. Press the space bar to anchor the range. A rectangle, called the *bounding box*, appears; use the arrow keys to stretch the box to encompass the area where you want the ellipse to appear. When you press Enter, the ellipse appears. The freehand line or ellipse has some dark squares superimposed on it, indicating that the line is a selected object. To change the thickness of the line, select **Edit Width 2**:Narrow.

To create the arrow pointing to the freehand line or ellipse, select **Add Arrow**. Move the pointer to the area where you want the tail of the arrow to appear. Hold down the left mouse button to drag the pointer and create a line, or press the space bar and use the arrow keys to move the pointer to where you want the arrow head. Complete the process by double-clicking the left mouse button or pressing Enter.

To add the text at the top of the graph, select **Add Text**, type **Our best quarter yet**, and press Enter. When the text appears, move it with the mouse or the arrow keys to the position shown in figure 7.16. Then click the left mouse button or press Enter. Select **Edit Font** and specify one of the smaller fonts (for example, Times 10-point).

To create more attractive legends than those created with the 1-2-3 /Graph commands, select **Add Rectangle** and move the pointer to just below the lower left corner of the graph. Hold down the left mouse button or press the space bar and stretch the bounding box to create a rectangle; then release the mouse button or press Enter. Select **Color Inside** and specify color **48**. To copy the rectangle, select **Rearrange Copy**.

A new rectangle appears, superimposed on the existing one (slightly lower and to the right). The new rectangle (not the one you copied) is the selected object.

Change the fill color of the new rectangle by selecting **Color Inside** and specifying color **1**. To move the new rectangle, move the pointer to it and drag it with the mouse, or select **Rearrange Move** and use the arrow keys to reposition the new rectangle. To add the legend text, select **Add Text**, enter **Stores**, position the text box to the right of the upper rectangle, and double-click or press Enter. Select **Add Text** again, enter **Mail Order**, and position this text box next to the lower rectangle.

Finally, enlarge the text in the graph by selecting **Options Font Magnification** and entering **125**. To return to the worksheet, select **Quit**.

Printing Graphs

After creating a graph, you usually want a hard copy of it. The Allways and Wysiwyg add-ins and the printing capability of Release 3.x provide more flexible printing options than those of PrintGraph, but the various methods have both advantages and disadvantages. The remainder of this chapter discusses the available options for getting printouts of your graphs.

Printing Graphs with Allways (Release 2.2)

The Allways add-in—included with Release 2.2 and available separately for Releases 2 and 2.01—prints graphs directly without using Print-Graph. You can print a graph that fills a page or include a smaller graph on the same page with worksheet data.

 PrintGraph prints graphs with a pleasing width-to-height ratio. If you use Allways, your graphs may need some work to produce appropriate width-to-height appearance.

To use Allways, save your graphs as PIC files with **/Graph Save**. Then change the current directory to the directory containing the PIC files. Invoke Allways and move the cell pointer to the upper left corner of the area that will contain the graph. Select **/Graph Add** and specify the desired PIC file, highlight the range that will contain the graph, and press Enter. Figure 7.18 shows a graph added to a worksheet with Allways.

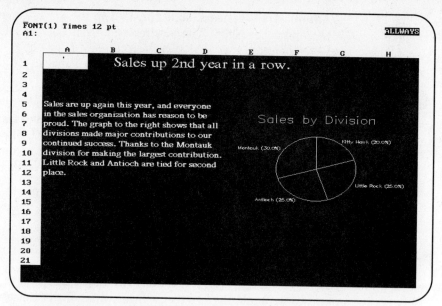

Fig. 7.18. *An Allways screen showing a graph (stored as a PIC file) added to a worksheet.*

To print a graph, select /**P**rint **R**ange **S**et and define a range that includes only the graph. To print a graph with worksheet data, assign a range that includes the graph and the data; then select **A**lign **G**o **P**age **Q**uit to print the selected range and return to the worksheet.

If you are unhappy with the size or shape of the printed graph, select /**G**raph **S**ettings **R**ange and adjust the size of the range containing the graph. For fine adjustments, change the width of one of the columns (Allways can set column widths in fractions of characters) or the height of one of the rows.

Printing Graphs with the /Print Menu (Release 3.x)

Releases 3 and 3.1 can print graphs directly from the worksheet, without any add-ins. You can print the current graph or a named graph in any open worksheet file.

To print a graph from the worksheet, select /**P**rint **P**rinter **I**mage and select **C**urrent or **N**amed-Graph. If you select **N**amed-Graph, highlight the graph name and press Enter; or highlight the name of an open file and press Enter, and then highlight the graph name and press Enter. Select **O**ptions **A**dvanced **I**mage **D**ensity. Specify **D**raft for a fast print or **F**inal for a more polished graph. Select **I**mage-**S**z **L**ength-**F**ill. Specify the number of lines for the graph area; 1-2-3 prints the largest graph possible that fills the number of lines you specify without changing the width-to-height ratio of the graph. Select **Quit Quit** to return to the main **/P**rint menu, line up the paper in your printer, and select **Align Go Page Quit** to print the graph and return to the worksheet.

If you select **Image-Sz Margin-Fill** rather than **Image-Sz Length-Fill**, 1-2-3 prints a graph that fills the space between the left and right margins. To vary the graph aspect ratio, select **Image-Sz Reshape** and enter the desired height and width.

*Select /**P**rint **P**rinter **I**mage **O**ptions **A**dvanced **I**mage **R**otate **Y**es to rotate a graph 90 degrees to the left.*

You can mix worksheet data and graphs on the same page but only vertically. You cannot have a graph beside worksheet data. To print data and graphs on the same page, select **/P**rint **P**rinter **R**ange, specify a worksheet range to print, and select **Align Go.** Don't select **P**age; instead select **Image Current** or **Image Named-Graph** (specify a graph name with this option). Change the settings as desired by selecting **Options Advanced Image.** When the settings are correct, select **Quit Quit** to return to the main **/P**rint menu. Don't select **Align;** select **Go.** You then can specify another graph or more worksheet data to print, or select **Quit** to return to the worksheet.

Printing Graphs with Wysiwyg (Releases 2.3 and 3.1)

With the Wysiwyg add-in included with Releases 2.3 and 3.1, you can print graphs large enough to fill a page or smaller ones mixed with worksheet data. You even can print text and graphs side by side.

With Wysiwyg attached, you add a graph to the worksheet by selecting **:Graph Add** and selecting **Current, Named, PIC, Metafile,** or **Blank** (**Blank** adds a place holder for a graphic image in the worksheet). If you select **Named,** enter or highlight a graph name in the current or any open file. If you select **PIC,** you can use a PIC file created with any version of 1-2-3. If you select **Metafile,** you can use a CGM file created by 1-2-3 Release 3.x or by one of many graphics programs.

When you have selected the graph you want to add, Wysiwyg prompts you for the range in which to place the graph. Specify the range and then select **Quit.**

To print the graph, select **:P**rint **R**ange **Set** and specify a range that includes only the graph or one that includes the graph and worksheet data. Select **Go** to print the selected range. Wysiwyg returns 1-2-3 to READY mode after printing.

Summary

Your graphing needs may range from occasional and simple to constant and complex. 1-2-3's graphing capabilities can help you to create quick graphs on-screen for analyzing relationships between numbers, or attractive printed graphs for use as presentation materials.

The next chapter discusses creating macros to simplify and improve your use of 1-2-3.

Chapter Eight

WRITING MACROS

This chapter discusses techniques for creating effective, efficient macros. Information in this chapter is based on the assumption that you already have some experience in writing basic macros.

Specifically, this chapter covers the following topics:

- Ways to name and run macros
- How to create macros by recording keystrokes
- Techniques for using advanced macro commands
- How to create and use subroutines
- How to run macros stored in macro libraries or open files

Naming and Starting Macros

The traditional way to name a macro is to assign its first cell a range name consisting of a backslash and a letter. You run such a macro by holding down the Alt key and pressing the letter (upper- or lowercase). This method is certainly the easiest way to start a macro, but limits you to a maximum of 26 combinations (one for each letter in the alphabet).

You may not need 26 macros in one worksheet, but you may want to use mnemonic Alt–*letter* combinations; a macro that prints a worksheet, for example, is often called \p. After you have used the \p combination for the printing macro, you cannot use the same combination for other macros.

Starting Macros with the Run Key (Alt-F3)

With Releases 2.2, 2.3, 3, and 3.1, you can use the Run key (Alt–F3) to start a macro that uses a descriptive range name for the first cell of the macro, rather than an Alt–*letter* combination. When you press the Run key, a list of range names appears in the control panel. To see the entire list, press Name (F3). You can highlight the name of a macro and press Enter, or highlight the name of an open file to see a list of its range names. You also can type a range name or file name.

With Releases 2.2 and 2.3, the list includes range names found in macro libraries. With Releases 3 and 3.1, the list includes the names of open files enclosed in less-than and greater-than signs (for example, <<PROGRAMS.WK3>>). Methods for using macro libraries and macros in open files are discussed later in this chapter.

To invoke a macro that has no name, enter the address of the first cell at the `Select the macro to run:` prompt. To execute the macro beginning at the current location of the cell pointer, press Esc once (unless the worksheet has no named ranges) and press Enter.

Using the Run Key (Alt-F3) in Macro Development

Using the Run key is helpful when you develop and debug macros. In figure 8.1, for example, after confirming that the instructions in range AB1..AB4 work correctly, you can test the rest of the macro starting from cell AB5 by pressing Run (Alt–F3) and entering AB5.

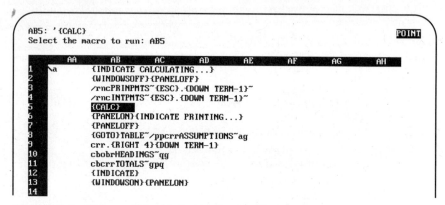

Fig. 8.1. Debugging a macro with the Run key, starting at an unnamed cell.

Simulating the Run Key (Alt-F3) in Release 2.01

If you use Release 2.01 (which does not support the Run key), you can place a *run macro* in your worksheet, as shown in figure 8.2. The run macro uses /xg (equivalent to the {GOTO} key name), included in all versions of 1-2-3 beginning with Release 1A. When you invoke the macro, 1-2-3 switches to NAMES mode and displays the worksheet's range names. Highlight or type a range name, type a cell address, or press Esc and then Enter to invoke the macro that starts at the current cell.

To create the run macro, enter the label shown in cell AB1 of figure 8.2, and assign the name \r (or a different name, if desired) to that cell.

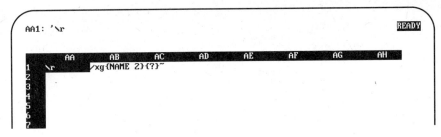

Fig. 8.2. *A Release 2.01 macro that simulates the action of the Run key in later versions.*

Organizing Macro Names

A drawback to using the Run key or the run macro is that all named ranges appear on the screen. 1-2-3 cannot distinguish between range names used for macros and range names used for data.

A good way to deal with this problem is to devise macro range names that are easy to find; for example, you can incorporate verbs into range names—GETNAMES and DO_SUMS are more likely to be names for macros than DATA or Q1SALES.

You also can isolate macros on the list of range names by assigning names that cause the macros to appear at the beginning or the end of the list. Macro names beginning with @ appear at the beginning of the list, as shown in figure 8.3.

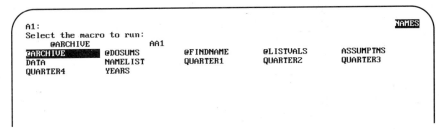

Fig. 8.3. *Range names with @ appearing at the beginning of the list of names.*

Range names that begin with a split vertical bar (¦) appear at the end of the list of range names from the current worksheet, but *before* range names in macro libraries and the names of open files. Figure 8.4 shows an example.

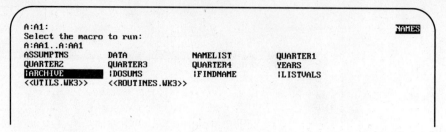

Fig. 8.4. Range names with ¦ appearing at the end of the list of range names, but before names of open files in the current file.

Creating Macros with the Learn Key in Release 2.2 and 2.3

With Release 2.2 and 2.3, you can create macros that duplicate user keystrokes by executing the keystrokes and recording them in a range of the worksheet. Begin by setting up a learn range, pressing Learn (Alt–F5), and executing the keystrokes to be recorded. Figure 8.5 shows a macro in range E1..E2 created with the Learn key. You can use this macro to sum contiguous columns of numbers.

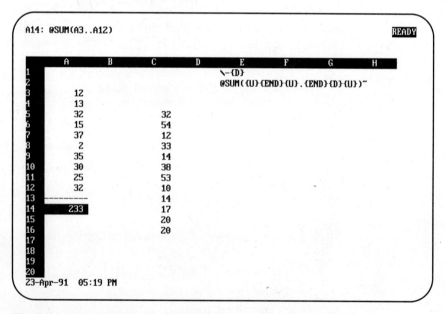

Fig. 8.5. A macro (in range E1..E2) created with the Learn key.

To set up the macro in figure 8.5, enter the numbers in range A3..A12, and establish a learn range by selecting /Worksheet Learn and specifying range **E1..E20** (always specify a larger learn range than you think is necessary). Position the cell pointer in cell A13 and press Learn (Alt–F5). Create a dashed line by typing **\–** and pressing the down-arrow key to complete the entry and move the cell pointer to the next line. Type **@SUM(** and move the cell pointer to the top of the column of numbers by pressing the up-arrow key, End, and the up-arrow key again. Anchor the range with a period and press End, the down-arrow key, and the up-arrow key to highlight the rest of the column (but not the dashed line). Type a closing parenthesis and press Enter. To stop recording key-strokes, press Learn (Alt–F5) again. This process creates the labels in cells E1 and E2 of figure 8.5.

You can use this macro to create summing formulas for other contiguous ranges of numbers; for example, if you assign the name \s to cell E1, position the cell pointer in cell C17 of figure 8.5, and press Alt–S, the macro enters `\-` in cell C17 and `@SUM(C5..C16)` in cell C18.

Shortening Recorded Macros in Release 2.2

One problem with using the Learn key with Release 2.2 is that each keystroke is recorded as a separate word. Suppose that you press the down-arrow key 10 times and the right-arrow key four times while creating a macro. You may get a macro like the one in figure 8.6, which runs perfectly, but doesn't need to be so long.

With Release 2.3, pressing the down-arrow key 10 times results in the instruction {D 10} in the learn range.

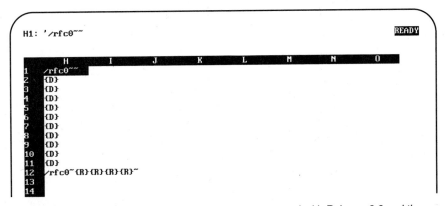

Fig. 8.6. *A macro containing a series of key names created with Release 2.2 and the Learn key.*

You can create a macro that replaces 10 {DOWN}s with {DOWN 10} or {D 10}, and four {RIGHT}s with {RIGHT 4} or {R 4}, and so on.

Arranging the Macro

Before using the repeat-eliminating utility, arrange the macro you want to modify in as few rows as possible with the **/R**ange **J**ustify command. Selecting **/R**ange **J**ustify and specifying range H1..M12, for example, changes the macro in figure 8.6 to look like the one in figure 8.7.

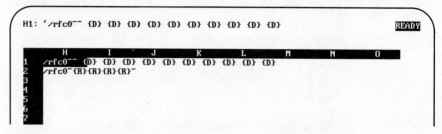

Fig. 8.7. *The macro from figure 8.6, rearranged with /Range Justify.*

Next you must take out all the spaces with the **/R**ange **S**earch command. Select **/R**ange **S**earch, specify the range **H1..H2**, enter a space at the String to search for: prompt, select **L**abels **R**eplace, press Enter at the Replacement string: prompt (press Esc if a default string appears) and select **A**ll. This process creates the macro shown in figure 8.8.

*If you created string-returning formulas when recording your macro, they may contain spaces that you need intact. Finish the /**R**ange **S**earch operation by selecting **R**eplace or **N**ext, rather than **A**ll, and remove spaces selectively.*

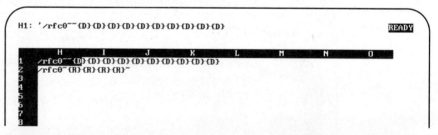

Fig. 8.8. *The macro from figure 8.7, with extra spaces removed using /Range Search.*

Using the Repeat-Eliminating Macro

Now you're ready to use the macro shown in figure 8.9. This macro replaces repeated key names (up to 10 repetitions) with a key name-number combination. If your recorded macro contains, for example, 15 {L}s in sequence, those key names are replaced with {L 10}{L 5}. You can replace this string with {L 15} if desired.

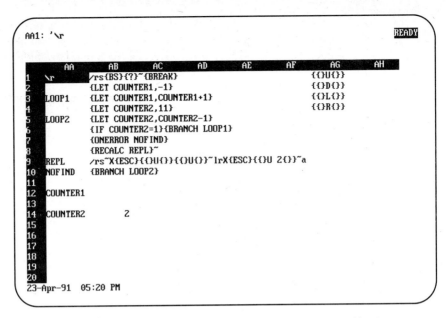

Fig. 8.9. *A macro that replaces multiple occurrences of a key name with a key name-number combination.*

Before considering the macro's instructions in order, look at cell AB9. This instruction replaces all occurrences of {U}{U} with {U 2}. Because 1-2-3 must *type* the characters {U} (instead of pressing the up-arrow key), the opening and closing braces are themselves encased in braces, hence the combinations {{} and {}}.

To create this macro, first enter all the labels in columns AA, AB, and AG (but don't enter anything in cell AB9 yet). Select **/R**ange **N**ame **La**bels **R**ight and specify range AA1..AA14. Assign the name KEYTABLE to range AG1..AG4. Enter the following string-returning formula in cell AB9:

```
+"/rs~X{ESC}"&@REPEAT(@INDEX(KEYTABLE,0,COUNTER1),COUNTER2)&
     "~1rX{ESC}"&@LEFT(@INDEX(KEYTABLE,0,COUNTER1),4)&
     " "&@STRING(COUNTER2,0)&"{}}~a"
```

Your result should match that shown in figure 8.9. This formula combines the keystrokes that operate the **/R**ange **S**earch command with a label from the range KEYTABLE repeated the number of times stored in COUNTER2, and with the same label from KEYTABLE combined with the string equivalent of the value in COUNTER2.

You invoke the macro by pressing Alt–R. The macro executes the **/R**ange **S**earch command, presses the Backspace key to clear any existing range, and waits for you to highlight a range. (For the example shown in figure 8.8, specify range H1..H2.) The BREAK command returns 1-2-3 to READY mode.

The next instruction initializes the cell named COUNTER1 by setting its value to –1. The instruction that follows is the beginning of a loop, increasing COUNTER1 by 1. COUNTER1 is used by the @INDEX function to determine which label from KEYTABLE is repeated in cell AB9.

The following step initializes COUNTER2 by setting its value to 11. A second loop follows, decreasing COUNTER2 by 1.

The next instruction, {IF COUNTER2=1}{BRANCH LOOP1}, tests whether COUNTER2 has been decreased to 1. If so, the macro branches back to LOOP1, which increases COUNTER1 by 1 and sets COUNTER2 back to 11.

{ONERROR NOFIND} forces the macro to continue to the next instruction (instead of triggering an error condition) if the /Range Search operation does not find a search string. {RECALC REPL}~ updates the string-returning formula in cell AB9, so that its result agrees with the current values in COUNTER1 and COUNTER2.

Cell AB9 executes the /Range Search command and presses Enter to accept the range established at the beginning of the macro. The search string is entered as X followed by Esc to clear any preexisting search string, and the macro types {U}, {D}, {L}, or {R} the number of times specified in COUNTER2, followed by Enter. Next the macro selects Label Replace, presses X followed by Esc, and types {U}, {D}, {L}, or {R} with the number in COUNTER2 inserted inside the braces, presses Enter, and selects All. The next step branches back to the range LOOP2, which decreases COUNTER2 by 1.

The macro replaces 10 {U}s with {U 10}, nine {U}s with {U 9}, and so forth, and repeats the process with 10 {D}s, nine {D}s, and so on. The macro works "backwards" because if it started with two and worked up, it would replace every pair of {U}s with {U 2}; thus every group of 10 {U}s would be replaced with 5 {U 2}s.

Notice that the macro contains no instruction to end when COUNTER1 reaches four. When COUNTER1 has a value above three, cell AB9 returns ERR, and the macro stops.

When used with the labels shown in figure 8.8, the \r macro creates the label shown in figure 8.10.

Creating Macros with the Record Feature in Release 3.x

Releases 3 and 3.1 also create keystroke macros by performing the tasks involved; instead of placing the keystrokes in a worksheet range, these versions constantly record keystrokes in a buffer in your computer's memory. You can create a macro by copying selected keystrokes to a worksheet range. You also can *play back* the keystrokes directly from the buffer.

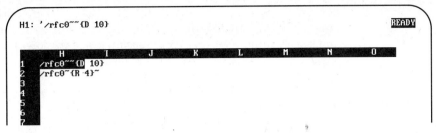

Fig. 8.10. *The macro in figure 8.6, with 10 {DOWN}s and four {RIGHT}s converted to {D 10} and {R 4}.*

Clearing the Buffer

When you plan to perform an operation with the express purpose of creating a macro, erase the buffer to make finding the captured keystrokes easier. Suppose that you want to create a summing macro. Begin by moving the cell pointer to the starting position, as shown in figure 8.11.

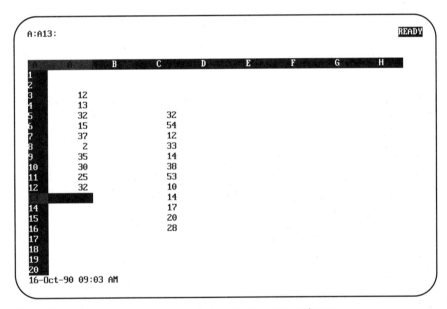

Fig. 8.11. *A worksheet, prior to recording a macro to sum columns.*

Erase the buffer by pressing Record (Alt–F2) and selecting **E**rase; then execute the keystrokes you want to record. For this example, begin by typing **\–** to create a dashed line. Press the down-arrow key, type **@SUM(**, and press the up-arrow key, End, and the up-arrow key again to move the cell pointer to the top of the range. Anchor the range with a period and highlight the rest of the column by pressing End, the down-arrow key, and the up-arrow key. Type a closing parenthesis and press Enter to complete the macro steps. Press Record (Alt–F2) again and select Copy. 1-2-3 displays the contents of the keystroke buffer, as shown in figure 8.12.

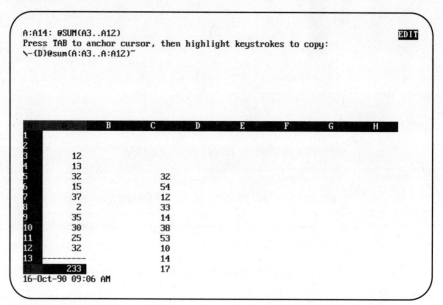

Fig. 8.12. *The keystrokes (used to create the dividing line and @SUM formula) contained in the buffer.*

Editing the Buffer

You can edit the buffer before copying it into the worksheet, in the same way you edit a cell. If you created the macro in figure 8.12, for example, 1-2-3 stored the exact coordinates of the range specified for the @SUM formula (A:A3..A:A12). Replacing the range with ({UP}{END}{UP}.{END}{DOWN}{UP}) makes the macro more generic for use with other columns of figures.

Copying Buffer Contents

With the buffer contents displayed, highlight the keystrokes you want to copy to the worksheet. To copy the entire buffer, just press Home, Tab (to anchor the highlight), End, and Enter. When you have highlighted the keystrokes to copy, specify the range in the worksheet where you want to place the keystrokes. Figure 8.13 shows the worksheet with the recorded macro in range E1..E5. If you assign the name \s to cell E1, you can move the cell pointer to cell C17 and press Alt–S to create a dividing line and a formula that sums range C5..C16.

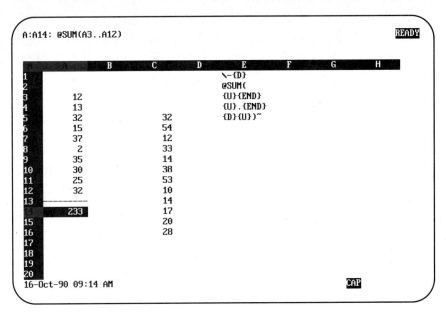

```
A:A14: @SUM(A3..A12)                                           READY

        A        B        C        D        E        F     G        H
1                                          \-{D}
2                                          @SUM(
3        12                                {U}{END}
4        13                                {U}.{END}
5        32               32               {D}{U})~
6        15               54
7        37               12
8         2               33
9        35               14
10       30               38
11       25               53
12       32               10
13     --------           14
14       233              17
15                        20
16                        28
17
18
19
20
16-Oct-90 09:14 AM                                             CAP
```

Fig. 8.13. *The edited buffer contents copied into the worksheet to create a macro.*

If you want to execute keystrokes in the buffer only (without copying them to the worksheet), move the cell pointer to the starting position. Press Record (Alt–F2) and select **P**layback, highlight the keystrokes you want to execute, and press Enter. Unlike Release 2.2, Release 3.x uses key name-number combinations to record multiple keystrokes. If you press the down-arrow key 15 times in sequence when recording keystrokes, the buffer contains the characters {D 15} rather than 15 {D}s.

Using Numeric Arguments with Key Names

As indicated previously in this chapter, several ways exist for telling 1-2-3 to press the same direction key several times. Of course, including the command {UP 7} or {U 7} in a macro is easier than typing {UP}{UP}{UP}{UP}{UP}{UP}{UP}.

Using Cell References for Repeating Key Names

You can devise a macro that places varying values in a cell named REPTNS (for "repetitions"). Or REPTNS may contain a live formula that returns different values based on changing conditions in the worksheet. The command {DOWN REPTNS} moves the cell pointer down the number of times stored in REPTNS.

If the value stored in REPTNS is not an integer, 1-2-3 drops the non-integer portion, rather than rounding it. If REPTNS contains the value 7.998, {DOWN REPTNS} moves the cell pointer down seven times.

Using Formulas for Repeating Key Names

You can use a formula as the numeric argument of a key name repetition command. Consider the problem of creating a macro that produces a range of formulas the same size as a specified source range, even if the size or location of the source range changes. In figure 8.14, an array of values constitutes the range B5..G13 (assigned the name DATA), and cell B5 is assigned the name DATA1.

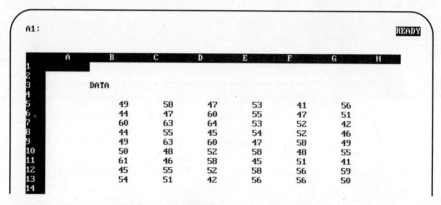

Fig. 8.14. A range that will be copied with a macro.

Figure 8.15 shows the solution to the macro copying problem, using @ROWS and @COLS commands. The macro creates a formula that reduces by 10 percent the value at the upper left corner of DATA, and executes the /Copy command, pressing Enter to use the current cell pointer location as the beginning of the source range. Then the macro anchors the range with a period, and moves {DOWN} and {RIGHT} the appropriate number of times to define a range the same size as DATA. Use this macro to create a new block of values, each one 10 percent less than the corresponding value in DATA.

This macro uses a label that includes the characters of the @ROWS and @COLS formulas. 1-2-3 calculates the current values of these formulas as it executes the instruction.

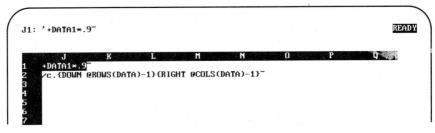

```
J1: '+DATA1*.9~                                                    READY

         J     K     L     M     N     O     P     Q
1  +DATA1*.9~
2  /c.{DOWN @ROWS(DATA)-1}{RIGHT @COLS(DATA)-1}~
3
4
5
6
7
```

Fig. 8.15. *A macro that uses @ROWS and @COLS as numeric arguments with key names to control the size of a copy range.*

If you are comfortable with the technique of including string-returning formulas in macros, you may have thought of replacing the label in cell J2 of figure 8.15 with a formula like the following:

```
+"/c~.{DOWN "&@STRING(@ROWS(DATA)-1,0)& "}
        {RIGHT "&@STRING(@COLS(DATA)-1,0)&"}~"
```

Given the size of the range DATA in figure 8.14, the formula returns `/c~.{DOWN 8}{RIGHT 5}~`. *This macro works, but it requires more memory and an additional instruction in the macro to recalculate the formula before executing it.*

If you want a macro to move the cell pointer to column A in the current row, use the following macro command:

```
{LEFT @CELLPOINTER("col")-1}
```

Using Advanced Macro Commands

The advanced macro commands make the difference between simple time savers and full-fledged programs. These commands enable you to create macros that accomplish objectives you cannot handle from the keyboard. Macros using advanced commands can display menus you have designed, read selected characters from disk files, or enhance the appearance of your applications by suppressing the 1-2-3 border. They even can display prompts in the control panel and accept input from the user.

Using GETLABEL and GETNUMBER

In Releases 2.2, 2.3, 3, and 3.1, you can use the advanced macro commands GETLABEL and GETNUMBER to accept an entry from the user and place the entry at the current location of the cell pointer. Use

@CELLPOINTER("address") as the *location* argument, as in the following example:

```
{GETNUMBER What is your age? ,@CELLPOINTER("address")}
```

This technique does not work in Release 2.01; if you want a macro to place entries in the current cell, the macro must place the entry in a named cell and then use the LET command to copy the entry to the current cell, as in the following example:

```
{GETNUMBER What is your age? ,RESPONSE}
{LET @CELLPOINTER("address"),RESPONSE}
```

Accepting Single Characters without the Enter Key

The GET command waits for a user to press a key, and stores that key in a cell as a character or a key name. The syntax for the GET command is {GET *address*}. Unlike GETLABEL and GETNUMBER, the GET command doesn't use a *prompt* argument, but you still can force a macro to display a prompt and accept a single character. The trick is to have the macro type a label without entering it, execute the GET command, and press Esc. Figure 8.16 shows an example of this type of macro.

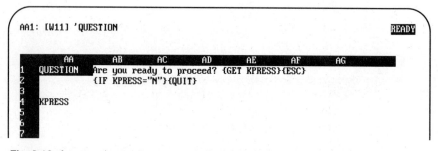

Fig. 8.16. *A macro that types an entry in the control panel without pressing Enter, waits for the user to press a key, and stores the key in the cell named KPRESS.*

Displaying Messages

Sometimes you want to display a message to the user without getting any information. A macro can display a message in the control panel by typing the message without pressing Enter, and then press Esc to clear the message. The WAIT command puts a time limit on the message. The GET command displays the message until the user presses a key. Following are two examples of such displayed message macros:

```
Assumptions are current as of 2/15/91
{WAIT @NOW+@TIME(0,0,15)}{ESC}
```

```
         This will overwrite files (press any key to continue)
         {GET XXX}{ESC}
```

The second example involves passing data into the worksheet (putting the character the user types in a cell named XXX). This character is irrelevant and can be ignored.

Understanding Subroutines

A subroutine is a set of instructions that a computer program branches to *temporarily*, after which the program returns to the same point in the routine and continues with its next instruction. Using subroutines allows several parts of the same program to use one routine.

Some inexperienced macro programmers waste time and computer memory by entering identical instructions in several different places in a macro. Others devise elaborate schemes in which a macro stores a marker in a cell to keep track of which section is currently executing, uses the BRANCH command to jump to a different routine, and uses the marker to find its way back to the "jumping-off point."

If a macro must process a specific set of instructions more than once, enter those instructions in an area of the worksheet separated from the main routine by at least one cell, and assign a descriptive name to the first cell of the subroutine. To make the main routine call the subroutine, enclose the subroutine's name in braces. Figure 8.17 shows a program that prompts the user for an order number and four item names and amounts. The macro assigns the currency format, amounts under $1,000.00 with two decimal places, and amounts at or over $1,000.00 with zero decimal places. The macro performs this task efficiently by calling the subroutine PLACES every time an amount is accepted.

When the macro is directed to PLACES, it jumps temporarily to cell AB17, processes the two instructions in cells AB17 and AB18, and returns to the point from which it left the main macro and continues with the next instruction.

Creating Commands with Subroutines

PLACES resembles a macro command; in fact, thinking about subroutines this way is useful. You can add to 1-2-3's macro-language vocabulary by creating generic subroutines that any of the worksheet's other macros can use.

WINDOWSOFF and PANELOFF are two commands that can speed up macros by preventing 1-2-3 from redrawing the screen and displaying menus and prompts in the control panel. It gets tedious, however, to type

{WINDOWSOFF}{PANELOFF} and {WINDOWSON}{PANELON}
repeatedly as you create your macros. Instead, you can create two routines, called FREEZE and SHOW, as shown in figure 8.18. With these
subroutines, any macro can use FREEZE to suppress updating the
screen and the control panel or SHOW to reenable updating, as if
FREEZE and SHOW were two macro commands.

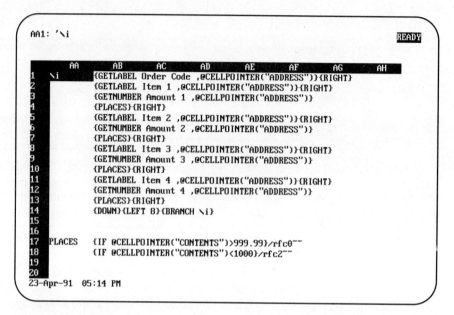

AA1: '\i   READY

```
        AA        AB          AC          AD          AE        AF        AG        AH
1    \i            {GETLABEL Order Code ,@CELLPOINTER("ADDRESS")}{RIGHT}
2                  {GETLABEL Item 1 ,@CELLPOINTER("ADDRESS")}{RIGHT}
3                  {GETNUMBER Amount 1 ,@CELLPOINTER("ADDRESS")}
4                  {PLACES}{RIGHT}
5                  {GETLABEL Item 2 ,@CELLPOINTER("ADDRESS")}{RIGHT}
6                  {GETNUMBER Amount 2 ,@CELLPOINTER("ADDRESS")}
7                  {PLACES}{RIGHT}
8                  {GETLABEL Item 3 ,@CELLPOINTER("ADDRESS")}{RIGHT}
9                  {GETNUMBER Amount 3 ,@CELLPOINTER("ADDRESS")}
10                 {PLACES}{RIGHT}
11                 {GETLABEL Item 4 ,@CELLPOINTER("ADDRESS")}{RIGHT}
12                 {GETNUMBER Amount 4 ,@CELLPOINTER("ADDRESS")}
13                 {PLACES}{RIGHT}
14                 {DOWN}{LEFT 8}{BRANCH \i}
15
16
17   PLACES        {IF @CELLPOINTER("CONTENTS")>999.99}/rfc0~~
18                 {IF @CELLPOINTER("CONTENTS")<1000}/rfc2~~
19
20
```
23-Apr-91 05:14 PM

Fig. 8.17. A macro that eliminates repetition by placing the instructions for formatting
cells in a subroutine called PLACES.

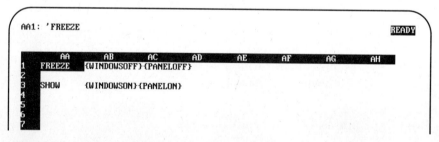

AA1: 'FREEZE   READY

```
        AA        AB          AC          AD          AE        AF        AG        AH
1    FREEZE        {WINDOWSOFF}{PANELOFF}
2
3    SHOW          {WINDOWSON}{PANELON}
4
5
6
7
```

Fig. 8.18. Subroutines used to add FREEZE and SHOW to 1-2-3's vocabulary.

Using Subroutines To Organize Programs

Subroutines are not just for invoking short utilities that many different
macros can use. By breaking a long routine designed to perform one
specific task into subroutines, you can modularize the program and write
a short master program that controls the entire operation.

Suppose that you want to create a macro that produces a quarterly sales report. The macro will consolidate ranges from several different worksheets, create a summary table from the consolidated data, produce graphs from the summary data, and use Allways or Wysiwyg to create a formatted report combining text and graphs.

To make this program easier to debug and maintain, you can break it into major sections. The first section can control the /File Combine operation consolidating the various worksheets, the second the /Data Table operation producing the summary report, and so forth. When you're reasonably sure that all of the sections are working correctly, you can write a master program that calls each of the sections, as shown in figure 8.19.

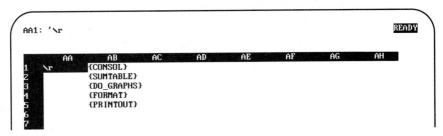

Fig. 8.19. A complex macro application modularized into subroutines called by a master program.

The master program controls the entire process of creating the report; you can see what the sections are, their operations, and the order in which they are executed.

Using Subroutines To Replay Stored Characters

A fairly common macro trick involves the macro "remembering" the starting location of the cell pointer and returning the cell pointer to the same location at a later time. Figure 8.20 shows a macro that displays a set of instructions and returns the cell pointer to its starting location.

The macro in figure 8.20 is self-modifying. Cell AB1 puts the current cell address (for example, $K$15) in cell AB7, so that by the time the macro gets to cell AB7 it finds keystrokes waiting. Cell AB6 presses the GoTo key, cell AB7 types the former address of the cell pointer, and cell AB8 presses Enter.

Figure 8.21 shows an alternate approach. Cell AB1 stores the current cell address in the cell named OLD_LOC. Cell AB6 presses the GoTo key, calls OLD_LOC as a subroutine, and presses Enter. This approach looks more polished, and you can see more easily what the macro is doing when the entire {GOTO} operation is in one cell instead of separated in three cells.

```
AA1: '\i                                                          READY

          AA        AB        AC        AD        AE        AF        AG        AH
1    \i        {LET OLD_LOC,@CELLPOINTER("ADDRESS")}
2              {GOTO}INSTR1~{WAIT @NOW+@TIME(0,0,20)}
3              {GOTO}INSTR2~{WAIT @NOW+@TIME(0,0,20)}
4              {GOTO}INSTR3~{WAIT @NOW+@TIME(0,0,20)}
5              {GOTO}INSTR4~{WAIT @NOW+@TIME(0,0,20)}
6              {GOTO}
7    OLD_LOC        ~
8
9              Do you want to see the instructions again? {GET KPRESS}{ESC}
10             {IF KPRESS="Y"}{BRANCH \i}
11
12   KPRESS
13
14
```

Fig. 8.20. *A macro that "remembers" the current location and returns the cell pointer to that location later.*

```
AA1: '\i                                                          READY

          AA        AB        AC        AD        AE        AF        AG        AH
1    \i        {LET OLD_LOC,@CELLPOINTER("ADDRESS")}
2              {GOTO}INSTR1~{WAIT @NOW+@TIME(0,0,20)}
3              {GOTO}INSTR2~{WAIT @NOW+@TIME(0,0,20)}
4              {GOTO}INSTR3~{WAIT @NOW+@TIME(0,0,20)}
5              {GOTO}INSTR4~{WAIT @NOW+@TIME(0,0,20)}
6              {GOTO}{OLD_LOC}~
7              Do you want to see the instructions again? {GET KPRESS}{ESC}
8              {IF KPRESS="Y"}{BRANCH \i}
9
10
11   OLD_LOC
12
13   KPRESS
14
```

Fig. 8.21. *An alternate version of the macro that stores the cell pointer location in an isolated cell and calls that label as a subroutine.*

The braces surrounding the range name OLD_LOC are very important. Without them, the macro would position the cell pointer at OLD_LOC, instead of using the cell contents as keystrokes.

Avoiding the use of QUIT and RETURN

If 1-2-3 is processing a macro and encounters a blank cell or a cell containing a value, the macro ends. As a general rule, use the QUIT command only as a way to stop a macro under certain circumstances. You can use the QUIT and IF commands in conjunction, for example, in the statement {IF *condition*}{QUIT}. If *condition* is TRUE, the macro ends. Otherwise the macro proceeds to the instruction in the next cell.

The RETURN command forces the termination of a subroutine and passes control back to the instruction following the subroutine call. Like

QUIT, RETURN is not always necessary; 1-2-3 ends a subroutine when it encounters an empty cell. Use RETURN with IF to end a subroutine only when a certain condition is met.

Techniques for Using Menu Macros

If a worksheet contains a half-dozen or so macro routines, don't give the user printed instructions saying, "Use Alt–A for this task, use Alt–B for that task." Instead, create a menu macro that enables the user to choose from among the worksheet's routines. 1-2-3's macro capabilities enable you to create menus that operate just like 1-2-3's built-in menus—most users feel right at home. This section discusses some strategies for creating menus.

A menu macro can display from one to eight items. If your worksheet has more than eight sections, you can use seven sections as the first seven menu items (selecting any of these items causes the appropriate section of the worksheet to be displayed). The eighth item (titled More Choices, for example) can display a second menu containing the names of the additional sections. This selection invokes another MENUBRANCH or MENUCALL command rather than performing a {GOTO} operation.

Another approach is to categorize the sections of the worksheet and use a hierarchical menu structure. Suppose that a worksheet contains a section for each of the 12 departments in a small company. Seven of the departments are profit centers; the other five are support departments. To help users find the worksheet sections, you can create a menu with two items: Profit Centers and Support Departments. If the user selects Profit Centers, a second menu appears, listing the seven profit centers. The Support Departments selection accesses a second menu listing the five support departments.

Making Custom Menus Safer To Use

In all of 1-2-3's regular menus, each option has a different first character. Following this example when you design your own macros is usually a good idea. On the other hand, sometimes you may want to make choosing a particular menu option more difficult. If selecting a menu option can have disastrous consequences, you can make the user think about the option before selecting it.

If your menu has two options starting with the same letter, pressing that letter selects the first of the two. To select the second, the user must highlight the option and press Enter. If possible, give a "dangerous" menu option the same letter as an option preceding it.

Suppose that you create a menu including the option **Delete**. You want the user to be careful when selecting this option. To make the user highlight **Delete** and see the prompt that the option displays, include another option beginning with D in the menu prior to **Delete**. Perhaps you can think of a task for the macro to perform that can be indicated by the word **Data**. If not, you can use the word **Dummy**, with the phrase **This option does nothing** as the prompt, and a MENUBRANCH command after the prompt to restart the same menu.

Another way to require users to select a menu option by highlighting is to begin the option name with a hard-to-type character. Instead of typing **Delete** for the menu option, type the formula **@CHAR(255)&"Delete"**, press CALC, and press Enter. With this method, the menu choice **Delete** is preceded by a solid box. Because no key exists for typing the box, the user must highlight the **Delete** option to select it.

Organizing Menu Macro Code Effectively

Many people set up menus in the format shown in figure 8.22. This method works, but the resulting menu can be hard to read and interpret because the code usually overlaps. A better way to organize the routines invoked by a menu is shown in figure 8.23. Each long prompt is followed by a BRANCH command or subroutine call, and the code for each menu option is arranged in a separate area of the worksheet.

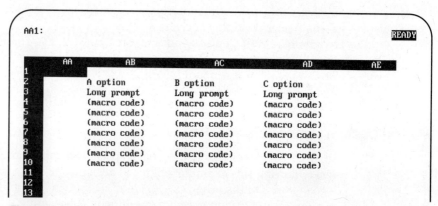

Fig. 8.22. A typical approach to creating menu macros, putting the macro programs under each option.

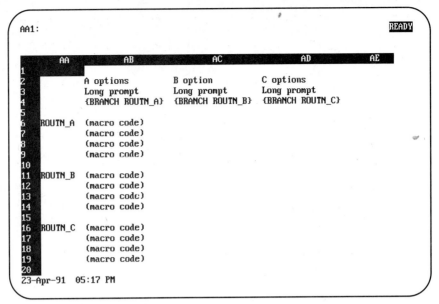

```
AA1:                                                              READY

         AA           AB              AC              AD           AE
1
2                A options       B option        C options
3                Long prompt     Long prompt     Long prompt
4                {BRANCH ROUTN_A}  {BRANCH ROUTN_B}  {BRANCH ROUTN_C}
5
6     ROUTN_A    (macro code)
7                (macro code)
8                (macro code)
9                (macro code)
10
11    ROUTN_B    (macro code)
12               (macro code)
13               (macro code)
14               (macro code)
15
16    ROUTN_C    (macro code)
17               (macro code)
18               (macro code)
19               (macro code)
20
23-Apr-91  05:17 PM
```

Fig. 8.23. A better approach to menu macros.

Creating Menu Trees

Because menu macros execute macro code, one menu can start another menu. Figure 8.24 shows how this process can work. The \m macro starts the first menu. If you select **W**iden, **M**oney, or **D**ate, a macro performs an operation on the current cell (the example contains none), and terminates. If you select **P**rint, the menu starting in cell AA12 appears.

The **P**rint menu has four options that perform some operations and then terminate. The fifth choice, **Q**uit, returns the user to the original menu. The **Q**uit option in the **P**rint menu thus behaves like the **Q**uit option in many of 1-2-3's regular menus. An alternate approach is to use the label **Return to READY mode** in cell AE13, leaving cell AE14 blank.

Notice the instruction {MENUBRANCH XMENU} in cell AB9. Using this instruction is another way to make menu systems behave like regular 1-2-3 menus. If the user starts the first menu, selects **P**rint, and presses Esc before choosing any of the **P**rint menu options, control is passed to the instruction following the MENUBRANCH or MENUCALL command. As the instruction restarts the first menu, the user can "back up" from the second menu to the first by pressing Esc.

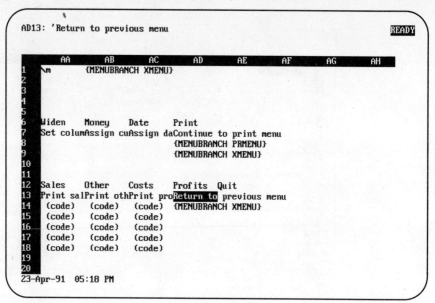

```
AD13: 'Return to previous menu                                    READY

      AA       AB       AC       AD       AE       AF       AG       AH
1   \m         {MENUBRANCH XMENU}
2
3
4
5
6   Widen    Money    Date     Print
7   Set columAssign cuAssign daContinue to print menu
8                              {MENUBRANCH PRMENU}
9                              {MENUBRANCH XMENU}
10
11
12  Sales    Other    Costs    Profits  Quit
13  Print salPrint othPrint proReturn to previous menu
14  (code)   (code)   (code)   {MENUBRANCH XMENU}
15  (code)   (code)   (code)
16  (code)   (code)   (code)
17  (code)   (code)   (code)
18  (code)   (code)   (code)
19
20
23-Apr-91  05:18 PM
```

Fig. 8.24. A menu that calls other menus, which in turn can restore earlier menus.

You can "daisy-chain" several menus to create a complex command structure. If every MENUBRANCH command is followed by an instruction to restart the menu in which the command occurs, you can back up from the last menu to the first by pressing Esc. Multilevel menu structures require planning and careful work, but they can result in wonderful user-friendly applications.

Using the Macro Library Manager with Releases 2.2 and 2.3

Releases 2.2 and 2.3 include a very useful add-in, the Macro Library Manager, that stores macro routines in "libraries." You can load the libraries into your computer's memory, where they stay regardless of which worksheet files you retrieve. You can use macro libraries to customize your 1-2-3 session with your own handy utilities, or you can use a library to "ride shotgun" on a complex application involving several different worksheet files. Chapter 12 explains how to attach and use the Macro Library Manager.

You can start a library routine in one of three ways. If you name a routine with an Alt–*letter* combination, you can start that routine by holding down the Alt key and pressing the letter, unless another macro supersedes it. A macro in the current worksheet always supersedes a macro with the same name in a library. If your worksheet contains a macro named \s, and a macro library in memory contains a macro with the same name, Alt–S starts the macro in the worksheet. If you have several libraries in memory, and two or more of them contain macros named \s (assuming the worksheet contains none by that name), Alt–S starts the macro in the library that was opened first.

The second way to invoke a macro from a macro library is to press the Run key (Alt–F3) and enter the name of the routine you want to run. Again, if the worksheet contains a macro with the same name, entering the name runs the macro in the worksheet. If two or more libraries contain macros with the same name, 1-2-3 runs the macro in the library that was opened first.

The only way to run a macro that is superseded by one in the worksheet or in another library is to press the Run key (Alt–F3), highlight the exact macro you want to run, and press Enter. When you press Run (Alt–F3) and then Name (F3), 1-2-3 lists all available range names on-screen. The range names in the worksheet appear first, followed by range names in the first library opened, the second library opened, and so on. As you highlight each range name, its address in the worksheet or the name of the library in which it is found appears at the top of the screen. Using this method, you can select the macro you want to run.

Running Macros in Open Release 3.x Files

Releases 3 and 3.1 do not include a Macro Library Manager add-in, but you can get some of the benefits of the Macro Library Manager by putting useful routines into a worksheet file, and opening that file *after* another worksheet.

Suppose that you create a set of macros to help you develop your Release 3.x applications, and save the macros in a worksheet named UTILS.WK3. To use these routines, retrieve a new worksheet, select /File Open After, and specify UTILS.WK3. Press Ctrl–PgDn to return the cell pointer to the original worksheet. To run the macros in UTILS.WK3, press Run (Alt–F3) followed by Name (F3). A list of range names in the current worksheet (if any) appears on-screen, followed by <<UTILS.WK3>>. Highlight <<UTILS.WK3>> and press Enter. The list of range names in your utilities file appears on-screen. Highlight the name of the macro you want to run and press Enter.

Saving the Current Worksheet

To save the worksheet you're developing, select /File Save. The message [ALL MODIFIED FILES] appears in the control panel. Assuming that you don't need to resave your utility file, type the name of the worksheet you're developing and press Enter.

Abandoning a Worksheet

To abandon a worksheet and start another (with your utilities still available), you cannot just select /Worksheet Erase as you can with the Release 2.2 and 2.3 Macro Library Manager. This command erases all open worksheets. Instead, select /Worksheet Delete File and enter the name of the worksheet you have been building with the utilities. This selection leaves your utilities worksheet on-screen. Select /File Open Before or /File New Before and enter the name of the new worksheet. This procedure opens the new file *before* the utilities worksheet. Another option is to select /File Retrieve and specify the new file, which replaces only the current file in memory. You then can work in the new worksheet, using the macros in the utilities file as desired.

Summary

This chapter has provided some hints for writing more efficient, unique, and functional macros, and some guidelines for managing macros, especially regarding naming and running macros. You have seen how to create macros by recording keystrokes, and learned some tricks to use when creating custom menus. Not every application needs a macro but, when used appropriately, macros greatly increase your productivity (and sense of accomplishment).

The next section of this book discusses using 1-2-3 for business presentations, financial and accounting applications, and databases.

Part Three

CREATING 1-2-3 APPLICATIONS

Chapter Nine

USING 1-2-3 FOR BUSINESS PRESENTATIONS

This chapter discusses *presentation documents*, one-page gems that communicate a world of information in a glance. Whether the page contains text, graphs, or both, you can create bold presentation documents using 1-2-3 with Allways or Wysiwyg.

After you create and print your documents, you can duplicate them as handouts or transparencies for large groups. Use a high-resolution output device, such as a laser, inkjet, or 24-pin dot-matrix printer. Most offices have quality copiers and you can find transparency stock for duplication at your local stationer. Using easily available equipment, you can create an impressive, professional-looking document for your next important meeting.

This chapter discusses the following elements of creating business presentations:

- Creating simple charts that represent detailed data
- Constructing attractive text charts using Allways and Wysiwyg
- Devising graphs that communicate your message
- Annotating graphs with text
- Illustrating longer passages of text with graphs

Creating Text-Only Charts

Sometimes your business presentations need only the printed word to communicate your message. When you choose this format for your presentation, you must choose your words carefully. When you report the preceding quarter's transactions to your boss or the accounting department, you must be thorough. But when you distribute or display a summary of the quarter's activity at a meeting, you must be concise. Study the information carefully, determine the important points, and use those points in your presentation.

Creating Simple Text Charts

Figure 9.1 shows weekly sales of a company's product. Each figure is important and should be recorded somewhere. But suppose that you have five minutes at the next quarterly meeting to tell management how sales of mango mashers have contributed to the firm's fortunes. Figure 9.1 clearly contains too much information; you must identify some key values and place those values in context. Figure 9.2 shows a simple table you can duplicate on paper handouts or copy to transparency.

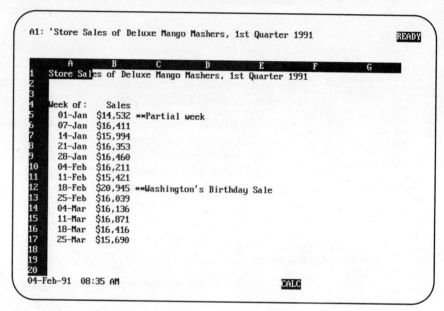

Fig. 9.1. *A worksheet containing important information but too many details for a presentation.*

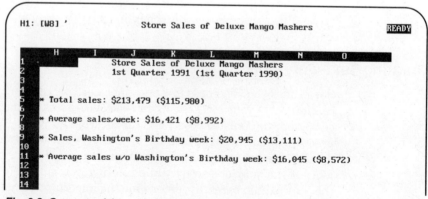

Fig. 9.2. *One area of the worksheet to be printed as a concise and organized presentation document.*

Figure 9.2 illustrates how you can create a clear and useful presentation document without using graphics or add-in programs. Enter a few labels and use the usual 1-2-3 print commands, using the best printer available to you.

If you create a chart that relies solely on words, pay attention to grammar. Looking up the rules governing subordinate clauses and verb tenses may not be necessary, but use common-sense grammar. Be consistent, because inconsistencies can distract your audience from the points under discussion. Use complete sentences for all or none of the bulleted items (see fig. 9.3). Don't use periods if you don't use complete sentences. Avoid using the word *and* in some cases and the ampersand (&) in others.

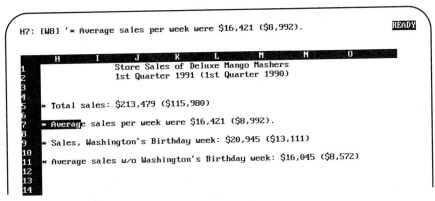

Fig. 9.3. A text chart containing complete and incomplete sentences.

A typeface *is a particular style of characters, such as Times or Triumvirate; a* font *is a typeface and its point size, such as Times 14 point or Times 17 point. Allways and Wysiwyg can mix fonts on a page, but avoid doing so unless you have a good reason. If you add a statement supporting a major point, for example, you can assign a smaller typeface to that text. Avoid small typefaces if you plan to use the chart as a transparency, however, or reading the finished product may be difficult.*

Creating Text-Only Charts with Allways (Release 2.2)

With Release 2.2, you can polish your text charts by using Allways to print the text in larger and more attractive characters (see fig. 9.4).

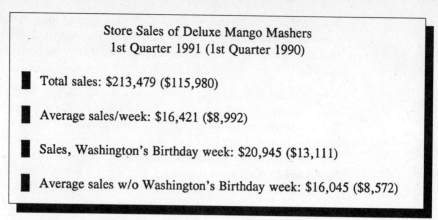

Store Sales of Deluxe Mango Mashers
1st Quarter 1991 (1st Quarter 1990)

■ Total sales: $213,479 ($115,980)

■ Average sales/week: $16,421 ($8,992)

■ Sales, Washington's Birthday week: $20,945 ($13,111)

■ Average sales w/o Washington's Birthday week: $16,045 ($8,572)

Fig. 9.4. *A text chart created with Allways.*

In figure 9.2, the labels are centered in the first two rows because the dates and figures are preceded by several spaces. To center text in Allways, you enter the text in the center column of the print range, preceded by a carat (^). In normal 1-2-3 mode, long labels don't appear centered because they spill into the cells to the right. If you switch to Allways mode, however, the text spills out of the cell in both directions (see fig. 9.5).

```
FONT(1) Times 14 pt                                                    ALLWAYS
M1: ^Store Sales of Deluxe Mango Mashers

    H I J   K      L        M        N         O        P        Q        R
 1                        Store Sales of Deluxe Mango Mashers
 2                        1st Quarter 1991 (1st Quarter 1990)
 3
 4      ■  Total sales: $213,479 ($115,980)
 5
 6      ■  Average sales/week: $16,421 ($8,992)
 7
 8      ■  Sales, Washington's Birthday week: $20,945 ($13,111)
 9
10      ■  Average sales w/o Washington's Birthday week: $16,045 ($8,572)
11
12
13
14
```

Fig. 9.5. *The worksheet used to create the text chart in figure 9.4.*

In the previous text charts in this chapter, the major points are preceded by a marker. Figure 9.2, for example, uses asterisks. Allways doesn't have a good way to create bullets, but you can use multiple asterisks, lowercase O's, or the delta character (Δ), which appears on the printout as a roughly equilateral triangle. To produce a delta, press Alt–F1 (Compose) and type the compose sequence **dd**.

In Figure 9.4, the major points are marked with black squares. To create these squares, insert or set aside three empty columns to the left of the text, setting the width of each column to 1. Create a "bullet" by coloring a cell in the middle column black. With Allways active, highlight the appropriate cell, select **/F**ormat **S**hade **S**olid, and press Enter. In figure 9.5, solid shades are assigned to cells I4, I6, I8, and I10.

Creating Text-Only Charts with Wysiwyg (Releases 2.3 and 3.1)

You can create the chart shown in figure 9.6 using the Wysiwyg add-in program included with Releases 2.3 and 3.1.

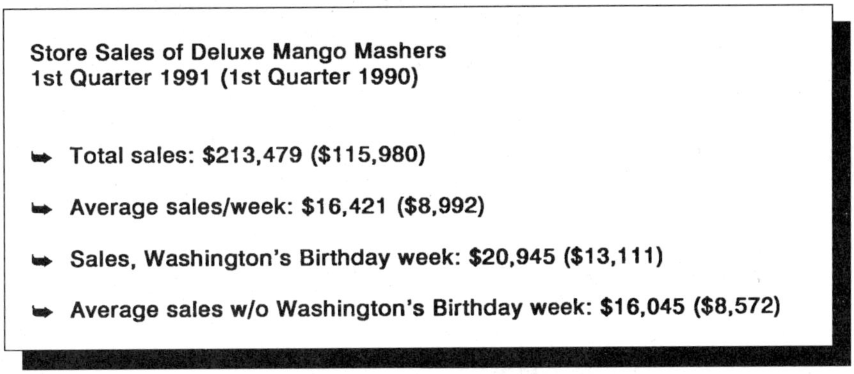

Store Sales of Deluxe Mango Mashers
1st Quarter 1991 (1st Quarter 1990)
Total sales: $213,479 ($115,980)
Average sales/week: $16,421 ($8,992)
Sales, Washington's Birthday week: $20,945 ($13,111)
Average sales w/o Washington's Birthday week: $16,045 ($8,572)

Fig. 9.6. A text chart created with Wysiwyg in Release 3.1.

Wysiwyg uses a different approach to centering text from the one used in Allways. Type the text you want to center in the extreme left column of the print range. Select **:T**ext **A**lign **C**enter and specify the range of columns with the text you want to center. In figure 9.7, the range is H1..O2.

A:H1: {Bold} [W3] ^Store Sales of Deluxe Mango Mashers
READY
A H I J K L M N O
1 re Sales of Deluxe Mango Mashers
2 1st Quarter 1991 (1st Quarter 1990)
5 Total sales: $213,479 ($115,980)
7 Average sales/week: $16,421 ($8,992)
9 Sales, Washington's Birthday week: $20,945 ($13,111)
11 Average sales w/o Washington's Birthday week: $16,045 ($8,572)

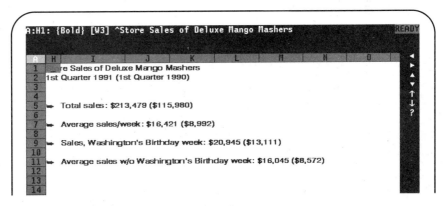

Fig 9.7. The worksheet used to create the chart in figure 9.6.

Wysiwyg doesn't offer an obvious way to create bullets, but you can make them using the raised period from 1-2-3's character set. Press Alt–F1 (Compose) and type a carat followed by a period (^.). The raised period character is larger in the Wysiwyg environment than in Allways. You can make raised periods even larger, more like bullets, by assigning a larger font to cells containing raised periods.

To mark points with other characters, you can use Wysiwyg symbols, one of which is shown in figure 9.6. In figure 9.7, the XSymbols 14-point font assigned to range H5..H10 converts the lowercase *e* in each cell to a curved arrow. To make 14-point **XSymbols** available, select **:Format Font Replace**. Type the number of an unused font, select **XSymbols**, and enter 14. Select **Quit Quit**. To turn *e*'s into curved arrows, select **:Format Font**, type the number associated with the XSymbol 14-point font, and specify the range containing the *e*'s.

Creating Graphs for Presentations

You can create a graph to solve the problem of the excess information in figure 9.1. The graph in figure 9.8 plots the values in range B5..B17 so that the information is condensed and presented pictorially. Chapter 7 of this book explains how easily you can create graphs in 1-2-3. Don't create as many graphs as possible each time you develop a worksheet, though. Creating a graph of weekly sales during a quarter, for example, is advantageous only if the sales exhibited a trend. Graphs should provide context for data, in addition to displaying the information in another form.

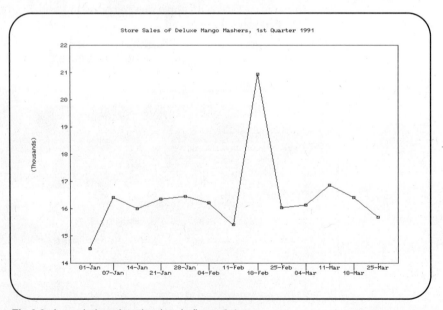

Fig 9.8. A graph that plots the data in figure 9.1.

Figure 9.9 shows a more meaningful graph. The bar graph instantly conveys how much the sales of mango mashers during the Washington's Birthday Sale exceeded the average and how the first quarter of this year compares to the same quarter of last year. Like the charts shown in figures 9.2, 9.4, and 9.6, this graph captures the important data without overwhelming the reader with details.

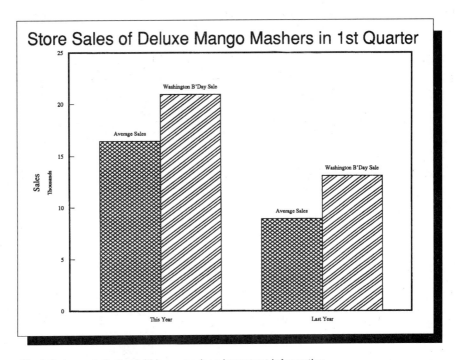

Fig 9.9. *A graph that quickly summarizes important information.*

Choosing the Correct Graph Type

Figure 9.10 is an exaggerated example of a line graph used incorrectly. Line graphs usually show how data changes over time, particularly when the data reveals a trend or cycle. In figure 9.10, the squares compare the sales of the various gadgets but the lines serve no purpose. Mango masher sales don't flow into dental-floss splicer sales. The sales of each product are discrete occurrences.

You can choose one of two graph types to represent the sales of the five gadgets. When you look at a bar graph (fig. 9.11), you can compare the values by the relative heights of the bars and see the real sales figures by comparing the bars to the scale on the left. Using the same figures in a pie graph format (fig. 9.12), you cannot discern the absolute values, but you easily can see how sales of the gadgets compare.

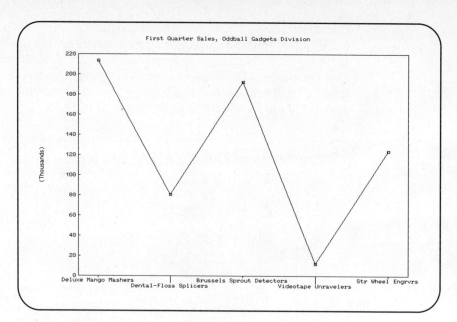

Fig 9.10. A line graph inappropriately comparing discrete categories.

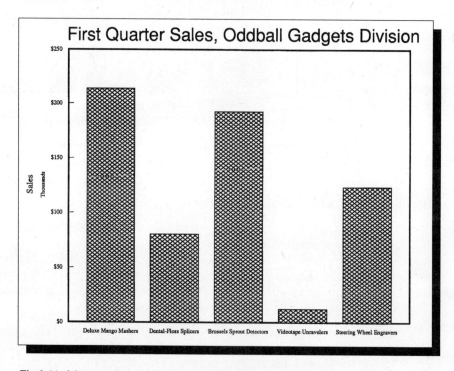

Fig 9.11. A bar graph that conveys relative sales and absolute sales.

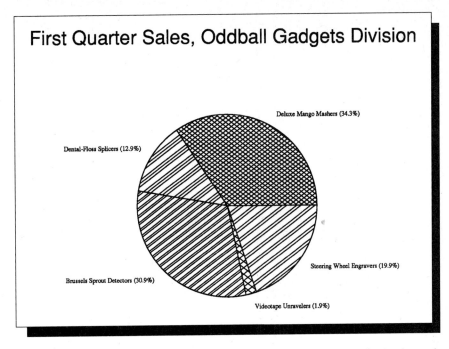

Fig 9.12. *A pie graph that shows relative sales but doesn't convey actual sales for each product.*

To choose between a bar graph and a pie graph, you must decide what information you want your audience to receive. Is it significant that mango mashers sold more than any other item and that videotape unraveler sales contributed only 1.9% of total gadget sales? Is it important that the audience learn that sales from each gadget range from $10,000 to $220,000?

1-2-3 can create a graph on the computer screen in several seconds; producing hard copy on a high-resolution printer takes time and ties up the hardware. When you prepare a presentation, preview each graph before printing and carefully consider whether it conveys the relevant information.

Adding Text to Graphs

Some presentations require only text, others only a pertinent graph. Sometimes, however, text needs support from a graph, or a graph can be made clearer with a short passage of text. In figure 9.13, the text under the graph explains to the reader why the company continues with the production and sale of videotape unravelers.

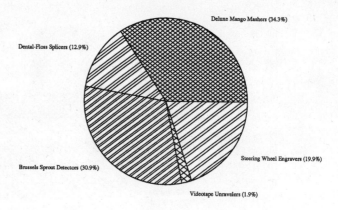

First Quarter Sales, Oddball Gadgets Division

Deluxe Mango Mashers (34.3%)

Dental-Floss Splicers (12.9%)

Steering Wheel Engravers (19.9%)

Brussels Sprout Detectors (30.9%)

Videotape Unravelers (1.9%)

NOTE: Although videotape unravelers seems to contribute little compared with sales of other gadgets, we are able to produce them more cheaply than our competitors. Given current market prices, this operation is quite profitable when considered on a per-piece basis.

Fig 9.13. A graph that incorporates text to explain the smallest pie wedge.

In the following sections, you learn how to create documents consisting of a graph with a brief passage of text. You have several options to choose, even if you don't have access to Allways or Wysiwyg, or you prefer not to use add-ins.

Combining Graphs and Text with Release 3.x /Print Commands

Releases 3 and 3.1 offer the most convenient way to create a text and graph combination, such as in figure 9.13. To create a graph and text combination, select **/P**rint and then **P**rinter or **E**ncoded. Select **I**mage and **C**urrent or **N**amed (for **N**amed, specify one of the worksheet's named graphs). Select **A**lign **G**o (don't select **P**age). Finally, select **R**ange and specify the range containing the text to be printed under the graph. Don't select **A**lign again; select **G**o **P**age **Q**uit.

Combining Graphs and Text with Allways (Release 2.2)

The most convenient way to print a text and graph combination with Release 2.2 is by using the Allways add-in program. To create a graph and text combination, you must save the graph as a PIC file. Start by selecting /Graph. If necessary, make the desired graph current by selecting **Name Use** and specifying the name. Then select **Save** and enter a file name.

After you create the PIC file, you can add the graph to the worksheet. With Allways active, select /Graph **Add**, specify the name of the PIC file, specify the range for the graph to occupy, and select **Quit**.

To print the graph and the block of text, select /Print **Range Set**, specify a range that includes the graph and the text, and select **Go**.

Combining Graphs and Text with Wysiwyg (Releases 2.3 and 3.1)

Printing a graph and text combination with Release 2.3 or 3.1 and Wysiwyg is similar to using Allways except you don't create a PIC file. With Wysiwyg, you can incorporate the current graph or a named graph into the worksheet. You also can incorporate a PIC file or a CGM (graphics metafile) file. Metafile is a standardized format created by many graphics products (including Lotus Freelance Plus).

To place a graph in the worksheet, select :Graph **Add** and then select **Current**, **Named**, **PIC**, or **Metafile**. If you select **PIC** or **Metafile** format, specify the path and name of the PIC or CGM file to use. Specify a range for the graph to occupy and then select **Quit**. To print the graph and the block of text, select :Print **Range Set**, specify a range that includes the graph and the text, and select **Go**.

Preserving the Shape of a Graph

A minor problem with using Allways or Wysiwyg is that getting a pleasing aspect ratio takes a bit of trial and error. You must practice to create perfectly round, nonelliptical pie graphs; therefore, you may prefer to use the regular Release 3.x /Print commands, as described earlier. If you use Release 2.x, you can use the included PrintGraph program with the regular /Print commands to add text to a graph. This task is somewhat inconvenient but preserves a graph's original aspect ratio.

To use PrintGraph, begin by saving the graph as a PIC file with /Graph **Save**. Save the worksheet that you used to create the graph by selecting /File **Save**. End your 1-2-3 session by selecting /Quit **Yes**, and start PrintGraph via the Access menu or by entering **PGRAPH** at the DOS prompt.

From the PrintGraph menu, select **Settings Image Size Half Quit Quit**, and then select **Action Eject No Quit Quit**. Select **Image-Select** and specify the PIC file you created with the 1-2-3 /Graph menu. Then select **Align Go**. PrintGraph prints the graph image. If you use a laser printer, you know the printing is finished when the mode indicator in the upper right corner of the screen stops flashing WAIT. When the graph finishes printing, select **Exit Yes**. Restart 1-2-3, retrieve the file containing the text to be printed, and print the text that you want to appear below the graph, using the regular 1-2-3 commands.

Adding Graphics to Existing Text

You can create a longer passage of text to illustrate with a graph by entering the text in 1-2-3 or by importing text from your word processing software (see fig. 9.14). To arrange text and graphs side-by-side, you must use Allways or Wysiwyg. Using PrintGraph or the Image option of the Release 3.x **/P**rint menu enables you to print graphs above or below text only.

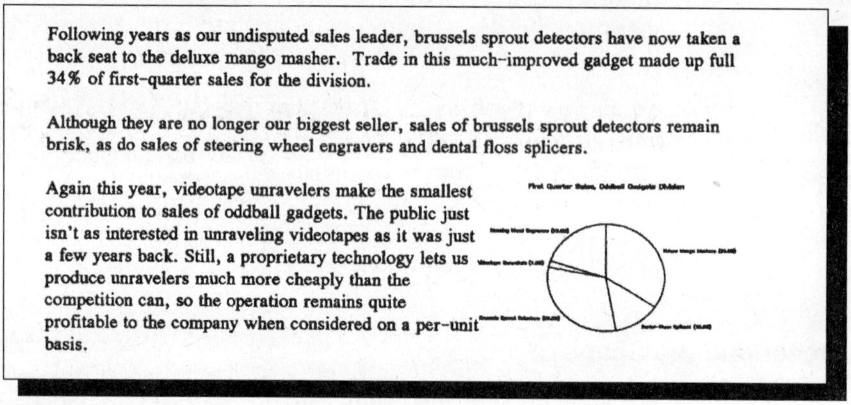

Following years as our undisputed sales leader, brussels sprout detectors have now taken a back seat to the deluxe mango masher. Trade in this much–improved gadget made up full 34% of first–quarter sales for the division.

Although they are no longer our biggest seller, sales of brussels sprout detectors remain brisk, as do sales of steering wheel engravers and dental floss splicers.

Again this year, videotape unravelers make the smallest contribution to sales of oddball gadgets. The public just isn't as interested in unraveling videotapes as it was just a few years back. Still, a proprietary technology lets us produce unravelers much more cheaply than the competition can, so the operation remains quite profitable to the company when considered on a per–unit basis.

Fig 9.14. *A printout created with Allways, featuring a long passage of text and a small pie graph.*

Mixing Text and Graphs with Allways (Release 2.2)

To create a text/graph combination like the one in figure 9.14 with Allways, enter or import the text, switch to Allways, and establish a print range (see fig. 9.15). Justify the text that will extend across the entire print range by selecting **/S**pecial **J**ustify and then specifying a range. Figure 9.16 was created by justifying range A1..H8. This justification leaves an extra line between the second and third paragraphs that is corrected in figure 9.17.

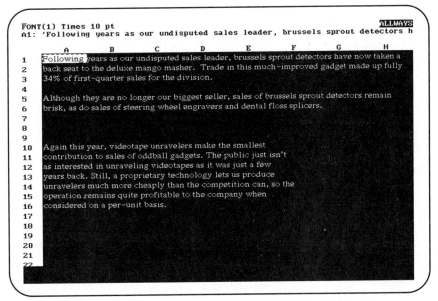

FONT(1) Times 10 pt   ALLWAYS
A1: 'Following years as our undisputed sales leader, brussels sprout

      A   B   C   D   E   F   G   H   I
1   Following years as our undisputed sales leader, brussels sprout
2   detectors have now taken a back seat to the deluxe mango masher.
3   Trade in this much-improved gadget made up fully 34% of
4   first-quarter sales for the division.
5
6   Although they are no longer our biggest seller, sales of
7   brussels sprout detectors remain brisk, as do sales of steering
8   wheel engravers and dental floss splicers.
9
10 Again this year, videotape unravelers make the smallest
11 contribution to sales of oddball gadgets. The public just isn't
12 as interested in unraveling videotapes as it was just a few
13 years back. Still, a proprietary technology lets us produce
14 unravelers much more cheaply than the competition can, so the
15 operation remains quite profitable to the company when
16 considered on a per-unit basis.
17
18
19
20
21
22
23
24
25
26

Fig 9.15. Text in the Allways environment before justification.

FONT(1) Times 10 pt   ALLWAYS
A1: 'Following years as our undisputed sales leader, brussels sprout detectors h

      A   B   C   D   E   F   G   H
1   Following years as our undisputed sales leader, brussels sprout detectors have now taken a
2   back seat to the deluxe mango masher. Trade in this much-improved gadget made up fully
3   34% of first-quarter sales for the division.
4
5   Although they are no longer our biggest seller, sales of brussels sprout detectors remain
6   brisk, as do sales of steering wheel engravers and dental floss splicers.
7
8
9
10 Again this year, videotape unravelers make the smallest
11 contribution to sales of oddball gadgets. The public just isn't
12 as interested in unraveling videotapes as it was just a few
13 years back. Still, a proprietary technology lets us produce
14 unravelers much more cheaply than the competition can, so the
15 operation remains quite profitable to the company when
16 considered on a per-unit basis.
17
18
19
20
21
22

Fig 9.16. The text from figure 9.15, after the first two paragraphs are justified.

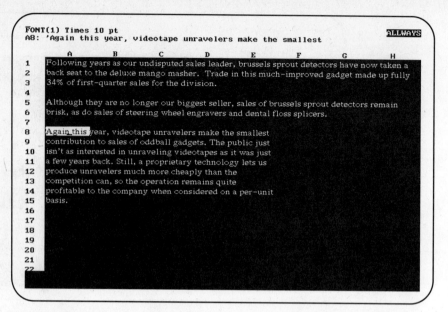

FONT(1) Times 10 pt
A8: 'Again this year, videotape unravelers make the smallest   ALLWAYS

	A	B	C	D	E	F	G	H
1	Following years as our undisputed sales leader, brussels sprout detectors have now taken a
2	back seat to the deluxe mango masher. Trade in this much-improved gadget made up fully
3	34% of first-quarter sales for the division.
4	
5	Although they are no longer our biggest seller, sales of brussels sprout detectors remain
6	brisk, as do sales of steering wheel engravers and dental floss splicers.
7	
8	Again this year, videotape unravelers make the smallest
9	contribution to sales of oddball gadgets. The public just
10	isn't as interested in unraveling videotapes as it was just
11	a few years back. Still, a proprietary technology lets us
12	produce unravelers much more cheaply than the
13	competition can, so the operation remains quite
14	profitable to the company when considered on a per-unit
15	basis.
16	
17	
18	
19	
20	
21	
22	

Fig 9.17. *The third paragraph, justified in a narrower range to accommodate a graph.*

You can move the third paragraph up one row without returning to the 1-2-3 environment. Specify a justification range that starts where you want the first row of text to appear. Justifying range A8..E16 creates the pattern shown in figure 9.17.

Now you can add the graph; in figure 9.18, the PIC file was added to the worksheet in range F8..H15. Print the text and graph using the Allways /Print commands.

Mixing Text and Graphs with Wysiwyg (Releases 2.3 and 3.1)

Arranging text and a graph within a print range is even easier with Release 2.3 or 3.1 and Wysiwyg. To combine text and graphs in Wysiwyg, add the graph to the print range; then justify the text by selecting :Text Reformat and specifying the range to contain the justified text
and the graph. In figure 9.19, a graph has been added to the worksheet in range F8..H15. In figure 9.20, range A1..H16 has been justified. Wysiwyg wraps the text around the graph. The figure 9.20 worksheet produces the printout in figure 9.21.

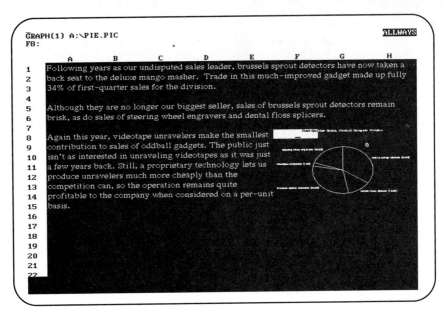

Fig 9.18. A graph added to the right of the third paragraph.

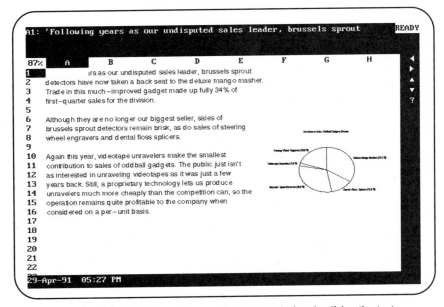

Fig 9.19. A graph added to the print range in Wysiwyg before justifying the text.

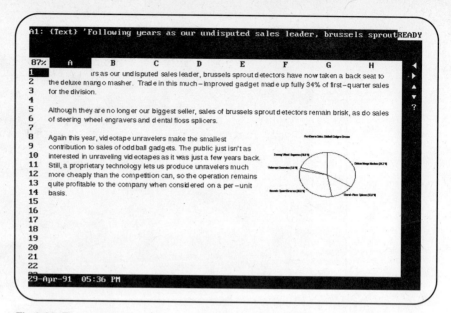

Fig 9.20. *The same print range after Wysiwyg justifies all three paragraphs around the pie graph.*

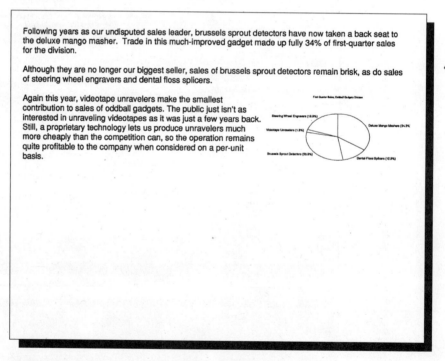

Fig 9.21. *A printed document created with Release 3.1 and Wysiwyg.*

Summary

In this chapter, you have seen some ways to create effective text charts and graphs. Experiment with ways to summarize and visualize data found in your own work environment. Always preview your work on-screen and in draft-quality printouts to judge its effectiveness. Then create high-quality output that gets the attention of your colleagues.

For more useful tips and information on creating presentation documents, see *1-2-3 Graphics Techniques*, Que Corporation, 1990.

The next chapter discusses ways to use 1-2-3 to simplify your financial and accounting applications.

Chapter Ten

USING 1-2-3 FOR FINANCIAL AND ACCOUNTING APPLICATIONS

T he original spreadsheet software, VisiCalc, was conceived as an aid to financial and accounting professionals. Indeed, the designation *electronic spreadsheet* comes from the fact that VisiCalc was designed as an electronic replacement for the large, ruled spreadsheets accountants use.

Over the years, spreadsheets have proved to be much more than mere financial tools. Still, the row-and-column structure and the selection of powerful financial functions make 1-2-3 ideal for financial and accounting tasks.

This chapter discusses the following aspects of using 1-2-3 in financial and accounting applications:

- Ways to work with financial functions
- How to perform financial calculations
- How to create loan-amortization tables
- How to create financial reports that conform to the interval of time covered
- How to date the rows of a financial report
- How to design financial worksheets that are easy to use

Modifying Financial Functions for Annuity-Due Calculations

The 1-2-3 financial functions that are related to equal periodic cash flows are based on ordinary annuity, in which cash flows occur at the ends of periods. These functions can be modified to account for annuity-due situations, in which cash flows occur at the beginnings of periods.

Suppose that you win $1 million in a lottery, to be paid at a rate of $40,000 for 25 years. If you can invest the money at 12 percent, you compute the present value of this arrangement by using the formula @PV(40000,0.12,25), which returns $313,725.56. But this formula assumes that you must wait a year to receive the first payment.

Suppose instead that the lottery commission issues the first check immediately. The first $40,000 doesn't lose any value by being delayed; in effect, you are receiving $40,000 plus $960,000 to be paid over 24 (not 25) years. To gauge the value of your winnings more accurately, you can use the following formula, which returns $351,372.63:

+40000+@PV(40000,0.12,24)

A different approach is to go back to the first formula but modify @PV by multiplying its result by 1 plus the interest rate, as in the formula @PV(40000,0.12,25)*1.12. This formula returns the same result.

You can modify other financial functions for annuity-due transactions in similar ways, using the following syntax:

@FV(*deposit*,*interest*,*term*)*(1+*interest*)

@TERM(*deposit*,*interest*,*future_value*/(1+*interest*))

@PMT(*principal*,*interest*,*term*)/(1+*interest*)

Using Financial Functions in Unusual Ways

The @PMT function returns the payment required to satisfy a loan, and several of the other financial functions compute values relating to annuities. With some small adjustments, you can use @PMT with annuities and use annuity-related functions with loans.

Calculating the Term of a Loan

@TERM computes the number of periods required for a fund to reach a desired future value when you know the interest rate and the per-period deposit. Consider the following formula:

@TERM(100,0.08/12,10000)

This formula returns 76.88, meaning that 77 months are required to acquire $10,000 by depositing $100 a month at 8% annual interest.

Normally, @TERM doesn't compute the term of a loan; however, if you use a minus sign before the function's third argument (*future_value*), the function returns the negative of a loan's term. Use another minus sign before the @ character, and the formula returns the term of a loan.

Suppose that you want to borrow $7,500, you can afford payments of $125 a month, and the interest rate at the local bank is 11 percent. The following formula returns 87.5, indicating that a $7,500 loan is repaid in 88 months:

– @TERM(125,0.11/12,–7500)

Calculating the Deposit Needed To Reach a Future Value

Use @PMT to compute the per-period deposit needed to reach a future value. Add a minus sign before the *term* argument and another before the function's @ character. The following formula, for example, indicates that you must deposit $144.50 per month in an account paying 8 percent per year to accumulate $50,000 in 15 years:

– @PMT(50000,0.08/12,–15*12)

Computing the Principal of a Loan

1-2-3 can compute the principal of a loan when you know the payment amount, the interest rate, and the term. Suppose that you want to know how large a mortgage you can get with payments of $750 per month, a current interest rate of 9.75%, and a 30-year term. One approach to getting this answer is to modify the @FV function, using the following formula:

– @FV(750,0.0975/12,–360)

This formula returns $87,295. Another way to arrive at this result is to remember that the amount the bank lends you is the present value of the stream of payments you will give to them. The following formula returns the same result ($87,295):

@PV(750,0.0975/12,360)

Computing Financial Values without a Designated Function

1-2-3 has no functions for determining the future value of a one-time investment or the present value of one payment to be made in the future. These values can be found with very simple formulas.

To determine the future value of a lump sum, add 1 to the interest rate, raise that sum to the power of the number of periods, and multiply the lump sum by that result. If you deposit $5,000 into an account paying 9 percent per year and leave the money for five years, the formula +5000*1.09^5 determines that your investment will reach a value of $7,693.12.

Keep the following points in mind. Use the monthly interest rate if the number of periods is in months. If you use a formula to compute the one-plus-interest portion of the formula, enclose the formula in parentheses. Figure 10.1 illustrates both points. The formula in cell C11 is +C5*(1+C7/12)^C9. The parentheses cause the formula to compute the interest rate before raising it to the seventh power; otherwise, the formula would raise 12 to the seventh power first.

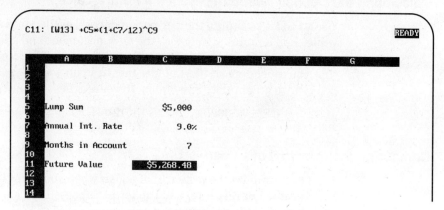

Fig. 10.1. *A formula (in cell C11) that computes the future value of a lump sum.*

Determining the present value of a one-time payment is the same except that you *divide* the payment amount by the exponential value. If someone who owes you $750 dollars offers to pay $1,000 in two years' time and you can invest money at 11% interest, the formula +1000/1.11^2 determines that the present value of $1,000 received two years from now is $811.62. The terms of the offer are therefore favorable to you.

Using the Release 3.x @VDB Function

Accountants use many methods for calculating depreciation. The @VDB function in Release 3.x enables you to calculate depreciation easily using the variable declining balance method. The following sections present ways to use the flexibility of @VDB and methods of applying this flexibility to the depreciation functions in Release 2.x.

The @VDB function includes options that enable you to customize the exact depreciation method used. The following examples illustrate methods you can use to specify fractional starting and ending years and varying depreciation rates, and to control the final period depreciation method.

The @VDB function is useful but complex; it requires five arguments and can accept up to seven. @VDB can compute depreciation based on factors other than 200 percent: use 150 percent, 300 percent, or any percentage you prefer. This function also can calculate depreciation for portions of years.

The syntax of @VDB is as follows:

@VDB(*cost*,*salvage*,*life*,*start_period*,*end_period*, *[depreciation]*,*[switch]*)

The last two arguments are optional. If you omit a depreciation factor, @VDB calculates depreciation based on double-declining balance (200 percent). The *switch* argument can be omitted, or it can be 0, 1, or any expression evaluating to 0 or 1.

The *switch* argument tells the function whether or not to switch to straight-line depreciation. If this argument is omitted or has a value of 0, @VDB switches to straight-line depreciation when that is greater than declining-balance depreciation. If the argument has a value of 1, the function never switches to straight-line depreciation.

The functions @SYD and @DDB can tell you only the depreciation occurring during an entire period. (Because depreciation periods are typically years, the remainder of this discussion of depreciation uses the term *year* instead of *period*.) The following formula, for example, returns the depreciation occurring in the third year in the life of a $50,000 asset with a $10,000 salvage value and a five-year life:

@DDB(50000,10000,5,3)

Because the depreciation factor is omitted, the following formula returns the same value:

@VDB(50000,10000,5,2,3)

@VDB offers more flexibility than @DDB because you can use fractional numbers for the *start_period* and *end_period* arguments. In the following formula, 1-2-3 returns the depreciation for only the last six months of the third year:

@VDB(50000,10000,5,2.5,3)

The *start_period* argument can be any value greater than or equal to zero but not greater than the *life* argument. The *end_period* argument can be any value greater than or equal to *start_period* but not greater than *life*.

You can think of @VDB as a variant of @DDB that enables you to specify portions of years. If you need to specify a different depreciation factor, however, you can use that factor as the sixth argument—for example, in the following formula (for 150% declining balance):

@VDB(50000,10000,5,2.5,3,1.5)

If your accounting practice is to continue depreciating at the declining-balance rate, add the value 1 as the seventh argument—for example, in the following formula:

@VDB(50000,10000,5,2.5,3,1.5,1)

Finally, if you want to use a switch value but let @VDB default to 200 percent, use two commas after the *end_period* argument, as in the following example:

@VDB(50000,10000,5,2.5,3,,1)

Figure 10.2 shows a worksheet that computes 150-percent declining-balance depreciation for each year in the life of a five-year asset.

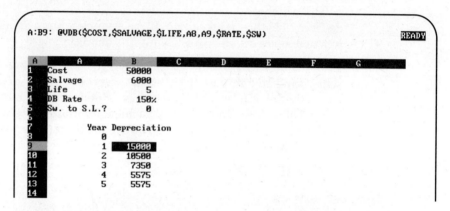

Fig. 10.2. A Release 3.x worksheet that calculates depreciation for a five-year asset based on 150 percent declining balance and a switch to straight-line depreciation.

Calculating Variable Depreciation with Releases 2.01 and 2.2

@VDB is not available with Releases 2.01 and 2.2, but you still can calculate depreciation (for entire years) using your choice of declining-balance rate, as the worksheet shown in figure 10.3 demonstrates.

You need one formula for the first period's depreciation and another for the remaining periods. In figure 10.3, the range names COST, SALVAGE, LIFE, and RATE are assigned to cells B1, B2, B3, and B4, respectively. The formula for the first period, in cell B7, is as follows:

```
@MIN(COST*RATE/LIFE,COST-SALVAGE)
```

The formula for the second period, in cell B8, is as follows:

```
@MIN(($COST-@SUM(B$7..B7))*$RATE/$LIFE,($COST-$SALVAGE)
  -@SUM(B$7..B7))
```

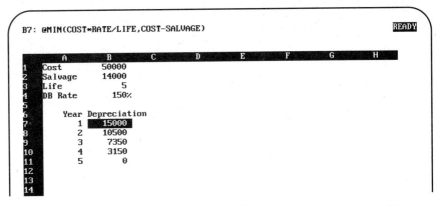

```
B7: @MIN(COST*RATE/LIFE,COST-SALVAGE)                         READY

         A          B          C      D      E      F      G      H
1   Cost         50000
2   Salvage      14000
3   Life             5
4   DB Rate       150%
5
6        Year Depreciation
7          1     15000
8          2     10500
9          3      7350
10         4      3150
11         5         0
12
13
14
```

Fig. 10.3. *A worksheet that (for any 1-2-3 version) calculates 150 percent declining-balance depreciation for a five-year asset.*

This formula is copied to range B9..B11.

As you copy the formula to the remaining cells, the @SUM function adjusts (because of the mixed reference B$7 in the first argument) to include all previous depreciation amounts. In cell B9, for example, the @SUM formula adjusts to `@SUM(B$7..B8)`. The overall formula thus applies the depreciation rate to the remaining nondepreciated balance.

The total depreciation is limited to the cost less the salvage value. In the fifth year, the sum of the previous years' depreciation amounts equals the cost less the salvage value, making the fifth year depreciation zero.

Creating an Amortization Table

You probably have seen worksheets that produce amortization tables. Such worksheets have appeared in other Que books, in *LOTUS* magazine, and in other places. When you got your computer, it probably came with a BASIC program to create amortization tables.

An *amortization table* analyzes a loan (often a mortgage) and computes how much of each payment goes to pay interest and how much goes to reduce the loan's outstanding principal. Figure 10.4 shows the first several rows of an amortization table. This information is important in business because accountants need to record amounts being spent to pay interest.

The math for amortization tables is simple but, if you don't have an amortization worksheet handy, you may find yourself hunting for a magazine article or book that explains how to build one. This section discusses some simple rules that can help you create an amortization worksheet from memory.

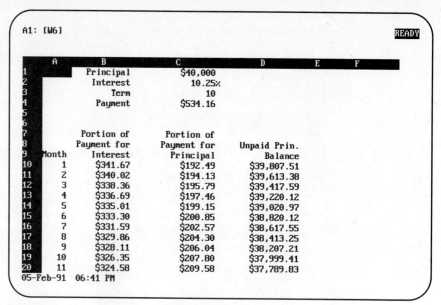

```
A1: [W6]                                                         READY

        A        B               C             D        E      F
1                Principal       $40,000
2                Interest        10.25%
3                   Term         10
4                Payment         $534.16
5
6
7                Portion of      Portion of
8                Payment for     Payment for
9      Month     Interest        Principal     Unpaid Prin.
                                               Balance
10      1        $341.67         $192.49       $39,807.51
11      2        $340.02         $194.13       $39,613.38
12      3        $338.36         $195.79       $39,417.59
13      4        $336.69         $197.46       $39,220.12
14      5        $335.01         $199.15       $39,020.97
15      6        $333.30         $200.85       $38,820.12
16      7        $331.59         $202.57       $38,617.55
17      8        $329.86         $204.30       $38,413.25
18      9        $328.11         $206.04       $38,207.21
19      10       $326.35         $207.80       $37,999.41
20      11       $324.58         $209.58       $37,789.83
05-Feb-91   06:41 PM
```

Fig. 10.4. *A simple loan-amortization table created in 1-2-3.*

Start by entering the principal, interest rate, term, and payment of the loan in a worksheet. How you organize these values is up to you, but the arrangement in figure 10.4 is as good as any.

If you don't know the amount of the payment, use the @PMT function to compute it. Remember to make any necessary adjustments to the *interest* and *term* arguments. If you enter an annual interest rate and a term expressed in years, for example, use the following formula to see the monthly payment:

@PMT(*principal,interest*/12,*term**12)

On the other hand, if you enter a monthly interest rate and a term in months, make no adjustments.

In the first month, the original principal of the loan accrues one month's interest, so multiply the principal by the monthly interest rate (or by the annual rate divided by 12). In figure 10.4, the formula in cell B10 is +C1*C2/12. The calculated amount of the first month's payment goes toward interest. Because the remainder goes toward principal, in the principal-payment column you subtract the first month's interest from the payment amount.

Be sure to use absolute cell references. In figure 10.4, the formula in cell C10 is +$C$4-B10.

The amount of the payment that goes toward principal also is the amount by which the unpaid principal is reduced. Subtract the principal portion of the first payment from the original principal to find the unpaid principal at the end of the first period. In figure 10.4, the formula in cell D10 is +C1-C10.

In the second and subsequent periods, the interest accrues on the preceding period's principal balance (not on the original principal). In the example, the formula in cell B11 is +D10*$C$2/12. Again, remember to use dollar signs to make the reference to the interest rate absolute. Copy the first period's principal-payment formula to the second period. Then create the second period's unpaid-balance formula using the previous balance instead of the original principal. In the example, cell D11 contains the formula +D10-C11.

Copy the second-period formulas into as many rows as necessary to get a complete table. In the example in figure 10.4, you copy range B11..D11 to range B12..B129.

These rules really are intuitive; take another minute or two to review them, and you always will have an instant loan-analysis table at your fingertips.

Creating Self-Sizing Financial Tables

Now that you understand the creation of the amortization table, you may want to build a deluxe version with design touches of your own, rather than an ad hoc table. You also may need to create a different kind of financial table with a layout resembling an amortization table.

You can devise a table that accommodates different lengths of time, such as varying loan terms. The following section demonstrates ways to build tables that take the term into account and avoid returning zeros, negative numbers, or ERRs beyond the last period. The amortization table is used as an example, but these techniques also apply to other kinds of tables.

Controlling the Size of a Table with Formulas

Figure 10.5 shows a table that uses formulas to "shut itself off." Because the formulas in columns A through D actually extend to row 370, the worksheet can accommodate loans with up to 360 periods (30 years). Because the loan in the example has a term of 10 years and starts in January of 1991, the table computes values through January of 2001 and returns empty character strings ("").

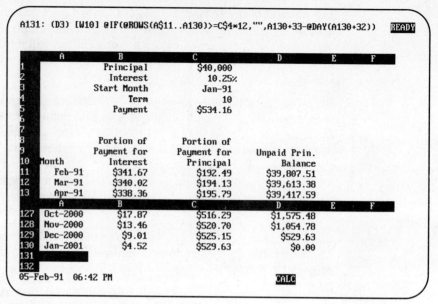

```
A131: (D3) [W10] @IF(@ROWS(A$11..A130)>=C$4*12,"",A130+33-@DAY(A130+32))        READY

           A          B              C             D          E      F
    1                Principal      $40,000
    2                Interest        10.25%
    3               Start Month     Jan-91
    4                 Term             10
    5                Payment       $534.16
    6
    7
    8              Portion of     Portion of
    9              Payment for    Payment for   Unpaid Prin.
   10  Month       Interest       Principal       Balance
   11   Feb-91      $341.67        $192.49       $39,807.51
   12   Mar-91      $340.02        $194.13       $39,613.38
   13   Apr-91      $338.36        $195.79       $39,417.59
           A          B              C             D          E      F
  127  Oct-2000     $17.87         $516.29        $1,575.48
  128  Nov-2000     $13.46         $520.70        $1,054.78
  129  Dec-2000      $9.01         $525.15          $529.63
  130  Jan-2001      $4.52         $529.63            $0.00
  131
  132
  05-Feb-91  06:42 PM                              CALC
```

Fig. 10.5. *A table that uses formulas returning empty strings to make the worksheet appear blank after the last period of the loan.*

The following formula is in cell A11:

    @DATEVALUE(C3)+33-@DAY(@DATEVALUE(C3)+32)

This formula converts the label in cell C3 to a date serial number and finds the first day of the following month. The formula in cell A12 reads as follows:

    @IF(@ROWS(A$11..A11)>=C$4*12,"",A11+33-@DAY(A11+32))

This formula returns an empty string if the number of rows from the top of the table to the preceding row equals or exceeds the term of the loan in months. If the formula doesn't return an empty string, it returns the value of the first day of the month following the month just above.

The cells in range B11..D11 use the first-period formulas (described earlier in this chapter) as follows:

Location	Formula
B11	+C1*C2/12
C11	+$C$5-B11
D11	+C1-C11

The remaining formulas in the table use the @IF function to determine whether the corresponding formula in column A returns a value. The individual cell formulas are as follows:

Location	Formula
B12	@IF(@ISNUMBER(A12),D11*$C$2/12,"")
C12	@IF(@ISNUMBER(A12),$C$5-B12,"")
D12	@IF(@ISNUMBER(A12),D11-C12,"")

After you have entered the formulas, copy range A12..D12 to range A13..A370. Now try entering different values in cell C4. The new values change the size of the area returning real numbers instead of empty strings.

Controlling the Size of a Table with Macros

You also can use a macro to copy the formulas into the appropriate number of rows. Enter the following formulas in row 12:

Location	Formula
A12	+A11+33-@DAY(A11+32)
B12	+D11*$C$2/12
C12	+$C$5-B12
D12	+D11-C12

Erase range A13..D370. Assign the name SECONDROW to range A12..D12 and the name TERM to cell C4. Enter the following macro in the worksheet:

```
{GOTO}SECONDROW~
/cSECONDROW~.{DOWN TERM*12-2}~
{CALC}
```

Assign the name \t to the first cell of the macro, and run the macro by pressing Alt–T. Assuming that cell C4 contains the number 10, this macro makes 118 copies of the second-period formulas, creating a table that accommodates 120 periods.

Still another approach is to use the simpler formulas, even if the table returns meaningless values after the last period of the loan. Then use a macro to print out the appropriate number of rows. Assign the name HEADER to range A1..D10 and enter the following macro in the worksheet:

```
{CALC}
/ppcrrHEADER~
r{DOWN TERM*12}~agpq
```

Assign the name \p to the macro's first cell, and run the macro by pressing Alt–P. Assuming that the term value is 10, 1-2-3 prints rows 1 to 10 of the worksheet plus 120 rows of the amortization table.

Dating Financial Tables Automatically

Many of the tables you create for financial and accounting reports show how values change at some regular interval of time. An amortization table is a good example. Typically, each row shows values for a calendar month; in other cases, you may need to create a column of dates a week apart.

As a general rule, enter a starting date in the top cell of the dates column, enter a formula in the second cell that computes the date for the second period, and copy that formula into the rest of the dates column. Or place in the top cell a formula that computes the starting date and use a different formula to compute the second and subsequent dates.

Several ways exist to date the rows of a table. The strategy you choose depends on your needs, but simple formulas usually can compute series of date values. Avoid using long @IF expressions that determine the number of days in the current month or determine if the current year is a leap year.

Creating Date Values at Weekly Intervals

Creating a series of dates a week apart is simple. After you have determined the date value for the starting date, increment that value by 7 with formulas or with /Data Fill.

Figure 10.6 shows a dummy table with weekly dates. Cell A7 contains the current date. Cell A8 contains the simple formula +A7+7 that is copied down column A.

To create the same stream of dates with the /Data Fill command, select /Data Fill, specify a fill range, enter @TODAY as the start value, enter 7 as the step value, and enter a very high number (for example, 100000) as the stop value. To use a different date as the start value, enter that date at the Enter start value: prompt. Use the formula @DATE (*year,month,day*) for Releases 2.01 and 2.2 or *MM/DD/YY* for Release 3.x.

You also can compute a starting date that falls on a given day of the week. If you want the dates in a table to be Mondays, for example, set the first cell in the dates column to compute the date number for the Monday following the current date (or a date entered elsewhere in the worksheet). Then enter the formula **+cellabove+7** and copy it to create a series of Mondays.

Assuming that you have entered a date (falling on any day of the week) in a cell named STARTDATE, use the following formula:

$$+\text{STARTDATE}+ 6 - @\text{MOD}(\text{STARTDATE}+x,7)$$

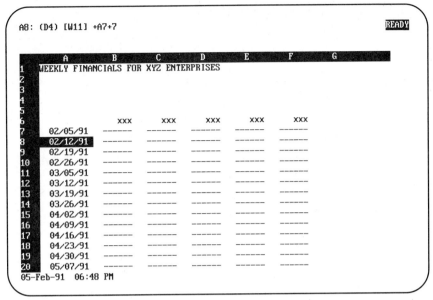

Fig. 10.6. *A worksheet that assigns dates a week apart to the rows of a financial table.*

(You can replace STARTDATE with any other expression evaluating to a date value, including @NOW or @TODAY.) Replace x with 6 for Saturdays, 5 for Sundays, 4 for Mondays, 3 for Tuesdays, 2 for Wednesdays, and 1 for Thursdays. Omit the $+x$ expression when creating a formula that returns the next Friday. If STARTDATE falls on the day of the week the formula is designed to return, the formula returns the value of STARTDATE.

To find the Monday following the current date, use the following formula (if the current date is a Monday, the formula returns the current date):

$$@TODAY+6 - @MOD(@TODAY+4,7)$$

To find the first Friday of the current year (this formula may be useful for payroll applications), use the following formula:

$$@DATE(@YEAR(@NOW),1,1)+6 - @MOD(@DATE(@YEAR(@NOW),1,1),7)$$

If you want the formula to compute the date of the first Thursday of the year, apply the rule discussed in the last paragraph and use the following formula:

$$@DATE(@YEAR(@NOW),1,1)+6 - @MOD(@DATE(@YEAR(@NOW),1,1)+1,7)$$

Creating Date Values at Monthly Intervals

When you want to date the rows of a table with months, the usual method is to write a series of formulas returning the first day of successive months and assign the month-and-year format to the formulas. Figure 10.7 shows an example of this type of formula.

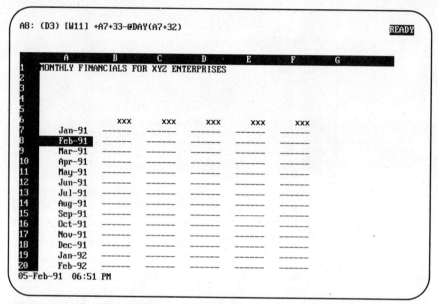

Fig. 10.7. *The rows of a table dated with the names of months, using the /Range Format Date 3 (month-and-year) format.*

The following short formula returns the first day of the month following the date in the cell above it:

$$+cellabove+33 - @DAY(cellabove+32)$$

If the table you're creating has many rows, use the preceding formula to save memory and shorten the worksheet's recalculation time. But be aware that the formula works reliably only when the date in *cellabove* falls early in the month. If you enter the formula @DATE(91,2,28) in cell B10, for example, the formula +B10+33−@DAY(B10+32) returns the date value for April 1, 1991, not March 1.

If you use the short formula, be sure that the first cell in the date column is the first of the month. One way to accomplish this objective is to use text in the worksheet to instruct the user to enter a date formula for the first of the month in the first cell of the dates column. Another alternative is to tell the user to enter any date during the starting month in a cell outside of the table, and (in the first cell of the dates column) use the formula +STARTDATE – @DAY (STARTDATE)+1. This formula always returns the first day of STARTDATE's month.

A third strategy has the user enter the date as a label in a cell outside the table. The label takes the format MMM–YY, for example Apr–91. With Releases 2.01 and 2.2, the formula in the first cell of the table would be @DATEVALUE(STARTDATE). The @DATEVALUE function converts the label Apr–91 to 33329, the value for April 1, 1991.

The following (longer) formula *always* returns the first day of the next month:

$$@DATE(@YEAR(cellabove)+(@MONTH(cellabove)=12,@MOD$$
$$(@MONTH(cellabove),12)+1,1)$$

Sometimes you may want the date column to state explicitly that the rows pertain to the first of each month. Use one of the approaches just discussed but assign the long Lotus standard or the long international date format to the formulas.

If only the name of the month is relevant, you can label the rows of the table with the months spelled out in full, as shown in figure 10.8. The trick is to set up a simple lookup table like the one shown in figure 10.9 and assign a name like NXTMONTH to it. Then use the following formula to return the name of the following month:

$$@VLOOKUP(cellabove,$NXTMONTH,1)$$

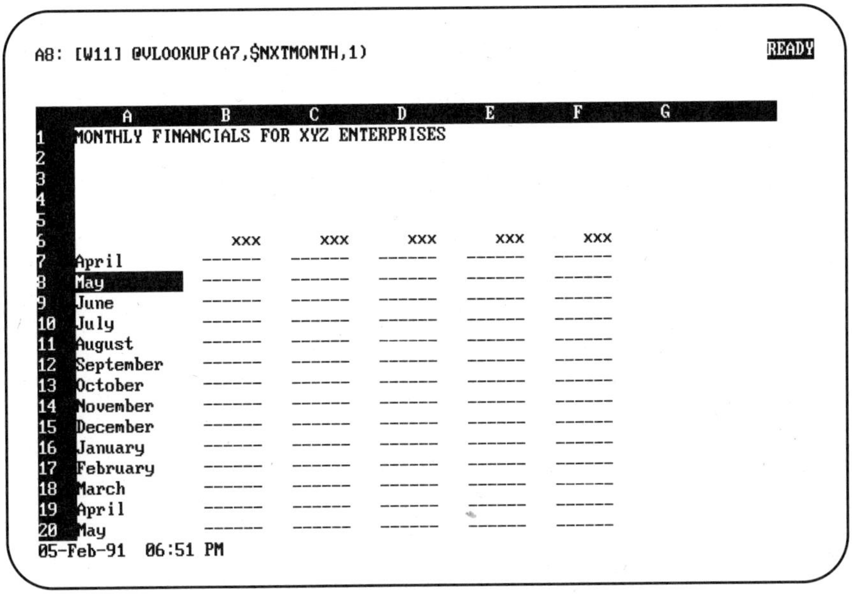

Fig. 10.8. *@VLOOKUP formulas (in column A) that return the full names of months (using any starting month in the first cell).*

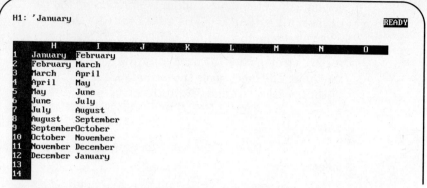

	H	I	J	K	L	M	N	O
1	January	February						
2	February	March						
3	March	April						
4	April	May						
5	May	June						
6	June	July						
7	July	August						
8	August	September						
9	September	October						
10	October	November						
11	November	December						
12	December	January						
13								
14								

Fig. 10.9. *A lookup table that lets a formula return the month following the month in the cell above it.*

You can enter the name of any month in the first cell of the date column to start the cycle. If you want the first cell to return the name of the current month, use the following formula:

@VLOOKUP(@MONTH(@NOW) –1,NXTMONTH,0).

In some cases, you may want to label the rows of a table with the *last* day of each month, as shown in figure 10.10. As long as the formula in the first cell returns the last day of the month, the formula +*cellabove*+33–@DAY(*cellabove*+33) returns the last day of the following month. In figure 10.10, the formula in cell A7 is @DATE(91,1,31).

Most daunting are the times when you want a column of formulas to return the same day from successive months but return the last day of a month where appropriate when the beginning date is after the 28th of the month. The formula for the second and subsequent cells is long but shorter than anything you can get if you try to compute such a date with @IF functions. The formula is as follows:

@DATE(@YEAR(*cellabove*)+(@MONTH(*cellabove*)=12),
    @MOD(@MONTH(*cellabove*),12)+1,@MIN(@DAY($*cellabove*),
        @DAY(*cellabove*+33–@DAY(*cellabove*+33))))

Note the absolute reference in this formula, before the first *cellabove* in the @MIN expression. Be sure to use an absolute reference for the range name (or both column and row of a cell reference) when you use this formula.

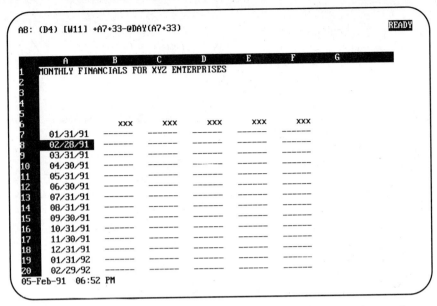

Fig. 10.10. Formulas (in column A) that return the last day of the respective month.

Using Formulas To Age Receivables

A common task in financial management is organizing outstanding accounts receivables into age categories. Most firms determine percentages of the amounts not yet due, zero to 30 days past due, 31 to 60 days past due, and so forth to write off as bad debt. A company may consider as a matter of accounting practice that one percent of monies not yet due ultimately will be uncollectible. By contrast, 12 percent of monies more than 90 days past due will be uncollectible. (The other categories fall somewhere between the two extremes.) The percentage to apply to each category varies from one firm to the next. If a company is owed $6,124 in accounts more than 90 days overdue and uses 12% for that category, accounting posts $735 to a category called Allowance for Doubtful Accounts.

Figure 10.11 shows a list of receivables. Column C contains the due dates and column D contains the amounts of the transactions. Each formula in column B subtracts the date in the cell to its right from the current date and uses the difference to look up a label in the lookup table (range E1..F5). The following formula, for example, is in cell B4:

```
@VLOOKUP(@TODAY-C4,$AGE_TABLE,1)
```

NOTE

If you enter the formula using **@TODAY**, *Release 2.x changes that expression to* @INT(@NOW).

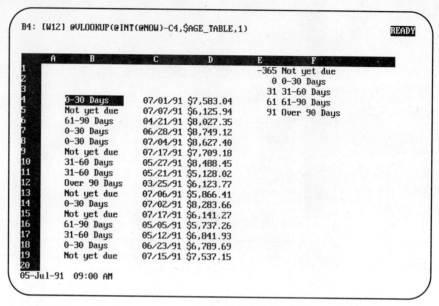

B4: [W12] @VLOOKUP(@INT(@NOW)-C4,$AGE_TABLE,1)   READY

	A	B	C	D	E	F
1					-365	Not yet due
2					0	0-30 Days
3					31	31-60 Days
4		0-30 Days	07/01/91	$7,583.04	61	61-90 Days
5		Not yet due	07/07/91	$6,125.94	91	Over 90 Days
6		61-90 Days	04/21/91	$8,027.35		
7		0-30 Days	06/28/91	$8,749.12		
8		0-30 Days	07/04/91	$8,627.40		
9		Not yet due	07/17/91	$7,709.18		
10		31-60 Days	05/27/91	$8,488.45		
11		31-60 Days	05/21/91	$5,128.02		
12		Over 90 Days	03/25/91	$6,123.77		
13		Not yet due	07/06/91	$5,866.41		
14		0-30 Days	07/02/91	$8,283.66		
15		Not yet due	07/17/91	$6,141.27		
16		61-90 Days	05/05/91	$5,737.26		
17		31-60 Days	05/12/91	$6,841.93		
18		0-30 Days	06/23/91	$6,789.69		
19		Not yet due	07/15/91	$7,537.15		
20						

05-Jul-91 09:00 AM

Fig. 10.11. *Formulas (in column B) that classify the list of receivables by age.*

After you have created a set of formulas telling you the age groups of the accounts, you have several ways to proceed. A very simple approach is to sort columns C and D by date in descending order and then recalculate the worksheet, as shown in figure 10.12. This method makes finding the totals for each category easy. (Chapter 11 describes a simple method for computing subtotals for a sorted list.)

When you have the subtotals for each age group, you can multiply them by the percentages in use in your company to determine the amount for Allowance for Doubtful Accounts.

Creating Bullet-Proof Financial Models

Using a sinking-fund worksheet as an example, the rest of this chapter discusses techniques for building easy-to-use, mistake-resistant financial templates. The sinking-fund model concepts also apply to loan-amortization tables and other financial and accounting applications.

A sinking fund is set up for the purpose of acquiring a certain amount of money by a certain time. Suppose that a company must make a $100,000 expenditure (or pay off a $100,000 balloon payment) in April of 1997 and sets up an interest-bearing account in which to make monthly deposits. Accounting needs to record the interest earned by the account each month, and creates the table shown in figure 10.13.

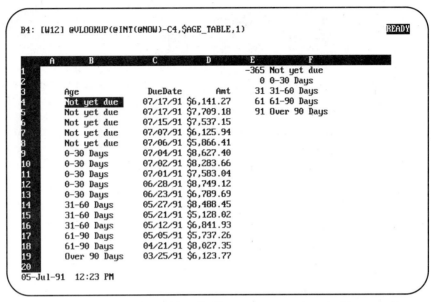

Fig. 10.12. Transaction amounts classified by age group and receivables sorted by due date.

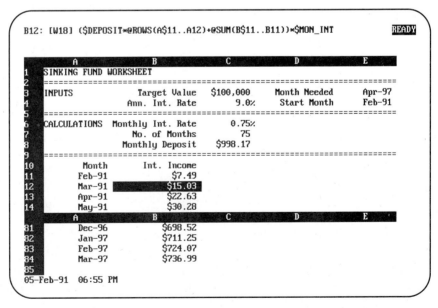

Fig. 10.13. A sinking fund table that computes the interest earned by an account each month.

The mathematics of this model are simple. To compute the interest earned in a given month, sum the deposits made through that month plus the interest earned in previous months, and multiply the result by the monthly interest rate.

Rows 3 and 4 of figure 10.13 are used for input values. The labels identifying the input cells tell the user what belongs in those cells; furthermore, the labels "ask for" values that most likely reflect the way you think about a sinking fund. Cell C4 is used for the annual interest rate; formulas in other parts of the worksheet use the monthly interest rate in their calculations. Banks generally don't quote monthly interest rates when describing their savings products. Having the user enter the annual rate is easier—and less prone to errors—than labeling the cell Monthly Interest Rate and expecting the user to mentally divide the bank's rate by 12, or to enter the annual rate followed by /12.

Similarly, cells E3 and E4 are used for information the user already knows: the month that the target value is needed and the month the deposits will start. The model doesn't expect you to know that 75 months exist from February 1991 through April 1997. In a loan-amortization model, because you probably know the term of the loan in years, the model includes a cell for the term next to a label reading Term (Yrs). For a 15-year loan, you enter **15**, not 180 or 15*12.

Rows 6 to 8 of figure 10.13 perform the arithmetic for you. Cell C6 computes the monthly rate with the formula +C4/12. This cell is named MON_INT.

Cell C7 calculates the number of months from the first deposit to withdrawal of the target amount, which is used to calculate the monthly deposit amount. Its formula is as follows:

```
(@YEAR(E3)*12+@MONTH(E3))-(@YEAR(E4)*12+@MONTH(E4))+1
```

Cell C8 computes the monthly deposit needed to reach the target amount, using the @PMT functions with modifications for annuities, as discussed earlier in this chapter. The following formula is in this cell (named DEPOSIT):

```
-@PMT(C3,MON_INT,-C7)
```

Cell A11 computes the first day of the starting month with the formula +E4-@DAY(E4)+1. The remaining formulas in column A return the date numbers for the first days of subsequent months. Cell A12's formula is +A11+33-@DAY(A11+32), copied to range A13..A84.

Cell B11 computes the interest earned in the first month by multiplying the monthly payment value in cell C8 by the monthly interest rate in cell C6. Cell B12 computes the interest in the second month. It starts by computing the sum of the deposits through the second month with the following expression:

```
DEPOSIT*@ROWS(A$11..A12)
```

The expression `@ROWS(A$11..A12)` returns 2. Because of the dollar sign in `A$11`, each copy of the formula references a larger range, and the `@ROWS` expressions in range A13..A84 evaluate to 3, 4, 5, 6, and so on.

The formula then adds the sum of the previous periods' interest earnings with the expression `@SUM(B$11..B11)`. Again, because this expression refers to a larger and larger range as it is copied down column B, it always returns the sum of the interest amounts from cell B11 to the cell one row above the formula. Finally, the sum of the payments to date and the previous interest is multiplied by the monthly interest rate in cell C6. The entire formula in cell B12 is as follows:

```
(DEPOSIT*@ROWS(A$11..A12)+@SUM(B$11..B11))*$MON_INT
```

You can use an @ROWS expression like the one in this formula anywhere you usually create a column of ascending values to be used as expressions in formulas.

Figure 10.14 shows a more common approach to a sinking-fund model.

```
A1: [W14] 'SINKING FUND WORKSHEET                                    READY

           A              B              C            D              E
1   SINKING FUND WORKSHEET
2   ===================================================================
3   INPUTS            Target Value   $100,000    Month Needed      Apr-97
4                     Ann. Int. Rate     9.0%    Start Month       Feb-91
5   ===================================================================
6   CALCULATIONS  Monthly Int. Rate     0.75%
7                 No. of Months            75
8                 Monthly Deposit     $998.17
9   ===================================================================
10       Period #      Int. Income
11           1           $7.49
12           2          $15.03
13           3          $22.63
14           4          $30.28
15           5          $38.00
16           6          $45.77
17           7          $53.60
18           8          $61.49
19           9          $69.43
20          10          $77.44
05-Feb-91  06:56 PM
```

Fig. 10.14. *An alternative sinking fund worksheet, where column A contains period numbers used to compute deposits to date.*

Instead of month-and-year combinations, this model uses a column of "period numbers," from 1 to 84. Rather than multiplying the deposit amount by an @ROWS expression, each formula in column B multiplies the deposit by the period number on its own row. The results are the same and the worksheet pictured in figure 10.14, when saved, creates a file almost 2,500 bytes smaller than the worksheet shown in figure 10.13. The worksheet in figure 10.13, however, is easier to interpret. You can tell at a glance how much interest the fund will earn in March of 1994.

Again, the techniques discussed here are intended to make the sinking fund model as "user-friendly" as possible. Even if you never need to create a sinking fund worksheet, you can apply these techniques in your other financial and accounting applications.

Summary

This chapter has focused on some of the specific tools used for creating worksheets for analyzing and managing financial undertakings (notably the financial functions). You have gained a broad view of two common financial models, the amortization table and the sinking fund table. You also have learned some strategies for dating and controlling the size of financial tables and for making such tables easy to use.

The next chapter of this book covers the use of 1-2-3 as a database manager, discussing efficient ways to store and retrieve your data.

Chapter Eleven

USING 1-2-3 AS A DATABASE MANAGER

W hen you organize and store large quantities of data in 1-2-3
files, you can use 1-2-3's database capabilities to gain specific
knowledge from the data. With a database, you can accomplish
anything from computing the average salary of a company's
minority employees to producing a detailed listing showing the activity of west
coast sales people.

This chapter covers all of the following topics:

- How to manipulate criteria ranges to get the exact information
you want

- How to devise output ranges that don't corrupt worksheet data

- How to make database statistical functions more flexible

- How to create larger disk-based databases with Release 3.x

- How to generate a variety of useful reports from your database

Selecting Criteria Ranges

When you perform the database operations **F**ind, **E**xtract, **U**nique, and
Delete, or use @D functions, you want the results to reflect the desired
records only. Criteria ranges give you control over which records are
selected.

The basic use of criteria ranges is simple. Suppose that you want to
perform a database operation to select records where the department is
Admin. In an empty area of the worksheet, enter the name of the department field; for example, type **Dept**. (Better yet, copy the field heading
from the top row of the database range to ensure an exact match between the field name in the database range and the one in the criteria
range.) Enter the label **Admin** directly under the field name. Specify

these two cells as the Criteria range when you perform a /Data Query operation or as the third argument in an @D formula. To select records with Admin or HR in the Dept field, enter **HR** in the cell directly below Admin and use all three cells as the criteria range.

A criteria range must be at least two rows high. The first row contains the field name or names and the second contains the first criterion. Unless you are using Release 3.x, the criteria range must contain exactly enough rows to accommodate the criteria you specify. With Release 2.2 and earlier, if the criteria range contains any empty rows, the database operation or @D function uses all records. Release 3.x disregards empty rows as long as at least one of the rows in the criteria range contains criteria.

Ensuring Accurate Record Selection

Suppose that your worksheet contains a database of company employees and you want to create a listing of female employees. Unless you are careful, you may get a list of *all* employees (male and female) or a list including female salaried employees only.

To get a listing of female employees, you typically need a criteria range containing the label F in the Sex field. All other fields in the criteria range must be blank, or the database operation may select some subset of the records for female employees. Figure 11.1 shows such a problematic criteria range. With the label Sal in cell AD2, you don't get a full listing of female employees when you issue the /Data Query Extract command. If you create macros to perform database operations, the likelihood of getting undesirable results increases.

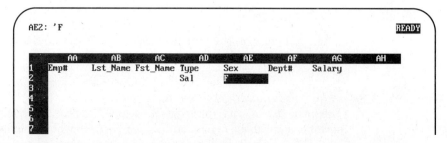

Fig. 11.1. *A criteria range resulting in a list of employees who are female and salaried.*

The simplest way to avoid problems is to use caution with the criteria range. After selecting /Data Query (but before selecting Extract, Unique or Delete), select Criteria and review the range that 1-2-3 highlights. Make sure that it includes the correct number of rows and no unwanted criteria.

Another strategy is to set up several areas to be used as criteria ranges for different types of reports; for example, set up a two-cell range containing the column heading for the `Sex` field and the letter `F` below it and assign the range name FCRIT to these cells. When you want a listing of female employees, select **/D**ata **Q**uery Criteria and specify FCRIT, or include in a macro the instruction `/dqcFCRIT~`.

You can use as many specialized criteria ranges as necessary. To create a list of salaried female employees, for example, use a range like the one in figure 11.2, with the name FSALCRIT assigned to the range AA1..AB2.

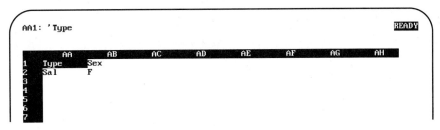

Fig. 11.2. *A specialized criteria range that produces a listing of salaried female employees.*

Specifying Multiple Criteria

You may want to select records satisfying several criteria or matching at least one of several criteria. For these operations, think of the criteria as statements connected by AND or OR.

To create a listing of male employees with salaries over $45,000, for example, you can instruct 1-2-3 to select records where the `Sex` field contains `M` AND the salary field contains a value greater than 45000.

Suppose that you want a listing of employees who are female and members of a racial minority. Don't be confused by the word *and* in the preceding sentence. What you want is records where the `Sex` field contains `F` OR the `Ethnic Group` field doesn't contain `Caucasian`. (Or both—when dealing with database queries, as a general rule, the idea of *or* doesn't include an implied "but not both.")

You can connect criteria with AND and OR in several ways, not necessarily involving the 1-2-3 operators #AND# and #OR#.

Connecting Criteria with AND

The simplest way to specify two or more criteria, all of which must be met, is to arrange the criteria on the same row of the criteria range.

Figure 11.3 shows a criteria range that produces a listing of male employees with salaries over $45,000. The criteria range is R1..S2. Cell R2 contains the label M. Cell S2 contains the formula +F8>45000. The formula assumes that cell F8 is the first cell below the field name Salary in the database. Using this criteria range, a database operation selects only records with M in the Sex field and values higher than 45000 in the Salary field.

In Release 3.x, you can enter the formula in cell S2 as **+SALARY>45000**, *or enter the label* **'>45000**.

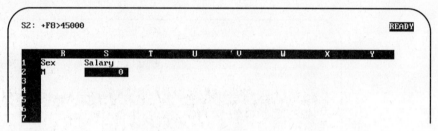

Fig. 11.3. *A criteria range that produces a listing of employees who are male AND have salaries over $45,000.*

With all versions, this approach selects records satisfying two or more criteria, each of which involves a *different* field.

Occasionally you may want to select records meeting two criteria related to the *same* field. Suppose that your database contains a column of identifier numbers using prefix letters and suffixes, as shown in figure 11.4. To extract all records in which the prefix is E AND the suffix is .3, use the formula shown in the control panel. This formula works with any version of 1-2-3.

With Release 2.x, you must use the #AND# operator. Under the heading Student ID in the criteria range, enter the following formula:

@LEFT (A8,1)= "E"#AND#@RIGHT(A8,1)="3"

If all of the entries in column A have the same number of characters, you also can use the label **E??????3**.

With Release 3.x, you can use the same method, or create a criteria range containing the same field more than once. Figure 11.5 shows an example. The criteria range, A4..B5, contains two Student ID field headings. Under the first is the label E*, which tells 1-2-3 to select all records where the student number begins with E. Under the second is the formula @RIGHT(A8,1)="3", which selects records where the student number ends with 3. A record must meet both criteria to be selected. This technique doesn't work in versions prior to Release 3; 1-2-3 ignores the second `Student ID` field and selects all records where the student number begins with E.

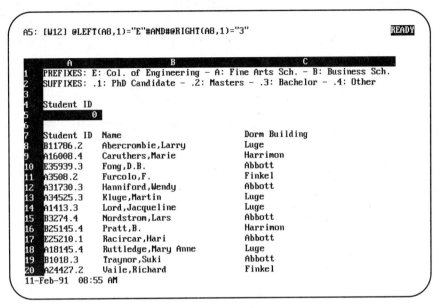

Fig. 11.4. A formula that selects records where one field meets two criteria.

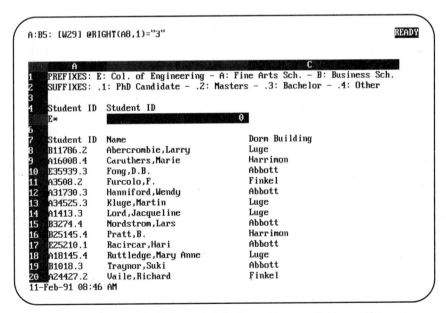

Fig. 11.5. A criteria range (in Release 3.x) that uses the same field more than once.

Connecting Criteria with OR

To select records matching at least one of several criteria, arrange the criteria on several rows of the criteria range. Figure 11.6 shows a criteria range that selects records where the `Sex` field contains F OR the `Ethnic Group` field contains a letter other than W. (The formula in cell S3 assumes that the first cell in the `Ethnic Group` field is cell J8.)

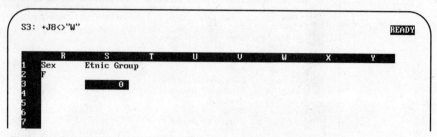

Fig. 11.6. *Criteria arranged on different rows to find records meeting any of the criteria.*

Connecting criteria with OR when the criteria pertain to the same field is not a problem in any version of 1-2-3. Figure 11.7 shows a criteria range that selects a record if the dorm building is Harrimon OR Abbott. If you prefer, enter the formula **+C8="Harrimon"#OR#C8="Abbott"** in cell C4 and specify range C3..C4 as the criteria range.

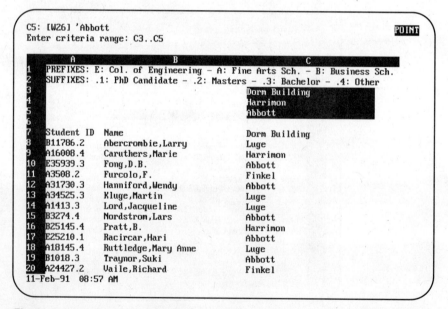

Fig. 11.7. *A criteria range that selects records where the* Dorm Building *field matches either of two criteria.*

Using Combinations of AND and OR

With a little planning, you can create criteria ranges that select any combination of records. Figure 11.8 shows a criteria range that selects records for female employees in department 4302 and employees of both sexes in department 4306. 1-2-3 selects a record if the department number is 4302 AND the sex is F OR if the department number is 4306.

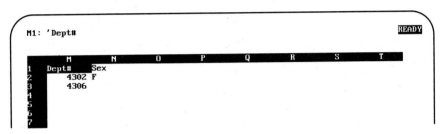

Fig. 11.8. Criteria connected with AND and OR logic.

Creating Safe Output Ranges

1-2-3 accepts two kinds of output ranges for use with the /Data Query Extract command. If you specify only the row containing the field names, 1-2-3 regards the output range as extending to the bottom of the worksheet (to row 8192). If you specify the row of field names and some rows below it, 1-2-3 limits the output range to the specified rows.

Choosing the latter option and performing an Extract operation that selects more records than rows existing in the output range causes 1-2-3 to copy as many records as possible to the output range and then display the error message Too many records for output range.

If you specify the row containing field names as the output range, 1-2-3 doesn't overfill the output range, but the Extract and Unique operations erase entries in the output range columns all the way down to row 8192.

One good way to avoid problems with choosing an output range is to use a macro that creates an output range tailored to the size of the extracted records.

Begin by creating a set of field names for the fields you want in the output range, arranged along one row at the top of an empty area of the worksheet. Assign the range name OUTPUTROW to the row containing these field names. Assuming that you have assigned the names DB to the database (input) range and CRIT to the criteria range, include the following instruction in a macro:

```
'/dqiDB~cCRIT~oOUTPUTROW~o{DOWN @DCOUNT(DB,x,CRIT)}~eq
```

Replace *x* with the number of a column in the database range containing no empty cells. This instruction establishes the row of field headings as the output range, reissues the Output command, and expands the range by pressing {DOWN} once for each record in the database matching the specified criteria. The output range exactly accommodates the records, and the Extract operation doesn't erase any entries below the output range.

Using Field Names in Database Functions

Releases 3 and 3.1 accept a field name enclosed in quotation marks as the column-offset argument in a database statistical function. To compute the average of salary-column values associated with records that match criteria, for example, you can use the formula @DAVG (DB,"SALARY",CRIT). In Releases 2.2 and earlier, the column-offset argument must be the number of the salary column or an expression evaluating to that number. If the salary column is the fourth column from the left, use the formula @DAVG(DB,3,CRIT). (You use 3 instead of 4 for the column number because the far left column is column 0.)

Using column names in Release 3.x is more than just convenient. With this option, you can adjust the database—adding, removing, or rearranging columns—without being forced to edit all of the @D formulas in the worksheet.

You can use field names in @D formulas in Release 2.x if you incorporate the name into an @HLOOKUP expression within the @D function, as in the following formula:

@DAVG(DB,@HLOOKUP("SALARY",DB,0),CRIT)

This formula works because @HLOOKUP returns position numbers when the offset row is 0 and contains labels (rather than values). The expression @HLOOKUP("SALARY",DB,0) returns the column number with the field name SALARY. This formula continues to work even if the salary column changes position within the database, like the @DAVG(DB,"SALARY",CRIT) formula in Release 3.x.

Managing Disk-Based Databases with Release 3.x

With the Release 3.x /Data External command, you can create and establish connections between 1-2-3 and external tables, use the /Data Query command to exchange data with these external tables and use the @D functions to extract data. You also can use any /Data Query Modify options supported by your database driver program.

These database driver programs are called *DataLens drivers*. Release 3.x comes with a DataLens database driver called SAMPLE that provides access to files stored in the dBASE III DBF file format. The SAMPLE database driver is described in Appendix 7 of the 1-2-3 Release 3.1 reference manual. Lotus sells another DataLens driver that provides access to SQL (Structured Query Language) database servers. You can get DataLens drivers for other database management products from the companies that make those products.

A database driver may not support all options of the **/D**ata **Q**uery command (particularly the **M**odify options) or all 1-2-3 @D functions. The SAMPLE driver, for example, doesn't support a number of important features. See the documentation for your driver to determine which 1-2-3 features are supported.

Because the 1-2-3 SAMPLE database driver can create dBASE III-compatible files, you can create Release 3.x applications to share data with dBASE III. You don't need a copy of dBASE III to create these files, modify the contents, or extract the data into your worksheet.

Accessing External Data Tables

To access an existing external data table, you must establish a connection to the table with the **/D**ata **E**xternal **U**se command. Specify the full table name, consisting of the name of the DataLens database driver and the name of the external table. For the sample EMPFILE.DBF database provided with Release 3.x, the database driver name is SAMPLE. The external database name is the name of the directory containing the DBF files. The **/D**ata **E**xternal command considers an external database to be all of the external tables of a particular format within a directory. All dBASE III-format DBF files in the directory C:\123R3\DBF, for example, constitute an external database. The name of the external table is EMPFILE.

When you select **/D**ata **E**xternal **U**se, 1-2-3 displays a list of all installed DataLens database drivers. Specify the driver you want and then select a subdirectory to serve as an external database. 1-2-3 displays a list of all external tables in the external database. By selecting the external table, you complete the full table name.

After selecting the external table, 1-2-3 displays the `Enter range name for table:` prompt. Enter a range name that 1-2-3 can use as a pointer for the external table. The default name appearing in the prompt is the same as the external table name. Accept the default range name by pressing Enter, or enter a different range name. Don't use a name already assigned to a range in your 1-2-3 worksheet unless you want to replace the existing range name. You use the range name with the /Data Query command and the @D functions to exchange data with the external table.

Some external-database drivers require an owner name between the external-database name and the external table name. The owner name is a name supplied for security purposes when the external table was created. Generally, the database owner has complete access to all database features and can override any assigned passwords. If the driver you are using prompts for an owner name, refer to the documentation provided with the driver.

Using /Data External List

After you have established a connection to an existing external database table, use the /Data External List command to obtain the information you need to access the external table.

Listing External Tables

If you need to find out which external tables are available for use with the current DataLens driver, use the /Data External List Tables command. 1-2-3 lists the available external tables, showing the table name in the first column, the owner name in the second column, and the table description in the third column. In most cases the second and third columns contain NA to indicate that the external table doesn't use an owner name or description.

/Data External List Tables and /Data External List Fields write over any existing data; make sure that the area below the cell you specify as the beginning of the definition table is empty.

Listing Fields from External Tables

The /Data External List Fields commands enable you to get table definition information so that you can exchange data with the external table. Because each external database driver uses a table definition to communicate with external database tables, you need that information to exchange data with the external table using /Data Query or the @D functions.

Select /Data External List Fields and specify a cell at the upper left corner of an empty area. This action places a definition table in the worksheet. The first column of the definition table shows the field names in the external table. The second column shows field types. The third shows the length and number of decimal places for numeric fields or the width for character fields. The fourth shows column labels, the fifth shows field descriptions, and the sixth shows field creation strings.

The last three columns are not used by dBASE III and so are filled with NA statements when you access external tables using the SAMPLE DataLens driver. Other database drivers use these three columns if the database products to which the drivers are related track additional field information.

Figure 11.9 shows the result of using both the **/D**ata **E**xternal **L**ist **T**ables and the **/D**ata **E**xternal **L**ist **F**ields commands.

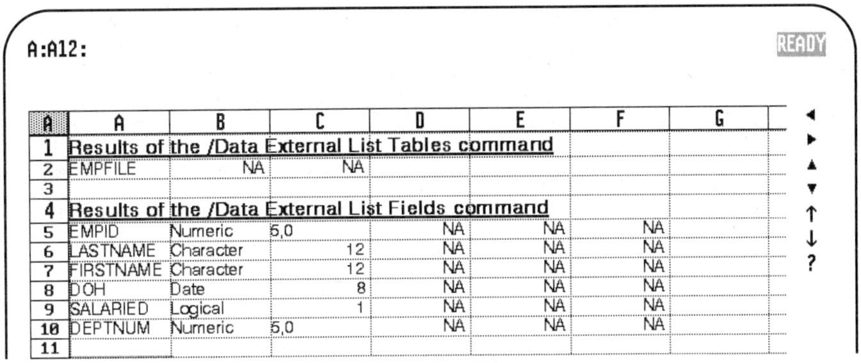

A	A	B	C	D	E	F	G
1	Results of the /Data External List Tables command						
2	EMPFILE	NA	NA				
3							
4	Results of the /Data External List Fields command						
5	EMPID	Numeric	5,0	NA	NA	NA	
6	LASTNAME	Character	12	NA	NA	NA	
7	FIRSTNAME	Character	12	NA	NA	NA	
8	DOH	Date	8	NA	NA	NA	
9	SALARIED	Logical	1	NA	NA	NA	
10	DEPTNUM	Numeric	5,0	NA	NA	NA	
11							

Fig. 11.9. *Lists of tables in a database and fields in a table produced with the /**D**ata **E**xternal **L**ist commands.*

Using /Data External Create

A DataLens driver enables you to create an external database, but the driver is not a replacement for a dedicated database management program, which has many useful features beyond those provided by the driver. Even without the product to which it relates, a database driver enables you to maintain a database too large to fit in your worksheet, yet still use 1-2-3's unique array of analytical tools. In addition to sharing 1-2-3 data with dBASE III, for example, the SAMPLE database driver included with Release 3.x helps you to create and use disk-based databases even if you don't have dBASE III.

You can create an external table from scratch, or produce a list of fields from an existing table in your worksheet, edit the list, and use the edited list to create a new external table. Suppose that you want to create an external table similar to the sample database table EMPFILE included with 1-2-3. Figure 11.9 shows EMPFILE's structure. By editing some or all of the entries, you can create the definition for a new table.

When you use a database driver, you must observe limitations that the external database program imposes on field names, field size, file size, data types, number of fields in a database, number of records in a database, and so on. With the SAMPLE driver for dBASE III files, these limitations include the following:

- The maximum number of fields in an external table is 128.

- A record cannot exceed 4,000 bytes.

- Field names must begin with a letter and cannot exceed 10 characters. (In 1-2-3, an external table name can use up to 15 characters, but the driver restricts table name length.)

- Only letters, numerals, and underscores can be used in field names.

- Table names cannot consist of a single letter between A and J.

To create an external table, select **/Data External Create Name** and specify a full external table name at the `Enter name of table to create:` prompt. The table name consists of the DataLens driver name, a space, the drive and directory where you want the database to be located, another space, and the new file name (for example, **SAMPLE C:\123R3 MYEMPL**).

1-2-3 displays the prompt `Enter range name for table:` followed by the name you entered as the table name (in this case, `MYEMPL`). To accept the default name, press Enter. (You use the range name in all references to the external table using **/Data Query** or **@D** functions.) After you provide the range name, the prompt `Enter table creation string (if required):` appears. For the SAMPLE driver, press Enter. The documentation for other database drivers indicates whether a table creation string is required.

Select **Definition** and then **Use-Definition**; highlight the entire table definition range (in fig. 11.9, the table definition range is A5..F10) and press Enter. Without leaving the **/Data External Create** menu (if you exit the menu, 1-2-3 "forgets" the preceding steps and you have to start over), select **Go**. 1-2-3 creates a new, empty external database table.

The process for exporting files to an external database is covered later in this chapter.

Creating External Databases from 1-2-3 Databases

Suppose that you have an address database like the one shown in figure 11.10, and the database has grown so large that you cannot keep it in memory all at once. You can use this database to structure a new, disk-based database.

	A	B	C	D	E	F
1	**NAME**	**ADDRESS**	**CITY**	**STATE**	**ZIP**	**PHONE**
2	Alderman, Minnis	4250 Muldoon St	Carnelian Bay	NV	89403	832–0462
3	Allen, Norman W.	POB 2259	S Lk Tahoe	NV	89503	832–0797
4	Alston, Gordon D	POB 8281	Gardnerville	NV	89503	832–3436
5	Anderson, Frank E.	POB 10286	Reno	NV	89509	832–7660
6	Anderson, Sarah	2650 Plumas St #20	S Lk Tahoe	NV	89434	836–0512
7	Ansert, William S.	2175 Skyline Blvd	Carson City	NV	89434	849–0619
8	Arthur, Jesse B.	3705 Brighton Way	McDermitt	NV	89502	849–1459
9	Belarmino, Antonio A Rev.	576 W Riverview Cir	Sparks	NV	89503	849–2430
10	Bellard, Anne–Marie	630 Travis Dr	Incline Village	NV	89506	851–0130
11	Bellard, Bret M.	POB 18698	Sparks	CA	89570	851–0938
12	Benelisha, Alan	1115 York Way	Reno	NV	89701	851–2000
13	Betts, Cynthia D.	747 W Seventh St #6	Reno	NV	89701	851–9331
14	Boessmann, Alan W.DR	6380 Stone Valley Dr	Reno	NV	89702	851–9331
15	Brien, Thomas P.	310 Arrowhead Dr	Carson City	NV	89703	852–2228
16	Brown, Barry D.	POB 1008	Carson City	NV	89703	852–7121
17	Brown, Milly A.	POB 7626	Carson City	CA	95730	853–6001
18	Bucher, Linda L.	POB 2143	Reno	NV	89506	246–3141
19	Byerman, David A.	1746 B St	Elko	NV	89701	246–5541
20	Campbell, Beth S.	632 13th St	Carson City	NV	89509	253–2138
21	Campbell, Richard H.,Jr.	10 Comstock Cir	Reno	NV	89315	253–3388
22	Cannon, Elizabeth	POB 261	Denio	NV	89512	257–3895
23	Carroll, Lois J.	40 Suzanne Way	Carson City	NV	89511	265–3055
24	Chamberlain, Fred R.	1208 Pinewood	Reno	NV	89410	265–3322
25	Chernock, William D.	963 5th St	Sparks	NV	89406	273–3219

Fig 11.10. A worksheet database that you can convert to a disk-based table using /Data External Create.

To create a new external database table using an existing 1-2-3 database as a model, begin by inserting a second worksheet for the table definition (select /Worksheet Insert Sheet After and press Enter to accept 1 as the number of worksheets). Press Ctrl–PgDn to return to worksheet A. Select /Data External Create Name and specify a full external table name at the Enter name of table to create: prompt; for example, type SAMPLE C:\123R3\DATA ADDRESS.

1-2-3 displays the prompt Enter range name for table: followed by the name you entered as the table name (in this case, ADDRESS). Because the range ADDRESS already exists in the database, change the range name to **ADDRESS_LIST** and press Enter. The prompt Enter table creation string (if required): appears. Because the SAMPLE driver doesn't require a table creation string, press Enter at this prompt. (If you are using a different driver, consult the driver documentation to learn whether a table creation string is required and how to create one.)

Select Definition and then Create-Definition. At the prompt Enter model table range: highlight the entire row of field names and the first row of data (in figure 11.10, highlight A:A1..A:F2) and press Enter. At the prompt Enter range for table definition: specify cell B:A1. Select Go to create a new, empty external database table named ADDRESS.DBF.

Exporting Data to an External Table

The next step is to export the data from your 1-2-3 database to the external table. With the data moved to a disk file, your 1-2-3 database has considerably more growing room because the database is no longer limited by memory, only by disk space.

You export data to an external table with the **/D**ata **Q**uery **E**xtract command. Before you can issue this command, however, you must perform a few preliminary steps.

Create a row of criteria range headings by copying range A:A1..A:F1 to cell B:A8. Select **/D**ata **Q**uery **I**nput and specify the entire database range. (In this example, the database range is A:A1..A:F178.) Don't forget to include the row of field names. Select **C**riteria and specify the range **B:A8..B:F9** and then select **O**utput and enter the range name **ADDRESS_LIST** (which you specified as the range name for the external table). Select **E**xtract to copy the database records to the external database table ADDRESS.DBF.

Adjusting Worksheet Data To Match Driver Field Lengths

If 1-2-3 beeps and displays the error message Data too long to fit in column — press HELP (F1), press the F1 key to view a screen similar to figure 11.11. Note the number of records processed successfully. Because figure 11.11 shows the number of records processed as 7, you know that record 8 contains too much information for the defined field length.

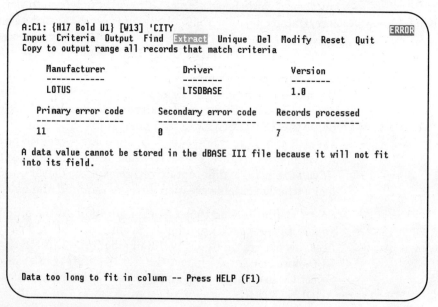

Fig 11.11. *The 1-2-3 error screen displayed if you export a database range to a DBF file and a label overflows its cell.*

The field lengths in the external table correspond to the column widths in the range used to create the external table. 1-2-3's database operations are not affected by labels that overflow their cells, but dBASE III (and the SAMPLE driver) fields cannot contain more characters than the field length. Press Ctrl–Break to clear the help screen and return to the /Data Query menu; then check the first record that 1-2-3 did not export for labels that overflow their cells.

If the labels in the 1-2-3 database don't appear longer than their respective cells, the Wysiwyg add-in may be attached and graphics mode enabled. Wysiwyg fonts are proportional; a cell in a 12-character-wide column, for example, can display more than 12 characters. If your screen shows Wysiwyg fonts, switch to text mode by issuing the Wysiwyg command sequence :Display Mode Text Quit.

To retain the current column widths and the current field lengths in the external table, truncate or condense those labels that overflow their cells. Then select /Data Query Extract again.

If don't want to change any of the data in the database range, you can create an external table file with longer field lengths. Select /System to exit to the operating system temporarily. At the operating system prompt, enter the command **ERASE ADDRESS.DBF** (or **ERASE** followed by the name of the external table file you created). To return to 1-2-3, type **EXIT** and press Enter. Select /Data External Reset and specify the range name **ADDRESS_LIST**. Correct the worksheet column widths so that the entire text of each record can be viewed within the cell (in regular text mode). Then repeat the steps listed previously for creating the external database table and extracting records to it.

Using /Data External Other Refresh

If you work in a network environment where someone else can update an external database table while you are using a 1-2-3 file connected to it, use /Data External Other Refresh Automatic to reexecute the current /Data Query and /Data Table commands and recalculate formulas at specified time intervals. This process ensures that your current file stays up-to-date even if someone else alters external database tables connected to the file.

By default, 1-2-3 uses a refresh interval of one second when Refresh is set to Automatic and /Worksheet Global Recalc is set to Automatic. To change this interval, use /Data External Other Refresh Interval.

*If worksheet recalculation is set to **Automatic**, the refresh cycle also updates @D formulas with range arguments that refer to the external table and other formulas referring to the data moved into the current worksheet by the refresh cycle. If recalculation is set to **Manual**, the refresh cycle reexecutes only /**Data Query** and /**Data Table** operations without user assistance. To update formulas when recalculation is set to manual, press the Calc key (F9).*

If you use a shorter refresh interval, you are more certain of being up-to-date at a specific moment, but refreshing at shorter intervals takes more time.

After you activate the /**Data External Other Refresh Automatic** command, you cannot select /**Data Query** or /**Data Table** unless you first select /**Data External Other Refresh Manual**. 1-2-3 "takes over" the /**Data Query** and /**Data Table** commands when automatic refresh is turned on, executing those command sequences once for every internal refresh process. If you activate **Refresh Manual**, you can control when the /**Data Query** or /**Data Table** command is used. If **Refresh** is set to **Manual**, issue the appropriate /**Data Query** or /**Data Table** commands one last time before printing a report.

Creating Reports

After you set up a database in a worksheet or disk file, you can create a variety of reports, from simple to complex. Because databases usually are large and finely detailed, you may need to summarize the database data into concise, meaningful reports.

To work through the examples in the rest of this chapter, set up the database shown in figure 11.12. (As a rule, the techniques discussed also work with external tables.)

Start setting up the employee database (use a new worksheet) by selecting /**Worksheet Global Format Currency 0**. Enter the labels in row 6 and then copy range A6..F6 to cell A1.

*Use the /**Copy** command to copy field headings to your **Input**, **Output**, and **Criteria** ranges instead of typing the labels. Most database operations don't work properly if the headings don't match exactly. Copying labels ensures an exact match.*

With the headings in place, enter the data shown in range A7..D31 (all data in this range is entered as labels, using the label prefix '). Enter the values shown in range E7..E31 and assign the General format to that range. Then enter the values shown in range F7..F31. To create the dashed line marking the end of the database, type \− in cell A32 and copy that cell to range B32..F32. Assign the name DB to range A6..F31 and the name CRIT to range A1..G2.

When the employee database is finished, you are ready to create some reports.

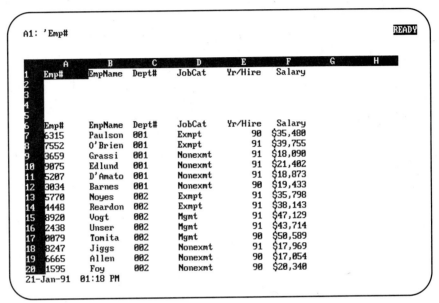

Fig. 11.12. *An employee database used for the examples in the remainder of this chapter.*

Creating Summary Reports with /Data Table

A summary report contains subtotals by category. For the employee database, you may want to see a listing of total salaries for each department number. Perhaps you want to subtotal the list by job category within departments (total salaries for exempt employees in department 001, for nonexempt employees in department 001, for exempt employees in department 002, and so on). Depending on the fields in the database, you can produce reports in varying levels of detail.

One of the easiest ways to create a summary report is to use the /Data Table commands. Figure 11.13 shows a table, created with the /Data Table commands, that lists salaries by department.

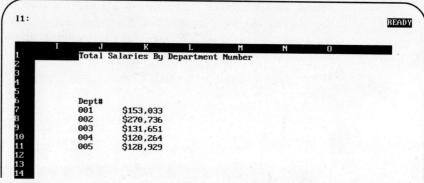

Fig. 11.13. *A summary table created with the /Data Table commands.*

Creating One-Way Data Tables

To create the report shown in figure 11.13, enter the title shown in cell J1. Create a list (in range J7..J11) of the different department numbers from column C of the employee database. The most accurate way to create the list is by using the /Data Query Unique command. Copy cell C6 to cell J6. Be sure that the second row of the criteria range (A2..F2) contains no entries. Select /Data Query Input, enter **DB**, select Criteria, enter **CRIT**, select Output, specify cell J6, and select Unique Quit. This procedure fills the area under cell J6 with one copy of each different department number.

Now create a formula for the /Data Table commands to use as a *template*. Enter **@DSUM(DB,5,CRIT)** in cell K6 and assign the Hidden format to that cell.

Select /Data Table 1, specify range **J6..K11** as the table range, and specify cell **C2** as input cell 1. In seconds, 1-2-3 fills range K7..K11 with the values shown in figure 11.13. These values are the results that the formula in cell K6 *would* return if the various labels in column J were placed in cell C2. If you enter the label **'001** in cell C2, for example, cell K6 returns the sum of all salaries for employees in department 001. When you issue the /Data Table 1 command, 1-2-3 swaps all of the entries in the table's left-hand column into the input cell.

You can get a grand total with the subtotals. Select /Data Table 1 again; 1-2-3 highlights the table range you specified earlier. Add a row to the range by pressing the down-arrow key once and then pressing Enter. Press Enter again to accept C2 as input cell 1. 1-2-3 fills range K7..K11 with the subtotals, placing the value $804,613 in cell K12. You can see what cell K6 returns if cell C2 contains 001, 002, and so on; if cell C2 is blank, K6 returns the sum of salaries for *all* records.

A one-way data table can contain several columns, each with different formulas in the top row. (Each formula is dependent on the input cell.) In figure 11.14, the table is modified to show average salaries and number of employees for each department.

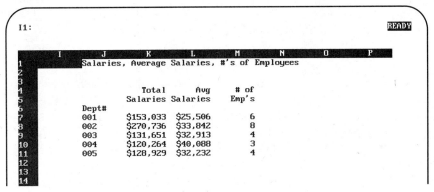

Fig. 11.14. A one-way data table with different formulas in each column.

Before creating this version of the table, enter the new label shown in cell J1 and erase the salary total from cell K12. Enter the formula **@DAVG(DB,5,CRIT)** in cell L6 and **@DCOUNT(DB,0,CRIT)** in cell M6. Assign the **Hidden** format to those cells and the **General** format to range **M7..M11**. Select **/D**ata Table **1**, specify range **J6..M11**, and press Enter to accept C2 as input cell 1.

Creating Two-Way Data Tables

1-2-3 also can set up a table that subtotals a database on two fields and arranges the results in a row-and-column format. Figure 11.15 shows an example. The salary total for exempt employees in department 001 ($75,235) appears in cell K7, cell L7 shows total salaries for nonexempt employees in department 001 ($77,798), and so on.

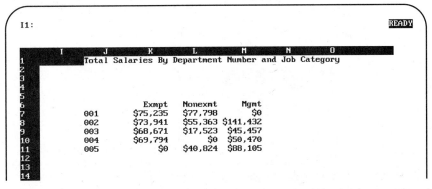

Fig. 11.15. A two-way data table showing the breakdown of salaries by department and job category.

To create this table, enter the new title shown in cell J1 and move cell K6 to cell J6. (A two-way data table always uses one formula, in the upper left corner of the table range.) Assign the General format to range **K6..M6**. Enter the labels **Exmpt**, **Nonexmt**, and **Mgmt** in cells K6, L6, and M6, respectively. Select **/Data Table 2**, specify range **J6..M11** as the table range, specify cell **C2** as input cell 1, and specify cell **D2** as input cell 2. The resulting table resembles figure 11.15.

You can include an extra row, an extra column, or both in the table range to see totals. Select **/Data Table 2**, extend the table range by one row and one column, and press Enter twice to accept the existing input cells. Cell K12 now contains $287,641, which is the total of all salaries for exempt employees. Cell N7 contains $153,033, the total of salaries for department 001. Cell N12 contains $804,613, the grand total of salaries for all departments and job categories.

Creating Three-Way Data Tables with Release 3.x

Because the worksheets in Release 3.x are three-dimensional, you can build data tables that produce subtotals on three fields. Consider the table in figure 11.16. This table is very much like the table in figure 11.15, with the data broken down into one more category (year of hire). The table in figure 11.16 is two worksheets deep, with subtotals for employees hired in 1990 in the first worksheet and employees hired in 1991 in the second worksheet.

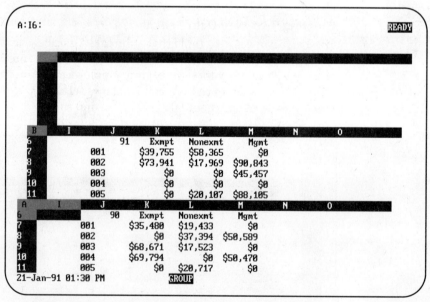

Fig. 11.16. Three-way data tables with subtotals on three fields.

To begin creating the table, add a new worksheet to your employee database worksheet. Select **/Worksheet Insert Sheet After** and enter **1**. Press Ctrl–PgDn to return to worksheet A and select **/Worksheet Global Group Enable**. Erase ranges A:K12..A:N12 and A:N7..A:N11 and move cell A:J6 to cell A:I4. Like two-way tables, three-way tables use one formula, but the formula must be separate from the table range.

Copy range A:J6..A:M11 to cell B:J6. Enter **90** in cell A:J6 and **91** in cell B:J6 and assign the General format to those two cells. Select **/Data Table 3** and specify range **A:J6..B:M11** as the table range. Specify cell **A:I4** as the formula cell, cell **A:C2** as input cell 1, cell **A:D2** as input cell 2, and cell **A:E2** as input cell 3. 1-2-3 builds the table shown in figure 11.16.

Creating Summary Reports with Formulas

One problem with creating data tables is that 1-2-3 fills the ranges with static values. If you modify the database, 1-2-3 doesn't update the data table automatically; you must remember to update the table by reissuing the **/Data Table** commands or by pressing the Table key (F8).

Using @DSUM formulas, you can create a block of formulas that return subtotals and continue to return correct values as the database changes. For the following example, use the worksheet shown in figure 11.15.

To set up a formula-based summary report, start by entering the title shown in cell J1 of figure 11.17. Erase everything shown in figure 11.15 *except* the list of department numbers in range J7..J11. Copy cell C6 to cell J6. This step is very important; the formulas don't work if cell J6 doesn't contain the field heading for the department number column.

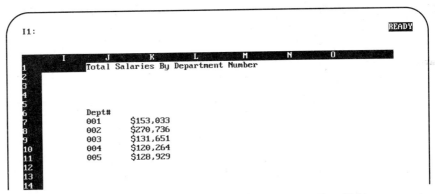

Fig. 11.17. A summary table created with formulas rather than /Data Table commands.

Enter the formula **@DSUM(DB,5,J6..J7)** in cell K7. This formula is the sum of salaries in the database for records satisfying the criteria range J6..J7 (in other words, all of the department 001 salaries). Enter the following formula in cell K8 (be sure to place the three dollar signs exactly as shown):

@DSUM($DB,5,J$6..J8)–@SUM(K$7..K7)

This formula sums the salaries for all records matching criteria range J6..J8 (department 001 *and* department 002) and subtracts the department 001 salaries computed in cell K7.

The last step is to copy cell K8 to range K9..K11. Your worksheet resembles figure 11.17. Each formula in range K9..K11 sums the salaries for all departments up to and including the one listed on the formula's row and then subtracts the salaries from previous departments.

This technique is best suited to the @DSUM and @DCOUNT formulas. You cannot compute averages by substituting @DAVG for @DSUM in the formulas in column K; however, you can create a table that computes averages if the table also computes sums and counts. Figure 11.18 illustrates this principle. Column K contains the @DSUM formulas listed in the preceding example. Cell M7 contains the formula `@DCOUNT (DB,5,J6..J7)`. Cell M8 contains the formula `@DCOUNT($DB,5,J$6..J8)-@SUM(M$7..M7)`. The formula is copied from cell M8 into range M9..M11. Column L divides the sums by the counts. Cell L7 contains the formula `+K7/M7`, and the formula is copied to range L8..L11.

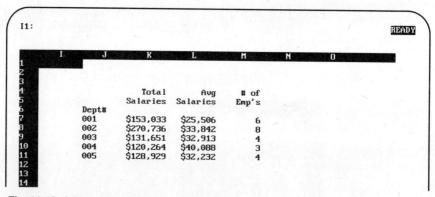

Fig. 11.18. *A formula-based table that computes sums, averages, and counts.*

Creating Multilevel Summary Reports

Besides providing an alternative for one-way data tables, the technique of using formulas enables you to set up a kind of summary table that you cannot create with the **/Data Table** commands. In the table in figure

11.19, each row shows the total salary for a job category within a department. Cell L7 sums the salaries for exempt employees in department 001, cell L8 sums the salaries for nonexempt employees in department 001, and so forth.

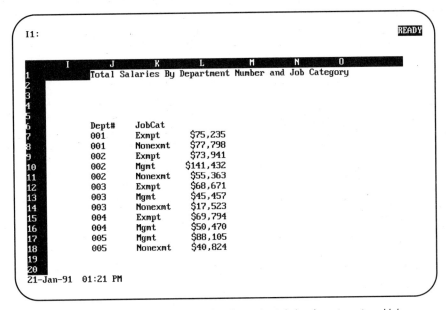

Fig. 11.19. *A formula-based summary showing subtotals by department and job category.*

This table is like the one shown in figure 11.17 except that the table in figure 11.19 uses formulas referring to two-field criteria ranges.

To create this table, start by erasing everything shown in figure 11.18. Copy range C6..D6 to cell J6. Confirm that the range A2..F2 contains no entries; then select /Data Query and make sure that DB and CRIT are still the operative Input and Criteria ranges. Specify range **J6..K6** as the **O**utput range and select **U**nique **Q**uit. This procedure creates (in columns J and K) a list of all possible pairings of department numbers and job categories.

Enter the formula **@DSUM(DB,5,J6..K7)** in cell L7. Enter the following formula in cell L8 and copy cell L8 to range L9..L18:

@DSUM($DB,5,J$6..K8)–@SUM(L$7..L7)

Creating Detailed Reports

A detailed report lists individual records; the simplest example of creating a detailed report is printing the entire database. You are more likely to want a detailed listing that includes selected records only.

The **/D**ata **Q**uery **E**xtract command copies selected records (records meeting specific criteria) to a separate range of the worksheet. Figure 11.20, for example, contains an extracted listing of all exempt employees.

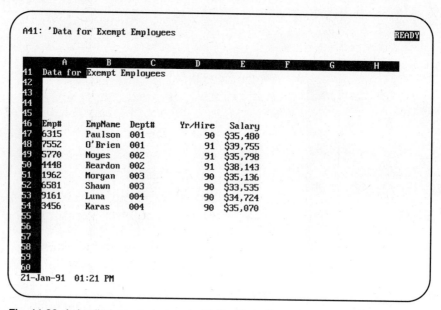

```
A41: 'Data for Exempt Employees                                    READY

            A        B        C        D         E        F        G        H
41    Data for Exempt Employees
42
43
44
45
46    Emp#     EmpName  Dept#    Yr/Hire   Salary
47    6315     Paulson  001           90   $35,480
48    7552     O'Brien  001           91   $39,755
49    5770     Noyes    002           91   $35,798
50    4448     Reardon  002           91   $38,143
51    1962     Morgan   003           90   $35,136
52    6581     Shawn    003           90   $33,535
53    9161     Luna     004           90   $34,724
54    3456     Karas    004           90   $35,070
55
56
57
58
59
60
21-Jan-91  01:21 PM
```

Fig. 11.20. *A detailed report produced with the /**D**ata **Q**uery **E**xtract commands.*

To create this table, copy range A6..C6 to cell A46 and range E6..F6 to cell D46. This procedure creates a row of field headings for the output range. Notice that the output range contains all of the fields from the database except `JobCat`. Because all of the extracted records are exempt employees, listing the job categories is redundant; however, you can include all fields in the output range. You also can use any other subset of the database fields.

Enter **Exmpt** in cell D2 and make sure that the range A2..F2 contains no other entries. Select **/D**ata **Q**uery and confirm that DB and CRIT are still the operative **I**nput and **C**riteria ranges. Select **O**utput, specify range **A46..E46**, and select **E**xtract **Q**uit. Your worksheet resembles figure 11.20.

Creating Detailed Extracts by Sorting

If your database is large and uses most of your computer's memory, you may not be able to extract records, especially if the criteria you specify cause a significant portion of the records to be selected. If you cannot extract records, try sorting the database to move all of the records that you want to print to a contiguous range.

To sort the database in figure 11.12, for example, group all of the Mgmt employees together, select /Data Sort Data-Range, specify range **A7..F31**, select **Primary-Key**, specify cell **D7**, enter **A**, and select **Go**. This process places all of the Mgmt employees in rows 15 to 21. To print these records and include the row of field names, select /Print **Printer Range**, specify range **A15..F21**, select **Options Borders Rows**, specify any range limited to row 6, and select **Quit Align Go Page Quit**.

When the data has been sorted, you can print the report by selecting /Print **Printer Range** and designating the desired block of records as the print range. Then select **Options Borders Rows** and specify the row containing the field headings. This option causes the field headings to appear on every page of the printout. To eliminate fields from the printout, leave the /Print menu and hide the appropriate worksheet columns before printing the range.

Creating Detailed Reports with Subtotals

Dedicated database management software such as dBASE or Paradox can produce detailed listings of databases or extracts of databases and print a subtotal every time the value of a field changes. Such a listing from the employee database may look like the following report.

Emp#	EmpName	Dept#	JobCat	Salary	
6315	Paulson	001	Exmpt	$28,377	
7552	O'Brien	001	Exmpt	$28,328	
Subtotal, Dept 001, Exmpt					$ 56,705
9075	Edlund	001	Nonexmt	$19,840	
3659	Grassi	001	Nonexmt	$22,371	
5207	D'Amato	001	Nonexmt	$19,370	
3034	Barnes	001	Nonexmt	$18,948	
Subtotal, Dept 001, Nonexmt					$ 80,529
Subtotal, Dept 001					$137,234
		⋮			
7906	Yarrow	005	Mgmt	$40,454	
6472	Quinn	005	Mgmt	$39,588	
Subtotal, Dept 005, Mgmt					$ 80,042
2546	Chang	005	Nonexmt	$19,270	
4839	Howard	005	Nonexmt	$22,714	
Subtotal, Dept 005, Nonexmt					$ 41,984
Subtotal, Dept 005					$122,026
Grand Total					$701,091

You can write macros to create this type of report, but the following section describes a simple, quick-and-dirty approach to computing database subtotals.

Creating Subtotaled Reports with Formulas

Figure 11.21 shows a portion of the employee database, plus a column of formulas that compute the subtotals of salaries for each department. Each formula returns an empty string ("") or, if the department number in the formula's row is different from the one in the next row, returns the subtotal. Notice that the database is sorted by department number as the primary key and job category as the secondary key.

```
G20: @IF(C20<>C21,@SUM(F$7..F20)-@SUM(G$7..G19),"")                  READY
```

	A	B	C	D	E	F	G	H
1	Emp#	EmpName	Dept#	JobCat	Yr/Hire	Salary		
2								
3								
4								
5							Dept#	
6	Emp#	EmpName	Dept#	JobCat	Yr/Hire	Salary	Subtot	
7	6315	Paulson	001	Exmpt	90	$35,480		
8	7552	O'Brien	001	Exmpt	91	$39,755		
9	3659	Grassi	001	Nonexmt	91	$18,090		
10	9075	Edlund	001	Nonexmt	91	$21,402		
11	5207	D'Amato	001	Nonexmt	91	$18,873		
12	3034	Barnes	001	Nonexmt	90	$19,433	$153,033	
13	5770	Noyes	002	Exmpt	91	$35,798		
14	4448	Reardon	002	Exmpt	91	$38,143		
15	8920	Vogt	002	Mgmt	91	$47,129		
16	2438	Unser	002	Mgmt	91	$43,714		
17	0079	Tomita	002	Mgmt	90	$50,589		
18	8247	Jiggs	002	Nonexmt	91	$17,969		
19	6665	Allen	002	Nonexmt	90	$17,054		
20	1595	Foy	002	Nonexmt	90	$20,340	$270,736	

21-Jan-91 01:21 PM

Fig. 11.21. The employee database, with formulas in column G that return subtotals in those rows where the department number changes.

These formulas are similar to the ones in the formula-based summary tables discussed earlier in this chapter. The first formula, in cell G7, is @IF(C7<>C8,F7,""). The second formula, in cell G8, is the following:

@IF(C8<>C9,@SUM(F$7..F8)-@SUM(G$7..G7),"")

This formula is copied to range G9..G31.

The formulas work in the following manner. If the label in the same row in column C is the same as the label in the next row in column C, the formula returns an empty string. If the column C label is *not* the same as the one below it, the formula sums the values in column F from row 7 to its own row, and then subtracts from the total the sum of the values in column G from row 7 to the row above the formula.

Because the database uses labels for department numbers, one more label must exist after the last department number for the last formula to work—in this case, the hyphens in row 32 (see figure 11.12). 1-2-3 considers a cell containing a label to be equal to an empty cell, because both cells have a numeric value of 0. If cell C32 contains no label, the formula in cell G31 treats cell C31 as being equal to cell C32 and returns an empty string instead of the final subtotal.

The database must be sorted by department numbers for these formulas to work. To find subtotals for job categories, sort the database by job category and modify the formulas to compare column D labels.

Figure 11.22 shows the employee database with formulas in column G that subtotal job categories within departments.

Figure 11.22 is shown with the /Worksheet Window Horizontal option set.

```
A32: \-                                                              READY

         A         B         C         D         E        F         G         H
1    Emp#      EmpName   Dept#     JobCat    Yr/Hire   Salary
2
3
4                                                                JobCat
5                                                                Subtot
6    Emp#      EmpName   Dept#     JobCat    Yr/Hire   Salary
7    6315      Paulson   001       Exmpt          90   $35,480
8    7552      O'Brien   001       Exmpt          91   $39,755   $75,235
9    3659      Grassi    001       Nonexmt        91   $18,090
         A         B         C         D         E        F         G         H
23   6806      Zucker    003       Mgmt           91   $45,457   $45,457
24   6493      Ilmer     003       Nonexmt        90   $17,523   $17,523
25   9161      Luna      004       Exmpt          90   $34,724
26   3456      Karas     004       Exmpt          90   $35,070   $69,794
27   7007      Waters    004       Mgmt           90   $50,470   $50,470
28   6472      Quinn     005       Mgmt           91   $45,422
29   7906      Yarrow    005       Mgmt           91   $42,683   $88,105
30   2546      Chang     005       Nonexmt        90   $20,717
31   4839      Howard    005       Nonexmt        91   $20,107   $40,824
32   ----------------------------------------------------------------------
21-Jan-91   01:21 PM
```

Fig. 11.22. *Formulas (in column G) that subtotal job categories within departments.*

If you want to create formulas to subtotal job categories *within* departments, keep in mind that the last record in one department can have the same job category as the first record in the next department. In figure 11.22, column G contains formulas that return job category subtotals within departments. Note the records for Waters and Quinn, rows 27 and 28. Waters is the last record in department 004 and must have a subtotal. But Quinn's job category also is management. If the formulas in column G compare job categories only, cell G27 returns an empty string.

To compare job category and department number, the formula in cell G7 is @IF(D7<>D8#OR#C7<>C8,F7,""). The formula in cell G8, @IF(D8<>D9#OR#C8<>C9,@SUM(F$7..F8)-@SUM(G$7..G7),""), is copied into the rest of the column. With this formula structure, if the job category *or* the department number changes, the formula returns a subtotal.

Using Macros To Create Subtotaled Reports

With a little effort, you can create professional-looking reports with subtotals using a macro. The macro program shown in figure 11.23 produces a subtotaled report from the employee database.

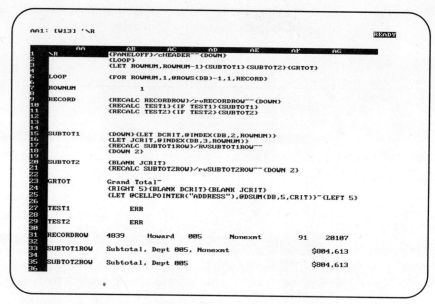

Fig. 11.23. *A macro that creates a subtotaled report from the employee database.*

To set up the macro, begin by entering all of the labels shown in column AA and range AB1..AB25. Enter **1** in cell AB7 (so that the formulas you enter return readable results) and assign the General format to that cell. Select **/R**ange Name **L**abels **R**ight and specify range **AA1..AA29**, and then assign the additional range names indicated in the following list. Assign the General format to the ranges ROWNUM, TEST1, and TEST2.

Range name	Location
DCRIT	C2
JCRIT	D2
HEADER	A6..F6
RECORDROW	AB31..AG31
SUBTOT1ROW	AB33..AG33
SUBTOT2ROW	AB35..AG35

After you finish naming ranges, enter the formulas indicated in the following list.

AB27   `@INDEX(DB,3,ROWNUM)<>@INDEX(DB,3,ROWNUM+1)`
       `#OR#@INDEX(DB,2,ROWNUM)<>@INDEX(DB,2,ROWNUM+1)`

AB29   `@INDEX(DB,2,ROWNUM)<>@INDEX(DB,2,ROWNUM+1)`

AB31   `@INDEX($DB,0,ROWNUM)`

AB33   `+"Subtotal, Dept "&@INDEX(DB,2,ROWNUM)&", "&`
       `@INDEX(DB,3,ROWNUM)`

AG33   `@DSUM(DB,5,CRIT)`

AB35   `+"Subtotal, Dept "&@INDEX(DB,2,ROWNUM)`

AG35   `@DSUM(DB,5,CRIT)`

Copy cell AB31 to range AC31..AG31. Then edit cell AC31 and change the second parameter to 1. For each formula in the remaining columns to the right, edit the second parameter, incrementing by one. The resulting formulas create a complete database record. Assign the General format to cell AF31. To start the macro, move the cell pointer to cell A41 and press Alt–R. The macro creates a series of entries in the worksheet, as shown in figure 11.24.

The macro copies the row of field headings from the database into the current row and moves the cell pointer down a row. Then it starts a loop, setting the value of ROWNUM at 1 and increasing that value by 1 until it reaches the number of rows in the range DB. Every time ROWNUM is increased by 1, the macro recalculates the formulas in the range RECORDROW, which returns values from the database based on the current value in ROWNUM. Then the macro uses the /Range Values command to bring those values to the current row and moves the cell pointer down.

```
A41: 'Emp#                                                              READY

         A          B         C          D          E          F         G
41  Emp#        EmpName   Dept#      JobCat     Yr/Hire    Salary
42  6315        Paulson   001        Exmpt          90      35480
43  7552        O'Brien   001        Exmpt          91      39755
44
45  Subtotal, Dept 001, Exmpt                             $75,235
46
47  3659        Grassi    001        Nonexmt        91      18090
48  9075        Edlund    001        Nonexmt        91      21402
49  5207        D'Amato   001        Nonexmt        91      18873
50  3034        Barnes    001        Nonexmt        90      19433
51
52  Subtotal, Dept 001, Nonexmt                           $77,798
53
54  Subtotal, Dept 001                                   $153,033
55
56  5770        Noyes     002        Exmpt          91      35798
57  4448        Reardon   002        Exmpt          91      38143
58
59  Subtotal, Dept 002, Exmpt                             $73,941
60
21-Jan-91  01:24 PM
```

Fig. 11.24. *Entries in the worksheet created by the macro shown in figure 11.23.*

If the macro reaches the last record in a department with a specific job category, it temporarily leaves the loop to run a routine that moves the cell pointer down and places a label and a subtotal in the current row. If it reaches the last record in a department, it runs another routine that places the department subtotal in the current row. After running one or both of these routines, the macro returns to the main loop and continues copying the current values in RECORDROW to the current row.

When the macro has brought all of the individual records to the report area, it creates one more job category subtotal, one more department subtotal, and a grand total.

Creating Formatted Reports

The detailed reports considered to this point have more or less retained the one-record-per-row format of 1-2-3 databases. But you can print a report that arranges the different fields for each record in a two-dimensional block, as in the following example.

Employee Number	9161	Dept Number	004
Employee Name	Luna	Year Hired	90
Job Category	Exmpt		
	Salary $34,724		
Employee Number	3456	Dept Number	004
Employee Name	Karas	Year Hired	90
Job Category	Exmpt		
	Salary $35,070		
Employee Number	7007	Dept Number	004
Employee Name	Waters	Year Hired	90
Job Category	Mgmt		
	Salary $50,470		

This report format requires a few formulas and a simple macro.

Setting Up the Report Format and Macro

Begin by setting up a report range as shown in figure 11.25. The first step is to erase the report created by the macro described in the last section. Enter the labels in columns A and E and the label **Salary** in cell C48. Enter \- in cell A49 and copy that cell to range B49..G49.

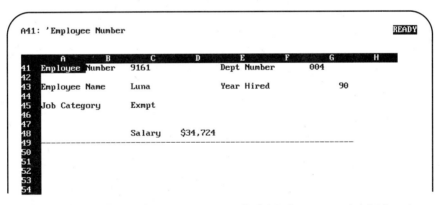

Fig. 11.25. *A report range that uses a macro to find data from a record, print it, and repeat the process for other records.*

Enter the following formulas:

Location	Formula
C41	@INDEX(DB,0,@CELLPOINTER("row") – @CELL("row",DB))
C43	@INDEX(DB,1,@CELLPOINTER("row") – @CELL("row",DB))
C45	@INDEX(DB,3,@CELLPOINTER("row") – @CELL("row",DB))
G41	@INDEX(DB,2,@CELLPOINTER("row") – @CELL("row",DB))
G43	@INDEX(DB,4,@CELLPOINTER("row") – @CELL("row",DB))
D48	@INDEX(DB,5,@CELLPOINTER("row") – @CELL("row",DB))

These formulas correctly return ERR when entered. The macro works by moving the cell pointer to various rows within the database range. When this area of the worksheet gets recalculated, the formulas return values from the cell pointer's current row.

Assign the name REPTRANGE to range A41..G49, assign the General format to cell G43, and create the macro by entering the labels shown in figure 11.26. Assign names to individual cells by selecting /**R**ange **N**ame Labels **R**ight and specifying range **AA41..AA47**.

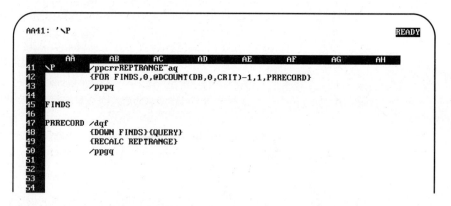

Fig. 11.26. A macro that creates a formatted report.

This macro uses a loop. For every pass through the loop, the macro finds one of the records matching the specified criteria, updates the report range, and prints the report range to the printer.

Printing the Report

To keep a report range from being split onto successive printed pages, adjust your printer settings so that one page accommodates a certain number of print ranges.

Because each report is nine rows in height, the printer settigs must accept 54 rows of text to fit six report ranges on a page. Most printers print 66 lines per page. 1-2-3 reserves six of the lines on each printed page for a header and a footer, leaving 60 lines you can use for your forms. Set the top and bottom margins to 3 (select /Print Printer Options Margins Top 3, Margins Bottom 3, and Quit Quit) and the report comes out correctly.

If you use a laser printer, check its control panel to make sure that the printer is set to print 66 lines per page, rather than 60.

Now set the criteria for the report. To print the records for nonexempt employees only, enter **Nonexmt** in cell D2. Make sure that your printer is turned on and the paper is lined up; then press Alt–P. The 10 records for nonexempt employees print in the format shown in figure 11.25.

The macro starts the /Print menu, establishes REPTRANGE as the print range, selects Align from the print menu, exits the print menu, and starts a loop. For each pass through the loop, the macro places a number in the cell named FINDS. These numbers start at 0, increase by 1 each time, and stop at the number of records in the database meeting the specified criteria. Every time the macro increases FINDS, it selects /Data Query Find and presses the down-arrow key x times, where x is the value stored in FINDS. Then the macro presses the Query key (F7). Normally, Query repeats the last /Data Query operation you performed. During a /Data Query Find operation, however, the Query key returns 1-2-3 to READY mode, leaving the cell pointer in its current location.

When 1-2-3 is back to READY mode, the macro recalculates the report range so that it returns the values for the cell pointer's current row. Then the macro accesses the /Print menu and sends the report range to the printer.

All of these operations are performed repeatedly until the macro has found and printed all of the records matching your criteria.

Summary

In this chapter, you have learned some ways to handle the data in your 1-2-3 worksheet databases, including methods for getting the most use out of criteria ranges, determining the best place for output ranges, and enhancing the utility of @D functions. You also have learned how to create and use external, disk-based databases with Release 3.x and how to create useful reports from your database.

The remainder of this book shows you how to add to 1-2-3's power and utility by using it with other software products.

Part Four

USING 1-2-3 WITH OTHER PROGRAMS

Chapter Twelve

USING ADD-INS WITH 1-2-3

This chapter examines some of the add-in programs that come with 1-2-3 Releases 2.2, 2.3, and 3.1. Other types of add-ins discussed include a new power tool for 1-2-3 users: the Macro Editor/Debugger.

Understanding Add-Ins

An add-in is a separate program that, when attached to 1-2-3, becomes a functional part of 1-2-3. In most cases add-ins use a menu structure similar to 1-2-3 and are designed to be easy to use.

1-2-3 has evolved considerably since its introduction in 1983, but both users and developers always have felt the need for more features than those offered by the basic package. For a time, the only options were templates—worksheets prebuilt for the user. While templates can help, they cannot expand on 1-2-3's basic features. A template, for example, cannot give 1-2-3 the ability to read and write dBASE files, add new functions, add new types of graphs, link worksheets, or enable worksheet viewing in different sizes and colors.

Add-ins may be *attached* (made available for use in 1-2-3) in two ways. You may either attach add-ins as needed, or set up the add-in manager to attach certain add-ins automatically. Each method has advantages. Automatic attachment guarantees that the add-ins are ready to use; you will not receive error messages for forgetting to attach add-ins before you try to use them. On the other hand, attaching add-ins with the add-in manager prevents them from wasting precious conventional memory when they are not in use—add-ins can use quite a bit of your system's memory.

Figure 12.1 shows the result of issuing the /Worksheet Global command in an empty 1-2-3 Release 2.2 worksheet with a typical add-in attached. Figure 12.2 shows the memory settings in the same worksheet when the add-in is not attached. As the figure shows, about 65K of conventional memory is used by the add-in.

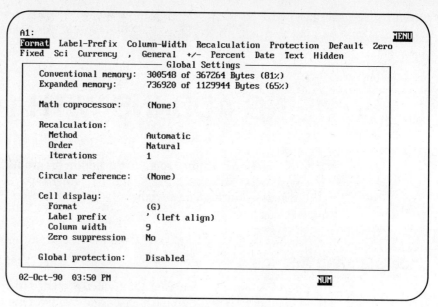

Fig. 12.1. *Conventional memory used by 1-2-3 add-ins.*

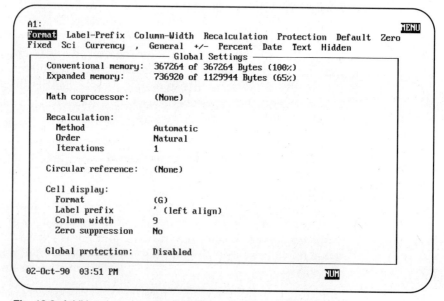

Fig. 12.2. *Additional memory available when add-ins are detached.*

Some add-ins present an interesting problem—they cannot be detached. Typically, those add-ins that add new functions cannot be detached during a 1-2-3 session. They can be detached only by exiting 1-2-3, then restarting 1-2-3 without attaching the add-in. Add-ins that cannot be detached also prevent you from recovering memory by detaching other existing add-ins, unless the add-ins that cannot be detached are attached before any other add-ins.

If memory is a concern, use care in selecting add-ins for automatic attachment. Be sure to attach add-ins that cannot be detached before add-ins that can be detached to allow recovery of the maximum amount of memory when an add-in is no longer needed.

When you load (or attach) add-ins, you can choose between assigning the add-in to a function key and starting (*invoking*) the add-in through the add-in manager menu. All versions of 1-2-3 enable you to assign add-ins to the key combinations of Alt–F7, Alt–F8, and Alt–F9. Releases 2.2 and 2.3—because they do not need to use Alt–F10 to start the add-in manager's menu—also enable you to assign an add-in to the Alt–F10 key combination. You can use any of the key combinations, as long as you remember which add-in is assigned to which function key.

*Add-ins for Release 2.x are not compatible with add-ins for Release 3.x. To allow the add-in manager to differentiate, add-ins for Release 2.x use the default file extension ADN and those for Release 3.x use PLC. If you use Release 3 or 3.1, therefore, the files displayed when you press Alt–F10 and select **L**oad have PLC extensions.*

Add-ins you use frequently may be good candidates for automatic attachment. If you keep in mind the considerations discussed earlier about add-ins that cannot be detached and how this problem affects the order in which add-ins should be attached, specifying certain add-ins that should always be loaded automatically when you start 1-2-3 may be easier.

The add-in manager built into Releases 3 and 3.1 enables you to specify add-ins that are loaded automatically when a particular *file* is retrieved. Although similar to the option that automatically loads certain add-ins when 1-2-3 is loaded, the **S**ettings **F**ile **S**et option (on the add-in menu) is specific to an individual file.

This feature is particularly useful if you develop worksheets that require certain add-ins for proper operation. By setting add-ins to load with the worksheet, you can distribute the worksheet to other users along with the add-in files. When the worksheet is retrieved, the proper add-ins also are loaded.

Because add-ins typically use conventional memory, you may need to detach certain add-ins when you load a different add-in or a very large worksheet. Keep in mind that add-ins providing new functions cannot really be detached; the memory used is not freed even if the add-in is no longer available. You can see if detaching an add-in frees its allocation of memory by issuing a /Worksheet Global command and noting the available memory before and after detaching an add-in. If the available memory is unchanged, detaching the add-in does not free memory. In this case, your only recourse is to exit and reload 1-2-3 without attaching the add-in.

All versions of the add-in manager can invoke (start) an add-in in two ways. If you assigned the add-in to an Alt–function key combination, hold down the Alt key and press the associated function key. If you selected No-Key, access the add-in manager menu to invoke an add-in.

All versions of the add-in manager also share a Clear command that removes add-ins from memory. Because the Clear command attempts to remove all add-ins, it acts immediately without any follow-up steps. Because the restrictions on removing certain add-ins also apply to the Clear command, however, this command may not accomplish the desired result if nondetachable add-ins are in use.

Using the Standard 1-2-3 Add-Ins

1-2-3 Release 2.2 includes two add-ins and Release 3.1 includes one add-in as part of the standard software package. These three add-ins increase the power of 1-2-3 by adding important new features. The following sections discuss each of these add-ins and 1-2-3 applications. These sections assume that the add-ins have been properly installed with your 1-2-3 software. The INSTALL program includes the standard add-ins when you install 1-2-3.

1-2-3 Release 2.3 includes five standard add-ins. One of these add-ins, Wysiwyg, replaces the Allways add-in included with Release 2.2, and is identical to the Release 3.1 Wysiwyg add-in. The Release 2.3 Macromgr add-in is identical to its Release 2.2 counterpart. Of the remaining Release 2.3 add-ins, Auditor and Viewer are discussed in the following sections. The Tutor add-in is not covered, as it is designed to teach the basics of 1-2-3.

Macro Library Manager (Releases 2.2 and 2.3)

The *Macro Library Manager* places macros in memory without actually taking up space in a worksheet. You can use the Macro Library Manager to load and run your macros; this add-in is activated using the menu provided with the /Add-In command. The Macro Library Manager enables you to use your macros independent of any individual worksheet.

The macro library conserves disk space by providing access to macros you use often; rather than repeatedly storing the same macros in different worksheets, you can save them once in the macro library. The Macro

Library Manager also can load several macro libraries in memory at the same time. Each library is kept separate from the others.

Suppose that you have an HP LaserJet printer connected to your computer. When you print worksheets, sometimes you need special fonts or landscape orientation. By creating a macro that selects fonts and modes and saving that macro in a macro library, you can use the macro to control your printer when using any of your worksheets.

This example demonstrates how to use the Macro Library Manager add-in with a macro that controls HP LaserJet printers, but macro libraries also are useful tools for many other purposes. The macros shown could easily be adapted to provide control codes for other printers, for example.

To begin using the Macro Library Manager, create the macros shown in figure 12.3. Create the range names for the \f and LJMENU macros by selecting **/R**ange **N**ame **L**abels **R**ight and specifying range **A5..A7**. Invoke the Macro Library Manager with the key combination you assigned to the add-in (or by selecting **/A**dd-in **I**nvoke and specifying **MACROMGR.ADN**) and select **S**ave. At the Enter name of macro library to save: prompt, type a name for the macro library (such as LJFONTS), and press Enter. Then specify a range for the macro library. At the Enter macro library range: prompt, use the arrow keys to highlight the macros (in this example, highlight **A1..E13**) and press Enter.

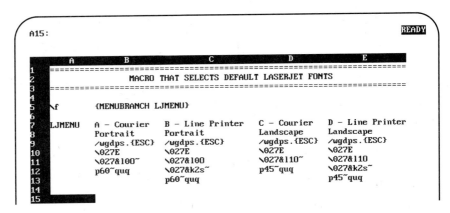

Fig. 12.3. A macro to be placed in a macro library.

The Macro Library Manager add-in also can password-protect your macro library. If you have a macro that uses sensitive material, for example, you may need to control access to the macro to prevent its modification. In such cases, select **Y**es to password-protect your macro library at the Use password to lock library? prompt. This prompt appears immediately after you enter the library range. If you do not need password-protection for the macro library, select **No**. For this example, select **No**.

A password-protected macro library can still be loaded and used. Password protection simply prevents the user from editing macros contained in the library.

Don't be alarmed when your macros suddenly disappear. The Macro Library Manager add-in moves the macros out of the worksheet into memory and, at the same time, saves them to a disk file with the name you specified earlier (such as LJFONTS.MLB). You can confirm that the macros are saved by retrieving another worksheet and pressing \f to execute the Alt–F macro still in memory. The macro is not in the new worksheet, but the menu shown in figure 12.3 appears at the top of the screen, and you can make your selection as if the macro were resident in the current worksheet.

Password-protecting libraries before distribution is an effective way to ensure that macros are not modified.

Loading Macro Libraries

As you have seen, when you save a macro library it is removed from the worksheet, placed in memory, and saved on disk. If you use the Macro Library Manager's **R**emove command, detach the Macro Library Manager add-in, or quit 1-2-3, the macro library disappears from memory. Each time you start using 1-2-3, you must load a macro library file before you can use the macros in that library. Invoke the Macro Library Manager add-in and select **L**oad. The following prompt appears:

```
Enter name of macro library to load:
```

All macro library files with the extension MLB are displayed. Select the macro library to load into memory and press Enter. The macro library is loaded, and 1-2-3 returns to the Macro Library Manager menu. Select **Q**uit to return to READY mode.

*If you have an existing library with the same name in memory, specify **Y**es to overwrite the library in memory or **No** to cancel the operation and return to the Macro Library Manager menu.*

Editing Macro Libraries

Occasionally you may need to edit macros in a macro library. You can accomplish this objective by placing the macros into a worksheet, making the necessary changes, and saving the macros again.

The best strategy when editing macros in a macro library is to begin with a fresh, blank worksheet. Load the macro library into memory and select Edit from the Macro Library Manager menu. Specify the macro library to edit and press Enter. If the library is password-protected, you are prompted to enter the password. The password must be entered exactly as it was entered when the library was saved. Because passwords are case-sensitive, *BRIAN* and *brian* are considered to be different passwords.

If you have named ranges in the current worksheet, 1-2-3 asks whether you want to Ignore or Overwrite. If you select Overwrite, range names in the worksheet that conflict with range names in the macro library are overwritten. Selecting Ignore preserves range names in the worksheet. For this example, select Ignore, position the cell pointer where you want the macros to be copied, and press Enter.

All macros, range names, and documentation contained in the macro library are written to the worksheet. Make any necessary changes; when you have finished editing, save the macro library. The following prompt appears:

```
Macro library already exists in memory and on disk.
Write over it?
```

Select Yes to overwrite the macro library on disk and in memory with the edited macros. If you select No, the Macro Library Manager does not overwrite the existing macro library. To keep both the existing macro library and the edited version, save the edited macros with a different name.

Saving edited macros with a different name creates two copies of the same range names in memory. If you invoke the macros, the Macro Library Manager uses the existing range names instead of the range names in the new, edited macro library. Use the Remove command to remove the original macro library from memory before attempting to test the edited macros.

Because macro libraries are separate from worksheets, they have many special uses. If you maintain worksheets used by several people, for example, you can create a macro library that updates formulas in worksheets without disturbing data. Rather than sending out new worksheets or a list of formula corrections, you can include the corrections in a macro library that you distribute to each user. When the user runs the macros in the library, the worksheet is corrected without requiring the user to make changes in the formulas.

Another advantage of saving your macros in a macro library is that the macros are protected from changes in the worksheet such as inserted or deleted rows or columns, or /File Combine operations.

Allways (Release 2.2)

The *Allways* add-in (included with Release 2.2) is used for spreadsheet publishing. Allways formats and incorporates graphs in worksheets, and prints with presentation quality. On systems with graphics displays, you can see Allways effects on-screen. For more information on using Allways with 1-2-3, see Chapter 9, "Using 1-2-3 for Business Presentations."

Wysiwyg (Releases 2.3 and 3.1)

1-2-3 Releases 2.3 and 3.1 include a sophisticated spreadsheet publishing add-in called *Wysiwyg*. This add-in is more closely integrated with Releases 2.3 and 3.1 than Allways is with Release 2.2. Allways requires you to return to the worksheet to edit cells or perform most worksheet operations, but Wysiwyg provides an alternative to working in text mode. You can switch to Wysiwyg mode and never use text mode.

Wysiwyg is a new version of an add-in called *Impress* (for Releases 2.01 and 2.2). When Impress was converted to Wysiwyg for Releases 2.3 and 3.1, the menu structure was modified to match the Allways menu structure. A primary reason for this change was to simplify users' transition from 1-2-3 Release 2.2 to Releases 2.3 and 3.1. A Release 2.2 user should have no trouble adapting to Wysiwyg in Releases 2.3 and 3.1. The major noticeable difference is how much easier Wysiwyg is to use than Allways.

With Wysiwyg, you can perform spreadsheet operations in graphics display mode, including entering formulas and data, editing cells, and creating graphs. For more information on using Wysiwyg with 1-2-3, see Chapter 9, "Using 1-2-3 for Business Presentations."

Auditor (Release 2.3)

The *Auditor* add-in included with Release 2.3 provides new power in examining worksheets. Auditor can show you considerable information about the formulas in a worksheet; for example, you can obtain the following information:

- All cells a formula depends on (its *precedents*)
- All formula cells that depend on a specified cell (its *dependents*)
- All formulas within a specified range

- The order in which all formulas in the worksheet are recalculated

- A pathway through any circular references in a worksheet

Because of the specialized nature of the Auditor add-in, you may want to attach it only when necessary and detach it immediately after you use it (to conserve memory). Auditor evaluates worksheet formulas so that you can find and correct erroneous assumptions in the formulas.

In figure 12.4, Auditor shows the precedent cells that affect the results produced by a formula. The formula in cell E10 depends on the results of four other cells, as indicated in cells A12..A16. Even in this simple example, a formula can depend on quite a few other worksheet cells.

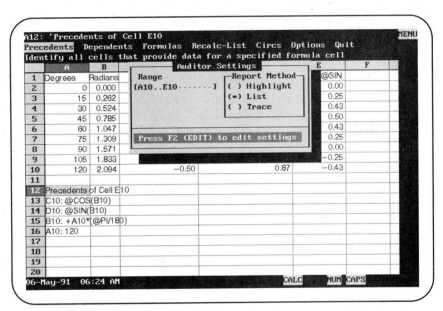

Fig. 12.4. Using the Auditor add-in to examine the precedents of a formula.

The Auditor add-in also performs a much more difficult task. Figure 12.5 shows the dependents of cell A10 (formulas that change if the cell's value is changed). If you have looked through the cells in a worksheet to find all of the formulas that depend on a given cell, you can see how this feature of Auditor is really useful.

The list in cells A12..A16 of figure 12.5 shows all formulas that refer, directly or indirectly, to cell A10. Notice that only the formula +A10*(@PI/180) refers directly to cell A10. If you examined a listing of worksheet formulas, you easily could miss one or more of the indirect references.

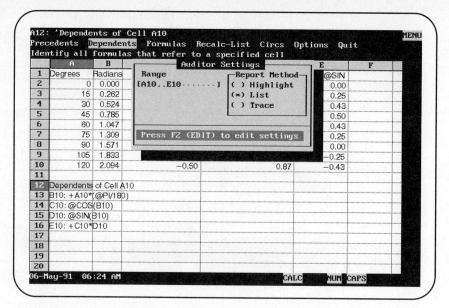

Fig. 12.5. *Using the Auditor add-in to find a cell's dependents.*

Figure 12.6 demonstrates how the Auditor add-in displays the formulas in a specified range. This list is similar to the list produced by the **/P**rint **P**rinter **O**ptions **O**ther **C**ell-Formulas command. By changing Auditor options, you can highlight formula cells instead of listing them. This option helps you to find formula cells (which otherwise can be difficult to distinguish from cells containing values).

1-2-3 generally recalculates formulas in the proper order to ensure that all precedent formulas are calculated before their dependents. Lotus Development calls this *natural order recalculation.* Usually you don't have to worry about the details, but in special cases, such as intentional circular references, knowing the order in which formulas are recalculated can make a difference. Figure 12.7 shows how the Auditor add-in lists the recalculation order.

The list shown in the figure extends many rows below the bottom of the screen; the recalculation order list includes all *worksheet formulas.*

Circular references are sometimes intentional, but they usually result from an error in entering a formula or in the logic used to design a formula. The 1-2-3 **/W**orksheet **S**tatus screen can show you one cell in the chain of a circular reference, but tracing all of the affected cells is sometimes difficult.

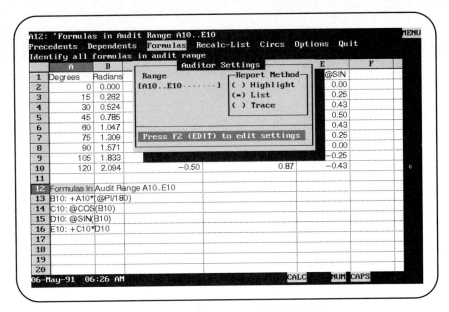

Fig. 12.6. *Using the Auditor add-in to find all formula cells within a range.*

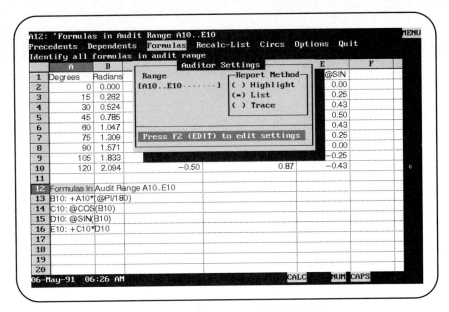

Fig. 12.7. *Displaying the recalculation order list with the Auditor add-in.*

Auditor expands the information provided by /**W**orksheet **S**tatus by displaying the complete list of cells involved in a circular reference. In figure 12.8, for example, Auditor shows a common mistake; the address of the formula cell (D12) is included in its argument range.

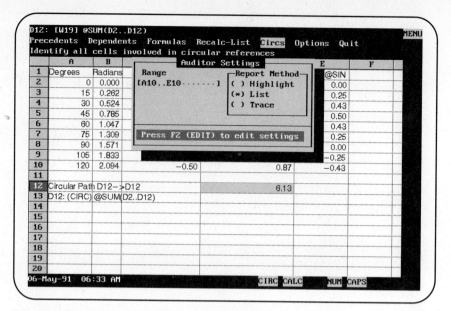

Fig. 12.8. Examining a circular reference with Auditor.

You can specify different operating modes for the Auditor add-in. As figure 12.9 shows, you can specify whether results are highlighted or listed, or cause the cell pointer to move only to result cells. Except for the recalculation order list, you can use the Audit-Range option to limit the cells reported.

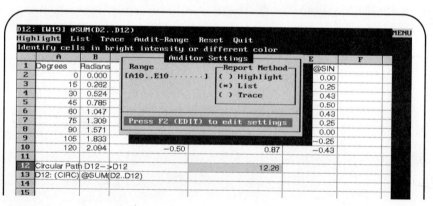

Fig. 12.9. The Auditor add-in options menu.

Viewer (Release 2.3)

1-2-3 Release 2.3 includes the *Viewer* add-in. Viewer (a simplified version of Lotus Magellan) includes the following major features:

- Display of worksheet files before retrieving; used to determine which file contains the desired worksheet
- Simplified worksheet linking; you can point to cells in external worksheets
- Browsing through files (including nonworksheet files)

Figure 12.10 shows the Viewer menu with the choices **R**etrieve, **L**ink, and **B**rowse. These selections are examined in the following sections.

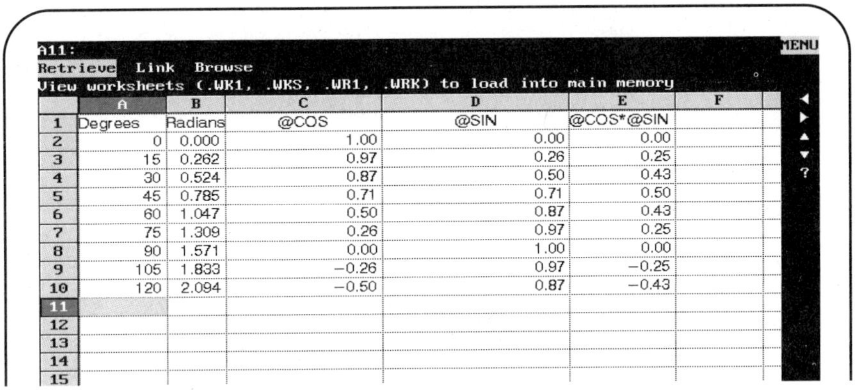
A11:   MENU
Retrieve   Link   Browse
View worksheets (.WK1, .WKS, .WR1, .WRK) to load into main memory

	A	B	C	D	E	F
1	Degrees	Radians	@COS	@SIN	@COS*@SIN	
2	0	0.000	1.00	0.00	0.00	
3	15	0.262	0.97	0.26	0.25	
4	30	0.524	0.87	0.50	0.43	
5	45	0.785	0.71	0.71	0.50	
6	60	1.047	0.50	0.87	0.43	
7	75	1.309	0.26	0.97	0.25	
8	90	1.571	0.00	1.00	0.00	
9	105	1.833	−0.26	0.97	−0.25	
10	120	2.094	−0.50	0.87	−0.43	
11						
12						
13						
14						
15						

Fig. 12.10. *The Viewer add-in menu.*

The Viewer add-in enables you to scan your worksheet files to select the exact file you want to retrieve. This feature can be handy when you are unsure of the name of the desired file. Because you can use the F5 key to sort the files by date and the F6 key to re-sort by name, you can narrow the search if you know the approximate date a worksheet was saved. Figure 12.11 shows how Viewer enables you to examine worksheet files before retrieving.

Worksheet linking provides the power to create master worksheets that consolidate data from a series of other worksheets. Unfortunately, creating the formulas that link worksheets can be a complex task. Linking formulas use the following syntax:

+<<external worksheet filename>>cell (or range) reference

To enter a linking formula in a worksheet, you must know the name of the file you want to link and the cell address or range name you want to link to the current cell.

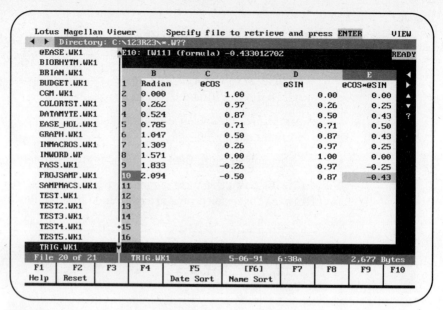

Fig. 12.11. *Examining worksheet files with the Viewer add-in.*

The Viewer add-in makes linking easier by enabling you to browse through your files to find the correct worksheet, point at the desired linking cell, and link a range of cells at the same time. Figure 12.12 shows how you select a range of cells in an external worksheet to be linked to an identically-sized range in the current worksheet. Figure 12.13 shows an example of the linking formula that Viewer enters in the current worksheet.

The **B**rowse option examines any type of file except password-protected worksheet and macro library files. This option is especially useful before importing text files with the **/F**ile **I**mport **T**ext command. In figure 12.14, Viewer is examining the AUTOEXEC.BAT file.

*Most files examined with the **B**rowse option on the Viewer menu contain unreadable "garbage." In most cases, what looks like garbage is actually program code—instructions only your computer can read.*

Using Other Add-Ins with 1-2-3

Many manufacturers produce add-ins for 1-2-3. These programs perform useful operations such as adding new functions, enabling multiple worksheets, and examining hidden trends and relationships in a worksheet. Following is a list of add-in manufacturers and their products. Many of the listed add-ins are discussed in detail later in this chapter.

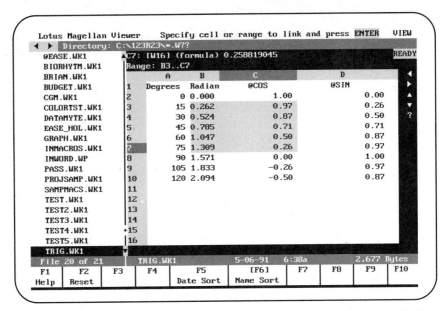

Fig. 12.12. *Using Viewer to specify a range of cells in an external worksheet for linking.*

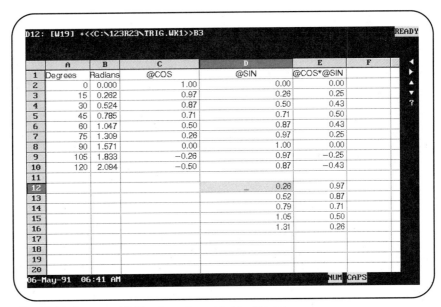

Fig. 12.13. *A range of linking formulas added by Viewer.*

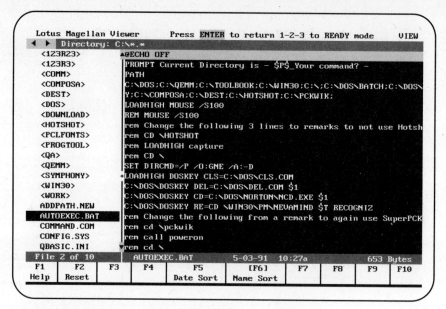

Fig. 12.14. *Browsing the AUTOEXEC.BAT file with Viewer.*

Many add-ins require a specific version of 1-2-3 and do not work with any other. The following listings indicate which versions were covered for each add-in at the time this book was published; many add-in manufacturers had not yet verified that their add-in products work properly with 1-2-3 Release 2.3. Some third-party add-ins are made obsolete by Release 2.3's standard add-ins. Before you buy, check with the manufacturer to verify that the add-in you want is fully compatible with your version of 1-2-3.

Personics Corporation
63 Great Road
Maynard, MA 01754
508-897-1575

Add-In Name	Releases Covered	Description
Macro Editor/ Debugger (MED)	2.x	Edits/debugs macros
SeeMORE	2.x	Shows extra rows and columns; creates multiple windows in worksheets
Look & Link	2.x	Enables browsing in one worksheet while working in another; links or consolidates worksheets on disk

Add-In Name	Releases Covered	Description
Instant Analyst	2.x	Uses ratio analysis and intelligent coloring to reveal hidden trends and relationships
@BASE	2.x	Full-featured database manager; enables use of dBASE files and converts 1-2-3 databases to dBASE databases

Frontline Systems, Inc.
140 University Avenue, Suite 100
Palo Alto, CA 94301
415-327-7297

Add-In Name	Releases Covered	Description
What-If Solver	2.x, 3.x	Solves "what-if" problems in reverse
Project Calc/ Resources	2.x	Project management with 1-2-3; creates Gantt and PERT charts
Decision Analyst	2.x	Creates decision trees within 1-2-3
3-2-1 GOSUB	2.x, 3.x	Creates individualized functions and subroutines

Funk Software
222 Third Street
Cambridge, MA 02142
617-497-6339

Add-In Name	Releases Covered	Description
The Worksheet Utilities	2.x	Formula editor, print utility, automatic save feature, search and replace utility, and file manager for 1-2-3
Sideways	2.x, 3.x	Prints large worksheets in landscape mode (sideways) on PC printers
InWord	2.x	Full-featured word processing software that runs in 1-2-3
Noteworthy	2.x	Cell annotation and documentation

Business Forecast Systems, Inc.
68 Leonard Street
Belmont, MA 02178
617-484-5050

Add-In Name	Releases Covered	Description
ForeCalc	2.x, 3.x	Creates forecasts within 1-2-3

Spreadsheet Solutions
600 Old Country Road
Garden City, NY 11530
516-222-1429

Add-In Name	Releases Covered	Description
@EASE	2.x, 3.x	Supplies functions that simplify everyday tasks

Intex Solutions
161 Highland Avenue
Needham, MA 02194
617- 449-6222

Add-In Name	Releases Covered	Description
3D-Graphics	2.x	Produces 3–D bar, line, and surface charts
Beyond 640	2.x	Frees memory for creating larger worksheets and using more add-ins
@Functions III	2.x, 3.x	Adds over 40 functions
Financial Toolkit	2.x, 3.x	Adds over 20 financial functions
JetSet	2.x	Controls laser printers, including margins, fonts, and paper feed

These popular 1-2-3 add-ins represent a very small sampling of the add-ins currently available for 1-2-3. Two additional sources of information are the *Lotus Selects* catalog (available free from Lotus Development Corporation; call 800-635-6887) and the Lotus Enhancements Products Directory. For further information on the latter publication, contact Lotus Development Corporation at the following location:

Lotus Development Corporation
55 Cambridge Parkway
Cambridge, MA 02142
617-577-8500

Macro Editor/Debugger (MED)

Personics Corporation's *Macro Editor/Debugger* (*MED*) for Releases 2, 2.01, and 2.2 truly can be called a 1-2-3 power tool. MED was designed to help users develop, debug, and maintain 1-2-3 macros. Using MED, you even can gain an understanding of how someone else's complex macros function (or why they don't function).

Finding and correcting errors in programs using complex languages such as C, Fortran, or Pascal can be difficult. Often a problem is caused by an event that occurred long before the program indicated an error condition. 1-2-3 macro users experience some of the same difficulties; the 1-2-3 macro programming does not provide tools that are powerful enough or helpful enough to debug properly. MED was designed to address 1-2-3's lack of sophisticated programming tools. Using MED, you can run macros at slow speed and watch the results; MED can alert you when variables reach specified values; you can specify conditions that halt the program; you even can edit a macro and restart it from that point. In short, MED provides complete control over the 1-2-3 macro programming environment.

Assume that you have installed MED and assigned the Alt–F7 key combination to invoke it. You load a worksheet that supposedly calculates payments on loans, but something seems to be wrong. Normally you press Alt–F2 to switch to STEP mode, follow the macro step-by-step, and see if you can find the error. With MED attached, when you step through the macro you see on-screen both the worksheet and the macro code as each instruction is executed. If the macro is named \ l, press Alt–F2 (Step) and then Alt–L to start the macro. The MED screen appears, showing the worksheet and the macros as in figure 12.15.

Following the macro, watching each instruction as it executes, you come to a {FOR} loop with three instructions, each of which executes every time the macro steps through the loop (100 times!). Notice the lower window in figure 12.16. Between row 11 and row 15 is the message `===> Next step is shown below, at cell B15`, which indicates that the macro is making a subroutine call to the macro in cell B15. This macro would require pressing the Enter key 300 times using 1-2-3's STEP mode. MED, however, enables you to press Ctrl–Enter to execute the 300 instructions in one step.

Because MED displays the worksheet and the macro code as the macro executes, you can see what the program is doing and find any errors.

Sometimes errors are not easy to locate. You may have a macro that appears to be correct, but the results just are not right. For this problem, you can set a breakpoint. A breakpoint halts a macro if a certain point (a subroutine, for example) is reached, or if a variable changes value or is changed to a specified value. MED uses several types of breakpoints and watchpoints (variables whose value is constantly displayed as macros execute).

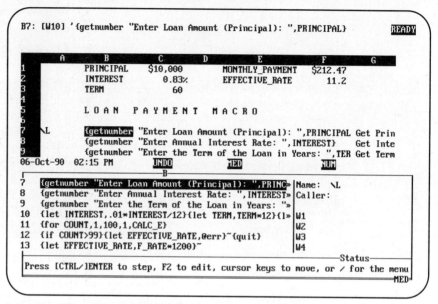

Fig. 12.15. Using MED to examine macros.

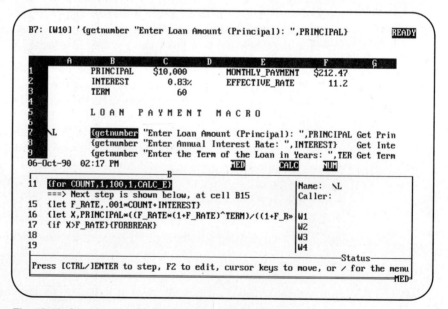

Fig. 12.16. Stepping through a macro loop with MED.

Often when you use breakpoints to debug macros, you want to run the macros at full speed instead of stepping through them. MED enables you to select the Run command instead of the Step command from the MED menu when you want the macro to run at nearly full speed. If you have set a breakpoint, MED stops the macro and informs you when the breakpoint condition is reached, as shown in figure 12.17.

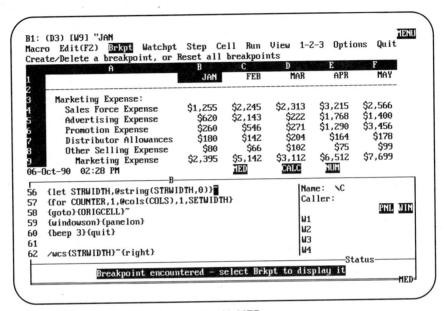

Fig. 12.17. Stepping a macro breakpoint with MED.

MED has many more features than those discussed in this short section. This program is a good example of the powerful add-ins available for 1-2-3, and certainly should be considered by anyone serious about creating 1-2-3 macros. You can get more information on MED from Personics Corporation.

SeeMORE

SeeMORE is a two-part 1-2-3 add-in that controls 1-2-3 colors, display size options, and window capabilities. SeeMORE was designed to work with many other 1-2-3 add-ins, such as MED and Look & Link.

Most users are interested in SeeMORE's ability to display additional information beyond 1-2-3's normal number of rows and columns. To use an add-in like SeeMORE, your system must be able to display graphs. Table 12.1 shows the many different screen sizes that SeeMORE can display (depending on the graphics adapter installed in your PC).

Table 12.1. *Graphics Mode Screen Sizes (number of columns by number of rows).*

	Big	Medium	Small	Very Small	Tiny	Presentation
CGA	80x25	91x28	106x33	128x25	128x33	40x25
MCGA	80x30	91x37	106x48	128x53	160x60	40x30
EGA	80x25	106x38	128x43	160x43	160x58	40x25
HIRes EGA	94x29	107x31	125x41	150x51	150x68	47x29
VGA	80x34	91x37	106x48	128x53	160x60	40x34
IBM 8514/a	80x34	91x37	106x48	128x53	160x60	40x34
Hercules	90x25	90x43	120x43	144x43	180x58	45x25
3270 PC	90x25	90x43	120x43	144x43	180x58	45x25
Gas Plasma	80x28	91x30	106x44	128x44	160x50	40x28
AT&T 6300	80x28	91x30	106x44	128x44	160x50	40x28

In addition to enabling you to select the graphics screen sizes, SeeMORE supports enhanced text mode displays on systems with EGA or VGA adapter types (as shown in table 12.2). These text mode display options are faster than the graphics modes, but cannot display graphs and worksheet data at the same time, display the menu lines in a larger character size, or use rule lines (horizontal lines below each worksheet row).

Table 12.2. *Text Mode Screen Sizes (number of columns by number of rows).*

	A	B	C	D
EGA	80x25	80x35	80x43	
VGA	80x25	80x40	80x50	
HIRes EGA	80x25	80x43	120x25	120x43
UltraVision	Supports all UltraVision extended screen sizes.			

The windows add-in that comes with SeeMORE gives 1-2-3 the capacity to display several windows on-screen at the same time. You can, for example, display your worksheet data in one window and a 1-2-3 graph in another window at the same time. This add-in also enhances your control over the appearance of windows by enabling you to select the size, layout, and type of border for each window.

The SeeMORE windows add-in also offers a very important option that has always existed in Symphony, but has never before been available to the 1-2-3 user—restriction of window ranges. When a window has a restricted range, the cursor can be moved only within that range. Suppose that you create a window called MACROS and restrict its range to IA1..IV8192. If you restrict the main window to the range

A1..HZ8192, the cell pointer cannot be moved into the main window's range (A1..HZ8192) while it is located in the MACROS window. To move the cursor outside of a window's restricted range, you must use the F6 (Window) key to move the cell pointer to the other window.

More important than the cell pointer movement restriction is the restriction on other actions. Suppose that your macros start in cell IA1 and continue down to cell IA50. Normally, 1-2-3 offers these macros no protection from row or column insertion or deletion. If the cell pointer is in cell A10, and you delete rows 10 through 15, the macros that were in rows 10 through 15 are deleted. If, however, you use the windows add-in and restrict the window ranges as described previously, your macros are protected from any changes you make in the main window.

Figure 12.18 shows how the SeeMORE and windows add-ins can enable you to see much more of your worksheet at one time. In this example, several tax forms are restricted to separate windows, preventing changes in one form from affecting the others.

Figure 12.19 shows another good use for SeeMORE. In this case, one window shows the worksheet data, the second shows a graph, and the third shows the worksheet's macros.

Like MED, SeeMORE is a product of Personics Corporation.

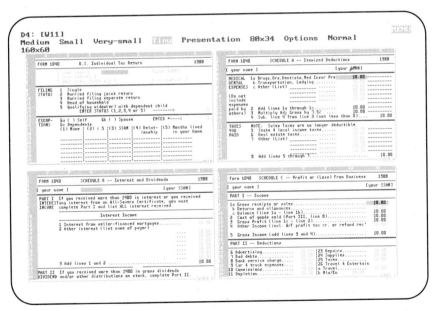

Fig. 12.18. Using the SeeMORE add-in to display more worksheet information.

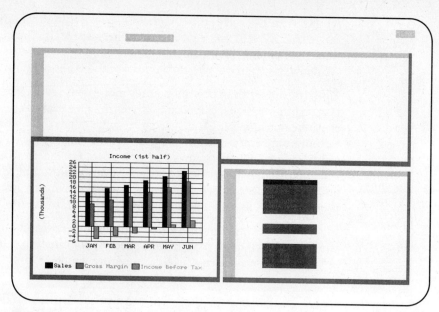

Fig. 12.19. *Displaying worksheet data and graphs at the same time with SeeMORE.*

Look & Link

The *Look & Link* add-in uses three modules (LOOK.ADN, LINK.ADN, and LINKFUN.ADN) that together enable you to look at multiple worksheets simultaneously, create linked worksheets, cut and paste between worksheets, and use 14 new functions.

With a worksheet on-screen, the LOOK module enables you to view another worksheet. In figure 12.20, an address database is shown in the viewing window while another worksheet is active. When you view another worksheet, LOOK displays the name of the worksheet being viewed. The LOOK menu offers options that control the size, positioning, and type of border for the view window.

In many ways the Release 2.3 Viewer add-in is similar to the LOOK module; however, the Look & Link add-in offers several features not included in Viewer.

When you use the 1-2-3 /File Combine Copy command, you can specify the entire file or a named range. You are out of luck if you want to copy an area that is not a named range or if you cannot remember the exact name (or coordinates of the range if you use Release 2.3). LOOK provides another option; while you are viewing a second worksheet, you can copy an area from it to the active worksheet with the LOOK /Combine command. Figure 12.21 shows the worksheet from figure 12.20 after some names in the address database worksheet are copied to the active worksheet.

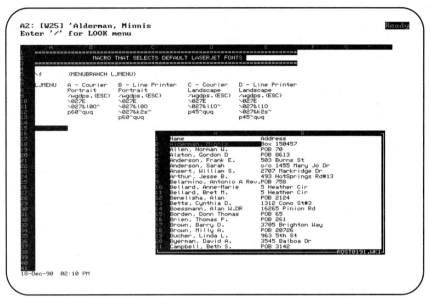

Fig. 12.20. Viewing a second worksheet with LOOK.ADN.

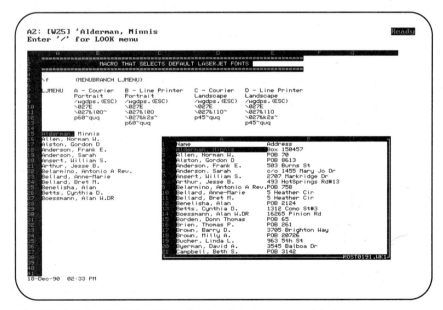

Fig. 12.21. Using LOOK.ADN to cut and paste between worksheets.

Suppose that you run a small business. To help you handle your business accounting reports, you have created several 1-2-3 worksheets that calculate the cost of buying goods, expenses for office space, taxes, and profits. You want to expand your business, but your banker will not lend you money unless you prepare a monthly report showing how the business is doing. Because this report requires information from several worksheets, it takes considerable work to prepare each monthly report. The LINK and LINKFUN add-in modules, however, make short work of consolidating the information.

As figure 12.22 shows, the report worksheet consolidates the data contained within the four individual worksheets. Rather than using static amounts, however, the report worksheet uses Look & Link to ensure that changes made in any of the four linked worksheets are reported.

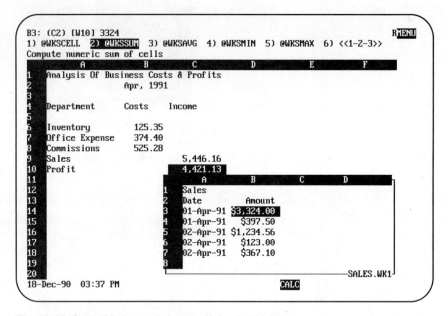

Fig. 12.22. Consolidating worksheets with Look & Link.

1-2-3 Releases 2.2 and 2.3 include a simple form of file linking. A single cell in one worksheet can refer to only a single cell in the linked worksheet. The LINKFUN module expands this file-linking capability by providing 14 new functions, divided into four types: group functions, worksheet functions, retrieval functions, and statistical functions.

The group functions define which worksheets are collected together and used as a unit.

The worksheet functions load part or all of a worksheet into memory. These functions improve the performance of linking formulas because worksheets can be accessed much faster in memory than on disk.

The retrieval functions retrieve information from worksheets. They return the value of a single cell.

The statistical functions retrieve information from a group of cells in an external worksheet. They are similar to the 1-2-3 statistical functions.

The individual functions within each type are described in Table 12.3.

Table 12.3. Functions in LINKFUN Module.

Function type	Function name	Action
Group	@SETGROUP	Creates an associated group of up to 24 worksheet files
	@ADDGROUP	Adds names to an existing group
	@CLEARGROUP	Removes a group name from memory
Worksheet	@WKSLOAD	Loads a worksheet into memory for access by LINK; the worksheet is not accessible to the user
	@WKSRELOAD	Reloads a worksheet
	@WKSUNLOAD	Removes a worksheet from memory
Retrieval	@WKSCELL	Returns the value of a specified cell
	@WKSBLANK	Determines if the specified cell is blank or contains an entry
	@WKSVLOOKUP	Performs a vertical lookup in an external worksheet (like @VLOOKUP within the current worksheet)
	@WKSHLOOKUP	Performs a horizontal lookup in an external worksheet (like @HLOOKUP within the current worksheet)
Statistical	@WKSSUM	Returns the sum of a range within an external worksheet; range does not have to be named
	@WKSAVG	Returns the average value of numeric cells within a range in an external worksheet

continues

Table 12.3. (continued)

Function type	*Function name*	*Action*
	@WKSMIN	Returns the minimum value of numeric cells within a range in an external worksheet
	@WKSMAX	Returns the maximum value of numeric cells within a range in an external worksheet

Look & Link provides the capacity to access and use values in related worksheets without using /File Combine, and helps consolidate information from many different worksheets without creating a single worksheet too large for available memory. Look & Link also can improve the performance of large applications because you can work with smaller, individual worksheets until you need to produce a consolidated worksheet.

Contact Personics Corporation for more information on Look & Link.

What-If Solver

Spreadsheets like 1-2-3 seem to be ideal for "what if" problems. When you develop a model application, you may change some of the numbers just to see the result. You may, for example, change the number of gizmos sold in a month to see how that change affects net profit. You may use several different figures until you arrive at a good-looking final figure. Trying all of the possibilities may be more difficult if you add in factors like changing your advertising budget, seasonal buying patterns, and so on. In fact, if you try to consider all possibilities in even a small model, you soon find that too many different combinations exist, and give up long before coming up with the best solution.

The *What-If Solver* add-in uses the *Generalized Reduced Gradient method* to provide an optimum solution of linear and nonlinear equations, handling up to 40 variables and 20 goals at the same time. Obviously, trying to solve problems this complex on your own by substituting values is difficult or even impossible!

Suppose that you run a small electronics manufacturing company that uses a mix of components to manufacture a series of consumer electronics products. Because your company is small, you don't have enough capacity to produce many components, and you want to optimize profits by producing the best combination of finished products. You also must take into account the fact that dealers expect better pricing as they sell more of your product; therefore, as your volume increases, your per unit profit decreases.

Figure 12.23 illustrates this problem. In this example, the components are divided to produce 100 each of three different finished products. The total profit from this mix of products is shown as $10,096.

	A	B	C	D	E	F	G
1	Example 1: Product mix problem with diminishing profit margin — Your						
2	company manufactures TVs, stereos and speakers, using a common parts						
3	inventory of power supplies, speaker cones, etc. Parts are in limited						
4	supply and you must determine the most profitable mix of products to						
5	build. But your profit per unit built decreases with volume because						
6	extra price incentives are needed to load the distribution channel.						
7							
8	Diminish by:		0.9		TV set	Stereo	Speaker
9		Number to Build—>		100	100	100	
10	Part Name	Inventory	# Used				
11	Chassis	400	200	1	1	0	
12	Picture Tube	200	100	1	0	0	
13	Speaker Cone	800	500	2	2	1	
14	Power Supply	400	200	1	1	0	
15	Electronics	600	400	2	1	1	
16							
17			Profit by Product	4732	3155	2208	
18			Total Profit	10095			
19							
20			Table Load From: B21..D31				
21			Lower	WhatifCell	Upper		
22			0	+$D$9	1.00E+30		
23			0	+$E$9	1.00E+30		
24			0	+$F$9	1.00E+30		
25			Lower	Constraint	Upper		
26			−1.0E+30	+$C$11	500		
27			−1.0E+30	+$C$12	200		
28			−1.0E+30	+$C$13	800		
29			−1.0E+30	+$C$14	400		
30			−1.0E+30	+$C$15	600		
31			Max	+$D$18	Max		

Fig. 12.23. A product mix example before optimizing.

You can adjust the quantities of each product, seeking the mix that produces the highest overall profit, but using the What-If Solver is more efficient. Look at the table of values that What-If Solver will use (B21..D31); the "what-if" cells are the quantities of each product (cells D9..F9). These quantities can be any value equal to or greater than zero, constrained by the available components (C11..C15). The upper limit of these values is equal to the inventory quantity. Finally, the value to be maximized, cell D18, is the total profit.

Figure 12.24 shows the result of using What-If Solver. Rather than producing 100 of each product, it optimizes the production by adjusting the individual quantities, improving the total profit to a figure of $14,917—again of over $4,800.

This example is simple, but What-If Solver can help you with problems that are much more complex. Because What-If Solver handles up to 40 variables while optimizing up to 20 goals, few business problems are too complex. Sample applications included with What-If Solver show you how to determine the least costly shipping routes; minimize the costs of staffing through optimal scheduling; maximize the return on investments; manage a stock portfolio; and solve electrical engineering problems. For more information on What-If Solver, contact Frontline Systems.

```
A:D17: (F0) [W10] 75*D9^$B$8                                          EDIT
Maximum value found: 14917.445683  Press ENTER to keep, ESC to discard_
```

	A	B	C	D	E	F	G
1	Example 1: Product mix problem with diminishing profit margin — Your						
2	company manufactures TVs, stereos and speakers, using a common parts						
3	inventory of power supplies, speaker cones, etc. Parts are in limited						
4	supply and you must determine the most profitable mix of products to						
5	build. But your profit per unit built decreases with volume because						
6	extra price incentives are needed to load the distribution channel.						
7							
8	Diminish by:	0.9		TV set	Stereo	Speaker	
9		Number to Build—>		160	200	80	
10	Part Name	Inventory	# Used				
11	Chassis	400	360	1	1	0	
12	Picture Tube	200	160	1	0	0	
13	Speaker Cone	800	800	2	2	1	
14	Power Supply	400	360	1	1	0	
15	Electronics	600	600	2	1	1	
16							
17		Profit by Product:		7220	5887	1811	
18		Total Profit:		14917			
19							
20		Table Load From:	B21..D31				
21		Lower	WhatIfCell	Upper			
22		0	+$D$9	1.00E+30			
23		0	+$E$9	1.00E+30			
24		0	+$F$9	1.00E+30			
25		Lower	Constraint	Upper			
26		−1.0E+30	+$C$11	500			
27		−1.0E+30	+$C$12	200			
28		−1.0E+30	+$C$13	800			
29		−1.0E+30	+$C$14	400			
30		−1.0E+30	+$C$15	600			
31		Max	+$D$18	Max			
32							

Fig. 12.24. The product mix example after optimizing with What-If Solver.

Project Calc/Resources

Project management with 1-2-3 is a specialized task that many users attempt, but this task requires resources that just are not part of the basic 1-2-3 package. Project management may bring to mind extremely complicated tasks like targeting, designing, prototyping, manufacturing, and selling a new car line. This field, however, has broader application. Anyone who manages projects needs to plan the allocation of resources such as staff and machinery. Two people, for example, often cannot use the same machine at the same time, and some tasks must be complete before others begin. You cannot mail a newsletter before the printer finishes the printing.

Project Calc/Resources adds to 1-2-3 a special menu, 47 functions, and three chart types. With these additions, you can plan projects and produce *Gantt*, *PERT* (Program Evaluation and Review Technique), and *Resource Histogram* charts to display the project plan graphically. Figure 12.25 shows a typical Gantt chart produced by Project Calc/Resources for a small project.

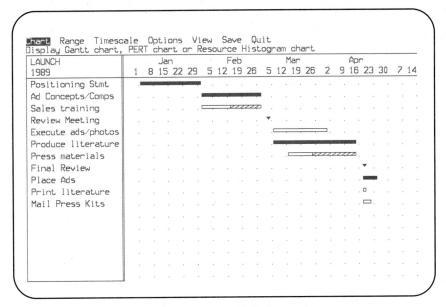

Fig. 12.25. *A Gantt chart produced by Project Calc/Resources.*

The Gantt chart shows in time-line style how each task fits into the overall project schedule. Sometimes a PERT chart, showing in network fashion how the project's tasks relate, may be more useful. Figure 12.26 shows the same project as a PERT chart.

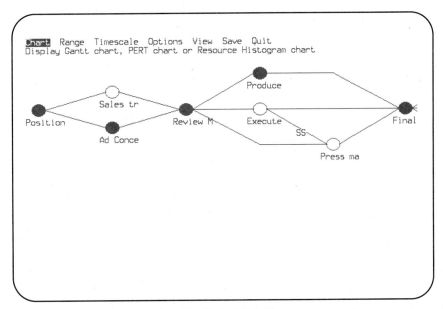

Fig. 12.26. *A PERT chart produced by Project Calc/Resources.*

Finally, Project Calc/Resources can produce a Resource Histogram chart (as shown in fig. 12.27) that combines a Gantt chart with a resource loading bar chart to show how a selected resource is being utilized.

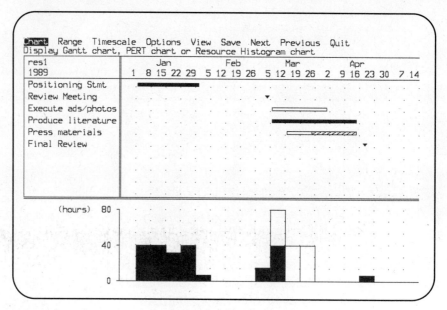

Fig. 12.27. *A Resource Histogram chart produced by Project Calc/Resources.*

The charts produced by Project Calc/Resources can be printed with the PrintGraph program in Release 2.x, but you also can use the Allways or Wysiwyg add-ins to enhance the printed result. One problem exists, however. Project Calc/Resources consists of two add-ins, PROJFUNC.ADN and PROJMENU.ADN. With both add-ins attached, too much conventional memory is used for Allways to be attached. Before you can use Allways or Wysiwyg to print one of Project Calc/Resources' charts, you must detach the PROJMENU.ADN add-in (1-2-3 add-ins that add functions cannot be detached without exiting 1-2-3).

Project Calc/Resources is available for 1-2-3 Release 2.x (and Symphony Release 2.x) from Frontline Systems.

The Worksheet Utilities

You probably don't have a pressing need for any of the features provided by Funk Software's *The Worksheet Utilities* add-in for 1-2-3. On the other hand, after you have used this collection of enhancements, you may wonder why 1-2-3 doesn't include them. You may, in fact, wonder how you ever used 1-2-3 without The Worksheet Utilities.

Unlike many 1-2-3 add-ins, The Worksheet Utilities uses overlays; only the feature you are using is loaded into memory. This capability justifies attaching The Worksheet Utilities modules automatically at the beginning of each 1-2-3 session, so that enhancements are always available.

The Worksheet Utilities consists of two add-ins. CELLWKS.ADN contains AutoSave, Formula Editor, Print Settings, Search and Replace, and Range Column Width functions. The second add-in, FILEWKS.ADN, is a file manager.

Figure 12.28 shows the pop-up CELLWKS menu in a 1-2-3 worksheet. From this menu you select the desired function.

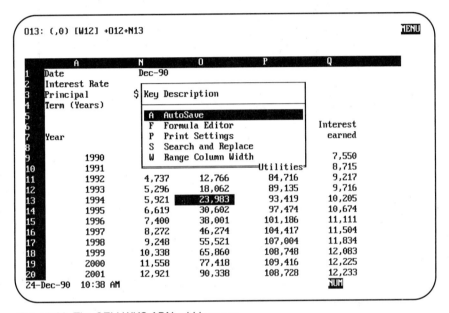

Fig. 12.28. The CELLWKS.ADN add-in menu.

The CELLWKS Add-In

The CELLWKS AutoSave module saves 1-2-3 worksheets at intervals you specify. When AutoSave saves a backup copy of your worksheet, it does not use the same file name you used when you created the file (unless you change the backup file name). This procedure protects your original worksheet in case you make changes that you don't want in the original. Figure 12.29 shows the AutoSave menu.

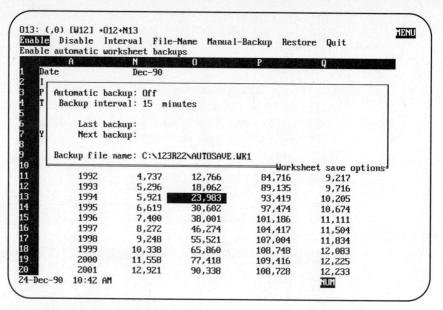

```
O13: (,0) [W12] +O12+N13                                    MENU
Enable  Disable  Interval  File-Name  Manual-Backup  Restore  Quit
Enable automatic worksheet backups
        A              N            O           P           Q
1   Date             Dec-90
2   I
3   P    Automatic backup: Off
4   T      Backup interval: 15   minutes
5
6            Last backup:
7   Y        Next backup:
8
9        Backup file name: C:\123R22\AUTOSAVE.WK1
10                                              ─Worksheet save options─
11        1992      4,737     12,766     84,716      9,217
12        1993      5,296     18,062     89,135      9,716
13        1994      5,921     23,983     93,419     10,205
14        1995      6,619     30,602     97,474     10,674
15        1996      7,400     38,001    101,186     11,111
16        1997      8,272     46,274    104,417     11,504
17        1998      9,248     55,521    107,004     11,834
18        1999     10,338     65,860    108,748     12,083
19        2000     11,558     77,418    109,416     12,225
20        2001     12,921     90,338    108,728     12,233
24-Dec-90   10:42 AM                                        NUM
```

Fig. 12.29. *The AutoSave menu.*

The Formula Editor module of the CELLWKS add-in helps you to enter, edit, and debug formulas in the 1-2-3 worksheet. The Formula Editor enables you to do all of the following tasks:

- View an entire formula on a multiline display
- See syntax errors and unmatched parentheses as you type
- Select functions, range names, and operators from a menu
- See a description of each function and the arguments it requires as you enter the arguments
- Convert addresses to range names and vice versa
- Create new range names as you enter formulas
- Highlight each level of parentheses
- Calculate a formula step-by-step and see results at every stage of its operation
- Refer to a complete on-line function reference through the Formula Editor help facility

Figure 12.30 shows the Formula Editor screen.

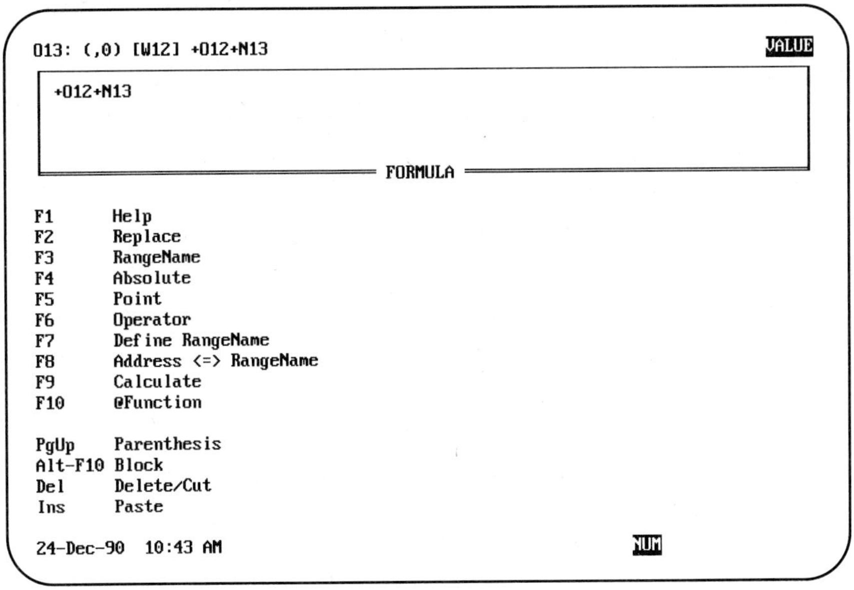

```
 013: (,0) [W12] +012+N13                                          VALUE

  +012+N13



 ═══════════════════════════ FORMULA ═══════════════════════════

 F1       Help
 F2       Replace
 F3       RangeName
 F4       Absolute
 F5       Point
 F6       Operator
 F7       Define RangeName
 F8       Address <=> RangeName
 F9       Calculate
 F10      @Function

 PgUp     Parenthesis
 Alt-F10  Block
 Del      Delete/Cut
 Ins      Paste

 24-Dec-90  10:43 AM                                      NUM
```

Fig. 12.30. *The Formula Editor screen.*

The Formula Editor can be used to enter and edit formulas, and can be invoked before you enter a formula or after you begin typing or editing an entry.

Suppose that you are entering a formula such as @SUM(MY_RANGE) in a cell, and 1-2-3 beeps and refuses to enter the formula when you press Enter. With such a simple formula, you can easily see that the likely error is that the range name MY_RANGE probably doesn't exist. Rather than pressing Esc, creating the range name, and retyping the formula, you can invoke the Formula Editor and create the range MY_RANGE, and then continue with the entry.

Sometimes you may not remember the exact syntax of a 1-2-3 function. The Formula Editor includes a complete on-line reference to all functions, and the option to select functions from a menu while you enter or edit a formula. This add-in also can show the entire formula, not just the part that fits in the top line of the control panel. Rather than printing long, complex formulas and trying to debug them from a printout, you can accomplish the task in one step on-screen with the Formula Editor.

The Print Settings module of CELLWKS.ADN controls 1-2-3 print options. You can, for example, store a group of print styles and their related printer control codes. Later, when you want to use one of the print styles, you select it from a list instead of entering a cryptic set of commands at the /Print menu. Figure 12.31 shows the Print Settings menu.

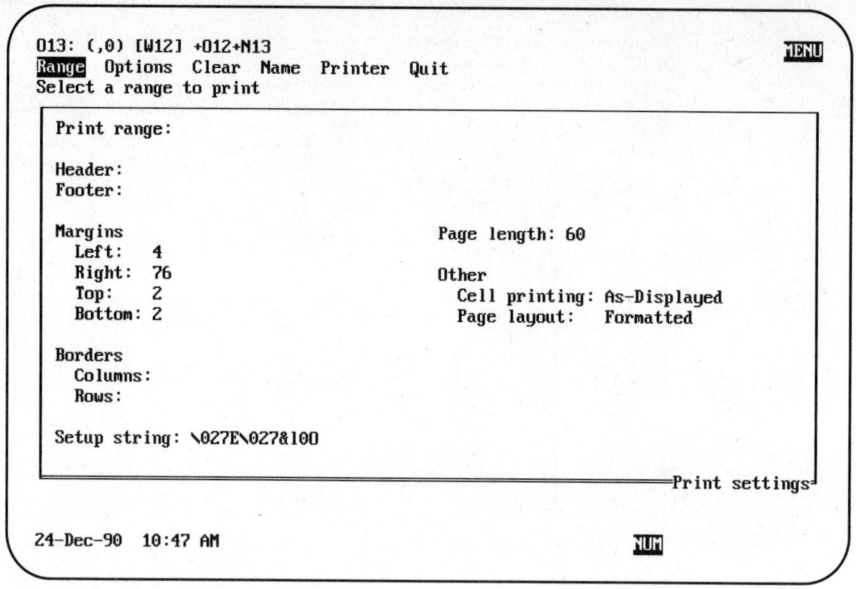

```
013: (,0) [W12] +012+N13                                              MENU
Range Options Clear Name Printer Quit
Select a range to print

  Print range:

  Header:
  Footer:

  Margins                          Page length: 60
    Left:    4
    Right:  76                      Other
    Top:     2                        Cell printing: As-Displayed
    Bottom: 2                         Page layout:   Formatted

  Borders
    Columns:
    Rows:

  Setup string: \027E\027&100

                                                      =Print settings=

 24-Dec-90  10:47 AM                                  NUM
```

Fig. 12.31. *The Print Settings menu.*

The Print Settings module includes one feature that can be quite useful. Because complete print settings information is saved in a file with the same name as your worksheet (but using a PSC extension), you can create master style sheets for different types of worksheet reports. You save each using a name that indicates the report style, and attach a copy of the style sheet to the worksheet.

The Print Settings module can read print settings information from a Symphony worksheet. This feature may be helpful if you use both 1-2-3 and Symphony and want to maintain consistent report styles.

The fourth CELLWKS module, Search and Replace, provides 1-2-3 with search-and-replace capability much like that of word processing software. You can search and (optionally) replace words, phrases, numbers, cell addresses, and function references. Figure 12.32 shows the Search and Replace menu.

The search-and-replace process enables you to replace selectively. If you select Once, the highlighted item is replaced and the worksheet returns. Selecting Continue results in the highlighted item being replaced and the search resuming. Skip instructs the program to ignore the highlighted item and continue the search. All-Remaining replaces the highlighted item and any others found in the specified search area. Quit ends the search and returns to 1-2-3. Symphony users may notice that the choices are identical to those of the DOC mode Replace command. This parallel offers an advantage if you use both Symphony and 1-2-3.

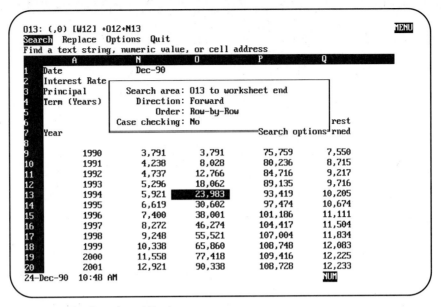

```
013: (,0) [W12] +012+N13                                        MENU
Search  Replace  Options  Quit
Find a text string, numeric value, or cell address
        A             N          O         P         Q
1  Date              Dec-90
2  Interest Rate┌────────────────────────────────────────────┐
3  Principal    │  Search area: 013 to worksheet end         │
4  Term (Years) │     Direction: Forward                     │
5             │         Order: Row-by-Row                    │
6             │  Case checking: No                    │rest
7  Year         └─────────────────────────────Search options┘rned
8
9          1990      3,791      3,791     75,759     7,550
10         1991      4,238      8,028     80,236     8,715
11         1992      4,737     12,766     84,716     9,217
12         1993      5,296     18,062     89,135     9,716
13         1994      5,921    ▐23,983▌    93,419    10,205
14         1995      6,619     30,602     97,474    10,674
15         1996      7,400     38,001    101,186    11,111
16         1997      8,272     46,274    104,417    11,504
17         1998      9,248     55,521    107,004    11,834
18         1999     10,338     65,860    108,748    12,083
19         2000     11,558     77,418    109,416    12,225
20         2001     12,921     90,338    108,728    12,233
24-Dec-90   10:48 AM                                    NUM
```

Fig. 12.32. *The Search and Replace menu.*

The CELLWKS Range Column Width module enables you to set the width of a range of columns with one command, as shown in figure 12.33. This feature is provided with 1-2-3 Releases 2.3 and 3.x, but not with versions earlier than 2.3.

```
013: (,0) [W12] +012+N13                                        MENU
Set-Width  Reset-Width  Quit
Set the width of one or more columns
        A             N          O         P         Q
1  Date              Dec-90
2  Interest Rate     11.20
3  Principal       $72,000
4  Term (Years)        20
5
6                     Year    Running    Balance    Interest
7  Year               Total     Total   remaining    earned
8
9          1990      3,791      3,791     75,759     7,550
10         1991      4,238      8,028     80,236     8,715
11         1992      4,737     12,766     84,716     9,217
12         1993      5,296     18,062     89,135     9,716
13         1994      5,921    ▐23,983▌    93,419    10,205
14         1995      6,619     30,602     97,474    10,674
15         1996      7,400     38,001    101,186    11,111
16         1997      8,272     46,274    104,417    11,504
17         1998      9,248     55,521    107,004    11,834
18         1999     10,338     65,860    108,748    12,083
19         2000     11,558     77,418    109,416    12,225
20         2001     12,921     90,338    108,728    12,233
24-Dec-90   10:50 AM                                    NUM
```

Fig. 12.33. *Using CELLWKS Range Column Width to set the width of several columns simultaneously.*

The FILEWKS Add-In

FILEWKS.ADN is a file manager that works within 1-2-3, providing the following features:

- Descriptions of up to 240 characters for each file
- Catalogs of files, listed by owner, keywords, file name pattern, or a pattern contained in the file description
- File list sorting by file name, extension, date, and size
- Saving and retrieving worksheets in compressed format (takes up less room on disk)
- Display of information from worksheets without retrieving
- Searching worksheets on disk for specific labels or range names
- Archiving files to keep a history of successive versions
- Using menus to perform DOS operations such as copying, moving, and deleting single files or many files
- Easy directory changes by pointing
- Directory management (creating, deleting, renaming)
- Searching for misplaced files throughout directories on disk

Figure 12.34 shows the main FILEWKS screen. Like other modules in The Worksheet Utilities, FILEWKS has features that are already available in 1-2-3 or at the DOS prompt without an add-in, but the add-in makes these features easier to use.

If you use a stand-alone utility to compress files and save disk space, you save your file, exit 1-2-3, run the compression utility, and delete the noncompressed file. To reload the compressed file into 1-2-3, you reverse this process. With the FILEWKS add-in, you can select File Save from the FILEWKS menu, and specify compressed or noncompressed format.

Because compressed files are usually considerably smaller than noncompressed versions, you may want to use compressed versions to transmit files over telephone lines or distribute them on diskette. Funk Software includes a program with FILEWKS (DECOMP.EXE) that you can distribute to users who do not use The Worksheet Utilities. This program eliminates the concern that someone else will be unable to read your compressed file.

The Worksheet Utilities are not the most complex 1-2-3 add-ins available, but they can help you overcome some of 1-2-3's shortcomings and make everyday tasks easier. More information on The Worksheet Utilities is available from Funk Software.

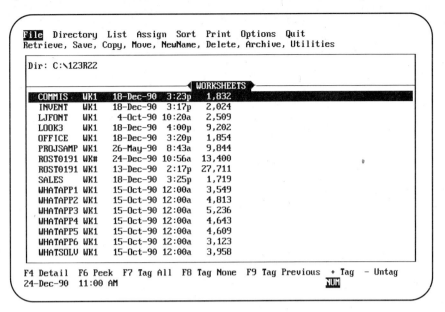

```
 File  Directory  List  Assign  Sort  Print  Options  Quit
 Retrieve, Save, Copy, Move, NewName, Delete, Archive, Utilities

 Dir: C:\123R22

                        ◄ WORKSHEETS ►
  COMMIS   WK1   18-Dec-90   3:23p    1,832
  INVENT   WK1   18-Dec-90   3:17p    2,024
  LJFONT   WK1    4-Oct-90  10:20a    2,509
  LOOK3    WK1   18-Dec-90   4:00p    9,202
  OFFICE   WK1   18-Dec-90   3:20p    1,854
  PROJSAMP WK1   26-May-90   8:43a    9,844
  ROST0191 WK#   24-Dec-90  10:56a   13,400
  ROST0191 WK1   13-Dec-90   2:17p   27,711
  SALES    WK1   18-Dec-90   3:25p    1,719
  WHATAPP1 WK1   15-Oct-90  12:00a    3,549
  WHATAPP2 WK1   15-Oct-90  12:00a    4,813
  WHATAPP3 WK1   15-Oct-90  12:00a    5,236
  WHATAPP4 WK1   15-Oct-90  12:00a    4,643
  WHATAPP5 WK1   15-Oct-90  12:00a    4,609
  WHATAPP6 WK1   15-Oct-90  12:00a    3,123
  WHATSOLV WK1   15-Oct-90  12:00a    3,958

 F4 Detail  F6 Peek  F7 Tag All  F8 Tag None  F9 Tag Previous  + Tag  - Untag
 24-Dec-90  11:00 AM                                          NUM
```

Fig. 12.34. The FILEWKS add-in menu.

Sideways

Sideways was one of the earliest 1-2-3 companion products. Before the introduction of 1-2-3 add-ins, Sideways was printing 1-2-3 worksheets and other files in landscape mode on dot matrix printers. Reports that were much too wide to print even on wide carriage printers were easy to print with Sideways.

The latest version of Sideways can be used as an add-in product with 1-2-3 Release 2.x and Symphony 2.x. It doesn't work as an add-in with 1-2-3 Release 3.x, but can print 3.x reports if they are first printed to a file.

Figure 12.35 shows how Sideways appears when you invoke it as a 1-2-3 add-in.

Sideways provides considerable control over the size of printed output; options vary with the installed printer's capabilities. Using an NEC P9XL printer, for example, Sideways offers nine character sizes from Miniscule (4x9 dot matrix) to Mammoth (9x21 dot matrix). Both character and line spacing are adjustable. Using the extreme settings, Sideways produces text as small as 22.5 characters per inch with 106 lines per page to as large as 5 characters per inch and 8 lines per page. The broad range between these extremes enables users to find settings in exactly the right size for each report.

Sideways also can print ASCII text files in landscape mode on a dot matrix printer. Because most PC programs can produce an ASCII file, Sideways is useful with other applications software besides 1-2-3. Contact Funk Software for more information on Sideways.

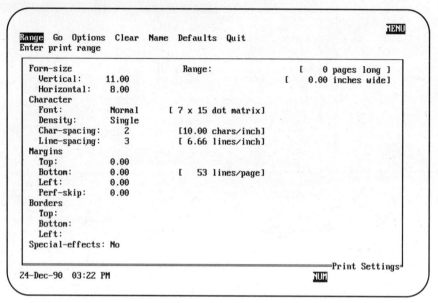

Fig. 12.35. The Sideways add-in for 1-2-3.

InWord

Before Lotus added Wysiwyg to Releases 2.3 and 3.1, word processing was always difficult with 1-2-3 for anything beyond a short note. With Funk Software's *InWord*, you can perform most common word processing tasks within 1-2-3 and even use links to a database in your worksheet to perform mail merge functions.

When you use InWord, any document you create is separate from your 1-2-3 worksheet. You can transfer information between 1-2-3 and the document in both directions, or you can switch back and forth between the two as if they were separate programs loaded simultaneously. You can, for example, use InWord while documenting a worksheet model. Because the document and the worksheet are independent, you can examine part of the worksheet, switch to the document to write documentation, and switch back without affecting the worksheet.

InWord offers many of the features found in word processing applications software such as formatting options, block operations, and cut-and-paste capability. Figure 12.36 shows a document with the final paragraph formatted to print in italics.

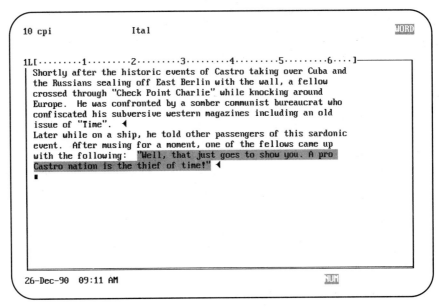

```
10 cpi                  Ital                                    WORD

1L[ ········1········2·········3·········4········5·········6····]──────────
   │ Shortly after the historic events of Castro taking over Cuba and
   │ the Russians sealing off East Berlin with the wall, a fellow
   │ crossed through "Check Point Charlie" while knocking around
   │ Europe.  He was confronted by a somber communist bureaucrat who
   │ confiscated his subversive western magazines including an old
   │ issue of "Time".  ◄
   │ Later while on a ship, he told other passengers of this sardonic
   │ event.  After musing for a moment, one of the fellows came up
   │ with the following:  "Well, that just goes to show you. A pro
   │ Castro nation is the thief of time!" ◄
   │ ▪



26-Dec-90  09:11 AM                                         NUM
```

Fig. 12.36. An InWord document.

Like 1-2-3, InWord uses function keys. With InWord attached, the only function key which works in 1-2-3's normal fashion is the F1 (Help) key. Figure 12.37 shows how InWord reassigns the function keys.

The InWord program disk includes several examples to help you learn how to use InWord. It also includes a worksheet of macros that you can use as shortcuts for such standard operations as setting paragraph justification, deleting characters, words, or larger blocks, and inserting the current date. While using InWord, you are limited to single-character macro names because InWord reassigns the function keys.

InWord is billed as a full-function word processing add-in, but its one major limitation is that it lacks a spell checking function. This lack limits InWord's value as a substitute for stand-alone word processing, but if you need the convenience of word processing while using 1-2-3, InWord may be appropriate for you. Further information on InWord is available from Funk Software.

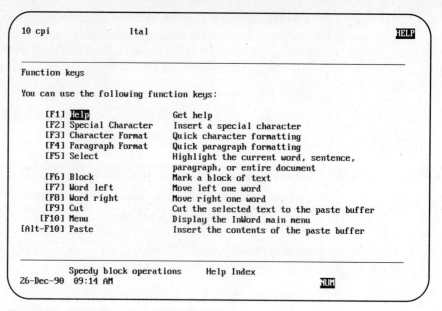

```
 10 cpi                  Ital                                          HELP


 Function keys

 You can use the following function keys:

         [F1] Help                Get help
         [F2] Special Character   Insert a special character
         [F3] Character Format    Quick character formatting
         [F4] Paragraph Format    Quick paragraph formatting
         [F5] Select              Highlight the current word, sentence,
                                  paragraph, or entire document
         [F6] Block               Mark a block of text
         [F7] Word left           Move left one word
         [F8] Word right          Move right one word
         [F9] Cut                 Cut the selected text to the paste buffer
        [F10] Menu                Display the InWord main menu
    [Alt-F10] Paste               Insert the contents of the paste buffer



          Speedy block operations      Help Index
 26-Dec-90  09:14 AM                                        NUM
```

Fig. 12.37. *How InWord uses the function keys.*

ForeCalc

ForeCalc is a forecasting add-in from Business Forecast Systems. The package includes add-ins for 1-2-3 Release 2.x, Release 3.x, and Symphony. ForeCalc uses a variety of methods to examine trends in existing historical data and predict future paths of the data. You may not be familiar with the forecasting models used by ForeCalc, but you still can use this add-in to analyze your data and make predictions.

If you are familiar with forecasting models, you can select from ForeCalc's catalog of models, including the following:

- Simple one parameter smoothing

- Holt two parameter smoothing

- Winters three parameter smoothing (multiplicative and additive)

- Trendless seasonal models

- Damped versions of Holt and Winters (for longer horizon forecasting)

If none of these terms is familiar to you, don't worry. ForeCalc examines the range of historical data, considers the specified parameters, and selects an appropriate model.

Suppose that you have been asked to prepare a forecast of the future trends in housing starts for a large construction company. This forecast is important because the company will use it to plan for land purchases, staffing levels, and financing needs. You have data covering the number of housing starts over the past ten years and must project five years into the future, taking into account any seasonal trends. Figure 12.38 shows the type of chart ForeCalc provides after examining the data set.

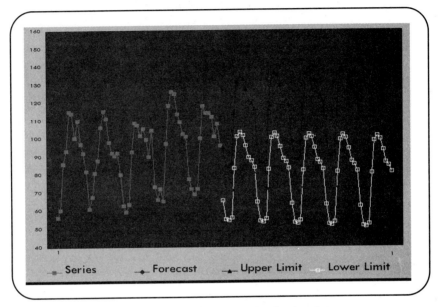

Fig. 12.38. *A ForeCalc prediction of five year construction trends.*

Forecasting is a complex subject because it incorporates so many factors. Making accurate forecasts can be difficult without considerable training unless you have tools like ForeCalc. The methods used by this add-in are much too complex to duplicate using 1-2-3 worksheet models, but using ForeCalc is easy, even if you have no training in statistical forecasting methods.

Additional information on the ForeCalc add-in for 1-2-3 and Symphony is available from Business Forecast Systems.

@EASE

The *@EASE* package includes add-ins for 1-2-3 Release 2.x and Release 3.x. While none of the functions break new ground, you may find that they offer a better way to handle 1-2-3 tasks.

The 1-2-3 carat (^) label prefix centers a label within a single column, but 1-2-3 without Wysiwyg provides no convenient means of centering a label over several columns, as you may want to do for report titles. One @EASE function provides the capability to center a heading over a range of columns.

Reports often include subtotals and grand totals. Suppose that cells A1..A12 contain monthly sales data for one year. You need a subtotal in cell A14. Next year's data appears in cells A16..A27, subtotaled in A29. To produce a grand total you can use one of the following formulas:

@SUM(A1..A12)+@SUM(A16..A27)

@SUM(A1..A12,A16..A27)

+A14+A29

Regardless of the method you select, you must be aware of the addresses of the subtotals contained within the A1..A29 range. As you add more years of data, the task of keeping track of the addresses becomes more difficult. @EASE, however, uses two functions that simplify this task. The @ST (subtotal) function replaces the @SUM functions in cells A14 and A29. The @GT (grand total) formula becomes @GT(A1..A29). The @GT function ignores any @ST values within its range. Because the @GT function also ignores any @GT totals within its range, you can have several levels of subtotals and grand totals.

The @GT function includes a variation, @GTSU, that subtracts unprotected values in the designated range. This feature is handy if values are shown as positive, but must be subtracted from the grand total.

The @SD, @GTD, and @GTDSU function of @EASE work like the functions just described except that they use displayed values, not 1-2-3's internal values. Suppose that a worksheet range is formatted to display integers (that is, zero digits after the decimal). If you enter 1.4 in three different cells in the range, 1-2-3 displays the number 1 in each cell, but an @SUM formula shows the value of 4. Using @SD shows the result as 3. If you have a specialized application that requires rounding, @SD is easier to use than adding the results of multiple @ROUND functions.

The @DI function provides the day of the week or the name of the month for a specified date. While you can duplicate this function using an @CHOOSE formula, @DI is a much simpler method.

Two functions, @SCOLS and @C_R, check the width of a range of columns. @SCOLS provides the total width of a given range, while @C_R checks to see if the specified range fits within the current print settings parameters.

@U helps you to design and lay out reports. @U works like the \ (repeating) label prefix, except that @U's repeated label stops one character short of the right edge of the column. You may find this function useful for producing lines above subtotals and grand totals, because the repeating label adjusts if you change the column width.

More information on @EASE is available from Spreadsheet Solutions.

Developing Your Own 1-2-3 Add-Ins

Despite the availability of hundreds of 1-2-3 add-ins, you may have a special need that isn't filled by any add-in on the market. If you are willing to expend the effort, you can develop your own add-ins with the help of a pair of tools from Lotus Development Corporation.

Developing 1-2-3 add-ins is not a task for everyone; it can require advanced programming skills. In fact, unless you develop add-ins for 1-2-3 Release 3.x, your only choice is to program in 8086 Assembly Language. Release 3.x add-in development uses the *Lotus Add-In Toolkit* with a language called *LPL* (Lotus Programming Language) that is similar to C or Pascal. Release 2 add-ins are developed with the *Lotus Developer Tools*.

They appear to the user to be functionally the same, but add-ins for Release 2.x are incompatible with add-ins for Release 3.x. You cannot, for example, use the Lotus Add-In Toolkit for 1-2-3 Release 3 to produce an add-in for Release 2.x.

The tools you use to create 1-2-3 add-ins differ between versions, but the development process is similar.

The Lotus Add-In Toolkit (Release 3.x)

Unlike most DOS programs, add-ins extend the functionality of other programs. Strict rules apply in developing add-ins; for example, the Lotus Add-In Toolkit for 1-2-3 Release 3.x requires that you write your program in LPL and adhere to the rules of LPL.

Add-ins can consist of new functions, new macro keywords, or complete applications. If your company provides financial services, for example, you can develop an add-in function that calculates optimum retirement benefits based upon a complex set of input factors. This new function, @BENEFIT, may replace a whole series of individual calculations. Using one custom function, you can reduce the chance of errors that may be introduced by a user who "adjusts" one of the interim calculations.

You can create a new macro keyword that displays a box in a contrasting color on-screen and prompts the user for input. This keyword enables you to produce 1-2-3 applications that are easier to use because users' attention is drawn to the prompt box.

Finally, you can combine all of the available techniques to create complete applications that don't look like 1-2-3. You can, for example, create an application that uses 1-2-3 as the front-end for a disk-based order-entry and inventory database. As the user keys in an order, your application can use 1-2-3's functions to perform necessary calculations, update database files, and print shipping tickets and invoices.

Toolkit Modules

The Lotus Add-In Toolkit for 1-2-3 Release 3.x contains a specialized compiler, an editor for entering and editing source files, a debugger to help you find and correct errors, and a library of routines that enable you to access 1-2-3.

The Toolkit compiler can be run from the editor or from the command line. It converts an LPL source code file with a PL extension into an add-in program with a PLC extension.

The Toolkit editor is similar to the integrated editors provided with Microsoft's language compilers. You can enter or edit your source code and then compile your program without leaving the editor. Because LPL source code is simple ASCII text, however, you can use any other text editor that produces straight ASCII files. (Most editors and word processing packages can be instructed to save an ASCII file—that is, one without any special formatting commands or special characters.)

The Toolkit debugger is an OS/2 program that enables you to find and correct errors in your add-ins. Because the debugger cannot be run under DOS, testing 1-2-3 Release 3.x add-ins is somewhat more difficult if your development system does not use OS/2 as an operating system. Even so, the Lotus Add-In Toolkit for 1-2-3 Release 3.x still can be used quite effectively on a DOS system.

The Toolkit library files consist of software routines provided by Lotus Development to assist you in accessing 1-2-3. These program modules provide services that you otherwise would have to develop and test on your own. The Cell module, for example, enables your add-in to determine a cell's contents and appearance (format, width, and color) and permit some manipulation of the cell. Other modules give your add-in access to external ASCII files, handle user input, access 1-2-3 ranges, and provide built-in functions.

Toolkit Considerations

If you use 1-2-3 Release 3.x and have a need for a specialized add-in that isn't already on the market, the Lotus Add-In Toolkit for 1-2-3 Release 3.x may be for you. You have to learn a new programming language and follow structured programming techniques, but if you are an advanced macro programmer or have programmed in other computer languages such as C, Pascal, or even BASIC, you shouldn't have too much difficulty. At the current list price of $395, however, the Lotus Add-In Toolkit for 1-2-3 Release 3.x really is not targeted at the individual 1-2-3 user.

For more information on the Lotus Add-In Toolkit for 1-2-3 Release 3.x, contact Lotus Development Corporation.

The Lotus Developer Tools for Release 2.x

The Lotus Developer Tools for Release 2 are not as easy to use as the Lotus Add-In Toolkit for 1-2-3 Release 3.x, but they still provide the means for developing Release 2 add-ins.

One big disadvantage of trying to develop Release 2 add-ins as opposed to Release 3.x add-ins is that the tools provided by Lotus Development for Release 2 require that you program in 8086 Assembly Language. Because assembly language programming is difficult for most programmers, this package is definitely not for the casual user.

Despite the language disadvantage, the Lotus Developer Tools provide everything you need to develop Release 2 add-ins and Symphony add-ins.

The Lotus Developer Tools for Release 2 are available for $150 from Lotus Development Corporation.

Using Other Developer Tools with 1-2-3

In addition to using predeveloped add-ins and developing your own add-ins, you can use two other types of 1-2-3 developer tools. Programs like @Tools, for example, provide simple methods for producing your own add-in functions. Others, like King Jaguar, develop stand-alone applications that start as 1-2-3 worksheets, but extend the application well beyond 1-2-3's capabilities.

@Tools

@Tools cannot produce new macro keywords and complete applications like the tools from Lotus Development, but it offers a method of developing functions using C language. If you program in C and use either Microsoft's or Borland's C compilers, the start-up routines and 70 library functions enable you to create functions.

@Tools includes 15 ready-to-use functions that you can use as examples or in 1-2-3. @Tools is available for $299.95 from PC Publishing, at the following address:

PC Publishing
1033 Massachusetts Avenue
Cambridge, MA 02138
617-661-8050

King Jaguar

Unlike the Lotus Add-In Toolkit for 1-2-3 Release 3.x, the Lotus Developer Tools for Release 2, and @Tools, King Jaguar's 1-2-3 enhancement tools enable you to develop 1-2-3 applications that don't require 1-2-3 for execution. Spreadsheet compilers like King Jaguar (Sheng Labs, Inc.) and Baler (Baler Software Corporation) change your 1-2-3 worksheet into stand-alone programs.

If King Jaguar only enabled users to run applications developed in 1-2-3 without a copy of 1-2-3, it still would be a worthwhile investment for many companies. King Jaguar also helps your applications to run much faster (for example, a report requiring two hours to produce in 1-2-3 may take only 10 minutes after being compiled) and enables you to add your own functions.

King Jaguar also enables your applications to use virtual memory; if your program becomes too large to fit in the available RAM, part of your hard disk is used as a memory extension. You don't have to worry that an application will grow too large.

Modern spreadsheet compilers like King Jaguar support all 1-2-3 Release 2.x built-in functions and macro keywords. The compilers cannot, however, support 1-2-3 add-ins, because add-ins are nonstandard extensions to 1-2-3. With the hundreds of available add-ins, it would be impossible to include support for those external programs. Instead, a spreadsheet compiler follows a different path by providing the tools to develop those added functions yourself, or by providing extra functions automatically. King Jaguar, for example, includes commands that print worksheets sideways. It also enables you to use several different types of menus, such as the pulldown menus shown in figure 12.39.

At the time this book was printed, Sheng Labs had begun work on a compiler for 1-2-3 Release 3.1. Contact Sheng Labs for further information on a release date.

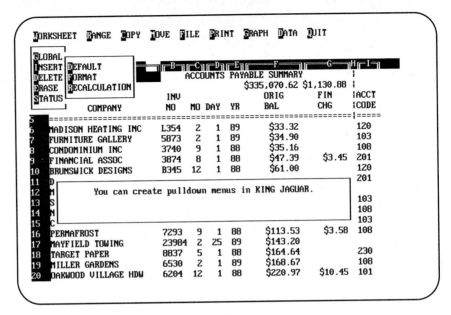

Fig. 12.39. *Creating pulldown menus with King Jaguar.*

Spreadsheet compilers are interesting and powerful alternatives to 1-2-3 add-ins and developer tools, providing economy, performance, and flexibility. King Jaguar is available for $595 (plus $6 shipping) from Sheng Labs, Inc., at the following address:

Sheng Labs, Inc.
4470 SW Hall Street, #282
Beaverton, OR 97005
503-646-3691

For more information on Baler 5.1 ($495) and BalerEx 1.0 ($795), contact Baler Software at the following address:

Baler Software Corporation
1400 Hicks Road
Rolling Meadows, IL 60008
708-506-9700

Summary

This chapter discussed a number of popular 1-2-3 aftermarket add-ins and some products offered by Lotus Development Corporation. You have seen how add-ins increase the capabilities and usefulness of an already powerful product (1-2-3). If the available add-ins cannot meet your needs, you have learned of alternative methods for developing applications with 1-2-3.

The next chapter discusses using 1-2-3 with presentation products to create high-quality documents with 1-2-3 data.

Chapter Thirteen

USING 1-2-3 WITH PRESENTATION PROGRAMS

H igh-quality business presentations and reports are more accessible today than ever before, due to the lower prices and increased power of PC graphics, hardware, and software. In this case, it may be true that a picture is worth a thousand words; executives who don't have time to search through a list of numbers for trends can see the story at a glance with a well-presented graph.

Lotus 1-2-3 is an excellent spreadsheet program but its graphics capabilities are more limited than those of a presentation program (such as Freelance Plus) or a desktop publishing program (such as Aldus Page-Maker). The built-in Lotus 1-2-3 graphing commands are adequate for some graphs, but you can accent 1-2-3 data with a presentation program by adding extra lines, figures, captions, and art, and by integrating your 1-2-3 data with related text. Figures 13.1 and 13.2 demonstrate the difference that a presentation program can make.

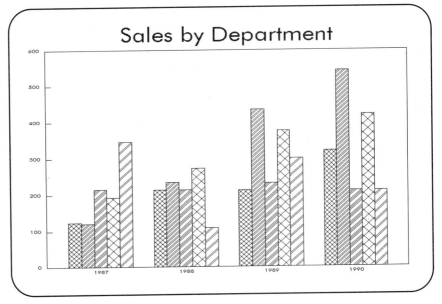

Fig. 13.1. A graph produced with 1-2-3 graphing commands.

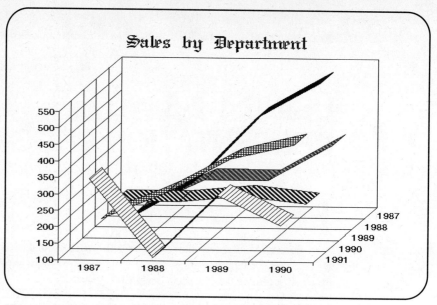

Fig. 13.2. The graph from figure 13.1, retouched with Freelance Plus.

This chapter explores the ways you can integrate 1-2-3 graphs and data with presentation and desktop publishing programs to create more appealing business reports and publications.

In this chapter, the visual representation of data shown in figure 13.1 is called a graph. *Some software documentation may refer to a graph as a* chart.

Using 1-2-3 with Freelance Plus

Freelance Plus 4.0 is a presentation graphics program that creates professional-looking business graphs, charts, and diagrams. Because Freelance Plus is a Lotus product, it is one of the few presentation programs that fully integrates 1-2-3 worksheets and works with every version of 1-2-3. You even can view the worksheet from within Freelance Plus. Freelance Plus has the added advantage of a menu interface familiar to 1-2-3 users.

Freelance Plus can import 1-2-3 worksheets and PIC files. You can link a Freelance Plus document to a worksheet so that imported graphs are updated when the original 1-2-3 data is changed. This section discusses the process of importing and using data from 1-2-3 in Freelance Plus.

Creating a Sample 1-2-3 Worksheet To Import

The worksheet in figure 13.3 is used by a jewelry store to show sales in individual departments, listed by staff member. Create the worksheet as shown to follow the importing examples in this section. In cell F8, type the formula **@SUM(B8..E8)**; then copy cell F8 to the range F9..F13. Format rows 8 and 15 as **C**urrency with **0** decimal places and the remaining values in the worksheet as **,** (Comma) format with **0** decimal places. Type **@SUM(B8..B13)** in cell B15 and copy it to the range C15..F15. Set the column width for column A as 16 characters and columns B through F as 11 characters.

```
A:F20: [W11]                                                      READY

                A          B         C         D         E
                                Jayne's Jewelry
                              Sales By Department

        Salespeople    Solitaires Bracelets  Pendants   Watches     Total
        ===============
        B. Drew          $5,128    $1,232    $1,321    $3,234    $10,907
        J. Murdoch        6,323     2,693     3,112     1,002     13,130
        S. Wiseman        3,432     3,234     2,744     4,190     13,600
        C. Ulmer          3,532     5,232     1,211     2,122     12,097
        G. Murphy         2,133     3,212     3,342     2,134     10,821
        J. Boyd           4,322     3,851     2,135     1,294     11,602
                       --------------------------------------------------
        Total Sales:    $24,862   $19,454   $13,865   $13,976    $72,157
                       ==================================================



JAYNE.WK1
```

Fig. 13.3. *A 1-2-3 worksheet to be imported into Freelance Plus.*

Create a series of ranges with the following command sequence:

/**R**ange Name Create

STAFF	A8..A13
SOLITAIRES	B8..B13
BRACELETS	C8..C13
PENDANTS	D8..D13
WATCHES	E8..E13
TOTAL	F8..F13

Save the worksheet to disk with the name JAYNE.WK3 (or JAYNE.WK1 if you use 1-2-3 Release 2.x). Then create a graph with the following command sequence:

/Graph Type Bar

X	B6..E6
A	B8..E8
B	B9..E9
C	B10..E10
D	B11..E11
E	B12..E12
F	B13..E13

Options Legend

A	B. Drew
B	J. Murdoch
C	S. Wiseman
D	C. Ulmer
E	G. Murphy
F	J. Boyd

Titles

First   Jayne's

Second Department Sales

Y-Axis Dollars

Grid Horizontal

B&W

Quit

Select View to see the graph on-screen, as shown in figure 13.4. Save the worksheet (in case you need to make a correction later) and save the graph as **JAYNE.PIC**. You are ready to import the worksheet data with Freelance Plus.

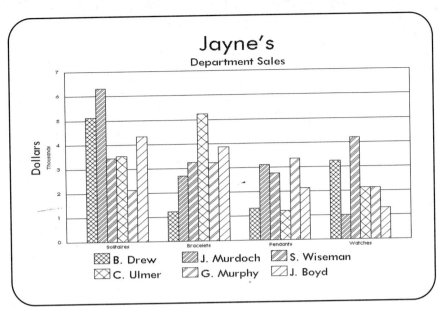

Fig. 13.4. *Viewing the graph in the JAYNE worksheet.*

Importing 1-2-3 Data

Freelance Plus can use worksheet data to create graphs. After you import the data, you can change the resulting graph in many ways. In the import process, formulas in the worksheet are converted to their numerical values and macros are ignored.

To import the worksheet, start Freelance Plus and select **Charts and Drawings**. Freelance Plus displays a horizontal menu of options. Select **Chart New-data**. The Chart form appears, as shown in figure 13.5.

Change the Chart Type by pressing the space bar and selecting the desired graph type. For this example, select **Bar – Vertical**. To add a heading, select **Headings** and enter the desired text. For this example, type **Jayne's Jewelry**. To enhance the heading, move the cursor to the HEADING STYLE field and press the space bar to display the Heading Style form shown in figure 13.6.

Depending on your output device, you may want to change the heading style options. If you use a color plotter, for example, you can add color to the heading lines by selecting a color other than **black** (the default). For this example, leave the color set to **black** and select **Font**.

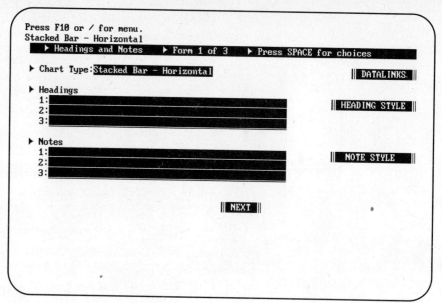

Fig. 13.5. The Freelance Plus Chart form.

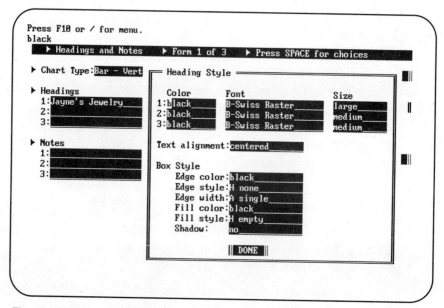

Fig. 13.6. The Heading Style form.

Press the space bar to see a list of available fonts. Depending on the fonts installed with Freelance Plus, you can select from five to ten fonts. Select **S**wiss for this example. (Swiss is one of the default fonts supplied with Freelance Plus.) When you finish specifying the heading style, move the cursor to DONE and press Enter to return to the Chart form.

To display information at the bottom of your graph or add notes directly from the worksheet, select **Notes**. (For this example, don't add any notes.)

To import the data, move the cursor to the DATALINKS field and press the space bar. Use the Datalinks form that appears (as shown in fig. 13.7) to specify the 1-2-3 worksheet file to import and to link the Freelance Plus graph to the source worksheet.

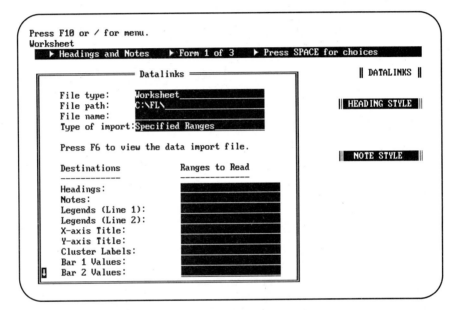

Fig. 13.7. The Datalinks form.

Always define Datalinks so that your Freelance Plus graph is linked to and updated by the source worksheet.

Leave the **File** type set to Worksheet to import 1-2-3 worksheets. Specify the full path name and file name of the 1-2-3 file you want to import; for example, type **C:\LOTUS**, press the down-arrow key, and type **JAYNE.WK3** (or **JAYNE.WK1**). If you prefer, you can press the space bar at the File name: prompt to see a list of files and select from the list.

Move the cursor down to the Type of import: prompt and select Specified Ranges or **Named Graph**. For this example, select **Specified Ranges**.

Link the ranges in the worksheet to the appropriate data groups in the Freelance Plus graph with the information in the Destinations and

`Ranges to Read` columns at the bottom of the Datalinks form. You can specify range names by typing (for example, type **STAFF**) or pressing F6 (to display the worksheet on-screen) and pointing to the range.

You needn't assign a range to every prompt in the `Ranges to Read` column. In this example, because you already specified a heading, you don't have to specify the heading again. You did not specify a note earlier, however, so press the down-arrow key to move the cursor to `Notes`. The `Notes` value (`Sales by Department`) is in cell C3 of the worksheet, but you don't have to remember the cell coordinates. Instead, press F6 to display the worksheet on-screen within Freelance Plus, as shown in figure 13.8.

```
Notes: Move to 1st corner and press PERIOD
A:A1
   ▶ View of Import File: JAYNE.WK3            ▶                    →
   A        A         B         C          D         E         F        G
   1                            Jayne's
   2
   3                            Sales By
   4
   5
   6  Salespeop Solitaire Bracelets Pendants_ Watches_  Total_
   7           ========= ========= ========= ========= =========
   8  B. Drew_ 5120      1232      1321      3234      10907
   9  J. Murdoc 6323     2693      3112      1002      13130
   10 S. Wisema 3432     3234      2744      4190      13600
   11 C. Ulmer_ 3532     5232      1211      2122      12097
   12 G. Murphy 2133     3212      3342      2134      10821
   13 J. Boyd_  4322     3851      2135      1294      11602
   14
   15 Total Sal 24862    19454     13865     13976     72157
   16           ========= ========= ========= ========= =========
   17
   18
   19
   20
   21
```

Fig. 13.8. *Displaying the worksheet from within Freelance Plus.*

Only the first nine characters of the data in each cell are displayed, but you can see a good representation of the worksheet. To specify a multicell range, press the period key to anchor the range and extend the range with the arrow keys. For this example, move the cursor to C3 to see `Sales by Department`. Press Enter. Freelance Plus returns to the Datalink screen and displays `C3..C3` in the Notes field.

Specify the remaining ranges for the graph. For this example, type the range name **STAFF** for the Cluster Labels field, **SOLITAIRES** for Bar 1, **BRACELETS** for Bar 2, **PENDANTS** for Bar 3, and **WATCHES** for Bar 4.

Instead of typing a range name for Bar 5, press the space bar. You see a list of worksheet ranges, as shown in figure 13.9. This method is helpful if you forget a range name. For this example, select TOTAL from the list of range names.

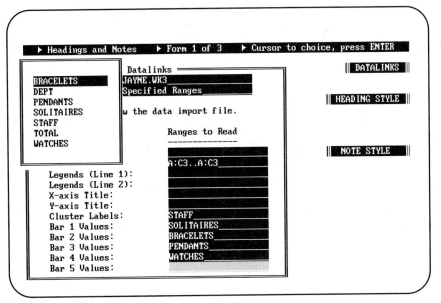

Fig. 13.9. *Viewing a list of range names from the worksheet.*

When you have specified all of the desired ranges for the graph, move the cursor to DONE and press Enter. Freelance Plus displays the following query:

     Update the chart form with data from the import file?

Respond **Yes** or **No**. (For this example, select **Yes**.) If you select **No**, you can change the options before Freelance Plus updates the chart form. Freelance Plus updates the graph and displays error messages for any incorrect information in the Chart form (such as a misspelled range name). If an error message appears, correct the error condition and update again. After you respond **Yes** or **No**, the Chart form returns to the screen.

To finish the graph, press Ctrl–PgDn twice to display the third Chart form and enter the legends for the graph. Move the cursor to the Legend 1 field and press F6 to display the worksheet. Move the cursor to the cell containing the first legend and press Enter twice to select it. Select the rest of the legends in the same manner. For this example, select cell C6 (containing the heading Solitaires) for the first legend, cell D6 for the second, and so on.

To view the finished graph, press F10 to display the menu, followed by Alt–F8. Press Enter to display the graph. The example graph in figure 13.10 shows sales by department for each staff member, along with that person's total sales.

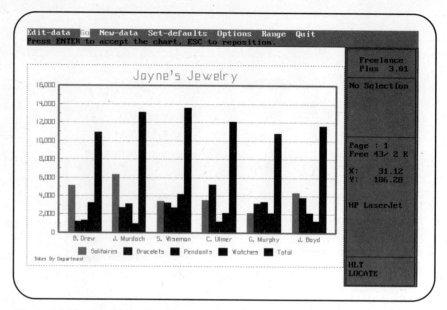

Fig. 13.10. *Viewing the graph of the worksheet data.*

You can save the graph at this point, or use the Freelance Plus editing tools to add captions or change other graph elements. Datalinks updates the Freelance Plus graph each time you change the worksheet data in 1-2-3. Because the worksheet is linked to the graph, any enhancements you have made apply to the changed worksheet data.

Importing 1-2-3 PIC Files

You don't have to re-create existing 1-2-3 graphs with Freelance Plus. Instead, you can import PIC files directly into Freelance Plus, change the graphs, and save them as Freelance Plus graphs. Freelance Plus preserves some settings from the original PIC file, such as ranges, fill patterns, colors, and titles. This example shows a bar graph being imported, but Freelance Plus can import any type of 1-2-3 graph.

To import a PIC file, select **Charts and Drawings**. Select **Chart New-Data**. The Chart form appears. Move the cursor to DATALINKS and press the space bar. The Datalinks form appears. Specify the full path name and file name; for example, type **C:\LOTUS\JAYNE.WK3** (or **JAYNE.WK1**).

Select **Type of Import** and press the space bar. Select **Named Graph** from the resulting menu. Specify the graph name at the `Name of Graph:` prompt. For this example, type **JAYNE**. Select `DONE`. Freelance Plus displays the following prompt:

> `Update the chart form with data from the import file?`

Select **Yes** to continue. Display the resulting Freelance Plus graph by pressing F10 and selecting **Go** (or press F10 followed by Alt–F8 and Enter). Figure 13.11 shows the example graph displayed within Freelance Plus.

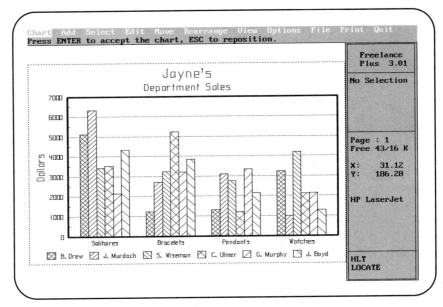

Fig. 13.11. *Viewing the 1-2-3 graph imported into Freelance Plus.*

Using 1-2-3 with Harvard Graphics

Software Publishing Corporation's *Harvard Graphics* 2.x, one of the easiest presentation graphics programs to use, can produce graphs from 1-2-3 worksheets or use 1-2-3 graphs saved with **/Graph Save**. You can choose from Harvard Graphics' wide assortment of predesigned graphs and modify your graph with several editing and font tools.

You cannot view a worksheet within Harvard Graphics. Before exiting your worksheet, record graph names and range names (or range addresses) so you can specify them when prompted by Harvard Graphics.

Creating a Sample 1-2-3 Worksheet To Import

The worksheet in figure 13.12 is used by a jewelry store to show sales in individual departments, listed by staff member. Create the worksheet as shown to follow the importing examples in this section. (This worksheet was used earlier in the chapter for importing to Freelance Plus.) In cell F8, type the formula **@SUM(B8..E8)**; then copy cell F8 to the range F9..F13. Format rows 8 and 15 as Currency with **0** decimal places and the remaining values in the worksheet as **,** (Comma) format with **0** decimal places. Type **@SUM(B8..B13)** in cell B15 and copy it to the range C15..F15. Set the column width for column A as 16 characters and columns B through F as 11 characters.

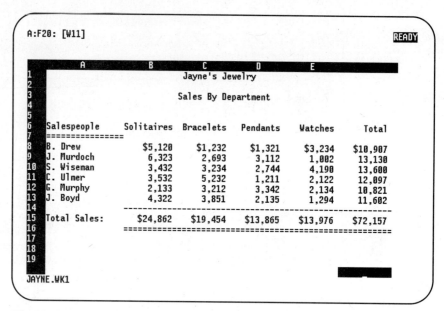

Fig. 13.12. A 1-2-3 worksheet to be imported into Harvard Graphics.

Create a series of ranges with the following command sequence:

/Range Name Create

STAFF	**A8..A13**
SOLITAIRES	**B8..B13**
BRACELETS	**C8..C13**
PENDANTS	**D8..D13**
WATCHES	**E8..E13**
TOTAL	**F8..F13**

Save the worksheet to disk with the name JAYNE.WK1 (even if you use Release 3.x). Harvard Graphics can import only 1-2-3 Release 2.x worksheets. Then create a graph with the following command sequence:

/Graph Type Bar

X	B6..E6
A	B8..E8
B	B9..E9
C	B10..E10
D	B11..E11
E	B12..E12
F	B13..E13

Options Legend

A	B. Drew
B	J. Murdoch
C	S. Wiseman
D	C. Ulmer
E	G. Murphy
F	J. Boyd

Titles

First	Jayne's
Second	Department Sales
Y-Axis	Dollars

Grid Horizontal

B&W

Quit

Select View to see the graph on-screen, as shown in figure 13.13. Save the worksheet (in case you need to make a correction later) and save the graph as **JAYNE.PIC**. You are ready to import the worksheet data with Harvard Graphics.

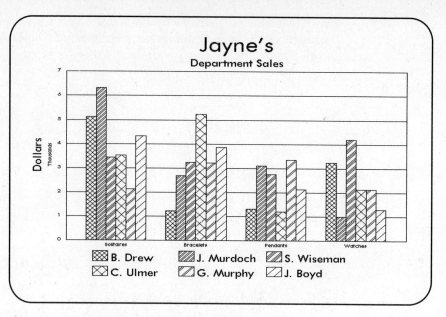

Fig. 13.13. *Viewing the graph in the JAYNE worksheet.*

Importing 1-2-3 Data

In the import process, Harvard Graphics converts worksheet formulas to their numerical values and ignores macros.

Harvard Graphics must know which type of graph you are creating *before* you import a worksheet from 1-2-3, or it doesn't format the incoming data properly.

To import the worksheet, select **Create new chart** from the Main Menu. The Create New Chart menu appears. Select the type of graph you want to create. For this example, select **Bar/Line**. The X Data Type menu appears with Name highlighted. Check the x-axis values. If the values are correct, press F10. If the values are incorrect, type new values. If the x-axis values are dates, months, weeks, or any of the other values in the X Data Type menu list, type the starting date, month, week, etc. and the increment Harvard Graphics will use between the values. In this example, because the x-axis values are department names, you can leave the screen as is and press F10 to continue. The Bar/Line Chart Data screen appears.

You need not define anything else until you import the 1-2-3 data. You can obtain all x-axis names and graph data from the worksheet. Press Esc to return to the Main Menu and select **Import/Export**. The Import/Export menu appears, as shown in figure 13.14.

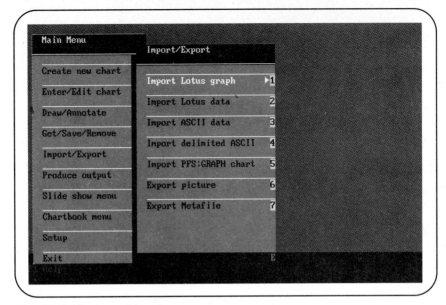

Fig. 13.14. The Import/Export menu.

Select **Import Lotus data.** Type the full path name at the `Directory` prompt; for example, type **C:\LOTUS**. A list of 1-2-3 files appears. If you use 1-2-3 Release 3.x, you may see WK3 extensions in the list, but you can import only files with WK1 and WKS extensions. Specify the desired file (for this example, JAYNE.WK1) by highlighting it and pressing Enter.

The Import Lotus Data screen appears. You can type the desired title, subtitle, and footnote at the appropriate prompts on the Import Lotus Data screen, or specify cells containing the information to be used in these fields. To type a cell address, begin with a backslash (\). For this example, type **\C1** at the `Title:` prompt and **\C3** at the `Subtitle:` prompt. Leave the `Footnote:` field blank for this example.

You cannot type range names at these prompts.

Type range names next to the `X-axis data` prompts (below the title information) to specify the cell contents used for legends in the graph. Use Tab and Shift–Tab to move between fields. For this example, use the values shown in figure 13.15.

After specifying titles and legends, select `Yes` at the `Append data:` prompt to add this data to existing graph data, or select `No` (by pressing the space bar). For this example, select `No` and press F10 to continue.

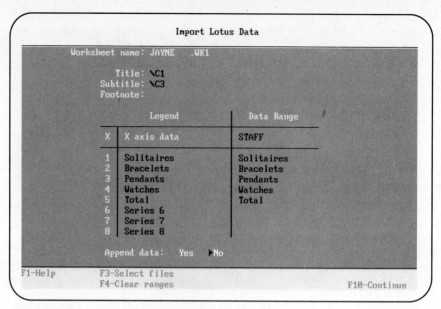

```
                          Import Lotus Data

        Worksheet name: JAYNE    .WK1

                 Title: \C1
              Subtitle: \C3
              Footnote:

                      Legend                Data Range

               X  │ X axis data            STAFF

               1  │ Solitaires             Solitaires
               2  │ Bracelets              Bracelets
               3  │ Pendants               Pendants
               4  │ Watches                Watches
               5  │ Total                  Total
               6  │ Series 6
               7  │ Series 7
               8  │ Series 8

               Append data:    Yes   ▶No

  F1-Help          F3-Select files
                   F4-Clear ranges                        F10-Continue
```

Fig. 13.15. *Specifying titles and legends for the graph.*

Harvard Graphics displays the message Reading worksheet while it imports the data and then displays the Bar/Line Chart Data screen showing the series values and titles for your review.

Harvard Graphics centers all titles. Because extra spaces can distort the centering, remove them before graphing the data in Harvard Graphics. In the JAYNE.WK1 worksheet, if you used an extra space to center the title Jayne's Jewelry *over* Sales By Department, *move the cursor to the title (on the Bar/Line Chart Data screen) and remove the extra space.*

When the values on the Bar/Line Chart Data screen are correct, press F2 to see the graph. Your graph should resemble figure 13.16. You can modify and accent the graph with Harvard Graphics' editing and presentation tools.

Draw Partner, *another software product included with Harvard Graphics, enables you to draw lines and place the graph over special symbols (such as a map).*

To save this file for later viewing, select **G**et/**S**ave/**R**emove **S**ave Chart. Type a file name and description for the graph (Harvard Graphics uses the graph's title as a default description). You can **G**et the graph later for viewing or printing.

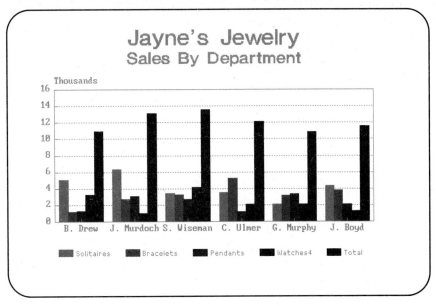

Fig. 13.16. *The JAYNE.WK1 worksheet imported as a Harvard Graphics graph.*

Streamlining the Importing Process

If you often import 1-2-3 worksheets with Harvard Graphics, you can streamline the importing process by changing default values, creating templates, and linking Harvard Graphics graphs to their source worksheets to keep data current.

To save time when importing a worksheet file, change Harvard Graphics' default settings. Select **Setup** from the Main Menu and **Defaults** from the Setup menu. The Default Settings screen appears. Type the full path name of the 1-2-3 directory at the Import directory prompt; for example, type **C:\LOTUS**. If you always import the same worksheet file, type the file name next to the Import file prompt. Press F10 to leave the Default Settings screen and save the specified defaults.

Before importing a worksheet file, change defaults as necessary (for example, if you specified a worksheet file as the default but plan to use a different file).

The graph created from the imported JAYNE.WK1 data in the preceding section is not linked to its source worksheet. If you change the worksheet in 1-2-3, the graph doesn't change until you import the worksheet file again. To create a real-time link between a Harvard Graphics graph and its source 1-2-3 worksheet, save the graph's *template*. The template stores the worksheet file name, data ranges, titles, and so on but not the actual data.

To save the graph template, select **S**ave template from the **G**et/Save/Remove option of the Main Menu. The Save Template screen appears, as shown in figure 13.17. Type a name for the template at the `Template Name:` prompt, using up to eight characters. Harvard Graphics supplies the TPL extension. Type a description if desired. To clear existing graph data before importing current worksheet information, respond **Y**es at the `Clear Values:` prompt. Specify `Lotus` at the `Import data link:` prompt. Press Enter to save the template and Esc to return to the Main Menu.

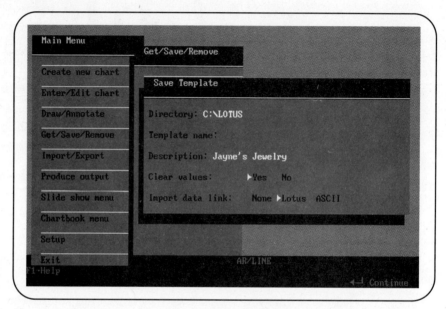

Fig. 13.17. *Specifying template information for imported data.*

To view a worksheet graph by loading its template, select **G**et/Save/Remove **G**et template. Harvard Graphics displays a list of files with the TPL extension. Select a template file and press F2 to preview the graph on-screen. The graph reflects the latest worksheet values.

Importing Named 1-2-3 Graphs

Harvard Graphics can directly import graphs created with 1-2-3's /**G**raph **N**ame **C**reate command. Harvard Graphics reads the named graph and interprets as much of the graph's appearance as possible without requiring you to re-create a graph from the raw worksheet data. This example shows a bar graph being imported, but Harvard Graphics can import any type of 1-2-3 graph.

To import a named graph, select the **Import/Export** option from the Main Menu. Select **Import Lotus graph**. The Select Worksheet screen appears, as shown in figure 13.18.

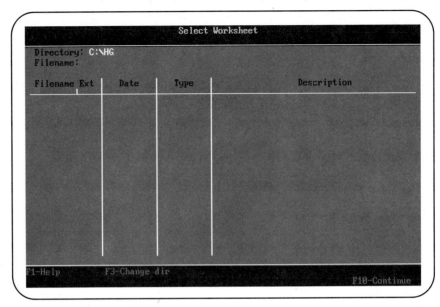

Fig. 13.18. The Select Worksheet screen.

Type the path name and file name for the worksheet containing the named graph; for example, type **C:\LOTUS\JAYNE.WK1**. The named graphs in the specified worksheet file appear on the Select Worksheet screen.

 All 1-2-3 worksheets except Release 1.x use a default graph called MAIN.

In this example, the graph names JAYNE and MAIN appear. Any other named graphs in the specified directory appear with MAIN on the Import Lotus graph screen.

Respond **No** at the `Import Data Only:` prompt to import graph settings with the data for the named graph. Select the desired named graph from the displayed list. Harvard Graphics reads the graph settings from the named graph and displays the Harvard Graphics equivalent, such as the graph shown in figure 13.19.

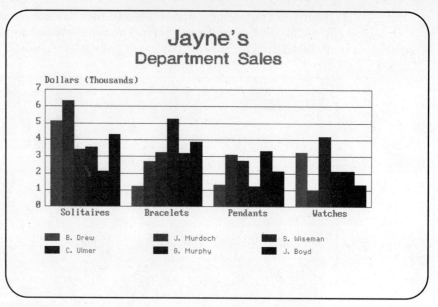

Fig. 13.19. *The Harvard Graphics equivalent of the named graph.*

Using 1-2-3 with CorelDRAW!

CorelDRAW! 2.0 is a drawing and presentation graphics program offering advanced artistic drawing, shading, and coloring capabilities and clip art libraries. CorelDRAW! imports 1-2-3 PIC files directly into drawings. After importing a PIC file, you can add to it, touch it up, or combine it with other drawn images. CorelDRAW! doesn't produce graphs; the import process combines 1-2-3's graphing capability with CorelDRAW!'s drawing tools.

Because CorelDRAW! offers several free-form drawing tools with many uses, covering all of the ways you can manipulate an imported 1-2-3 graph in CorelDRAW! is impossible. (The most common usage is highlighting and accenting the graphs.) This section discusses only the procedure for importing 1-2-3 PIC files with CorelDRAW!.

Creating a Sample 1-2-3 Graph To Import

The worksheet in figure 13.20 is used by a jewelry store to show sales in individual departments, listed by staff member. (This worksheet was used earlier in the chapter for importing to Freelance Plus.) Create the worksheet as shown to follow the importing examples in this section. In cell F8, type the formula **@SUM(B8..E8)**; then copy cell F8 to the range F9..F13. Format rows 8 and 15 as **Currency** with **0** decimal places and the remaining values in the worksheet as , (Comma) format with **0** decimal places. Type **@SUM(B8..B13)** in cell B15 and copy it to the range C15..F15. Set the column width for column A as 16 characters and columns B through F as 11 characters.

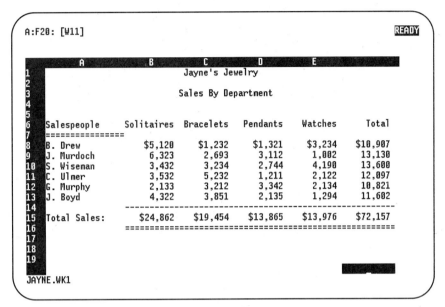

Fig. 13.20. A 1-2-3 worksheet to be used with CorelDRAW!.

Save the worksheet to disk with the name JAYNE.WK3 (or JAYNE.WK1 if you use 1-2-3 Release 2.x). Then create a graph with the following command sequence:

/Graph Type Bar

X	B6..E6
A	B8..E8
B	B9..E9
C	B10..E10
D	B11..E11
E	B12..E12
F	B13..E13

Options Legend

A	B. Drew
B	J. Murdoch

C	S. Wiseman
D	C. Ulmer
E	G. Murphy
F	J. Boyd

Titles

First **Jayne's**

Second **Department Sales**

Y-Axis **Dollars**

Grid Horizontal

B&W

Quit

Select View to see the graph on-screen, as shown in figure 13.21. Save the worksheet (in case you need to make a correction later) and save the graph as **JAYNE.PIC**. You are ready to import the graph with CorelDRAW!.

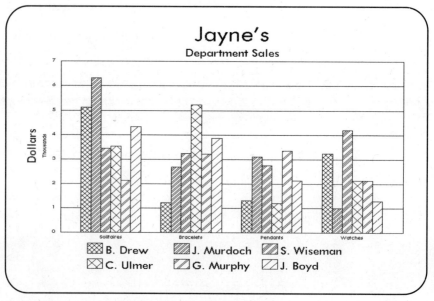

Fig. 13.21. Viewing the graph in the JAYNE worksheet.

Importing 1-2-3 PIC Files

To take advantage of CorelDRAW!'s tools, you must understand how a 1-2-3 PIC file is imported. CorelDRAW! converts the imported data to the CorelDRAW! format to match surrounding art and text and treats the imported data as a group of objects that you can edit as CorelDRAW! objects. You can expand or resize portions of the graph using Corel-DRAW! tools. Colors defined in the PIC file are retained in the CorelDRAW! image; text in the imported data can be edited using CorelDRAW!'s text-editing tools. (Most programs that import PIC files treat the entire section of imported data—text and art—as a single graphic image that cannot be changed separately.)

The first font in the CorelDRAW! list of fonts (generally the Avalon font) is applied to the title of the imported graph (if any). CorelDRAW! converts the remaining text to the second font in the list, usually Aardvark. You can change the order of fonts before importing the PIC file, or change the applied fonts after importing as with other CorelDRAW! text.

Figure 13.22 shows a simple drawing in CorelDRAW!. The dynamic appearance of the text is a common format in CorelDRAW!. Prepare as much of your drawing as possible before importing. Because Corel-DRAW! imports a PIC file as a group of objects, you can move and resize the imported data without affecting surrounding art or text.

Fig. 13.22. A CorelDRAW! image ready for an imported PIC file.

The procedure for importing a PIC file with CorelDRAW! is straight-forward, requiring only a few steps. For this example, create the text as shown in figure 13.22. To import the PIC file, position the cursor at the place in the drawing where you want the graph to appear. Select **F**ile Import. The Import selection screen appears, as shown in figure 13.23.

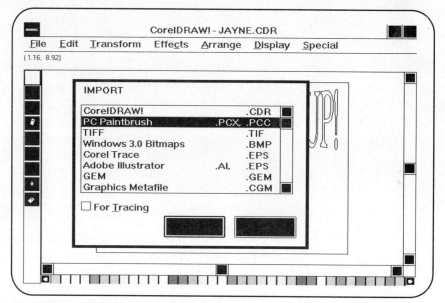

Fig. 13.23. *The Import selection screen.*

Select the import format (Lotus PIC) from the displayed list on the Import selection screen. The Import file screen appears; specify the desired PIC file. You can type the full path name for the file (for example, type **C:\LOTUS\JAYNE.PIC**) or select the file from the list. CorelDRAW! imports the specified file, displaying the hourglass "wait" symbol. When the PIC file is imported, CorelDRAW! displays the graph surrounded by grab handles, as shown in figure 13.24. This example shows a bar graph being imported, but CorelDRAW! can import any type of 1-2-3 graph.

Because CorelDRAW! imports the graphs in a small size (relative to the rest of the drawing page), you must enlarge most imported graphs by clicking on the graph area with the mouse and pulling a handle outward. After enlarging the graph, press F9 to see a preview of the drawing on-screen before changing fonts or modifying the graph.

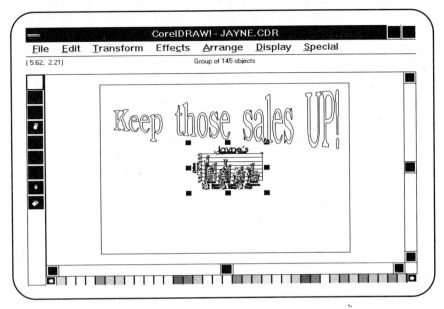

Fig. 13.24. The imported 1-2-3 graph, surrounded by grab handles.

You may need to use CorelDRAW!'s text-editing tools to adjust the text in the graph, as long labels in the legend can overlap. (Fig. 13.25 shows an editing session for the imported graph from the JAYNE worksheet.) After you finish adjusting the graph and surrounding art, save the drawing.

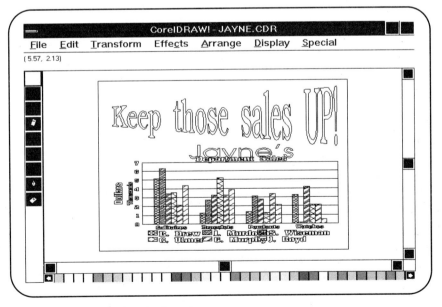

Fig. 13.25. Editing the imported graph.

After importing a 1-2-3 graph into CorelDRAW!, you can enhance the graph in many ways. You can change the graph colors or add new ones, or add text (or change existing text that doesn't overlap any of the graph, such as titles) in a large variety of font styles and sizes. After you add text, you can use CorelDRAW! tools to add stretching effects to words on or around your graphs (as shown in fig. 13.25), or superimpose clip art images over the graph. With these art images in place, 3-D tools are available to make your graph more appealing and visual.

 Keep in mind that—despite the wide variety of tools you get with CorelDRAW!—less is more; the simpler your message, the better it comes across. Don't clutter the graph by using a lot of special effects. One well-placed clip art icon can mean much more to your audience than five or six pictures that take the reader's eyes away from the important graph data. CorelDRAW! makes adding effects easy, but use these art tools to express and not impress.

CorelDRAW! doesn't have linking capability; if your 1-2-3 data changes, you must re-create the PIC file and import it again.

Using 1-2-3 with First Publisher

First Publisher 3.0's popularity stems from its low price and ease of use. Its features are designed for users who want to publish newsletters, flyers, and simple business reports.

Like most desktop publishing and presentation programs, First Publisher lacks numerical and graphing capabilities. First Publisher cannot read worksheet data directly but can import worksheets saved as ASCII print files or art captured with the SNAPSHOT facility. This section discusses procedures for importing 1-2-3 information by both methods.

Importing 1-2-3 Data

The worksheet in figure 13.26 is used by a jewelry store to show sales in individual departments, listed by staff member. (This worksheet was used earlier in the chapter for importing to Freelance Plus.) Create the worksheet as shown to follow the importing examples in this section. In cell F8, type the formula **@SUM(B8..E8)**; then copy cell F8 to the range F9..F13. Format rows 8 and 15 as **Currency** with **0** decimal places and the remaining values in the worksheet as , (Comma) format with **0** decimal places. Type **@SUM(B8..B13)** in cell B15 and copy it to the range C15..F15. Set the column width for column A as 16 characters and columns B through F as 11 characters.

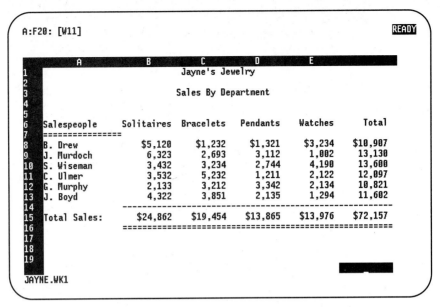

```
A:F28: [W11]                                                    READY

        A           B          C          D          E
1                           Jayne's Jewelry
2
3                         Sales By Department
4
5
6   Salespeople   Solitaires  Bracelets  Pendants   Watches     Total
7   ================
8   B. Drew          $5,120     $1,232     $1,321    $3,234    $10,907
9   J. Murdoch        6,323      2,693      3,112     1,002     13,130
10  S. Wiseman        3,432      3,234      2,744     4,190     13,600
11  C. Ulmer          3,532      5,232      1,211     2,122     12,097
12  G. Murphy         2,133      3,212      3,342     2,134     10,821
13  J. Boyd           4,322      3,851      2,135     1,294     11,602
14                 ------------------------------------------------------
15  Total Sales:    $24,862    $19,454    $13,865   $13,976    $72,157
16                 ======================================================
17
18
19

JAYNE.WK1
```

Fig. 13.26. *A 1-2-3 worksheet to be imported into First Publisher.*

To save the worksheet to an ASCII text file, select **/P**rint **F**ile and specify the full path name and file name for the new file. Select **R**ange and specify the entire worksheet. Select **G**o to print the worksheet to the specified file name (in this example, JAYNE.TXT) and **Q**uit to leave the **/P**rint menu. Exit 1-2-3 and start First Publisher.

*Use the First Publisher directory in the path name and TXT extension in the file name when saving your 1-2-3 worksheet to ASCII; for example, type **C:\ PUB\ JAYNE.TXT**.*

When you import a worksheet file, First Publisher reads it as a text file and attempts to retain column and alignment settings. (Some adjustment is usually required, however.)

Use First Publisher's font commands to add eye-catching detail to a publication.

Before importing the 1-2-3 worksheet file, move the cursor to the place where you want the imported data to appear and specify the First Publisher fonts for the incoming data. Press F4 to display the Font menu and select the desired font (for this example, select Geneva). Press F5 to display the Style pull-down menu and select the desired style (for this example, select 12-point and Normal). These options already may be selected, depending on your First Publisher environment. For this example, First Publisher uses the 12-point Geneva font for the imported worksheet data.

To import the worksheet data, press F3 to display the Text menu. Select Get Text and specify the desired file at the `Filename` prompt. For this example, type **JAYNE** and press Enter. You don't need to type the TXT extension. First Publisher recognizes that the file is not in First Publisher text format and displays the menu shown in figure 13.27; specify the format of the incoming data (ASCII). First Publisher imports the worksheet, as shown in figure 13.28.

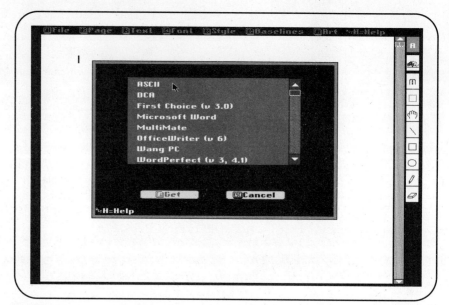

Fig. 13.27. *Specifying the format of the file to be imported.*

As figure 13.28 shows, the imported worksheet requires some alignment and editing before it has a finished look in First Publisher. The fonts in First Publisher are proportionally spaced and don't align properly without adjustment. By using the text tool to add a few spaces before some of the data, and deleting some spaces between other parts, you can align the worksheet properly. You may want to change the style of the title or some of the data; the text is imported into First Publisher directly onto the baselines so you can move the cursor directly to any of the worksheet's text.

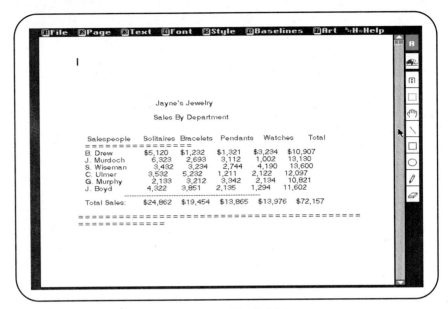

Fig. 13.28. *The imported worksheet data in First Publisher.*

Importing 1-2-3 PIC Files

First Publisher's SNAPSHOT is a memory-resident utility program that "photographs" images on-screen. The resulting "snapshot" is easily converted into a First Publisher art file that can be modified as desired.

Before starting 1-2-3 to create or retrieve your graph, change to the First Publisher directory, type **SNAPSHOT** at the DOS prompt, and press Enter. The SNAPSHOT copyright message appears, indicating that the program is loaded properly.

If you often import worksheet data into your First Publisher publications, include the SNAPSHOT command in your AUTOEXEC.BAT file. This procedure causes SNAPSHOT to be loaded each time you start your computer.

Creating a Sample 1-2-3 Graph To Import

This example uses the JAYNE.WK1 (or WK3) worksheet created earlier in this section. Start 1-2-3 and retrieve JAYNE.WK1 (or WK3). Then create a graph with the following command sequence:

/Graph Type **B**ar

X   **B6..E6**

A   **B8..E8**

B	B9..E9
C	B10..E10
D	B11..E11
E	B12..E12
F	B13..E13

Options Legend

A	B. Drew
B	J. Murdoch
C	S. Wiseman
D	C. Ulmer
E	G. Murphy
F	J. Boyd

Titles

First	Jayne's
Second	Department Sales
Y-Axis	Dollars

Grid Horizontal

B&W

Quit

Select View to see the graph on-screen, as shown in figure 13.29. Save the worksheet (in case you need to make a correction later). You are now ready to take a SNAPSHOT picture of the graph. This example shows a bar graph being imported, but First Publisher can import any type of 1-2-3 graph.

Taking a SNAPSHOT of the Graph

With the graph on-screen, press Shift–PrtSc. SNAPSHOT beeps to indicate that you correctly captured the graph. Press Esc to exit SNAP-SHOT; then exit 1-2-3.

You must "develop" the SNAPSHOT image with a program in your First Publisher directory called *SNAP2ART* before transferring the graph into First Publisher. To develop the graph into an art file, type **SNAP2ART** at the DOS prompt in the First Publisher directory. The SNAP2ART program displays the graph and a choice of menu options. You can shrink the graph by moving the sides of the graph toward the center.

For this example, don't modify the graph. Press **E** to exit SNAP2ART and return to the DOS prompt. Upon exiting, SNAP2ART saves the graph in a First Publisher art file image and calls it SNAP.ART.

If the SNAP.ART file exists, SNAP2ART displays the following message:

```
The file snap.art already exists, delete it or use a new name
```

If you want to save the existing SNAP.ART file, you must rename it to another file and reshoot the 1-2-3 graph. If you don't want to save the existing file, you can overwrite it with the 1-2-3 graph snapshot.

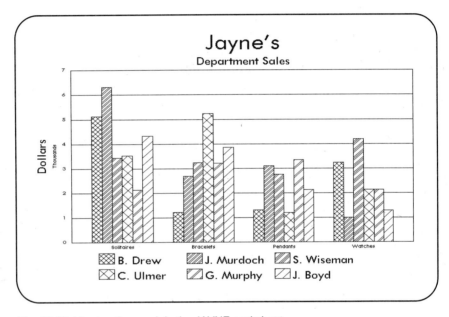

Fig. 13.29. Viewing the graph in the JAYNE worksheet.

Importing the Graph

To import the graph, press F7 to display the Art menu. Select Get Art and specify the desired file at the Filename prompt (for example, type **SNAP.ART**). The First Publisher hand tool appears. Move the hand tool to the location where you want the graph to appear and press F10 (or a mouse button). The graph appears as an inverted image (white lines on a black background).

To reverse the image, select Invert from the Art menu. Figure 13.30 shows the example after the imported graph is reversed.

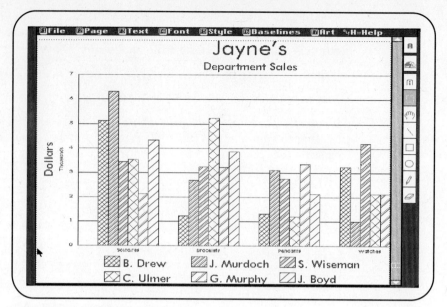

Fig. 13.30. *The imported graph after reversing the image.*

Imported SNAPSHOT images may be too large for your publication's settings. To resize the image, press Alt–R. You may want to draw lines to surround the graph and separate it from the text (making it stand out). To see a page preview of the publication, press Alt–Z. Make any additional adjustments necessary.

Because the imported graph lies on the graphics layer, you can edit it with any of the graphics tools (except the high-resolution tool, which is reserved for a different type of art). Be sure to save your publication with the imported picture before exiting First Publisher.

Using 1-2-3 with PageMaker

One of the leaders in the high-end desktop publishing market is *PageMaker* 4.0 from Aldus. PageMaker can import 1-2-3 graphs and worksheets (from 1-2-3 Releases 2.x and 3.x) directly into a publication with very little effort.

Creating a Sample 1-2-3 Worksheet To Import

The worksheet in figure 13.31 is used by a jewelry store to show sales in individual departments, listed by staff member. Create the worksheet as shown to follow the importing examples in this section. (This worksheet was used earlier in the chapter for importing to Freelance Plus.) In cell F8, type the formula **@SUM(B8..E8)**; then copy cell F8 to the range F9..F13. Format rows 8 and 15 as Currency with **0** decimal places and the remaining values in the worksheet as **,** (Comma) format with **0** decimal places. Type **@SUM(B8..B13)** in cell B15 and copy it to the range C15..F15. Set the column width for column A as 16 characters and columns B through F as 11 characters.

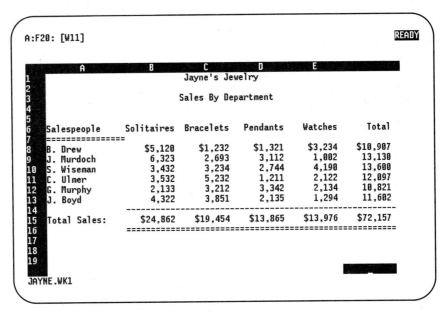

Fig. 13.31. *A 1-2-3 worksheet to be imported into PageMaker.*

Create a series of ranges with the following command sequence:

/Range Name Create

STAFF	**A8..A13**
SOLITAIRES	**B8..B13**
BRACELETS	**C8..C13**
PENDANTS	**D8..D13**
WATCHES	**E8..E13**
TOTAL	**F8..F13**

Save the worksheet to disk with the name JAYNE.WK3 (use the extension WK1 if you use Release 2.x). Then create a graph with the following command sequence:

/Graph Type Bar

X	B6..E6
A	B8..E8
B	B9..E9
C	B10..E10
D	B11..E11
E	B12..E12
F	B13..E13

Options Legend

A	B. Drew
B	J. Murdoch
C	S. Wiseman
D	C. Ulmer
E	G. Murphy
F	J. Boyd

Titles

First	Jayne's
Second	Department Sales
Y-Axis	Dollars

Grid Horizontal

B&W

Quit

Select View to see the graph on-screen, as shown in figure 13.32. Save the worksheet (in case you need to make a correction later) and save the graph as **JAYNE.PIC**. You are ready to import the worksheet data with PageMaker.

Importing 1-2-3 Data

Before importing the worksheet, you must create a publication or open an existing one. Start PageMaker from the Windows environment. (To add a worksheet to an existing publication, load the publication and display the page where you want to place the imported worksheet data. The example that follows creates a new publication.)

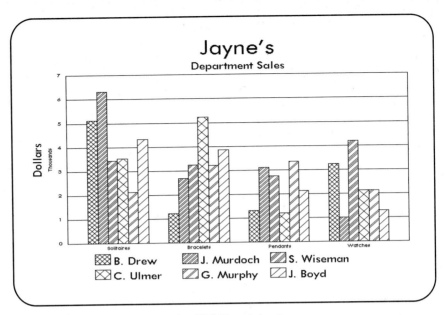

Fig. 13.32. Viewing the graph in the JAYNE worksheet.

PageMaker imports macros as cell contents. If your worksheet includes macros and the cells containing the macros are imported, the macro contents appear in the resulting publication. Because the macros are meaningless to PageMaker, you must use the text tools of PageMaker to remove this macro data from the imported worksheet.

PageMaker tries to reproduce your original worksheet formatting in the imported data. Other than the decimal tab alignment (which you can specify), PageMaker's imported worksheet looks just as it did in 1-2-3.

Open a new publication by selecting New from the File menu. Accept the defaults of the Page Setup dialog box. A blank publication page appears. To import the worksheet, select Place from the File menu; the Place File dialog box appears, as shown in figure 13.33. Type your 1-2-3 path name at the Name prompt (for example, type **C:\LOTUS**) and press Enter to see a list of worksheet files.

Select the JAYNE worksheet you created earlier. (Because PageMaker recognizes 1-2-3 Release 2.x and 3.x file formats, you can select JAYNE.WK1 or JAYNE.WK3.) PageMaker recognizes the 1-2-3 format and gives you the option of importing all or only a portion of the worksheet. The Place a 1-2-3 or Symphony Range dialog box appears, as shown in figure 13.34.

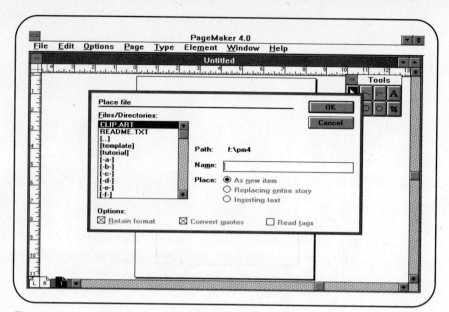

Fig. 13.33. Viewing the Place File dialog box.

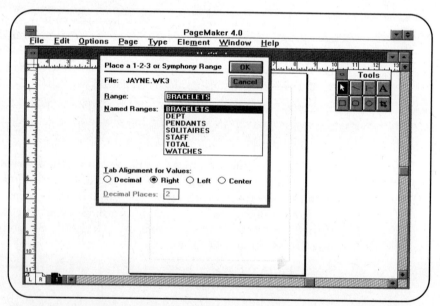

Fig. 13.34. Specifying the worksheet range to import.

The dialog box shows a list of all ranges assigned to the worksheet. If you elect to import a portion of the worksheet, only one range can be imported at a time (to import more than one range, repeat these steps for each range). To import the entire worksheet, type the range address for the entire worksheet in the **R**ange field. If you use 1-2-3 Release 3.x, you can have multiple worksheets in the same file; PageMaker requires that you append the worksheet name (or names if more than one exists in memory) to the range values. To import the entire JAYNE worksheet, type **A1..F16** for 1-2-3 Release 2.x, or **A:A1..A:F16** for 1-2-3 Release 3.x.

You specify the way that PageMaker aligns numbers when importing the worksheet. If a worksheet uses the **D**ecimal format, select the Decimal option from the **T**ab Alignment for Values field. This process ensures that all numbers are aligned by decimal point. If you select this option, type the number of decimal places used by the majority of values in the worksheet at the **D**ecimal Places prompt (even if the number of decimal places varies). The default is 2. The JAYNE worksheet doesn't use decimal places; for worksheets of this type, specify how you want the numbers to be aligned after PageMaker imports them. If the values in the original worksheet were right-aligned, for example, select the Right option from the **T**ab Alignment for Values field.

After you specify the tab alignment and select OK or press Enter, Page-Maker imports the data. When the import process is complete, an Auto-flow pointer appears; use the pointer to place the data at the desired location. (For this example, place the worksheet at the top of the publication.) A thumbnail sketch of the imported worksheet appears, as shown in figure 13.35. Use the handles to stretch or shrink the worksheet, as with other graphic images in PageMaker.

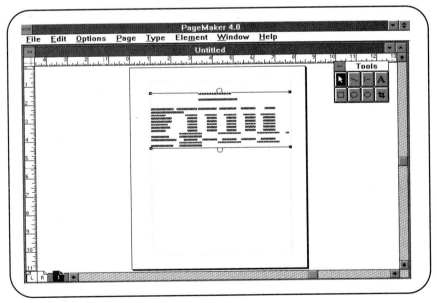

Fig. 13.35. *Placing the imported worksheet in the publication.*

The imported worksheet data is treated as regular text in the publication. You can apply all of the available text tools and fonts in PageMaker to modify the numbers or titles of the worksheet. Depending on how the worksheet was created in 1-2-3, you may have to adjust some of the underlining by adding or removing spaces and underlines. If you used the 1-2-3 repeat prefix (\) to underline a cell instead of typing dashes or underscores, add underscores to the imported data. Very little of this kind of editing is necessary, however, because PageMaker does a good job of placing the data correctly.

To make your editing easier, select a larger view size (for example, 200% *or* 400%*) from the* **Page** *menu.*

After you adjust the alignment of the imported data, save the publication to disk and continue working with the tools available in PageMaker.

Importing 1-2-3 PIC Files

PageMaker can import 1-2-3 PIC files as easily as worksheets. The steps for importing PIC files are similar to those discussed in the preceding section: open or create a publication and place the PIC file in the publication. Because PageMaker recognizes the PIC file format, you can apply all of PageMaker's art tools to the imported graph.

To import the sample PIC file, open a new publication by selecting **New** from the **File** menu. Accept the defaults of the Page Setup dialog box and select **Place** from the **File** menu. Specify the JAYNE.PIC file you created earlier. The message in the **Name** field changes to As independent graphic to indicate that PageMaker recognizes the PIC file format. Press Enter or select OK. PageMaker imports the data and places grab handles around it, as shown in figure 13.36.

Move the graph to the desired location (for this example, place the graph at the top of the new publication). After placing the graph, save the publication to disk and continue working on the publication using the tools available in PageMaker.

Using 1-2-3 with Ventura Publisher

Ventura Publisher 3.0 produces multiple-page publications and can use imported data from several different software programs. No direct way exists to import a 1-2-3 worksheet, but you can save a worksheet to a PRN file and read it into Ventura Publisher. A little extra editing is needed to clean up the imported worksheet data, but that process usually is much simpler than typing the data from scratch. You can import 1-2-3 PIC files directly into Ventura Publisher.

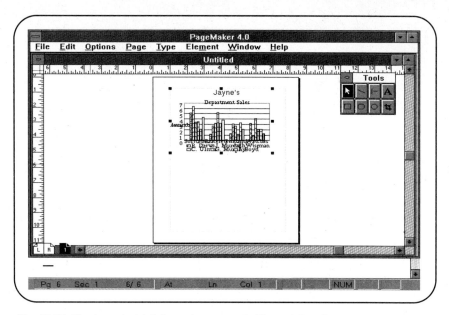

Fig. 13.36. *The imported 1-2-3 graph, surrounded by grab handles.*

Importing 1-2-3 Data

Because Ventura Publisher can import only PRN worksheet data, the format of the data when you create the PRN file dictates the look of the imported data in Ventura Publisher. Decimal places and column widths are retained, but alignment problems occur because 1-2-3 inserts spaces instead of tabs when printing columns of data to the PRN file. A proportional font may make the imported data look off-center in places; adjust these sections of data with Ventura Publisher's text tools. Any macros in your worksheet are ignored by the import process.

Creating a Sample 1-2-3 Worksheet To Import

The worksheet in figure 13.37 is used by a jewelry store to show sales in individual departments, listed by staff member. Create the worksheet as shown to follow the importing examples in this section. (This worksheet was used earlier in the chapter for importing to Freelance Plus.) In cell F8, type the formula **@SUM(B8..E8)**; then copy cell F8 to the range F9..F13. Format rows 8 and 15 as **Currency** with **0** decimal places and the remaining values in the worksheet as **,** (Comma) format with **0** decimal places. Type **@SUM(B8..B13)** in cell B15 and copy it to the range C15..F15. Set the column width for column A as 16 characters and columns B through F as 11 characters.

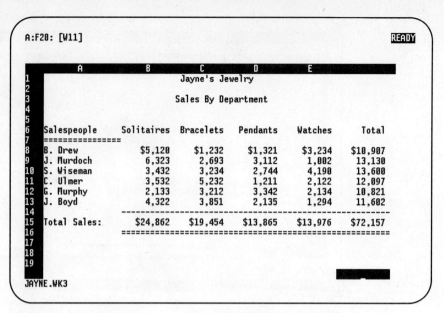

```
A:F20: [W11]                                                   READY

          A           B          C          D          E
1                        Jayne's Jewelry
2
3                      Sales By Department
4
5
6   Salespeople   Solitaires  Bracelets   Pendants   Watches      Total
7   =================
8   B. Drew          $5,120     $1,232     $1,321     $3,234    $10,907
9   J. Murdoch        6,323      2,693      3,112      1,002     13,130
10  S. Wiseman        3,432      3,234      2,744      4,190     13,600
11  C. Ulmer          3,532      5,232      1,211      2,122     12,097
12  G. Murphy         2,133      3,212      3,342      2,134     10,821
13  J. Boyd           4,322      3,851      2,135      1,294     11,602
14                 -----------------------------------------------------
15  Total Sales:    $24,862    $19,454    $13,865    $13,976    $72,157
16                 =====================================================
17
18
19
                                                        ███████████

JAYNE.WK3
```

Fig. 13.37. A 1-2-3 worksheet to be imported into Ventura Publisher.

Create a series of ranges with the following command sequence:

/Range Name Create

STAFF	**A8..A13**
SOLITAIRES	**B8..B13**
BRACELETS	**C8..C13**
PENDANTS	**D8..D13**
WATCHES	**E8..E13**
TOTAL	**F8..F13**

Save the worksheet to disk with the name JAYNE.WK3 (use the extension WK1 if you use Release 2.x). Then create a graph with the following command sequence:

/Graph Type Bar

X	**B6..E6**
A	**B8..E8**
B	**B9..E9**
C	**B10..E10**
D	**B11..E11**

E	B12..E12
F	B13..E13

Options Legend

A	B. Drew
B	J. Murdoch
C	S. Wiseman
D	C. Ulmer
E	G. Murphy
F	J. Boyd

Titles

First **Jayne's**

Second **Department Sales**

Y-Axis **Dollars**

Grid Horizontal

B&W

Quit

Select View to see the graph on-screen, as shown in figure 13.38. Save the worksheet (in case you need to make a correction later) and save the graph as **JAYNE.PIC**. You are ready to print the worksheet to a PRN file that you will later read into Ventura Publisher.

Preparing the PRN File

To import a 1-2-3 worksheet file into Ventura Publisher, you must print the file to an ASCII PRN disk file from 1-2-3 before starting Ventura Publisher. With your worksheet on-screen, select **/P**rint File, type **JAYNE**, and press Enter (1-2-3 adds the PRN extension). Select **R**ange, type **A1..F16**, and press Enter. This procedure tells 1-2-3 to send the entire worksheet to the PRN file; to import a range, specify the range name or range address. Select Go **Q**uit; 1-2-3 prints the worksheet data to JAYNE.PRN.

 To speed up the import process, create several small PRN files using different worksheet ranges rather than creating one large PRN file.

After creating the PRN file, exit 1-2-3 and start Ventura Publisher from the Windows environment.

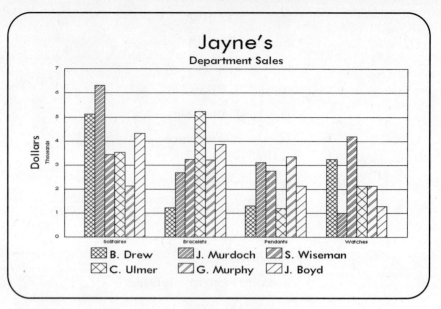

Fig. 13.38. *Viewing the graph in the JAYNE worksheet.*

Importing the Data

To import the PRN file, you must open an existing publication or create a new one. This example assumes that you are creating a new publication from scratch and loading the PRN file at the top of the blank publication. To import worksheet data into the middle of an existing publication, display the desired page and position the cursor before importing the data.

Set your left and right margins at 0, the number of columns at 1, and the width of the first column at 8 inches (the standard setting for a one-column page). If your defaults are set to a different value, change the margin information from within the **Frame** menu before importing the worksheet data.

Select **L**oad Text/Picture from the **F**ile menu. The LOAD/TEXT PICTURE dialog box appears, as shown in figure 13.39. Select **T**ext from the `File Type` field and highlight `WordStar 3` in the **Format** field. *This step is very important.* Although the 1-2-3 PRN file is in ASCII format, Ventura Publisher cannot use the `ASCII` option to perform the import because 1-2-3 PRN files have a carriage return at the end of each line and the ASCII import doesn't read this type of file properly. The `PRN to Table` option imports data into a Ventura table of values (not the best way to import 1-2-3 worksheet data).

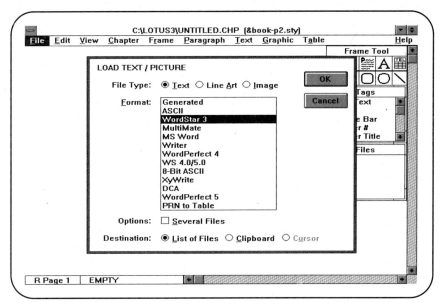

Fig. 13.39. *The LOAD/TEXT PICTURE dialog box.*

After you specify the information in the LOAD TEXT/PICTURE dialog box, specify the PRN file to import from the OPEN FILE dialog box. At the File Name prompt, type the path name of your 1-2-3 directory followed by the name of the file you want to import (for example, type **C:\LOTUS\JAYNE.PRN**). Select Open; Ventura Publisher begins importing the PRN file. When the import process is complete, your screen should resemble figure 13.40. After importing the data, save the publication; then modify it by enhancing fonts or adding art with Ventura Publisher's tools.

If your worksheet doesn't look like figure 13.40 because the imported data is out of alignment, make sure that your publication is set to one column, not multiple columns (the JAYNE worksheet is too wide to fit in a multiple-column publication).

To import a wide worksheet into a multiple-column publication, make the worksheet import area one column and don't change the rest of the publication. For more information on formatting, refer to your Ventura Publisher manual or to Que's Using Ventura Publisher.

If the data is in one column but still out of alignment, check the font. With a proportional font, the tabular data of a worksheet doesn't align properly because some numbers and characters are wider than others. You can change the entire worksheet to a nonproportional font using the font tools available in Ventura, or adjust by adding and removing spaces throughout the imported data.

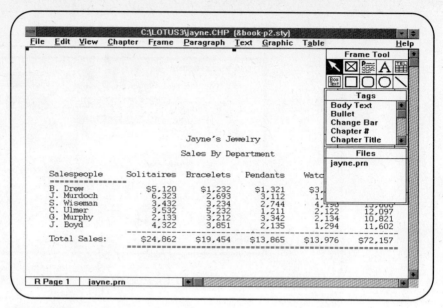

Fig. 13.40. *The imported worksheet data.*

Importing 1-2-3 PIC Files

The procedure for importing 1-2-3 PIC files is simple. Open a publication (or create a new one) and import the PIC file as a line art image. To import the JAYNE.PIC file created earlier in this chapter, open a new publication and select **L**oad Text/Picture from the **F**ile menu. Select Line **Art** at the `File Type:` prompt. The rest of the options change to the line art options, as shown in figure 13.41.

Select `Lotus .PIC` from the LOAD TEXT/PICTURE dialog box and then select OK. The OPEN FILE dialog box appears. Type the full path name and file name of the PIC file to import (for example, type the path name **C:\LOTUS\JAYNE.PIC**). The import process begins when you click on OK.

You don't see the imported graph immediately; the file name of the graph is listed in the `Files` box so that you can place it where and when you want. For this example, click on the `JAYNE.PIC` file name in the `Files` box; the graph appears in the publication, as shown in figure 13.42.

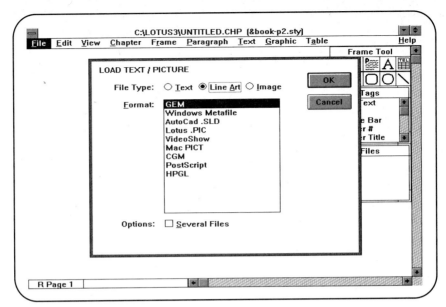

Fig. 13.41. Selecting from the Line Art options.

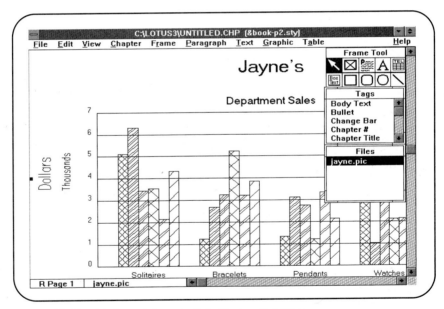

Fig. 13.42. The 1-2-3 graph imported into Ventura Publisher.

When the graph is correctly positioned, save the publication; then modify and enhance the imported graph with the tools available in Ventura Publisher.

Summary

In this chapter, you learned many ways that 1-2-3 can be used with presentation and graphics programs such as CorelDRAW! and PageMaker. 1-2-3's built-in graphics are sometimes not enough to reproduce in a publication; the presentation and graphics programs described in this chapter can help you to enhance your 1-2-3 worksheets and graphs, adding flair to your information.

The next chapter discusses the use of 1-2-3 with a number of popular word processing software programs, showing you ways to add text to graphs and worksheet data and graphs to word processing documents.

Chapter Fourteen

USING 1-2-3 WITH WORD PROCESSING PROGRAMS

Sometimes you need to include worksheet data in a letter or report. 1-2-3 doesn't have the text-formatting capabilities of dedicated word processing software, but many popular word processing programs processing software, but many popular word processing programs enable you to import 1-2-3 worksheets directly into text.

This chapter discusses commands and concepts for using 1-2-3 worksheets with word processing documents in WordPerfect, Microsoft Word, Word for Windows, and Professional Write. The powerful importing features of these software packages enable you to use worksheet data without retyping, transferring information easily between 1-2-3 and your word processing package.

Some popular word processing packages (such as WordPerfect and Word for Windows) can import 1-2-3 graphs directly into documents. This chapter also explores techniques for that process.

This chapter calls these visual representations graphs, *but some software documentation may refer to them as* charts.

Using 1-2-3 with WordPerfect

WordPerfect is the most widely used word processing program sold today. The latest version, WordPerfect 5.1, directly imports 1-2-3 worksheets and PIC files. After importing worksheet data into WordPerfect, you can use text formatting features to highlight key figures and wrap text around graphs. WordPerfect's Link feature continuously updates the data in your document as you change worksheet data in 1-2-3.

This section discusses the process of importing worksheet data and graphs into WordPerfect documents.

Importing 1-2-3 Data

The worksheet in figure 14.1 illustrates yearly expenses for a small apartment building. Create the worksheet as shown to follow the importing examples in this section. Enter the formula **@SUM(B10..B12)** in cell B14 and copy it to the rest of row 14. Enter **+B7–B14** in cell B16 and copy it to the rest of row 16. Format rows 11 and 12 as **F**ixed with no decimal places and rows 7, 10, 14, and 16 as **C**urrency with no decimal places. Assign the range name RENTS to the range B7..E7 and save the worksheet with the file name RENTAL.WK1 (even if you use Release 3.x). WordPerfect can import only 1-2-3 Release 2.x worksheets.

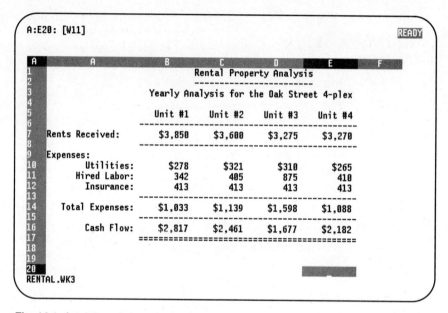

Fig. 14.1. *A 1-2-3 worksheet that will be imported into WordPerfect.*

Before importing a worksheet into WordPerfect, type as much of the document text as possible to give you a better idea of where the worksheet will appear in the document. This method helps you to position the worksheet with minimal moving and resizing.

For this example, start WordPerfect and type the text in the following paragraph. Leave blank space between the text and the incoming worksheet.

> **Despite the current housing slump and rental market glut, I have been successful with my apartment building. The following table shows my positive cash flow figures for the last twelve months:**

To import the worksheet, press Ctrl–F5 to select Text In/Out. WordPerfect displays the Text In/Out menu at the bottom of the screen, as shown in figure 14.2.

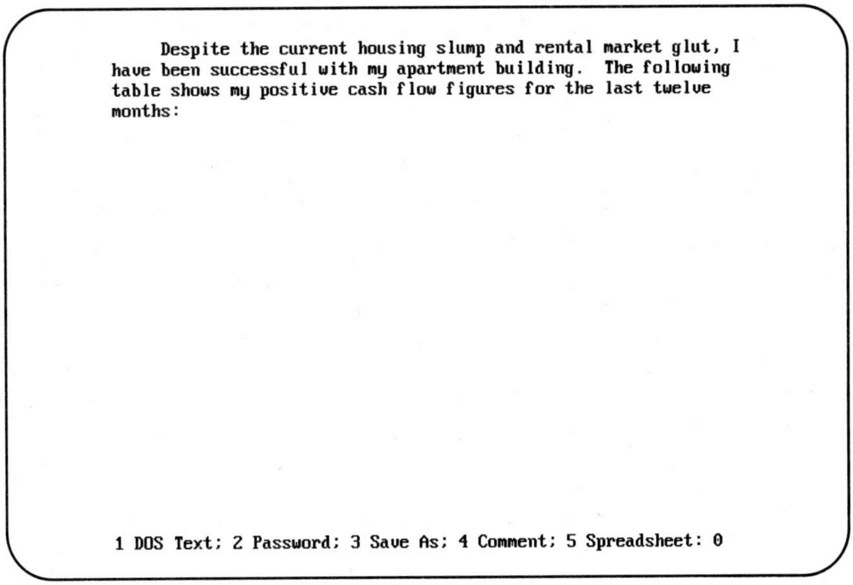

```
        Despite the current housing slump and rental market glut, I
   have been successful with my apartment building.  The following
   table shows my positive cash flow figures for the last twelve
   months:




   1 DOS Text; 2 Password; 3 Save As; 4 Comment; 5 Spreadsheet: 0
```

Fig. 14.2. *The sample WordPerfect document with the Text In/Out menu displayed.*

Select **Spreadsheet** (**5**). The Spreadsheet menu appears. The following table explains the options on the Spreadsheet menu.

Selection	Action
Import	Imports a worksheet file into the document
Create Link	Imports a worksheet file and links the document to the worksheet; worksheet changes cause parallel updates in the linked document
Edit Link	Changes a defined worksheet link
Link Options	Changes the way a worksheet is linked to a document

Select **Import** (**1**). The Spreadsheet: Import menu appears. Select **Filename** (**1**) and specify the full path name of the worksheet; for example, type the path name **C:\LOTUS\RENTAL.WK1**. By default, WordPerfect imports entire worksheets; to import a specified range, select **Range** (**2**) and specify the range coordinates or the range name.

By default, WordPerfect imports worksheet data to table format, retaining the proportionate column sizes of the source worksheet. If you prefer to import the data as text, select Type (**3**) from the Spreadsheet: Import menu, and then select Text (**2**). (For this example, don't import the data as text; the figures in this section assume a table format in WordPerfect.)

If you import the worksheet data as Text (**2**), WordPerfect inserts tabs and hard returns to retain the row and column orientation of the source worksheet, and you may need to adjust column alignment.

1-2-3 worksheets imported to WordPerfect cannot exceed 32 columns for table view, or 20 columns if you import the data as regular text.

WordPerfect imports the data from 1-2-3 in a manner appropriate to retain the column widths from the source worksheet.

Select Perform Import (**4**) from the Spreadsheet: Import menu. Figure 14.3 shows the imported worksheet.

```
      Despite the current housing slump and rental market glut, I
   have been successful with my apartment building.  The following
   table shows my positive cash flow figures for the last twelve
   months:
```

		Rental Property Analysis		
		-----------	-----------	--
	Yearly Analysis for the Oak Street 4-plex			
	Unit #1	Unit #2	Unit #3	Unit #4
	-----------	-----------	-----------	-----------
Rents Received:	$3,850	$3,600	$3,275	$3,270
	-----------	-----------	-----------	-----------
Expenses:				

Doc 1 Pg 1 Ln 2" Pos 1"

Fig. 14.3. *The RENTAL.WK1 worksheet imported into WordPerfect.*

If WordPerfect displays the message WARNING: Table extends beyond right margin, *the worksheet you imported doesn't fit within the current margins. You may have to adjust the WordPerfect margins or import a smaller worksheet.*

To see how the table of worksheet data fits into your WordPerfect text, preview the document on-screen. Press Shift–F7 to display the Print menu. Select View Document (**6**). WordPerfect displays a preview of the final printed page, as shown in figure 14.4. To exit the preview and return to the document, press F7.

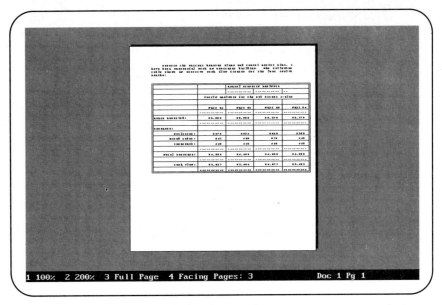

Fig. 14.4. *A preview of the WordPerfect document.*

WordPerfect converts all formulas to their computed values before importing them. The full precision of each worksheet cell is retained; if the worksheet has numbers formatted to five decimal places, the imported data retains the five place format. You can edit the imported data as if you had typed the numbers in WordPerfect. No macros are imported because WordPerfect doesn't use macro commands like 1-2-3.

As figure 14.4 shows, titles and data that were centered or justified in 1-2-3 are positioned the same way after importing. Because WordPerfect draws table lines between the cells when importing the worksheet into table view (but not text view), you may prefer to remove underlines from worksheet totals before importing the data from 1-2-3.

Linking a Worksheet to a Document

If you use the import process described in the preceding section, the WordPerfect document contains the 1-2-3 worksheet data *as it appeared at the time of importing*. Changes made in the worksheet after importing don't affect the WordPerfect document. If you establish a *link* between the worksheet and the WordPerfect document, however, WordPerfect updates the document when you change the worksheet.

To create a link between a WordPerfect document and a 1-2-3 worksheet, press Ctrl–F5 to select Text In/Out. Select **S**preadsheet (**5**) from the Text In/Out menu. Select the **C**reate Link option (**2**) from the Spreadsheet menu. WordPerfect displays the Create Link screen, where you can select **F**ilename, **R**ange, **T**ype, and **P**erform Link.

Select **F**ilename and specify the full path name of the file; for example, type **C:\LOTUS\RENTAL.WK1**. By default, WordPerfect imports the entire worksheet; if you prefer to import a range, select **R**ange and specify the range coordinates or range name. (For this example, import the whole RENTAL.WK1 worksheet.) To start the linking process, select **P**erform Link (**4**).

WordPerfect imports the worksheet into the document in table view, as shown in figure 14.5.

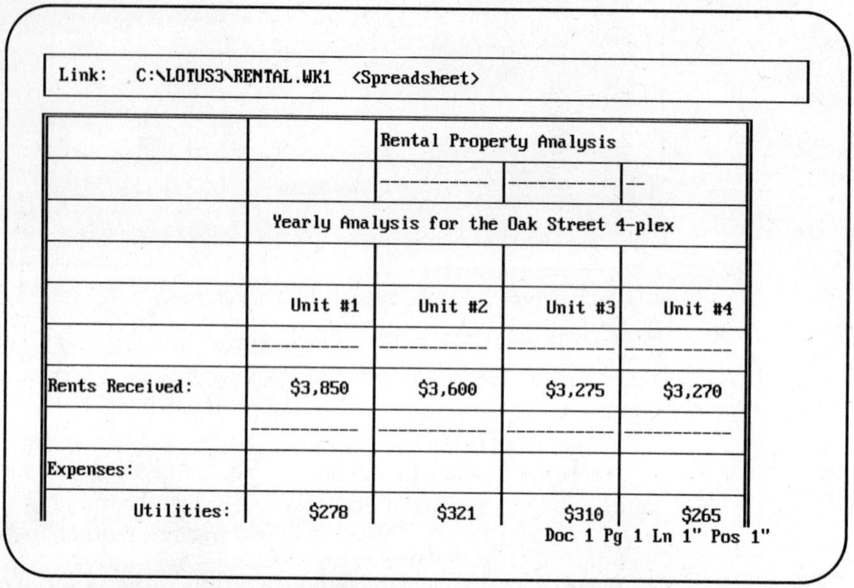

Link:	C:\LOTUS3\RENTAL.WK1 <Spreadsheet>			
		Rental Property Analysis		
		-----------	-----------	--
		Yearly Analysis for the Oak Street 4-plex		
		Unit #1	Unit #2	Unit #3	Unit #4
		-----------	-----------	-----------	-----------
Rents Received:		$3,850	$3,600	$3,275	$3,270
		-----------	-----------	-----------	-----------
Expenses:				
Utilities:		$278	$321	$310	$265

Doc 1 Pg 1 Ln 1" Pos 1"

Fig. 14.5. A WordPerfect document linked to a 1-2-3 worksheet file.

WordPerfect inserts special link codes into your document before and after the worksheet data. (The beginning link code is shown at the top of figure 14.5.) The link codes don't print with the document.

You cannot edit link codes, but you can modify the link. Position the cursor between the link codes and press Ctrl–F5 to display the Text In/Out menu. Select **S**preadsheet (**5**) and **E**dit Link (**3**). When the Edit Link screen appears, change the **F**ilename, **R**ange, **T**ype, and **P**erform Link options as necessary (for example, if you want to remove a file link).

Changing the Link Options

By changing the link options, you can specify when links are updated, or turn the link code display on or off. To change the link options, press Ctrl–F5, select **S**preadsheet (**5**), and select **L**ink Options (**4**). The Link Options menu appears, as shown in figure 14.6.

```
Link Options:

    1 - Update on Retrieve          No

    2 - Show Link Codes             Yes

    3 - Update All Links
```

Fig. 14.6. *The Link Options menu.*

To ensure that the WordPerfect document contains the most current data from 1-2-3, select Update on **R**etrieve (**1**) **Y**es. With this option selected, when you load the WordPerfect document into memory a new copy of the worksheet or range is imported. If Update on **R**etrieve is set to **N**o, the linked data is updated only when you select the Update All Links option (**3**).

To hide the link codes, change the **S**how Link Codes option to **N**o. The link codes are still in the document but not visible on-screen. If you have several linked worksheets in your document, all of the link codes disappear when you change the **S**how Link Codes option to **N**o.

Importing 1-2-3 PIC Files

WordPerfect imports 1-2-3 PIC files with no conversion necessary. The most difficult aspect of using PIC files with WordPerfect is preparing the document to receive the graph. Before importing a PIC file, you must set up a figure box or a user box within the text. WordPerfect places the graph in this box. You cannot change the text or design of the graph within WordPerfect, but you can move the graph, resize it, or preview it on-screen.

You cannot link WordPerfect documents and PIC files. After you import a graph into WordPerfect, the graph remains the same in the document—even if the original graph is changed in 1-2-3—until you import it again.

Creating a Sample 1-2-3 PIC File To Import

For this example, retrieve the RENTAL.WK1 worksheet and create a graph with the following 1-2-3 commands:

/Graph Type Bar

X   B5..E5

A   B7..E7

B   B10..E10

C	B11..E11
D	B12..E12
E	B14..E14
F	B16..E16

Options Legend

A	Rents
B	Utilities
C	Hired Labor
D	Insurance
E	Expenses
F	Cash Flow

Titles

First   Rentals

Second Current 12 Months

X-Axis Units

Y-Axis Dollars

Grid Horizontal

B&W

Quit

Select View to see the graph on-screen. Your graph should resemble figure 14.7. This graph is a typical 1-2-3 bar graph, but WordPerfect can import any of 1-2-3's graph types.

Save the graph to a PIC file; select /Graph Save, type **RENTAL** (1-2-3 supplies the PIC extension), and press Enter. (If you use 1-2-3 Release 2.3 or 3.1, you can enhance the graph with Wysiwyg before saving it.) Exit 1-2-3 and start WordPerfect. Retrieve the WordPerfect document you created earlier. You now can place the graph at the bottom of the imported worksheet data.

Preparing the Text for the Imported Graph

Before importing the PIC file, you must make a place for it in your document. You can place a PIC graph inside a figure box or a user box. To create a box for the graph, press Alt–F9 to select the Graphics command. Select **Figure** (**1**) and select **Create** (**1**). The Definition: Figure menu appears, as shown in figure 14.8.

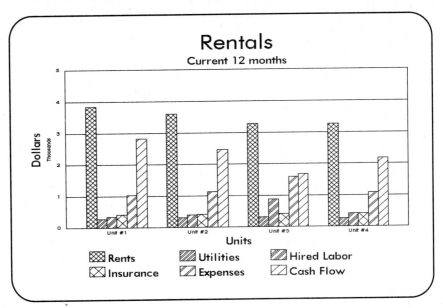

Fig. 14.7. Viewing the graph in RENTAL.WK1.

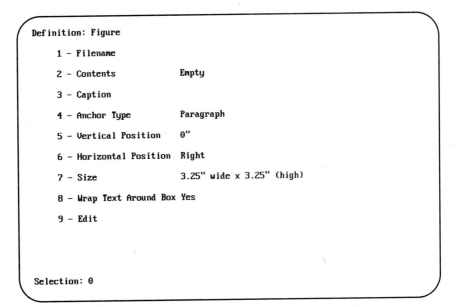

Fig. 14.8. The Definition: Figure menu.

Select Filename (**1**) and specify the full path name of the PIC file; for example, type **C:\LOTUS\RENTAL.PIC**. WordPerfect loads the graph into memory and replaces several of the Definition: Figure menu items with appropriate values. For this example, select Horizontal Position (**6**) to change the graph's position, and then select Full (**4**) to see the fully-expanded graph.

Press Enter to return to the document. WordPerfect displays figure codes to show where the graph will appear when you print the document. You cannot see the graph in the document on-screen; to see what the graph and text will look like when printed, press Shift–F7 and select View Document (**6**). Press F7 to return to the document. The link codes appear as shown (earlier in this chapter) in figure 14.5.

Adjusting the Graph

You can control the exact size and placement of an imported graph within a document. The Definition: Figure menu described in the preceding section lists many options you can change. If your graph doesn't contain a caption, for example, select Caption (**3**) and type a caption.

The Anchor Type option (**4**) specifies how the graph relates to its surrounding text. If you select Paragraph (**1**), the graph appears within the preceding paragraph. Selecting Page (**2**) keeps the graph at the same location on the page, no matter how you change or move surrounding text and paragraphs. Selecting Character (**3**) makes the figure code behave like an ordinary text character; you can move it or copy it anywhere in the document.

The Vertical Position option (**5**) specifies how far from the preceding paragraph (in inches) the figure box appears. The Horizontal Position option (**6**) specifies how the graph is placed between the left and right margins of the document. When you select Horizontal Position (**6**), you can select from the following options:

Selection	Graph Alignment
Left	Left document margin
Right	Right document margin
Center	Centered between the left and right margins
Full	Stretched to match its left and right edges with the left and right margins

The Size option (**7**) defines the size of the imported graph. The dimensions of the graph extend (or shrink) to fit the size you specify. The size is measured in inches.

The Wrap Text Around Box option (**8**) wraps text around the box, instead of stopping above the box and starting again below it. This feature enables you to create a "newsletter" appearance. If the **Horizontal Position** of the figure box is specified as **Left**, **Right**, or **Center**, WordPerfect wraps the text around the figure (on the *left* side only for **Center**).

WordPerfect can wrap text around a maximum of 20 figure boxes.

Editing the Graph

You cannot change the imported graph with WordPerfect (you must modify the original image in 1-2-3 and import it again), but you can change the way the graph appears within the document. Press Alt–F9 to use the Graphics command. Select **F**igure if you imported the graph into a figure box or **U**ser if you imported the graph into a user box.

Select **E**dit (**9**) from the Definition: Figure menu. WordPerfect displays the graph on-screen, as shown in figure 14.9.

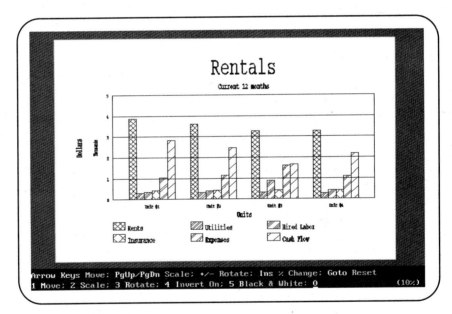

Fig. 14.9. Editing the graph on-screen.

From this screen, you can raise or lower the graph within the box (the top or bottom of the graph is truncated accordingly), invert the image (black background with white lines), shrink or expand the graph within the box, and/or rotate the graph 45 degrees at a time. WordPerfect changes the graph on-screen as you type the editing commands. Press F7 to exit this screen and return to the document. You can preview the entire document (including the text, worksheet data, and graph) by pressing Shift–F7 and then **6**.

Using 1-2-3 with Microsoft Word

Microsoft Word 5.5 is designed for users who need advanced text-formatting capability. Microsoft Word directly imports 1-2-3 worksheets and PIC files into documents; after importing a 1-2-3 file into a document, you can edit and format the text.

This section explores the process of importing 1-2-3 worksheet data and PIC files into Microsoft Word documents.

 Microsoft Word can import only 32K of data at one time. To import a large worksheet, split it into smaller worksheets and import them sequentially.

Importing 1-2-3 Data

The worksheet in figure 14.10 illustrates yearly expenses for a small apartment building. (This worksheet was used earlier in this chapter for importing to WordPerfect.) Create the worksheet as shown to follow the importing examples in this section. Enter the formula **@SUM(B10..B12)** in cell B14 and copy it to the rest of row 14. Enter **+B7–B14** in cell B16 and copy it to the rest of row 16. Format rows 11 and 12 as **F**ixed with no decimal places and rows 7, 10, 14, and 16 as **C**urrency with no decimal places. Save the worksheet with the file name RENTAL.WK1 (even if you use Release 3.x). Microsoft Word can import only 1-2-3 Release 2.x worksheets.

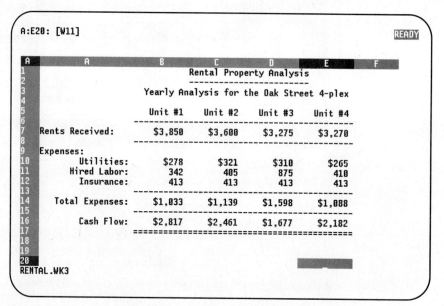

Fig. 14.10. *A 1-2-3 worksheet that will be imported into Microsoft Word.*

Before importing a worksheet into Microsoft Word, type as much of the document text as possible to give you a better idea of where the worksheet will appear in the document. This method helps you to position the worksheet with minimal moving and resizing.

For this example, start Microsoft Word and type the text in the following paragraph. Leave blank space between the text and the incoming worksheet.

Despite the current housing slump and rental market glut, I have been successful with my apartment building. The following table shows my positive cash flow figures for the last twelve months:

To import the worksheet, select Insert File from the menu. Specify the full path name of the 1-2-3 worksheet; for example, type the following **C:\LOTUS\RENTAL.WK1**. (To import a range, move the cursor to the **R**ange text box and type the range address or name. If you have several ranges, retrieve them individually; move the cursor to the desired location in the document before retrieving each range.) For this example, leave the **R**ange text box blank. Press Enter to import the worksheet data. Formulas are converted to their numerical values and macros are ignored during the import process. Figure 14.11 shows the Microsoft Word editing screen after importing the RENTAL.WK1 worksheet.

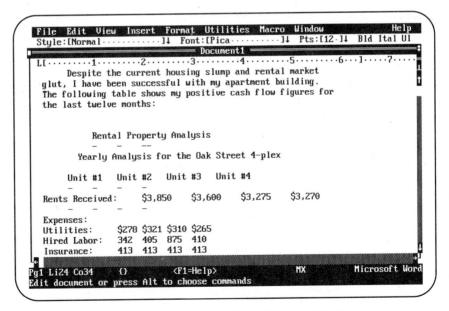

Fig. 14.11. The RENTAL.WK1 data imported into a Microsoft Word document.

Because Microsoft Word inserts tab characters before each cell, your tab stop settings may align the columns differently than in 1-2-3.

Adjusting the Column Alignment

If the worksheet is out of alignment you can fix it easily. By default, Microsoft Word sets tab stops at half-inch intervals. 1-2-3 cells typically are not 1/2-inch wide; therefore, you usually must adjust the tab stops of the imported section. To set up new tabs, select Format Tabs and specify the desired tab spacing, use the mouse on the ruler line, or use Ctrl–Shift–F10 and the arrow keys to mark the tabs on the ruler.

If you use DOS 2.0 or 2.1, Microsoft Word places a dollar sign ($) before any numbers formatted as Currency in the 1-2-3 worksheet. If you use DOS 3.0 or later, Microsoft Word checks the operating system currency format (from the *COUNTRY* = line in the CONFIG.SYS file, if one exists) for the proper currency format.

You may need to make other minor changes in the worksheet data if you want it to look exactly as it did in 1-2-3. Some of the titles (such as Utilities:) must be right-aligned and others (such as Expenses:) left-aligned. Insert appropriate spaces to align the titles properly. After you make these changes, your document should resemble figure 14.12.

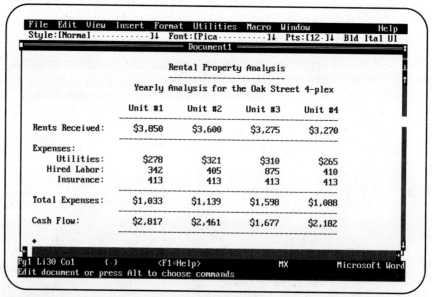

Fig. 14.12. *The Microsoft Word document with adjusted text and tab settings.*

Updating the Imported Data

If you save the Microsoft Word document and then change the worksheet data in 1-2-3, those changes are not updated in your document. When you load the document into Microsoft Word again, the worksheet data appears *as it did when you imported it.*

If you want the 1-2-3 worksheet data to stay current, select the **Link** option when you select **Insert File**. Microsoft Word inserts *.L.* codes before and after the worksheet data as it imports the file, linking the document to the worksheet for updating later (if desired). The .L. codes block the worksheet section; to see these hidden codes in the text, select **View Preferences Hidden Text** (if you want the codes to print with the text, select **File Print Options Hidden Text**). You can delete the linking codes from your Microsoft Word document when you no longer need the link.

Microsoft Word can update the document to reflect changes in the worksheet (or multiple worksheets, if several are imported into the document). To update the worksheet data from within Microsoft Word, select the worksheet paragraph. If you imported multiple worksheets and want to update all of them, select the entire document (press Shift–F10). Select **Insert File Update** and press Enter. Don't specify a file name or a range.

Microsoft Word highlights each imported paragraph separately and displays the following prompt:

```
Do you want to update this link? Choose YES to update
or NO to go on.
```

Press **Y** or **N** for each worksheet paragraph when prompted. Pressing Esc cancels the update request and returns the cursor to the document. The update occurs as you answer each prompt. Because the update can affect the paragraph's format, you may need to reformat the paragraph to reflect the new worksheet data.

Importing 1-2-3 PIC Files

Microsoft Word imports 1-2-3 PIC files with no conversion necessary. You cannot change the graph within Microsoft Word, but you can move it, resize it, and preview it on-screen. Microsoft Word inserts a *.G.* code that identifies the PIC file's path name, size, and format. To delete a graph from a document, delete the .G. code.

Microsoft Word continually updates the imported graph. If you make changes in the PIC file in 1-2-3, the changes are updated in Microsoft Word when you retrieve the document (if you did not delete the .G. code).

Creating a Sample 1-2-3 PIC File To Import

For this example, retrieve the RENTAL.WK1 worksheet and create a graph with the following 1-2-3 commands:

/Graph Type Bar

X	B5..E5
A	B7..E7
B	B10..E10
C	B11..E11
D	B12..E12
E	B14..E14
F	B16..E16

Options Legend

A	Rents
B	Utilities
C	Hired Labor
D	Insurance
E	Expenses
F	Cash Flow

Titles

First	Rentals
Second	Current 12 Months
X-Axis	Units
Y-Axis	Dollars

Grid Horizontal

B&W

Quit

Select View to see the graph on-screen. Your graph should resemble figure 14.13. (This graph was used earlier in this chapter to import to WordPerfect.) This example uses a bar graph, but Microsoft Word can import any type of graph created with 1-2-3.

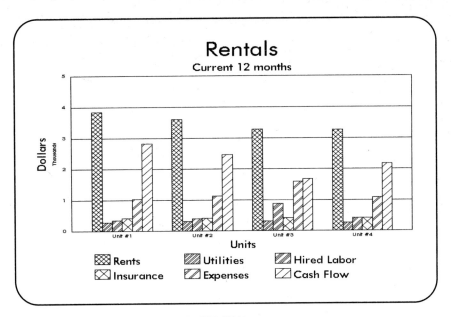

Fig. 14.13. *Viewing the graph in RENTAL.WK1.*

Save the graph to a PIC file; select /Graph Save, type **RENTAL** (1-2-3 supplies the PIC extension), and press Enter. (If you use 1-2-3 Release 2.3 or 3.1, you can use Wysiwyg to enhance your graph before saving it.) Exit 1-2-3 and start Microsoft Word. Retrieve the Microsoft Word document that you created earlier and delete the imported worksheet data by removing its link code and data.

Importing the PIC File

To import the PIC file into the Microsoft Word document, select Insert Picture and specify the full path name of the PIC file; for example, type **C:\LOTUS\RENTAL.PIC**. Because Microsoft Word understands and interprets PIC files, you can ignore the remaining fields. Press Enter to start the import process.

A .G. code appears at the location of the imported graph and the cursor returns to the editing screen. If you cannot see the .G. code, change your Microsoft Word settings to show hidden text.

Microsoft Word uses the current margin settings, with 1/6 inch of white space surrounding the graph. You can add more space by typing values into the Space Before and Space After fields when linking the PIC file.

Previewing the Graph in the Document

You cannot see the graph when editing the document, but you can preview the graph and text by selecting File Print Preview. Figure 14.14 shows a preview version of the example document with the imported graph.

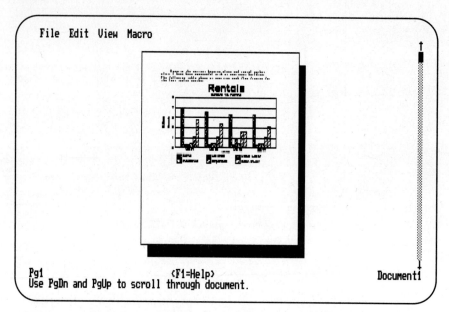

Fig. 14.14. *Previewing the imported graph in the Microsoft Word document.*

If your margins are not wide enough, part of the graph may be truncated in the preview; if this problem occurs, adjust the margins as necessary.

Press Esc to leave the preview screen and return to the document.

Adjusting the Graph

You can add a caption, borders, and shading to the graph. To add a caption, press Shift–Enter after the last character of the .G. code and type the caption in the paragraph following the graph. You must keep the caption with the graph, or the caption doesn't "follow" if you move the graph to another location. Press Enter after typing the caption paragraph.

You can make further adjustments, such as adding borders or lines, by selecting options from the Format Borders menu.

Using 1-2-3 with Word for Windows

Microsoft's *Word for Windows* offers word processing features with total WYSIWYG text and graphics integration and one of the industry's most complete macro languages and document merging capabilities. Word for Windows easily imports 1-2-3 worksheets and PIC files.

Importing 1-2-3 Data

The worksheet in figure 14.15 illustrates yearly expenses for a small apartment building. (This worksheet was used earlier in this chapter to import to WordPerfect.) Create the worksheet as shown to follow the importing examples in this section. Enter the formula **@SUM(B10..B12)** in cell B14 and copy it to the rest of row 14. Enter **+B7−B14** in cell B16 and copy it to the rest of row 16. Format rows 11 and 12 as **F**ixed with no decimal places and rows 7, 10, 14, and 16 as **C**urrency with no decimal places. Assign the range name RENTS to the range B7..E7 and save the worksheet with the file name RENTAL.WK1 (even if you use Release 3.x). Word for Windows can import only 1-2-3 Release 2.x worksheets.

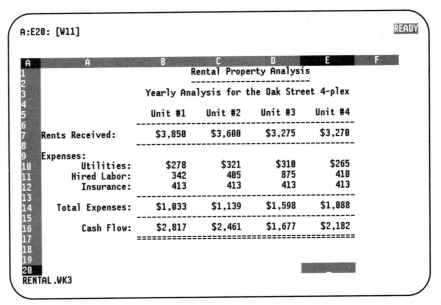

Fig. 14.15. A 1-2-3 worksheet that will be imported into Word for Windows.

Before importing a worksheet into Word for Windows, type as much of the document text as possible to give you a better idea of where the worksheet will appear in the document. This method helps you to position the worksheet with minimal moving and resizing.

For this example, start Word for Windows and type the text in the following paragraph. Leave blank space between the text and the incoming worksheet.

Despite the current housing slump and rental market glut, I have been successful with my apartment building. The following table shows my positive cash flow figures for the last twelve months:

To import the worksheet, select Insert File. Word for Windows prompts you for the file name, as shown in figure 14.16.

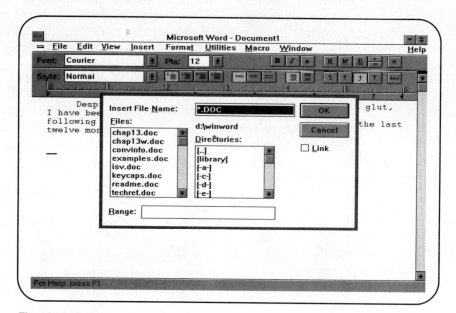

Fig. 14.16. *Getting ready to insert the worksheet.*

Specify the RENTAL.WK1 file. You can type the full path name, such as **C:\LOTUS\RENTAL.WK1**, or select the path name and file name by pointing with the mouse or arrow keys.

You can import a range from the worksheet. To import a range, type the range in the Insert File Name Range blank; for example, type **B7..E7** or **RENTS**. If you have several ranges in the worksheet, you can retrieve them individually; move the cursor to the desired location in the document before retrieving the range.

Just as when you import the entire worksheet, you may need to adjust the font and point size of the incoming data.

After you specify the worksheet file name, Word for Windows displays the Convert File From menu (because the worksheet is not in Word for

Windows format) and highlights WKS. Press Enter or click with the mouse to confirm that Word for Windows is importing from the worksheet (WKS) format.

Word for Windows converts the worksheet data and inserts it into your document, as shown in figure 14.17. Formulas are converted to their numerical values and macros are ignored in the import process. All cells formatted as Currency are displayed with two decimal places, even if the source worksheet did not show decimal places.

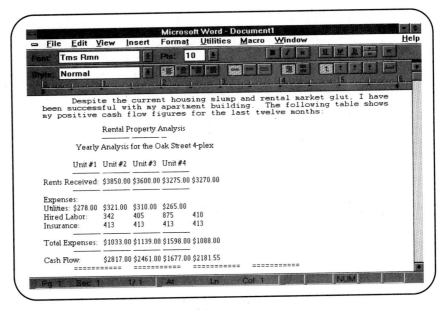

Fig. 14.17. The imported worksheet data.

Because Word for Windows inserts tab characters before each cell, your tab stop settings may align the columns differently than in 1-2-3.

Adjusting the Column Alignment

Before fixing the column alignment, make sure that Word for Windows imported the worksheet with the same font and point size as the surrounding document. Most LaserJet owners, for example, use the Courier 12 point font. If the font and point size values (indicated at the top of the screen) change when you move the cursor within the worksheet data (for example, to a Times Roman 10 point font), you may want to adjust the settings.

To change a font or point size, highlight the portion of the worksheet data section that you want to change. Select Format Character from the menu and change the font and point size of the paragraph to match the surrounding text.

Word for Windows' default tab stops are set at half-inch intervals. 1-2-3 cells typically are not one-half inch wide; therefore, you usually must adjust the tab stops of the imported section. Place the cursor within the imported data and select Format **P**aragraph Tabs. The Tab Position menu appears.

Enter new tab stop numbers in the Tab Position box. For each tab, select the type of alignment; for example, press Alt–R to select **R**ight. Then set the tab by selecting **S**et. To match the original worksheet settings, set right-aligned tabs at 2.5 inches, 3.5 inches, 4.5 inches, and 5.5 inches; then select OK.

Make any other desired format adjustments, such as adding spaces before the Utilities title. After you make these changes, your Word for Windows document should resemble figure 14.18.

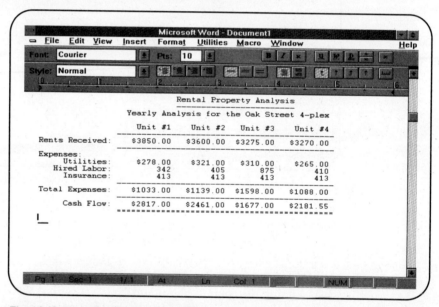

Fig. 14.18. The adjusted worksheet data.

Updating the Imported Data

You can link a 1-2-3 worksheet to a Word for Windows document instead of importing the worksheet directly. If the worksheet file and document are linked, changes in the worksheet are reflected in the document when you retrieve it in Word for Windows. To link a worksheet, select the Link box when you insert the worksheet file.

Word for Windows includes the linked worksheet file as a field in the document. Select View Preferences Show All to see the field (the worksheet data doesn't appear). If you link the sample worksheet, for example, the field resembles the following statement:

```
"{INCLUDE C:\\LOTUS\\RENTAL.WK1}"
```

To switch from field view to a view of the worksheet data, turn off Show All in the View Preferences menu. Each time you load the document into Word for Windows, it reflects the most recent changes made in the worksheet.

Importing 1-2-3 PIC Files

Word for Windows is one of the few word processing programs that can display an imported graph while you edit the document (versus showing the graph in a preview mode). You cannot change the imported graph within Word for Windows, but you can adjust it.

Creating a Sample 1-2-3 PIC File To Import

For this example, retrieve the RENTAL.WK1 worksheet and create a graph with the following 1-2-3 commands:

/Graph Type Bar	
X	B5..E5
A	B7..E7
B	B10..E10
C	B11..E11
D	B12..E12
E	B14..E14
F	B16..E16
Options Legend	
A	Rents
B	Utilities
C	Hired Labor
D	Insurance
E	Expenses
F	Cash Flow

Titles

First   **Rentals**

Second **Current 12 Months**

X-Axis **Units**

Y-Axis **Dollars**

Grid Horizontal

B&W

Quit

Select View to see the graph on-screen. Your graph should resemble figure 14.19. (This graph was used earlier in this chapter to import to WordPerfect.) The example uses a bar graph, but Word for Windows can import any type of 1-2-3 graph.

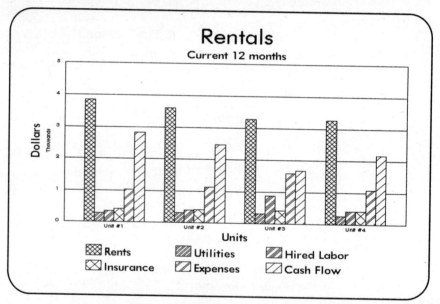

Fig. 14.19. *Viewing the graph in RENTAL.WK1.*

Save the graph to a PIC file; select /Graph Save, type **RENTAL** (1-2-3 supplies the PIC extension), and press Enter. (If you use 1-2-3 Release 2.3 or 3.1, you can enhance your graph with Wysiwyg before saving it.) Exit 1-2-3 and start Word for Windows.

Preparing To Import the PIC File

Before you import a graph into a Word for Windows document, the Lotus PIC filter must be loaded into your Word for Windows environment. If you loaded the PIC filter once, you need never reload it. To load this filter (and several other programs' graphics filter files), load the document called EXAMPLES.DOC. (When you installed Word for Windows, the installation routine placed this file in the Word for Windows subdirectory.)

Scroll down the screen with PgDn or the scroll bar until you see an entry labeled InstallGraphicsFLTs. This macro places the graphics filter files into your copy of WIN.INI. Your screen should resemble figure 14.20.

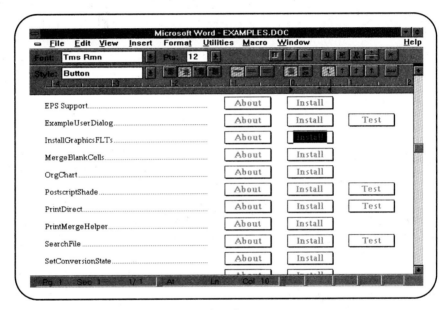

Fig. 14.20. *Selecting a graphics filter to install.*

Select the Install option. After a brief pause (while Word for Windows loads the graphics filters), the message All graphics filters installed appears at the bottom of the screen.

Before importing a PIC file into a document, turn on the full menu display. Select View from the menu. If the bottom option of the View menu reads Full Menus, select this item with the mouse or keyboard. This procedure sets the display for full menus (every menu option is available). You can now access the Insert Picture menu option. (If the bottom option of the View menu reads Short Menus, you don't have to change anything, as Full Menus is already set.)

Importing the PIC File

After you load the graphics filters (if necessary) and turn on the full menu display, retrieve the Word for Windows document you created earlier. Delete the worksheet data that you imported and remove the link code if you linked the document to the source 1-2-3 worksheet file. Place the cursor where you want the graph to appear. Select Insert Picture. At the Picture File Name prompt, specify the full path name for the desired PIC file; for example, type **C:\LOTUS\RENTAL.PIC**. Word for Windows searches for the file and imports it.

If Word for Windows displays a warning that LOTUSPIC.FLT is not loaded, the PIC filter file described in the preceding section was not loaded successfully. Load the PIC filter file before continuing.

After you import it, the graph may not appear exactly as you expected. In figure 14.21, for example, a preview of the sample document shows that the title Rentals is not centered. Word for Windows is not always able to reproduce 1-2-3 fonts, especially title fonts. You can insert a title with Word for Windows after cropping the imported graph (see the next section for details).

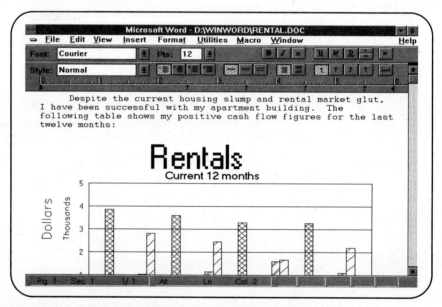

Fig. 14.21. *Previewing the document with the imported graph.*

Adjusting the Graph

You cannot edit the graph, but you can change its placement and size and add borders. To change (*scale*) the size of the graph you use *handles*.

Handles are eight small black boxes appearing around the perimeter of a graph. You display these handles by clicking the mouse within the graph frame.

To scale the graph, click on a handle while holding down a Shift key. Move the handle toward the center of the graph to reduce its size, or away from the center to increase its size. If you know the exact scale you want, select Format Picture and type the actual scaling percentages in the Height and Width fields.

To crop the picture, click on a handle and drag it toward the center of the graph. To crop the graph's title, for example, click on the center handle above the title and drag it down until the title disappears. Or you can select Format Picture and type new Crop From values for the Top, Bottom, Left, and Right margin fields. You then can type a new title, using one of the Word for Windows fonts for better integration in your document.

Word for Windows offers four kinds of borders to place around your graph. You can add a thin line (one point thickness), a two point line, two parallel one point lines (a double border), or a shadowed box (to give the graph a raised appearance). To add a border (or remove one), select Format Picture. As shown in figure 14.22, you can make several adjustments to the graph from this menu.

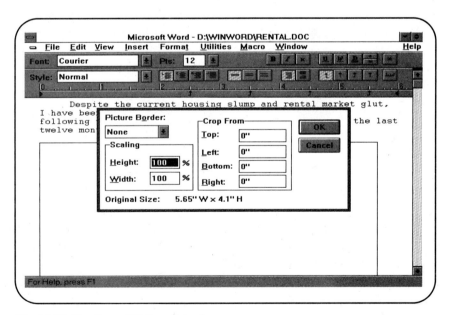

Fig. 14.22. The Format Picture dialog box.

Using 1-2-3 with Professional Write

Professional Write offers easy-to-use word processing at an affordable price for those users who want to get started without a time-consuming learning curve. Professional Write doesn't include a way to import 1-2-3 PIC files but offers a smooth importing feature for 1-2-3 worksheets.

Worksheets you import into Professional Write cannot exceed 250 characters in width. If your worksheets are wider, you may have to split them up and import them separately.

The worksheet in figure 14.23 illustrates yearly expenses for a small apartment building. (This worksheet was used to import to WordPerfect earlier in this chapter.) Create the worksheet as shown to follow the importing examples in this section. Enter the formula **@SUM(B10..B12)** in cell B14 and copy it to the rest of row 14. Enter **+B7–B14** in cell B16 and copy it to the rest of row 16. Format rows 11 and 12 as **F**ixed with no decimal places and rows 7, 10, 14, and 16 as **C**urrency with no decimal places. Assign the range name RENTS to the range B7..E7 and save the worksheet with the file name RENTAL.WK1 (even if you use Release 3.x). Professional Write can import only 1-2-3 Release 2.x worksheets.

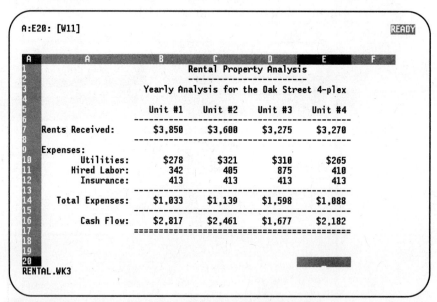

Fig. 14.23. *A 1-2-3 worksheet that will be imported into Professional Write.*

Before importing a worksheet into Professional Write, type as much of the document text as possible to give you a better idea of where the worksheet will appear in the document. This method helps you to position the worksheet with minimal moving and resizing.

For this example, start Professional Write and type the text in the following paragraph. Leave blank space between the text and the incoming worksheet.

> **Despite the current housing slump and rental market glut, I have been successful with my apartment building. The following table shows my positive cash flow figures for the last twelve months:**

To import the worksheet, select **Insert file** from the File/Print menu. Specify the complete path name of the worksheet file; for example, type **C:\LOTUS\RENTAL.WK1**. Professional Write displays the Get/Insert Worksheet Data menu. Press **1** to import the entire worksheet or **2** to import a range. If you select **2**, Professional Write displays a list of all named ranges named in the worksheet file. Select a name from the list, or type the range address or range name.

Professional Write imports the worksheet at the cursor's current location. As shown in figure 14.24, Professional Write approximates the look of the original worksheet. Formulas are converted to their numerical values and macros are ignored during the import process. You can edit the imported data as if you had typed it in Professional Write.

```
 F1-Help  F2-File/Print  F3-Edit  F4-Format  F5-Spell/Grammar  F6-Addresses
              Despite the current housing slump and rental market
           glut, I have been successful with my apartment building.  The
           following table shows my positive cash flow figures for the
           last twelve months:

                                   Rental Property Analysis
                                   ----------- ----------- --
                          Yearly Analysis for the Oak Street 4-plex

                             Unit #1      Unit #2     Unit #3     Unit #4
                          ----------- ----------- ----------- -----------
          Rents Received:    $3,850      $3,600      $3,275      $3,270
                          ----------- ----------- ----------- -----------

          Expenses:
                Utilities:     $278        $321        $310        $265
              Hired Labor:      342         405         875         410
                Insurance:      413         413         413         413
                          ----------- ----------- ----------- -----------
           Total Expenses:   $1,033      $1,139      $1,598      $1,088
                          ----------- ----------- ----------- -----------
               Cash Flow:    $2,817      $2,461      $1,677      $2,182
   └┴┴┴┴┴┴┴┴┴┴┴┴┴┴┴┴2┴┴┴┴┴┴┴┴3┴┴┴┴┴┴┴┴4┴┴┴┴┴┴┴┴5┴┴┴┴┴┴┴┴6┴┴┴┴┴┴┴┴7┴┴┴┴┴┴┘
   Working Copy  Inserting                                1%    Line 7 of Pg 1
   Esc-Main Menu  Courier P 12
```

Fig. 14.24. The document with the worksheet data imported.

You can change the appearance of the worksheet with the tools available in Professional Write.

Summary

This chapter discussed methods for importing 1-2-3 worksheets and PIC files into several popular word processing programs. By importing data, you can combine the number-crunching and graphical power of 1-2-3 with the extensive text and formatting capabilities of word processing software.

The next chapter discusses how you can use financial programs with 1-2-3; you learn methods for using tax and accounting information accumulated in 1-2-3 with other software to produce tax statements and printed reports and to perform analyses.

Chapter Fifteen

USING 1-2-3 WITH FINANCIAL PROGRAMS

L otus 1-2-3 offers virtually every financial analysis tool you need. With 1-2-3, you can create budgets, tax worksheets, home and business financial records, graphs, and much more. 1-2-3's macro programming language helps you to create any feature Lotus did not build into 1-2-3.

Despite the comprehensive commands and features included with 1-2-3, you may need to use another financial program occasionally. Rather than creating a different tax worksheet for every form available, you may prefer to use a tax program with the latest tax tables built in, such as TurboTax. You may want to use the word processing or data communications features of Symphony, or to share 1-2-3 spreadsheets with a friend or co-worker who uses Quattro Pro or Excel. Another financial package—Quicken—provides an audited home and business record-keeper that is hard to beat.

You can transfer files between each of these programs and 1-2-3. This chapter discusses the concepts and commands for successful integration of 1-2-3 data with other financial programs. By arming yourself with these tools, you can create a complete financial modeling system with 1-2-3 as the central hub and analysis program.

Using 1-2-3 with Symphony

Lotus *Symphony* was designed to continue where 1-2-3 stops. Symphony offers spreadsheet, graphing, and database capabilities, with a forms data entry system, word processing, and communications. All functions of the package are integrated in a format very much like 1-2-3.

Symphony 2.2 reads and writes 1-2-3 files with little conversion needed, using the WR1 extension to retain compatibility with 1-2-3 Release 2.x and 3.x files. Depending on your 1-2-3 version, you may not be able to transfer *all* of your macros, but data and some macros transfer correctly.

(Many macros consist of 1-2-3 keystrokes that are not equivalent to Symphony keystrokes; those macros don't transfer correctly.) 1-2-3 graphs don't translate into Symphony because of graphing differences between the two programs.

This section guides you through the process of transferring files between 1-2-3 and Symphony. The method for translating 1-2-3 worksheets to Symphony files varies, depending on whether you use 1-2-3 Release 3.x or 2.x. Read the appropriate section that follows.

Creating a Sample 1-2-3 Worksheet To Import

The 1-2-3 worksheet in figure 15.1 shows a credit card listing of charges and payments and includes formulas and a printing macro. The worksheet is used in this section to demonstrate transferring 1-2-3 files to Symphony.

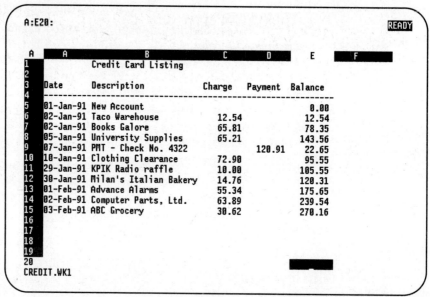

Fig. 15.1. A 1-2-3 worksheet that will be transferred to Symphony.

Create the worksheet as indicated in the figure, entering the formula **+E5+C6–D6** in cell E6 and copying it down the rest of column E. Create the following print macro in cell G1: **/ppra1..i15~agq**. Name the macro with the command sequence **/Range Name Create \p**. After creating the worksheet, save it under the file name **CREDIT.WK1** or **CREDIT.WK3** (depending on your 1-2-3 version).

Importing Symphony Worksheets with 1-2-3

1-2-3 users can retrieve Symphony worksheets directly; no conversion is necessary. All Symphony files use the WR1 extension.

To retrieve a Symphony worksheet in 1-2-3, select **/F**ile **R**etrieve, press Esc to clear the path, and enter the full path name for your Symphony files (for example, type **C:\SYMPHONY*.WR1**). To see a list of files in the specified directory, press F3 (Name). Highlight or type the name of the desired file and press Enter.

After you retrieve a Symphony worksheet, save it as a 1-2-3 file with **/F**ile **S**ave, using the WK3 extension for Release 3.x or the WK1 extension for Release 2.x. This process preserves the original file for use in Symphony.

Using 1-2-3 Release 3.x with Symphony

Symphony is one of the few programs available that can use 1-2-3 Release 3.x files. You must translate the files with the 1-2-3 Translate Utility before importing them into Symphony.

1-2-3 functions with no corresponding function in Symphony are translated to labels. The following functions don't exist in Symphony: @DGET, @DQUERY, @DSTDS, @DVARS, @D360, @VDB, @ISRANGE @SUMPRODUCT, @COORD, @INFO, @SHEETS, @STDS, and @VARS.

Because 1-2-3 Release 3.x uses extended memory, a 1-2-3 worksheet may be too large to fit within Symphony's memory space.

To translate the CREDIT file into a Symphony file, start at your DOS prompt. Type **LOTUS** to access the 1-2-3 Access Menu, and then select **T**ranslate. The 1-2-3 Translate Utility screen appears, as shown in figure 15.2.

Specify the source program of the file you want to translate by highlighting 1-2-3 Release 3 in the FROM box and pressing Enter. Specify the target (TO) program by highlighting the appropriate Symphony version number and pressing Enter. Translate displays two warning screens describing possible translation problems; to continue the translation, press Esc.

A file selection screen appears with a list of Release 3 files. Highlight the desired file name and press Enter. Translate displays the same file name with a WR1 extension as the target file name; to accept this name, press Enter. To use a different name or directory for the translated file, type the desired path name and file name; for example, type the path name **C:\SYMPHONY\CREDIT.WR1**. (Be sure to use the WR1 extension.)

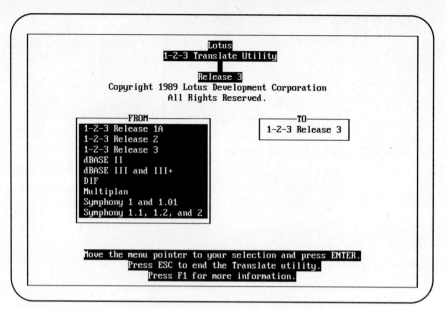

```
                          ┌─────┐
                          │Lotus│
                    ┌──────────────────────┐
                    │1-2-3 Translate Utility│
                    └──────────────────────┘
                             ┌─────────┐
                             │Release 3│
                             └─────────┘
             Copyright 1989 Lotus Development Corporation
                         All Rights Reserved.

          ┌────────FROM────────┐          ┌──────TO──────┐
          │1-2-3 Release 1A    │          │1-2-3 Release 3│
          │1-2-3 Release 2     │          └──────────────┘
          │1-2-3 Release 3     │
          │dBASE II            │
          │dBASE III and III+  │
          │DIF                 │
          │Multiplan           │
          │Symphony 1 and 1.01 │
          │Symphony 1.1, 1.2, and 2│
          └────────────────────┘

          ┌──────────────────────────────────────────────────┐
          │Move the menu pointer to your selection and press ENTER.│
          │Press ESC to end the Translate utility.           │
          │Press F1 for more information.                     │
          └──────────────────────────────────────────────────┘
```

Fig. 15.2. The 1-2-3 Translate Utility screen.

Translate asks whether you want to translate all worksheets or just one worksheet in the selected 1-2-3 file. Press Enter to select all worksheets. If you elect to translate one worksheet in the file, Translate displays the prompt Enter the letter of the worksheet to translate: with the default A. Enter the desired worksheet letter.

Translate then displays the prompt Proceed with translation and the options **Yes**, **No**, and **Quit**. Confirm the translation by pressing Enter or typing **Y**. The message Translation successful appears when the conversion is complete. Select another file to translate or press Esc. To return to the DOS prompt, respond **Yes** at the Do you want to end Translate? prompt and select **Exit** at the 1-2-3 Access Menu.

Symphony can retrieve the CREDIT.WR1 worksheet without further conversion, but the macro must be corrected. To retrieve the converted file, press F9 to display the Symphony Services menu. Select **File Re-**trieve and specify the desired file, selecting from the list of Symphony files that appear on-screen, or typing the file name (for example, **CREDIT.WR1**).

You now can correct the macro. The content of the macro appears in the Symphony worksheet, and the name is the same (\ p), but the key-strokes must be changed to Symphony's equivalent keystrokes to make it work correctly.

Using 1-2-3 Release 2.x with Symphony

You can import data between 1-2-3 Release 2.x and Symphony. Because the file name extensions must be compatible to import the files, save Symphony worksheets with the WR1 extension and 1-2-3 Release 2.x worksheets with the WK1 extension.

To save time, you can save the worksheet with the file extension appropriate to the target program, rather than the extension of the source program. To import the CREDIT.WK1 worksheet to Symphony, for example, save it as CREDIT.WR1. This procedure also protects the original CREDIT.WK1 file in 1-2-3.

Before saving the file, convert keystroke macros to the format used by the target program. If you import the 1-2-3 CREDIT.WK1 sample worksheet to Symphony, for example, change the \ p print macro to use Symphony's menu keystrokes rather than 1-2-3's menu keystrokes.

1-2-3 Release 2.x users can import worksheets to Symphony without using the Translate Utility. Column widths and range formats are preserved in the imported worksheet. To import the CREDIT.WK1 worksheet, start Symphony and press F9 to display the Services menu. Select **/F**ile **R**etrieve and type the full path name of the 1-2-3 file; for example, type **C:\LOTUS\CREDIT.WK1**.

Symphony retrieves and displays the worksheet as shown in figure 15.3.

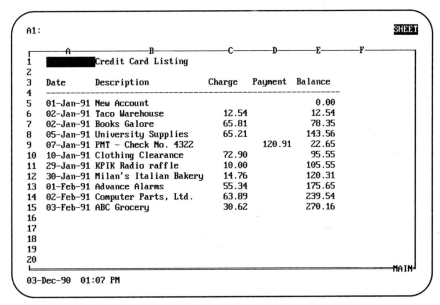

Fig. 15.3. *The 1-2-3 CREDIT.WK1 worksheet retrieved in Symphony.*

Using 1-2-3 with Quattro Pro

Borland's *Quattro Pro* 3.0 provides advanced spreadsheet presentation and publishing capabilities, including easy transfer of data and macros with 1-2-3. If you want to share data with a friend or co-worker who uses Quattro Pro, or use some Quattro Pro features not included in 1-2-3, you must know how to transfer your worksheet data from 1-2-3 into Quattro Pro.

Creating a Sample 1-2-3 Worksheet To Import

The 1-2-3 worksheet in figure 15.4 shows a credit card listing of charges and payments and includes formulas and a printing macro. This is the same CREDIT.WK1 worksheet created earlier in this chapter; it is used in this section to demonstrate transferring 1-2-3 files to Quattro Pro.

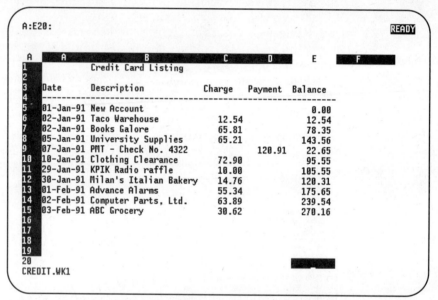

Fig. 15.4. A 1-2-3 worksheet that will be transferred to Quattro Pro.

If you have not already created the worksheet, enter the data as indicated in figure 15.4, placing the formula **+E5+C6–D6** in cell E6 and copying it down the rest of column E. Create the following print macro in cell G1: **/ppra1..i15~agq**. Name the macro with the command sequence **/Range Name Create \p**. After creating the worksheet, save it under the file name **CREDIT.WK1**. Quattro Pro cannot read 1-2-3 Release 3.x files unless you use the Translate utility to change the file into Release 2.x format. (Some formulas may not translate.)

Using 1-2-3 Menus in Quattro Pro

Quattro Pro can display its own standard menus or 1-2-3 menus. The 1-2-3 menus in Quattro Pro are pull-down style but each choice is the same as in 1-2-3. 1-2-3 macros imported into Quattro Pro work correctly if you change to the 1-2-3 menu system in Quattro Pro. Figures 15.5 and 15.6 show the difference between the standard main menu and the 1-2-3 main menu in Quattro Pro.

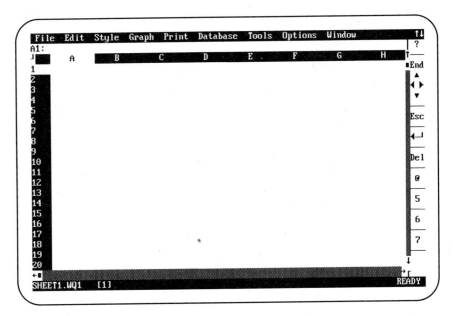

Fig. 15.5. *The standard Quattro Pro main menu.*

You can set Quattro Pro to display 1-2-3 menus permanently, or select the 1-2-3 menu option while using Quattro Pro. (This option is particularly useful if you use someone else's computer who may not want 1-2-3 menus as the default.)

To change Quattro Pro to the 1-2-3 menu setup, select /Options Startup Menu 123. If you want the 1-2-3 menus permanently displayed, select /Worksheet Global Default Update. To change back to the standard Quattro Pro menus, select /Worksheet Global Default Files Menu Quattro.

You also can use the 1-2-3 menus in Quattro Pro by starting Quattro Pro with the **Q123** batch command from the DOS prompt, rather than the usual **Q** command. This command causes Quattro Pro to use the 1-2-3 menus for one session without changing any permanent default settings.

All commands in this section assume you are working in Quattro Pro with the 1-2-3 menu structure.

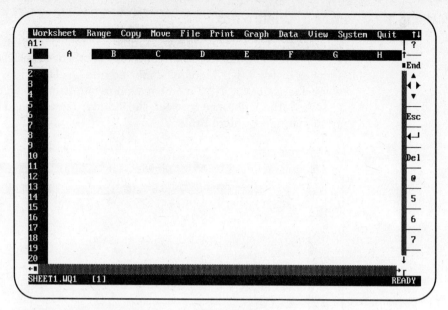

Fig. 15.6. *The 1-2-3 look-alike main menu in Quattro Pro.*

Importing and Exporting Files

Quattro Pro imports and exports 1-2-3 worksheets with little or no translation needed by examining the file extension to determine how to read or write the file. When saving or retrieving 1-2-3 worksheets, use the extension WK1 to indicate Release 2.x. Quattro Pro retains all formulas, column widths, cell formats, and macros.

To import the CREDIT.WK1 worksheet, select **/**F**ile** **R**etrieve and type the full path name of the 1-2-3 worksheet file; for example, type **C:\LOTUS2\CREDIT.WK1**.

Figure 15.7 shows the CREDIT.WK1 worksheet retrieved in Quattro Pro.

To save a Quattro Pro spreadsheet in 1-2-3 format, use the appropriate WK1 extension when saving the spreadsheet. Quattro Pro formulas, macros, functions (such as @DEGREES and @RADIANS) and features (such as shading and data entry blocks) that are not available in 1-2-3 are stripped out by the Quattro Pro conversion process before saving. When you create spreadsheets in Quattro Pro that you intend to use with 1-2-3, use 1-2-3 commands and functions to ensure that the spreadsheets transfer properly.

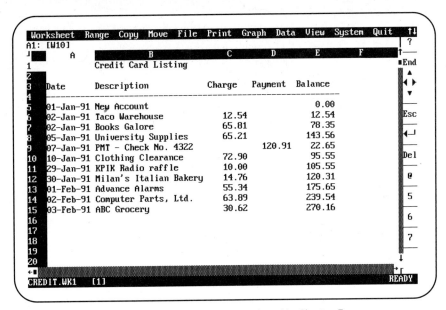

```
Worksheet  Range  Copy  Move  File  Print  Graph  Data  View  System  Quit  ↑↓
A1: [W10]                                                                    ?
J     A             B              C       D        E       F    ↑
1              Credit Card Listing                                   ■End
2                                                                     ▲
3    Date        Description       Charge  Payment  Balance       ◀ ▶
4    ─────────────────────────────────────────────────              ▼
5    01-Jan-91 New Account                           0.00
6    02-Jan-91 Taco Warehouse      12.54            12.54         Esc
7    02-Jan-91 Books Galore        65.81            78.35
8    05-Jan-91 University Supplies 65.21           143.56         ↵
9    07-Jan-91 PMT - Check No. 4322        120.91   22.65
10   10-Jan-91 Clothing Clearance  72.90            95.55         Del
11   29-Jan-91 KPIK Radio raffle   10.00           105.55
12   30-Jan-91 Milan's Italian Bakery 14.76        120.31         @
13   01-Feb-91 Advance Alarms      55.34           175.65
14   02-Feb-91 Computer Parts, Ltd. 63.89          239.54         5
15   03-Feb-91 ABC Grocery         30.62           270.16
16                                                                    6
17
18                                                                    7
19
20                                                                    ↓
◀■                                                                ▶┌
CREDIT.WK1    [1]                                               READY
```

Fig. 15.7. *The 1-2-3 CREDIT.WK1 worksheet retrieved in Quattro Pro.*

Using 1-2-3 with Excel

Microsoft Excel 3.0 is a Windows-based worksheet program similar to
1-2-3. Because Excel can read and write 1-2-3 Release 2.x and 3.x worksheet files, sharing data with an Excel user is easy. Some macros require
translation, but Excel offers tools to aid in the macro-translation process.
One advantage of using Excel is its true integration with Microsoft Windows. If you need to transfer data from a DOS-based version of 1-2-3 to a
Windows-based software program, you can transfer the 1-2-3 data into
Excel and from Excel to the other program.

Excel was designed with 1-2-3 users in mind. To use an Excel worksheet
in 1-2-3, save the Excel worksheet in 1-2-3 format, using the correct
1-2-3 extension (WK1 for Release 2.x and WK3 for Release 3.x). To import a 1-2-3 worksheet into Excel, type its name at the Excel file name
prompt. The following sections illustrate the process for transferring
data between 1-2-3 and Excel.

Creating a Sample 1-2-3 Worksheet

The 1-2-3 worksheet in figure 15.8 shows a credit card listing of charges
and payments and includes formulas and a printing macro. This is the
same CREDIT.WK1 worksheet created earlier in this chapter; it is used
in this section to demonstrate transferring 1-2-3 files to Excel.

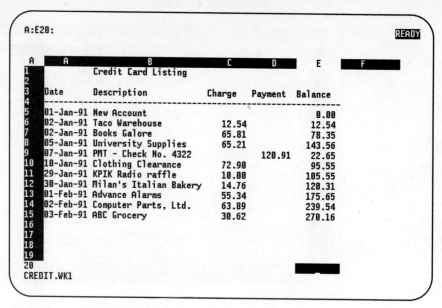

```
A:E20:                                                         READY

A      A                 B           C       D       E        F
1                 Credit Card Listing
2
3      Date      Description         Charge  Payment Balance
4      -----------------------------------------------------
5      01-Jan-91 New Account                           0.00
6      02-Jan-91 Taco Warehouse      12.54            12.54
7      02-Jan-91 Books Galore        65.81            78.35
8      05-Jan-91 University Supplies 65.21           143.56
9      07-Jan-91 PMT - Check No. 4322        120.91   22.65
10     10-Jan-91 Clothing Clearance  72.90            95.55
11     29-Jan-91 KPIK Radio raffle   10.00           105.55
12     30-Jan-91 Milan's Italian Bakery 14.76        120.31
13     01-Feb-91 Advance Alarms      55.34           175.65
14     02-Feb-91 Computer Parts, Ltd. 63.89          239.54
15     03-Feb-91 ABC Grocery         30.62           270.16
16
17
18
19
20
CREDIT.WK1
```

Fig. 15.8. *A 1-2-3 worksheet that will be transferred to Excel.*

If you have not already created the worksheet, enter the data as indicated in figure 15.8, placing the formula **+E5+C6–D6** in cell E6 and copying it down the rest of column E. Create the following print macro in cell G1: **/ppra1..i15~agq**. Name the macro with the command sequence **/Range Name Create \p**. After creating the worksheet, save it under the file name **CREDIT.WK1**. If you are a 1-2-3 version 3.x user, save the worksheet with the WK3 extension.

Understanding 1-2-3 and Excel Differences

Because the basic worksheet concepts of 1-2-3 and Excel are similar, moving between the two programs isn't difficult, but be aware of the conceptual differences. Excel takes full advantage of the Windows environment. If you are familiar with Windows, you will have little trouble selecting commands in Excel; the pull-down menus and dialog boxes are like those in Windows. If you are comfortable with the 1-2-3 DOS-based menu structure, you may have to accustom yourself to the way you choose commands in Excel. Microsoft eases 1-2-3 users into the Excel environment by including a 1-2-3 menu help system (described in the following section).

Figure 15.9 shows an Excel screen with a dialog box for changing print options. Notice that some of the options (such as margin settings, headers, and footers) are similar to 1-2-3, except that these options are selected with the Windows dialog box instead of the 1-2-3 menu bar.

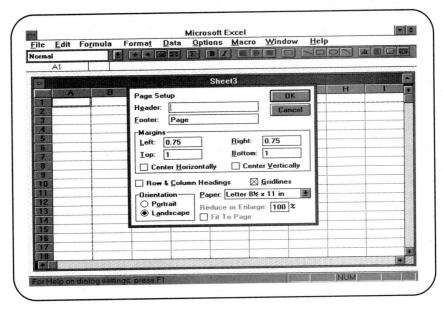

Fig. 15.9. *Using the Excel dialog box to set print options.*

The other differences between the two programs are outlined in the Excel user manuals and on-line help. The rest of this section discusses how to use the on-line 1-2-3 menu help in Excel and how to import and export worksheets between the programs.

Using the Excel Help Lotus 1-2-3 Menu System

If you need Excel for only a few tasks, using Excel's Help Lotus 1-2-3 menu system may save time. To turn on the help system, select Options Workspace to display the Workspace dialog box shown in figure 15.10. Select Alternate Menu or Help Key, type a slash (/), and select the Lotus 1-2-3 Help option. To make the integration from 1-2-3 even easier, select Alternate Navigation Keys, changing Excel's cursor-movement keystrokes to match the direction key patterns of 1-2-3. With the Help Lotus 1-2-3 menu system turned on, Excel uses a mixture of Excel and 1-2-3 commands. When you press the slash key, Excel brings up the Help for Lotus 1-2-3 Users dialog box shown in Figure 15.11.

When you don't know the Excel equivalent of a 1-2-3 command, press the slash key to display the 1-2-3 Help screen. Notice that the commands from the 1-2-3 menu bar appear in the left column of the help screen. For each of the familiar 1-2-3 commands you select (such as **/R**ange Format), the equivalent Excel commands appear in the middle of the Help screen. After you are familiar with Excel's command structure, you can turn off the Help Lotus 1-2-3 menu system.

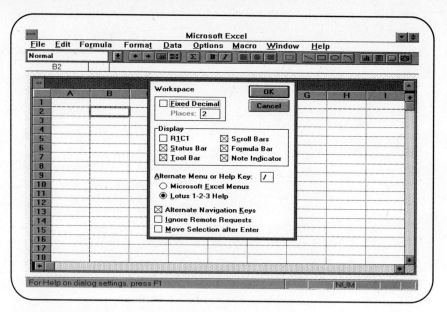

Fig. 15.10. *Turning on Excel's* **H**elp **L**otus 1-2-3 *menu system.*

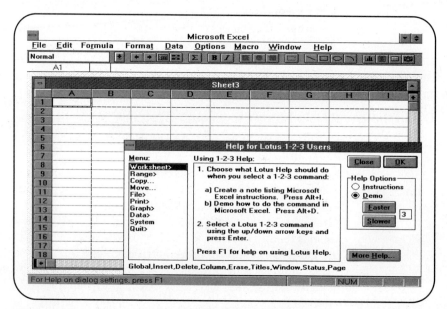

Fig. 15.11. *Excel's Help for Lotus 1-2-3 Users dialog box.*

Importing Files from 1-2-3

To import a 1-2-3 worksheet into Excel, open the file as if it were an Excel worksheet. To import the CREDIT worksheet created earlier, select the File Open command and type the full path name of the 1-2-3 worksheet file in the File Name text box; for example, type the path name **C:\LOTUS2\CREDIT.WK1**. Figure 15.12 shows the CREDIT.WK1 worksheet retrieved in Excel.

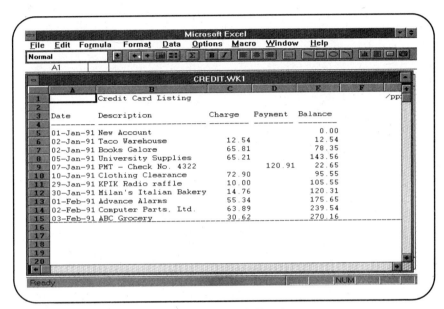

Fig. 15.12. The 1-2-3 CREDIT.WK1 worksheet in Excel.

Importing 1-2-3 worksheets with Excel rarely creates problems. If a cell is referenced differently, for example, Excel converts the cell during the import process. All formulas in Excel begin with an equal sign (=); when importing the CREDIT.WK1 worksheet, Excel adds the equal sign prefix to each formula in column E. In the same manner, because function names in Excel don't begin with the @ sign, Excel removes this symbol from 1-2-3 functions as it imports. In formulas including cell ranges, Excel substitutes a colon (:) for the 1-2-3 periods (..).

Excel includes the Macro Translation Assistant to help convert 1-2-3 macros to Excel format. Because 1-2-3's menus are different from Excel's, 1-2-3 command macros must be converted to work with Excel.

To translate a 1-2-3 macro to Excel format, select **Control Run** from the Windows control box in the upper left corner of the screen. Excel displays four choices of programs to run. Select the **Macro Translator** option. At the macro Translator box, select **Translate Lotus 1-2-3**. Excel displays a list of worksheets containing potential macros to convert. Select the CREDIT.WK1 worksheet; after saving the macro in its macro file (by clicking on OK at the **F**ile name prompt), the converted macro sheet appears, as shown in figure 15.13. You now can run the macro from the **Macro Run** menu selection as if it were an Excel macro.

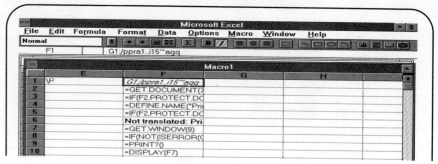

Fig. 15.13. *The converted 1-2-3 macro.*

Exporting Files to 1-2-3

Exporting Excel worksheets to 1-2-3 is even easier than going from 1-2-3 to Excel. After creating your Excel worksheet, select **F**ile Save **A**s to display the Save Worksheet As dialog box. Select **O**ptions to specify the 1-2-3 file format. Select WK1 or WK3, depending on the version of 1-2-3 you use; type a name with extension (and path name, if necessary) for the new 1-2-3 worksheet. When you select OK, Excel translates the file to 1-2-3 format and saves it to the disk. Exit Excel, start 1-2-3, and re-trieve the file with **/F**ile **R**etrieve. Excel macros don't translate to 1-2-3; you must re-create them after retrieving the worksheet in 1-2-3.

Using 1-2-3 with Quicken

Quicken has become one of the most popular home and business account-ing programs available. Part of Quicken's success comes from ease of use and numerous features at a low price. Quicken automates checking and savings account transactions, keeps track of budgets, provides flexible reporting and audit trails, and reconciles bank accounts.

You may want to use Quicken data in 1-2-3, or send Quicken reports to 1-2-3 to be analyzed in a worksheet format. (You cannot transfer 1-2-3 worksheet data to Quicken.) Two methods for transferring data from Quicken versions 3 and 4 to 1-2-3 are described in the following sections.

Using Quicken Reports in 1-2-3

You can send any report that Quicken generates to a 1-2-3 PRN file. After entering your Quicken data, view the report on-screen to make sure that it is complete before exiting Quicken. Then start 1-2-3 and load the report file.

To save a Quicken file in the 1-2-3 PRN format, for example, start Quicken and specify an account. Select **3** Reports, **2** Business Reports, and **2** Cash Flow. Type an appropriate title and specify dates on the Cash Flow Report screen. After collecting the appropriate data, Quicken displays a cash flow report on-screen. Press F8 to access the Print menu and the Print Report options menu appears, as shown in figure 15.14. Select **5** Disk (1-2-3 file).

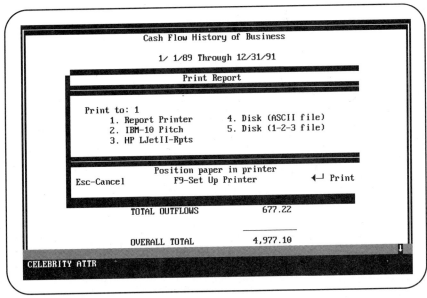

Fig. 15.14. The Quicken Print Report options menu.

At the File prompt, type the complete path name for the 1-2-3 print file you want Quicken to create; for example, type **C:\LOTUS2\ QREPORT**. Quicken supplies the PRN extension. After printing the file, exit Quicken and start 1-2-3.

To import the Quicken report in 1-2-3, select /File Import Numbers and specify the Quicken report; for example, type **QREPORT.PRN**. (You must type the PRN extension.) 1-2-3 imports the file into the worksheet as shown in figure 15.15. The report looks out-of-adjustment but is easy to fix.

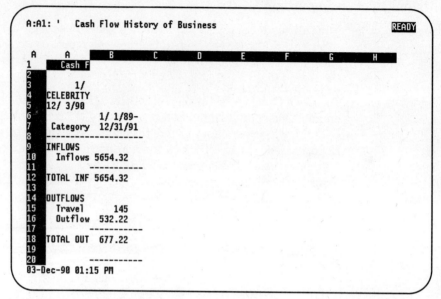

Fig. 15.15. *The Quicken report, imported into 1-2-3.*

Select /Worksheet Column Set-Width and widen the first few columns of the worksheet. After adjusting the column widths, you can see that 1-2-3 imported the Quicken report completely. If you want each report field separated into different worksheet cells, use /Data Parse. Save the worksheet as a 1-2-3 file if you want to use it again later.

Using the Transfer Utility

Intuit—the manufacturer of Quicken—offers an additional program called *Quicken Transfer Utility* that can create 1-2-3 Release 2.x compatible worksheets. The Transfer Utility transfers detail and summary data from Quicken to 1-2-3; you don't have to import and parse the data. Once transferred, all formats (such as commas and dollar signs) remain with the numbers in 1-2-3.

Detail Transfers

The Transfer Utility transfers Quicken detail transactions for any specified account into an existing 1-2-3 worksheet. (The worksheet can be blank.) Quicken transfers the date, account, check number, amount, payee, memo, and cleared status into seven separate columns of the worksheet beginning at cell A1. Before starting the Transfer Utility, save a blank 1-2-3 worksheet (for this example, use the file name QUIKDATA.WK1) and exit 1-2-3.

Even if you use 1-2-3 Release 3.x, you must save the worksheet with the WK1 extension to use the Transfer Utility.

Start the Transfer Utility from the DOS prompt by typing **QT**. (If you loaded the RAM-resident version, press Alt–T.) The Quicken Transfer Main Menu appears, as shown in figure 15.16.

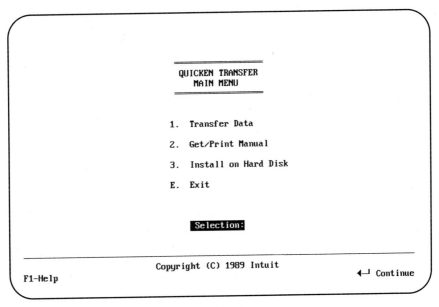

```
              QUICKEN TRANSFER
                 MAIN MENU


       1.   Transfer Data

       2.   Get/Print Manual

       3.   Install on Hard Disk

       E.   Exit


              Selection:


         Copyright (C) 1989 Intuit
 F1-Help                                    ← Continue
```

Fig. 15.16. *The Quicken Transfer Utility Main Menu.*

Select **1** Transfer Data. The Select Spreadsheet screen appears, displaying a list of files. (You may have to change the directory to match your 1-2-3 path name.) Enter the number of the file to use for the transfer. If more than twelve files appear, you can press PgDn to see more of the list. After you choose a file, the Transfer Utility displays the Select Account Group screen shown in figure 15.17.

Type one or more account groups (separated by commas) to transfer. The Transfer Utility displays the Time period screen. Enter the time periods of the data to transfer and press **Y** at the `Transfer Entire Items` prompt. Press F10 to begin the transfer.

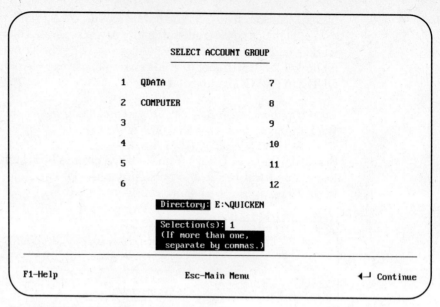

```
                    SELECT ACCOUNT GROUP
                    _____

              1   QDATA                  7

              2   COMPUTER               8

              3                          9

              4                         10

              5                         11

              6                         12

                 Directory: E:\QUICKEN

                 Selection(s): 1
                 (If more than one,
                  separate by commas.)



   F1-Help                  Esc-Main Menu              ↵ Continue
```

Fig. 15.17. *The Select Account Group screen.*

Quicken modifies the file name you specified, using the first six letters of the file name, an underscore, a number, and the WK1 extension. The file QUIKDATA, for example, becomes QUIKDA_1.WK1. This process ensures that you don't overwrite the original 1-2-3 file. Each time you transfer the detail (up to nine times), Quicken creates a different spreadsheet, using the numbers 1–9 in the file name. After the ninth file is created, Quicken overwrites the first file.

To see the transferred file, exit the Transfer Utility by pressing **E** at the Main Menu, start 1-2-3, and retrieve the new file. The data is separated into category columns as shown in figure 15.18. Modify the 1-2-3 format as necessary to display all of the information in each column.

Summary Transfers

Transferring Quicken summary data requires more effort than the detail data. You must make entries called *transfer labels* in the worksheet indicating the transactions you want to use. Quicken totals those transactions and transfers the results. The following list describes the codes used in the transfer labels.

Code	Group
m	Memo
p	Payee

Code	Group
c	Category/Class
d	Date
a	Account
n	Unmatched (any transaction NOT in code list)

If the transfer label is preceded by a plus sign (+), the Transfer Utility transfers the positive amounts (deposits) matching the transfer label only. Transfer labels preceded by a minus sign (–) cause the Transfer Utility to transfer negative amounts (payments) to the worksheet.

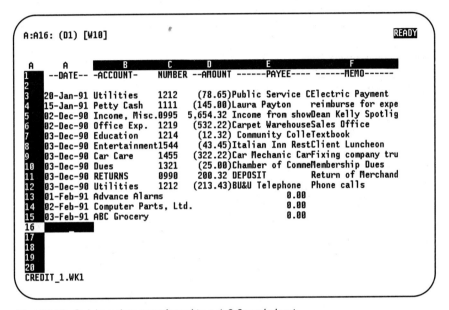

Fig. 15.18. *Quicken data transferred to a 1-2-3 worksheet.*

The transfer code can be followed by brackets indicating the desired transaction; the brackets can include dates or categories. The Transfer Utility places the summary data in the matching area of the worksheet. The worksheet in figure 15.19, for example, is structured to receive five category totals for the last six months of 1990. The Transfer Utility transfers these values to cells C2..H6.

After you create the spreadsheet with the transfer labels, exit 1-2-3 and start the Transfer Utility from DOS by typing **QT**. (If you loaded the RAM-resident version, press Alt–T instead.) The Quicken Transfer Main Menu appears.

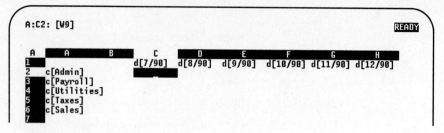

Fig. 15.19. *A worksheet structured to receive summary data.*

Select **1** Transfer Data. The Select Spreadsheet screen appears, displaying a list of files. (You may have to change the directory to match your 1-2-3 path name.) Enter the number of the file to use for the transfer. If more than twelve files appear, you can press PgDn to see more of the list. After you select a file, the Transfer Utility displays the Select Account Group screen.

Type one or more account groups (separated by commas) to transfer. The Transfer Utility displays the Time period screen. Enter the time periods of the data to transfer; press **N** at the `Transfer Entire Items` prompt as you want only the totals transferred. Press F10 to begin the transfer.

Exit the Transfer Utility, return to 1-2-3, and retrieve the worksheet to see the summary values placed in the worksheet by the Transfer Utility. You may have to press the Calc key (F9) to update calculations in the worksheet that rely on the imported numbers. The Transfer Utility doesn't format the summary data with commas or dollar signs as it does the detail data.

You may need to create several transfer template worksheets over time. Because transferring is easy, transferring Quicken data into a worksheet for further analysis may become a common practice.

Using 1-2-3 with TurboTax

One of the best-selling tax preparation programs is *TurboTax*. TurboTax offers yearly updated tax tables, tax form preparation, and tax planning. TurboTax handles tax preparation well, but many people prefer to keep records in 1-2-3 because of its flexibility and analyzing capabilities. At tax time, however, 1-2-3 worksheet data can be transferred into TurboTax.

No direct link exists between TurboTax and 1-2-3 data, but you can import worksheet data to TurboTax by converting to an ASCII file and importing the ASCII file into TurboTax. This section describes the steps for transferring worksheet data to TurboTax.

Preparing the Data

When importing worksheet data into TurboTax, use the table of *Import Data Codes* found in the appendix of the TurboTax reference manual. Because TurboTax can import ASCII data only, each value you import must be preceded by a data code. You can type the data codes in upper- or lowercase letters.

You are limited to one data code and data value per line. Figure 15.20 shows a sample ASCII file, ready for importing into TurboTax. The file was created in 1-2-3 and a selected range of the file was printed to the TAX.PRN file for TurboTax to import.

```
C:\>TYPE TAX.PRN
=TPAA= Murphy
=TPAC= Glen
=TPAE= 543-09-5012
=TPAG= Retired
=TPAP= 1983
=NPEE= 32443.22
=NPEM= 1092.85
=TBAA= YMCA Credit Union
=NBAC= 321.46
SchC01
=TCAA= Murphy Trust
=TCAB= Yes
=TDAA= SFDD Stock Sold, 100 shares
=TDAB= 02/12/89
=TDAC= 12/31/90
=NDAD= 5434.32
=NDAE= 4349.61


C:\>
```

Fig. 15.20. *An ASCII print file created in 1-2-3 for use in TurboTax.*

Before you attempt to transfer 1-2-3 data into TurboTax, plan your use of the tax data. You may have one worksheet containing income data with one row per check received and another worksheet with tax-deductible expenses. Insert appropriate @SUM formulas to produce end-of-the-year totals in each worksheet. Figure 15.21 shows an example worksheet listing income and payroll taxes paid during the year. These values are totaled in row 15. The TurboTax codes are listed at the bottom of the worksheet, starting in row 16; in column B, the appropriate total for each code is copied from row 15.

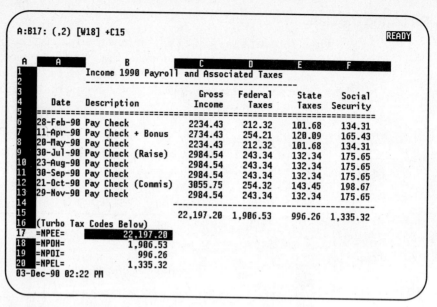

Fig. 15.21. *Worksheet data prepared for importing into TurboTax.*

To create an import file for TurboTax from the worksheet, print the data codes and their values to a disk file. Select /Print File and type a file name (1-2-3 supplies the PRN extension). Select the range to print and select Go to begin printing to the disk. Repeat this process for each worksheet containing tax data (for example, income worksheets, depreciation worksheets, and expense worksheets), creating several ASCII PRN files.

Use sequentially numbered names for the disk files; for example, use the file names IMPORT1.PRN, IMPORT2.PRN, and so on. TurboTax places the values appropriately when you import the files.

If you use 1-2-3 Release 3.x, you can save several steps in the transfer process. Use cell-linking formulas to combine the necessary worksheet data, listing all data codes in column A and the corresponding values from their respective worksheets in column B. This process enables you to create one PRN file with all of the appropriate data and to import the data in one step.

Using Multiple Copy Forms

You may require several copies of some TurboTax forms, depending on your tax data. You can have up to four of Schedule C and two each of Schedule F, Form 2106, and Form 4137. When transferring 1-2-3 data to these forms, you must use the appropriate import data codes and indicate which copy of the form the data represents. All data for these forms must be preceded with the appropriate *Form Copy Code* from the following table.

Schedule C	*Schedule F*	*Form 2106*	*Form 4137*
SchC01	SchF01	Fm210601	Fm413701
SchC02	SchF02	Fm210602	Fm413702
SchC03			
SchC04			

If you have two businesses, for example "Doc's Chimney Cleaning," and "Doc's Heating and Air," you can import each business name into a separate copy of Schedule C with the following PRN file:

```
SchC01
=TCAF= Doc's Chimney Cleaning
SchC02
=TCAF= Doc's Heating and Air
```

"=TCAF=" is the Data Import Code for a Schedule C Business Name. After importing the preceding file, you have two copies of Schedule C, each with the correct Business Name.

Importing Data into TurboTax

After creating your PRN files, exit 1-2-3 and start TurboTax. You must create a return before importing worksheet data. To create a return, select **Create Return** from the **Files** pull-down menu. Type a description of the return; for example, type **Bob's 1990 Tax Return**. After a brief pause, TurboTax begins a new return. Select **Import data** from the **Files** menu. Specify the 1-2-3 directory where the incoming data is located by selecting Import **Directory**. Specify the worksheet's file name by selecting Import **File** and typing the file name (for example, **IMPORT.PRN**). TurboTax is ready to import the PRN file. Select **Go To Import**. TurboTax displays the Import Summary screen shown in figure 15.22.

Press Enter to start importing the data. When the import process is complete, TurboTax calculates the return with the imported data and returns to the tax form screen shown in figure 15.23. Look over the imported data carefully, making sure that you imported the proper data into the right fields of the correct form.

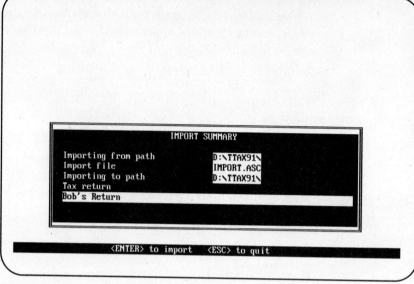

```
                        IMPORT SUMMARY

   Importing from path          D:\TTAX91\
   Import file                  IMPORT.ASC
   Importing to path            D:\TTAX91\
   Tax return
   Bob's Return


           <ENTER> to import    <ESC> to quit
```

Fig. 15.22. The TurboTax Import Summary screen.

```
                TurboTax Personal Information Worksheet        1990

  FileID Bob's Return_____
  Your Name:                         Spouse Name:
    Last Name......Smith_____   Last Name..Smith_____
    First Name.....John_____     First Name.Jayne_____
  Social Sec No....212-33-2122           Spouse SSN...222-55-6544
  Occupation.......Lawyer_____         Spouse Occup.Homemaker_____
  Address..........131 Mockingbird Lane_____
  City.............Kansas City_____    State......KS  Zip Code 21223_____

  FEDERAL FILING STATUS:

  Using the following codes, enter 1, 2, 3, 4 or 5 for your
      Federal Filing Status...................................>>          2.

          1- Single
          2- Married Filing Joint Return
          3- Married Filing Separate Return [_] Enter 'X' if you did not live
                                                 with your spouse for the entire
                                                 year
          4- Head of Household:  If the qualifying person is your child but
                                 not your dependent, enter the child's name:
  F1-Help          PERSONAL INFORMATION WORKSHEET          Form Text
  F2-Edit  F3-Xref  F4-Back  F5-GoTo  F6-Form  F7-Menu  F8-IRS  F9-Calc  F10-Save
```

Fig. 15.23. The TurboTax worksheet after importing the 1-2-3 data.

Handling Import Errors

The first time you import worksheet data, you may make mistakes. You must type the import data codes as shown in the TurboTax Appendix, enclosed between two equal signs (=). If you make an error and misspell a data code, TurboTax warns you by displaying ***Invalid Interface Code*** after importing the rest of the file. If you import data that is already in the tax return (for example, the Social Security Number), TurboTax indicates that this data exists by displaying ***Text Field Is Already Used*** and ignoring the duplicate data.

TurboTax displays all error listings on-screen after the import process is finished. You also can look at these errors in an error file TurboTax creates with the name TTAXIMP.ERR.

Summary

This chapter discussed many ways that you can use 1-2-3 worksheet data with other financial programs. The general-purpose design of 1-2-3 enables you to gather tax information throughout the year and merge this data into TurboTax at tax season, or to combine 1-2-3 data with the features of your financial management program (such as Quicken). You also can transfer spreadsheet data between 1-2-3 and Symphony, Excel, and Quattro Pro.

Integrating financial programs requires planning before transferring data, but being able to import and export data between programs is almost always easier and faster than retyping.

The next chapter discusses methods for using 1-2-3 data with Paradox, Q&A, and dBASE.

Chapter Sixteen

USING 1-2-3 WITH DATABASE PROGRAMS

L otus 1-2-3's built-in database commands sort and retrieve data, but occasionally you may need a full-functioning database program with more extensive data management and reporting capabilities. This chapter discusses methods for transferring 1-2-3 data to and from the database programs dBASE, Paradox, and Q&A.

Using 1-2-3 with dBASE

One of the first database programs developed for the PC, *dBASE* is now the industry leader. dBASE IV, the latest version, is Ashton-Tate's flagship product. You can transfer data between 1-2-3 and dBASE without translation if you use 1-2-3 Release 2.3 or earlier versions. For Release 3.x worksheets, use the Lotus Translate Utility to translate worksheets into dBASE format.

This section describes the process of transferring data between 1-2-3 and dBASE.

Preparing the Data

The 1-2-3 worksheet shown in figure 16.1 is a college professor's list of semester grades. The professor needs to combine this semester's grades with semester grades previously stored in a dBASE file.

To follow the transfer examples in this section, create the sample 1-2-3 database from figure 16.1. Enter the student numbers (StdNo) as labels and format the homework and test score numbers with the command sequence /Range Format Fixed 0. Assign the range name SCORES to range A4..J20; in this example, you import only the data from the worksheet and not the first three rows. Use the column widths from the following table.

Column	Width
A	5 characters
B	16 characters
C through I	6 characters
J	9 characters

```
A:A2: [W5]                                                          READY

        B             C     D     E     F     G     H     I     J
1  Class: Computer Concepts, #CSC1202
                              - Homework -              - Tests -  - Final -
3                      +---------------------------+------------+---------+
4  StdNoStdName        HW1   HW2   HW3   HW4   HW5 Test1 Test2   Final
5  -------------------------------------------------------------------------
6  5754 Austin, Lee     7     6     9     8    10    87    91    87.2%
7  2123 Barker, Larry   5     8     8     8     9    91    94    89.2%
8  6753 Barkley, Jess  10     9    10    10     9    98   100    98.4%
9  3234 Chambers, Chris 9    10    10     9    10    99    94    96.4%
10 4257 Costner, Angela 10   10     9    10    10    98    96    97.2%
11 4323 Drew, Harry     8     9     9     9     9    89    88    88.4%
12 7897 Gregg, Bettye   0     5     0     0     6    76    80    66.8%
13 5434 Kelley, Susie   4     8     6     7     8    65    75    69.2%
14 4322 Kemp, Sally     9    10     9    10     9    88    98    93.2%
15 5445 Majors, Steve  10    10     9    10     9   100   100    99.2%
16 4333 Murphy, Barbara 9    10    10     9     9    98    96    96.4%
17 7654 Owens, Heath    8     9     9    10     9    93    84    88.8%
18 1266 Peters, Jayne   9    10     9    10    10    72    89    83.6%
19 7667 Seavers, C.J.  10    10     9    10     9    91    87    90.4%
20 4321 Smith, Steve    6     7     6     7     7    56    81    68.0%
STUDENT.WK3
```

Fig. 16.1. A worksheet to be transferred to dBASE.

Compute the final averages in column J by entering the formula **@SUM(C6..I6)/250** in cell J6 and copying the formula to range J7..J20. Format column J using the command **/R**ange **F**ormat **P**ercent **1**. Save the worksheet with the file name STUDENT and exit 1-2-3.

Worksheets converted to dBASE are limited to 128 columns. Because dBASE uses column labels as database field names, the column labels must conform to dBASE's field naming rules. Make sure that all fields are set wide enough to display all of the data in every cell; dBASE truncates any remaining data. The method for converting worksheet data to dBASE varies with 1-2-3 versions; read the section in the following text that is appropriate for your 1-2-3 version.

Importing 1-2-3 Release 3.x Data with dBASE

The Translate Utility from the 1-2-3 Access Menu converts 1-2-3 worksheets to dBASE format. You can translate an entire worksheet file or a named range. Translate converts all column labels in the worksheet or range to dBASE field names and all data in the worksheet or range to dBASE data.

Before translating, delete any worksheet contents that don't conform to the standard 1-2-3 database format. In the STUDENT sample worksheet, for example, delete the titles in the first few rows and the dashed line in the fifth row. If you don't remove this extraneous information, Translate converts it to data.

dBASE cannot import all of 1-2-3's data formats. The data in each column must be uniform; remove labels or notes from numeric columns. Because dBASE has no equivalent field formats, your worksheets cannot use **Sci** (scientific), **Hidden**, **Color**, or **Parentheses** formats.

When the worksheet is ready for translation, exit 1-2-3. Type **LOTUS** at the DOS prompt to access the 1-2-3 Access Menu and select **Translate**. The 1-2-3 Translate Utility menu appears. Specify the source program of the file you want to translate by highlighting 1-2-3 Release 3 in the FROM box and pressing Enter. Specify the target (TO) program by highlighting dBASE III and dBASE III+ and pressing **Enter**.

Select the same options for dBASE IV; dBASE IV can read these translated worksheets.

Translate displays warning screens describing possible translation problems; to continue the translation, press Esc.

A file selection screen appears with a list of Release 3 files. Highlight the desired file name and press Enter. Translate displays the same file name with DBF (the dBASE extension) as the target file name; to accept this name, press Enter. To use a different name or directory for the translated file, type the desired path name and file name; for example, type **C:\DBASE\STUDENT.DBF**. (Be sure to use the DBF extension.)

Translate prompts you to specify whether you are translating the entire worksheet or a named range. For this example, select **Named** range. If you elect to translate a range, Translate prompts you for the name of the range. For this example, type **SCORES** to use the SCORES range from the STUDENT worksheet. Your screen should resemble figure 16.2.

After typing the range name, press Enter. Translate asks whether you want to translate all worksheets or one worksheet from the selected 1-2-3 file. Select All worksheets or One worksheet. If you elect to translate one worksheet in the file, Translate displays the prompt Enter the letter of the worksheet to translate: with the default A. Enter the desired worksheet letter.

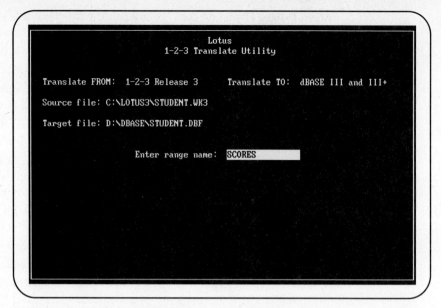

```
                            Lotus
                     1-2-3 Translate Utility


      Translate FROM:  1-2-3 Release 3     Translate TO:  dBASE III and III+

      Source file: C:\LOTUS3\STUDENT.WK3

      Target file: D:\DBASE\STUDENT.DBF


                     Enter range name:  SCORES
```

Fig. 16.2. *Selecting a worksheet range to translate to dBASE.*

Translate displays the prompt Proceed with translation and the options Yes, No, and **Q**uit. Confirm the translation by pressing Enter or typing **Y**. If Translate finds errors (such as bad field names) in the file, a warning appears, and you must correct the worksheet before continuing the translation. The message Translation successful appears when the conversion is complete. Select another file to translate or press Esc. To return to the DOS prompt, respond **Yes** at the Do you want to end Translate? prompt and select **Exit** at the 1-2-3 Access Menu.

You can access the STUDENT.DBF database file in the same way as any database created in dBASE.

Importing 1-2-3 Release 2.x Data with dBASE

To import data from a 1-2-3 Release 2.x worksheet, you must use the dBASE **Import** command. The **Import** command is available from the dot prompt and from the Control Center's **Tools** menu.

You can convert only 1-2-3 Release 2.x worksheet files with the dBASE Import command. For Release 3.x worksheets with the WK3 extension, use the Lotus Translate Utility.

Before importing a worksheet, remove everything except the data and column labels. You can import only entire worksheets with the dBASE Import command. To import the STUDENT sample worksheet into dBASE, use **/R**ange **D**elete **R**ow to remove rows 1–3 and row 5. If you leave these rows in the worksheet, dBASE attempts to use them as data values. When importing, dBASE converts formulas to their numerical values and ignores worksheet macros.

dBASE cannot import all of 1-2-3's data formats. The data in each column must be uniform; remove labels or notes from numeric columns. Because dBASE has no equivalent field formats, your worksheets cannot use **S**ci (scientific), **H**idden, **C**olor, or **P**arentheses formats.

To import a 1-2-3 Release 2.x worksheet into dBASE, select **I**mport from the Tools menu. dBASE displays a list of import formats; select **L**otus 1-2-3. dBASE opens a disk selection menu. To specify the path name, select **<parent>**. A list of files in the root directory appears, as shown in figure 16.3.

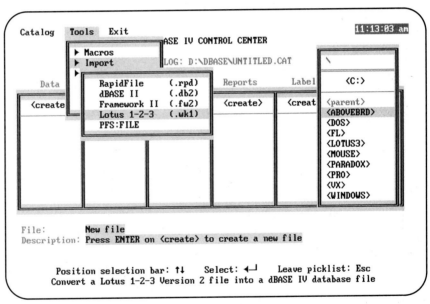

Fig. 16.3. *Specifying the path name for a 1-2-3 worksheet to import into dBASE.*

Select the subdirectory where your 1-2-3 files are stored. dBASE displays a list of WK1 worksheets; select the desired worksheet. For this example, select STUDENT.WK1. dBASE starts the import operation and displays a status report on its progress.

When prompted, type a description of the new database file. dBASE supplies this description when you search a list of database files. After you have finished typing the description, dBASE returns to the Control Center, where you can view the database file using normal dBASE commands or menus.

Display the new data in table view to check the conversion of labels to field names. After importing, always view the data to make sure that it was converted correctly. Figure 16.4 shows the STUDENT database after importing to dBASE.

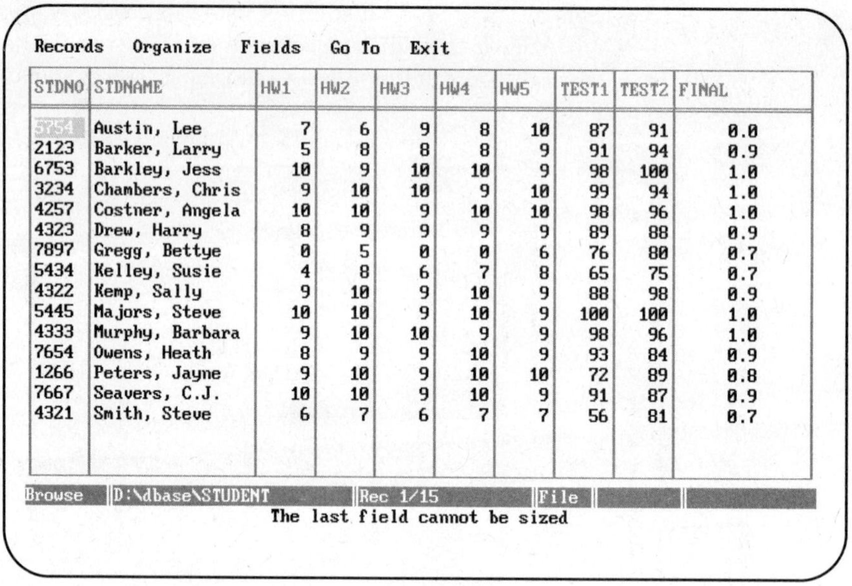

Records	Organize	Fields	Go To	Exit					

STDNO	STDNAME	HW1	HW2	HW3	HW4	HW5	TEST1	TEST2	FINAL
5754	Austin, Lee	7	6	9	8	10	87	91	0.0
2123	Barker, Larry	5	8	8	8	9	91	94	0.9
6753	Barkley, Jess	10	9	10	10	9	98	100	1.0
3234	Chambers, Chris	9	10	10	9	10	99	94	1.0
4257	Costner, Angela	10	10	9	10	10	98	96	1.0
4323	Drew, Harry	8	9	9	9	9	89	88	0.9
7897	Gregg, Bettye	0	5	0	0	6	76	80	0.7
5434	Kelley, Susie	4	8	6	7	8	65	75	0.7
4322	Kemp, Sally	9	10	9	10	9	88	98	0.9
5445	Majors, Steve	10	10	9	10	9	100	100	1.0
4333	Murphy, Barbara	9	10	10	9	9	98	96	1.0
7654	Owens, Heath	8	9	9	10	9	93	84	0.9
1266	Peters, Jayne	9	10	9	10	10	72	89	0.8
7667	Seavers, C.J.	10	10	9	10	9	91	87	0.9
4321	Smith, Steve	6	7	6	7	7	56	81	0.7

Browse	D:\dbase\STUDENT		Rec 1/15		File		

The last field cannot be sized

Fig. 16.4. *Viewing the imported file in dBASE.*

Importing 1-2-3 Release 2.x Data from the dBASE Dot Prompt

You also can import 1-2-3 worksheets from the dot prompt. This method enables you to import worksheet files from within a dBASE program. The format of the command is **IMPORT FROM *filename* TYPE WK1**. You must type the complete path name when specifying the file name. dBASE imports the file into database format with the extension DBF. To import the STUDENT worksheet from the dot prompt, for example, type **IMPORT FROM C:\LOTUS\STUDENT.WK1 TYPE WK1**. If the resulting database file name already exists, dBASE prompts you to overwrite it or cancel the import operation.

Exporting Data from dBASE to 1-2-3

You can convert a dBASE database file to 1-2-3 with the **Export** command. This command mirrors the **Import** command described in the preceding section. dBASE III and IV can export only to 1-2-3 Release 1 format, using the WKS extension. This limitation poses no problem, however, because Releases 2.x and 3.x read WKS worksheets. After retrieving the WKS worksheet in 1-2-3, you can save it in the newer format.

To export a dBASE database file to 1-2-3, select **Export** from the **Tools** menu. Select **Lotus 1-2-3** from the list of file formats. dBASE displays a list of database files; select the desired file. dBASE starts the export operation and displays a status report showing its progress. When the export is complete, the Control Center screen returns.

You cannot export data to a 1-2-3 worksheet by using the dot prompt.

Figure 16.5 shows an exported dBASE database file; the database was created with the same field names, widths, and data as in the STUDENT worksheet. The dBASE field names become the first row in the resulting worksheet. The worksheet has the original dBASE file name with the WKS extension. Notice that all data gets exported and numbers retain full precision.

```
A:A20: [W5]                                              READY

              B          C     D     E     F     G     H     I     J
1  StdNoStdName         HW1   HW2   HW3   HW4   HW5   Test1 Test2 Average
2   5754Austin, Lee      7.00  6.00  9.00  8.00 10.00 87.00 91.00  0.872
3   2123Barker, Larry    5.00  8.00  8.00  8.00  9.00 91.00 94.00  0.892
4   6753Barkley, Jess   10.00  9.00 10.00 10.00  9.00 98.00100.00  0.984
5   3234Chambers, Chris  9.00 10.00 10.00  9.00 10.00 99.00 94.00  0.964
6   4257Costner, Angela 10.00 10.00  9.00 10.00 10.00 98.00 96.00  0.972
7   4323Drew, Harry      8.00  9.00  9.00  9.00  9.00 89.00 88.00  0.884
8   7897Gregg, Bettye    0.00  5.00  0.00  0.00  6.00 76.00 80.00  0.668
9   5434Kelley, Susie    4.00  8.00  6.00  7.00  8.00 65.00 75.00  0.692
10  4322Kemp, Sally      9.00 10.00  9.00 10.00  9.00 88.00 98.00  0.932
11  5445Majors, Steve   10.00 10.00  9.00 10.00  9.00100.00100.00  0.992
12  4333Murphy, Barabara 9.00 10.00 10.00  9.00  9.00 98.00 96.00  0.964
13  7654Owens, Heath     8.00  9.00  9.00 10.00  9.00 93.00 84.00  0.888
14  1266Peters, Jayne    9.00 10.00  9.00 10.00 10.00 72.00 89.00  0.836
15  7667Seavers, C.J.   10.00 10.00  9.00 10.00  9.00 91.00 87.00  0.904
16  4321Smith, Steve     6.00  7.00  6.00  7.00  7.00 56.00 81.00  0.680
17
18
19
STUDENT1.WKS
```

Fig. 16.5. *The STUDENT database, exported from dBASE into 1-2-3 format as a WKS file.*

Because dBASE exports to the WKS format only, retrieve the exported data with the **/F**ile **R**etrieve command and immediately save it with your usual 1-2-3 extension (WK1 or WK3). After you save the worksheet in the new file format, all of that version's commands function properly.

Using 1-2-3 with Paradox

Borland's *Paradox* 3.5 has become a popular database program because of its ease of use, relational data capabilities, and powerful Paradox Application Language (PAL). Paradox can read and write 1-2-3 worksheets (Releases 1 through 2.2), but 1-2-3 users usually need to edit worksheet data before transferring it. Paradox converts 1-2-3 worksheets to tables but ignores macros and graphs. Paradox imports worksheet data correctly only if extra titles and underlines are removed from the 1-2-3 database.

This section describes the process of transferring data between 1-2-3 and Paradox.

Preparing the Data

The 1-2-3 worksheet shown in figure 16.6 is a college professor's list of semester grades. The professor needs to combine this semester's grades with semester grades previously stored in a Paradox file. (This database is virtually identical to the one in figure 16.1 but without titles.)

```
A:J20: [W9]                                                    READY

      A          B         C     D     E     F     G     H     I
1   StdNoStdName           HW1   HW2   HW3   HW4   HW5 Test1 Test2  Final
2   5754 Austin, Lee        7     6     9     8    10    87    91   87.2%
3   2123 Barker, Larry      5     8     8     8     9    91    94   89.2%
4   6753 Barkley, Jess     10     9    10    10     9    98   100   98.4%
5   3234 Chambers, Chris    9    10    10     9    10    99    94   96.4%
6   4257 Costner, Angela   10    10     9    10    10    98    96   97.2%
7   4323 Drew, Harry        8     9     9     9     9    89    88   88.4%
8   7897 Gregg, Bettye      0     5     0     0     6    76    80   66.8%
9   5434 Kelley, Susie      4     8     6     7     8    65    75   69.2%
10  4322 Kemp, Sally        9    10     9    10     9    88    98   93.2%
11  5445 Majors, Steve     10    10     9    10     9   100   100   99.2%
12  4333 Murphy, Barbara    9    10    10     9     9    98    96   96.4%
13  7654 Owens, Heath       8     9     9    10     9    93    84   88.8%
14  1266 Peters, Jayne      9    10     9    10    10    72    89   83.6%
15  7667 Seavers, C.J.     10    10     9    10     9    91    87   90.4%
16  4321 Smith, Steve       6     7     6     7     7    56    81   68.0%
17
18
19
STUDENT.WK1
```

Fig. 16.6. *A worksheet to be transferred to Paradox.*

To follow the transfer examples in this section, create the sample 1-2-3 database from figure 16.6. Enter the student numbers (StdNo) as labels and format the homework and test score numbers with the command sequence /Range Format Fixed 0. Assign the range name SCORES to range A4..J20; in this example, you import only the data from the worksheet and not the first three rows. Use the column widths from the following table.

Column	Width
A	5 characters
B	16 characters
C through I	6 characters
J	9 characters

Compute the final averages in column J by entering the formula @SUM(C2..I2)/250 in cell J3 and copying the formula to range J3..J16. Format column J using the command /Range Format Percent 1. Save the worksheet with the file name STUDENT.WK1 (even if you use Release 3.x); exit 1-2-3 and start Paradox.

Column Labels

If you intend to use a 1-2-3 worksheet in Paradox, type the column labels in the first row. Paradox uses these labels as field names after importing the worksheet. If the first row contains no labels, Paradox finds the first row with a label and uses that row's labels as field names, assuming that all data falls directly below the field names. Figure 16.7 shows a worksheet that can be misinterpreted—Paradox regards the dashed line in row 2 as values. To use this worksheet in Paradox, delete row 2 before importing the worksheet.

Paradox cannot import formulas, only their values. Column J contains a list of formulas, but only the computed results are imported to Paradox. If you want the Paradox field values to contain calculations, add the formulas in Paradox.

To ensure that you import the correct information, press the Calc (F9) key before importing worksheets containing formulas to Paradox.

Data Formats

Before transferring worksheet data, you must understand the format Paradox uses. 1-2-3 provides more freedom than Paradox in formatting data; in Paradox, an entire column (field) must use the same format. Paradox converts columns with two or more date, number, or alphanumeric values, in any combination, to alphanumeric fields. The following table shows how Paradox formats 1-2-3 data.

1-2-3 Column Format	Paradox Field Format
Labels	Alphanumeric (A)
Currency	Currency ($)
Numbers containing 2 decimal places	Currency ($)
Numbers	Numeric (N)
Dates	Date

```
A:J28: [W9]                                              READY

     A         B          C     D     E     F     G     H     I
 1 StdNoStdName            HW1   HW2   HW3   HW4   HW5 Test1 Test2  Final
 2 ----------------------------------------------------------------------
 3 5754 Austin, Lee          7     6     9     8    10    87    91  87.2%
 4 2123 Barker, Larry        5     8     8     8     9    91    94  89.2%
 5 6753 Barkley, Jess       10     9    10    10     9    98   100  98.4%
 6 3234 Chambers, Chris      9    10    10     9    10    99    94  96.4%
 7 4257 Costner, Angela     10    10     9    10    10    98    96  97.2%
 8 4323 Drew, Harry          8     9     9     9     9    89    88  88.4%
 9 7897 Gregg, Bettye        8     5     8     8     6    76    80  66.8%
10 5434 Kelley, Susie        4     8     6     7     8    65    75  69.2%
11 4322 Kemp, Sally          9    10     9    10     9    88    98  93.2%
12 5445 Majors, Steve       10    10     9    10     9   100   100  99.2%
13 4333 Murphy, Barbara      9    10    10     9     9    98    96  96.4%
14 7654 Owens, Heath         8     9     9    10     9    93    84  88.8%
15 1266 Peters, Jayne        9    10     9    10    10    72    89  83.6%
16 7667 Seavers, C.J.       10    10     9    10     9    91    87  90.4%
17 4321 Smith, Steve         6     7     6     7     7    56    81  68.0%
18
19
                                                      ███████████

STUDENT.WK1
```

Fig. 16.7. *A 1-2-3 worksheet with lines that Paradox can misinterpret.*

Scan your worksheet before importing to ensure that every column contains "pure" data—numbers, dollar amounts, or labels. If Paradox uses the alphanumeric format in a field, you cannot perform calculations on the field.

Importing the Data

Paradox imports worksheet data only into new tables. You cannot add worksheet data to an existing table.

To add a worksheet to the end of an existing Paradox table, import the worksheet to a new table and merge the two tables.

To import a 1-2-3 worksheet into a new table, select **Tools ExportImport Import**. Paradox displays a list of import formats; select **1-2-3**. Because Paradox imports worksheets from Releases 1 through 2.x, you must specify the 1-2-3 version used. Paradox requests the file name to import. Enter the complete path and file name, for example **C:\LOTUS\STUDENT.WK1**. If you forget the file name, type the full path name (with the drive letter). Paradox displays a list of all 1-2-3 worksheet files, as shown in figure 16.8.

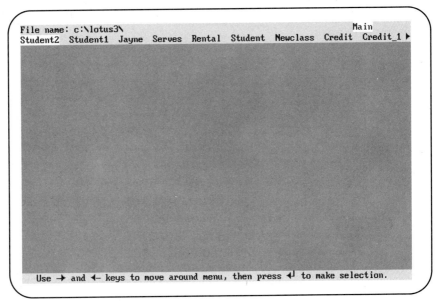

```
File name: c:\lotus3\                                          Main
Student2  Student1  Jayne  Serves  Rental  Student  Newclass  Credit  Credit_1 ▶




















     Use → and ← keys to move around menu, then press ↵ to make selection.
```

Fig. 16.8. *Selecting a worksheet file to import in Paradox.*

After selecting a file, specify a name for the new table Paradox will create with the 1-2-3 data. To replace an existing table with the newly created one, type the name of the existing table. For this example, name the table **Student**. After you specify the table name, Paradox begins importing and displays a status report showing the progress of the import operation. If Paradox encounters any errors while importing, it places the questionable record in a separate table called problems. If a table called problems already exists, Paradox overwrites it.

If worksheet columns are missing field names, Paradox creates its own field names (using Field-1, Field-2, and so on). If field names are duplicated (for example, two columns in the worksheet have the label ADDRESS), Paradox names the first ADDRESS-1 and the second ADDRESS-2 in the resulting table.

When Paradox completes the import operation it displays the newly created table, as shown in figure 16.9.

```
Viewing Student table: Record 1 of 15                              Main

STUDENT    Stdno          Stdname              Hw1        Hw2        Hw3
     1     5754      Austin, Lee                7          6          9
     2     2123      Barker, Larry              5          8          8
     3     6753      Barkley, Jess             10          9         10
     4     3234      Chambers, Chris            9         10         10
     5     4257      Costner, Angela           10         10          9
     6     4323      Drew, Harry                8          9          9
     7     7897      Gregg, Bettye              0          5          0
     8     5434      Kelley, Susie              4          8          6
     9     4322      Kemp, Sally                9         10          9
    10     5445      Majors, Steve             10         10          9
    11     4333      Murphy, Barbara            9         10         10
    12     7654      Owens, Heath               8          9          9
    13     1266      Peters, Jayne              9         10          9
    14     7667      Seavers, C.J.             10         10          9
    15     4321      Smith, Steve               6          7          6




                                                      15 records converted
```

Fig. 16.9. *The imported worksheet data.*

You can view the new table in the same way as any other Paradox table. After checking the table for errors, press F10 to return to the Paradox menu.

Exporting Paradox Tables to 1-2-3

To use a Paradox table in 1-2-3, export it to a worksheet file. Paradox exports table data to new worksheets; it cannot export to an existing worksheet.

To add Paradox data to an existing worksheet, export the data to a new worksheet and merge the new and existing worksheets.

The process of exporting data mirrors the import process described in the preceding section. To export the table you just created to a new 1-2-3 worksheet, select **Tools ExportImport Export** from the Main menu. Paradox displays a list of export formats; select **1-2-3**. Specify the appropriate 1-2-3 version and type the name of the table you want to export. If you don't know the name, press Enter to see a list of tables available.

Type a path and file name for the new worksheet; for example, type **C:\LOTUS\NEWDATA.WK1**. Paradox begins exporting and displays a status report showing the progress of the export operation. Formulas in the database are not exported; only the computed values are translated to 1-2-3 format.

The first row of the resulting worksheet contains column labels matching the Paradox field names in the original table. Each column label is followed by the data from the table. Paradox sets the 1-2-3 column widths to match the width of the original table fields. Figure 16.10 shows how the Student table looks after Paradox exports it to a 1-2-3 worksheet.

```
A:A1: [W7] 'Stdno                                          READY

                    B          C        D        E        F        G
     Stdno  Stdname         Hw1      Hw2      Hw3      Hw4      Hw5
2    5754   Austin, Lee       7        6        9        8       10
3    2123   Barker, Larry     5        8        8        8        9
4    6753   Barkley, Jess    10        9       10       10        9
5    3234   Chambers, Chris   9       10       10        9       10
6    4257   Costner, Angela  10       10        9       10       10
7    4323   Drew, Harry       8        9        9        9        9
8    7897   Gregg, Bettye     0        5        0        0        6
9    5434   Kelley, Susie     4        8        6        7        8
10   4322   Kemp, Sally       9       10        9       10        9
11   5445   Majors, Steve    10       10        9       10        9
12   4333   Murphy, Barbara   9       10       10        9        9
13   7654   Owens, Heath      8        9        9       10        9
14   1266   Peters, Jayne     9       10        9       10       10
15   7667   Seavers, C.J.    10       10        9       10        9
16   4321   Smith, Steve      6        7        6        7        7
17
18
19
20
STDOUT.WK1
```

Fig. 16.10. The Student table exported from Paradox to a 1-2-3 worksheet.

Using 1-2-3 with Q&A

Symantec's *Q&A* 4.0 offers powerful database management and word processing capabilities. One highlight of Q&A is a natural language interface that accepts data retrieval queries and report requests in English. 1-2-3 users may prefer this natural language system over the more cryptic commands of the 1-2-3 database.

Q&A can import data from and export data to 1-2-3. With this two-way data structure, you can perform worksheet analysis on your data in 1-2-3 and data retrieval and reporting in Q&A—without having to re-type data. This method maintains consistency and data integrity.

This section describes the process of transferring data between 1-2-3 and Q&A.

Preparing the Data

The 1-2-3 worksheet shown in figure 16.11 is a college professor's list of semester grades. The professor needs to combine this semester's grades with semester grades previously stored in a Q&A file. (This database is similar to the one in figure 16.1 but the range address for SCORES is different.)

```
A:A2: [W5]                                                            READY

              B        C    D    E    F    G    H    I      J
1   Class: Computer Concepts, #CSC1202
2                              - Homework -          - Tests - - Final -
3         +----------------------------------+-----------+--------+
4   StdNoStdName     HW1  HW2  HW3  HW4  HW5 Test1 Test2  Final
5   ------------------------------------------------------------------
6   5754 Austin, Lee   7    6    9    8   10   87    91   87.2%
7   2123 Barker, Larry 5    8    8    8    9   91    94   89.2%
8   6753 Barkley, Jess 10   9   10   10    9   98   100   98.4%
9   3234 Chambers, Chris 9  10   10    9   10   99    94   96.4%
10  4257 Costner, Angela 10 10    9   10   10   98    96   97.2%
11  4323 Drew, Harry   8    9    9    9    9   89    88   88.4%
12  7897 Gregg, Bettye 0    5    0    0    6   76    80   66.8%
13  5434 Kelley, Susie 4    8    6    7    8   65    75   69.2%
14  4322 Kemp, Sally   9   10    9   10    9   88    98   93.2%
15  5445 Majors, Steve 10  10    9   10    9  100   100   99.2%
16  4333 Murphy, Barbara 9 10   10    9    9   98    96   96.4%
17  7654 Owens, Heath  8    9    9   10    9   93    84   88.8%
18  1266 Peters, Jayne 9   10    9   10   10   72    89   83.6%
19  7667 Seavers, C.J. 10  10    9   10    9   91    87   90.4%
20  4321 Smith, Steve  6    7    6    7    7   56    81   68.0%
    STUDENT.WK3
```

Fig. 16.11. A worksheet to be transferred to Q&A.

To follow the transfer examples in this section, create the sample 1-2-3 database from figure 16.11. Enter the student numbers (StdNo) as labels and format the homework and test score numbers with the command sequence /Range Format Fixed 0. Assign the range name SCORES to range A6..J20; you don't import the first five rows of the worksheet in this example. Use the column widths from the following table.

Column	Width
A	5 characters
B	16 characters
C through I	6 characters
J	9 characters

Compute the final averages in column J by entering the formula **@SUM(C6..I6)/250** in cell J6 and copying the formula to range J7..J20.

Format column J using the command **/R**ange Format Percent **1**. Save the worksheet with the file name STUDENT.WK1 (even if you use Release 3.x); exit 1-2-3 and start Q&A.

Q&A can read 1-2-3 worksheets only in Release 2 format; use the WK1 extension for files you intend to import to Q&A.

Creating the Database File

You must create a Q&A database file before importing the 1-2-3 data. When you are learning to import 1-2-3 data, use a database with the same number of fields as your 1-2-3 worksheet.

After you are comfortable with importing 1-2-3 data, you can create Q&A merge specs to import into a database with fields that don't exactly match the worksheet. For more information on using merge specs, consult your Q&A manual.

To create the database file, select **F**ile from the Q&A Main Menu, **D**esign file from the File Menu, and **D**esign a new file from the Design Menu. Q&A displays a `Data file:` prompt to request a file name, as shown in figure 16.12.

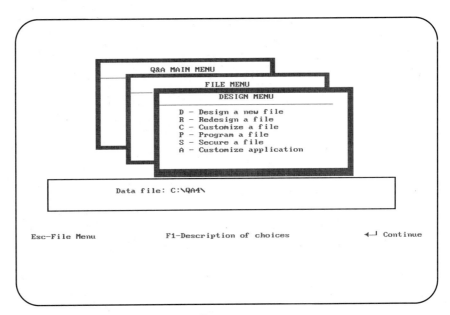

Fig. 16.12. Naming a new Q&A data file.

Type the name of the file and press Enter. For this example, use the file name **STUDENT**; Q&A supplies the default DTF extension.

Set up fields in the STUDENT database to match the fields in the 1-2-3 worksheet. For this example, use the following field names in the database to match the columns in the STUDENT.WK1 worksheet:

Student Number

Student Name

HW #1

HW #2

HW #3

HW #4

HW #5

Test #1

Test #2

Final Score

End each field name with a colon (:). You can use titles and separating lines and spaces in the database design, as shown in figure 16.13. The title, lines, and spaces don't affect the field names.

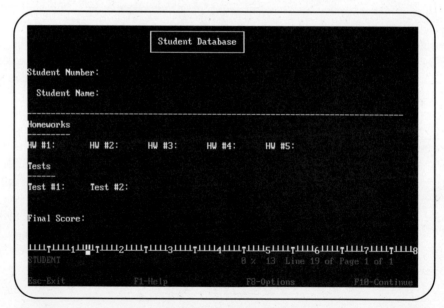

Fig. 16.13. Designing the STUDENT database with field names that match the 1-2-3 worksheet.

Press F10 to save the database design and set up attributes for the data fields. In the STUDENT database, the Student Number and Student Name fields are set up as Text fields and the remaining worksheet fields are Numeric. Press Enter in the Student Number and Student Name fields to accept the default designation (Text). Enter **N** (Numeric) in the remaining fields to ensure that Q&A imports all numbers and formulas correctly. Press F10 to continue.

If your database contains fields with numbers on which you never perform math, designate them as Text fields. In the STUDENT database, for example, the Student Number field is designated as Text.

The Global Format Options screen appears (you can specify how Q&A interprets currency and date fields with this screen). For importing worksheets, accept the default options by pressing F10. After a brief pause, the File Menu reappears; the design is complete and you can import the data.

Importing the Data

Each row in the 1-2-3 worksheet becomes a separate record in the database file. Q&A evaluates formulas and displays the results in the database if you import cells containing formulas into numeric fields. In the sample worksheet, column J is computed and formatted as percentages with one decimal place, but Q&A stores the data with full precision (to seven decimal places).

Q&A imports the first column of the worksheet to the first field in the database, the second column to the second field (to the right or down), and so on. To import a 1-2-3 worksheet, select **U**tilities from the File Menu and **I**mport data from the File Utilities Menu. Press **L** to select the 1-2-3/Symphony menu option from the Import Menu, specifying the format of the file to be imported.

Type the full path name for the 1-2-3 worksheet; for example, type **C:\LOTUS\STUDENT.WK1**. Type the Q&A database file name; for example, type **STUDENT** (Q&A supplies the DTF extension). Q&A displays the Define Range screen shown in figure 16.14.

Specify on this screen whether you want to import the whole worksheet or a range. In this example, you can type the range A6 through J20 at the FROM and TO prompts. An easier alternative is to press Tab until the cursor is positioned at the type the name of a range: prompt, and press PgDn. The range names in the selected worksheet file appear successively when you press PgDn. When the range name SCORES appears, press F10 to start the import operation. After a brief pause, the 1-2-3 data appears in the database file.

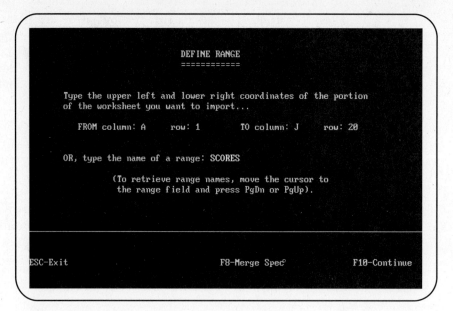

```
                           DEFINE RANGE
                           ============


          Type the upper left and lower right coordinates of the portion
          of the worksheet you want to import...

             FROM column: A      row: 1        TO column: J      row: 20


          OR, type the name of a range: SCORES

                          (To retrieve range names, move the cursor to
                           the range field and press PgDn or PgUp).




    ESC-Exit                             F8-Merge Spec          F10-Continue
```

Fig. 16.14. *Specifying the worksheet range to import.*

If your worksheet contains more columns than the Q&A database contains fields, Q&A ignores the remaining columns. If the worksheet contains fewer columns, Q&A inserts spaces in every field that doesn't have a corresponding column in the worksheet.

Figure 16.15 shows the Q&A database created from the imported worksheet. Notice that the column widths are sufficient to handle the largest worksheet column. You can scroll to the right to see the remaining fields in the database.

Don't attempt to import a password-protected worksheet. Q&A detects the password and aborts the import operation. You must save the worksheet in 1-2-3 without a password to import the data to Q&A.

Exporting Q&A Data to 1-2-3

You can export data from a Q&A database to ASCII format for use in 1-2-3, but you must adjust the worksheet (column widths, cell formats) to use the data after retrieving it in 1-2-3.

If you imported the STUDENT.WK1 data to Q&A in the preceding section, you can export the same data to 1-2-3. Before starting the export process, start 1-2-3 and enter the first six lines (the title and header rows) of the worksheet shown in figure 16.16.

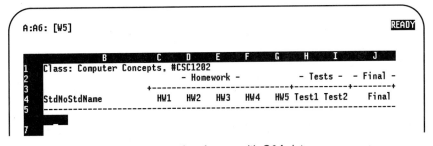

```
┌─────────────────────────────────────────────────────────────────────────────┐
│ Student Number   Student Name        HW #1          HW #2          HW #3      │
│                                                                               │
│ 5754             Austin, Lee             7              6              9       │
│ 2123             Barker, Larry           5              8              8       │
│ 6753             Barkley, Jess          10              9             10       │
│ 3234             Chambers, Chris         9             10             10       │
│ 4323             Drew, Harry             8              9              9       │
│ 7897             Gregg, Bettye           0              5              0       │
│ 5434             Kelley, Susie           4              8              6       │
│ 4322             Kemp, Sally             9             10              9       │
│ 5445             Majors, Steve          10             10              9       │
│ 4333             Murphy, Barbara         9             10             10       │
│ 7654             Owens, Heath            8              9              9       │
│ 1266             Peters, Jayne           9             10              9       │
│ 7667             Seavers, C.J.          10             10              9       │
│ 4321             Smith, Steve            6              7              6       │
│ 4257             Costner, Angela        10             10              9       │
│                                                                               │
│ STUDENT.DTF      Retrieved record 1      of 15         Total records: 15      │
│ Esc-Exit  F1-Help   { ↓ ↑ → ← Home End PgUp PgDn }-Navigate      F10-Show form │
└─────────────────────────────────────────────────────────────────────────────┘
```

Fig. 16.15. *The imported worksheet data.*

```
A:A6: [W5]                                                           READY

        B          C     D     E     F     G      H     I      J
1   Class: Computer Concepts, #CSC1202
2                            - Homework -              - Tests -  - Final -
3                      +---------------------------+-----------+--------+
4   StdNoStdName       HW1   HW2   HW3   HW4   HW5  Test1 Test2   Final
5   --------------------------------------------------------------------
7
```

Fig. 16.16. *A 1-2-3 worksheet template for use with Q&A data.*

Set the column widths as indicated in the following table.

Column	Width
A	5 characters
B	16 characters
C through I	6 characters
J	9 characters

Save the worksheet as NEWCLASS.WK1. This procedure prepares a template file to receive the incoming Q&A data.

Exit 1-2-3 and start Q&A. To export a Q&A database file, load the file into memory. Select File from the Main Menu, Utilities from the File Menu, Export Data from the File Utilities Menu, and the Standard ASCII option from the Export Menu. Specify the name of the Q&A file you want to export; for example, type **STUDENT**. Q&A supplies the DTF extension. Type the full path name of the destination file; for example, type **C:\LOTUS\NEWCLASS.WK1**.

Q&A can export only to a new file. If the file you specify exists, Q&A overwrites it.

The Retrieve Spec screen appears. To export all records in the database, press F10. To export specific records, use the Retrieve Spec to select the appropriate records.

The Merge Spec screen appears. Press F10 again to export the records in the same order as the database file, or specify the desired order with the Merge Spec and press F10.

The Merge Spec defines the order of the export; last field in the database to first column in the 1-2-3 worksheet, for example. Exporting the data in the same order as the database file is easier and less error-prone.

Q&A displays the ASCII Options screen shown in figure 16.17. When you export Q&A data to an ASCII file, you can place quotes around text fields or commas between fields, insert carriage returns between fields, and so on.

Press F10 to accept the default values. Q&A starts the export operation and displays each exported record in succession. When the export process is complete, exit Q&A and start 1-2-3.

Using the Exported Q&A Data

Use /File Retrieve to access the NEWCLASS.WK1 template worksheet you created earlier. To finish the exporting process, move the cell pointer to the upper left cell in the area of the worksheet where you want to place the Q&A data. For this example, move the cell pointer to cell A6. Select /File Import Numbers and specify the ASCII text file created by the Q&A export operation (for example, NEWCLASS.TXT). 1-2-3 imports the ASCII data into the worksheet. Reformat the worksheet as necessary; in this example, use /Range Format Percent 1 to format column J. Figure 16.18 shows the result of the import process.

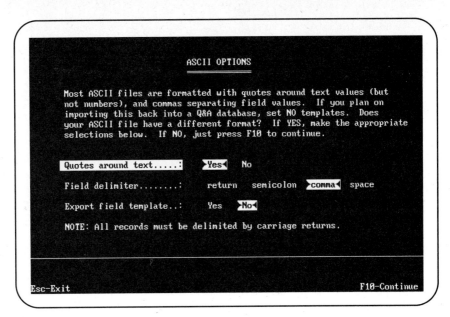

```
                        ASCII OPTIONS


     Most ASCII files are formatted with quotes around text values (but
     not numbers), and commas separating field values.  If you plan on
     importing this back into a Q&A database, set NO templates.  Does
     your ASCII file have a different format?  If YES, make the appropriate
     selections below.  If NO, just press F10 to continue.


     Quotes around text.....:   ►Yes◄   No

     Field delimiter........:   return   semicolon  ►comma◄  space

     Export field template..:   Yes    ►No◄

     NOTE: All records must be delimited by carriage returns.



Esc-Exit                                                    F10-Continue
```

Fig. 16.17. The ASCII Options screen.

```
A:A2: [W5]                                                          READY

            B          C    D    E    F    G    H    I      J
1  Class: Computer Concepts, #CSC1202
                              - Homework -              - Tests -  - Final -
3                         +------------------------+----------+---------+
4  StdNoStdName       HW1  HW2  HW3  HW4   HW5 Test1 Test2    Final
5                  ---------------------------------------------------
6  5754 Austin, Lee     7    6    9    8    10   87    91      87.2%
7  2123 Barker, Larry   5    8    8    8     9   91    94      89.2%
8  6753 Barkley, Jess  10    9   10   10     9   98   100      98.4%
9  3234 Chambers, Chris 9   10   10    9    10   99    94      96.4%
10 4323 Drew, Harry     8    9    9    9     9   89    88      88.4%
11 7897 Gregg, Bettye   8    5    8    8     6   76    80      66.8%
12 5434 Kelley, Susie   4    8    6    7     8   65    75      69.2%
13 4322 Kemp, Sally     9   10    9   10     9   88    98      93.2%
14 5445 Majors, Steve  10   10    9   10     9  100   100      99.2%
15 4333 Murphy, Barbara 9   10   10    9     9   98    96      96.4%
16 7654 Owens, Heath    8    9    9   10     9   93    84      88.8%
17 1266 Peters, Jayne   9   10    9   10    10   72    89      83.6%
18 7667 Seavers, C.J.  10   10    9   10     9   91    87      90.4%
19 4321 Smith, Steve    6    7    6    7     7   56    81      68.0%
20 4257 Costner, Angela 10  10    9   10    10   98    96      97.2%
NEWCLASS.WK1
```

Fig. 16.18. The Q&A database data exported to 1-2-3 worksheet format.

Summary

In this chapter, you learned how to integrate 1-2-3 worksheets with many popular database software programs. Most databases import and export 1-2-3 worksheet data with little intervention needed on your part. By importing your worksheets into a database program, you can perform more extensive searching and reporting than the built-in 1-2-3 database commands provide.

USING 1-2-3 ON A NETWORK

L otus 1-2-3 is available in single-user and network versions. *Networking* provides the advantage of printer and disk sharing and a lower cost alternative to buying individual copies of 1-2-3 for each PC in your organization. With a networked PC system running Novell SFT NetWare version 2.12 or 2.15, for example, you can create, modify, and print 1-2-3 worksheets as if you were using a single-user computer.

This appendix focuses on using 1-2-3 with Novell's NetWare. The following sections describe the network environment, installation of 1-2-3 on a network, and the operation of 1-2-3 with Novell's NetWare Operating System (NOS). If 1-2-3 is already installed on your network, you can skip the section entitled "Installing 1-2-3 on a Network."

If you are new to networking or need more network-specific information than that supplied in this section, consult Que's *Using Novell NetWare*, Second Edition. This book provides in-depth coverage of how to set up, manage, and use a networking environment.

Understanding Networking

A *Local Area Network (LAN)* connects two or more personal computers together. In a network environment, one computer is designated as the *file server* and the remaining computers (sometimes called *workstations*) are called *nodes*. Networks can include more than one file server; many file servers also act as nodes when the number of computers is insufficient to *dedicate* one as the file server.

Networked computers can share peripherals such as printers and disks. One printer attached to the file server can provide printing access for every computer in your organization.

Typically, the file server has more disk space than any of the nodes; it can hold programs and data shared by the rest of the node computers. Figure A.1 shows a typical local area network.

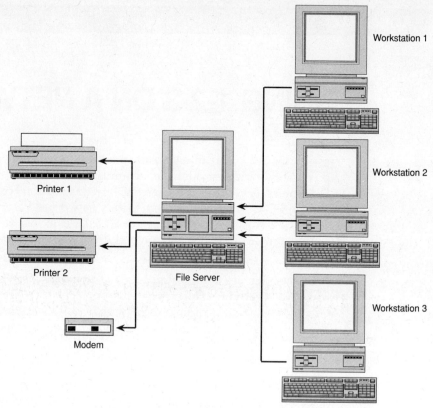

Fig. A.1. *A typical network configuration.*

Network file sharing provides true data integrity and integration between multiple users. If you and your co-workers update the same worksheets on separate computers (without a network), you must save the worksheets to disk and update each PC with the new files. If two of you make changes in separate copies of the same worksheet, you immediately lose data integrity—neither computer has both changes of data. A network system prevents this problem because the server holds the original worksheet data. Because the data is shared and updated by every node on the network, the latest changes are instantly available to everyone.

You can use your PC independently of the network if you choose not to *login* (obtain access) to the network. You can run 1-2-3, Freelance Plus, or other software that your computer has on disk. You cannot, however, use one of the server's programs unless you login to the network and access the programs.

Network systems include network hardware and software. The hardware consists of cables between computers and network boards installed in each server and node. Network software maintains the network security, user access, and privileges (a list of the files and peripherals that each user can or cannot view or modify), and transfers data and programs between computers on the network, staying in memory with DOS to handle any network requests. The network software is often called the *network operating system*.

The industry standard for network operating systems today is Novell's *NetWare*. NetWare has provided reliable data sharing and network operations since the first IBM PC was sold. The general user of Netware doesn't need to be completely familiar with the operation of the network to take advantage of networked applications software such as 1-2-3.

Installing 1-2-3 on a Network

In a network environment, one copy of 1-2-3 exists, residing on the server. You can keep worksheets on the server or on your node, but the 1-2-3 program stays on the server. Before using the network version of 1-2-3, you must purchase network site licenses for each person on the network.

Installing 1-2-3 on a network takes a little more time than installing on a single-user system. The installer must have full *access privileges* to the server and nodes within the network. This task is best handled by the designated *network supervisor*, the person responsible for maintaining the server's files and access privileges of each user on the network.

Installing the 1-2-3 network version requires the following steps:

1. Create directories on the server to hold programs, license information, and data.

2. Assign access rights, map the 1-2-3 directory, and initialize the 1-2-3 system disk.

3. Transfer the 1-2-3 program files to the server.

4. Set the maximum number of users on the network as defined by your license agreement.

5. Set up access to 1-2-3 programs and shared data for each user in the network.

These steps are described in detail in the following sections.

Creating Server Directories

1-2-3 requires that you create several directories on the server disk using the DOS *make directory (MD)* command. The primary directory is called LOTUS. You also create subdirectories of the LOTUS directory. The following table lists contents and recommended names for the directories.

Directory	Contents
\LOTUS\123R23	1-2-3 program files (for Release 3.x, 123R3 or 123R31)
\LOTUS\123R23\ALLWAYS	Allways program files
\LOTUS\123R23\WYSIWYG	Wysiwyg program files
\LOTUS\123R23\WYSYGO	Wysiwyg tutorial directory
\LOTUS\123R23\TUTOR	1-2-3 tutorial files
\LOTSHARE\123.V23	License information; use the server's root directory (for Release 3.x, 123.V3 or 123.V31)

All shared data must reside in one directory. Lotus doesn't recommend a particular directory name, but you may want to store the data in a subdirectory of the \USERS directory, perhaps with the name \USERS\SHARED.

If you are creating directories with the MD command and receive the DOS message Unable to create directory, *the directories already exist or you need to obtain full access privileges to the server disk.*

In addition to the required directories, set up *personal directories* as subdirectories of a directory called \USERS in the root directory. The personal directories can store each user's personal worksheets, configuration files, and driver files. To set up personal directories for three users named Adams, Barkley, and Connors, for example, name them \USERS\ADAMS, \USERS\BARKLEY, and \USERS\CONNORS.

You cannot use the DOS MD command to create personal directories. See the section entitled "Creating Personal Directories" later in this appendix for help in creating personal directories.

Users who store their worksheets on the workstation disks don't need special server privileges. The best practice is for each user to create his or her personal directory on the server, following the layout of the directory structure on the workstation. When saving worksheets, the user can decide whether to store them on the workstation or on the server.

Figure A.2 shows the structure for a typical 1-2-3 network directory configuration. Set up your directory structure in a similar fashion, with the personal directories named for users in your network.

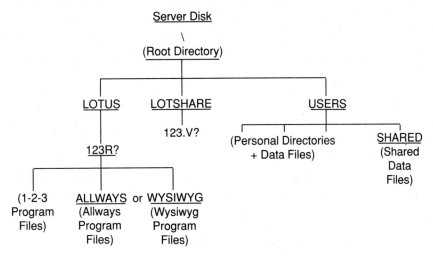

Fig. A.2. A typical 1-2-3 server directory structure.

Assigning Access Rights

Because only the PUBLIC directory is shared by default, you must run the SYSCON utility program to enable sharing in the 1-2-3 directories. Start SYSCON by typing **SYSCON** from the server's DOS prompt. Assign Read-Open-Search *access trustee rights* to the program directory (for example, \LOTUS\123R23). Assign All access trustee rights to the remaining directories.

You must assign access trustee rights to each user after creating personal directories. If you define all 1-2-3 users as a group (for example, the group EVERYONE), you can assign access trustee rights to the group, rather than assigning them individually. Use the up-arrow and down-arrow keys or PgUp and PgDn to scroll through the groups.

To assign access trustee rights to a group, select Group Information from the SYSCON Available Topics menu. Specify the group name you are using (for example, EVERYONE). Select Trustee Directory Assignments from the Group Information menu. The Trustee Directory Assignments screen appears, as shown in figure A.3.

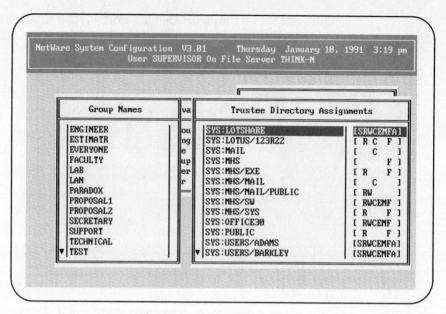

```
NetWare System Configuration   V3.01        Thursday  January 10, 1991  3:19 pm
                     User SUPERVISOR On File Server THINK-N

        Group Names          va        Trustee Directory Assignments

     ENGINEER              ou      SYS:LOTSHARE              [SRWCEMFA]
     ESTIMATR              ng      SYS:LOTUS/123R22          [ R C   F ]
     EVERYONE              e       SYS:MAIL                  [   C     ]
     FACULTY               up      SYS:MHS                   [       F ]
     LAB                   er      SYS:MHS/EXE               [ R     F ]
     LAN                   r       SYS:MHS/MAIL              [   C     ]
     PARADOX               =       SYS:MHS/MAIL/PUBLIC       [ RW      ]
     PROPOSAL1                     SYS:MHS/SW                [ RWCEMF  ]
     PROPOSAL2                     SYS:MHS/SYS               [ R     F ]
     SECRETARY                     SYS:OFFICE30              [ RWCEMF  ]
     SUPPORT                       SYS:PUBLIC                [ R     F ]
     TECHNICAL                     SYS:USERS/ADAMS           [SRWCEMFA]
   ▼ TEST                        ▼ SYS:USERS/BARKLEY         [SRWCEMFA]
```

Fig. A.3. *Assigning directory access rights.*

If the directory assignments have not been made, you must add them. Press the Ins key and type the name of the 1-2-3 program directory; for example, type **SYS:LOTUS\123R23**. Press Enter. The directory is added to the trustee directory listing.

Highlight the 1-2-3 directory and press Enter. To add the Read-Open-Search access to this directory, press Enter again. Select each option not assigned to the directory. If the directory already has Read and Search (sometimes called *File Scan*) assignments, you need only select Open (or Create, depending on your version of NetWare).

Add all access rights to the remaining 1-2-3 license and shared directories. If you are adding access trustee rights to a group, you are finished after the first pass. To add access trustee rights to individual users, you must repeat these steps after creating the personal directory for each person who uses 1-2-3. After you finish adding access rights, press Esc to exit SYSCON.

Mapping the 1-2-3 Directory

Users must map a *logical drive* letter to the 1-2-3 directory to access the file server with the access trustee rights just assigned. Use a logical drive that is not currently in use. (For more information on using logical drives, consult your DOS or NetWare manual.) To connect the 1-2-3 program directory on the server to the logical drive S, for example, each user must login to the network and type the following command at the DOS prompt (replacing *SERVER* with the name of your server):

MAP S:=*SERVER*/SYS:LOTUS\123R23

Your users probably don't want to type the MAP command each day before starting 1-2-3. You can add the MAP command to each 1-2-3 user's login script. Be sure to use a logical drive that is not already in use. If no more logical drives are available, you must remap one. (For information on creating a login script, consult your NetWare manual.)

Initializing the Disk

You must initialize your system disk before copying the 1-2-3 network files onto the server. The initialization process writes your server name and your company's name onto the original 1-2-3 system disk so that the disk can be used only with the server specified on the system disk. This procedure ensures that the system is installed on one network server. If you are installing from 3 1/2-inch disks, use the disk labeled "System, Help, and PrintGraph Disk." If you are installing from 5 1/4-inch disks, use the disk labeled "System Disk."

The initialization procedure described here assumes you are using drive A for the system disk (substitute another disk drive if necessary).

To initialize the system disk, insert the system disk in drive A. Type **A:** and press Enter to make drive A the default. Type **INIT** and press Enter. The initialization screen appears, as shown in figure A.4.

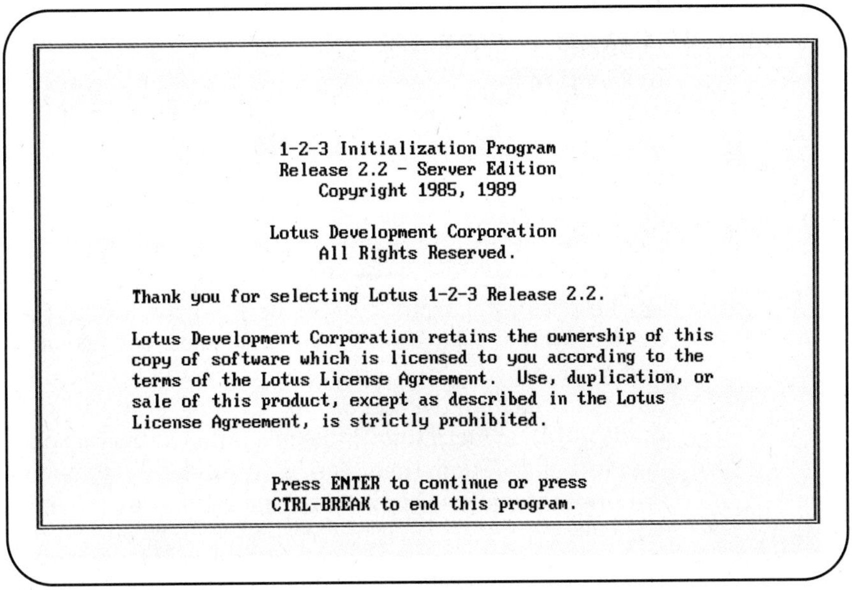

```
                1-2-3 Initialization Program
                Release 2.2 - Server Edition
                   Copyright 1985, 1989

                Lotus Development Corporation
                    All Rights Reserved.

   Thank you for selecting Lotus 1-2-3 Release 2.2.

   Lotus Development Corporation retains the ownership of this
   copy of software which is licensed to you according to the
   terms of the Lotus License Agreement.  Use, duplication, or
   sale of this product, except as described in the Lotus
   License Agreement, is strictly prohibited.



                Press ENTER to continue or press
                CTRL-BREAK to end this program.
```

Fig. A.4. The system disk initialization screen.

Press Enter twice. 1-2-3 prompts you for the server name; type the name of your server and press Enter. Press **Y** and Enter to confirm the server name. Type your company name and press Enter; press **Y** and Enter to confirm your company name.

1-2-3 displays the Final Confirmation Screen, which repeats the information you typed and adds the serial number and version number of the system disk. If everything is correct, press Enter twice to end the session. If any information is incorrect, press Ctrl–Break and repeat the entire process.

Because you can initialize the system disk only once, be sure that the information is correct—the system disk can be installed only on the server you named in the initialization process.

Copying the Files

The next step is to copy the 1-2-3 and ALLWAYS files to the 1-2-3 program directory on the server disk. Make the server disk drive (which can be a logical drive) the default by typing its name and pressing Enter at the DOS prompt. Change to the 1-2-3 program directory; for example, type **CD\LOTUS\123R23** and press Enter. Copy the 1-2-3 disks to the program directory by inserting each one and typing **COPY A:*.*** at the DOS prompt. Each file name appears on-screen as the file is being copied.

After copying the 1-2-3 program files, copy the ALLWAYS and Wysiwyg files to their directories on the server.

Some hardware devices, such as special high-resolution video boards, come with their own 1-2-3 drivers. Using a network presents no new problems in installing these drivers. Copy the drivers to the server's 1-2-3 program directory, run **INSTALL** from the Lotus Access menu and add the drivers to the Install library.

Initializing the Count

To ensure that the number of 1-2-3 users doesn't exceed the number of site licenses you purchased, you must set the licence count before you use the system. The 1-2-3 *Count Utility* sets the license count; you can update this facility if you purchase more site licenses. The total number initialized includes the server and the nodes. If you set your license count to 15, no more than 14 people (and the server) can use 1-2-3 on the network at the same time. You can install 1-2-3 on more than 15 nodes but Count monitors the network and allows only 15 at a time to access 1-2-3.

Because you must have full server access privileges before using the Count utility, connect the 1-2-3 license directory on the server to a logical drive with the MAP command. To map the logical drive T, for example, use the following command at the DOS prompt (replacing *SERVER* with the name of your server):

MAP T:=*SERVER*/SYS:LOTSHARE\123.V23

Change to the 1-2-3 program directory (for example, by typing **CD\LOTUS\123R23** and pressing Enter). Type **COUNT** and press Enter to start the Count utility. The Count opening screen appears. Press Enter to begin using the program; your screen should resemble figure A.5. Other Lotus network products (such as Symphony) also are listed under the `Number of Licenses` heading. Notice the 1-2-3-style menu on the top of the screen—Count has several functions that you can activate from this menu.

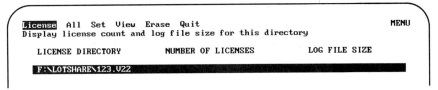

```
License  All  Set  View  Erase  Quit                          MENU
Display license count and log file size for this directory

   LICENSE DIRECTORY          NUMBER OF LICENSES        LOG FILE SIZE

   F:\LOTSHARE\123.V22
```

Fig. A.5. *Accessing the Count utility program.*

Specifying the Count

Highlight the license directory name (for example, 123.V23) and select Set from the menu. The Count utility displays the current license count. (If you have not run Count before, the license count shows 0.) Type the number of licenses you are entitled to use (purchased node site licenses plus the server) at the prompt.

Modifying the License Overflow Message

If one more user than the limit tries to access 1-2-3, the License Overflow Message appears. The message indicates that the potential user must wait for a current user to exit the system. You can modify the message or create a different message with word processing or text editor software. You can create a personalized message such as the following:

```
You cannot access 1-2-3 at this time. Please wait for another
person to exit 1-2-3. Contact James Larson at extension 303
if you have any questions.
```

Save the desired message (up to 2,048 characters) in an ASCII file called LOTUS.LOM in the 1-2-3 program directory (such as \LOTUS\123R23).

Viewing the 1-2-3 Log File

Any person with full access rights to the 1-2-3 program directory can view the 1-2-3 network *log file*. The log file contains a listing of the dates and times people attempted to use 1-2-3 and were denied due to the number of users already in 1-2-3.

1-2-3 maintains the log file. When you install 1-2-3, the log file is empty; over time, many records may be added to this file showing attempts to access 1-2-3 on a full network. The log file doesn't track users who attempt access but instead tracks dates and times of the attempts to help you decide whether you need more site licenses.

To see the log file, select **View** from the Count utility's main menu. If the log file is empty, 1-2-3 displays the message There are no more entries in this LOTUS.LOG file.

If the log file gets too large, you can erase it by selecting **Erase** from the Count utility's main menu.

Erase the log file each time you add site licenses to track how the newly-purchased licenses affect your users.

Using 1-2-3 on a Network

With the network version of 1-2-3 installed, you and your users are ready to use the system.

If you want to store your 1-2-3 worksheets on your workstation's disk, no special steps are required, but type the full path and file name when saving the file. Storing your worksheets on the server's hard disk offers advantages, however. Because a network server disk usually has a large amount of storage available, you can save space on your computer's disk by storing files on the server. Only you can access files saved in your personal directory, unless your system is configured to allow others access to your personal directory.

Saving worksheets in a shared data directory on the server enables anyone else using the network to load the worksheets and share them but doesn't allow more than one user to be in a worksheet at any time.

Creating Personal Directories

A utility called *NewUser* is supplied with the network 1-2-3 program. NewUser creates personal directories on the server. This utility also is useful for copying the 1-2-3 driver set, configuration file, and PrintGraph configuration file to the server. Without these files, users cannot run 1-2-3 on the network.

You must have full access rights to use the NewUser utility.

To create the personal directories, change to the 1-2-3 program directory. Type **NEWUSER** followed by the complete directory name of the personal directory. To add a personal directory called ADAMS to the \USERS directory on drive F, for example, type the following command at the DOS prompt:

NEWUSER F:\USERS\ADAMS

Figure A.6 shows the NewUser utility verifying personal directory file names before creating the files.

```
                 NewUser Program

              Release 2.2 - Server Edition

                 Copyright (C) 1989
            Lotus Development Corporation
                 All Rights Reserved.


NewUser will create the following files:

   f:\users\adams\123.CNF        (1-2-3 configuration file)
   f:\users\adams\123.SET        (1-2-3 driver set)
   f:\users\adams\PGRAPH.CNF     (PrintGraph configuration file)

If the displayed directory name is incorrect, or if you don't
want to continue, press CTRL-C or CTRL-BREAK, and then type Y
at the "Terminate batch job (Y/N)?" prompt.

Press any other key to continue.
```

Fig. A.6. *Creating a personal directory with the NewUser utility.*

When the displayed directory name is correct, press any key to start the utility. NewUser creates the personal directory, copies the configuration files to that directory, and displays a confirmation message.

Be sure to add the personal directory's full path name to each user's AUTOEXEC.BAT file PATH statement. After creating a personal directory, you must add access rights for that directory with the network's SYSCON utility, in the same way that you added access rights for the program directories earlier in this chapter.

Installing 1-2-3

To start the network version of 1-2-3, change to the program directory (such as F:\LOTUS\123R23), type **LOTUS** at the DOS prompt, and press Enter. If you normally start 1-2-3 by typing **123** (bypassing the 1-2-3 Access Menu), you can use that method after accessing 1-2-3 the first time.

Select Install the first time you start the 1-2-3 Access Menu to install your workstation's monitor and printer. The Install program requests the path name and file name of your driver. Type the full path name of your personal directory, followed by the driver name you want to use (usually 123). Figure A.7 shows a user configuration being installed.

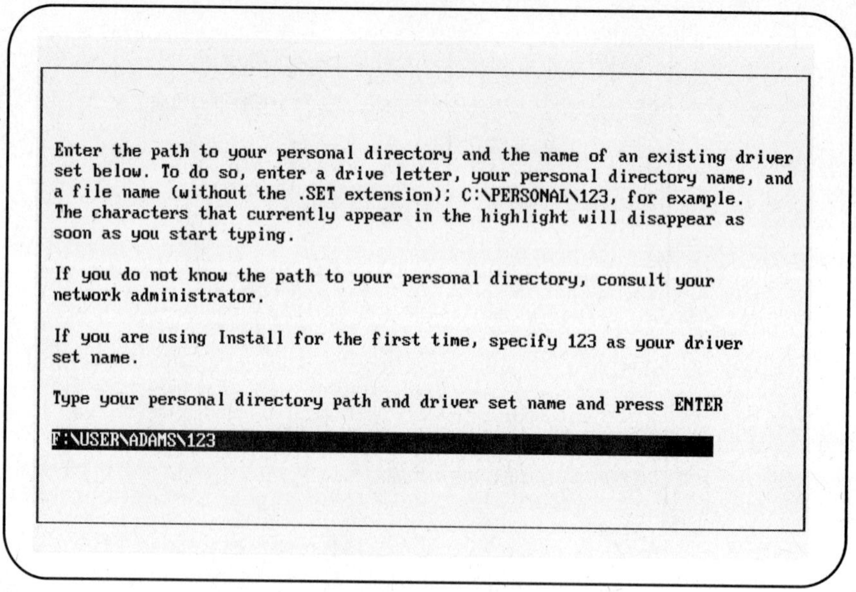

```
Enter the path to your personal directory and the name of an existing driver
set below. To do so, enter a drive letter, your personal directory name, and
a file name (without the .SET extension); C:\PERSONAL\123, for example.
The characters that currently appear in the highlight will disappear as
soon as you start typing.

If you do not know the path to your personal directory, consult your
network administrator.

If you are using Install for the first time, specify 123 as your driver
set name.

Type your personal directory path and driver set name and press ENTER

F:\USER\ADAMS\123
```

Fig. A.7. *Specifying the 1-2-3 driver.*

After specifying the driver path and file name, specify the equipment connected to your workstation and exit the install procedure. You now can select 1-2-3 from the 1-2-3 Access Menu. If 1-2-3 is installed correctly on your network, the server version of the 1-2-3 copyright screen appears (as shown in fig. A.8), followed by the familiar 1-2-3 worksheet.

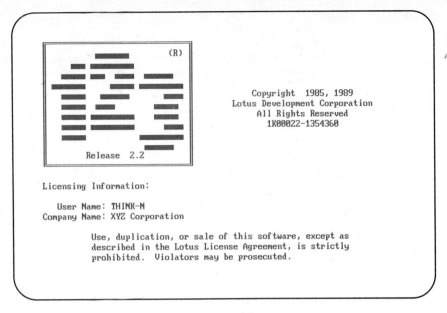

```
                                                          (R)
                    ▬▬▬▬▬▬
          ▬▬  ▬▬▬▬▬
     ▬▬▬▬   ▬▬   ▬▬▬▬▬
     ▬▬▬▬▬▬   ▬▬   ▬▬▬▬▬▬
     ▬▬▬▬▬   ▬▬   ▬▬▬▬▬
     ▬▬▬▬▬▬▬
     ▬▬▬▬▬▬      ▬▬▬▬▬▬
                ▬▬▬▬▬

        Release  2.2
```

                          Copyright 1985, 1989
                          Lotus Development Corporation
                          All Rights Reserved
                          1K00022-1354360

Licensing Information:

   User Name: THINK-N
Company Name: XYZ Corporation

          Use, duplication, or sale of this software, except as
          described in the Lotus License Agreement, is strictly
          prohibited. Violators may be prosecuted.

Fig. A.8. The server version of the 1-2-3 copyright screen.

Changing the Directory

Before creating a worksheet, specify the file directory to use. Select /Worksheet Global Default Directory and type the full path name of your personal directory or shared directory; for example, type **F:\USER\ADAMS**. Your worksheets are saved to and retrieved from the specified directory.

You are not limited to this directory for your worksheets.

You can change the directory at any time in the network version of 1-2-3 (just as in the single-user version) or enter a different path when you save or retrieve worksheets.

Most users keep their worksheets in their personal directories. Because company-wide worksheets can be shared, however, use caution when saving files in the SHARED directory to avoid overwriting another person's files. Your network supervisor may impose naming conventions for shared files, such as tagging a person or department code to the end of a worksheet file name, or making shared worksheet files read-only (for 1-2-3 worksheets, this safety method may be too confining). Whether access restrictions or naming conventions are imposed, be aware of the potential problems of sharing worksheet files and be especially careful when deleting files from the SHARED directory.

Printing on a Network

All printer output created with /Print Printer is routed to the workstation's local printer. To use the server's printer, you must change the 1-2-3 printer interface, specifying the server's printer.

To route worksheet printing to the server's printer, select /Worksheet Global Default Printer Interface. Select a number (corresponding to the server's printer port) from the following table.

Server Printer Port	Interface Number
LPT1	5
LPT2	6
LPT3	7
LPT4	8

If your network uses a serial printer, such as a LaserJet, it should be routed to one of the parallel printer ports on the server (if not, contact your network supervisor for assistance).

After selecting the appropriate port, select Quit Update Quit to save your changes and return to the worksheet.

Ending the 1-2-3 Session

After saving your worksheets, exit from the 1-2-3 session by selecting Quit Yes to return to the 1-2-3 Access Menu or to the DOS prompt.

Typically, the network supervisor regularly backs up the server; therefore, if you accidently erase a file in 1-2-3, exit the system and contact your network supervisor to see if the file can be restored from an earlier backup. Make sure that your personal directory is backed up regularly or you may overwrite or delete an important worksheet file and be unable to restore it.

Index

Symbols

@BASE add-in, 345
@EASE add-in, 371-372
@functions
  see functions
@Functions III add-in, 346
@Tools add-in, 376
\ (backslash) repeat-character
  prefix, 19
^ (caret)
  exponentiation operator, 20
  label prefix, 74
' label prefix, 74
" label prefix, 74
~ (tilde), 44
1-2-3
  installing on Local Area Network
    (LAN), 505-512
  main menu, 22
  starting, 11-13
3-2-1 GOSUB add-in, 345
3D-Graphics add-in, 346

A

Abs (F4) function key, 95-96
absolute references, 95
  copying, 98-99
  mixing with relative references, 96
access rights, assigning, 507-508
accessing external data tables, 301-302
add-in programs, 329-332, 342,
  345-346

add-in manager (Rel. 3.x), 331
attaching, 329-331
compatibility, 331
detaching, 330
developer tools, 373
  @Tools, 375-376
  Baler, 377
  King Jaguar, 376-377
  Lotus Add-in Toolkit, 373-375
  Lotus Developer Tools, 375
standard, 332
  Allways, 175-177, 336
  Auditor, 336-340
  Macro Library Manager, 248-249,
    332-334
  Viewer, 144-145, 341-342
  Wysiwyg, 336
third-party
  @BASE, 345
  @EASE, 371-372
  @Functions III, 346
  3-2-1 GOSUB, 345
  3D-Graphics, 346
  Beyond 640, 346
  Decision Analyst, 345
  Financial Toolkit, 346
  ForeCalc, 370-371
  Instant Analyst, 345
  InWord, 368-370
  JetSet, 346
  Look & Link, 352-356
  Macro Editor/Debugger (MED),
    344, 347-349
  Noteworthy, 345
  Project Calc/Resources, 358-360
  SeeMORE, 349-352

Sideways, 367-368
The Worksheet Utilities, 360-367
What-If Solver, 356-357
adding
entry forms to database ranges,
89-90
graphics to text, 264-266
text to graphs, 261-262
Undo feature to earlier releases of
1-2-3, 118
addressing modes
changing, 95-96
in formulas, 99-101
adjusting worksheet data to match
driver field lengths, 306-307
advanced macro commands
see macros, commands
Allways add-in, 175, 336
copying formats with Release 2.2,
102-103
creating charts, 255-257
graphs,
combining with text, 263
printing, 223-224
amortization tables, 277
#AND# operator, 189, 296
{APPENDBELOW} advanced macro
command, 89-90
applications, designing, 67
ASCII
codes, 158-159
numbers, 176
text files, saving worksheets to, 405
assigning access rights, 507-508
Auditor add-in, 336-340
@AVG function, 195-196

B

backslash (\) label prefix, 19, 74
Backspace key, 33
Backup option, 126
BAK file extension, 126
Baler, 377

bar graphs, 207
Beyond 640 add-in, 346
boolean expressions, 190-192
borders, 163-167, 183
{BRANCH} advanced macro
command, 241
buffer, 116
copying contents, 236-237
editing, 236
erasing, 235-236

C

/c command, 92, 104, 108
Calc (F9) function key, 32, 38
CALC indicator, 31-32
calculating
annuity-due, 271-272
deposit for future value, 273
depreciation, 276-277
financial values, 273
loan principal, 273
recalculating worksheets, 31-32
roots, 197
term of a loan, 272
what-if analysis, 29-30
caret (^)
exponentiation operator, 20
label prefix, 74
@CELL function, 200
@CELLPOINTER function, 201
cell pointer, 15
establishing cell references, 21
navigating worksheets, 16
cells, 15
addresses, 163-164
copying, 23-24
copying formats, 102
editing, 32-33
erasing, 34
formatting, 23
linking to named, 145-146
noncontiguous, 112-115
pointing to, 21

printing formulas, 168-170
references, 162
removing formats, 83
characters
    changing with /rs command, 118
    composed, 217
    replaying stored, 243-244
    searching for in ranges, 118
charts
    see also graphs
    Gantt, 359-360
    Resource Histogram, 360
columns
    border, 163-165
    widths, 28, 44-45
combining files, 127-137
commands
    /c, 92, 104, 108-109
    /de, 300-301
    /decn, 303-304
    /del, 302
    /delf, 302-303
    /deora, 307-308
    /deu, 301-302
    /df, 77-80, 281-283
    /dp, 141
    /dpf, 140
    /dq, 41-44
    /dqc, 295
    /dqe, 306, 315-316
    /dqm, 300-301
    /dt, 309-314
    /fal, 150
    /fc, 98-99
    /fca, 130-134
    /fcc, 127-130, 352
    /fccn, 110
    /fcs, 134-137
    /fd, 121
    /fi, 137
    /fin, 141
    /fit, 370
    /fll, 150-152
    /fo, 124
    /foa, 71

/fr, 111
/fs, 99
/fx, 126-127
/fxf, 71
/ga, 223
/gg, 212
/gnc, 218
/gnu, 218-219
/grg, 207, 218
/gs, 389
/gsr, 224
/gtb, 205, 214-215
/m, 108-109
macro
    see macros, advanced commands
/pb, 171
/pe, 171
/pf, 170, 173
/pp, 171
/ppi, 224
/ppof, 161
/ppoh, 161
/ppooa, 170
/ppooc, 168, 337-338
/ppoof, 167
/ppoou, 167
/ppos, 158-159
/ppr, 163-165, 225
/pprb, 167
/re, 34
/rfd, 284
/rfdt, 80
/rfo, 75
/rfp, 23
/ri, 85-87
/rj, 143
/rnc, 37, 381, 390, 411, 418
/rnlr, 320-322, 333
/rs, 99-101, 118
/rt, 79-80, 105, 109
/ru, 61
/rv, 104-105, 111
/s, 25
selecting from menus, 22-23
/wcr, 28

/wcs, 28
/wds, 71
/wg, 329-331
/wgc, 28
/wgdd, 122
/wgdgm, 220
/wgdoci, 162
/wgdoic, 84
/wgdoid, 84
/wgdoip, 83
/wgdoud, 116
/wgdpi, 516
/wgfc, 24-25
/wgfl, 75
/wgge, 68
/wgdgr, 213
/wgpe, 61
/wgrm, 31
/wisa, 71
/wl, 230
/ws, 340
/wt, 61-63
/wtb, 64-65
commas, changing format
    appearance, 83
Compose (Alt–F1) key combination,
    256, 258
control panel, 15
converting formulas to values, 104-105
copying
    absolute references, 98-99
    Allways formats with Release 2.2,
        102-103
    between files and worksheets, 110
    buffer contents, 236-237
    cell formats, 102
    cells, 23-24
    data between files, 111
    files to server disk, 510
    formulas
        to cells, 95
        to worksheets, 101
        without inserting dollar sign, 97
    from file on disk, 110
    protection status, 102

ranges, 105-107
    to rows, 92-94
    to noncontiguous cells, 112-115
    to/from files in memory, 111
CorelDRAW!, 398
    importing PIC files, 401-404
@COUNT function, 194-196
Count utility, 510-512
criteria
    specifying, 295-299
    criteria ranges, 41-42, 293-295
Ctrl-← key combination, 17
Ctrl-→ key combination, 17
Ctrl-Break key combination, 23
Ctrl-Home key combination, 16
Ctrl-PgDn key combination, 16
Ctrl-PgUp key combination, 16
currency
    changing
        format appearance, 83
        symbols, 84
cursor, 15

D

data
    adjusting in worksheets, 306-307
    copying between files, 111
    entering into data forms, 87
    exporting to external table, 306
    importing, 137
        converting, 138-140
        into Microsoft Word, 436-439
        into Professional Write, 452-454
        into Word for Windows, 443-447
        into WordPerfect, 426-431
data formulas, entering into ranges, 80
data input (restricting), 85-86
data tables, 301-302
    three-way, 312-313
    two-way, 312
database drivers, 303-304
databases, 40-43
    disk-based, 300-301

external, creating from 1-2-3
  databases, 304-305
programs
  dBASE, 481-488
  Paradox, 488-493
  Q&A, 493-501
sorting, 316-317
using field names in database
  functions, 300
DataLens drivers, 303-304
Datalinks, 386
date values, 282-285
date-and-time indicator, 15
dates
  changing format appearance, 84
  entering, 90-91
  in headers and footers, 162
@DATEVALUE function, 203-204
dBASE, 481-488
  exporting to 1-2-3, 487-488
  importing 1-2-3 worksheets, 481-486
@DDB function, 275
/de command, 300-301
debugging macros, 228
Decision Analyst add-in, 345
/decn command, 303-304
default settings, 82-83
Del key, 33
/del command, 302
/delf command, 302-303
/deora command, 307-308
depreciation, calculating, 276-277
/deu command, 301-302
/df command, 77-80, 282-283
directories
  changing, 121-122
    in network systems, 515-516
  creating, 25-26
    personal, 512-513
  mapping 1-2-3, 508-509
  searching, 122-123
  server, 506-507
disabling Undo, 116
disk-based databases, 300-301
disks, initializing system, 509-510

dollar ($) sign, 97
DOS MD command, 26
{DOWN} macro instruction, 237-238
down-arrow key, 19, 33
/dp command, 141-142
/dpf command, 140-141
/dq command, 41-44
/dqc commands, 295
/dqe command, 306, 315-316
/dqm command, 300-301
drivers, DataLens, 303-304
@DSUM formula, 313-314
/dt command, 309-314

E

@EASE add-in, 372
Edit (F2) function key, 32, 89
EDIT mode, 32-33
editing
  buffer, 236
  cells, 32-33
  macro libraries, 334-335
End key, 32
ending macros and subroutines,
  244-245
entering
  data into entry forms, 87
  date formulas, 80
  label prefixes, 74-75
  labels, 17-19, 73
  numeric series, 77-78
  time formulas into ranges, 80-82
  values, 19, 75
entry forms
  adding to database ranges, 89-90
  entering data, 87
  restricting data input, 85-86
  using macros, 87
erasing
  buffer, 235-236
  cells, 34
Esc key, 23, 33

Excel, 463
    importing 1-2-3 worksheets, 463-468
exiting network sessions, 516
exponentiation (^) operator, 20, 188
exporting
    data to external tables, 306
    with /Print File, 173-174
exporting to 1-2-3
    dBASE files, 487-488
    Excel files, 468
    Paradox tables, 492-493
    Q&A files, 498-500
    Quattro Pro files, 462
    Quicken Transfer Utility, 470-474
    Symphony files, 457-459
external databases
    creating from 1-2-3 databases,
      304-305
    updating, 307-308
external tables, 301-302
    creating, 303-304
    exporting data to, 306
    listing, 302
    listing fields, 302-303
    updating, 307-308
extracts, detailed, 316-317

F

/fal command, 151, 155
/fc command, 98-99, 127, 356
/fca command, 130-134
/fcc command, 127-130, 134, 352
/fccn command, 110
/fcs command, 135-137
/fd command, 121
/fi command, 137
fields, database, 40
    headings, 41
    listing from external tables, 302-303
    using field names in database
      functions, 300
File does not exist message, 144
file servers, 503

files
    ASCII text, saving worksheets
      to, 405
    combining, 127-137
    copying
      data between files, 111
      from disk, 110
      to server disk, 510
      to/from, in memory, 111
    creating new, from old, 124
    exporting
      dBASE, 487-488
      Excel, 468
      Paradox, 492-493
      Q&A, 498-500
      Quattro Pro, 462
      Quicken Transfer Utility, 470-474
      Symphony, 457-459
    extensions
      BAK, 126
      WK1, 27
      WK3, 27
    importing
      dBASE, 481-486
      Excel, 463-468
      Microsoft Word, 436-442
      Paradox, 488-492
      Professional Write, 452-454
      Q&A, 494-498
      Quattro Pro, 460-462
      Quicken, 469-470
      Symphony, 456-459
      TurboTax, 475-477
      Word for Windows, 443-451
      WordPerfect, 426-435
    linking, 143-155
    opening multiple, 123-124
    PIC, 388-389
      importing with CorelDRAW!,
        401-404
      importing with First
        Publisher, 407
      importing with PageMaker, 416
      importing with Ventura Publisher,
        422-423

PRN, 417
  importing with Ventura Publisher,
    419-421
  protecting existing, 124
  retrieving, 122
  running macros in, 249-250
  saving, 26-27, 124
    by highlighting, 125
    with Backup option, 126
    with passwords, 125-126
  searching for
    in current directory, 122
    in subdirectories, 123
    with wild-card characters, 123
/fin command, 141-143
financial programs
  Excel, 463-468
  Quattro Pro, 460-462
  Quicken, 468-474
  Symphony, 455-459
  TurboTax, 474-477
Financial Toolkit add-in, 346
First Publisher, 404
  importing PIC files, 407
  importing worksheet files, 405-406
  SNAPSHOT memory-resident utility
    program, 407-409
    importing graphs, 409-410
/fit command, 137-139, 342
/fll command, 151, 155
/fo command, 124
/foa command, 71
fonts, 255
footers, 161-164, 179, 183
  dates in, 162
  page numbers in, 162
ForeCalc add-in, 370-371
{FORM} advanced macro command,
  87-90
  optional arguments, 88-89
formats
  comma, 83
  currency, 83
  date, 84
  macro, 323-324

native, 137
report, 322-324
formatting
  cells, 23
  imported text, 138
  multiple worksheets, 68-70
  removing
    from cells, 83
    from ranges, 83
  values, 82-83
  worksheets, 24-25
formulas, 20-21
  @IF
    nested, 200
    repeating, 199
  addressing, 99-100
  cell references, 21
  combining with worksheets, 128-130
  controlling table size, 279-280
  converting to values, 104-105
  copying
    into worksheets, 101
    to cells, 95
    without inserting dollar sign, 97
  @DSUM function, 313-314
  linking, 143-145
    compound, 153
  protecting, 59-61
  recalculating, 31-32
  simplifying, 193-194
  to age receivables, 287-288
  to compare data, 215
/fr command, 27, 111, 122-123
Freelance Plus, 380
  importing PIC files, 388-389
/fs command, 26, 99-101, 124-125
function keys
  Alt–F1 (Compose), 256-258
  Alt–F2 (Record), 235-237
  Alt–F3 (Run), 227-229
  Alt–F4 (Undo), 115-116
  Alt–F5 (Learn), 230-231
  F1 (HELP), 306
  F2 (Edit), 32, 89
  F3 (Name), 37, 122

F4 (Abs), 95-96
F5 (GoTo), 16
F7 (Query), 42
F9 (Calc), 32, 38
F10 (Graph), 89, 211-212
functions
 @AVG, 195-196
 @CELL, 200
 @CELLPOINTER, 201
 @COUNT, 194-196
 @DATEVALUE, 203-204
 @DDB, 275
 @FV, 272
 @HLOOKUP, 201-203
 @IF, 189-190, 285
 @INFO, 200
 @LOG, 199
 @MAX, 193
 @MIN, 193
 @MOD, 163-164, 197-198
 @NOW, 163-164
 @PMT, 272-273
 @ROUND, 194
 @ROWS, 291-292
 @SUM, 187, 194 195, 207, 381, 390, 404, 411, 417
 @SYD, 275
 @TERM, 272
 @TODAY, 282-283, 287-288
 @VDB, 274
 @VLOOKUP, 201-203
 using in formulas, 21-22
@FV function, 272
/fx command, 126-127
/fxf command, 71

G

/ga command, 223
Gantt chart, 359-360
General format, 82-83
{GET} advanced macro command, 240
{GETLABEL} advanced macro command, 218, 239-240

{GETNUMBER} advanced macro command, 239-240
/gg command, 212
/gnc command, 218
/gnu command, 219
GoTo (F5) function key, 16
Graph (F10) function key, 89, 211-212
graphics, 177
 adding to text, 264-266
 ASCII characters, 176
{GRAPHOFF} advanced macro command, 218
{GRAPHON} advanced macro command, 218
graphs, 38-40, 208-210
 adding text, 261-262
 automatic, 212-213
 bar, 207
 capturing, 408-409
 choosing type, 259-261
 combining with text, 262-263
 composed characters, 217
 creating, 205-207, 213, 258-259, 382, 391, 399-400, 407-409, 411, 418
 displaying with macros, 218
 enhancing with Wysiwyg, 220-223
 HLCO (high-low-close-open), 210
 importing
  Harvard Graphics, 396-397
  Microsoft Word, 439-442
  SNAPSHOT, 409-410
  Word for Windows, 447-451
  WordPerfect, 431-435
 line, 207
 mixed, 210
 naming, 217-218
 pie, 207-208
 printing, 223-225
 saving, 219-220
 shape, 263
 stack-bar, 208
 xy, 208
/grg command, 207, 218
GROUP mode, 68-71

/gs command, 389
/gsr command, 224
/gtb command, 205, 214-215, 382,
    399-400, 412, 418

H

hard disks, logical drives, 121
Harvard Graphics, 389
    importing graphs, 396-397
    importing worksheets, 392-396
headers, 161-164, 179, 183
    dates in, 162
    page numbers in, 162
headings, field, 41
HELP (F1) function key, 306-307
HLCO (high-low-close-open) graph, 210
@HLOOKUP function, 201-203
Home key, 16, 32

I-J

@IF function, 189-190, 285
importing
    blocks of text, 137-139
    data, 137-141
    graphs
        with Harvard Graphics, 396-397
        with SNAPSHOT, 409-410
    numbers, 141-143
    PIC files, 388-389
        CorelDRAW!, 401-404
        First Publisher, 407
        Microsoft Word, 439-442
        PageMaker, 416
        Ventura Publisher, 422-423
        Word for Windows, 447-451
        WordPerfect, 431-435
    PRN files with Ventura Publisher,
        419-421
    worksheets, 381-382, 395-396
        dBASE, 481-486
        Excel, 463-468

First Publisher, 405-406
Freelance Plus, 383-388
Harvard Graphics, 392-394
Microsoft Word, 436-439
PageMaker, 413-416
Paradox, 488-492
Professional Write, 452-454
Q&A, 494-498
Quattro Pro, 460-462
Quicken, 469-470
Symphony, 456-459
TurboTax, 475-477
Word for Windows, 443-447
WordPerfect, 426-431
indicators
    CALC, 31-32
    date-and-time, 15
    mode, 15
@INFO function, 200
initializing
    license count, 510-512
    system disks, 509-510
input areas, 86
Ins key, 33
installing 1-2-3 on a network, 505-512
Instant Analyst add-in, 345
InWord add-in, 368-369
JetSet add-in, 346

K

key names
    macros, 45-46
    repeating, 237-239
keyboard, 76
keys
    arrow, 19
    Ctrl-←, 17
    Ctrl-→, 17
    Ctrl-Break, 23
    Ctrl-Home, 16
    Ctrl-PgDn, 16
    Ctrl-PgUp, 16
    editing, 32-33

Esc, 23
Home, 16
PgDn, 17
PgUp, 17
Shift-Tab, 17
Tab, 17
King Jaguar, 376-377

L

LABEL mode, 17
labels
  documenting worksheets with, 53-55
  entering, 17-19, 73
    prefixes, 18, 74-75
  formats, 75
Learn (Alt–F5) key combination,
  230-231
left-arrow key, 19, 33
license count, initializing, 510-512
line graphs, 207
linking
  files, 143-155
  worksheets
    and Microsoft Word
      documents, 439
    and Word for Windows
      documents, 446-447
    and WordPerfect documents,
      429-431
listing
  external tables, 302
  fields from external tables, 302-303
loading macro libraries, 334
loans, calculating, 272-273
@LOG function, 199
log files, 512
logical drives, 121, 508
logical operators, 189
Look & Link add-in, 352-356
Lotus Add-in Toolkit, 373-375
Lotus Developer Tools, 375

M

/m command, 108-109
Macro Editor/Debugger (MED) add-in,
  347-349
Macro Library Manager, 248-249,
  332-334
macros, 43
  advanced commands, 46, 239
    {APPENDBELOW}, 89-90
    {BRANCH}, 241
    {DOWN} macro instruction,
      237-238
    {FORM}, 87-90
    {GET}, 240
    {GETLABEL}, 218, 239-240
    {GETNUMBER}, 239-240
    {GRAPHOFF}, 218
    {GRAPHON}, 218
    {MENUBRANCH}, 245
    {MENUCALL}, 245
    {PANELOFF}, 241
    {QUIT}, 244
    {RETURN}, 244
    {WINDOWSOFF}, 241
  controlling flow, 200
  creating, 44-45, 230-231, 234-237
  creating with subroutines, 241-242
  debugging, 228
  displaying graphs with, 218
  ending, 244-245
  importing to Excel, 467-468
  key names, 45-46
    numeric arguments, 237-239
  libraries
    editing, 334-335
    loading, 334
  menu, 245-248
    to navigate worksheets, 57-58
  naming, 227
    organizing, 229-230
  password protecting, 333-334
  protecting in worksheets, 59-66
  replaying stored characters, 243-244

running in open files, 249-250
setting up for formatted reports, 323-324
shortening recorded, 231-235
starting, 227-229
starting library routines, 248-249
storing in separate worksheets, 70-71
mapping 1-2-3 directories, 508-509
margins, 160-161, 178, 183
@MAX function, 193
memory
copying to/from files in memory, 111
saving, 116
`Memory full` message, 134
menu macros, 245
creating trees, 247-248
making safer to use, 245-246
organizing codes, 246
{MENUBRANCH} advanced macro command, 245
{MENUCALL} advanced macro command, 245
menus
1-2-3 main, 22
macros, 57-58
print, 163-165
selecting commands, 22-23
messages
displaying, 240-241
`File does not exist`, 144
`Memory full`, 134
@MIN function, 193
minimal recalculation, 31
mixed references, 95
@MOD function, 163-164, 197-198
mode indicators, 15
models, creating, 288-290
modes
addressing, 95-96
EDIT, 32-33
GROUP, 68-71
LABEL, 17
overtype, 33
READY, 18, 23, 62
VALUE, 18

modifying linked files, 153
mouse
moving cell pointer, 15-16
selecting menu commands, 22
specifying ranges, 38
multilevel summary reports, 314-315
multiple criteria, 295
multiple worksheets, 67-68
formatting concurrently, 68-70
opening screens, 71
storing macros, 70-71

N

Name (F3) function key, 37, 122
naming
graphs, 217-218
macros, 227-230
ranges, 37
native formats, 137
NetWare, 503-505
network operating systems, 505
networks, 503-505
changing directories, 515-516
creating personal directories, 512-513
exiting sessions, 516
installing 1-2-3, 505
assigning access rights, 507-508
copying files, 510
creating server directories, 506-507
individual workstations, 514-515
initializing license count, 510-512
initializing system disks, 509-510
mapping 1-2-3 directories, 508-509
printing on, 516
saving worksheets, 512
NewUser utility, 512-513
nodes, 503
noncontiguous cells, 112-115
#NOT# operator, 189
Noteworthy add-in, 345
Novell NetWare, 503-505
@NOW function, 163-164

numbers, importing, 141-143
numeric keypad, 76
numeric series, 77-78

O

opening multiple files, 123-124
operators
  #AND#, 189
  #NOT#, 189
  #OR#, 189
  addition (+), 187
  division (/), 187
  equal to (=), 187-189
  exponentiation (^) (caret), 188
  greater than (>), 189
  greater than or equal to (>=), 189
  less than (<), 189
  less than or equal to (<=), 189
  not equal to (<>), 189
  multiplication (*), 187
  precedence, 187-189
  subtraction (-), 187
output ranges, 299-300
overtype mode, 33

P

page breaks, 137
page numbers, 162
PageMaker, 410
  importing PIC files, 416
  importing worksheets, 413-416
{PANELOFF} advanced macro
  command, 241
Paradox, 488-493
  exporting to 1-2-3 worksheets,
    492-493
  importing 1-2-3 worksheets, 488-492
passwords
  saving files with, 125-126
  protecting macro library, 333-334

/pb command, 172
/pe command, 171
/pf command, 170, 173-174, 405
PgDn key, 17
PgUp key, 17
PIC files, importing, 388-389
  into Microsoft Word, 439-442
  into Word for Windows, 447-451
  into WordPerfect, 431-435
  with CorelDRAW!, 401-404
  with First Publisher, 407
  with PageMaker, 416
  with Ventura Publisher, 422-423
pie graphs, 208
@PMT function, 272-273
pointing to cell references, 21
/pp command, 172
/ppi command, 224
/ppof command, 161
/ppoh command, 161
/ppooa command, 170
/ppooc command, 168, 337-338
/ppoof command, 168
/ppoou command, 168
/ppos command, 158-159
/ppr command, 38, 163-165, 225
/pprb command, 167
prefixes
  entering, 74
  labels, 74
preselecting ranges, 36
printing
  background, 171-172
  codes, 158-159
  controlling printers, 158
  default settings, 157-161
  dividing lines, 174-177
  formulas, 168-170
  graphs, 223-225
  margins, 160-161
  on a network, 516
  pages, 184
  printer types, 157
  ranges, 161, 179-184
  reports, 324

to disk files, 170
to encoded files, 171
with Allways, 178-181
with Wysiwyg, 182
worksheets, 38
PRN files, 417
importing with Ventura Publisher, 419-421
Professional Write, 452-454
programming subroutines, 241-244
Project Calc/Resources add-in, 358-360
protecting
existing files when saving, 124
formulas, 59-61
restricted zones, 61-63
worksheets, 65-66
arranging diagonally, 63-64
combining restricted zones and
diagonal arrangement, 64
protection status, copying, 102
:PRS command, 224

Q

Q&A, 493
exporting to 1-2-3, 498-500
importing 1-2-3 worksheets, 494-498
Quattro Pro, 460-462
importing 1-2-3 worksheets, 460-462
Query (F7) function key, 42
Quicken, 468-469
importing 1-2-3 worksheets, 469-470
Quicken Transfer Utility, 470
detail transfers, 470-473
summary transfers, 472-474
{QUIT} advanced macro command, 244

R

ranges
column widths, 28
combining worksheets with, 127-128
copying, 105-107
from files on disk, 110
from rows, 92-94
creating series of, 381-382, 390, 411, 418
criteria, 41-42, 293-295
entering
date formulas, 80
series of values, 78
time formulas, 80-82
erasing, 34
formatting, 23
linking to named, 145-146
naming, 37
output, 299-300
preselecting, 36
printing, 161, 179-184
recalculating, 104
rectangular, 78-80
removing formatting, 83
saving extracted, 126-127
searching for characters, 118
source, 92-94, 108
specifying, 34-35, 38, 92
target, 92-94, 108
three-dimensional, 36
transposing, 105-107
/re command, 34
READY mode, 15, 18, 23, 62
recalculating
ranges, 104
worksheets, 31-32
receivables, aging with formulas, 287-288
Record (Alt–F2) key combination, 235-237
records, database, 40
relative references, 95
mixing with absolute references, 96
repeat-character (\) prefix, 19
reports
creating, 308
detailed, 315-317
formatted, 322-323
printing, 324

subtotaled, 318-322
summary, 309-314
Resource Histogram charts, 360
restricted zones, 61-63
  combining with diagonal worksheet
    arrangements, 64
retrieving files, 27, 122
{RETURN} advanced macro
  command, 244
/rfd command, 284
/rfdt command, 80-82
/rfo command, 75
/rfp command, 23
/ri command, 85-87
right-arrow key, 19, 33
/rj command, 138-142, 232
/rnc command, 37, 381, 390, 411, 418
/rnlr command, 320-322, 333
roots, computing, 197
@ROUND function, 194
rounding numbers, 194
rows, 168, 183
  border, 166-167
  copying to ranges, 92-94
  designing worksheets in blocks,
    56-57
@ROWS function, 291-292
/rs command, 118, 232
/rt command, 79-80, 105-107
/ru command, 61
Run (Alt–F3) key combination, 227-229
/rv command, 104-105, 111

S

/s command, 25
saving
  files, 26-27, 124, 405, 512
    by highlighting, 125
    with Backup option, 126
    with passwords, 125-126
  graphs, 219-220
  memory, 116
  parts of worksheets, 126-127

screens
  Access System, 12-13
  elements, 14-15
  fitting worksheets on one, 54-58
  opening for three-dimensional
    worksheets, 71
  opening worksheet, 12-14
searching for files
  in current directory, 122
  in subdirectories, 123
  with wild-card characters, 123
SeeMORE add-in, 349-352
selecting
  criteria ranges, 293-295
  menu commands, 22-23
server directories, 506-507
Shift-Tab key, 17, 32
Sideways add-in, 367-368
SNAPSHOT memory-resident utility
  program, 407-409
  importing graphs, 409-410
sorting
  creating detailed extracts, 316-317
  databases, 316-317
source ranges, 92-94, 108
:Special Copy command, 103
specifying
  criteria, 295-299
  multiple criteria, 295
  ranges, 34-35, 92
    with mouse, 38
stack-bar graphs, 208
starting
  1-2-3, 11-13
  macro library routines, 248-249
  macros, 227-229
  new files, 27
storing macros in separate
  worksheets, 70
subroutines, 241
  creating commands with, 241-242
  ending, 244-245
  organizing programs, 242-243
  replaying stored characters, 243-244
subtotaled reports, 318-322

@SUM function, 187, 194-195, 207, 381, 390, 404, 411, 417
summary reports, 309-311
   creating with formulas, 313-314
   multilevel, 314-315
@SYD function, 275
Symphony, 455-456
   importing 1-2-3 worksheets, 456-459
SYSCON utility, 507-508

T

Tab key, 17, 32
tables
   amortization, 277
   controlling size
      with formulas, 279-281
      with macros, 281
   data, 301-302
   dating automatically, 282
   external, 302
   self-sizing, 279
target ranges, 92-94, 108
@TERM function, 272
text
   adding
      graphics, 264-266
      to graphs, 261-262
   combining with graphs, 262-263
   importing blocks, 137-139
   labels, 17-19
The Worksheet Utilities add-in, 360-367
   CELLWKS, 361-365
   FILEWKS, 366
three-dimensional
   ranges, 36
   worksheets, 67-71
three-way data tables, 312-313
tilde (~), 44
time
   changing format appearance, 84
   entering, 90-91
@TIME function, 81

@TODAY function, 282-283, 287-288
@Tools add-in, 376
tracking default file names, 125
transposing ranges, 105-107
TurboTax, 474
   importing 1-2-3 worksheets, 475-477
two-way data tables, 312
typefaces, 255

U

Undo (Alt-F4) key combination, 115-116
undo feature, adding to earlier releases of 1-2-3, 118
undoing macros with Undo, 117
up-arrow key, 19, 33
updating file links, 150-151, 154-155
updating external database tables, 307-308
user entries, placing in cells, 239-240

V

VALUE mode, 18
values
   combining in worksheets, 130-133
   converting formulas, 104-105
   displayed versus actual, 30
   entering, 19, 75
      into rectangular ranges, 78-80
      using a macro to automate, 76
   formatting, 82-83
   subtracting, 134-137
@VDB function, 275
Ventura Publisher, 416-417
   importing PIC files, 422-423
   importing PRN files, 419-421
Viewer add-in, 341-342
   linking files, 144-145
@VLOOKUP function, 201-203

W

/wcr command, 28
/wcs command, 28
/wds command, 71
/wg command, 329-331
/wgc command, 28
/wgdd command, 122
/wgdgm command, 220
/wgdoci command, 162
/wgdoic command, 84
/wgdoid command, 84
/wgdoip command, 83
/wgdoud command, 116
/wgdpi command, 516
/wgfc command, 24-25
/wgfl command, 75
/wgge command, 68
/wggr command, 213
/wgpe command, 61
/wgrm command, 31
what-if analysis, 29-30
What-If Solver add-in, 356-357
wild-card characters, 123
{WINDOWSOFF} advanced macro
   command, 241
/wisa command, 71
WK1 file extension, 27
WK3 file extension, 27
/wl command, 230
Word for Windows
   importing PIC files, 447-451
   importing worksheets, 443-447
word processing
   Microsoft Word, 436-442
   Professional Write, 452-454
   Word for Windows, 443-451
   WordPerfect, 425-435
WordPerfect, 425
   importing 1-2-3 PIC files, 431-435
   importing 1-2-3 worksheets, 426-431

worksheets
   cells
      editing, 32-33
      erasing, 34
   column widths, 28
   combining, 127-137
   copying
      data, 92
      formulas, 101
   designing, 51-52
   elements, 14-15
   exporting to 1-2-3
      dBASE, 487-488
      Excel, 468
      Paradox, 492-493
      Q&A, 498-501
      Quattro Pro, 462
      Quicken Transfer Utility, 470-474
      Symphony, 457-459
   fitting on one screen, 54-58
   formatting, 24-25
   formulas
      combining with, 128-130
      protecting, 59-61
   importing, 381-382
      blocks of text, 137-139
      into dBASE, 481-486
      into Excel, 463-468
      into Microsoft Word, 436-439
      into Paradox, 488-492
      into Professional Write, 452-454
      into Q&A, 494-498
      into Quattro Pro, 460-462
      into Quicken, 469-470
      into Symphony, 456-459
      into TurboTax, 475-477
      into Word for Windows, 443-447
      into WordPerfect, 426-431
      numbers, 141-143
      with First Publisher, 405-406
      with Freelance Plus, 383-388
      with Harvard Graphics, 392-396
      with PageMaker, 413-416

labels
  documenting with, 53-55
  entering, 17-19
linking, 143-155
navigating, 15-17
opening screen, 12-14
printing, 38
protecting, 65-66
  arranging diagonally, 63-64
  restricted zones, 61-63
ranges, combining with, 127-128
recalculating, 31-32
retrieving and starting new, 27
running macros, 249-250
saving, 26-27
  on network systems, 512
  parts, 126-127
saving to ASCII text files, 405
three-dimensional, 67-71
values
  combining in, 130-133
  displayed versus actual, 30
  entering, 19
  subtracting combined, 134-137
what-if analysis, 29-30

workstations, 503, 514-515
/ws command, 338-340
/wt command, 61-63
/wtb command, 64-65
Wysiwyg, 336
  copying formats, 103
  creating charts, 257-258
  enhancing graphs, 220-223
  graphs, combining with text, 263
  printing graphs, 225
  printing with, 182

X-Z

/xg run macro, 228-229
xy graphs, 208
y-axes, graphing with two, 214-215

Free Catalog!

Mail us this registration form today, and we'll send you a free catalog featuring Que's complete line of best-selling books.

Name of Book _____

Name _____

Title _____

Phone ( ) _____

Company _____

Address _____

City _____

State _____ ZIP _____

Please check the appropriate answers:

1. Where did you buy your Que book?
   - [ ] Bookstore (name: _____)
   - [ ] Computer store (name: _____)
   - [ ] Catalog (name: _____)
   - [ ] Direct from Que
   - [ ] Other: _____

2. How many computer books do you buy a year?
   - [ ] 1 or less
   - [ ] 2-5
   - [ ] 6-10
   - [ ] More than 10

3. How many Que books do you own?
   - [ ] 1
   - [ ] 2-5
   - [ ] 6-10
   - [ ] More than 10

4. How long have you been using this software?
   - [ ] Less than 6 months
   - [ ] 6 months to 1 year
   - [ ] 1-3 years
   - [ ] More than 3 years

5. What influenced your purchase of this Que book?
   - [ ] Personal recommendation
   - [ ] Advertisement
   - [ ] In-store display
   - [ ] Price
   - [ ] Que catalog
   - [ ] Que mailing
   - [ ] Que's reputation
   - [ ] Other: _____

6. How would you rate the overall content of the book?
   - [ ] Very good
   - [ ] Good
   - [ ] Satisfactory
   - [ ] Poor

7. What do you like *best* about this Que book?

   _____

   _____

8. What do you like *least* about this Que book?

   _____

   _____

9. Did you buy this book with your personal funds?
   - [ ] Yes   [ ] No

10. Please feel free to list any other comments you may have about this Que book.

    _____

    _____

    _____

qualified — que

Order Your Que Books Today!

Name _____

Title _____

Company _____

City _____

State _____ ZIP _____

Phone No. ( ) _____

Method of Payment:

Check [ ]   (Please enclose in envelope.)

Charge My: VISA [ ]   MasterCard [ ]

American Express [ ]

Charge # _____

Expiration Date _____

Order No.	Title	Qty.	Price	Total

You can **FAX** your order to **1-317-573-2583**. Or call **1-800-428-5331, ext. ORDR** to order direct.

Please add $2.50 per title for shipping and handling.

Subtotal _____

Shipping & Handling _____

Total _____

que

BUSINESS REPLY MAIL
First Class Permit No. 9918   Indianapolis, IN

Postage will be paid by addressee

11711 N. College
Carmel, IN 46032

NO POSTAGE
NECESSARY
IF MAILED
IN THE
UNITED STATES

BUSINESS REPLY MAIL
First Class Permit No. 9918   Indianapolis, IN

Postage will be paid by addressee

11711 N. College
Carmel, IN 46032